Gender and Social Life

Gender and Social Life

ROBERTA SATOW, EDITOR
Brooklyn College

ALLYN AND BACON
Boston • London • Toronto • Sydney • Tokyo • Singapore

Series Editor: Sarah L. Kelbaugh
Editor in Chief, Social Science: Karen Hanson
Editorial Assistant: Lori Flickinger
Composition Buyer: Linda Cox
Manufacturing Buyer: Julie McNeill
Editorial-Production Service: P. M. Gordon Associates
Production Administrator: Deborah Brown
Cover Administrator: Jenny Hart

Copyright © 2001 by Allyn and Bacon
A Pearson Education Company
160 Gould Street
Needham Heights, Massachusetts 02494

Internet: www.abacon.com

Library of Congress Cataloging-in-Publication Data

Gender and social life / edited by Roberta Satow.
　　p.　cm.
　　Includes bibliographical references.
　　ISBN 0–321–03421–X
　　1. Sex role.　2. Women—Social conditions.　3. Men—Social conditions.　I. Satow,
Roberta.
　　HQ1075.G42　2000
　　305.3—dc21
　　　　　　　　　　　　　　　　　　　　　　　　　　　　　　　　　　　　　99–057652

Printed in the United States of America

10 9 8 7 6 5 4 3 2 1   05 04 03 02 01 00

For Richard, Matthew, and Jason

CONTENTS

PART FOUR
Gender and Education   143

PART FIVE
Gender, Math, and Science   167

PART SIX
Gender and Religion   211

PREFACE

For years my students have been persistent in challenging me on two different levels. First, they question my basic assumptions about the nature of gender inequality or if it even exists. "My mother earns more than my father." The second challenge goes to the heart of sociological perspective—they question whether it is possible to make generalizations about social groups at all. "My father cooks and cleans." These are the kind of comments that inevitably arise in my Sociology of Gender class. I used to get annoyed at them and view them as my students' refusal to take in the great insights I was offering them about the social construction of gender roles and the patriarchal social structure. But I have come to realize that my students are bringing up important issues. Instead of wishing they would stop being so annoying, I have tried to create a curriculum package that addresses these fundamental issues. Each section of this reader contains articles that represent different and often conflicting theoretical approaches to a subject area. The articles also use a variety of methodologies—some are historical, others are based on participant observation, others use quantitative data, and still others are based on personal experiences. I hope that the variety of perspectives will encourage students to think about the assumptions of each of the authors as well as their own.

Oftentimes, students do not realize the assumptions they are making about the causes of gender inequality or that they are challenging mine. When I talk about gender and parenting, for example, the biological determinists emerge. Someone always says: "Women want to be mothers because of maternal instinct. It's biological." At first, they're reticent to say it out loud to me. They say what they really think under their breath: "Women are the ones who have the babies." When I encourage them to speak up and promise not to grade them on their opinions, their real ideas start to flow: "Males have more aggression, that's why they're dominant" or "males are stronger, that's why they're dominant" or "males were the hunters, that's why they're dominant."

This group of students are bioevolutionists or sociobiologists, although they don't know it. Essentially, the bioevolutionary view makes no distinction between sex and gender, or animals and human beings. To understand gender as an eminently *human* social institution, it is important to distinguish human action from animal behavior. For animals, physiological maturity and the ability to reproduce marks adult status; for human beings, the onset of physiological puberty is often marked by rites of passage, but it is distinct from adult status. Among animals, siblings mate and so do parents and children; humans have incest taboos. Mating in animals is determined by instinct; human mating involves rules that encourage or discourage mating between members of different groups (Lorber 1994).

In contrast to this group, which argues that gender inequality is biologically based and unchangeable, another group rejects the notion that culture molds them in any way, insisting on their individuality and free choice. They are, unknowingly, taking the human capital theory approach. Human capital consists of the things workers can do to make themselves more productive, that is, educational level and skills. Wage differences are seen as a function of variables over which individuals are presumed to have control. When applied to gender inequality, the male-female wage gap is seen as a result of individual choices men and women make, such as leaving the labor market to have children. Some of my students say: "Some women want to work and some don't." What I hear is: "We're all individuals." After I give a spirited lecture on occupational gender segregation, these students always say: "That's just your opinion. I don't want to be a teacher because I am a woman, I just love children." What I hear is: "I have not been shaped by social forces, I made an individual choice."

Of course, they are right. Gender categories are not pure—neither are sex categories. Sociologists traditionally distinguished between *sex* and *gender* by saying that gender is a social construction, whereas sex is based on genes and genitalia. However, even sex categories are not neatly divided into two and only two categories—there are wide variations within each of the groups that are sometimes greater than the difference between the groups. For example, menstruation, lactation, and pregnancy do not distinguish males and females because many females do not get pregnant or lactate; some have hysterectomies or reach menopause and do not menstruate. Men cannot be defined as sperm producers because some men do not produce sperm. Having a penis or vagina cannot distinguish the sexes because there are babies born with anomalous genitals. Even chromosomes cannot distinguish males and females perfectly because there are women who have XY chromosomes but do not have male anatomies because of a genetic defect (Lorber 1997).

Although genes and hormones that determine sex come in more than two combinations, in most societies there are only two genders assigned. The gender usually overlaps with the genetic or biological sex—but not always. In the case of hermaphrodites (individuals who possess full sets of both male and female genitals and reproductive organs at birth), transsexuals (individuals who have sex change operations as adults), and accidents (such as a boy who was castrated at seven months), gender and biological sex do not overlap. Masculine and feminine identity is not *always* consistent with biological sex (Lorber 1994).

My students are correct in pointing out that it is also important to be able to distinguish differences among women and men and not view women as a homogenous group united in its victimization by men. On the other hand, while it is clear that the biological aspect of gender, which is usually referred to as *sex*, is *not* unchangeable as most of us assume, once gender is ascribed, to what extent does the social order hold individuals to strongly gendered norms and expectations? I used to think that my students should accept my view that the division of the social world into men and women *is* pervasive. Many of them reject the premise that it is possible to make probability statements about gender groups. Their desire to be individuals and their fear of stereotypes make them reluctant to accept social patterns that may not always reflect their personal experience. They have taught me that my job is to help *them* find out the degree to which their personal experiences are "personal."

In order to facilitate that process, Gina Vastola and I have created a workbook and disk—*Gender and Social Life: A Workbook* to supplement this book. It allows students to test the hypotheses put forward in many of the articles in this reader. Sometimes students will find the data support the author's position; other times, some aspects of the author's position are supported, and occasionally students will find that hypotheses must be rejected because the probability of error is too high.

ABOUT THIS BOOK

The readings in this book offer students a wide variety of ideas—many of them quite provocative—about how gender structures our feelings about ourselves, expectations of ourselves and others, choices we make, and the opportunities available to us. The accompanying workbook and data disk, *Gender and Social Life: A Workbook,* will then give students the opportunity to test the extent to which those propositions are "just opinions"—that is, supported or rejected depending on their probability of error. Students will have to grapple with themselves (instead of me) when they find that many of their own personal experiences are not "personal" at all. They will find that sometimes their assumptions about gender and/ or racial differences cannot be supported by the data, while other times they will find differences they never thought about.

The perspectives most commonly held by my students—human capital theory and bioevolutionary theory—are only two of several theoretical perspectives that are presented in the reader and tested in *Gender and Social Life: A Workbook.* Although the workbook emphasizes quantitative methods, some of the chapters use qualitative methods. Each section of the reader presents contrasting theoretical perspectives as well as an assortment of methodologies and issues.

In Part One, Gender Socialization and Parenting, five readings focus on various aspects of the process of gender construction for men and women in the family and present different theoretical perspectives as well as methodologies. Combining a psychoanalytic object relations perspective with a social structural perspective, Nancy Chodorow's theoretical essay argues that women's mothering contributes to different relational and nurturing capacities in men and women. David D. Gilmore agrees that women's mothering makes "becoming a man" a difficult developmental process. However, based on his anthropological research, he concludes that the process serves an important function for society. In contrast to Chodorow and Gilmore, Barbara J. Risman takes a microstructural approach, contending that situational demands are better predictors of mothering behaviors than gender-typed internalized personality traits. She designed a study to disentangle the individual and microstructural determinants of mothering behaviors using single-father, single-mother, married two-paycheck, and traditional mother-at-home families. Risman used questionnaires to study a large sample of parents, whereas Ann Willard used two in-depth interviews with twenty women to study women's decision-making process about parenting and working outside the home for her article, "Cultural Scripts for Mothering."

Whereas the articles above deal with the processes of constructing gender and how it gets reproduced in the family, Patricia Hill Collins uses a historical perspective to examine the way that race and gender have interacted in the development of community-based child care in the African American culture. Collins points out that "othermothers," women who assist bloodmothers by sharing mothering responsibilities, traditionally have been part of the institution of black motherhood.

Part Two, Gender and Work, examines the role of gender in determining what type of work one does and whether it is defined as "work." The six articles in this section trace the historical development of women's participation in the labor force and their attitudes toward participation from the beginnings of industrial capitalism to the present. Barbara F. Reskin and Irene Padavic's historical description of the doctrine of separate spheres, which relegated women to the home and family and men to work outside the home in the middle of the nineteenth century, is poignantly revealed in Charlotte Perkins Gilman's autobiographical short story, "The Yellow Wallpaper." Betty Friedan's journalistic article, "The Problem That Has No Name," demonstrates that in the 1950s the doctrine of separate spheres was still alive and well. Arlie Hochschild and Anne Machung's study of two-pay-check couples, written twenty years after Friedan's piece, illustrates that when women began entering the workforce in large numbers, they were still expected (and expected themselves) to be the primary parent and take care of the home. Barbara R. Bergmann's article focuses on the continuing need for affirmative action as a remedy for occupational segregation. She discusses the motives for affirmative action and distinguishes it from quotas. Elizabeth Higginbotham's article deals specifically with the effects of race and gender on black professional and managerial women. She points out that they are subject to occupational segregation by race as well as gender.

Part Three, Gender and Sexuality, explores several themes. Deborah L. Tolman and Michael Messner focus on the social construction of sexuality—for adolescent girls and boys. Lillian B. Rubin examines the nature of heterosexual intimacy—contending that men and women are "intimate strangers." Benjamin P. Bowser and Becky W. Thompson deal with the importance of race and class in the process of developing sexuality. Bowser focuses on black male sexuality, while Thompson discusses girls' attitudes toward their bodies. John D'Emilio and Arlene Stein in separate articles discuss homosexuality from two different perspectives. D'Emilio takes a historical approach—analyzing the relationship between capitalism and the development of gay identity. Stein's article, based on extensive interviews, is about lesbians' experience of being "different."

Part Four, Gender and Education, examines how educational institutions create and reinforce gender distinctions. Barrie Thorne uses a microstructural perspective similar to Risman's (in Part One) to describe how gender is constructed in schools. Peggy Orenstein discusses girls' attitudes toward math in middle school and how their wish to be attractive to boys undermines their confidence.

Part Five, Gender, Math, and Science includes two readings that examine our cultural assumptions about the "neutrality" and "objectivity" of science. Men are most likely to define what is "objective" and the priorities for research and funding. Ruth Hubbard's theoretical essay discusses how assumptions about gender affect the process by which "facts" are constructed. Ruth Bleier criticizes the "man the hunter" theory, which is commonly used as an explanation of contemporary gender inequality. The third article, by Henry Etzkowitz et al., is an empirical study of the barriers to women in academic science and engineering.

The three articles in Part Six, Gender and Religion, discuss how religion reflects and reinforces dominant attitudes about gender and gender inequality. Susan A. Farrell examines the Catholic Church; Judith Plaskow looks at Judaism; and Fatima Mernissi explores Muslim attitudes toward female sexuality.

Part Seven, Gender, Health, and Illness, has three articles that examine the role of gender in defining "health" and "illness" as well as its being a determinant in getting sick. Roberta Satow's article provides a historical perspective on hysteria as a woman's "illness." Hortensia Amaro discusses the vulnerability of minority women to contracting HIV, and Vicki S. Helgeson explains that men's gender roles make them more vulnerable to coronary heart disease than women.

Part Eight, Gender and Reproductive Technology, calls attention to new reproductive technologies. Technology is not inherently good or bad—it affects different groups differently. Jennifer Strickler contrasts the views of physicians, consumers, and feminist critics of reproductive technology. Laura R. Woliver is concerned about women's increasing invisibility in a medical system in which women's bodies are simply producers of a commodity—babies. She believes women are increasingly marginal in the new reproductive arrangements—especially surrogacy.

Part Nine, Gender and Politics, has two articles exploring quite disparate themes. Linda Gordon discusses the evolution of the birth control movement. Margaret Sanger's original goal was to give working-class women more control over their lives. The birth control movement is now dominated by male physicians who want to control the population of immigrants and minorities. Sally Avery Bermanzohn's article, which was written for this reader, examines the conservative assumptions underlying the passing of the 1996 welfare reform law and its effect on women—particularly women of color.

Laws are created by legislatures that are dominated by men and upheld or thrown out by courts that are dominated by men. Part Ten, Gender and the Law, provides a brief introduction to how the law can be used to protect women (such as sexual harassment laws) or to deny them basic rights (such as making abortion illegal). Rosemarie Skaine describes the legal meaning of sexual harassment, and Rosalind Pollack Petchesky addresses the rightward drift in the Supreme Court's decisions on abortions. The anonymous article, "Nora," is a personal story by a woman who had three abortions before *Roe* v. *Wade* made abortion legal in 1973.

Part Eleven, Gender and Violence, explores violence as a way of dominating women. The articles discuss rape, pornography, and wife battering as ways that men control and devalue women. The article about fraternities and rape by Patricia Yancey Martin and Robert A. Hummer was chosen because it exemplifies the reality that most rapes are perpetrated by men who are known by their victims. Alan Soble's article on pornography was chosen because a Marxist approach to pornography is unique and provocative. I chose Kimberly A. Huisman's article on wife battering from among many articles on the topic because students often have stereotyped ideas about Asian Americans as well as who is at risk for domestic violence.

Each section of the reader is introduced by a brief review of relevant research and theory and a short summary of each reading. The introductions and readings should make it clear to students that gender categories are socially constructed and reinforced in all of the social institutions of our society—family, workplace, school, religion, law, and so on. Indeed, it is difficult to distinguish the impact of gender on any one institution without considering its overlapping effects. Law cannot be separated from politics, for example, because politics determines what becomes law and which laws are upheld by the courts. The social construction of gender in the family cannot be clearly separated from the workplace because one of the rationales for women's mothering is that they earn less than men in the workplace. Yet, one of the rationales for paying women less is the assumption that they have men to support them and that their loyalty to the job is undermined by their child care responsibilities.

In addition to my students, I would like to thank the many people who have helped me during the process of working on this book. My husband Richard Wool, Josephine Dobkin, Elizabeth Ruskin, Mary Howard, and Tatiana Billik each edited several of the introductions. Edie Mencher and Susan Farrell were extremely helpful with the introduction to Gender and Religion. My son, Matthew, and Maggie Nemser were my college student guinea pigs—reading the introductions to let me know what they did not understand. Matthew also made many trips to the library on my behalf. I am also grateful to the following reviewers, whose comments greatly improved the final product: Barbara Arrighi, Northern Kentucky University; Jason Blank, Rhode Island College; Janet Bogdan, LeMoyne College; Judith DiIorio, Indiana University–Purdue University at Ft. Wayne; Patricia Dorman, Boise State University; Barbara Feldman, Seton Hall University; Juanita Firestone, University of Texas at San Antonio; Carol Brooks Gardner, Indiana University–Purdue University at Indianapolis; Susan Marshall, University of Texas at Austin; Jane Prather, California State University at Northridge; Jennifer Solomon, Winthrop University; Theodore Wagenaar, Miami University of Ohio; Susan Weeks, ITT Technical Institute, Washington; Lois West, Florida International University; and Amy Wharton, Washington State University.

I hope that students will come to understand that gender is a major social status that is part of a structure of domination and subordination and shapes individual opportunities for education, work, sexuality, reproductive freedom, and shaping and changing the law.

REFERENCES

Lorber, Judith. 1994. *Paradoxes of Gender*. New Haven: Yale University Press.
Lorber, Judith. 1997. "Believing Is Seeing: Biology as Ideology." Pp. 13–22 in *Through the Prism of Difference*, edited by Maxine Baca Zinn, Pierrette Hondagneu-Sotelo, and Michael Messner. Boston: Allyn and Bacon.

Gender and Social Life

PART ONE

Gender Socialization and Parenting

Gender socialization is the process by which different behaviors and attitudes are encouraged or discouraged in men and women. Most of us like to think of ourselves as individuals. However, research shows that the process of gender-role socialization is quite pervasive and effective. Studying patterns of gender socialization does not deny that there are individual differences among us, but points to the common experiences shared by girls and boys as they become women and men (Andersen 1997). In this section, you will be presented with a variety of perspectives on the nature of gender socialization and its relationship to parenting—psychoanalytic object relations and microstructural and social learning. Nancy Chodorow and David D. Gilmore take a psychoanalytic object relations perspective—they both emphasize the importance of a woman as primary caregiver in raising children with internalized identities as "masculine" and "feminine." Sociologists and anthropologists who are object relations theorists view the most basic aspects of personality development as the result of a boy or girl's earliest social relationships (Chodorow 1989). In contrast, Barbara J. Risman's microstructural perspective argues that most differences between men and women as parents are not the result of psychic structure, but rather of differing experiences and adaptation to different opportunities.

This is an important issue because women's secondary status in the paid labor force is often justified by the assumption that women's devotion to child care makes them ineligible for top-level positions requiring long hours and travel. From that point of view, the gender wage gap is a result of an individual woman's "choice" to mother (be the primary parent). Most women want to mother. Most men do not. Why? The most common explanation is the biological one—if females are the primary parents in the animal kingdom, then it must be "natural." Yet, animals feed their young only until they can feed themselves; humans feed, clothe, and shelter their young long after they are able to do so for themselves (Lorber 1994). Similarly, animals do not have breast pumps and baby formula, which free the woman from the physical necessity of being in constant proximity to her infant for feeding purposes. In addition, we are constantly reading and hearing about mothers who murder or abandon their children—mothers clearly missing "maternal instinct." The concept of maternal instinct does not seem to be a human instinct: For humans, to a large extent, culture replaces instinct. What we view as natural actually grows out of our participation in certain social arrangements.

Philippe Aries (1962), in his classic study *Centuries of Childhood,* pointed out that culture shapes our view of children and good parenting. In Europe in the Middle Ages, children were not kept at home, but were sent into service for another family at age 7 or 8. In the sixteenth and seventeenth centuries, urban mothers did not nurse their own infants—they were sent to wet nurses in the country. The modern family, with parents and children living together as an isolated group, evolved in the eighteenth century, but was, at first, limited to the nobles, the middle class, the richer artisans, and the richer laborers. It was not until the late eighteenth and early nineteenth centuries, in England, that agricultural laborers set up family life with their own children (Aries 1962).

Nancy Chodorow in *The Reproduction of Mothering* (1978) views the change in the organization of production from home to production out of the home (e.g., in factories) as central to the change in family life. Women's emotional role in the family and their psychological mothering role grew just as their economic role decreased. Industrial capitalism removed men from family life and excluded most married women from economic life.

As we see in her article in this section, Chodorow argues that women's mothering is reproduced across generations through social, structurally induced psychological processes. In her view, women as mothers produce daughters with mothering capacities and desires and sons without mothering capacities or any desire to mother. This is built into the mother-daughter and mother-son relationship. Women as mothers produce sons whose nurturant capacities are curtailed and whose need for emotional connection has been repressed because of the necessity to differentiate from their mothers in order to stabilize their core gender identity.

In contrast to Chodorow, many feminists believe that girls are taught to be mothers, trained for nurturance, and told they ought to mother. She rejects this social learning argument, claiming that mothering is a psychologically based role—it consists of a psychological and personal experience of self in relation to a child. It is not just a set of behaviors. Chodorow says that those who believe in the role-training argument make it sound as if teaching girls to mother is conscious and intentional She argues that women's capacities for mothering and their ability to get gratification from it is built in intrapsychically because women mothered *them.*

Chodorow is one of the feminists who began to reinterpret Freud in the 1970s (Lorber 1994). Whereas Freud had emphasized the importance of the father in the psychosexual development of boys, psychoanalytic feminists focused on the importance of the mother as the primary parent for both boys and girls. Freud linked the devaluation of women by both sexes to their anatomy—not having a penis. He claimed that girls are contemptuous of their mothers for their penis-less state and suffer from penis envy. Many feminists, such as Juliet Mitchell (1974) reinterpreted the concept of penis envy, rather than rejecting it.

They claimed Freud brilliantly described the intrapsychic results for women of living in a patriarchy. But Freud ascribed women's psychic development to biology instead of social structure. Feminists argue that man's power does not depend on having a penis. The phallus is not *intrinsically* powerful, rather it is a *symbol* of power in the traditional patriarchal society. The father represents the outside world, freedom, novelty, stimulation, and excitement; the mother represents home, regression, and loss of autonomy for *both* the boy and the girl.

Psychoanalytic feminists such as Harriet Goldhor Lerner (1988) argue that devaluation of an envied object is a typical defensive maneuver, for as long as the object is devalued it need not be envied. Lerner argues that male stereotypes of women (e.g., dependency, passivity, and fragility) involve a reversal for males of their own early helplessness and dependency on a powerful female—mother.

Chodorow agrees that males' early dependency on a woman perpetuates the devaluation of women. She claims that as long as women mother, boys and girls will develop different relational capacities, preparing men and women to assume gender roles that perpetuate gender inequality. Men's work varies across cultures both in actual type and in the kinds of personality characteristics it requires; women mother in addition to whatever else they do in all societies. Women are the primary socializers. Thus, a boy's natural identification with the person to whom he is closest and on whom he is most dependent, that is, the mother, according to cultural values, is unnatural, and works against his attainment of a stable masculine identity. Girls' socialization is less conflicted and more continuous than the socialization of boys (Chodorow 1989).

Like Chodorow, David D. Gilmore uses a psychoanalytic object relations perspective to explain the nature of masculinity while rejecting some of Freud's basic assumptions. Freud assumed that everyone would want a penis and girls feel castrated without one. The superiority of the penis over the clitoris was obvious to him—he made that the keystone for the psychic development of both sexes. Freud argued that both boys and girls are born masculine and girls must achieve femininity by giving up their active masculine aims and becoming passive and receptive. He claimed that when the girl finds out that she does not have a penis, she feels castrated and gives up her masculine identification. She turns to femininity in disappointment—deciding to get someone with a penis to love her, because she does not have one of her own (Stockard and Johnson 1979:201). Freud's perspective is called "phallocentric" because of the centrality of the penis (phallus) in his theory.

In contrast, Chodorow and Gilmore use "gynocentric" (woman-centered) theory. Two themes are central to gynocentric accounts of early development. One involves boys' unconscious fear and envy of the mother; the other concerns the difficulty in developing a secure sense of masculine gender identity. Both aspects stem from the primacy of the mother or other females in early child care when the child is in a state of total dependence.

The earliest gynocentric theorists (e.g., Melanie Klein and Karen Horney) emphasized the "fear and envy" hypothesis. Klein argued that the fear of the mother is a defense against the child's aggressive impulses toward the mother. Horney claimed that both sexes see superiority in women's capacity for motherhood, rather than the male genital; boys defend themselves against this envy by devaluing women. More recently Robert Stoller has emphasized the idea that males have a less secure gender identity than females because their first close relationship is with the mother. Based on his work with trans-sexuals (people who have operations to change their sex), Stoller concluded that masculinity is not a "core-gender identity" as Freud supposed, but rather it is achieved by males only after they have separated themselves from the femininity of the mother. In other words, in order to feel masculine boys must "disidentify" from the mother in a way that women need not do to feel feminine (Stockard and Johnson 1979).

Gilmore also believes that masculinity is more problematic than feminin-ity. He argues that although the content of what is masculine may differ, there is a constantly recurring notion in all cultures that real manhood is different from simple anatomical maleness. It is not a natural condition that comes about through biological maturation, but rather is a hard-won state that boys must win against powerful odds. Gilmore views the real task as separating from the mother—renouncing his bond to her and entering into a new and in-dependent social status recognized as different, even opposite, from hers. He claims that this recurrent cultural phenomenon that boys must be tested is found at all levels of sociocultural development—among hunters, fishermen, and peasants as well as sophisticated urbanized peoples. Moreover, Gilmore argues that this universal view of masculinity represents a major difference from the view of femininity—which is more likely construed as a biological given and rarely involves tests or proofs of action. From this point of view, men are not born but made—"manhood" is a product of culture. Gilmore views the need to achieve manhood as a moral force that culture erects against the temptation of men to regress to being one with mother. Chodorow would agree. However, while Gilmore believes manhood serves a positive social function, Chodorow would view it as reproducing gender inequality. Unlike Chodorow, Gilmore does not question the inevitability of women do-ing the mothering and producing sons who have to prove their manhood.

Barbara J. Risman's article is an empirical test of whether the set of behav-iors called mothering is a result of women being psychologically drawn to mothering, as Chodorow argues, or is a result of situational factors. Risman argues that most sociological explanations of gender inequality are either macroinstitutional (i.e., structure of the economy or structure of occupations) or individualistic (personality traits that are internalized through socializa-tion). Individualistic explanations, from her point of view, suggest that by adulthood, men and women have developed very different personalities— women have become nurturant and child-centered, while men have become competitive and work-oriented. As opposed to the macroinstitutional and the individualistic approaches, Risman takes a microstructural perspective.

Rosabeth Moss Kanter (1977) applied a similar perspective with regard to gender in the workplace in *Men and Women of the Corporation,* arguing that what are called "female" characteristics are actually adaptations to powerlessness and lack of opportunity. The style is the *result* of women's position in the organization rather than a *cause* of it. Kanter claimed that individualistic models absolve organizations of responsibility for manufacturing the psychology of their workers. They assume that organizations take people as they find them and that all the molding has gone on before the workers are hired.

The structural characteristics of bureaucracies tend to produce symptoms of powerlessness in lower to middle managers, supervisors, bureaucrats, and professionals—positions in which most women are located. The chance to engage in the nonroutine, to show discretion, to take risks or become known are less available in a large bureaucracy. However, Kanter argues that power wipes out sex as an issue. A woman who does acquire organizational power stops arousing the same level of concern about whether she will be wanted as a leader. Thus, once there is a critical mass of women in powerful positions, expectations of them will change and they will behave differently. Kanter claims that many of the negative stereotypes of women bosses, for example, are perfect pictures of people who are powerless. The notion that "women are too rigid and controlling to make good bosses" is an example of powerlessness leading to overcontrol. Lack of power produces women bosses who anticipate resistance rather than cooperation. Thus, Kanter argues, what looks like sex differences may really be power differences.

Whereas Kanter applies microstructural theory to the leadership behavior of men and women in corporations, Risman applies it to parenting behavior. Risman hypothesizes that if individualist factors are the key to parental behavior, single fathers would not have the skills or motivation to provide primary care for their children. On the other hand, if microstructural factors are the most important determinants of parental behavior, the continuing expectations of the children to be nurtured would produce mothering by men that is indistinguishable from the behavior of women in the same situation.

In contrast to Chodorow, Gilmore, and Risman, Ann Willard takes a social learning perspective, arguing that cultures provide a "script" or rather specific set of ideas about how members of that culture can be guided through major life events. Social learning theorists point out that socialization is a constant part of our lives—a continuing process. It begins at the birth of the baby with: "Is it a boy or a girl?" Clearly, the sex of the baby is a salient feature from the earliest moments of life. Most parents create different worlds for boys and girls—beginning with naming and birth announcements. Studies of babies' rooms have found that pink, yellow, flowers, ruffles, and lace are used exclusively in girls' rooms, while boys' rooms are usually blue or red, with transportation or outer-space themes. Parents also provide different types of toys and play objects for boy and girl babies—and they respond differently to boys and girls. Research shows that with girls, mothers work to create and sustain an ongoing exchange, while boys are allowed to be independent. In one study that points to early differences in the treatment of babies, mothers were asked to play with a six-month-old child. Two female infants and two male infants appeared equally often as actor babies, sometimes dressed as their own sex and

sometimes as the other. In the play period, "boys" more than "girls" were verbally encouraged to engage in large-muscle motor activities such as crawling.
Fathers, on the other hand, cultivate a rough-and-tumble style of play with
sons and spend more time with them than with their daughters. Fathers tend
to be rigid about sex roles, being especially critical of any sign of feminine behavior in their sons and reinforcing their daughters' sex-typed behavior
(Richmond-Abbott 1992).

In her contribution to social learning theory, Willard explains that the cultural script for gender roles works well when clear cultural expectations are
supported by institutional arrangements. However, in times of social change
the cultural scripts for mothering diverge from the realities of the lives of
women who mother. She points out that we live in a time of conflicting views
of what women "ought" to do—American culture offers *several* scripts to
women who become mothers. Willard is interested in the process by which
women make decisions about combining motherhood with employment outside the home.

In contrast to Willard who studied white, college-educated, middle-class,
married women, Patricia Hill Collins focuses on the "cultural scripts" for African American mothers. She argues that three competing perspectives or
"scripts" about motherhood (the dominant Eurocentric view of motherhood,
the Eurocentric view of black motherhood, and African perspectives on
motherhood) intersected to produce a distinctly Afrocentric ideology of
motherhood. She goes on to discuss the African American mother-daughter
relationship from the psychoanalytic and social learning theory perspectives.

We can see that the five articles in this section are quite different from
each other in focus and method as well as theoretical perspective. Four of the
articles are about the United States. Gilmore, as an anthropologist, does a
cross-cultural analysis in his article to distill what he views as the essential in-
gredient in masculinity. Whereas Chodorow's article is purely theoretical,
Willard's is based on in-depth interviews that she coded to test three hypotheses. Despite these differences, all five authors point out that gender is produced and maintained by identifiable processes and built into our individual
identities as well as the social structure (Lorber 1994).

REFERENCES

Andersen, Margaret. 1997. *Thinking about Women: Sociological Perspectives on Sex and Gender.* Boston: Allyn and Bacon.

Aries, Philippe. 1962. *Centuries of Childhood: A Social History of Family Life.* New York:
Vintage Books.

Chodorow, Nancy. 1978. *The Reproduction of Mothering: Psychoanalysis and the Sociology of
Gender.* Berkeley: University of California Press.

Chodorow, Nancy. 1989. *Feminism and Psychoanalytic Theory.* New Haven: Yale University Press.

Kanter, Rosabeth Moss. 1977. *Men and Women of the Corporation.* New York: Basic Books.

Lerner, Harriet Goldhor. 1988. *Women in Therapy.* Northvale, NJ: Jason Aronson Inc.

Lorber, Judith. 1994. *Paradoxes of Gender.* New Haven: Yale University Press.

Mitchell, Juliet. 1974. *Psychoanalysis and Feminism.* New York: Pantheon Books.

Richmond-Abbott, Marie. 1992. *Masculine and Feminine: Gender Roles over the Life Cycle.* New York: McGraw-Hill.

Stockard, Jean, and Miriam Johnson. 1979. "The Social Origins of Male Dominance." *Sex Roles* 5:199–218.

1

The Sexual Sociology
of Adult Life

NANCY CHODOROW

Hence, there is a typically asymmetrical relation of the marriage pair to the occupational structure.

This asymmetrical relation apparently both has exceedingly important positive functional significance and is at the same time an important source of strain in relation to the patterning of sex roles.
—Talcott Parsons, "The Kinship System of the Contemporary United States"

Girls and boys develop different relational capacities and senses of self as a result of growing up in a family in which women mother. These gender personalities are reinforced by differences in the identification processes of boys and girls that also result from women's mothering. Differing relational capacities and forms of identification prepare women and men to assume the adult gender roles which situate women primarily within the sphere of reproduction in a sexually unequal society.

GENDER IDENTIFICATION AND GENDER ROLE LEARNING

All social scientists who have examined processes of gender role learning and the development of a sense of identification in boys and girls have argued that the asymmetrical organization of parenting in which women mother is the basic cause of significant contrasts between feminine and masculine identification processes.[1] Their discussions range from concern with the learning of appropriate gender role behavior—through imitation, explicit training and admonitions, and cognitive learning processes—to concern with the development of basic gender identity. The processes these people discuss seem to be universal, to the extent that all societies are constituted around a structural split, growing out of women's mothering, between the private, domestic world of women and the public, social world of men.[2] Because the first identification for children of both genders has always been with their mother, they argue, and because children are first around women, women's family roles and being feminine are more available and often more intelligible to growing children than masculine roles and being masculine. Hence, male development is more complicated than female because of the difficult shifts of identification which a boy must make to attain his expected gender identification and gender role assumption. Their view contrasts sharply to the psychoanalytic stress on the difficulties inherent in feminine development as girls make their convoluted way to heterosexual object choice.*

Because all children identify first with their mother, a girl's gender and gender role identification processes are continuous with her earliest identifications and a boy's are not. A girl's oedipal identification with her mother, for instance, is continuous with her earliest primary identification (and also in the context of her early dependence and attachment). The boy's oedipal crisis, however, is supposed to enable him to shift in favor of an identification with his father. He gives up, in addition to his oedipal and preoedipal attachment to his mother, his primary identification with her.

What is true specifically for oedipal identification is equally true for more general gender identification and gender role learning. A boy, in order to feel himself adequately masculine, must distinguish and differentiate himself from others in a way that a girl need not—must categorize himself as someone apart. Moreover, he defines masculinity negatively as that which is not feminine and/or connected to women, rather than positively.[3] This is another way boys come to deny and repress relation and connection in the process of growing up.

*The extent of masculine difficulty varies, as does the extent to which identification processes for boys and girls differ. This variance depends on the extent of the public-domestic split in a subculture or society—the extent to which men, men's work, and masculine activities are removed from the home, and therefore masculinity and personal relations with adult men are hard to come by for a child.

These distinctions remain even where much of a girl's and boy's socialization is the same, and where both go to school and can participate in adulthood in the labor force and other nonfamilial institutions. Because girls at the same time grow up in a family where mothers are the salient parent and caretaker, they also can begin to identify more directly and immediately with their mothers and their mothers' familial roles than can boys with their fathers and men. Insofar as a woman's identity remains primarily as a wife/mother, moreover, there is greater generational continuity in role and life-activity from mother to daughter than there can be from father to son. This identity may be less than totally appropriate, as girls must realistically expect to spend much of their life in the labor force, whereas their mothers were less likely to do so. Nevertheless, family organization and ideology still produce these gender differences, and generate expectations that women much more than men will find a primary identity in the family.

Permanent father-absence, and the "father absence" that is normal in our society, do not mean that boys do not learn masculine roles or proper masculine behavior, just as there is no evidence that homosexuality in women correlates with father absence.[4] What matters is the extent to which a child of either gender can form a personal relationship with his or her object of identification, and the differences in modes of identification that result from this. Mitscherlich, Slater, Winch, and Lynn all speak to these differences.[5] They suggest that girls in contemporary society develop a personal identification with their mother, and that a tie between affective processes and role learning—between libidinal and ego development—characterizes feminine development. By contrast, boys develop a positional identification with aspects of the masculine role. For them, the tie between affective processes and role learning is broken.

Personal identification, according to Slater and Winch, consists in diffuse identification with someone else's general personality, behavioral traits, values, and attitudes. Positional identification consists, by contrast, in identification with specific aspects of another's role and does not necessarily lead to the internalization of the values or attitudes of the person identified with. According to Slater, children preferentially choose personal identification because this grows out of a positive affective relationship to a person who is there. They resort to positional identification residually and reactively, and identify with the perceived role or situation of another when possibilities for personal identification are not available.

In our society, a girl's mother is present in a way that a boy's father, and other adult men, are not. A girl, then, can develop a personal identification with her mother, because she has a real relationship with her that grows out of their early primary tie. She learns what it is to be womanlike in the context of this personal identification with her mother and often with other female models (kin, teachers, mother's friends, mothers of friends). Feminine identification, then, can be based on the gradual learning of a way of being familiar in everyday life, exemplified by the relationship with the person with whom a girl has been most involved.

A boy must attempt to develop a masculine gender identification and learn the masculine role in the absence of a continuous and ongoing personal relationship to his father (and in the absence of a continuously available masculine role model). This positional identification occurs both psychologically and sociologically. Psychologically, as is clear from descriptions of the masculine oedipus complex, boys appropriate those specific components of the masculinity of their father that they fear will be otherwise used against them, but do not as much identify diffusely with him as a person. Sociologically, boys in father-absent and normally father-remote families develop a sense of what it is to be mas-

culine through identification with cultural images of masculinity and men chosen as masculine models.

Boys are taught to be masculine more consciously than girls are taught to be feminine. When fathers or men are not present much, girls are taught the heterosexual components of their role, whereas boys are assumed to learn their heterosexual role without teaching, through interaction with their mother.[6] By contrast, other components of masculinity must be more consciously imposed. Masculine identification, then, is predominantly a gender role identification. By contrast, feminine identification is predominantly *parental*: "Males tend to identify with a cultural stereotype of the masculine role; whereas females tend to identify with aspects of their own mother's role specifically."[7]

Girls' identification processes, then, are more continuously embedded in and mediated by their ongoing relationship with their mother. They develop through and stress particularistic and affective relationships to others. A boy's identification processes are not likely to be so embedded in or mediated by a real affective relation to his father. At the same time, he tends to deny identification with and relationship to his mother and reject what he takes to be the feminine world; masculinity is defined as much negatively as positively. Masculine identification processes stress differentiation from others, the denial of affective relation, and categorical universalistic components of the masculine role. Feminine identification processes are relational, whereas masculine identification processes tend to deny relationship.

These distinctions do not mean that the development of femininity is all sugar and spice for a girl, but that it poses different *kinds* of problems for her than the development of masculinity does for a boy. The feminine identification that a girl attains and the masculine identification about which a boy remains uncertain are valued differently. In their unattainability, masculinity and the masculine role are fantasized and idealized by boys (and often by girls), whereas femininity and the feminine role remain for a girl all too real and concrete. The demands on women are often contradictory—for instance, to be passive and dependent in relation to men, and active and independently initiating toward children....It is clear that mother-identification presents difficulties. A girl identifies with and is expected to identify with her mother in order to attain her adult feminine identification and learn her adult gender role. At the same time she must be sufficiently differentiated to grow up and experience herself as a separate individual—must overcome primary identification while maintaining and building a secondary identification.

Studies suggest that daughters in American society have problems with differentiation from and identification with their mothers.[8] Slater reports that all forms of personal parental identification (cross-gender and same-gender) correlate with freedom from psychosis or neurosis except personal identification of a daughter with her mother. Johnson reports that a boy's identification with his father relates to psychological adjustment, whereas a girl's with her mother does not. The implication in both accounts is that for a girl, just as for a boy, there can be too much of mother. It may be easy, but possibly too easy, for a girl to attain a feminine gender identification.*

Gender and gender-role identification processes accord with my account of the development of psychic structure. They reinforce and replicate the object-relational and ego outcomes which I have described. Externally, as internally, women grow up and remain more connected to others. Not only are the roles which girls learn more interpersonal, particularistic, and affective than those which

boys learn. Processes of identification and role learning for girls also tend to be particularistic and affective—embedded in an interpersonal relationship with their mothers. For boys, identification processes and masculine role learning are not likely to be embedded in relationship with their fathers or men but rather to involve the denial of affective relationship to their mothers. These processes tend to be more role-defined and cultural, to consist in abstract or categorical role learning rather than in personal identification.

FAMILY AND ECONOMY

Women's relatedness and men's denial of relation and categorical self-definition are appropriate to women's and men's differential participation in nonfamilial production and familial reproduction. Women's roles are basically familial, and concerned with personal, affective ties. Ideology about women and treatment of them in this society, particularly in the labor force, tend to derive from this familial location and the assumptions that it is or should be both exclusive and primary for women, and that this exclusivity and primacy come from biological sex differences. By contrast, men's roles as they are defined in our society are basically not familial. Though men are interested in being husbands and fathers, and most men do occupy these roles during their lifetime, ideology about men and definitions of what is masculine come predominantly from men's nonfamilial roles. Women are located first in the sex-gender system, men first in the organization of production.

We can reformulate these insights to emphasize that women's lives, and beliefs about women, define them as embedded in social interaction and personal relationships in a way that men are not. Though men and women participate in both the family and the nonfamilial world, the sexual division of labor is such that women's first association is within the family, a relational institution, and men's is not. Women in our society are prima-

---

*Recall also Deutsch's description of the prepubertal girl's random attempts to break her identification with her mother.

rily defined as wives and mothers, thus in particularistic relation to someone else, whereas men are defined primarily in universalistic occupational terms. These feminine roles and women's family functions, moreover, stress especially affective relationship and the affective aspects of family life. Being a mother and wife are increasingly centered on emotional and psychological functions—women's work is "emotion work."[9] By contrast, men's occupational roles, and the occupational world in general, are increasingly without room for affect and particularistic commitments. Women's two interconnected roles, their dual relatedness to men and children, replicate women's internalized relational triangle of childhood—preoccupied alternately with male-female and mother-child issues.

The definitional relatedness of being a wife and mother, and women's intrafamilial responsibility for affectively defined functions, receive further support from the way the family is related socially to the extrafamilial world. Parsons and many feminist theorists point out that it is the husband/father whose occupational role is mainly determinant of the class position and status of the whole family, and sociologists who measure socioeconomic status by *paternal* occupation and education seem to concur. The husband/father thus formally articulates the family in the larger society and gives it its place. And although families increasingly depend on income from both spouses, class position derives ideologically from what the male spouse does. The wife, accordingly, is viewed as deriving her status and class position mainly from her husband, even if she also is in the labor force and contributes to the maintenance of the family's lifestyle. She is seen as a representative of her family, whereas her husband is seen as an independent individual.

The wife/mother role draws on women's personality in another way, as a result of the fundamentally different modes of organization of the contemporary sex-gender system and contemporary capitalism. The activities of a wife/mother have a nonbounded quality. They consist, as countless housewives can attest and as women poets, novelists, and feminist theorists have described, of diffuse obligations. Women's activities in the home involve continuous connection to and concern about children and attunement to adult masculine needs, both of which require connection to, rather than separateness from, others. The work of maintenance and reproduction is characterized by its repetitive and routine continuity, and does not involve specified sequence or progression. By contrast, work in the labor force—"men's work"—is likely to be contractual, to be more specifically delimited, and to contain a notion of defined progression and product.

Even when men and women cross into the other's sphere, their roles remain different. Within the family, being a husband and father is different from being a wife and mother; as women have become more involved in the family, men have become less so. Parsons's characterization of men's instrumental role in the family may be too extreme, but points us in the right direction. A father's first responsibility is to "provide" for his family monetarily. His emotional contribution is rarely seen as of equal importance. Men's work in the home, in all but a few households, is defined in gender-stereotyped ways. When men do "women's" chores—the dishes, shopping, putting children to bed—this activity is often organized and delegated by the wife/mother, who retains residual responsibility (men "babysit" their own children; women do not). Fathers, though they relate to their children, do so in order to create "independence."[10] This is facilitated by a father's own previous socialization for repression and denial of relation, and his current participation in the public nonrelational world. Just as children know their fathers "under the sway of the reality principle,"*[11]

---

*Conscious of him as a separate person, verbally rather than preverbally.

so also do fathers know their children more as separate people than mothers do.

Outside the family, women's roles and ideology about women are more relational than nonfamilial male roles and ideology about men. Women's work in the labor force tends to extend their housewife, wife, or mother roles and their concern with personal, affective ties (as secretaries, service workers, private household workers, nurses, teachers). Men's work is less likely to have affective overtones—men are craft workers, operatives, and professional and technical workers.

Rosaldo claims that all these aspects of women's position are universal.[12] She suggests that feminine roles are less public or "social," that they exhibit less linguistic and institutional differentiation, and that the interaction they involve is more likely to be kin-based and to cross generations, whereas men's interaction remains within a single generation and cuts across kin units on the basis of universalistic categories. Women's roles are thus based on what are seen as personal rather than "social" or "cultural" ties. The corollary to this is that women's roles typically tend to involve the exercise of influence in face-to-face, personal contexts rather than legitimized power in contexts which are categorical and defined by authority. Finally, women's roles, and the biological symbolism attached to them, share a concern with the crossing of boundaries: Women mediate between the social and cultural categories which men have defined; they bridge the gap and make transitions—especially in their role as socializer and mother—between nature and culture.

Women's role in the home and primary definition in social reproductive, sex-gender terms are characterized by particularism, concern with affective goals and ties, and a diffuse, unbounded quality. Masculine occupational roles and men's primary definition in the sphere of production are universalistically defined and recruited, and are less likely to involve affective considerations. This non-relational, economic and political definition informs the rest of their lives. The production of feminine personalities oriented toward relational issues and masculine personalities defined in terms of categorical ties and the repression of relation fits these roles and contributes to their reproduction.

MOTHERING, MASCULINITY, AND CAPITALISM

Women's mothering in the isolated nuclear family of contemporary capitalist society creates specific personality characteristics in men that reproduce both an ideology and psychodynamic of male superiority and submission to the requirements of production. It prepares men for participation in a male-dominant family and society, for their lesser emotional participation in family life, and for their participation in the capitalist world of work.

Masculine development takes place in a family in which women mother and fathers are relatively uninvolved in child care and family life, and in a society characterized by sexual inequality and an ideology of masculine superiority. This duality expresses itself in the family. In family ideology, fathers are usually important and considered the head of the household. Wives focus energy and concern on their husbands, or at least think and say that they do. They usually consider, or at least claim, that they love these husbands. Mothers may present fathers to children as someone important, someone whom the mother loves, and may even build up their husbands to their children to make up for the fact that these children cannot get to know their fathers as well as their mothers. They may at the same time undercut their husbands in response to the position he assumes of social superiority or authority in the family.

Masculinity is presented to a boy as less available and accessible than femininity, as represented by his mother. A boy's mother is his primary caretaker. At the same time, masculinity is idealized or accorded superiority, and thereby becomes even more desirable. Although fathers are not as salient as mothers in daily interaction, mothers and children often idealize them and give them ideological primacy, precisely because of their absence and seeming inaccessibility, and because of the organization and ideology of male dominance in the larger society.

Masculinity becomes an issue in a way that femininity does not. Masculinity does not become an issue because of some intrinsic male biology, nor because masculine roles are inherently more difficult than feminine roles, however. Masculinity becomes an issue as a direct result of a boy's experience of himself in his family—as a result of his being parented by a woman. For children of both genders, mothers represent regression and lack of autonomy. A boy associates these issues with his gender identification as well. Dependence on his mother, attachment to her, and identification with her represent that which is not masculine; a boy must reject dependence and deny attachment and identification. Masculine gender role training becomes much more rigid than feminine. A boy represses those qualities he takes to be feminine inside himself, and rejects and devalues women and whatever he considers to be feminine in the social world.

Thus, boys define and attempt to construct their sense of masculinity largely in negative terms. Given that masculinity is so elusive, it becomes important for masculine identity that certain social activities are defined as masculine and superior, and that women are believed unable to do many of the things defined as socially important. It becomes important to think that women's economic and social contribution cannot equal men's. The secure possession of certain realms, and the insistence that these realms are superior to the maternal world of youth, become crucial both to the definition of masculinity and

to a particular boy's own masculine gender identification.[13]

Freud describes the genesis of this stance in the masculine oedipal crisis. A boy's struggle to free himself from his mother and become masculine generates "the contempt felt by men for a sex which is the lesser"[14]— "What we have come to consider the normal male contempt for women."[15]

Both sexes learn to feel negatively toward their mother during the oedipal period. A girl's negative feelings, however, are not so much contempt and devaluation as fear and hostility: "The little girl, incapable of such contempt because of her own identical nature, frees herself from the mother with a degree of hostility far greater than any comparable hostility in the boy."[16] A boy's contempt serves to free him not only from his mother but also from the femininity within himself. It therefore becomes entangled with the issue of masculinity and is generalized to all women. A girl's hostility remains tied more to her relationship to her mother (and/or becomes involved in self-depreciation).

A boy's oedipus complex is directly tied to issues of masculinity, and the devaluation of women is its "normal" outcome. A girl's devaluation of or hostility toward her mother may be a part of the process, but its "normal" outcome, by contrast, entails acceptance of her own femininity and identification with her mother. Whatever the individual resolution of the feminine oedipus complex, however, it does not become institutionalized in the same way.

Freud "explains" the development of boys' contempt for mothers as coming from their perception of genital differences, particularly their mother's "castration." He takes this perception to be unmediated by social experience, and not in need of explanation. As many commentators have pointed out, it did not occur to Freud that such differential valuation and ensuing contempt were not in the natural order of things. However, the analysis of "Little Hans," which provides the most direct (reported) evidence that Freud had for such an assumption, shows that in fact Hans's father perpetuated and created such beliefs in his son—beliefs about the inferiority of female genitalia, denial of the feminine role in gestation and parturition, views that men have something and women have nothing, rather than having something different."[17]

Karen Horney, unlike Freud, does take masculine contempt for and devaluation of women as in need of interactive and developmental explanation.[18] According to her, these phenomena are manifestations of a deeper "dread of women"—a masculine fear and terror of maternal omnipotence that arises as one major consequence of their early caretaking and socialization by women. Psychoanalysts previously had stressed boys' fears of their fathers. Horney argues that these fears are less severe and therefore less in need of being repressed. Unlike their fears of a mother, boys do not react to a father's total and incomprehensible control over his child's life at a time when the child has no reflective capacities for understanding: "Dread of the father is more actual and tangible, less uncanny in quality."[19] Moreover, since their father is male like them, boys' fears of men do not entail admission of feminine weakness or dependency on women: "Masculine self-regard suffers less in this way."[20]

Dread of the mother is ambivalent, however. Although a boy fears her, he also finds her seductive and attractive. He cannot simply dismiss and ignore her. Boys and men develop psychological and cultural/ideological mechanisms to cope with their fears without giving up women altogether. They create folk legends, beliefs, and poems that ward off the dread by externalizing and objectifying women: "It is not . . . that I dread her; it is that she herself is malignant, capable of any crime, a beast of prey, a vampire, a witch, insatiable in her desires . . . the very personification of what

is sinister."[21] They deny dread at the expense of realistic views of women. On the one hand, they glorify and adore: "There is no need for me to dread a being so wonderful, so beautiful, nay, so saintly."[22] On the other, they disparage: "It would be too ridiculous to dread a creature who, if you take her all round, is such a poor thing."[23]

Unfortunately, Horney does not point to developmental implications of the mother's overwhelming power for girls. Although a girl may well develop a fear or dread of her mother, this dread does not become tied up for her with the assertion of genderedness. Because she is also female, and presumably does not feel herself dreadful or fearsome, but rather the reverse, it is likely that a girl will not generalize her dread to all females. Moreover, because women's and girls' experiences take place in a male-dominant society, whatever fear or dread individual women do experience is less likely to gain cultural or normative import.

Horney's article implicitly claims that fear and disparagement of women and assertions of masculine superiority are universal. This claim needs further specification, since the extent of men's "dread of women and need to assert masculine superiority varies widely among different societies.[24] Horney noticed the dread of women because it was salient in her own society. Tendencies in contemporary family organization have produced a mother-son relationship that leads to disparagement and fear of women. Direct patriarchal authority and paternal salience in the family have declined as a result of men's steady loss of autonomy in work, and the growing submission of their lives to work requirements (whether the work of bureaucratized and salaried professionals and managers, or of proletarianized craft workers and small entrepreneurs).[25]

Grete Bibring provides a suggestive clinical account. She describes the fathers and mothers in "matriarchal" families in the

United States.*[26] As described by their grown sons and daughters (Bibring's patients), the mothers in these households were active and strong, efficient household managers, and generally seemed superior and more competent than their husbands. Fathers were generally ineffectual in the home and uninvolved in family life. (Bibring seems to be talking about professional, middle- and upper-middle-class husbands. What she says, however, would seem to apply equally to working-class households, where fathers have jobs which keep them away even longer hours, may exhaust them even more, and where much social life is sex-segregated.) Bibring summarizes the situation:

> At closer investigation it seems evident that in all these cases the father did not participate essentially in the upbringing of his children, that social as well as moral standards, religious and aesthetic values were mostly conveyed by the mother. The same holds true of praise and reprimands. The setting of goals and the supervision of the boy's development lay in her hands. The father appears in all these instances as a friendly onlooker rather than as an important participant.[27]

The sons in these families considered their mothers to be rejecting, punitive, ambitious, and cold. But the women who grew up in this "matriarchal" setting were less likely to reject the feminine role than female patients coming from patriarchal family settings. Bibring concludes, guided by the sons' concrete descriptions of their mothers' behavior, that the mothers were thoughtful and responsible and that the fathers' "absence," rather than anything the mother actually did, was the "major factor in determining these attitudes in the sons."[28] For these sons, whatever the social reality and however their mother acted, there was simply "too much of mother."[29]

*Horkheimer suggests, in contrast to Bibring, that in Germany at least this decline in real paternal authority and power was accompanied by a rise in what we might call pseudoauthority.

Sons in this situation inevitably experience their mother as overwhelming and resent her for this. They both admire and fear her, experience her as both seductive and rejecting. In such a situation, mothers themselves may also reciprocate and encourage their sons' incestuous wishes as well as their infantile dependence. As Bibring puts it, they are "as much in need of a husband as a son is of his father."[30] Moreover, because there is no mediator to his oedipal wishes—no father to protect him—a boy's wishes also build. He often projects both these and the fears they engender onto his mother, making her both a temptress and hostile punisher. Sons take these fears with them into adulthood and experience the world as filled with "dangerous, cold, cutting women."[31]

Too much of mother results from the relative absence of the father and nearly exclusive maternal care provided by a woman isolated in a nuclear household. It creates men's resentment and dread of women, and their search for nonthreatening, undemanding, dependent, even infantile women—women who are "simple, and thus safe and warm."[32] Through these same processes men come to reject, devalue, and even ridicule women and things feminine.

Women's mothering produces a psychological and ideological complex in men concerning women's secondary valuation and sexual inequality. Because women are responsible for early child care and for most later socialization as well, because fathers are more absent from the home, and because men's activities generally have been removed from the home while women's have remained within it, boys have difficulty in attaining a stable masculine gender-role identification. Boys fantasize about and idealize the masculine role and their fathers, and society defines it as desirable.

Given that men control not only major social institutions but the very definition and constitution of society and culture, they have the power and ideological means to enforce these perceptions as more general norms, and to hold each other accountable for their enforcement. (This is not solely a matter of force. Since these norms define men as superior, men gain something by maintaining them.[33]) The structure of parenting creates ideological and psychological modes which reproduce orientations to and structures of male dominance in individual men, and builds an assertion of male superiority into the definition of masculinity itself.

The same repressions, denials of affect and attachment, rejection of the world of women and things feminine, appropriation of the world of men and identification with the father that create a psychology of masculine superiority also condition men for participation in the capitalist work world. Both capitalist accumulation and proper work habits in workers have never been purely a matter of economics. Particular personality characteristics and behavioral codes facilitated the transition to capitalism. Capitalists developed inner direction, rational planning, and organization, and workers developed a willingness to come to work at certain hours and work steadily, whether or not they needed money that day.

Psychological qualities become perhaps even more important with the expansion of bureaucracy and hierarchy: In modern capitalism different personality traits are required at different levels of the bureaucratic hierarchy.[*34] Lower-level jobs are often directly and continuously supervised and are best performed by someone willing to obey rules and conform to external authority. Moving up the hierarchy, jobs require greater dependability and predictability, the ability to act without direct and continuous supervision. In technical, professional, and managerial positions, workers must on their own initiative carry out the goals and values of the organization for which they work, making those goals and values their own. Often they must be able to draw on their interpersonal capacities as a skill. Parental child-rearing values and practices (insofar as these latter reflect parental values) reflect these differences: Working-class parents are more likely to value obedience, conformity to external authority, neatness, and other "behavioral" characteristics in their children; middle-class parents emphasize more "internal" and interpersonal characteristics such as responsibility, curiosity, self-motivation, self-control, and consideration.[35]

These behavioral and personality qualities differentiate appropriately according to the requirements of work in the different strata. But they share an important commonality. Conformity to behavioral rules and external authority, predictability and dependability, the ability to take on others' values and goals as one's own, all reflect an orientation external to oneself and one's own standards, a lack of autonomous and creative self-direction. The nuclear, isolated, neolocal family in which women mother is suited to the production in children of these cross-class personality commitments and capacities.

Parsonians and theorists of the Frankfurt Institute for Social Research have drawn on psychoanalysis to show how the relative position of fathers and mothers in the contemporary family helps to create the foundations of men's psychological acquiescence in capitalist domination.** They discuss how the family prepares men for subordination to authority, for participation in an alienated work world,

---

*... The work I am drawing on has investigated only the capitalist West, and especially the United States.

**I do not mean to suggest here that a psychological account gives a complete explanation for the reproduction of workers. The main reason people go to work is because they need to in order to live. The family creates the psychological *foundations* of acquiescence in work and of work skills. But even reinforced by schools and other socializing institutions, it is clear that socialization for work never works well enough to prevent all resistance.

for generalized achievement orientation.[36] These complementary and overlapping accounts discuss personality traits required of all strata, centering on lack of inner autonomy and availability to manipulation. Yet their differences of emphasis point to variation among strata as well. Parsonians discuss more how middle-class families prepare boys to be white-collar bureaucrats, professionals, technicians, and managers; Frankfurt theorists discuss more the genesis of working-class character traits. Parsonians start from the growing significance of the mother, and her sexualized involvement with her male infant. Frankfurt theorists start from the historical obverse, from the decline in the father's role and his growing distance, unavailability, and loss of authority in the family.

In American families, Parsons argues, where mothers tend not to have other primary affective figures around, a mutual erotic investment between son* and mother develops—an investment the mother can then manipulate. She can love, reward, and frustrate him at appropriate moments in order to get him to delay gratification and sublimate or repress erotic needs. This close, exclusive, preoedipal mother-child relationship first develops dependency in a son, creating a motivational basis for early learning and a foundation for dependency on others. When a mother "rejects" her son or pushes him to be more independent, the son carries his still powerful dependence with him, creating in him both a general need to please and conform outside of the relationship to the mother herself and a strong assertion of independence. The isolated, husband-absent

mother thus helps to create in her son a pseudoindependence masking real dependence, and a generalized sense that he ought to "do well" rather than an orientation to specific goals. This generalized sense can then be used to serve a variety of specific goals— goals not set by these men themselves. The oedipus complex in the contemporary family creates a "'dialectical' relationship between dependency, on the one hand, independence and achievement on the other."[37]

In an earlier period of capitalist development, individual goals were important for more men, and entrepreneurial achievement as well as worker discipline had to be based more on inner moral direction and repression. Earlier family arrangements, where dependency was not so salient nor the mother-child bond so exclusive, produced this greater inner direction. Today, with the exception of a very few, individual goals have become increasingly superseded by the goals of complex organizations: "Goals can no longer be directly the individual's responsibility and cannot be directly specified to him as a preparation for his role."[38] The contemporary family, with its manipulation of dependency in the mother-child relationship, and its production of generalized achievement orientation rather than inner goals and standards, produces personalities "that have become a fully fluid resource for societal functions."[39]

Slater extends Parsons's discussion. People who start life with only one or two emotional objects, he argues, develop a "willingness to put all [their] emotional eggs in one symbolic basket."[40] Boys who grow up in American middle-class nuclear families have this experience.** Because they received such

---

*Parsons and his colleagues talk of the "mother-child" relationship. However, they focus on erotic, oedipal attachment as motivating, and on the development of character traits which are appropriate to masculine work capacity and not to feminine expressive roles. It is safe to conclude, therefore, that the child they have in mind is male.

**Again, girls do as well, and both genders transfer it to monogamic, jealous tendencies. But Slater is talking about the sexually toned oedipal/preoedipal relationship that is more specific to boys.

a great amount of gratification from their mother relative to what they got from anyone else, and because their relationship to her was so exclusive, it is unlikely that they can repeat such a relationship. They relinquish their mother as an object of dependent attachment and deny their dependence on her, but, because she was so uniquely important, they retain her as an oedipally motivated object to win in fantasy—they retain an unconscious sense that there is one finally satisfying prize to be won. They turn their lives into a search for a success that will both prove their independence and win their mother. But because they have no inner sense of goals or real autonomy apart from this unconscious, unattainable goal from the past, and because success in the external world does not for the most part bring real satisfactions or real independence, their search is likely to be neverending. They are likely to continue to work and to continue to accept the standards of the situation that confronts them.

This situation contrasts to that of people who have had a larger number of pleasurable relationships in early infancy. Such people are more likely to expect gratification in immediate relationships and maintain commitments to more people, and are less likely to deny themselves now on behalf of the future. They would not be the same kind of good worker, given that work is defined in individualist, noncooperative, outcome-oriented ways, as it is in our society.

Horkheimer and other Frankfurt theorists focus on the oedipal relationship of son to father, rather than son to mother, and on the internalization of paternal authority. The family in every society transmits orientation to authority. However, the nature of this orientation changes with the structure of authority in the economic world. During the period of early capitalist development, when independent craftspeople, shopkeepers, farmers, and professionals were relatively more important, more fathers had some economic power in the world.* This paternal authority expressed itself also in the family. Sons could internalize their father's authority through a classic oedipal struggle. They could develop inner direction and self-motivation and accept "realistic" limits on their power: "Childhood in a limited family [became] an habituation to authority."[41] But with the growth of industry, fathers became less involved in family life. They did not just physically leave home, however. As more fathers became dependent on salaries and wages, on the vagaries of the labor market and the authority of capitalists and managers, the material base for their family authority was also eroded. Fathers reacted by developing authoritarian modes of acting. But because there was no longer a real basis for their authority, there could be no genuine oedipal struggle. Instead of internalizing paternal authority, and developing a sense of self with autonomous inner principles, sons remained both fearful of and attracted to external authority. These characteristics were appropriate to obedience and conformity on the job and in the world at large.

Contemporary family structure produces not only malleability and lack of internalized standards, but often a search for manipulation. These character traits lend themselves to the manipulations of modern capitalism—to media and product consumerism, to the attempt to legitimate a polity that serves people unequally, and finally to work performance. The decline of the oedipal father creates an orientation to external authority and behavioral obedience. Exclusive maternal involvement and the extension of dependence create a generalized need to please and to "succeed," and a seeming independence. This need to succeed can help to make someone dependable and re-

---

*The Frankfurt theorists are not explicit and in their implicit account are inconsistent about class. The reading of their account that is to me most consistent with the changes in work and the family they describe is that they are talking about the proletarianization of the traditionally independent middle strata.

liable. Because it is divorced from specific goals and real inner standards but has involved the maintenance of an internal dependent relationship, it can also facilitate the taking of others' goals as one's own, producing the pseudoindependent organization man.

An increasingly father-absent, mother-involved family produces in men a personality that both corresponds to masculinity and male dominance as these are currently constituted in the sex-gender system, and fits appropriately with participation in capitalist relations of production. Men continue to enforce the sexual division of spheres as a defense against powerlessness in the labor market. Male denial of dependence and of attachment to women helps to guarantee both masculinity and performance in the world of work. The relative unavailability of the father and overavailability of the mother create negative definitions of masculinity and men's fear and resentment of women, as well as the lack of in-

ner autonomy in men that enables, depending on particular family constellation and class origin, either rule-following or the easy internalization of the values of the organization.

Thus, women's and men's personality traits and orientations mesh with the sexual and familial division of labor and unequal ideology of gender and shape their asymmetric location in a structure of production and reproduction in which women are in the first instance mothers and wives and men are workers. This structure of production and reproduction requires and presupposes those specific relational modes, between husband and wife, and mother and children, which form the center of the family in contemporary society. An examination of the way that gender personality is expressed in adulthood reveals how women and men create, and are often committed to creating, the interpersonal relationships which underlie and reproduce the family structure that produced them.

NOTES

1. For a review of the literature which argues this, see Biller, 1971, *Father, Child*. See also Stoller, 1965, "The Sense of Maleness." For a useful recent formulation, see Johnson, 1975, "Fathers, Mothers."

2. See Mead, 1949, *Male and Female*; Michelle Z. Rosaldo, 1974, "Woman, Culture, and Society"; Nancy Chodorow, 1971, "Being and Doing," and 1974, "Family Structure and Feminine Personality," in Rosaldo and Lamphere, eds., *Woman, Culture and Society*, pp. 43–66; Beatrice Whiting, ed., 1963, *Six Cultures*; Beatrice B. Whiting and John W. M. Whiting, 1975, *Children of Six Cultures*; John Whiting, 1959, "Sorcery, Sin"; Burton and Whiting, 1961, "The Absent Father."

3. See Richard T. Roessler, 1971, "Masculine Differentiation and Feminine Constancy," *Adolescence*, 6, #22, pp. 187–196; E. M. Bennett and L. R. Cohen, 1959, "Men and Women, Personality Patterns and Contrasts," *Genetic Psychology Monographs*, 59, pp. 101–155; Johnson, 1963, "Sex Role Learning," and 1975, "Fathers, Mothers"; Stoller, 1964, "A Contribution to the Study," 1965, "The Sense of Male-

ness," and 1968, "The Sense of Femaleness," *Psychoanalytic Quarterly*, 37, #1, pp. 42–55.

4. See Biller, 1971, *Father, Child*.

5. Mitscherlich, 1963, *Society Without the Father*; Philip E. Slater, 1961, "Toward a Dualistic Theory of Identification," *Merrill-Palmer Quarterly of Behavior and Development*, 7, #2, pp. 113–126; Robert F. Winch, 1962, *Identification and Its Familial Determinants*; David B. Lynn, 1959, "A Note on Sex Differences," and 1962, "Sex Role and Parent."

6. Johnson, 1975, "Fathers, Mothers," and Maccoby and Jacklin, 1974, *The Psychology of Sex Differences*, point this out.

7. D. B. Lynn, 1959, "A Note on Sex Differences," p. 130.

8. See Slater, 1961, "Toward a Dualistic Theory," and Johnson, 1975, "Fathers, Mothers."

9. This phrase is Arlie Hochschild's. (See Arlie Russell Hochschild, 1975b, "The Sociology of Feeling and Emotion: Selected Possibilities," in Marcia Millman and Rosabeth Moss Kanter, eds., *Another Voice*, pp. 280–307.) She uses it to refer to the internal

work women do to make their feelings accord with how they think they ought to feel. My usage here extends also to work for and upon other people's emotions.

10. See, for example, Johnson, 1975, "Fathers, Mothers"; Parsons and Bales, 1955, *Family, Socialization*; Deutsch, 1944, *Psychology of Women*.

11. Alice Balint, 1939, "Love for the Mother."

12. Rosaldo, 1974, "Women, Culture and Society."

13. On these issues, see Lynn, 1959, "A Note on Sex Differences," and 1962, "Sex Role and Parent"; Parsons, 1942, "Age and Sex"; Mitscherlich, 1963, *Society Without the Father*; Slater, 1968, *The Glory of Hera*; Mead, 1949, *Male and Female*.

14. Freud, 1925, "Some Psychical Consequences," p. 253.

15. Brunswick, 1940, "The Preoedipal Phase," p. 246.

16. Ibid.

17. Freud, 1909, "Analysis of a Phobia."

18. Horney, 1932, "The Dread of Women."

19. Ibid., p. 351.

20. Ibid.

21. Ibid., p. 135.

22. Ibid., p. 136.

23. Ibid.

24. Slater (1968, *The Glory of Hera*, p. 19) points this out. For cross-cultural comparisons of the relationship between family structure and men's preoccupation with masculinity, see, in addition to Slater, Whiting et al., 1958, "The Function of Male Initiation Rites"; Whiting, 1959, "Sorcery, Sin"; and Burton and Whiting, 1961, "The Absent Father."

25. On the relation of proletarianization to the decline of the oedipal father, see Horkheimer, 1936, "Authority and the Family," and Mitscherlich, 1963, *Society Without the Father*.

26. Bibring, 1953, "On the 'Passing of the Oedipus Complex.'"

27. Ibid, p. 280.

28. Ibid, p. 281.

29. Ibid.

30. Ibid.

31. Ibid., p. 282.

32. Ibid.

33. But for discussions of ways that this accountability is actively maintained, see Joseph H. Pleck and Jack Sawyer, 1974, *Men and Masculinity*, and Marc F. Fasteau, 1974, *The Male Machine*.

34. My formulation of the personality requirements of the hierarchical firm follows Edwards, 1975, "The Social Relations of Production."

35. See Melvin L. Kohn, 1969, *Class and Conformity*.

36. Frankfurt Institute, 1972, *Aspects*; Horkheimer, 1936, "Authority and the Family"; Mitscherlich, 1963, *Society Without the Father*; Parsons, 1964, *Social Structure and Personality*; Parsons and Bales, 1955, *Family, Socialization*; Slater, 1970, *The Pursuit of Loneliness*, and 1974, *Earthwalk*.

37. Talcott Parsons with Winston White, 1961, "The Link Between Character and Society," in *Social Structure and Personality*, p. 218.

38. Ibid., p. 203.

39. Ibid., p. 233.

40. Slater, 1974, *Earthwalk*, p. 131. See also Slater, 1970, *The Pursuit of Loneliness*.

41. Horkheimer, 1936, "Authority and the Family," p. 108.

REFERENCE

Parsons, Talcott. 1964. "The Kinship System of the Contemporary United States" in Talcott Parsons, ed., *Essays in Sociological Theory*. New York: Free Press.

2

The Manhood Puzzle

DAVID D. GILMORE

There are continuities of masculinity that transcend cultural differences.
—Thomas Gregor, *Anxious Pleasures*

Are there continuities of masculinity across cultural boundaries, as the anthropologist Thomas Gregor says (1985:209)? Are men everywhere alike in their concern for being "manly?" If so, why? Why is the demand made upon males to "be a man" or "act like a man" voiced in so many places? And why are boys and youths so often tested or indoctrinated before being awarded their manhood? These are questions not often asked in the growing literature on sex and gender roles. Yet given the recent interest in sexual stereotyping, they are ones that need to be considered if we are to understand both sexes and their relations.

Regardless of other normative distinctions made, all societies distinguish between male and female; all societies also provide institutionalized sex-appropriate roles for adult men and women. A very few societies recognize a third, sexually intermediary category, such as the Cheyenne *berdache*, the Omani *xanith*, and the Tahitian *mahu*, but even in these rare cases of androgynous genders, the individual must make a life choice of identity and abide by prescibed rules of sexual comportment. In addition, most societies hold consensual ideals—

guiding or admonitory images—for conventional masculinity and femininity by which individuals are judged worthy members of one or the other sex and are evaluated more generally as moral actors. Such ideal statuses and their attendant images, or models, often become psychic anchors, or psychological identities, for most individuals, serving as a basis for self-perception and self-esteem (D'Andrade 1974:36).

These gender ideals, or guiding images, differ from culture to culture. But, as Gregor and others (e.g., Brandes 1980; Lonner 1980; Raphael 1988) have argued, underlying the surface differences are some intriguing similarities among cultures that otherwise display little in common. Impressed by the statistical frequency of such regularities in sexual patterning, a number of observers have recently argued that cultures are more alike than different in this regard. For example, Gregor (1985:200) studied a primitive Amazonian tribe and compared its sex ideals to those of contemporary America. Finding many subsurface similarities in the qualities expected of men and women, he concludes that our different cultures represent only a symbolic veneer masking a bedrock of sexual thinking. In another study, the psychologist Lonner (1980:147) echoes this conclusion. He argues that culture is "only a thin veneer covering an essential universality" of gender dimorphism. In their comprehensive survey of sex images in thirty different cultures, Williams and Best (1982:30) conclude that there is "substantial similarity" to be found "panculturally in the traits ascribed to men and women."

Whether or not culture is only a thin veneer over a deep structure is a complicated question: As the rare third sexes show, we must not see in every culture "a Westerner struggling to get out" (Munroe and Munroe 1980:25). But most social scientists would agree that there do exist striking regularities in standard male and female roles across cultural boundaries regardless of other social arrangements (Archer and Lloyd 1985:283–284). The one regularity that concerns me here is the often dramatic ways in which cultures construct an appropriate manhood—the presentation or "imaging" of the male role. In particular, there is a constantly recurring notion that real manhood is different from simple anatomical maleness, that it is not a natural condition that comes about spontaneously through biological maturation but rather is a precarious or artificial state that boys must win against powerful odds. This recurrent notion that manhood is problematic, a critical threshold that boys must pass through testing, is found at all levels of sociocultural development regardless of what other alternative roles are recognized. It is found among the simplest hunters and fishermen, among peasants and sophisticated urbanized peoples; it is found in all continents and environments. It is found among both warrior peoples and those who have never killed in anger.

Moreover, this recurrent belief represents a primary and recurrent difference from parallel notions of femaleness. Although women, too, in any society are judged by sometimes stringent sexual standards, it is rare that their very status as woman forms part of the evaluation. Women who are found deficient or deviant according to these standards may be criticized as immoral, or they may be called unladylike or its equivalent and subjected to appropriate sanctions, but rarely is their right to a gender identity questioned in the same public, dramatic way that it is for men. The very paucity of linguistic labels for females echoing the epithets "effete," "unmanly," "effeminate," "emasculated," and so on, attest to this archetypical difference between sex judgments worldwide. And it is far more assaultive (and frequent) for men to be challenged in this way than for women.

Perhaps the difference between male and female should not be overstated, for "femininity" is also something achieved by women who seek social approval. But as a social icon, femininity seems to be judged differently. It usually involves questions of body ornament or sexual allure, or other essentially cosmetic behaviors that enhance, rather than create, an inherent quality of character. An authentic femininity rarely involves tests or proofs of action, or confrontations with dangerous foes: win-or-lose contests dramatically played out on the public stage. Rather than a critical threshold passed by traumatic testing, an either/or condition, femininity is more often construed as a biological given that is culturally refined or augmented. . . .

REFERENCES

Archer, John, and Barbara Lloyd. 1985. *Sex and Gender.* Cambridge: Cambridge University Press.

Brandes, Stanley H. 1980. *Metaphors of Masculinity: Sex and Status in Andalusian Folklore.* Philadelphia: University of Pennsylvania Press.

D'Andrade, Roy G. 1974. Sex differences and cultural institutions. In *Culture and Personality: Contemporary Readings,* ed. Robert A. LeVine, pp. 16–19. Chicago: Aldine.

Gregor, Thomas. 1985. *Anxious Pleasures: The Sexual Life of an Amazonian People.* Chicago: University of Chicago Press.

Lonner, Walter J. 1980. The search for psychological universals. In *Handbook of Cross-Cultural Psychology,* ed. Harry C. Triandis and William W. Lambert, 1:143–204. Boston: Allyn and Bacon.

Munroe, Robert L., and Ruth H. Munroe. 1980. Perspectives suggested by anthropological data. In *Handbook of Cross-Cultural Psychology,* ed. Harry C. Triandis and William W. Lambert, 1:253–317. Boston: Allyn and Bacon.

Raphael, Ray. 1988. *The Men from the Boys: Rites of Passage in Male America.* Lincoln, Nebr.: University of Nebraska Press.

Williams, John E., and Deborah L. Best. 1982. *Measuring Sex Stereotypes: A Thirty-Nation Study.* Beverly Hills: Sage Publs.

Necessity and the Invention of Mothering

BARBARA J. RISMAN

What happens when individuals find themselves in ambiguous situations, when gendered selves are socialized for traditional family life but current interactional contexts shift? How flexible are we? Can men mother even if they have never dressed or bathed a doll? Male mothering isn't common, not now and not in the past. But is it possible?

All three levels of the gender structure push most men and women toward gendered lives and choices. Sometimes, however, this structure is disrupted; the planned courses of family lives are changed by unexpected circumstances (see, e.g., Gerson 1993). In this chapter, I acknowledge the macro-institutional aspects of the gender structure, which organize both family and work so as to support male advantage in the marketplace and female responsibility in the home. I focus on how individuals fare when the parental roles that men are socialized for (in this case, to be breadwinner fathers) are radically altered and men find themselves the sole caretakers of young children. Do gendered selves make "mothering" problematic for men? Or do the interactional expectations of their roles as custodial parents shape their lives more directly?

Although men have been involved at some places and times in the rearing of children—particularly boys old enough to be incorporated in economic labor—we use the phrase "mothering" because the nurturing of children has mostly been women's work.[1] This responsibility for the day-to-day nurturing that we have come to call mothering is, perhaps, the aspect of gender structure most constant across time and cultures.

Although I call mothering women's work, I do not mean to imply that it has not also been women's joy. The word "work" sometimes calls forth negative connotations: hard, unpleasant, performed only as an obligation. I use the word quite differently. Work must get done for a society to exist, yet working—doing what needs to ensure collective and individual survival—can and should be fun, fulfilling, and able to provide meaning for our very existence. Perhaps mothering is the best example of that positive kind of work—work that involves the shaping of human beings can be especially creative and fulfilling. And such work is of course critical to the survival of any society.

Can only women do this work well? Can only women be effective as primary nurturers? The answer is crucial, for no one would want to abolish gender structure at the cost of harming our children. But I do not believe that sexual equality and a post-gendered society would hurt future generations of children. My research suggests that men *can* mother.

Scholars and researchers who work at the individual level of analysis do not agree on this issue. Socialization theorists and feminists who adhere to a revisionist psychoanalytic tradition argue that childhood experiences determine the psychic predisposition to mothering (Chodorow 1978; Gilligan 1982). If we change the way we treat our sons and daughters, they argue, we could rear a generation of boys and girls who are equally capable as nurturers. Biosocial theorists, however, use evolutionary, genetic, and hormonal evidence to suggest that women have a biological predisposition to bonding with and caring for infants, although compensatory training is sometimes suggested to overcome these biological impediments to male nurturing (see Rossi 1984 for this argument). But all individual-level theories maintain that the desire to mother (or not) is the result of an internalized gendered identity. The implicit presumption often made by those who study individuals is that this internalized psychological motivation is why women nurture their children so intensively and men do not.

INTERACTIONAL BASES OF MOTHERING

Rules that are part of the gender structure at the interactional level can be conceptualized as folklore or as cognitive images that must be attended to when considering one's own actions. We face such images in every interpersonal relationship. There is rarely any sociological ambivalence in the cognitive images of parenthood, even today. Mothers, employed or not, are still expected to nurture their children emotionally and physically. Fathers are still expected to earn a family wage, even when that is not possible. Fathers are also expected to help mothers with nurturing, but they are not judged incompetent if they do not help very much as long as they continue to earn a good living.

Not all mothers or fathers turn this folk story into reality, but all are aware of the nor-matively accepted cognitive images. And the research on dual-earner couples shows that these images are indeed powerful organizers of many lives. Even when both parents work for pay the children and the home remain primarily the wife's responsibility (Brines 1994; Berardo, Shehan, and Leslie 1987; Berk 1985; Coverman 1983). Hochschild (1989) estimates that employed wives spend the equivalent of a month a year doing the "second shift" at home, thus adding appreciably to their work time. Such inequity exists only because it is invisible, hidden by the strong cultural beliefs about the natural bases of nurturance and mothering. Fathers are not usually expected to nurture their children intensively, but because children demand such nurturing, the cognitive images blur somewhat for single fathers. The status of single parent overrides sex category for the expectations of and demands made on single fathers not only by their children but also by friends, family members, and the educational system. The gender theory that I propose predicts that the consequences of gender structure at the interactional level, the situational demands, and the clearly expressed need of young children to be nurtured will create behaviors in men that are usually called "mothering." My hypothesis is that the consequences of gender structure at the interactional level are more powerful predictors of gendered parenting than are gendered selves.

To test these ideas I compared the parental behaviors and household strategies of single fathers with those of single mothers, dual-paycheck couples, and traditional mother-at-home families. If individual-level factors like socialization or biology are the keys to parental behavior, single fathers would have neither the motivation nor the skills to provide appropriate primary care for children; their care would not be equivalent to that provided by mothers. If, however, interactional factors are more influential, the father can take on the primary caretaker role and fulfill expectations for adequate care made by extended family,

schools, and neighbors and the children themselves. He will produce mothering that is very
similar to that provided by a woman in the
same situation.

My own study on single fathers was designed to test the relative power of individual-level versus interactional explanations for
empirically observable sex differences in
parenting styles (Risman 1987).... [In the following section,] I will mention what we know
about single fathers from other sources.

REVIEW OF THE LITERATURE ON SINGLE FATHERS

There has been much debate over the important question of how children who live in
single-parent households thrive versus those
who live with both parents. That is not my
concern here. Instead, I focus on how single
fathers and single mothers are similar and different, and why.

Descriptive findings about single fathers
are remarkably consistent across studies
(Chang and Deinard 1982; Gasser and Taylor
1976; George and Wilding 1972; Greenberg
1979; Hanson 1981; Mendes 1979; Orthner,
Brown, and Ferguson 1976; Risman 1986;
Rosenthal and Keshet 1981). Homemaking
does not appear to be a problem for single
fathers—few recruit female kin or paid help
to perform the "female" tasks of housekeeping. And although American single fathers do
report some problems, such as worrying because their daughters lack a female role
model, most respondents generally feel satisfied with their perceived competence as single parents and single adults.

Unfortunately, much of the research on
American men who are single fathers does
not compare them with other men or with single mothers. It simply describes small samples of predominantly white, middle-class
fathers (Ambert 1982; Defrain and Eirick
1981; Gasser and Taylor 1976; Greenberg 1979;
Hanson 1981; Mendes 1979; Orthner, Brown,
and Ferguson 1976; Risman 1986; Rosenthal

and Keshet 1981; Santrock and Warshak
1979). The fathers in these samples usually are
identified from such sources as parent organizations, media advertisements, and referrals,
and they frequently have similar incomes and
reasons for custody.

It is particularly problematic that American research has been based on such homogeneous samples, because English and
Australian studies, which include more economically deprived families, suggest that financial status is a key factor in men's
performance and satisfaction as single fathers (e.g., Ferri 1973; Hipgrave 1982; Murch
1973). In one large sample (George and Wilding 1972), fathers who reported financial
problems also felt less competent as parents.
Similarly, researchers whose samples include
many financially deprived families (Katz
1979; O'Brien 1982) tend to report more serious problems in both father-child relationships and father's role satisfaction.

There is a small body of research that
does explicitly compare single fathers and
single mothers concerning their parental behaviors and their children's development
(Ambert 1982; Defrain and Eirick 1981;
Downey and Powell 1993; Grief 1985; Hanson 1986; Luepnitz 1986; Pett and Vaughan-
Cole 1986; Rosen 1979; Santrock and Warshak
1979; Warshak 1986; Schnayer and Orr 1989).
These studies can be used to address the relative causal importance of individualist and
interactional factors on parenting behaviors.
Although the studies vary greatly in scope
and methodological strength, they all suggest that variables other than parental sex
greatly affect parent-child relationships in
single-parent homes.[2] The results are remarkably consistent: there are few differences in
either parental satisfaction or child's development based on the sex of the parent. The
results are similar whether the findings are
based on small samples with an intensive
study of each child's development (Santrock
and Warshak 1979; Rosen 1979) or on somewhat larger studies using primarily quantita-

tive measures of parents' attitudes and children's development (Luepnitz 1986).

One study reports an important and significant difference between children living with single mothers and with single fathers. Hanson (1986) found that children in single-father homes were slightly less physically healthy than those living with their mothers. The reverse was true for the parents: the fathers were healthier than the mothers. This finding, which seems to contradict most of the rest of the evidence, is based on a nonrepresentative sample of forty-two custodial parents recruited by the author. Still, it is the only study I know of that deals with health issues, and it indicates a need for further study on this topic.

Downey and Powell (1993) have provided a methodologically sophisticated study based on a nationally representative sample. Unfortunately, their question is even narrower than mine: Do children do better living with same-sex or opposite-sex parents after divorce? Still, I have found in their tables important information that sheds light on the more general question about gender differences in single parenting. Downey and Powell collected data from parents and their eighth-grade children. They found that when children living with single mothers and single fathers are compared with one another, the eighth-graders living with their *fathers* appeared to be doing better on social-psychological and educational standardized tests. But what was really happening was that children living with more well-to-do parents were scoring better on these tests, and most of the fathers were doing better economically than were the mothers. Given the well-documented gender gap in wages (Reskin and Padavic 1994) it should not be surprising that fathers earn higher salaries, on average, than do mothers. Once the effect of income was controlled statistically, however, the fathers' advantage disappeared. There are, instead, a few developmental advantages for children living with their mothers. Still, the major finding from this research is that there are few differences between single fathers and mothers as parents at least as measured by their children's development. (This does not differ whether the parent and child are the same or the opposite sex.)

In sum, the comparative research offers strong support for the importance of the interactional context in explaining gender-typed behavior. Nearly all the research published by others indicates that when fathers cannot depend on wives for child care, those fathers develop parenting behaviors similar to those of women. My own research was designed to further substantiate this hypothesis....

NOTES

1. Pruett (1987) argues that there may be more married nurturing fathers than we know because they are an "underground" phenomenon. He suggests that because societal expectations teach men that they ought to keep their distance from infants and focus on economic security, men who do otherwise might choose to hide their involvement. Nevertheless, Pruett's interview study is based on a small sample of married fathers referred to him from his own and others' pediatric practices.

2. There is some debate on whether there is interaction between parent's and child's sex; that is, whether boys do better living with their fathers and girls with their mothers. Santrock, Warshak, and El-

liot (1982) found that children living with same-sex parents were more socially competent, less angry, less demanding, and warmer than those living with opposite-sex custodial parents, but Rosen's research (1979) did not replicate these findings. Downey and Powell (1993) designed a study with a random sample of American teenagers and their parents and report absolutely no data to support the notion that children do better with same-sex parents. My own reading of this research is that there is no indication that children, as a rule, do better with one parent or another simply on the basis of whether the child is the same or the opposite sex.

REFERENCES

Ambert, A. 1982. "Differences in Children's Behavior Toward Custodial Mothers and Custodial Fathers." *Journal of Marriage and the Family* 44(1):73–86.

Berardo, Donna, Constance Shehan, and Gerald Leslie. 1987. "A Residue of Tradition: Jobs, Careers, and Spouse's Time in Housework." *Journal of Marriage and the Family* 49:381–390.

Berk, Sarah Fenstermaker. 1985. *The Gender Factory.* New York: Plenum.

Brines, Julie. 1994. "Economic Dependency and the Division of Labor." *American Journal of Sociology* 100(3):652–688.

Chang, Pi Nian, and Amos S. Deinard. 1982. "Single Father Caretakers: Demographic Characteristics and Adjustment Processes." *American Journal of Orthopsychiatry* 53:236–243.

Chodorow, Nancy. 1978. *The Reproduction of Mothering: Psychoanalysis and the Sociology of Gender.* Berkeley: University of California Press.

Coverman, Shelley. 1983. "Gender, Domestic Labor Time, and Wage Inequality." *American Sociological Review* 48:623–637.

Downey, Douglas B., and Brian Powell. 1993. "Do Children in Single-Parent Households Fare Better Living with Same-Sex Parents?" *Journal of Marriage and the Family* 55:55–71.

Defrain, John, and Rod Eirick. 1981. "Coping as Divorced Parents: A Comparative Study of Fathers and Mothers." *Family Relations* 30:265–273.

Ferri, E. 1973. "Characteristics of Motherless Families." *British Journal of Social Work* 3(1):91–100.

Gasser, R. D., and C. H. Taylor. 1976. "Role Adjustment of Single Fathers with Dependent Children." *Family Coordinator* 25(4):397–402.

George, V., and P. Wilding. 1972. *Motherless Families.* London: Routledge and Kegan Paul.

Gerson, Kathleen. 1993. *No Man's Land: Men's Changing Commitments to Family and Work.* New York: Basic Books.

Gilligan, Carol. 1982. *In a Different Voice: Psychological Theory and Women's Development.* Cambridge, Mass.: Harvard University Press.

Greenberg, J. B. 1979. "Single Parenting and Intimacy: A Comparison of Mothers and Fathers." *Alternative Lifestyles* 2(3):308–330.

Grief, Geoffrey. 1985. *Single Fathers.* Lexington, Mass.: Lexington Books.

Hanson, Shirley M. H. 1981. "Single Custodial Fathers and the Parent-Child Relationship." *Nursing Research* 30:202–204.

———. 1986. "Healthy Single-Parent Families." *Family Relations* 35:125–132.

Hipgrave, T. 1982. "Lone Fatherhood: A Problematic Status." In *The Father Figure,* 171–183, edited by L. McKee and M. O'Brien. London: Tavistock.

Hochschild, Arlie Russell. 1989. *The Second Shift: Working Parents and the Revolution at Home.* New York: Viking.

Katz, A. J. 1979. "Lone Fathers: Perspectives and Implications for Family Policy." *Family Coordinator* 28(4):521–528.

Luepnitz, Deborah Anna. 1986. "A Comparison of Maternal, Parental, and Joint Custody: Understanding the Varieties of Post-Divorce Family Life." *Journal of Divorce* 9(3):1–12.

Mendes, H. A. 1979. "Single-Parent Families—A Typology of Lifestyles." *Social Work* 24(3):193–200.

Murch, M. 1973. "Motherless Families Project: Bristol Council of Social Service Report on First Year's Work." *British Journal of Social Work* 3(3):365–376.

O'Brien, Mary. 1982. "Becoming a Lone Father: Differential Patterns and Experiences." In *The Father Figure,* 184–207, edited by L. McKee and M. O'Brien. London: Tavistock.

Orthner, Dennis K., Terry Brown, and Dennis Ferguson. 1976. "Single-Parent Fatherhood: An Emerging Family Lifestyle." *Family Coordinator* 25:429–437.

Pett, Marjorie A., and Beth Vaughan-Cole. 1986. "The Impact of Income Issues and Social Status on Post-Divorce Adjustment of Custodial Parents." *Family Relations* 35:1.

Pruett, Kyle D. 1987. *The Nurturing Father.* New York: Warner Books.

Reskin, Barbara, and Irene Padavic. 1994. *Women and Men at Work.* Thousand Oaks, Calif.: Pine Forge Press.

Risman, Barbara. 1986. "Can Men 'Mother'?: Life as a Single Father." *Family Relations* 35:95–102.

———. 1987. "Intimate Relationships from a Microstructural Perspective: Mothering Men." *Gender & Society* 1:6–32.

Rosen, R. 1979. "Children of Divorce." *Canadian Journal of Family Law* 2:403–415.

Rosenthal, K., and H. F. Keshet. 1981. *Fathers Without Partners.* Totowa, N.J.: Rowan and Littlefield.

Rossi, A. 1984. "Gender and Parenthood." *American Sociological Review* 49:1–19.

Santrock, J., and R. A. Warshak. 1979. "Father Custody and Social Development in Boys and Girls." *Journal of Social Issues* 35(4):112–125.

Santrock, J., R. Warshak, and G. Elliot. 1982. "Social Development and Parent-Child Interaction in Father Custody and Stepmother Families." In *Nontraditional Families: Parenting and Child Development,* edited by Michael E. Lamb. Hillsdale, N.J.: Erlbaum.

Schnayer, Reuben, and R. Robert Orr. 1989. "A Comparison of Children Living in Single-Mother and Single-Father Families." *Journal of Divorce* 12:171–184.

Warshak, Richard A. 1986. "Father-Custody and Child Development: A Review and Analysis of Psychological Research." *Behavioral Science and the Law* 4:185–202.

Cultural Scripts for Mothering

ANN WILLARD

No job is more important than raising a child in the first three years of life.
—Burton White, *The First Three Years*

*If you have someone you're counting on to do the job, your expectations
don't change just because a child has entered the picture.*
—Ron Greene, senior advisor for human relations training for Alcoa (quoted in the *Wall Street Journal*, September 19, 1984)

The quotations above represent two current viewpoints about employment and mothering. Conflicting views of what women "ought" to do permeate the media, the child development literature, and the emerging literature on adult development. These views are embodied in "cultural scripts" for motherhood, messages from the culture about the "right way" to be a mother.

Women, upon becoming mothers, are subject to numerous voices, each representing a different point of view—that of the child, as represented by a substantial literature, and that of friends, relatives, and often the institutions or businesses that employ women. Women are, thus, informed about what is good for the company, what is good for the baby, even, to some extent, what is good for the marriage.

Increasingly, there is a literature telling women what is "good for them." Studies have focused on whether or not it is good for mothers to work, and women have been advised that work is good for their mental health. Recently, some professional women have discovered the satisfaction of spending more time with their children and they advise women that it is better for them to stay at home (Fallows, 1985). Such global advice cannot take into account the situation of individual mothers who need, in fact, to make these decisions for themselves. This article outlines a process that women have found helpful in making decisions about employment and mothering.

Rather than seeking a rule that women should follow, it examines ways of making decisions, which take into consideration the complexity of women's lives and choices.

This study presents the viewpoint of women who are mothers of young children and who face often difficult decisions about motherhood and employment outside the home. In the midst of the many and conflicting voices which tell women what they should be doing as mothers, this study listens for the voice of the mother herself. For some women, their own voice is clear and strong as they make decisions about their lives and their mothering. For others, the cultural scripts, and the many voices which convey them, drown out the woman's own voice, leaving her vulnerable to the conflicts which are inherent in our culture's mixed messages about how to mother.

Cross-cultural evidence indicates that there is tremendous variation in the way work and mothering are organized. Cultures provide a script or a rather specific cultural set of ideas about how events should take place so that members of that culture can be guided through major life events and changes. Though there is never one-to-one correspondence between individual behavior and cultural prescriptions for how and what should take place, the script functions as a map for people in a culture, helping to guide their choices. A script works well when clear cultural expectations are supported by social structures that make it possible for people to carry out their roles in accord with the culture's expectations. When the script is not supported by appropriate social structures, it cannot serve as a useful guide. In a period of rapid social change, there may be a shared belief that following certain scripts continues to be possible and desirable, even though the script has come to contain inherent contradictions.

Japanese and Swedish cultures, for example, present women with very different scripts about how to carry out their roles as mothers, but the two cultures are similar in that they present women with a clear, non-conflictual script of how to deal with employment and mothering, and they provide social structures which support women in carrying out these roles. In Sweden, for example, the general availability of daycare means that the existence of a cultural script that calls for employment on the part of mothers is supported by provision of the means for carrying out the role. Japanese mothers have a very different script to follow in that they are expected to be responsible for not only nurturing their children but also for actively supporting their education. The existence of highly structured learning activities that demand the participation of the mothers—such as Suzuki violin lessons and preparations for children's school examinations—provide the vehicles through which mothers can meet those cultural expectations. Although conforming to such dominant cultural scripts can present problems for individual women whose interests are not compatible with these roles, the existence of a single dominant script and of social structures that support the script leave most women able to fulfill role expectations without experiencing a great deal of conflict.

American culture, in contrast, offers several scripts to women who become mothers. This range of choice can offer opportunities for personal development, but at the same time, the existence of more than one script can pose a dilemma or even a crisis, especially when the scripts are in conflict with one another or are not tied to the realities of women's lives because supportive social structures have not been developed. While many mothers are in the work force, structural supports for employed mothers, such as daycare, flexible work schedules, and adequate maternity and paternity leaves, are only beginning to be developed.

The cultural scripts for mothering in this culture are, increasingly, divergent from new realities of the lives of women who mother. A woman is left with three alternatives in this situation. First, she can try to follow a culturally prescribed script such as the traditional script that calls for the role of selfless wife and mother. Or she can try to follow the newer "superwoman" script that focuses on development of the self in the workplace in addition to being an ideal mother. The third possibility is to try to create ways of mothering that respond, not to a script, but to the reality of one's own family and situation. In order to follow this course, a woman must be able to define her "own terms" in the decision.

SCRIPT 1: SELFLESS WIFE AND MOTHER

There are volumes written on mothering. A virtual flood of literature has focused on mothers and their infants, and developmental psychologists from Bruner to Mahler have emphasized the early years as a time of tremendous importance in a child's development. In this literature on mother–child interaction, however, the mother appears as a shadowy figure. Beside the vivid, detailed descriptions of the developing infant is a woman who encourages or discourages the child's development, who smiles approvingly, offers a toy, appreciates or fails to recognize that her child's fingerpainting with the orange juice is a scientific exploration.

The reader of the literature on child development sees a picture of an unidimensional mother figure who appears to exist only in relation to her child. Turning to the literature on women's experience of motherhood, one would expect to find a representation of a multifaceted individual who has, among other relationships, this singularly important relationship with her child. Instead, the literature that looks most directly at women as mothers confuses the woman herself with her role as mother, and our sense of the maternal self disappears. There is, in fact, little study of the mother's self because the maternal role, generally, has been seen to be *selfless* (Attanucci, 1982). By this defini-

tion, it was only a bad, selfish mother who had a self to be studied.

Various schools of thought within psychology have contributed to this notion in different ways. The child development literature, concentrating on how the child can optimally develop, views other members of the child's environment only as instrumental to the child. The mother's self in this body of work is invisible. Other researchers recognized that the mother did, in fact, exist as an individual, and they designed studies intended to describe her experience. Traditionally, the study of women's experience of first-time mothering has followed women through the transition to motherhood and measured their adaptation to their new role. Since the cultural definition of motherhood remained relatively static for a number of years, researchers measuring adaptation seldom stopped to ask the question, "Adaptation to what?"

The focus on adaptation to the role of mother led to an emphasis on looking at intrapsychic variables to explain the variation that was found on such measures of adaptation as depression and self-esteem. Inevitably, when women appeared poorly adapted, the tendency was to see what was wrong with *them* rather than question the conditions of the role to which they were adapting. As long as the emphasis was on adaptation, the distinction between self and role was blurred.

Early studies of women's experience of motherhood came out of the psychoanalytic tradition and were influenced by assumptions that came with that theory and that period. One of the earliest writers to look directly at women's experience of mothering through a psychoanalytic lens was Deutsch (1945). She describes pregnancy as a time of extreme introversion during which psychic energies are diverted from the outside world. "With this step," she states, "the polarity between individual existence and service to the species changes its balance in favor of the latter" (p. 138). Given this belief, it is no wonder that she found that "the psychologic difficulty that stands in the way of direct realization of motherhood can have various causes; their most frequent common denominator [is] woman's fear of losing her personality in favor of the child" (p. 47). This tradition is important not only because in describing motherhood through its own lens, it prescribed a correct way to be a mother, but because it has had a powerful and lasting influence on the way that more recent empirical studies of motherhood have been framed.

SCRIPT 2: IMAGES OF SUPERWOMAN

An alternative that has been presented to the selfless mother script has been the "superwoman" script. The predominant characteristic of the superwoman has been her success in the workplace and her ability to "do it all." The superwoman is seen as making decisions by asking the question, "What is best for me?" In some cases this is really a narrower question that means, "What is best for my career?" "Me" is narrowly defined and, in fact, may simply be instrumental to different others than those whom the selfless mothers serve. This woman may serve the needs of the workplace rather than the needs of her family.

For example, Harragan, a business consultant and author of the book, *Games Mother Never Taught You,* sympathizes with companies that are losing experienced and productive female employees for any amount of time. "I hear stories of women who become pregnant and don't feel very well and so don't work very hard. Then they go off on maternity leave for weeks or even months. That can be hard for the organization." Harragan says she recommends that women not take the fully allowable leave time. "The really ambitious, committed women get back between two weeks to one month" (*Wall Street Journal,* September 19, 1984). Such advice assumes that what is good for the company is good for a woman's career and, thus, is best for her.

While some women succeed in following the superwoman script for a number of years,

the advent of motherhood introduces a complication. In order to continue to be successful as superwoman, the same commitment to the workplace that would get a woman back to work within "two weeks to one month" also needs to be made to the baby.

A number of researchers and psychologists, having seen the risks that women experienced in trying to follow the "selfless woman" script, have seen work as the answer for women. Baruch, Barnett, and Rivers (1983), on completion of a large study of mid-life women, advise that, "The best 'preventive medicine' for women against depression is fostering their sense of mastery. The confident, autonomous woman is likely to be less vulnerable to depression" (p. 22). The authors point out that because their findings are based on mid-life women, only 20 percent of their sample have a child under the age of seven. And they caution the reader that "If we had interviewed them at an earlier time, perhaps those with full-time careers would have shown a greater sense of role strain" (p. 149).

Since the cohort of women for whom the superwoman script has been an important formative influence is still rather young, there is less data to turn to in understanding the risks of that position. Baruch et al., for example, found that the major regret of their sample of mid-life women was that they had not taken their work more seriously. The cohort they interviewed had only a few women who had put themselves at risk of making work too central. It is important here to take seriously Giele's (1982) caution that "past negative experiences of middle-aged and older women do not automatically reveal an obverse set of positive developmental steps that each young woman should try in the future" (p. 121).

AN ALTERNATIVE FRAMEWORK

In order to understand the reality of women in their multiple roles, it will be necessary to turn our focus away from those cultural scripts that are increasingly unconnected to the realities of women's lives and turn toward the experience of women themselves as they make decisions about their lives in relation to cultural expectations and realities. Recognizing that people's lives are "permeated with cultural meanings ...the focus of interest becomes how people make sense of their lives with ideas drawn from their cultural environment, what kind of order they find there, and how they are affected by conclusions they draw from their culturally-guided introspection" (LeVine 1982, p. 290). As Gilligan (1982) has pointed out, "The meaning of mid-life events for a woman is contextual in the sense that it arises from the interaction between structures of her thought and the realities of her life."

Gilligan has recognized a general developmental progression in the way that women think about moral choices in their lives. She found that, within the context of an ethic of care, women move through a progression of (1) orientation to individual survival, (2) understanding of goodness as self-sacrifice, (3) a move from goodness to truth. It is in the move away from an understanding of goodness as self-sacrifice that women find their own voice and begin to define their own terms.

Attanucci has elaborated the concept of "own terms" in the lives of women who are mothers. Her work develops the understanding that thinking in one's own terms involves defining one's terms in the context of caring both for others and for oneself. My study is an application of that concept to a situation of choice and possible conflict in women's lives. It asks the question, "in whose terms" do mothers make decisions about employment and mothering? This conception calls into question the notions of self and development that are implicit in the motherhood scripts described previously, which place care of self and care of others in opposition.

Mothering, which brings with it the necessity to make choices that involve the well-being of oneself and others, provides an opportunity to redefine one's understanding of the place of the self in such decisions. The activity of mothering is a particularly interesting place to look at women's thinking about such choices, because cultural definitions of self as autonomous and separate often lead people to encounter the choices in the experience of mothering as being associated with self *or* other. Because mothering presents women with an opportunity to experience care of others as self-enhancing, it highlights the possibility of finding ways to think about self *and* other. Care of self and care of others need not be seen as opposing choices.

The focus of this chapter is on women's thinking about combining motherhood with employment outside the home. This focus was chosen because such issues come up so frequently when women are asked about what choices stand out for them as mothers. In addition, because employment holds a central place in each of the cultural scripts for mothering, it points out the importance of reaching new understandings about the relationship of maternal self and maternal role as defined by cultural scripts for mothering. While the ideal mother is supposed to place home above outside work, the superwoman is expected to add total commitment to mothering to total commitment to her job, an obvious contradiction in terms.

THE STUDY

This study is based on two in-depth interviews with twenty women, all residents of the greater Boston area. All of the participants in the study were white, college-educated, middle class, married women who were first-time mothers. They were interviewed around the end of their first year of mothering. This period was chosen because the women had been mothers long enough to reflect on their experience of the transition to motherhood and the changes it had brought to their lives. There had been time to adjust to some of the demands of motherhood. The infants were becoming mobile and assertive. The employed women had returned from maternity leave and, for the most part, had been back in the work force for a period of time.

The average age of the children at the time of the first interview was just under fourteen months, with a range of nine to eighteen months. A number of the women spontaneously commented that the end of the first year had seemed to be a kind of marker for them, causing them to reflect on their mothering and to evaluate the way their mothering fit into the other parts of their lives.

The sample was recruited to consist of women who had been in school or employed full-time outside their homes before they became mothers. It was divided so that there were three groups: one was employed full-time, one part-time, and one was at home full-time at the time of the interviews.

In order to have a sample of women who had been in the work force long enough to have some identity as "workers," it was necessary to recruit a sample that is somewhat older than the average first-time mother in our culture. The average age of the women in this sample was 31.4 years, with a range of 26 to 35 years. The respondents were interviewed twice, with each interview lasting between an hour and a half and two hours. The time lapse between interviews allowed both interviewer and respondent time to reflect on the responses. Often the women elaborated on their first week's responses at the second meeting.

The rest of the interview was modeled on the semi-structured clinical interview. The semi-structured clinical interview has been particularly valuable in formative research on adult development, where the goal is to obtain the respondent's perspective on his or her life. This was of paramount importance in this research, as reviews of the literature made it very clear that women's own perspective on the experience of mothering is glaringly absent. Since this study was designed to explore the ways women think about decisions in

their lives and, in particular, the way they think about themselves in those decisions, an interview which allowed the researcher to look at the women's own construction of their experience was needed. This part of the interview focused on questions about choice, self-concept, and change. Women were asked specifically about employment-related decisions and their responses were probed. Because higher depression has been seen as accompanying the transition to motherhood, the Center of Epidemiological Studies depression scale (CES-D) was administered at the end of the second interview.

The narratives in which women described their decisions about employment were analyzed in order to determine whether "own terms" and "not own terms" could be reliably coded in a decision-making process and to allow the testing of three hypotheses. The first hypothesis is derived from the self-less mother script. The work of Deutsch, for example, suggests that women give up their own personality in favor of that of the child when they become mothers. This implies that it is in responding to the child that women's voices are lost.

The second hypothesis is derived from the superwoman script, which places a woman in the professional work world as a way of reinforcing her sense of self. The third hypothesis suggests that women who use "own terms" thinking to make the employment decision would be less vulnerable to depression than women who rely on the current cultural scripts for mothering. Before turning to the coding, I will present four of the women and their thinking about decisions regarding whether and how much to work.

BECKY

In Becky's thinking about her decision to stay at home full-time, she measured herself against the superwoman cultural norms that she feels dominate the media but which conflict with her husband's belief that mothers should be at home with their children. In response to the question, "Looking back over the year since Heather was born, what are the choices that stand out for you?" Becky said,

> Deciding to stay with Heather more, be with her more than the average woman today. I think we measure ourselves against the norm, against other people a lot, especially with this issue. There's always a talk show about daycare ... It's come up every time I answer but it's the one thing I've fought with myself about.

Asked if she considered any other ways of doing it, Becky continued:

> I felt I wasn't being a supermother and that's the only kind of mother there is these days ... I had the TV on and it made me feel meaningless. What would eat away at me was that I didn't have any more choices. We had decided this was what I had to do. I felt this was what I had to do, that I didn't have any control. I didn't have money, didn't have choices. I really fought with myself about it ... I had to finally say. "I'm tired, this is enough for me."

As she tried to resolve the conflict between the superwoman script that she felt dominates the culture and the script that her husband believed was right for her to follow, she adopted the terms of his script. He had pointed out that not only did he think it was right for her to be with Heather, but also that they would be worse off financially if she had an outside job at this point. This left Becky with some unresolved contradictions. When asked who she thought about in making the decision to stay at home, she explained:

> My husband is pretty conservative. He believes I should be home with Heather ... and I do too. You're fighting yourself also with what's in vogue, with what's expected in society and want to be as contemporary as possible. But I've resolved that and it's fine, just fine. Sometimes I'd say I don't care about the money. Dan saw it in a practical, logical way, but I felt for my own peace of mind I needed to work, so perhaps I felt he wasn't thinking of me, only of the practical view, and sometimes I'd think he's not even thinking of Heather. All he cares

> about is the money. But he did have Heather in mind so she was thought of and perhaps he could see so to be convincing about that.

MONICA

The outlines of Monica's days and the ways she spent her time were very similar to Becky's. The way Monica thought about the decision to spend her time that way, however, was quite different from Becky's. Asked to describe her decision to stay at home full-time, leaving a responsible and challenging job, she replied:

> It wasn't a hard decision at all. We thought it was real important for one of us to be here. Bill's job is not suited, nor is he ... Bill makes enough money. I look at that as a luxury these days. I didn't want to miss a day of Tim's growing up, and I felt career and work would be there. I viewed this as a precious time for my child and myself. I wanted to be able to put energy into this and not be split. I didn't feel comfortable with the idea of a day-care center. I wanted to be with him, I wanted to raise him, I wanted to get to know him. I feel now that my relationship with him is so solid.

Monica's clarity about the fact that it is her own desire to care for her child helps her acknowledge the benefits of her decision, both for her child and for herself. Though she also recognizes that there are difficulties that come with her decision, she is not experiencing conflict about the difficulties she faces.

HELEN

Helen described her decision to take a full-time job that she didn't really want when her child was three months old. In response to the question, "Looking back over the year since Sally was born, what are the choices that stand out for you?" she said:

> Getting called back to work, to a job I didn't really want, to me was a very big point. I felt I would have to put in that year to get back to the school system I wanted. It's an unfortunate thing that women

have to do that, to prove they're serious about work. If I had stayed home I would have not looked serious to them about my work.

Knowing that her career was very important to her, and also recognizing that her family needed the income, she decided to take a calculated risk, recognizing the trade-offs. She described the considerations in the following way:

The superintendent (from my old job) had recommended me and I really wanted to show them I was a person they'd want back. I was thinking of my career. I saw it as a way of proving myself. I took it as a calculated risk. If I'd stayed home they might have wondered if I was the kind of person they wanted. We needed the money with the expenses of my husband's dissertation, and his job is not full-time. And fortunately, I found someone I really liked and who really liked Sally. For Sally it worked out fine. I had a terrible year because I hated the job. Coming home to Sally was always the light at the end of the tunnel.

PAT

Pat had one of the longest working days of anyone in the sample. She was an attorney and estimated that she worked about fifty hours a week. Pat found that her work really took off at the time her son was born and demanded many more hours from her than she originally had bargained for. Asked to think of a situation during the previous year where she didn't know what was the right thing to do, Pat responded: "There's plenty of those. Actually the most classic one is the one I've been describing" (how many hours to devote to her work and how to set up good child care) She described the conflicts in that situation for her:

In many ways it's a conflict of my growing up in the 50s, and later the influence of the 70s, and that typical conflict I'm sure you're looking at between the pulls of career and the pulls of being a mother and the responsibilities of each . . . Another conflict is the selfish me versus the giving me . . . we're talk-

ing about, you know, my career versus his life. I don't want to be selfish, but on the other hand, I'm being selfish . . .

Asked at this point to explain what she meant by "selfish," she responded:

When I've always been number one, having to look at someone else as number one. And I'm not doing such a great job I might add. There's this whole . . . you're supposed to feel all this giving and oh, I'm a mother and ergo, you know, my child comes first and I can float down this little path and it's a bunch of bull.

Asked how she evaluated the decision to continue to work and whether she now felt it was the right one, Pat replied:

Yes. It's the only decision . . . There's a lot of reasons . . . that have to do with self-image also as to why I chose . . . I guess it's the right decision, even though I feel guilty. Is all this stuff worth more than his well-being? . . . I'm putting all these things ahead of him, and he's my son and mothers aren't supposed to do that. You know, mothers are supposed to put their, especially their nine-month-old, babies first. Then, once kids get older, that's when you go back and do that. There's this feeling, you know, that even though a lot of women are working, there aren't that many working with little tiny babies. And there aren't that many working the amount of hours and the amount of stress and energy that I have to put into the job which, you know . . . there's a limited amount of energy, . . . he's not going to get what I spend. It's the guilt over, I mean, it's the same selfishness that I'm putting myself or all womankind ahead of him.

Because there is not a single, clear cultural script for mothering in this culture, women's conceptions of cultural norms varied within the sample. Becky sees herself as out of the mainstream because she is not employed and spends a great deal of time with her child. Pat, on the other hand, worries that her pattern of working away from her home for many hours a week is not in accord with cultural standards, as exemplified in her statement, "there's this feeling that, you know, even though a lot of women are working, there aren't that many working with little tiny babies."

In the descriptions of decisions about employment, it was possible to see the women's orientation toward the judgment of others. In some of the dilemmas the women's investment in what others thought and their wish to please others overshadowed, or even prevented, them from finding and hearing their own voices as they thought about the decisions they faced. These women, struggling to see the self in others' definitions and in others' expectations, were characterized by an inability to hear the self's own voice in the self's own terms. For other women, the awareness of others' views was accompanied by the woman's awareness of her own needs and desires and by a willingness and ability to hear and be guided by her own voice.

THE CODING

In order to be able to code systematically for whether or not women made the decision about employment in "their own terms," a coding system was developed to examine this aspect of women's thinking. It asks the question, "Is the decision ultimately made in a way that allows the woman to include her voice (own terms), or is her voice drowned out so that the decision cannot include the woman's own terms?"

A critical distinction in this coding system is made between women's vulnerability to allowing themselves to be judged in others' terms and women's needs to respond to and care for others. Traditionally, in this culture women have been at risk of losing their own voices in the process of being submerged in caring for others in the other's own terms, a risk of following the selfless mother script. In this time of cultural change, however, other voices are also defining women. In a culture where self has been equated with autonomy, women are also at risk of not hearing and responding to the voice which emphasizes their

own need to be in relationships and to care for others. It is this part of a woman's terms that may be lost in attempts to follow a superwoman script.

Deciding in One's Own Terms

The women who made the employment decision by listening to their own voices and including their own terms were characterized by either one or a combination of the following:

1. The entire decision was described in a voice which the coder could see was clearly the woman's own. The use of the first person was most prominent, as was the use of active verbs (I want, it's my choice, I see myself, I know). The presence of the woman's own voice by no means excluded her awareness of the needs and desires of others. Others' needs were considered along with the needs of the self, neither voice drowning out the other. For example, looking back at Monica's decision to stay at home full-time to care for her son, this kind of clarity could be heard: "I wanted to be with him, I wanted to raise him, I wanted to get to know him."

2. In the woman's description of the decision-making process, the coder could see that the process was one in which she discovered her own terms. The respondent was able to seek an inclusive solution, recognizing the terms of connection to others as well as her own individual needs. Connection does not mean subordination of one's own terms to others, but an engagement with the other that seeks to find an accommodation of the terms of both. The solution sought is an inclusive solution.

With Helen's decision to take the job so that she would not have to sacrifice her career, she was able to contribute to the financial support of the family and, with good daycare, she could still be assured that her child was happy and well cared for. She took the needs of all three of the family members into account. Though there were other things that they have given up for the time being (time to see friends, reading novels, and maintaining as clean a home as they were used to doing), this decision was made as the best way to care for everyone in an inclusive way, without the sense that someone had been sacrificed.

Deciding in Others' Terms

The women who did not make the decision in their own voice were characterized by one or more of the following:

1. A nonreflective quality in which other people's terms were accepted and acted upon. The description was characterized by language in the third person ("He says I could," "You have to be," "You just get used to it"), by language of obligation, guilt, and judgment ("Mothers are supposed to," "You're supposed to feel"), and by the use of passive verbs.

2. Hints of the woman's own voice entering into the decision were drowned out by external voices or lost because she herself could not identify her own voice. For example, in listening to Becky, one can hear her sense of what society in general expects mothers to do. "I felt I wasn't being a supermother and that's the only kind of mother there is these days." Equally strong was her husband's voice and his beliefs about the maternal role. "He believes I should be home with Heather." Her own voice, concerned about the fact that she felt she "didn't have any choices" was silenced, as she "had to finally say, 'I'm tired, this is enough for me.'"

3. There was frequently an unconscious denial of the constraints that limited the woman's choices. This denial of the limitations within which she was operating led to internal contradictions within the decision. For example, Becky's statement that "it's fine, just fine" was belied by concerns that she was "fighting with herself" over this decision, that she "felt she didn't have any choices."

FINDINGS

In this sample of twenty women, twelve were coded as having made the decision about outside employment primarily in their own terms. Eight made the decision predominantly in others' terms. "Own terms" or "not own terms" decisions were coded at 80% reliability. In response to the first hypothesis, it was found that most women were not, in fact, likely to lose their own terms in responding to the needs of their infant. All the mothers who were coded as making the decision about employment in their own terms did consider the needs of the infant in an integral way.

In order to address the second hypothesis, a second part of the coding system was developed to determine what other voices the women considered in making their decision. In the inner dialogue about whether or not to work outside the home, mothers of infants consider the perspectives of a number of other people. Other voices can either drown out the voice of the self or they can inform it. The second part of the coding process asked the coder to look for the presence or absence of any of the following voices in the woman's thinking: (1) self in relation to child, (2) self in relation to husband, (3) self in relation to work, (4) self in relation to own mother, (5) self in relation to authorities on childrearing, (6) self in relation to society and to others in general.

For all of the women in this sample the decision about employment clearly involved the needs both of adults and of the baby: The women described listening to the voice of some adult in the decision-making process, and 90 percent of the sample described thinking about the self in relation to the child. It was not considerations of the baby's needs that led the women to lose their own voice in the decision but the voice of other adults, very often adults who were not directly involved in the decision. Of the eight cases where the decision was not made in the woman's own terms, it was the voices of society, husband,

and childrearing experts that defined the terms of the decision. Thus, it was not a woman's perceived needs of her infant that drowned out her own voice in the decision but the voices of others. The others were either directly described by women as "they" or as "society," expressing the terms of a cultural script, or they came through the voice of an important person in the woman's life, as in "my husband thinks I should be home with the baby"—also a cultural script.

Spearman correlations were used in order to see whether there was a correlation between having made the decision about employment in one's own terms and measures of well-being. The women who made the decision in their own terms had lower depression scores on the CES-D ($\rho = 0.4$, $p < 0.05$). Thus, it appears that making the decision about outside employment and mothering in one's own terms can provide some protection against depression.

DISCUSSION

Women who have made the decision about employment and mothering in their own terms describe a mode of thinking that no longer fits into either script. While cultural scripts for mothering see the self of the mother and the self of the child as competing forces, women who are able to make the decision in their own terms recognize their own need to care for the child as aligned with the child's need for care. In this framework the question changes from, "Who do I put first, the child or me?" to "How can I best care for this child and for myself?"

Current cultural scripts for mothering offer definitions of the self that ask the mother to either "give up" the self or sacrifice care of the child in order to develop the self. Since these are the terms of choice which our culture presents to women, it is not surprising that women who try to make choices within that framework appear to be more vulnerable

to depression. In fact, the terms of the superwoman script for mothering demand that a woman add self-sacrifice to self-fulfillment. Unless women come to think in their own terms, they are left vulnerable to increasing distance between a self-ideal which embodies conflicting understandings of self, and the reality which they experience. When the distance between self-concept and self-ideal is great, depression is a likely outcome.

Making decisions in her own terms does not eliminate conflict or dilemmas from the woman's relationship with her child; her own needs can still be at odds with those around her. Because the activity of caring in the relationship with an infant is by definition unequal, and the child's needs for care are immediate and compelling, the challenge for the women in this group is to balance the needs of the self with the needs of the child in a way that does not deny the legitimacy of either. This way of thinking offers a framework within which to consider decisions; it does not offer solutions.

While the role-defined way of caring offers an automatic rule to rely upon in resolving conflicts that arise between the needs of the child and the self—the needs of the child always come first—the cost of this ready formula for conflict resolution is that the legitimacy of the self in the relationship is lost. Alternatively, women who do not follow a script by subordinating the self, experience the legitimacy of the self in the relationship and have access to a process for resolving the inevitable conflicts that exist in a relationship between two legitimate selves. Conflicts that arise need to be resolved by attention to both the needs of the self and others, requiring that a woman resist easy answers and live with the ambiguity of judging the rightness of her own response without reference to a ready-made rule.

The power of the cultural scripts for mothering was such that for some women, the scripts dictated not only the way women should care for others, but the way they should care for themselves. Caught in a contradiction that saw care of self as separate, several women described going to dance classes or taking lessons that they hated and were not good at. For one woman these activities were described as "what you're supposed to do to take care of yourself." Real pleasure came into her voice as she described walks that she and her friends took with their children, but these were not seen in her framework as a way of caring for both herself and her child.

The equating of care and selflessness, and the dichotomy which that equation creates between care of self and care of others leaves some women without a forum within which to resolve conflicts between their desires and a role-defined definition of the "right" way to care. The women who experienced the most conflict about the employment decision talked about the way mothers were "supposed to feel." Pat could not get away from seeing herself as "selfish" for working because she has absorbed the role-defined idea of care: "You're supposed to feel all this giving and oh, I'm a mother and ergo, you know,

my child comes first and I can float down this little path…" She goes on to describe herself as experiencing constant conflict between the "selfish me and the giving me…we're talking about, you know, my career versus his life."

Women who were clear about their own terms—those who had made their employment decision in terms of their own and their families' needs rather than by trying to meet the demands of a script—were able to work out a variety of arrangements for mothering that worked for them and their families. In fact, this study found that women who could recognize their own terms were less depressed even when they had limited choices. A woman who could hear her own voice was less at the mercy of cultural prescriptions about how she ought to think and act and was better able to make choices within the constraints of her particular life situation. Given the difficult choices that many women now need to make, these research findings have far-reaching implications and offer hope for innovative solutions to difficult but common problems experienced by many women and families.

REFERENCES

Attanucci, J. *How Would You Describe Yourself to Yourself: Mothers of Infants Reply.* Unpublished qualifying paper, Harvard Graduate School of Education, Cambridge, Mass. (1982).

Baruch, G. & Barnett R., & Rivers C. *Lifeprints: New Patterns of Love and Work for Today's Women.* New York: McGraw-Hill (1983).

Deutsch, H. *The Psychology of Women* (2nd ed.). New York: Grune & Stratton (1945).

Fallows, D. *A Mother's Work.* Boston: Houghton Mifflin (1985).

Giele, J., ed. *Women in the Middle Years.* New York: Wiley–Interscience Publications, John Wiley & Sons (1982).

Gilligan, C. *In a Different Voice: Psychological Theory and Women's Development.* Cambridge, Mass.: Harvard University Press (1982).

LeVine, R. *Culture, Behavior, and Personality* (2nd ed.). Chicago: Aldine de Gruyter Publishing (1982).

White, B. *The First Three Years of Life.* Englewood Cliffs, N.J.: Prentice Hall (1975).

Black Mother-Daughter Relationships

PATRICIA HILL COLLINS

BLACK MOTHER-DAUGHTER RELATIONSHIPS

In her discussion of the sex-role socialization of Black girls, Pamela Reid identifies two complementary approaches in understanding Black mother-daughter relationships.[1] The first, psychoanalytic theory, examines the role of parents in the establishment of personality and social behavior. This theory argues that the development of feminine behavior results from the girls' identification with adult female role models. This approach emphasizes how an Afrocentric ideology of motherhood is actualized through Black mothers' activities as role models.

The second approach, social learning theory, suggests that the rewards and punishments attached to girls' childhood experiences are central in shaping women's sex-role behavior. The kinds of behaviors that Black mothers reward and punish in their daughters are seen as key in the socialization process. This approach examines specific experiences that Black girls have while growing up that encourage them to absorb an Afrocentric ideology of motherhood.

African-American Mothers as Role Models

Feminist psychoanalytic theorists suggest that the sex-role socialization process is differ-

ent for boys and girls. While boys learn maleness by rejecting femaleness via separating themselves from their mothers, girls establish feminine identities by embracing the femaleness of their mothers. Girls identify with their mothers, a sense of connection that is incorporated into the female personality. However, this mother-identification is problematic because, under patriarchy, men are more highly valued than women. Thus, while daughters identify with their mothers, they also reject them, since in patriarchal families, identifying with adult women as mothers means identifying with persons deemed inferior.[2]

While Black girls learn by identifying with their mothers, the specific female role with which Black girls identify may be quite different than that modeled by middle-class White mothers. The presence of working mothers, extended family othermothers, and powerful community othermothers offers a range of role models that challenge the tenets of the cult of true womanhood.

Moreover, since Black mothers have a distinctive relationship to White patriarchy, they may be less likely to socialize their daughters into their proscribed role as subordinates. Rather, a key part of Black girls' socialization involves incorporating the critical posture that allows Black women to cope with contradictions. For example, Black girls have long had to learn how to do domestic work while rejecting definitions of themselves as Mammies. At the same time they've had to take on strong roles in Black extended families without internalizing images of themselves as matriarchs.

In raising their daughters, Black mothers face a troubling dilemma. To ensure their daughters' physical survival, they must teach their daughters to fit into systems of oppression. For example, as a young girl in Mississippi, Black activist Ann Moody questioned why she was paid so little for the domestic work she began at age nine, why Black women domestics were sexually harassed by their White male employers, and why Whites had so much more than Blacks. But her mother refused to answer her questions and actually became angry whenever Ann Moody stepped out of her "place."[3] Black daughters are raised to expect to work, to strive for an education so that they can support themselves, and to anticipate carrying heavy responsibilities in their families and communities because these skills are essential for their own survival as well as for the survival of those for whom they will eventually be responsible.[4] And yet mothers know that if daughters fit too well into the limited opportunities offered Black women, they become willing participants in their own subordination. Mothers may have ensured their daughters' physical survival at the high cost of their emotional destruction.

On the other hand, Black daughters who offer serious challenges to oppressive situations may not physically survive. When Ann Moody became involved in civil rights activities, her mother first begged her not to participate and then told her not to come home because she feared the Whites in Moody's hometown would kill her. In spite of the dangers, many Black mothers routinely encourage their daughters to develop skills to confront oppressive conditions. Thus, learning that they will work, that education is a vehicle for advancement, can also be seen as ways of preparing Black girls to resist oppression through a variety of mothering roles. The issue is to build emotional strength, but not at the cost of physical survival.

This delicate balance between conformity and resistance is described by historian Elsa Barkley Brown as the "need to socialize me one way and at the same time to give me all the tools I needed to be something else."[5] Black daughters must learn how to survive in interlocking structures of race, class, and gender oppression while rejecting and transcending those very same structures. To develop these skills in their daughters, mothers demonstrate varying combinations of behaviors devoted to ensuring their daughters' survival—such as providing them with basic necessities and ensuring their protection in dangerous environments to helping their daughters go farther than mothers themselves were allowed to go.

The presence of othermothers in Black extended families and the modeling symbolized by community othermothers offer powerful support for the task of teaching girls to resist White perceptions of Black womanhood while appearing to conform to them. In contrast to the isolation of middle-class White mother/ daughter dyads, Black women-centered extended family networks foster an early identification with a much wider range of models of Black womanhood, which can lead to a greater sense of empowerment in young Black girls.

Social Learning Theory and Black Mothering Behavior

Understanding this goal of balancing the needs of ensuring their daughters' physical survival with the vision of encouraging them to transcend the boundaries confronting them sheds some light on some of the apparent contradictions in Black mother-daughter relationships. Black mothers are often described as strong disciplinarians and overly protective parents; yet these same women manage to raise daughters who are self-reliant and assertive.[6] Professor Gloria Wade-Gayles offers an explanation for this apparent contradiction by suggesting that Black mothers "do not socialize their daughters to be passive or irrational. Quite the contrary, they socialize their daughters to be independent, strong and self-confident. Black mothers are suffocatingly protective and domineering precisely because they are determined to mold their daughters into whole and self-actualizing persons in a society that devalues Black women."[7]

Black mothers emphasize protection either by trying to shield their daughters as long as possible from the penalties attached to their race, class, and gender or by teaching them how to protect themselves in such situations. Black women's autobiographies and fiction can be read as texts revealing the multiple strategies Black mothers employ in preparing their daughters for the demands of being Black women in oppressive conditions. For example, in discussing the mother-daughter relationship in Paule Marshall's *Brown Girl, Brownstones*, Rosalie Troester catalogues some of these strategies and the impact they may have on relationships themselves:

> Black mothers, particularly those with strong ties to their community, sometimes build high banks around their young daughters, isolating them from the dangers of the larger world until they are old and strong enough to function as autonomous women. Often these dikes are religious, but sometimes they are built with education, family, or the restrictions of a close-knit and homogeneous community...this isolation causes the currents between Black mothers and daughters to run deep and the relationship to be fraught with an emotional intensity often missing from the lives of women with more freedom.[8]

Black women's efforts to provide for their children also may affect the emotional intensity of Black mother-daughter relationships. As Gloria Wade-Gayles points out, "Mothers in Black women's fiction are strong and devoted...but...they are rarely affectionate."[9] For far too many Black mothers, the demands

of providing for children are so demanding that affection often must wait until the basic needs of physical survival are satisfied.

Black daughters raised by mothers grappling with hostile environments have to confront their feelings about the difference between the idealized versions of maternal love extant in popular culture and the strict, assertive mothers so central to their lives.[10] For daughters, growing up means developing a better understanding that offering physical care and protection is an act of maternal love. Ann Moody describes her growing awareness of the personal cost her mother paid as a single mother of three children employed as a domestic worker. Watching her mother sleep after the birth of another child, Moody remembers:

> For a long time I stood there looking at her. I didn't want to wake her up. I wanted to enjoy and preserve that calm, peaceful look on her face. I wanted to think she would always be that happy...Adline and Junior were too young to feel the things I felt and know the things I knew about Mama. They couldn't remember when she and Daddy separated. They had never heard her cry at night as I had or worked and helped as I had done when we were starving.[11]

Renita Weems's account of coming to grips with maternal desertion provides another example of a daughter's efforts to understand her mother's behavior. In the following passage, Weems struggles with the difference between the stereotypical image of the super-strong Black mother and her own alcoholic mother, who decided to leave her children:

> My mother loved us. I must believe that. She worked all day in a department store bakery to buy shoes and school tablets, came home to curse out neighbors who wrongly accused her children of any impropriety (which in an apartment complex usually meant stealing), and kept her house cleaner than most sober women.[12]

Weems concludes that her mother loved her because she provided for her to the best of her ability.

Othermothers often play central roles in defusing the emotional intensity of relationships between bloodmothers and their daughters and in helping daughters understand the Afrocentric ideology of motherhood. Weems describes the women teachers, neighbors, friends, and othermothers that she turned to for help in negotiating a difficult mother-daughter relationship. These women, she notes, "did not have the onus of providing for me, and so had the luxury of talking to me."[13]

June Jordan offers one of the most eloquent analyses of a daughter's realization of the high personal cost Black women have paid as bloodmothers and othermothers in working to provide an economic and emotional foundation for Black children. In the following passage, Jordan captures the feelings that my Black women students struggled to put into words:

As a child I noticed the sadness of my mother as she sat alone in the kitchen at night...Her woman's work never won permanent victories of any kind. It never enlarged the universe of her imagination or her power to influence what happened beyond the front door of our house. Her woman's work never tickled her to laugh or shout or dance. But she did raise me to respect her way of offering love and to believe that hard work is often the irreducible factor for survival, not something to avoid. Her woman's work produced a reliable home base where I could pursue the privileges of books and music. Her woman's work invented the potential for a completely different kind of work for us, the next generation of Black women: huge, rewarding hard work demanded by the huge, new ambitions that her perfect confidence in us engendered.[14]

Jordan's words not only capture the essence of the Afrocentric ideology of motherhood so central to the well-being of countless numbers of Black women. They simultaneously point the way into the future, one where Black women face the challenge of continuing the mothering traditions painstakingly nurtured by prior generations of African-American women.

NOTES

1. Pamela Reid, "Socialization of Black Female Children," in *Women: A Developmental Perspective,* ed. Phyllis Berman and Estelle Ramey (Washington, DC: National Institutes of Health, 1983).

2. For works in the feminist psychoanalytic tradition, see Nancy Chodorow, "Family Structure and Feminine Personality," in *Woman, Culture, and Society,* ed. Rosaldo and Lamphere, 1974; Nancy Chodorow, *The Reproduction of Mothering* (Berkeley, CA: University of California, 1978); and Jane Flax, "The Conflict Between Nurturance and Autonomy in Mother-Daughter Relationships and Within Feminism." *Feminist Studies* 4 (1978):171–89.

3. Ann Moody, *Coming of Age in Mississippi* (New York: Dell, 1968).

4. Joyce Ladner, *Tomorrow's Tomorrow* (Garden City, NY: Doubleday, 1971); Gloria Joseph, "Black Mothers and Daughters: Their Roles and Functions in American Society," in *Common Differences,* ed. Gloria Joseph and Jill Lewis (Garden City, NY: Anchor, 1981), pp. 75–126; Lena Wright Myers, *Black Women, Do They Cope Better?* (Englewood Cliffs, NJ: Prentice-Hall, 1980).

5. Elsa Barkley Brown, "Hearing Our Mothers' Lives," paper presented at fifteenth anniversary of African-American and African Studies at Emory College, Atlanta, 1986. This essay appeared in the Black Women's Studies issue of *SAGE: A Scholarly Journal on Black Women,* vol. 6, no. 1:4–11.

6. Joseph, "Black Mothers and Daughters"; Myers, 1980.

7. Gloria Wade-Gayles, "The Truths of Our Mothers' Lives: Mother-Daughter Relationships in Black Women's Fiction," *SAGE: A Scholarly Journal on Black Women* 1 (Fall 1984):12.

8. Rosalie Riegle Troester, "Turbulence and Tenderness: Mothers, Daughters, and 'Othermothers' in *Brown Girl, Brownstones* by Paule Marshall. *SAGE: A Scholarly Journal on Black Women* (Fall 1984):13.

9. Wade-Gayles, "The Truths," p. 10.

10. Joseph, "Black Mothers and Daughters."

11. Moody, *Coming of Age,* p. 57.

12. Renita Weems, "'Hush. Mama's Gotta Go Bye Bye': A Personal Narrative," *SAGE: A Scholarly Journal on Black Women* 1 (Fall 1984):26.

13. Ibid, p. 27.

14. June Jordan, *On Call, Political Essays* (Boston: South End Press, 1985), p. 145.

PART TWO

GENDER AND WORK

When we think of *work*, we tend to think about one type of work: participation in the paid labor force. Of course, our economy depends on labor force participation to provide many of the goods and services that we consume. However, not all work involves participation in the paid labor force. Women's work includes productive labor, both paid and unpaid, as well as reproductive labor which is entirely unpaid (Stromberg and Harkess 1988). Factors such as the stage of economic development determine what is considered "work," the degree of female labor force participation, and the gender-based division of labor. Every society has some gender-based division of labor and believes that it is "natural." Other societies have completely different ways of dividing work between the sexes—and view *their* ways as "natural."

The selections in this section trace the changes in women's work and the dominant ideas about it in the United States from the middle of the nineteenth century to the 1980s. The first article, by Barbara F. Reskin and Irene Padavic, illustrates that economic and ideological change were closely tied together. Industrial capitalism had several consequences for middle-class women. It led to the destruction of the home economy; a gendered division of labor between unpaid work (e.g., care of home and family) and paid work outside the home; and created a new degree of dependence on men (Epstein 1986).

Prior to industrialization in Europe, both genders produced goods for their households. In the medieval European pattern, family and work life were intertwined. Peasant women played an essential role in agriculture and home industries such as weaving, silk making, and brewing. In eighteenth-century English villages, women still worked on family farms and were involved in craft production and small trade businesses. But as the Industrial Revolution gathered steam in the middle of the century, middle-class urban women became increasingly excluded from economic production and the feminine ideal of idleness became widespread among the bourgeois class. Having a wife who did not work outside the home and whose physical frailty allowed her to do little inside the home became a status symbol (Harris 1980).

Colonial America's economy in the middle of the eighteenth century, on the other hand, was characterized by small-scale agriculture and small crafts. This way of life fostered economic cooperation between husbands and wives and allowed women to carry on after their husbands' deaths as independent traders and entrepreneurs. Much of this was due to an extreme labor shortage—women were taught crafts such as printing and carpentry from fathers and brothers and husbands—but they were always considered secondary to men (Harris 1980).

In rural areas at the beginning of the nineteenth century, conditions remained as they had been in the Colonial era—women were still involved in agriculture and crafts. But single women in New England were recruited to take factory jobs in the textile mills. However, jobs were still distributed by sex; the small number of men supervised the girls and men were the skilled mechanics while women spun and wove. Even though women were at the bottom of the industrial hierarchy, the mills still offered single white women the possibility of economic independence. Black women were still slaves at the time and later when they were free labor, they worked as seamstresses and laundresses and domestic servants, continuing the kind of work they did as slaves. In 1820, the majority of industrial wage earners were single white women who were told that their economic independence was good for their families and the republic.

The depression from 1837 to 1839 caused many men to sell or lose their farms, so they started competing for industrial jobs. There was also an influx of immigrants willing to work cheaply. By 1840, the ideology had started to change; women were being discouraged from factory work and told that their duty was to stay home (Kessler-Harris 1982).

By the second half of the century, the ideological justification for keeping women out of the labor market had taken hold—"the doctrine of separate spheres." Women had to confront a variety of widely held prejudices. First, was the idea that women were unfit for any vocation that relied predominantly on mental abilities and the ability to make decisions. The second conviction was that respectable married women should not work outside the home. Women who had to work were scorned; it reflected poorly on a man to have a wife who worked outside the home. In addition, females were equated with their reproductive organs and anything other than ordinary domestic routine was considered a danger to their fragile nervous systems. The higher the class, it seemed, the more fragile the nervous system (Harris 1980).

By the end of the nineteenth century, the doctrine of separate spheres was so integrated into American life that fewer than one in twenty married women worked for pay outside the home. The doctrine of separate spheres had succeeded in creating an ideological barrier to wage work for all but the poorest married women.

As we see in Charlotte Perkins Gilman's (1860–1935) autobiographical short story "The Yellow Wallpaper," (1892) even writing was unacceptable for a woman. Intellectual discourse was considered too strenuous for a woman. The main character in the story is encouraged to do nothing and have no contact with the world outside the house so much so that she starts to have delusions about the wallpaper and about escaping the imprisonment of her life. Although Gilman is best known today for "The Yellow Wallpaper," in her own day she was recognized as a leading feminist thinker (Lengermann and Niebrugge-Brantley 1998).

Before she married, Gilman was writing poetry and fiction, studying German and French, and was an avid feminist, but nevertheless she felt that marriage was a woman's inescapable fate. She married Walter Stetson in 1884 despite her feelings of foreboding about married life. Soon after the birth of her daughter Katharine in 1885, Gilman became increasingly desperate to escape from being a wife and mother. Both her mother and her husband agreed that she was "sick" and they sent her to the most famous "nerve specialist" in the country, Dr. S. Weir Mitchell (Hill 1980).

Dr. Mitchell prescribed his standard therapy—no books, no conversations with friends, no taxing pressures of "inappropriate" ambition. Dr. Mitchell said Gilman suffered from hysteria; his recommended cure was designed to teach aggressive, dominating women how to be more "feminine" and domestic. His prescription was the following: "Live as domestic a life as possible. Have your child with you all the time.... Lie down an hour after each meal. Have but two hours' intellectual life a day. And never touch a pen, brush, or pencil as long as you live." Gilman later wrote that she followed the directions for months and came perilously close to losing her mind (Hill 1980).

In 1890, Gilman wrote "The Yellow Wallpaper," a fictional account of the progressive insanity that resulted from being treated by Dr. S. Weir Mitchell. In the story, Gilman presents insanity as a form of rebellion and a crucial turning point toward independence. Gilman herself escaped her heroine's fate and went on to divorce her husband and leave her daughter in his care (Hill 1980).

This was quite a radical step for a nineteenth-century woman—Gilman rebelled against the doctrine of separate spheres in a major way. She became a writer and feminist sociologist. In addition to her fiction, she published five major books of social theory between 1898 and 1911: *Women and Economics* (1890), an analysis of the "sexuo-economic relation," a condition existing only among human beings, in which one sex, the female, is economically dependent on the other sex, the male; *Concerning Children* (1900), a discussion of socialization; *The Home* (1903), a critical analysis of the home as a site of production; *Human Work* (1904), a study of the relationship between work and consciousness; and *The Man-Made World; or, Our Androcentric Culture* (1911), an exploration of patriarchal culture (Lengermann and Niebrugge-Brantley 1998).

Unlike Gilman, most middle-class white married women succumbed to the doctrine of separate spheres. For those women who needed to remain in the workforce because they were widowed or abandoned or needed to supplement their husbands' incomes, the doctrine of separate spheres legitimated the exclusion of women from many jobs. Since women were viewed as fragile by this new ideology, protective legislation played a major part in institutionalizing women's secondary labor force position. The need to protect women provided justification for regulating their working conditions as well as prohibiting women from certain occupations.

Conversely, African American, Latino, Asian American, and Native American women have never been put on a pedestal—the doctrine of separate spheres was not applied to them. People of color were brought to the United States to work. During slavery, black women were forced to work along with the men and after slavery they were expected to work. Men of color were not paid a family wage, as white men were, because their women were supposed to work. Nevertheless, women of color were excluded from many jobs because of protective legislation and paid less than white women for the same work (Higginbotham 1986).

By the beginning of the twentieth century, special protection for women legally imposed rules on the kind of work women could do. They were not allowed to sell liquor because it might expose them to lewd men; they could not be messengers because Western Union could not guarantee who might open the door to them; and they were not allowed to work at night because they would be too tired to take care of their children during the day (Kessler-Harris, 1982).

Trade unions supported protective legislation for women because it discouraged employers from hiring women and opened up more jobs for union men. Thus, protectionist legislation used the doctrine of separate spheres as justification and itself reinforced the notion that women were not full-fledged wage earners and that their primary role was in the home. It also justified paying women less than men because they were "protected" from many high-paying jobs and it was presumed that men were supporting them (Kessler-Harris 1982).

The Reskin and Padavic article, together with Gilman's short story, illustrates both the social and personal consequences of the doctrine of separate spheres for white women in the nineteenth-century United States. Reskin and Padavic focus on how the ideology (i.e., the doctrine of separate spheres) developed as a result of industrial capitalism and then they demonstrate the effect of that ideology on female labor force participation. Gilman, on the other hand, focuses on the personal experience of a middle-class white woman whose life was constrained by the doctrine of separate spheres. In these selections we can see that the way economic life is organized leads to the development of an ideology and then that ideology gets internalized by people and affects their attitudes about everyday life.

One of the most basic questions in social science is "What is the relationship between economic life and ideas?" In this case, we are particularly interested in the relationship between capitalism, which is a particular form of economic life, and a set of ideas about women, which is variously called "the doctrine of separate spheres," "the cult of domesticity," and "the domestic code." One of the most important theorists to write about the relationship between economic life and ideas was Karl Marx. Marx believed economic life determined ideas and that the dominant ideas of a particular historical period, which he called an "ideology," reflected the interests of the dominant class, which he called "the owners of production." Some Marxist feminists have modified Marx's position, arguing that the doctrine of separate spheres was not necessarily in the interests of the owners of production (the capitalists), but rather it was in the interest of all men-capitalists as well as wage earners (Hartmann 1979).

Although the doctrine of separate spheres created a barrier to wage work for women, the World Wars offered brief periods of change in attitude about women working outside the home. Married as well as single women were recruited to take over defense jobs that were left open by men going to war;

once again there was a change in the ideology about women. At the beginning of World War II, women were told it was their patriotic duty to leave their homes and their children and go to work in factories to save the nation. But when the war was over, women were expected to have babies and tend their homes and families. After World War II there was a baby boom, and beginning in the 1950s, young white families left the cities in large numbers to buy homes in the new suburbs. The ideology of womanhood had reverted back to the doctrine of separate spheres.

Suburbanization and the baby boom added to the isolation of white, middle-class married women. Each woman cooked meals, vacuumed, and did the laundry in her own separate house. The stark contrast between Betty Friedan's misery in the suburbs in the late 1950s and her college and labor union experience in the 1940s and early 1950s probably led her to write *The Feminine Mystique* and become one of the leaders of the women's movement in the 1960s.

The doctrine of separate spheres was still intact in the 1950s when Betty Friedan was writing her book. Sixty-three percent of families in 1950 were composed of a wage-earning dad, a stay-at-home mom, and one or more children (Catalyst 1997). However, many of the daughters of those 1950s housewives were partners in dual-earner couples a generation later. They were the subject of Arlie Hochschild's research which formed the basis for *The Second Shift* (1989). What happened in the United States in the almost twenty years between Friedan's and Hochschild's books? There was the Women's Movement, the Sexual Revolution, and more women going to work outside the home.

American women, even those with dependent children, started entering the labor force in large numbers in the 1970s. Presently, 70 percent of women with children under age eighteen participate in the paid labor force (Galinsky and Bond 1997). Dual-earner couples represent 60 percent of all marriages and only 17 percent of all families conform to the tradition of a wage-earning dad, a stay-at-home mom, and one or more children (Catalyst 1997). These changes have led sociologists to examine the impact of female labor force participation on the division of labor within the household and, more generally, on women's and men's gender roles.

The study of the relationship between paid labor and the household has led to a reexamination of what is "natural" and what constitutes real "work." Sociologists now routinely recognize that work may be paid (that is, accomplished in the labor market) or unpaid (that is, accomplished within the household by a household member). There are many perspectives on what are the most important factors determining the division of household labor. However, despite their disagreement about the causal factors, they all seem to come to the same basic conclusion: Even if women work for wages outside the home, they are still expected to take primary responsibility for the care of their home and children (Shelton 1992).

Many sociologists have tested hypotheses about the decisive factors in determining the household labor allocation in dual-earner families. Marxist theorists assume that the inequality in the division of labor in the household when both parents work outside the home is a result of class position. However, a study of dual-earner households in Sweden and the United States found that location within the class structure has little effect on the unequal division of household labor (Wright, Shire, Hwang, Dolan, and Baxter 1992). Other theorists take the power perspective which claims that household labor time is a function of one's resources relative to one's spouse's resources (Shelton 1992). However, Sanchez (1993) examined whether the relative resources of each partner affects husbands' domestic labor using data from five Southeast and East Asian countries and the United States. She found that the income of the wife does not uniformly predict husbands' domestic labor, and advanced industrialization does not signal gender egalitarianism Indeed, three of the five Southeast and East Asian countries had higher proportions of regular husband participation than the United States.

Other theorists have argued that sex-role ideology is the most salient factor in determining the household division of labor. Starrels (1994) argues that it is a combination of all these factors. She found that in the United States, the wife's earnings, employment status, gender role attitudes, and the husband's age at first birth are the strongest correlates of husbands' cross-gender housework. Nevertheless, working women do the majority of traditionally female household chores; only one-fifth of husbands are involved fully in these activities (Starrels 1994). As Hochschild points out in *The Second Shift* (1989), working women are more likely than their husbands to keep track of doctor and dentist appointments, haircuts, Halloween costumes, PTA meetings, birthday presents for friends, buying clothes, and so on.

Women in the labor force are subject to a gendered division of labor at their jobs as well as in their homes. Occupational segregation by gender exists on two different levels. First, there is segregation by occupation. For example, most teachers and librarians and nurses are women. Second, within any occupation, women and men are not distributed equally across the occupational hierarchy. There is occupational stratification with women clustered at the lower levels and men at the upper ones—even in occupations which are predominantly female. Women are clustered in the lower-paying occupations and they are paid less than men even when they are in the same profession (Beller 1984).

Cultural assumptions about the appropriate activities for the sexes play a large part in occupational segregation and wage inequality, yet they are often invisible. These unquestioned assumptions that have been used to exclude women from certain occupations and pay them less than men are remnants of the doctrine of separate spheres: Women are supported by men (therefore, they should be paid less); women's primary commitment is to their family not to their job (therefore, they should be paid less); women lack aggressiveness and capacity for abstract thought (therefore, they should not be given high-powered jobs); women are nurturing (therefore, they belong in jobs that require nurturing such as social work, nursing, and elementary school teaching) (Reskin and Hartmann 1986).

In this section, the readings are quite varied. Reskin and Padavic offer a historical perspective on the development of the doctrine of separate spheres, while Gilman's autobiographical short story illustrates its personal impact. Friedan's is a journalistic account of white married women's experiences in the 1950s, while Hochschild's work is qualitative sociology, based on extensive interviewing of working couples. Barbara Bergmann discusses the need for the continuation of affirmative action as a remedy to occupational segregation and wage inequality based on gender and race. She points out that the results of affirmative action have been limited because companies with less than fifty employees are exempt and they employ about one-third of American workers. In addition, she argues that while the government officially promotes affirmative action, its application has been largely voluntary. Elizabeth Higginbotham argues that although the degree of occupational segregation declined for the professional labor market, the majority of black professional and managerial women is employed in the public sector, while the majority of white professional and managerial women is in the private sector. Since public sector managerial and professional jobs tend to be female-dominated, black professional women remain in lower-paying, female-dominated occupations in contrast to white professional women.

REFERENCES

Beller, Andrea. 1984. Trends in Occupational Segregation by Sex and Race, 1960–1981. Pp. 11–25 in *Sex Segregation in the Workplace: Trends, Explanations and Remedies,* edited by Barbara Reskin. Washington, D.C.: National Academy Press.

Catalyst. 1997. *Two Careers, One Marriage: Making It Work in the Workplace.* New York: Catalyst.

Epstein, Barbara Leslie. 1986. *The Politics of Domesticity: Women, Evangelism and Temperance in Nineteenth Century America.* Middletown, CT: Wesleyan University Press.

Friedan, Betty. 1983. *The Feminine Mystique.* New York: Laurel Books.

Galinsky, Ellen, and James T. Bond, 1997. "Work and Family: The Experiences of Mothers and Fathers in the U.S. Labor Force." Pp. 80–103 in *The American Woman, 1996–97: Where We Stand.* Washington, D.C.: The Women's Research and Education Institute.

Harris, Barbara. 1980. *Beyond Her Sphere: Women and the Professions in American History.* Westport, CT: Greenwood Press.

Hartmann, Heidi. 1979. "Capitalism, Patriarchy and Job Segregation by Sex." Pp. 206–247 in *Capitalist Patriarchy and the Case for Socialist Feminism,* edited by Zilah Eisenstein. New York: Monthly Review Press.

Higginbotham, Elizabeth. 1986. "We Were Never on a Pedestal: Women of Color Continue to Struggle with Poverty, Racism, and Sexism." Pp. 99–110 in *For Crying Out Loud: Women and Poverty in the United States,* edited by Rochelle Lefkowitz and Ann Withorn. New York: Pilgrim Press.

Hill, Mary A. 1980. *The Making of a Radical Feminist: 1860–1896.* Philadelphia: Temple University Press.

Hochschild, Arlie, and Anne Machung. 1989. *The Second Shift: Working Parents and the Revolution at Home.* New York: Viking.

Kessler-Harris, Alice. 1982. *Out to Work.* New York: Oxford University Press.

Lengermann, Patricia Madoo, and Jill Niebrugge-Brantley. 1998. *The Women Founders: Sociology and Social Theory, 1830–1930.* New York: McGraw-Hill.

Reskin, Barbara F., and Heidi Hartmann. 1986. *Women's Work, Men's Work: Sex Segregation on the Job.* Washington, D.C.: National Academy Press.

Sanchez, Laura. 1993. "Women's Power and the Gendered Division of Labor in the Third World." *Gender & Society* 7:434–459.

Shelton, Beth Anne. 1992. *Women, Men and Time.* Westport, CT: Greenwood Press.

Starrels, Marjorie E. 1994. "Husbands' Involvement in Female Gender-Typed Household Chores." *Sex Roles* 31:473–491.

Stromberg, Ann Helton, and Shirley Harkess, eds. 1988. *Women Working: Second Edition.* Mountain View, CA: Mayfield Publ.

Wright, Erik Olin, K. Shire, S. Hwang, M. Dolan, and J. Baxter. 1992. "The Non-Effects of Class on the Gender Division of Labor in the Home: A Comparative Study of Sweden and the United States." *Gender & Society* 6:252–282.

The Doctrine of Separate Spheres

BARBARA F. RESKIN
IRENE PADAVIC

The *doctrine of separate spheres* which was born among the English upper-middle classes, called for the separation of work and family life. It held that a woman's proper place was in the home and not in the workplace; a man's natural sphere was in the world of commerce—or, at any rate, at his job—and not at home (Davidoff and Hall 1987:364–367; Skolnick 1991:30–31). These ideas encouraged male workers who had some voice in the matter to work away from home. Reinforcing these beliefs were stereotypes of men as strong, aggressive, and competitive and of women as frail, virtuous, and nurturing, images that depicted men as naturally suited to the highly competitive nineteenth-century workplace and women as too delicate for the world of commerce.

To earn respect, married women had two responsibilities: creating a haven to which their husbands could retreat from the world of work and demonstrating their husbands' ability to support their families. An employed wife was a sign of her husband's failure (Westover 1986). As one British woman who worked as a tailor recalled:

I never went out to work after I was married. There wasn't many who did. They used to cry shame on them in them days when they were married if they went to work. They used to say your husband should keep you.

The doctrine of separate spheres led to extremes. The tiny waists that women achieved through tightly laced corsets both ensured and symbolized their incapacity to do any work. Middle- and upper-class families hid the parts of the house devoted to productive work (cooking, bathing, laundry) out of sight from the areas of relaxation (parlor, dining room), furthering the illusion that the home was not a place of work (Davidoff and Hall 1987:359).

In reserving paid jobs for men, the doctrine of separate spheres especially victimized working-class wives whose families needed their earnings. Many employers refused to hire married women for "respectable" jobs; indeed, some firms enforced rules against employing married women until World War II (Goldin 1990). As a result, working-class women had to find ways to earn money at home, such as taking in laundry, sewing, or boarders. Conforming to the social standard meant doing piecework at home, which paid less for more hours of work (Westover 1986).

Around the turn of the twentieth century, the movement of people into and within the United States significantly affected patterns of paid labor. One such population shift was the migration to northern cities of 2 million African Americans from the rural South. After Emancipation, most former slaves in the South became sharecroppers, with entire families working in the fields. But in the late nineteenth century and early twentieth century, many sharecroppers sought to move North, where both the women and the men hoped to get paid jobs. Another population shift occurred in the early decades of the twentieth century, when the United States recruited families from Mexico for temporary agricultural jobs. Mexican women worked alongside their husbands at back-breaking work on huge "factory farms" in the Southwest (Amott and Matthaei 1991:75).

As these examples indicate, even during the heyday of the doctrine of separate spheres, thousands of women worked for pay: minority women, young single women, widows, and married women whose husbands had deserted their families or could not earn enough to support them. Employers in the market for cheap female labor did not care whether the women were married. Married immigrant women and former slaves were particularly likely to be employed. They labored in sweatshops, factories, offices, schools, and other families' homes, and some did paid work in their own homes. For sharecropping women who plowed the fields and for many immigrant and African-American women who worked 14-hour days as servants, staying out of the labor force would have meant starvation.

Nevertheless, the doctrine of separate spheres helped to drive all but the poorest married women out of the labor force. By 1890, fewer than one in 20 married American women worked for pay (U.S. Bureau of the Census 1961:72). But racial and ethnic background made a difference. In 1920, for example, only 7 percent of married European-American women were in the labor force, compared to one-third of married African-American women

and 18 percent of married Asian-American women. The labor force participation rate for unmarried European-American women was 45 percent; for African-American women, 59 percent; and for Asian-American women, 39 percent (Amott and Matthaei 1991:table 9.2). Even the Great Depression (1929–1937), which brought record unemployment among American men, did not draw large numbers of married women into the labor force. Families sent their children to work before mothers took jobs outside the home.

The doctrine of separate spheres contributed to the gendering of work in the twentieth century in several ways. First, men gained social approval as workers, but women's work became invisible because it was done at home. Second, social values that encouraged employers to ban women from many jobs made sex discrimination commonplace. Third, employers could justify low pay for women because men presumably supported them. Indeed, people came to define pay as what one earned for going to work; women's relegation to the home put them outside the system of pay for labor.

Finally, the sexual division of labor that assigned men to the labor force and women to the home encouraged employers to structure jobs on the assumptions that all permanent workers were men and that all men had stay-at-home wives. These assumptions freed workers (that is, male workers) from domestic responsibilities so they could work 12- to 14-hour days. These assumptions also bolstered the belief that domestic work was women's responsibility, even for women who were employed outside the home....

THE CONVERGENCE IN WOMEN'S AND MEN'S LABOR FORCE PARTICIPATION

The legacy of the doctrine that married women should not work outside the home has haunted us throughout the twentieth century. Not until the 1970s did married women's likelihood of paid employment catch up with that of single and divorced women. Moreover, the doctrine of separate spheres has not entirely disappeared. . . . Although society now expects married women to participate in the labor force, it continues to define domestic work as women's sphere.

As public support for the doctrine of separate spheres has waned, the gap between men's and women's labor force participation rates has narrowed, as Figure 1 shows. In 1890, 84.3 percent of males over the age of 14 were in the labor force, compared to only 18.2 percent of similar females.[1] Over the next hundred years, women's participation in the labor force climbed steadily. In contrast, men's labor force participation fell slightly. By 1992, 76 percent of men and 58 percent of women were in the labor force. More than three-quarters of women between the ages of 35 and 44 were in the labor force. Experts project that women's and men's labor force participation will continue to converge.

Although a substantial sex gap remains between men's and women's labor force participation, it has declined sharply, as Figure 2 shows. In 1870, during the heyday of the doctrine of separate spheres, fewer than 15 workers out of every 100 were female. In 1992, out of every 100 persons in the U.S. labor force, over 46 were women.

PERCENT IN LABOR FORCE

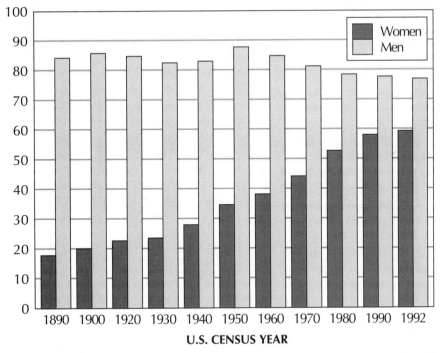

U.S. CENSUS YEAR

FIGURE 1 Trends in U.S. Labor Force Participation Rates by Sex, 1890 to 1992

Source: Data from U.S. Bureau of the Census 1975:131–132; U.S. Bureau of the Census 1992d: table 609; U.S. Women's Bureau 1993:1.

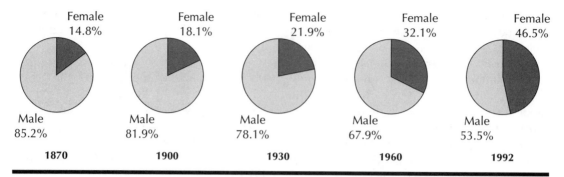

FIGURE 2   Composition by Sex of the U.S. Labor Force, 1870 to 1992

Source: Data from U.S. Bureau of the Census 1975:131–132; U.S. Bureau of Labor Statistics 1993d:table 1.

THE DEVALUATION OF WOMEN'S WORK

The shift of production from homes to shops and factories during the Industrial Revolution transformed men into wage laborers who left home each day for jobs in factories, shops, and offices. These jobs expanded men's contribution to their families: They became both the producers of the products their families needed and the earners who could pay for these products. The decline of domestic production, in turn, left women with the invisible and socially devalued tasks of housekeeping and child rearing. Thus, in the wake of industrialization, women found themselves in a no-win situation. Social norms and discrimination by employers reduced their participation in the labor force. As a result, women's path to economic security and respectability was through a husband, and women who worked at home were denied the esteem that society grants those who are economically productive. In sum, the definition of "real" work as paid activities performed away from home and the idealization of the home as a refuge from work rendered unpaid domestic work economically insignificant.

The devaluation of unpaid work in industrialized countries was exported by colonialists to Africa and Asia (Schrijvers 1983). Nowadays, no country counts as "employed" those people who do unpaid work in their own homes. Women who work in subsistence agriculture or who work without pay in a family business are also usually counted as nonemployed. Because laws often stipulate that only men can own farms or other property, in households engaged in farming, census takers tend to list the husband as a farmer and the wife as nonemployed. These practices underestimate women's economic contributions in developing countries, where most people work on family farms. Thus, as an indirect consequence of the Western doctrine of separate spheres, a twentieth-century Iranian peasant woman—who may harvest grain every day for her family's meals, tend animals, and haul water and wood for cooking and laundry—would officially be counted as nonemployed.

WOMEN'S AND MEN'S LABOR FORCE PARTICIPATION AROUND THE WORLD

Today, countries differ widely in the degree to which they enforce a sexual division of labor. The economically active, like the employed, exclude people engaged in unpaid family work that is important in developing countries, such as gathering fuel or water, processing crops, raising animals, keeping a kitchen garden, and laboring in cottage industry (United Nations 1991:85). The large sex differences in some countries thus stem from the undercounting of women's economic activities and sexual division of labor that limits women's access to paid work and confines them to unpaid domestic work.

We can draw some conclusions about the global sexual division of labor. Women's formal labor force participation is lowest in Muslim societies that strictly segregate the sexes (such as Saudi Arabia and Algeria). In developing countries that are not Muslim (such as Egypt and Brazil), men also greatly outnumber women in the labor force, because men tend to monopolize the paid jobs in developing labor markets, just as they did in earlier times in Western Europe and the United States. In fully developed capitalist societies (such as the United States, South Africa, Japan, and Canada), women's rates of labor force participation are somewhat closer to men's. They are even closer in Scandinavian countries (such as Sweden and Iceland), which provide paid leave for new parents and childcare for those who are employed. Finally, the gap between women's and men's labor participation rates is smallest in communist, for-

merly communist, and socialist societies (China, East Germany, the former Soviet Union, Mozambique, Poland, and Vietnam), reflecting the Marxist ideology that all able-bodied adults have both a right and an obligation to work. We see in these patterns the influence of economic development, social policies, and cultural norms.

Women's labor force participation in industrializing countries has been on the rise in the latter half of the twentieth century, at least until the economic recession of the 1980s.[2] In developing countries, transnational corporations have drawn women into the labor force as a source of cheap labor; transnational corporations pay these women between 5 and 25 percent of what Western workers earn for similar jobs (Safa 1990:77). Moreover, developing countries have few if any laws against exploitative conditions for workers. But women work for transnational corporations for the same reasons they left agricultural work and cottage industries in Western societies: These women want jobs that pay more than domestic work, farming, or jobs in the service sector.

NOTES

1. If the Census Bureau had counted farm wives on the same basis as it counted farmers, and if it had counted women who ran boardinghouses, women's labor force participation rate for 1890 would have been about 28 percent (Goldin 1990:44–45).

2. Women are generally the last to benefit from job expansion and the first to suffer from job contraction, so the recent recession has slowed the growth in women's labor force participation in developing countries (United Nations 1991:chart 6.7).

REFERENCES

Amott, Teresa and Julie A. Matthaei. 1991. *Race, Gender, and Work: A Multicultural Economic History of Women in the United States.* Boston: South End Press.

Davidoff, Leonore and Catherine Hall. 1987. *Family Fortunes.* London: Hutchinson.

Goldin, Claudia. 1990. *Understanding the Gender Gap.* New York: Oxford University Press.

Safa, Helen I. 1990. "Women and Industrialization in the Caribbean." Pp. 72–97 in Sharon Stichter

and Jane L. Parpart (eds.), *Women, Employment, and the Family in the International Division of Labour.* Philadelphia: Temple University Press.

Schrijvers, Joke. 1983. "Manipulated Motherhood: The Marginalization of Peasant Women in the North Central Province of Sri Lanka." *World Quarterly* 14:185–209.

Skolnick, Arlene. 1991. *Embattled Paradise: The American Family in an Age of Uncertainty.* New York: Basic Books.

United Nations. 1991. *The World's Women: Trends and Statistics, 1970–1990.* New York: United Nations Publications.

U.S. Bureau of the Census. 1961. *Historical Statistics of the United States: Colonial Times to 1957.* Washington, DC: U.S. Government Printing Office.

Westover, Belinda. 1986. "'To Fill the Kids' Tummies': The Lives and Work of Colchester Tailoresses, 1880–1918." Pp. 54–75 in Leonore Davidoff and Belinda Westover (eds.), *Our Work, Our Lives, Our Words.* London: Macmillan.

The Yellow Wallpaper

CHARLOTTE PERKINS GILMAN

It is very seldom that mere ordinary people like John and myself secure ancestral halls for the summer.

A colonial mansion, a hereditary estate, I would say a haunted house, and reach the height of romantic felicity—but that would be asking too much of fate!

Still I will proudly declare that there is something queer about it.

Else, why should it be let so cheaply? And why have stood so long untenanted?

John laughs at me, of course, but one expects that in marriage.

John is practical in the extreme. He has no patience with faith, an intense horror of superstition, and he scoffs openly at any talk of things not to be felt and seen and put down in figures.

John is a physician, and *perhaps*—(I would not say it to a living soul, of course, but this is dead paper and a great relief to my mind)—*perhaps* that is one reason I do not get well faster.

You see he does not believe I am sick!

And what can one do?

If a physician of high standing, and one's own husband, assures friends and relatives that there is really nothing the matter with one but temporary nervous depression—a slight hysterical tendency—what is one to do?

My brother is also a physician, and also of high standing, and he says the same thing.

So I take phosphates or phosphites—whichever it is, and tonics, and journeys, and air, and exercise, and am absolutely forbidden to "work" until I am well again.

Personally, I disagree with their ideas.

Personally, I believe that congenial work, with excitement and change, would do me good.

But what is one to do?

I did write for a while in spite of them; but it *does* exhaust me a good deal—having to be so sly about it, or else meet with heavy opposition.

I sometimes fancy that in my condition if I had less opposition and more society and stimulus—but John says the very worst thing I can do is to think about my condition, and I confess it always makes me feel bad.

So I will let it alone and talk about the house.

The most beautiful place! It is quite alone, standing well back from the road, quite three miles from the village. It makes me think of English places that you read about, for there are hedges and walls and gates that lock, and lots of separate little houses for the gardeners and people.

There is a *delicious* garden! I never saw such a garden—large and shady, full of box-bordered paths, and lined with long grape-covered arbors with seats under them.

There were greenhouses, too, but they are all broken now.

There was some legal trouble, I believe, something about the heirs and co-heirs; anyhow, the place has been empty for years.

That spoils my ghostliness, I am afraid, but I don't care—there is something strange about the house—I can feel it.

I even said so to John one moonlight evening, but he said what I felt was a *draught*, and shut the window.

I get unreasonably angry with John sometimes. I'm sure I never used to be so sensitive. I think it is due to this nervous condition.

But John says if I feel so, I shall neglect proper self-control; so I take pains to control myself—before him, at least, and that makes me very tired.

I don't like our room a bit. I wanted one downstairs that opened on the piazza and had roses all over the window, and such pretty old-fashioned chintz hangings! but John would not hear of it.

He said there was only one window and not room for two beds, and no near room for him if he took another.

He is very careful and loving, and hardly lets me stir without special direction.

I have a schedule prescription for each hour in the day; he takes all care from me, and so I feel basely ungrateful not to value it more.

He said we came here solely on my account, that I was to have perfect rest and all the air I could get. "Your exercise depends on your strength, my dear," said he, "and your food somewhat on your appetite, but air you can absorb all the time." So we took the nursery at the top of the house.

It is a big, airy room, the whole floor nearly, with windows that look all ways, and air and sunshine galore. It was nursery first and then playroom and gymnasium, I should judge; for the windows are barred for little children, and there are rings and things in the walls.

The paint and paper look as if a boys' school had used it. It is stripped off—the paper—in great patches all around the head of my bed, about as far as I can reach, and in a great place on the other side of the room low down. I never saw a worse paper in my life.

One of those sprawling flamboyant patterns committing every artistic sin.

It is dull enough to confuse the eye in following, pronounced enough to constantly irritate and provoke study, and when you follow the lame uncertain curves for a little distance they suddenly commit suicide—plunge off at outrageous angles, destroy themselves in unheard of contradictions.

The color is repellent, almost revolting; a smouldering unclean yellow, strangely faded by the slow-turning sunlight.

It is a dull yet lurid orange in some places, a sickly sulphur tint in others.

No wonder the children hated it! I should hate it myself if I had to live in this room long.

There comes John, and I must put this away,—he hates to have me write a word.

We have been here two weeks, and I haven't felt like writing before, since that first day.

I am sitting by the window now, up in this atrocious nursery, and there is nothing to hinder my writing as much as I please, save lack of strength.

John is away all day, and even some nights when his cases are serious.

I am glad my case is not serious!

But these nervous troubles are dreadfully depressing.

John does not know how much I really suffer. He knows there is no *reason* to suffer, and that satisfies him.

Of course it is only nervousness. It does weigh on me so not to do my duty in any way!

I meant to be such a help to John, such a real rest and comfort, and here I am a comparative burden already!

Nobody would believe what an effort it is to do what little I am able,—to dress and entertain, and order things.

It is fortunate Mary is so good with the baby. Such a dear baby!

And yet I *cannot* be with him, it makes me so nervous.

I suppose John never was nervous in his life. He laughs at me so about this wall-paper!

At first he meant to repaper the room, but afterwards he said that I was letting it get the better of me, and that nothing was worse for a nervous patient than to give way to such fancies.

He said that after the wall-paper was changed it would be the heavy bedstead, and then the barred windows, and then that gate at the head of the stairs, and so on.

"You know the place is doing you good," he said, "and really, dear, I don't care to renovate the house just for a three months' rental."

"Then do let us go downstairs," I said, "there are such pretty rooms there."

Then he took me in his arms and called me a blessed little goose, and said he would go down cellar, if I wished, and have it whitewashed into the bargain.

But he is right enough about the beds and windows and things.

It is an airy and comfortable room as any one need wish, and, of course, I would not be so silly as to make him uncomfortable just for a whim.

I'm really getting quite fond of the big room, all but that horrid paper.

Out of one window I can see the garden, those mysterious deep-shaded arbors, the riotous old-fashioned flowers, and bushes and gnarly trees.

Out of another I get a lovely view of the bay and a little private wharf belonging to the estate. There is a beautiful shaded lane that runs down there from the house. I always fancy I see people walking in these numerous paths and arbors, but John has cautioned me not to give way to fancy in the least. He says

that with my imaginative power and habit of story-making, a nervous weakness like mine is sure to lead to all manner of excited fancies, and that I ought to use my will and good sense to check the tendency. So I try.

I think sometimes that if I were only well enough to write a little it would relieve the press of ideas and rest me.

But I find I get pretty tired when I try.

It is so discouraging not to have any advice and companionship about my work. When I get really well, John says we will ask Cousin Henry and Julia down for a long visit; but he says he would as soon put fireworks in my pillow-case as to let me have those stimulating people about now.

I wish I could get well faster.

But I must not think about that. This paper looks to me as if it *knew* what a vicious influence it had!

There is a recurrent spot where the pattern lolls like a broken neck and two bulbous eyes stare at you upside down.

I get positively angry with the impertinence of it and the everlastingness. Up and down and sideways they crawl, and those absurd, unblinking eyes are everywhere. There is one place where two breadths didn't match, and the eyes go all up and down the line, one a little higher than the other.

I never saw so much expression in an inanimate thing before, and we all know how much expression they have! I used to lie awake as a child and get more entertainment and terror out of blank walls and plain furniture than most children could find in a toy-store.

I remember what a kindly wink the knobs of our big, old bureau used to have, and there was one chair that always seemed like a strong friend.

I used to feel that if any of the other things looked too fierce I could always hop into that chair and be safe.

The furniture in this room is no worse than inharmonious, however, for we had to bring it all from downstairs. I suppose when this was used as a playroom they had to take the nursery things out, and no wonder! I never saw such ravages as the children have made here.

The wall-paper, as I said before, is torn off in spots, and it sticketh closer than a brother—they must have had perseverance as well as hatred.

Then the floor is scratched and gouged and splintered, the plaster itself is dug out here and there, and this great heavy bed which is all we found in the room, looks as if it had been through the wars.

But I don't mind it a bit—only the paper.

There comes John's sister. Such a dear girl as she is, and so careful of me! I must not let her find me writing.

She is a perfect and enthusiastic housekeeper, and hopes for no better profession. I verily believe she thinks it is the writing which made me sick!

But I can write when she is out, and see her a long way off from these windows.

There is one that commands the road, a lovely shaded winding road, and one that just looks off over the country. A lovely country, too, full of great elms and velvet meadows.

This wallpaper has a kind of sub-pattern in a different shade, a particularly irritating one, for you can only see it in certain lights, and not clearly then.

But in the places where it isn't faded and where the sun is just so—I can see a strange, provoking, formless sort of figure, that seems to skulk about behind that silly and conspicuous front design.

There's sister on the stairs!

Well, the Fourth of July is over! The people are all gone and I am tired out. John thought it might do me good to see a little company, so we just had mother and Nellie and the children down for a week.

Of course I didn't do a thing. Jennie sees to everything now.

But it tired me all the same.

John says if I don't pick up faster he shall send me to Weir Mitchell in the fall.

But I don't want to go there at all. I had a friend who was in his hands once, and she says he is just like John and my brother, only more so!

Besides, it is such an undertaking to go so far.

I don't feel as if it was worth while to turn my hand over for anything, and I'm getting dreadfully fretful and querulous.

I cry at nothing, and cry most of the time.

Of course I don't when John is here, or anybody else, but when I am alone.

And I am alone a good deal just now. John is kept in town very often by serious cases, and Jennie is good and lets me alone when I want her to.

So I walk a little in the garden or down that lovely lane, sit on the porch under the roses, and lie down up here a good deal.

I'm getting really fond of the room in spite of the wallpaper. Perhaps *because* of the wallpaper.

It dwells in my mind so!

I lie here on this great immovable bed—it is nailed down, I believe—and follow that pattern about by the hour. It is as good as gymnastics, I assure you. I start, we'll say, at the bottom, down in the corner over there where it has not been touched, and I determine for the thousandth time that I *will* follow that pointless pattern to some sort of a conclusion.

I know a little of the principle of design, and I know this thing was not arranged on any laws of radiation, or alternation, or repetition, or symmetry, or anything else that I ever heard of.

It is repeated, of course, by the breadths, but not otherwise.

Looked at in one way each breadth stands alone, the bloated curves and flourishes—a kind of "debased Romanesque" with *delirium tremens*—go waddling up and down in isolated columns of fatuity.

But, on the other hand, they connect diagonally, and the sprawling outlines run off in great slanting waves of optic horror, like a lot of wallowing seaweeds in full chase.

The whole thing goes horizontally, too, at least it seems so, and I exhaust myself in trying to distinguish the order of its going in that direction.

They have used a horizontal breadth for a frieze, and that adds wonderfully to the confusion.

There is one end of the room where it is almost intact, and there, when the crosslights fade and the low sun shines directly upon it, I can almost fancy radiation after all,—the interminable grotesques seem to form around a common centre and rush off in headlong plunges of equal distraction.

It makes me tired to follow it. I will take a nap I guess.

I don't know why I should write this.

I don't want to.

I don't feel able.

And I know John would think it absurd. But I *must* say what I feel and think in some way—it is such a relief!

But the effort is getting to be greater than the relief.

Half the time now I am awfully lazy, and lie down ever so much.

John says I mustn't lose my strength, and has me take cod liver oil and lots of tonics and things, to say nothing of ale and wine and rare meat.

Dear John! He loves me very dearly, and hates to have me sick. I tried to have a real earnest reasonable talk with him the other day, and tell him how I wish he would let me go and make a visit to Cousin Henry and Julia.

But he said I wasn't able to go, nor able to stand it after I got there; and I did not make out a very good case for myself, for I was crying before I had finished.

It is getting to be a great effort for me to think straight. Just this nervous weakness I suppose.

And dear John gathered me up in his arms, and just carried me upstairs and laid me on the bed, and sat by me and read to me till it tired my head.

He said I was his darling and his comfort and all he had, and that I must take care of myself for his sake, and keep well.

He says no one but myself can help me out of it, that I must use my will and self-control and not let any silly fancies run away with me.

There's one comfort, the baby is well and happy, and does not have to occupy this nursery with the horrid wallpaper.

If we had not used it, that blessed child would have! What a fortunate escape! Why, I wouldn't have a child of mine, an impressionable little thing, live in such a room for worlds.

I never thought of it before, but it is lucky that John kept me here after all, I can stand it so much easier than a baby, you see.

Of course I never mention it to them any more—I am too wise,—but I keep watch of it all the same.

There are things in that paper that nobody knows but me, or ever will.

Behind that outside pattern the dim shapes get clearer every day.

It is always the same shape, only very numerous.

And it is like a woman stooping down and creeping about behind that pattern. I don't like it a bit. I wonder—I begin to think—I wish John would take me away from here!

It is so hard to talk to John about my case, because he is so wise, and because he loves me so.

But I tried it last night.

It was moonlight. The moon shines in all around just as the sun does.

I hate to see it sometimes, it creeps so slowly, and always comes in by one window or another.

John was asleep and I hated to waken him, so I kept still and watched the moonlight on that undulating wallpaper till I felt creepy.

The faint figure behind seemed to shake the pattern, just as if she wanted to get out.

I got up softly and went to feel and see if the paper *did* move, and when I came back John was awake.

"What is it, little girl?" he said. "Don't go walking about like that—you'll get cold."

I thought it was a good time to talk, so I told him that I really was not gaining here, and that I wished he would take me away.

"Why darling!" said he, "our lease will be up in three weeks, and I can't see how to leave before.

"The repairs are not done at home, and I cannot possibly leave town just now. Of course if you were in any danger, I could and would, but you really are better, dear, whether you can see it or not. I am a doctor, dear, and I know. You are gaining flesh and color, your appetite is better, I feel really much easier about you."

"I don't weigh a bit more," said I, "nor as much; and my appetite may be better in the evening when you are here, but it is worse in the morning when you are away!"

"Bless her little heart!" said he with a big hug, "she shall be as sick as she pleases! But now let's improve the shining hours by going to sleep, and talk about it in the morning!"

"And you won't go away?" I asked gloomily.

"Why, how can I, dear? It is only three weeks more and then we will take a nice little trip of a few days while Jennie is getting the house ready. Really dear you are better!"

"Better in body perhaps—" I began, and stopped short, for he sat up straight and looked at me with such a stern, reproachful look that I could not say another word.

"My darling," said he, "I beg of you, for my sake and for our child's sake, as well as for your own, that you will never for one instant let that idea enter your mind! There is nothing so dangerous, so fascinating, to a temperament like yours. It is a false and foolish fancy. Can you not trust me as a physician when I tell you so?"

So of course I said no more on that score, and we went to sleep before long. He thought I was asleep first, but I wasn't, and lay there for hours trying to decide whether that front pattern and the back pattern really did move together or separately.

On a pattern like this, by daylight, there is a lack of sequence, a defiance of law, that is a constant irritant to a normal mind.

The color is hideous enough, and unreliable enough, and infuriating enough, but the pattern is torturing.

You think you have mastered it, but just as you get well underway in following, it turns a back-somersault and there you are. It slaps you in the face, knocks you down, and tramples upon you. It is like a bad dream.

The outside pattern is a florid arabesque, reminding one of a fungus. If you can imagine a toadstool in joints, an interminable string of toadstools, budding and sprouting in endless convolutions—why, that is something like it.

That is, sometimes!

There is one marked peculiarity about this paper, a thing nobody seems to notice but myself, and that is that it changes as the light changes.

When the sun shoots in through the east window—I always watch for that first long, straight ray—it changes so quickly that I never can quite believe it.

That is why I watch it always.

By moonlight—the moon shines in all night when there is a moon—I wouldn't know it was the same paper.

At night in any kind of light, in twilight, candlelight, lamplight, and worst of all by moonlight, it becomes bars! The outside pattern I mean, and the woman behind it is as plain as can be.

I didn't realize for a long time what the thing was that showed behind, that dim sub-pattern, but now I am quite sure it is a woman.

By daylight she is subdued, quiet. I fancy it is the pattern that keeps her so still. It is so puzzling. It keeps me quiet by the hour.

I lie down ever so much now. John says it is good for me, and to sleep all I can.

Indeed he started the habit by making me lie down for an hour after each meal.

It is a very bad habit I am convinced, for you see I don't sleep.

And that cultivates deceit, for I don't tell them I'm awake—O no!

The fact is I am getting a little afraid of John.

He seems very queer sometimes, and even Jennie has an inexplicable look.

It strikes me occasionally, just as a scientific hypothesis,—that perhaps it is the paper!

I have watched John when he did not know I was looking, and come into the room suddenly on the most innocent excuses, and I've caught him several times *looking at the paper!* And Jennie too. I caught Jennie with her hand on it once.

She didn't know I was in the room, and when I asked her in a quiet, a very quiet voice, with the most restrained manner possible, what she was doing with the paper—she turned around as if she had been caught stealing, and looked quite angry—asked me why I should frighten her so!

Then she said that the paper stained everything it touched, that she had found yellow smooches on all my clothes and John's, and she wished we would be more careful!

Did not that sound innocent? But I know she was studying that pattern, and I am determined that nobody shall find it out but myself!

Life is very much more exciting now than it used to be. You see I have something more to expect, to look forward to, to watch. I really do eat better, and am more quiet than I was.

John is so pleased to see me improve! He laughed a little the other day, and said I seemed to be flourishing in spite of my wallpaper.

I turned it off with a laugh. I had no intention of telling him it was *because* of the wall-paper—he would make fun of me. He might even want to take me away.

I don't want to leave now until I have found it out. There is a week more, and I think that will be enough.

I'm feeling ever so much better! I don't sleep much at night, for it is so interesting to watch developments; but I sleep a good deal in the daytime.

In the daytime it is tiresome and perplexing.

There are always new shoots on the fungus, and new shades of yellow all over it. I cannot keep count of them, though I have tried conscientiously.

It is the strangest yellow, that wall-paper! It makes me think of all the yellow things I ever saw—not beautiful ones like buttercups, but old foul, bad yellow things.

But there is something else about that paper—the smell! I noticed it the moment we came into the room, but with so much air and sun it was not bad. Now we have had a week of fog and rain, and whether the windows are open or not, the smell is here.

It creeps all over the house.

I find it hovering in the dining-room, skulking in the parlor, hiding in the hall, lying in wait for me on the stairs.

It gets into my hair.

Even when I go to ride, if I turn my head suddenly and surprise it—there is that smell!

Such a peculiar odor, too! I have spent hours in trying to analyze it, to find what it smelled like.

It is not bad—at first, and very gentle, but quite the subtlest, most enduring odor I ever met.

In this damp weather it is awful, I wake up in the night and find it hanging over me.

It used to disturb me at first. I thought seriously of burning the house—to reach the smell.

But now I am used to it. The only thing I can think of that it is like is the *color* of the paper! A yellow smell.

There is a very funny mark on this wall, low down, near the mopboard. A streak that runs round the room. It goes behind every piece of furniture, except the bed, a long, straight, even *smooch*, as if it had been rubbed over and over.

I wonder how it was done and who did it, and what they did it for. Round and round and round—round and round and round—it makes me dizzy!

I really have discovered something at last.

Through watching so much at night, when it changes so, I have finally found out.

The front pattern *does* move—and no wonder! The woman behind shakes it!

Sometimes I think there are a great many women behind, and sometimes only one, and she crawls around fast, and her crawling shakes it all over.

Then in the very bright spots she keeps still, and in the very shady spots she just takes hold of the bars and shakes them hard.

And she is all the time trying to climb through. But nobody could climb through that pattern—it strangles so; I think that is why it has so many heads.

They get through, and then the pattern strangles them off and turns them upside down, and makes their eyes white!

If those heads were covered or taken off it would not be half so bad.

I think that woman gets out in the daytime!

And I'll tell you why—privately—I've seen her!

I can see her out of every one of my windows!

It is the same woman, I know, for she is always creeping, and most women do not creep by daylight.

I see her in that long shaded lane, creeping up and down. I see her in those dark grape arbors, creeping all around the garden.

I see her on that long road under the trees, creeping along, and when a carriage comes she hides under the blackberry vines.

I don't blame her a bit. It must be very humiliating to be caught creeping by daylight!

I always lock the door when I creep by daylight. I can't do it at night, for I know John would suspect something at once.

And John is so queer now, that I don't want to irritate him. I wish he would take another room! Besides, I don't want anybody to get that woman out at night but myself.

I often wonder if I could see her out of all the windows at once.

But, turn as fast as I can, I can only see out of one at one time.

And though I always see her, she *may* be able to creep faster than I can turn!

I have watched her sometimes away off in the open country, creeping as fast as a cloud shadow in a high wind.

If only that top pattern could be gotten off from the under one! I mean to try it, little by little.

I have found out another funny thing, but I shan't tell it this time! It does not do to trust people too much.

There are only two more days to get this paper off, and I believe John is beginning to notice. I don't like the look in his eyes.

And I heard him ask Jennie a lot of professional questions about me. She had a very good report to give.

She said I slept a good deal in the daytime.

John knows I don't sleep very well at night, for all I'm so quiet!

He asked me all sorts of questions, too, and pretended to be very loving and kind.

As if I couldn't see through him!

Still, I don't wonder he acts so, sleeping under this paper for three months.

It only interests me, but I feel sure John and Jennie are secretly affected by it.

Hurrah! This is the last day, but it is enough. John to stay in town over night, and won't be out until this evening.

Jennie wanted to sleep with me—the sly thing! But I told her I should undoubtedly rest better for a night all alone.

That was clever, for really I wasn't alone a bit! As soon as it was moonlight and that poor thing began to crawl and shake the pattern, I got up and ran to help her.

I pulled and she shook, I shook and she pulled, and before morning we had peeled off yards of that paper.

A strip about as high as my head and half around the room.

And then when the sun came and that awful pattern began to laugh at me, I declared I would finish it to-day!

We go away to-morrow, and they are moving all my furniture down again to leave things as they were before.

Jennie looked at the wall in amazement, but I told her merrily that I did it out of pure spite at the vicious thing.

She laughed and said she wouldn't mind doing it herself, but I must not get tired.

How she betrayed herself that time!

But I am here, and no person touches this paper but me—not *alive*!

She tried to get me out of the room—it was too patent! But I said it was so quiet and empty and clean now that I believed I would lie down again and sleep all I could; and not to wake me even for dinner—I would call when I woke.

So now she is gone, and the servants are gone, and the things are gone, and there is nothing left but that great bedstead nailed down, with the canvas mattress we found on it.

We shall sleep downstairs to-night, and take the boat home to-morrow.

I quite enjoy the room, now it is bare again.

How those children did tear about here!

This bedstead is fairly gnawed!

But I must get to work.

I have locked the door and thrown the key down into the front path.

I don't want to go out, and I don't want to have anybody come in, till John comes.

I want to astonish him.

I've got a rope up here that even Jennie did not find. If that woman does get out, and tries to get away, I can tie her!

But I forgot I could not reach far without anything to stand on!

This bed will *not* move!

I tried to lift and push it until I was lame, and then I got so angry I bit off a little piece at one corner—but it hurt my teeth.

Then I peeled off all the paper I could reach standing on the floor. It sticks horribly and the pattern just enjoys it! All those strangled heads and bulbous eyes and waddling fungus growths just shriek with derision!

I am getting angry enough to do something desperate. To jump out of the window would be admirable exercise, but the bars are too strong even to try.

Besides I wouldn't do it. Of course not. I know well enough that a step like that is improper and might be misconstrued.

I don't like to *look* out of the windows even—there are so many of those creeping women, and they creep so fast.

I wonder if they all come out of that wall-paper as I did?

But I am securely fastened now by my well-hidden rope—you don't get *me* out in the road there!

I suppose I shall have to get back behind the pattern when it comes night, and that is hard!

It is so pleasant to be out in this great room and creep around as I please!

I don't want to go outside. I won't, even if Jennie asks me to.

For outside you have to creep on the ground, and everything is green instead of yellow.

But here I can creep smoothly on the floor, and my shoulder just fits in that long smooch around the wall, so I cannot lose my way.

Why there's John at the door!

It is no use, young man, you can't open it!

How he does call and pound!

Now he's crying for an axe.

It would be a shame to break down that beautiful door!

"John dear!" said I in the gentlest voice, "the key is down by the front steps, under a plantain leaf!"

That silenced him for a few moments.

Then he said—very quietly indeed, "Open the door, my darling!"

"I can't," said I. "The key is down by the front door under a plantain leaf!"

And then I said it again, several times, very gently and slowly, and said it so often that he had to go and see, and he got it of course, and came in. He stopped short by the door.

"What is the matter?" he cried. "For God's sake, what are you doing?"

I kept on creeping just the same, but I looked at him over my shoulder.

"I've got out at last," said I, "in spite of you and Jane. And I've pulled off most of the paper, so you can't put me back!"

Now why should that man have fainted? But he did, and right across my path by the wall, so that I had to creep over him every time!

The Problem That Has No Name

BETTY FRIEDAN

The problem lay buried, unspoken, for many years in the minds of American women. It was a strange stirring, a sense of dissatisfaction, a yearning that women suffered in the middle of the twentieth century in the United States. Each suburban wife struggled with it alone. As she made the beds, shopped for groceries, matched slipcover material, ate peanut butter sandwiches with her children, chauffeured Cub Scouts and Brownies, lay beside her husband at night—she was afraid to ask even of herself the silent question—"Is this all?"

For over fifteen years there was no word of this yearning in the millions of words written about women, for women, in all the columns, books, and articles by experts telling women their role was to seek fulfillment as wives and mothers. Over and over women heard in voices of tradition and of Freudian sophistication that they could desire no greater destiny than to glory in their own femininity. Experts told them how to catch a man and keep him, how to breastfeed children and handle their toilet training, how to cope with sibling rivalry and adolescent rebellion; how to buy a dishwasher, bake bread, cook gourmet snails, and build a swimming pool with their own hands; how to dress, look, and act more feminine and make marriage more exciting; how to keep their husbands from dying young and their sons from growing into delinquents. They were taught to pity the neurotic, unfeminine, unhappy women who wanted to be poets or physicists or presidents. They learned that truly feminine women do not want careers, higher education, political rights—the independence and the opportunities that the old-fashioned feminists fought for. Some women, in their forties and fifties, still remembered painfully giving up those dreams, but most of the younger women no longer even thought about them. A thousand expert voices applauded their femininity, their adjustment, their new maturity. All they had to do was devote their lives from earliest girlhood to finding a husband and bearing children.

By the end of the nineteen-fifties, the average marriage age of women in America dropped to 20, and was still dropping, into the teens. Fourteen million girls were engaged by 17. The proportion of women attending college in comparison with men dropped from 47 percent in 1920 to 35 percent in 1958. A century earlier, women had fought for higher education; now girls went to college to get a husband. By the mid-fifties, 60 percent dropped out of college to marry, or because they were afraid too much education would be a marriage bar. Colleges built dormitories for "married students," but the students were almost always the husbands. A new degree was instituted for the wives—"Ph.T." (Putting Husband Through).

Then American girls began getting married in high school. And the women's magazines, deploring the unhappy statistics about these young marriages, urged that courses on marriage, and marriage counselors, be installed in the high schools. Girls started going steady at twelve and thirteen, in junior high. Manufacturers put out bràssieres with false bosoms of foam rubber for little girls of ten. And an advertisement for a child's dress, sizes 3–6x, in the *New York Times* in the fall of 1960, said: "She Too Can Join the Man-Trap Set."

By the end of the fifties, the United States birthrate was overtaking India's. The birth-control movement, renamed Planned Parenthood, was asked to find a method whereby women who had been advised that a third or fourth baby would be born dead or defective might have it anyhow. Statisticians were especially astounded at the fantastic increase in the number of babies among college women. Where once they had two children, now they had four, five, six. Women who had once wanted careers were now making careers out of having babies. So rejoiced *Life* magazine in a 1956 paean to the movement of American women back to the home.

In a New York hospital, a woman had a nervous breakdown when she found she could not breastfeed her baby. In other hospitals, women dying of cancer refused a drug which research had proved might save their lives: its side effects were said to be unfeminine. "If I have only one life, let me live it as a blonde," a larger-than-life-sized picture of a pretty, vacuous woman proclaimed from newspaper, magazine, and drugstore ads. And across America, three out of every ten women dyed their hair blonde. They ate a chalk called Metrecal, instead of food, to shrink to the size of the thin young models. Department-store buyers reported that American women, since 1939, had become three and four sizes smaller. "Women are out to fit the clothes, instead of vice-versa," one buyer said.

Interior decorators were designing kitchens with mosaic murals and original paintings, for kitchens were once again the center of women's lives. Home sewing became a million-dollar industry. Many women no longer left their homes, except to shop, chauffeur their children, or attend a social engagement with their husbands. Girls were growing up in America without ever having jobs outside the home. In the late fifties, a sociological phenomenon was suddenly remarked: a third of American women now worked, but most were no longer young and very few were pursuing careers. They were married women who held part-time jobs, selling or secretarial, to put their husbands through school, their sons through college, or to help pay the mortgage. Or they were widows supporting families. Fewer and fewer women were entering professional work. The shortages in the nursing, social work, and teaching professions caused crises in almost every American city. Concerned over the Soviet Union's lead in the space race, scientists noted that America's greatest source of unused brainpower was women. But girls would not study physics: it was "unfeminine." A girl refused a science fellowship at Johns Hopkins to take a job in a real-estate office. All she wanted, she said, was what every other American girl wanted—to get married, have four children and live in a nice house in a nice suburb.

The suburban housewife—she was the dream image of the young American women and the envy, it was said, of women all over the world. The American housewife—freed by science and labor-saving appliances from the drudgery, the dangers of childbirth and the illnesses of her grandmother. She was healthy, beautiful, educated, concerned only about her husband, her children, her home. She had found true feminine fulfillment. As a housewife and mother, she was respected as a full and equal partner to man in his world. She was free to choose automobiles, clothes, appliances, supermarkets; she had everything that women ever dreamed of.

In the fifteen years after World War II, this mystique of feminine fulfillment became the cherished and self-perpetuating core of contemporary American culture. Millions of women lived their lives in the image of those pretty pictures of the American suburban housewife, kissing their husbands goodbye in front of the picture window, depositing their stationwagonsful of children at school, and smiling as they ran the new electric waxer over the spotless kitchen floor. They baked their own bread, sewed their own and their children's clothes, kept their new washing machines and dryers running all day. They changed the sheets on the beds twice a week instead of once, took the rug-hooking class in adult education, and pitied their poor frustrated mothers, who had dreamed of having a career. Their only dream was to be perfect wives and mothers; their highest ambition to have five children and a beautiful house, their only fight to get and keep their husbands. They had no thought for the unfeminine problems of the world outside the home; they wanted the men to make the major decisions. They gloried in their role as women, and wrote proudly on the census blank: "Occupation: housewife."

For over fifteen years, the words written for women, and the words women used when they talked to each other, while their husbands sat on the other side of the room and talked shop or politics or septic tanks, were about problems with their children, or how to keep their husbands happy, or improve their children's school, or cook chicken, or make slipcovers. Nobody argued whether women were inferior or superior to men; they were simply different. Words like "emancipation" and "career" sounded strange and embarrassing; no one had used them for years. When a Frenchwoman named Simone de Beauvoir wrote a book called *The Second Sex,* an American critic commented that she obviously "didn't know what life was all about," and besides, she was talking about French women. The "woman problem" in America no longer existed.

If a woman had a problem in the 1950's and 1960's, she knew that something must be wrong with her marriage, or with herself. Other women were satisfied with their lives, she thought. What kind of a woman was she if she did not feel this mysterious fulfillment waxing the kitchen floor? She was so ashamed to admit her dissatisfaction that she never knew how many other women shared it. If she tried to tell her husband, he didn't understand what she was talking about. She did not really understand it herself. For over fifteen years women in America found it harder to talk about this problem than about sex. Even the psychoanalysts had no name for it. When a woman went to a psychiatrist for help, as many women did, she would say, "I'm so ashamed," or "I must be hopelessly neurotic." "I don't know what's wrong with women today," a suburban psychiatrist said uneasily. "I only know something is wrong because most of my patients happen to be women. And their problem isn't sexual." Most women with this problem did not go to see a psychoanalyst, however. "There's nothing wrong really," they kept telling themselves. "There isn't any problem."

But on an April morning in 1959, I heard a mother of four, having coffee with four other mothers in a suburban development fifteen miles from New York, say in a tone of quiet desperation, "the problem." And the others knew, without words, that she was not talking about a problem with her husband, or her children, or her home. Suddenly they realized they all shared the same problem, the problem that has no name. They began, hesitantly, to talk about it. Later, after they had picked up their children at nursery school and taken them home to nap, two of the women cried, in sheer relief, just to know they were not alone.

Gradually I came to realize that the problem that has no name was shared by countless women in America. As a magazine writer I often interviewed women about problems with their children, or their marriages, or their houses, or their communities. But after a while I began to recognize the telltale signs of this other problem. I saw the same signs in suburban ranch houses and split-levels on Long Island and in New Jersey and Westchester County; in colonial houses in a small Massachusetts town; on patios in Memphis; in suburban and city apartments; in living rooms in the Midwest. Sometimes I sensed the problem, not as a reporter, but as a suburban housewife, for during this time I was also bringing up my own three children in Rockland County, New York. I heard echoes of the problem in college dormitories and semi-private maternity wards, at PTA meetings and luncheons of the League of Women Voters, at suburban cocktail parties, in station wagons waiting for trains, and in snatches of conversation overheard at Schrafft's. The groping words I heard from other women, on quiet afternoons when children were at school or on quiet evenings when husbands worked late, I think I understood first as a woman long before I understood their larger social and psychological implications.

Just what was this problem that has no name? What were the words women used when they tried to express it? Sometimes a woman would say "I feel empty somehow ...incomplete." Or she would say, "I feel as if I don't exist." Sometimes she blotted out the feeling with a tranquilizer. Sometimes she thought the problem was with her husband, or her children, or that what she really needed was to redecorate her house, or move to a better neighborhood, or have an affair, or another baby. Sometimes, she went to a doctor with symptoms she could hardly describe: "A tired feeling...I get so angry with the children it scares me ...I feel like crying without any reason." (A Cleveland doctor called it "the housewife's syndrome.") A number of women told me about great bleeding blisters that break out on their hands and arms. "I call it the housewife's blight," said a family doctor in Pennsyl-

vania. "I see it so often lately in these young women with four, five and six children who bury themselves in their dishpans. But it isn't caused by detergent and it isn't cured by cortisone."

Sometimes a woman would tell me that the feeling gets so strong she runs out of the house and walks through the streets. Or she stays inside her house and cries. Or her children tell her a joke, and she doesn't laugh because she doesn't hear it. I talked to women who had spent years on the analyst's couch, working out their "adjustment to the feminine role," their blocks to "fulfillment as a wife and mother." But the desperate tone in these women's voices, and the look in their eyes, was the same as the tone and the look of other women, who were sure they had no problem, even though they did have a strange feeling of desperation.

A mother of four who left college at nineteen to get married told me:

> *I've tried everything women are supposed to do— hobbies, gardening, pickling, canning, being very social with my neighbors, joining committees, running PTA teas. I can do it all, and I like it, but it doesn't leave you anything to think about—any feeling of who you are. I never had any career ambitions. All I wanted was to get married and have four children. I love the kids and Bob and my home. There's no problem you can even put a name to. But I'm desperate. I begin to feel I have no personality. I'm a server of food and a putter-on of pants and a bedmaker, somebody who can be called on when you want something. But who am I?*

A twenty-three-year-old mother in blue jeans said:

> *I ask myself why I'm so dissatisfied. I've got my health, fine children, a lovely new home, enough money. My husband has a real future as an electronics engineer. He doesn't have any of these feelings. He says maybe I need a vacation, let's go to New York for a weekend. But that isn't it. I always had this idea we should do everything together. I can't sit down and read a book alone. If the children are napping and I have one hour to myself I just*

walk through the house waiting for them to wake up. I don't make a move until I know where the rest of the crowd is going. It's as if ever since you were a little girl, there's always been somebody or something that will take care of your life: your parents, or college, or falling in love, or having a child, or moving to a new house. Then you wake up one morning and there's nothing to look forward to.

A young wife in a Long Island development said:

I seem to sleep so much. I don't know why I should be so tired. This house isn't nearly so hard to clean as the cold-water flat we had when I was working. The children are at school all day. It's not the work. I just don't feel alive.

In 1960, the problem that has no name burst like a boil through the image of the happy American housewife. In the television commercials the pretty housewives still beamed over their foaming dishpans and *Time*'s cover story on "The Suburban Wife, an American Phenomenon" protested: "Having too good a time...to believe that they should be unhappy." But the actual unhappiness of the American housewife was suddenly being reported—from the *New York Times* and *News-*

week to *Good Housekeeping* and CBS Television ("The Trapped Housewife"), although almost everybody who talked about it found some superficial reason to dismiss it. It was attributed to incompetent appliance repairmen (*New York Times*), or the distances children must be chauffeured in the suburbs (*Time*), or too much PTA (*Redbook*). Some said it was the old problem—education: more and more women had education, which naturally made them unhappy in their role as housewives. "The road from Freud to Frigidaire, from Sophocles to Spock, has turned out to be a bumpy one," reported the *New York Times* (June 28, 1960). "Many young women—certainly not all—whose education plunged them into a world of ideas feel stifled in their homes. They find their routine lives out of joint with their training. Like shut-ins, they feel left out. In the last year, the problem of the educated housewife has provided the meat of dozens of speeches made by troubled presidents of women's colleges who maintain, in the face of complaints, that sixteen years of academic training is realistic preparation for wifehood and motherhood."

Marriage in the Stalled Revolution

ARLIE HOCHSCHILD
ANNE MACHUNG

Each marriage bears the footprints of economic and cultural trends which originate far outside marriage. A rise in inflation which erodes the earning power of the male wage, an expanding service sector which opens up jobs for women, new cultural images—like the woman with the flying hair—that make the working mother seem exciting, all these changes do not simply go on *around* marriage. They occur *within* marriage, and transform it. Problems between husbands and wives, problems which seem "individual" and "marital," are often individual experiences of powerful economic and cultural shock waves that are not caused by one person or two. Quarrels that erupt...result mainly from a friction between faster-changing women and slower-changing men, rates of change which themselves result from the different rates at which the industrial economy has drawn men and women into itself.

There is a "his" and "hers" to the economic development of the United States. In the latter part of the nineteenth century, it was mainly men who were drawn off the farm into paid, industrial work and who changed their way of life and their identity. At that point in history, men became more different from their fathers than women became from their mothers. Today the economic arrow points at women; it is women who are being drawn into wage work, and women who are undergoing changes in their way of life and identity. Women are departing more from their mothers' and grandmothers' way of life, men are doing so less.*

Both the earlier entrance of men into the industrial economy and the later entrance of women have influenced the relations *between* men and women, especially their relations within marriage. The former increase in the number of men in industrial work tended to increase the power of men, and the present growth in the number of women in such work has somewhat increased the power of women. On the whole, the entrance of men into industrial work did not destabilize the family whereas *in the absence of other changes, the rise in female employment has gone with the rise in divorce....* Here I'll focus on the current economic story, that which hangs over the marriages I describe....Beneath the image

---

*This is more true of white and middle-class women than it is of black or poor women, whose mothers often worked outside the home. But the trend I am talking about—an increase from 20 percent of women in paid jobs in 1900 to 55 percent in 1986—has affected a large number of women.

---

of the woman with the flying hair, there has been a real change in women without much change in anything else.

The exodus of women into the economy has not been accompanied by a cultural understanding of marriage and work that would make this transition smooth. The workforce has changed. Women have changed. But most workplaces have remained inflexible in the face of the family demands of their workers and at home, most men have yet to really adapt to the changes in women. This strain between the change in women and the absence of change in much else leads me to speak of a "stalled revolution."

A society which did not suffer from this stall would be a society *humanely* adapted to the fact that most women work outside the home. The workplace would allow parents to work part time, to share jobs, to work flexible hours, to take parental leaves to give birth, tend a sick child, or care for a well one. As Delores Hayden has envisioned in *Redesigning the American Dream*, it would include affordable housing closer to places of work, and perhaps community-based meal and laundry services. It would include men whose notion of manhood encouraged them to be active parents and share at home. In contrast, a stalled revolution lacks social arrangements that ease life for working parents, and lacks men who share the second shift.

If women begin to do less at home because they have less time, if men do little more, if the work of raising children and tending a home requires roughly the same effort, then the questions of who does what at home and of what "needs doing" become key. Indeed, they may become a source of deep tension in the marriage, tensions I explore here one by one.

The tensions caused by the stall in this social revolution have led many men and women to avoid becoming part of a two-job couple. Some have married but clung to the tradition of the man as provider, the woman as homemaker. Others have resisted marriage itself. In *The Hearts of Men*, Barbara Ehrenreich describes a "male revolt" against the financial and emotional burden of supporting and raising a family. In *Women and Love*, Shere Hite describes a "female revolt" against unsatisfying and unequal relationships with men. But the couples I focused on are not in traditional marriages and not giving up on marriage. They are struggling to reconcile the demands of two jobs with a happy family life. Given this larger economic story, and given the present stalled revolution, I wanted to know how the two-job family was progressing.

As I drove from my classes at Berkeley to the outreaching suburbs, small towns, and inner cities of the San Francisco Bay to observe and ask questions in the homes of two-job couples, and back to my own two-job marriage, my first question about who does what gave way to a series of deeper questions: What leads some working mothers to do all the work at home themselves—to pursue what I call a supermom strategy—and what leads others to press their husbands to share the responsibility and work of the home? Why do some men genuinely want to share housework and childcare, others fatalistically acquiesce, and still others actively resist?

How does each husband's ideas about manhood lead him to think he "should feel" about what he's doing at home and at work? What does he really feel? Do his real feelings conflict with what he thinks he should feel? How does he resolve the conflict? The same questions apply to wives. What influence does each person's consequent "strategy" for handling his or her feelings and actions with regard to the second shift affect his or her children, job, and marriage? Through this line of questioning, I was led to the complex web of ties between a family's needs, the sometime quest for equality, and happiness in modern marriage, the real topic of this book.

We can describe a couple as rich or poor and that will tell us a great deal about their two-job marriage. We can describe them as Catholic, Protestant, Jewish, black, Chicano, Asian, or white and that will tell us something more. We can describe their marriage as a combination of two personalities, one "obsessive compulsive," say, and the other "narcissistic," and again that will tell us something. But knowledge about social class, ethnicity, and personality takes us only so far in understanding who does and doesn't share the second shift, and whether or not sharing the work at home makes marriages happier.

When I sat down to compare one couple that shared the second shift with another three that didn't, many of the answers that would seem obvious—a man's greater income, his longer hours of work, the fact that his mother was a housewife or his father did little at home, his ideas about men and women—all these factors didn't really explain why some women work the extra month a year and others don't. They didn't explain why some women seemed content to work the extra month, while others were deeply unhappy about it. When I compared a couple who was sharing and happy with another couple who was sharing but miserable, it was clear that purely economic or psychological answers were not enough. Gradually, I felt the need to explore how *deep* within each man and woman gender ideology goes. I felt the need to understand the ways in which some men and women seemed to be egalitarian "on top" but traditional "underneath," or the other way around. I tried to sensitize myself to the difference between shallow ideologies (ideologies which were contradicted by deeper feelings) and deep ideologies (which were reinforced by such feelings). I explored how each person reconciled ideology with his or her own behavior, that of a partner, and with the other realities of life. I felt the need to explore what I call loosely "gender strategies."

THE TOP AND BOTTOM OF GENDER IDEOLOGY

A gender strategy is a plan of action through which a person tries to solve problems at hand, given the cultural notions of gender at play. To pursue a gender strategy, a man draws on beliefs about manhood and womanhood, beliefs that are forged in early childhood and thus anchored to deep emotions. He makes a connection between how he thinks about his manhood, what he feels about it, and what he does. It works in the same way for a woman.

A woman's gender ideology determines what sphere she *wants* to identify with (home or work) and how much power in the marriage she wants to have (less, more, or the same amount). I found three types of ideology of marital roles: traditional, transitional, and egalitarian. Even though she works, the "pure" traditional wants to identify with her activities at home (as a wife, a mother, a neighborhood mom), wants her husband to base his at work and wants less power than he. The traditional man wants the same. The "pure" egalitarian, as the type emerges here, wants to identify with the same spheres her husband does, and to have an equal amount of power in the marriage. Some want the couple to be jointly oriented to the home, others to their careers, or both of them to jointly hold some balance between the two. Between the traditional and the egalitarian is the transitional, any one of a variety of types of blending of the two. But, in contrast to the traditional, a transitional woman wants to identify with her role at work as well as at home. Unlike the egalitarian, she believes her husband should base his identity more on work than she does. A typical transitional wants to identify *both* with the caring for the home, and with helping her husband earn money, but wants her husband to focus on earning a living. A typical transitional man is all for his wife working, but expects her to take the main responsibility at home too. Most men and women I talked with were "transitional." At least, transitional ideas came out when I asked people directly what they believed.

In actuality, I found there were contradictions between what people said they believed about their marital roles and how they seemed to *feel* about those roles. Some men seemed to me egalitarian "on top" but traditional "underneath." Others seemed traditional on top and egalitarian underneath.[1] Often a person attached deep feelings to his or her gender ideology in response to what I call early "cautionary tales" from childhood, as well as in response to his or her present situation. Sometimes these feelings *reinforced* the surface of a person's gender ideology. For example, the fear Nancy Holt was to feel of becoming a submissive mother, a "doormat," as she felt her mother had been, infused emotional steam into her belief that her husband Evan should do half the second shift.

On the other hand, the dissociation Ann Myerson was to feel from her successful career undermined her ostensible commitment both to that career and to sharing the second shift. Ann Myerson's surface ideology was egalitarian; she *wanted* to feel as engaged with her career as her husband was with his. This was her view of the "proper experience" of her career. She thought she *should* love her work. She *should* think it mattered. In fact, as she confessed in a troubled tone, she didn't love her work and didn't think it mattered. She felt a conflict between what she thought she ought to feel (according to her surface ideology)—emotionally involved in her career—and what she did feel—uninvolved with it. Among other things, her gender strategy was a way of trying to resolve that conflict.

The men and women I am about to describe seem to have developed their gender ideology by unconsciously synthesizing certain cultural ideas with feelings about their past. But they also developed their ideology by taking opportunity into account. Sometime in adolescence they matched their personal assets against the opportunities available to men or women of their type; they saw which gender ideology best fit their circumstances, and— often regardless of their upbringing—they identified with a certain version of manhood or womanhood. It "made sense" to them. It felt like "who they were." For example, a woman sizes up her education, intelligence, age, charm, sexual attractiveness, her dependency needs, her aspirations, and she matches these against her perception of how women like her are doing in the job market and the "marriage market." What jobs could she get? What men? What are her chances for an equal marriage, a traditional marriage, a happy marriage, any marriage? Half-consciously, she assesses her chances—chances of an interesting, well-paid job are poor? her courtship pool has very traditional men? She takes these into account. *Then* a certain gender ideology, let's say a traditional one, will "make sense" to her. She will embrace the ideology that suits her perception of her chances. She holds to a certain version of womanhood (the "wilting violet," say). She identifies with its customs (men opening doors), and symbols (lacy dress, long hair, soft handshakes, and lowered eyes). She tries to develop its "ideal personality" (deferential, dependent), not because this is what her parents taught her, not because this corresponds to how she naturally "is," but because these particular customs now *make sense* of her resources and of her overall situation in a stalled revolution. The same principle applies to men. However wholehearted or ambivalent, a person's gender ideology tends to fit their situation.

GENDER STRATEGIES

When a man tries to apply his gender ideology to the situations that face him in real life, unconsciously or not he pursues a gender strategy.[2] He outlines a course of action. He might become a "superdad"—working long hours and keeping his child up late at night to spend time with him or her. Or he might cut back his hours at work. Or he might scale back housework and spend less time with his children. Or he might actively try to share the second shift.

The term "strategy" refers both to his plan of action and to his emotional preparations for pursuing it. For example, he may require himself to suppress his career ambitions to devote himself more to his children, or suppress his responsiveness to his children's appeals in the course of steeling himself for the struggle at work. He might harden himself to his wife's appeals, or he might be the one in the family who "lets" himself see when a child is calling out for help.

… I have tried to be sensitive to the fractures in gender ideology, the conflicts between what a person thinks he or she ought to feel and what he or she does feel, and to the emotional work it takes to fit a gender ideal when inner needs or outer conditions make it hard.

As this social revolution proceeds, the problems of the two-job family will not diminish. If anything, as more couples work two jobs these problems will increase. If we can't return to traditional marriage, and if we are not to despair of marriage altogether, it becomes vitally important to understand marriage as a magnet for the strains of the stalled revolution, and to understand gender strategies as the basic dynamic of marriage.

THE ECONOMY OF GRATITUDE

The interplay between a man's gender ideology and a woman's implies a deeper interplay between his gratitude toward her, and hers toward him. For how a person wants to identify himself or herself influences what, in the back and forth of a marriage, will seem like a gift and what will not. If a man doesn't think it fits the kind of "man" he wants to be to have his wife earn more than he, it may become his "gift" to her to "bear it" anyway. But

a man may also feel like the husband I interviewed, who said, "When my wife began earning more than me I thought I'd struck gold!" In this case his wife's salary is the gift, not his capacity to accept it "anyway." When couples struggle, it is seldom simply over who does what. Far more often, it is over the giving and receiving of gratitude.

FAMILY MYTHS

As I watched couples in their own homes, I began to realize that couples sometimes develop "family myths"—versions of reality that obscure a core truth in order to manage a family tension.[3] Evan and Nancy Holt managed an irresolvable conflict over the distribution of work at home through the myth that they now "shared it equally." Another couple unable to admit to the conflict came to believe "we aren't competing over who will take responsibility at home; we're just dreadfully busy with our careers." Yet another couple jointly believed that the husband was bound hand and foot to his career "because his work demanded it," while in fact his careerism covered the fact that they were avoiding each other. Not all couples need or have family myths. But when they do arise, I believe they often manage key tensions which are linked, by degrees, to the long hand of the stalled revolution.

After interviewing couples for a while, I got into the practice of offering families who wanted it my interpretations of how they fit into the broader picture I was seeing and what I perceived were their strategies for coping with the second shift. Couples were often relieved to discover they were not alone, and were encouraged to open up a dialogue about the inner and outer origins of their troubles.

Many couples worked long hours at their jobs and their children were very young: in this way their lot was unusually hard. But in one crucial way they had it far easier than most two-job couples in America: most were middle class. Many also worked for a company that embraced progressive policies toward personnel, generous benefits and salaries. If *these* middle-class couples find it hard to juggle work and family life, many other two-job families across the nation—who earn less, work at less flexible, steady, or lucrative jobs, and rely on poorer daycare—are likely to find it much harder still.

Anne Machung and I began interviewing in 1976, and accomplished most of our interviews in the early 1980s. I finished in 1988. About half of my later interviews were follow-up contacts with couples we'd talked to earlier; the other half were new.

How much had changed from 1976 to 1988? In practical terms, little: most women I interviewed in the late 1980s still do the lion's share of work at home, do most of the daily chores and take responsibility for running the home. But something was different, too. More couples *wanted* to share and imagined that they did. Dorothy Sims, a personnel director, summed up this new blend of idea and reality. She eagerly explained to me that she and her husband Dan "shared all the housework," and that they were "equally involved in raising their nine-month-old son Timothy." Her husband, a refrigerator salesman, applauded her career and "was more pleased than threatened by her high salary"; he urged her to develop such competencies as reading ocean maps, and calculating interest rates (which she'd so far "resisted learning") because these days "a woman should." But one evening at dinner, a telling episode occurred. Dorothy had handed Timothy to her husband while she served us a chicken dinner. Gradually, the baby began to doze on his father's lap. "When do you want me to put Timmy to bed?" Dan asked. A long silence followed during which it occurred to Dorothy—then, I think, to her husband—that this seemingly insignificant question hinted

to me that it was *she,* not he, or "they," who usually decided such matters. Dorothy slipped me a glance, put her elbows on the table, and said to her husband in a slow, deliberate voice, "So, what do *we* think?"

When Dorothy and Dan described their "typical days," their picture of sharing grew even less convincing. Dorothy worked the same nine-hour day at the office as her husband. But she came home to fix dinner and to tend Timmy while Dan fit in a squash game three nights a week from six to seven (a good time for his squash partner). Dan read the newspaper more often and slept longer.

Compared to the early interviews, women in the later interviews seemed to speak more often in passing of relationships or marriages that had ended for some other reason but of which it "was also true" that he "didn't lift a finger at home." Or the extra month alone did it. One divorcee who typed part of this manuscript echoed this theme when she explained, "I was a potter and lived with a sculptor for eight years. I cooked, shopped, and cleaned because his art 'took him longer.' He said it was fair because he worked harder. But we both worked at home, and I could see that if anyone worked longer hours I did, because I earned less with my pots than he earned with his sculpture. That was *hard* to live with, and that's really why we ended."

Some women moved on to slightly more equitable arrangements in the early 1980s, doing a bit less of the second shift than the working mothers I talked to in the late 1970s. Comparing two national surveys of working couples, F. T. Juster found the male slice of the second shift rose from 20 percent in 1965 to 30 percent in 1981, and my study may be a local reflection of this slow national trend.[4] But women like Dorothy Sims, who simply add to their extra month a year a new illusion that they aren't doing it, represent a sad alternative to the woman with the flying hair—the woman who doesn't think that's who she is.

NOTES

1. In a 1978 national survey, Joan Huber and Glenna Spitze found that 78 percent of husbands think that if husband and wife both work full time, they should share housework equally (*Sex Stratification: Children, Housework and Jobs*. New York: Academic Press, 1983). In fact, the husbands of working wives at most average a third of the work at home.

2. The concept of "gender strategy" is an adaptation of Ann Swidler's notion of "strategies of action." In "Culture in Action—Symbols and Strategies," *American Sociological Review* 51 (1986): 273–86, Swidler focuses on how the individual uses aspects of culture (symbols, rituals, stories) as "tools" for constructing a line of action. Here, I focus on aspects of culture that bear on our ideas of manhood and womanhood, and I focus on our emotional preparation for and the emotional consequences of our strategies.

3. For the term *family myth* I am indebted to Antonio J. Ferreira, "Psychosis and Family Myth," *American Journal of Psychotherapy* 21 (1967): 186–225.

4. See F. T. Juster, "A Note on Recent Changes in Time Use." In *Studies in the Measurement of Time Allocation*, edited by F. T. Juster and F. Stafford. Ann Arbor, Michigan: Institute for Social Research, 1986.

What Is Affirmative Action?

BARBARA R. BERGMANN

Affirmative action is planning and acting to end the absence of certain kinds of people—those who belong to groups that have been subordinated or left out—from certain jobs and schools. It is an insurance company taking steps to break its tradition of promoting only white men to executive positions. It is the admissions office at the University of California at Berkeley seeking to boost the number of blacks in the freshman class beyond a smattering by looking for a few black kids who may not have learned to do well on multiple choice tests but are nevertheless very smart. It is a lily-white all-male trucking company hiring a black female driver and then coping with the anger of the other drivers. It is the Detroit Police Department striving to overcome the obstacles that capable blacks and women experience in making sergeant. Affirmative action can be a formal program with a written, multipart plan and a special staff to carry it out, or it can be the activities of one manager who has consulted his conscience and decided to do things differently. The concept of affirmative action has been extended to ensuring that a share of government contracts go to minority-owned firms and to helping black groups or women's groups to buy broadcasting facilities.

Government has taken the lead in pushing affirmative action. The employers and schools with affirmative action plans may be public or private, but all have been mandated or encouraged by government regulations to achieve diversity. Nevertheless, there is no government agency that has closely monitored affirmative action activities and has cracked down on the noncompliant; the pace of affirmative action for the most part has been left to the discretion of individual workplaces and schools, whether private or public. Private companies with fewer than fifty employees are exempt from affirmative action regulations; they employ about one-third of American workers.[1] Larger employers are seldom if ever called to account for their staffing patterns by a government agency; the continuance of segregation almost never brings serious penalties. For example, the Ford Motor Company sells to the federal government and thus has been under a mandate to hire fairly for decades. Yet in 1992 only 4 percent of its managerial jobs were occupied by women; at many other large companies, 30 to 50 percent of managers performing similar functions were women.[2]

Thus, while the government officially promotes affirmative action, it is not an exaggeration to say that its application has been largely voluntary. As a result, desegregation of employment by race and sex has been uneven. While some public- and private-sector employers have made strides in increasing workforce diversity, many others have accomplished little or nothing. The condition of the American labor market suggests that much remains to be done. Abolishing, curtailing, or forbidding affirmative action anytime soon, particularly in employment, might abort further progress and cause the resegregation of some workplaces.

THE MOTIVES BEHIND
AFFIRMATIVE ACTION

We can cite three major motives for affirmative action. The most obvious one is the need to make systematic efforts to fight the discrimination that still exists in many workplaces against African Americans, Hispanics, and white women. Exhortation against discrimination, which can be ignored, has not inspired much progress, nor have expensive lawsuits against a handful of discriminators—these can take decades to work their way through the courts. Affirmative action provides a series of practical steps for dismantling discrimination: rounding up promising candidates, getting rid of artificial barriers, outflanking influential people who do not want to see change, shoehorning capable candidates into positions not previously held by people of their race or gender, and grooming the best of them for larger roles.

A second motive for affirmative action is the desire for integration—for achieving racial and gender diversity in certain activities. Diversity has positive value in many situations, but in some its value is crucial. To give an obvious example, a racially diverse community needs a racially diverse police force if the police are to gain the trust of all parts of the community and if one part of the community is not to feel dominated by the other part. While education and physical fitness are certainly aspects of "merit" in police officers, and while an appropriate floor on merit needs to be set and adhered to, efforts to get a corps of officers who are as educated and fit as possible should not be allowed to produce a police

force that fails to include significant parts of its community. In such cases, it is legitimate to take account of what a candidate contributes to diversity.

A third motive for affirmative action is to reduce the poverty of certain groups marked out by race or gender. Those who advocate this reason for affirmative action are sometimes derided as wanting equality of results rather than equality of opportunity. The derision seems to arise from a belief that the high rate of poverty among blacks is of no interest whatsoever to anybody with any sense. However, the United States is now experiencing how dysfunctional and divisive the concentration of poverty in the African-American community is.

Discrimination in the job market is an important cause of high poverty rates among U.S. children. It denies many single mothers, both black and white, access to jobs that would allow them to cover their health care and child care needs and to live at a decent standard. Their inability to keep their children out of poverty is a source of much present suffering and will lead to much grief in the future, as today's poor children mature and become one-quarter of America's adult population.[3]

AFFIRMATIVE ACTION AND QUOTAS

Opponents of affirmative action have been working hard for decades to make *quota* into a word that signifies something bad, wrong, indefensible. The measure of their success in demonizing quotas is that many people who favor affirmative action feel compelled to express assent to that view of quotas. They say that, of course, they too are against quotas, and that affirmative action and quotas are not the same thing.

Affirmative action plans, designed to get qualified women and minority people into jobs they have rarely if ever held, entail important activities that have nothing to do with quotas. The typical plan calls for efforts to get applications for each kind of job in reasonable numbers from qualified people from previously excluded groups. The office administering the plan looks at the process used to select candidates for hiring or promotion, trying to remove any source of bias. It tries to see that people from previously excluded groups are treated fairly and protected from harassment once they are on the job. Under an affirmative action plan, an employer may send supervisors—the employees who have a big say in hiring and promotion and whose past decisions have resulted in segregating jobs by race and sex—for training about racism, sexism, and sexual harassment and the laws and regulations against discrimination.

However, such activities are not all there is to affirmative action. The heart of an affirmative action plan is its numerical hiring goals, based on an assessment of the availability of qualified minority people and women for each kind of job. If progress is to be made toward those goals, some break with past practices is generally required. Those implementing the plan inevitably have to pay attention to the race and sex of appointees and exert pressure on or bypass those who have previously controlled the selection process. It is this aspect of affirmative action that draws the accusation that affirmative action is the same thing as a quota system.

There may be cases in which pressure to achieve a numerical goal is unnecessary—as when the appearance of the first good black or female candidate in the list of applicants for a previously segregated job generates an enthusiastic response among those doing the selecting. But there are many situations in which a female candidate or a nonwhite candidate, regardless of qualifications, has little chance of getting the job without such pressure. Those who say that affirmative action means "quotas" are talking about those goals and that pressure to fulfill them.

Advocates of affirmative action have argued that the numerical goals of affirmative action programs are not quotas because these goals are provisional, not hard and fast. The goals can be reduced or abandoned if no suitable African American or white female candidates can be found.[4] This defense does not really address the issue that makes affirmative action goals objectionable to many people. They want hiring and selection systems that reward merit and are fair to all candidates. They worry that racial or gender goals, whether rigid or soft, are incompatible with such systems.

The cause of honest debate over the costs and benefits of affirmative action is probably served if those defending affirmative action acknowledge that such programs do have quotalike aspects. The argument that has to be made to justify affirmative action goals is that under present conditions the merits of black and female candidates are habitually overlooked, that we cannot achieve diversity without numerical goals, and that having them does less harm than not having them. Of course, that defense is premised on the belief that the absence of certain kinds of people from certain places in our society is not due to their lack of competence, that such absences are an important source of grief and harm for many, and that those absences ought to be repaired if the process of doing so is tolerable on ethical grounds. . . .

NOTES

1. U.S. Bureau of the Census, *Statistical Abstract of the United States: 1994,* 114th ed. (Washington, D.C.: U.S. Government Printing Office, 1994), p. 546.

2. Data on Ford and other government contractors are based on company reports to the Equal Employment Opportunity Commission.

3. See Barbara R. Bergmann, "Curing Child Poverty in the United States," *American Economic Review* (May 1994): 76–80.

4. Others reject the use of the word *quota* in the context of affirmative action on the grounds that it falsely suggests an analogy between affirmative action goals and the quotas limiting the number of Jews admitted to elite schools prior to World War II. See the discussion of this issue in chap. 4 [of *In Defense of Affirmative Action* by Barbara R. Bergmann (Basic Books, 1996)]; see also Gertrude Ezorsky, *Racism and Justice: The Case for Affirmative Action* (Ithaca, N.Y.: Cornell University Press, 1991), p. 38.

11

Black Professional Women
Job Ceilings and Employment Sectors

ELIZABETH HIGGINBOTHAM

Myths and stereotypes about the success of educated Black women, many promoted by misleading news reports of major trends, mask important employment problems faced by members of this group (Sokoloff 1992). The limited social science research on the plight of middle-class Black women makes fertile ground for myths about their success and stereotypes about their abilities to handle all situations. In reality, this is not a population exempt from problems on the job. Research on the employment status of educated Black women can be important in addressing the nature of contemporary racism in America and how it impacts people of color who are members of the middle class.

This article explores the employment status of Black professional women.[1] Throughout the twentieth century, there has been a tiny elite of educated Afro-American women employed in professional and managerial positions. Since the 1970s, this population has experienced significant growth. In 1984, 14.3 percent of full-time, year-round employed Black women were in professional, technical, and kindred specialties, and 5.4 percent were managers, officials, and proprietors (U.S. Department of Labor 1984). They constituted nearly a fifth of all full-time, year-round employed Black women sixteen years and older. They are employed in a variety of occupations, but the majority—even today—are primary and secondary teachers, social workers, librarians, school counselors, and nurses. Since the 1970s, the number of Black women in traditionally male professions, such as attorney, accountant, physician, dentist, and minister, has increased, but the majority continue to be clustered in traditionally female professional and managerial positions (Kilson 1977; Sokoloff 1987, 1992; Wallace 1980).

The more education a woman has, the more likely she is to be employed. Thus, while a minority of Black women have college educations—about 5 percent of Black women over twenty-five years of age—this is the group most likely to be in the labor force (Jones 1986).

Some scholars might argue that the size of this group of Black women in professional and managerial positions is evidence that racial and sexual barriers can be scaled by the talented. From another perspective, educated Black women's employment patterns reveal a history of racial discrimination. During most of this century, the majority of employed professional and managerial Black women have worked either in the public sector (city,

From *Women of Color in U.S. Society* edited by Maxine Baca Zinn and Bonnie Thornton Dill, pp. 113–131. Reprinted by permission of Temple University Press. Copyright © 1994 by Temple University. All rights reserved.

county, state, and federal government) or for small independent agencies and employers in the Black community (Higginbotham 1987; Hine 1989).

This article provides details of the contemporary employment patterns of Black and White women to illustrate segmentation or clustering of professional and managerial women along racial lines. It addresses the question: What form does racial stratification take in this post–Civil Rights era? The concepts of job ceilings and employment sectors are used to illustrate shifting patterns of racism in the labor market options of professional and managerial Black women. These concepts are useful in evaluating the recent progress made by Black women.

THE BLACK MIDDLE CLASS

The traditional social science practice is to view social class as status rankings. New scholarship offers a definition that views social class as opposing structural positions in the social organization of production. Different social classes do not represent different ranks in a social hierarchy but denote shared structural positions with regard to ownership of the means of production, level and degree of authority in the workplace, or the performance of mental or manual labor. From this perspective, the middle class is defined to include the small traditional groups of self-employed shopkeepers and independent farmers, and the numerically larger group of professionals, managers, and administrators. This group, frequently referred to as the professional-managerial class (see Walker 1979), performs the mental labor necessary to control the labor and lives of the working class. In the modern industrial capitalist state, it is designated as middle class because of its position between labor and capital. The primary role of the middle class is to plan, manage, and monitor the work of others. Its members have greater incomes, prestige, and education than other workers, but the social relations of dom-

inance and subordination are key in defining their social class position (Braverman 1974; Poulantzas 1974; Ehrenreich and Ehrenreich 1979; Vanneman and Cannon 1987).

While Black women and men in middle-class positions enjoy many class advantages, they are still members of a racially devalued group. Understanding the middle class of a racially oppressed group requires a perspective that can investigate how both race and class interact to shape the lives of males and females. Racial oppression may be shared within the racial minority community but mediated by one's position within the class hierarchy (Barrera 1979). Both working-class and middle-class Afro-Americans are segmented and limited to the least remunerative and prestigious occupations, relative to Whites within their social class. Working-class Black men and women were denied access to many industrial, clerical, and sales jobs because these positions were reserved for Whites. Black men and women were readily able to find work in jobs that White people did not want. In the case of Black women, in the first half of the century they were employed primarily as domestics, and later gained access to service work, factory work, and some clerical and sales jobs (Amott and Matthaei 1991; Jones 1986).

Historically, Black middle-class men and women who occupied professional positions served their racial communities. These positions are often shunned by White professionals. Even today, most middle-class Black people teach and provide health and human services, and professional and managerial services to other Black people. The size and affluence of the Black community is a factor in the growth of the Black middle class (Drake and Cayton 1970; Landry 1987). Gender also plays a significant role in access to professional occupations.

GENDER DIFFERENCES IN JOB CEILINGS FOR BLACK AMERICANS

As noted previously, patterns of discrimination are evident in the history of employment for educated Black women and men. The concept of job ceilings helps clarify practices prior to the 1960s. Contrasting employment patterns between the public and private sectors best describes discriminatory patterns after the passage of Civil Rights legislation.

Job ceilings are the racially specific caps or ceilings placed on the occupational mobility of targeted groups. This form of economic oppression can be maintained by formal or informal practices. The results are the same. Black people are denied the opportunity to fill certain jobs, even if they are qualified, because employers have decided that this particular work is closed to Black Americans. Over the years, Black Americans have learned to watch for subtle changes or cracks in this ceiling.

Job ceilings, institutionalized early in this century, were instrumental in excluding Black people from many industrial jobs—both positions they might have held in the past and new jobs that were opening up. Job ceilings were very effective means of keeping Black people in low-wage manual jobs—the lowest of all working-class employment.

In *Black Metropolis*, St. Clair Drake and Horace Cayton (1970) talked in detail about the job ceiling in Chicago in the 1920s and 1930s:

> Between the First World War and the Depression, the bulk of the Negro population became concentrated in the lower-paid, menial, hazardous, and relatively unpleasant jobs. The employment policy of individual firms, trade-union restrictions, and racial discrimination in training and promotion made it exceedingly difficult for them to secure employment in the skilled trades, in clerical and sales work, and as foremen and managers. Certain entire industries had a "lily-white" policy—notably the public utilities, the electrical manufacturing industry, and the city's banks and offices. (p. 112)

The job ceiling was not unique to Chicago. It was a fundamental part of the labor market in urban and rural communities, both in the North and in the South (Hine 1989). Its existence prohibited Black males and females from following occupational mobility patterns open to both native-born White Americans and White immigrants. Over time, even first- and second-generation White immigrants were able to move from menial jobs into unskilled and semiskilled factory work. The next generation might proceed into skilled industrial work and sometimes eventually into white-collar positions.

With this established channel closed to them, Black American men and women had to find alternative routes out of the low-wage jobs in private household work, janitorial and custodial services, laundry work, and the other positions in which they could seek employment. A few Black men and women, with the support of their families or through their own efforts, were able to carve out an alternative course to better employment. They struggled to get an education, most often in traditionally Black institutions.

Acquiring a college education was often a route around the job ceiling for Black males and females. An education gave the credentials to qualify for middle-class positions. In this way, some Black people could bypass the ceiling and move to the next floor. That floor consisted of white-collar professional and managerial positions, primarily within the minority community.

For Black women, a college education did not guarantee a better livelihood than domestic or other low-wage service work. The Black females who obtained a college education, even an advanced degree, found another layer of obstacles in front of them. In a racially segmented society, even middle-class occupational positions are shaped by racism (and in the case of women, also sexism). So Black women who had the education to merit employment in middle-class professional jobs still faced race and sex barriers to securing satisfying and economically rewarding work in the middle class.

Prior to World War II, gender restrictions shaped the professions for which Black women could prepare and practice. Black women seeking higher education were steered into primary and secondary school teaching, nursing, social work, and library sciences (Hine 1989; Jones 1985). Gender also shaped the options of Black men. They were directed into medicine and dentistry, the ministry and business, as well as teaching. These gender-specific trends were noted by earlier social science researchers (Cuthbert 1942; Johnson 1969; Noble 1956). Black males and females were expected to practice their gender-specific professions within a racially segregated society.

On the whole, educational training equipped Black men for professional occupations in which they could be self-employed or work within Black institutions. With medical or dental training, they could set up independent or joint practices as physicians and dentists, in which they saw mostly Black patients—and in large communities, they were able to develop successful enterprises. As ministers, Black men were directly responsible to a congregation—if it was a large congregation, they could gain economic security. Some Black men moved into providing insurance and other services to the Black population. And other Black men found employment in traditionally Black educational institutions, where they were somewhat removed from the racist policies and practices in the White-dominated labor market.

College-educated Black women faced a different prospect. They were discouraged from pursuing traditionally male occupations and directed into developing female professions (Hine 1989). Thus, Black women were not educated for professions that enabled them to set up their own businesses or independent practices. Nurses do not set up individual practices; they are hired to work for doctors or employed in hospitals or clinics. Teachers do not recruit their own students; they are hired by public or private school systems. Librarians do not run their own institutions; they are hired to work in libraries operated by the city, the county, or an educational facility. And social workers do not go

into business for themselves; they are hired by human service agencies in the private or public sector. Gender barriers, along with race and class obstructions in both educational institutions and the labor market, complicated Black women's securing professional employment (Higginbotham 1987; Hine 1989; Jones 1985). A college education often prepared them for occupations where they still faced a racial job ceiling.

And Black women did confront rigid job ceilings. Many Northern cities did not hire Black people for professional positions in their schools, clinics, hospitals, libraries, and other agencies. In the South, some public sector jobs were set aside for Black people, because Jim Crow policies dictated segregated facilities. This was particularly the case in the teaching field, where Afro-Americans had a monopoly on positions in Black schools, and during the Depression in public health and voluntary health operations (Hine 1989). North of the Mason-Dixon Line, city and county employment policies regarding Black professionals were very mixed. De facto segregation was usually the rule for designating where children were schooled, but cities differed in whether they would hire Black teachers to staff the facilities used to educate Black children (Tyack 1974). Black nurses could not find employment outside of Black hospitals and private homes. Because they were not trained for professions that could be translated into independent entrepreneurial practices, Black females were dependent on salaries and wages. Thus, employment prospects for educated Black women were contingent upon city and county hiring policies to staff public institutions.

For these reasons, the numbers of Black professional and managerial women remained small and lagged behind the percentages of White women in these occupations. The percentage of Black women employed as professional, technical, or kindred workers increased from 4.3 in 1940 to 5.3 in 1950, 7.7 in

1960, and to 15.3 percent by 1980. Despite the increase among professionals, the number of Black women in managerial positions did not exceed 1.4 percent until 1980, when it reached 4.2 percent (Higginbotham 1987)....

NOTE

1. This discussion does not include Black women who are in the middle class solely by virtue of marriage. Black women married to professional and managerial men but not employed in the labor force faced different circumstances.

REFERENCES

Amott, Teresa, and Julie A. Matthaei. 1991. *Race, Gender, and Work: A Multicultural Economic History of Women in the United States.* Boston: South End Press.

Barrera, Mario. 1979. *Race and Class in the Southwest.* Notre Dame, Ind.: University of Notre Dame Press.

Braverman, Harry, 1974. *Labor and Monopoly Capital.* New York: Monthly Review Press.

Cuthbert, Marion. 1942. *Education and Marginality.* New York: Stratford Press.

Drake, St. Clair, and Horace Cayton. 1970. *Black Metropolis.* New York: Harper Torchbooks.

Ehrenreich, Barbara, and John Ehrenreich. 1979. "The Professional and Managerial Class." Pp. 5–25 in *Between Labor and Capital,* Pat Walker, ed. Boston: South End Press.

Higginbotham, Elizabeth. 1987. "Employment for Black Professional Women in the Twentieth Century." Pp. 73–91 in *Ingredients for Women's Employment Policy,* Christine Bose and Glenna Spitze, eds. Albany: State University of New York Press.

Hine, Darlene Clark. 1989. *Black Women in White: Racial Conflict and Cooperation in the Nursing Profession, 1890–1950.* Bloomington: Indiana University Press.

Johnson, Charles, 1969. *The Negro College Graduate.* College Park, Md.: McGrath.

Jones, Barbara A. P. 1986. "Black Women and Labor Force Participation: An Analysis of Sluggish Growth Rates." Pp. 11–31 in *Slipping Through the Cracks: The Status of Black Women,* Margaret C. Simm and Julianne Malveaux, eds. New Brunswick, N.J.: Transaction Press.

Jones, Jacqueline. 1985. *Labor of Love, Labor of Sorrow: Black Women, Work and the Family from Slavery to the Present.* New York: Basic Books.

Kilson, Marion. 1977. "Black Women in the Professions." *Monthly Labor Review* 100(May):38–41.

Landry, Bart. 1987. *The New Black Middle Class.* Berkeley: University of California Press.

Noble, Jeanne. 1956. *The Negro Women's College Education.* New York: Teachers College, Columbia University.

Poulantzas, Nicos. 1974. *Classes in Contemporary Society.* London: New Left Books.

Sokoloff, Natalie. 1987. "Black and White Women in the Professions: A Contradictory Process." Pp. 53–72 in *Ingredients for Women's Employment Policy,* Christine Bose and Glenna Spitze, eds. Albany: State University of New York Press.

———. 1992. *Black Women and White Women in the Professions.* New York: Routledge.

Tyack, David B. 1974. *The One Best System: A History of American Education.* Cambridge, Mass.: Harvard University Press.

United States Department of Labor, Bureau of Labor Statistics. 1984. *Employment and Earnings* 31 (December). Washington, D.C.: U.S. Government Printing Office.

Vanneman, Reeve, and Lynn Weber Cannon. 1987. *The American Perception of Class.* Philadelphia: Temple University Press.

Walker, Pat, ed. 1979. *Between Labor and Capital.* Boston: South End Press.

Wallace, Phyllis. 1980. *Black Women in the Labor Force.* Cambridge, Mass.: MIT Press.

PART THREE

Gender and Sexuality

"The personal is political" was an important insight of the women's movement in the 1960s. It communicates the notion that even the most intimate details of our lives are actually structured by larger social relations. While sexuality is biological, it is always shaped by culture. Even biological events such as menstruation and fertility are strongly influenced by sociocultural factors; we consider menstruating every twenty-eight days as biological fact, but women in foraging societies rarely menstruate because they are so physically active. Even in our society, we know that female athletes, gymnasts, dancers, as well as anorexics often stop menstruating. Clearly, then, physical activity and diet, which are socially determined, greatly affect menstrual cycles (Hubbard 1990; Ross and Rapp 1983).

Social definitions of sex are also changeable and transform the very experience of sex itself (Ross and Rapp 1983). For example, the frequency of articles with the term "impotence" in the title has increased dramatically since 1970. The increased use of the stigmatizing and stress-inducing label of impotence reflects the increasing importance of life-long sexual activity in one's life, the insatiability of mass media for sexual topics, the expansionist needs of specialty medicine and new medical technology (Tiefer 1987).

Psychologically, male sexual performance has as much to do with male gender role confirmation and homosocial status as with pleasure, intimacy, or tension release (Tiefer 1987). For example, Michael Messner's article focuses on young men, claiming that high school and college athletics create an atmosphere which encourages the use of women as objects of conquest and impoverishes young males' relationship with females. Benjamin Bowser's article in this section argues that black males feel sexual activity as the defining quality of masculinity to an even greater degree than white males.

Some writers claim there is not one "masculinity," but several kinds of "masculinities." Robert Staples claims that blocked opportunity structures make hypersexuality and sexual aggression the only measure of "masculinity" that lower-income black men can attain (Staples 1986). Bowser claims that it is not only lower-income black males that have more sexual partners than whites. He argues that even when black and white men have the same educational level, income, and occupational status, they are not necessarily in the same social class. Common measures of social class do not include information about stock ownership, inheritance, or parents' education. He claims that middle-class black men are more comparable to white working-class men, but when they are compared to white middle-class men the difference in sexual behavior gets erroneously attributed to culture or race instead of class.

Just as masculinity is socially constructed, so are attitudes toward female sexuality and the way women experience their sexuality. In this section of the reader, Deborah Tolman argues that social scientists studying adolescent sexuality have been reinforcing cultural stereotypes about female adolescent sexuality—assuming that girls do not want sex, but intimacy and a relationship. Lillian Rubin's article, in contrast to Tolman's, claims that for a woman there is no satisfactory sex without an emotional connection, while for a man the two are more easily separable.

Views of women's sexuality and what their bodies should look like vary according to class or race of the women. Becky Thompson's article points out that girls who do not fit the dominant view, whatever it is, internalize the negative assessments. Thompson explores different cultural, racial, and religious attitudes about girls' bodies and how they make girls more or less vulnerable to eating problems.

Attitudes about female sexuality vary between and among social groups and also change in different historical periods. In the nineteenth century, black women were seen as actively sexual, while white women, particularly in the middle classes, were viewed as having to bear sex as a duty in order to procreate. The ideal American girl was not only a virgin until she got married, but was also supposed to have pure thoughts—unsullied by familiarity with her own body or anyone else's. Thus, the hymen, a thin mucous membrane at the juncture of the vulva and the vagina, had both social and emotional value; an intact hymen was considered proof of virginity and was a prerequisite to a good middle-class marriage. Parents had a vested interest in its preservation because future husbands felt that a bride without an intact hymen was damaged goods (Brumberg 1997).

Attitudes about virginity changed dramatically in the Roaring Twenties, when the United States had its first sexual revolution. While a third of the women before 1900 usually remained clothed during sex, of those born in the 1920s, only 8 percent did. At the end of the nineteenth century, gynecologists were sometimes called in to verify that the potential bride was a virgin. In contrast, in the 1920s and 1930s many women went to the gynecologist for premarital hymenectomies, a surgical procedure that cut the hymen, in order to improve the quality of sex on the wedding night (Brumberg 1997).

Reverence for the hymen dissipated further with the widespread use of tampons, a sanitary product that was first used by women and later adolescents. Because tampons are worn internally, their use involves distinguishing the urethra from the vagina and touching the vagina in order to insert the tampon (Brumberg 1997).

Sexual activity among teenagers began to escalate in the 1960s as a result of the birth control pill and the Vietnam war. Yet, most states still had laws, based on the nineteenth-century model of "joint ownership" of girls' bodies, that made it illegal to prescribe birth control to minors without parental consent. In 1972, in *Eisenstadt* v. *Baird,* the Supreme Court upheld the right of minors to seek and obtain contraceptives without parental approval (Brumberg 1997).

In an environment in which open sexual expression was more acceptable, the social and sexual meaning of women's ties to one another became a burning intellectual question (Schneider and Gould 1987). This was facilitated both by the women's movement and the emergence of an openly gay movement (Brumberg 1997). In one of the most important and controversial essays about lesbianism, Adrienne Rich suggested that heterosexuality is a political institution that preserves male dominance. Since women are the earliest sources of emotional caring and physical nurturing for boys as well as girls, what is most "natural" for women is to love women, not men (Rich 1983). Arlene Stein's article in this section is based on extensive interviews with lesbians. She points out that "coming out" involves two processes—the development of a personal sense of self as a lesbian and the development of a social identity as a lesbian.

Rich (1983) argues that heterosexuality is socially constructed and women have married because it was necessary to survive economically and avoid social ostracism. John D'Emilio would probably agree. In his article in this section, he contends that it was only when men began to make their living through wage labor, instead of as part of an interdependent family unit, was it possible for male homosexual desire to coalesce into personal identity and lifestyle outside the heterosexual family. Capitalism, he claims, created the material conditions for gay communities to develop, but it took many generations until there was adequate ideological change to make it easier for people to make the choice to be part of those communities.

Although sexuality feels individual and personal, our feelings about it and the ways we express it incorporate the roles, meanings, and symbols of our cultural surroundings (Ross and Rapp 1983). By examining how notions about female and male sexuality have changed over time and how they vary in different cultural populations, it becomes clearer that even in this most private area, our experience is socially constructed.

REFERENCES

Brumberg, Joan Jacobs. 1997. *The Body Project: An Intimate History of American Girls*. New York: Random House.

Hubbard, Ruth. 1990. *The Politics of Women's Biology*. New Brunswick, NJ: Rutgers University Press.

Rich, Adrienne. 1983. "Compulsory Heterosexuality and Lesbian Existence." Pp. 177–205 in *Powers of Desire: The Politics of Sexuality*, edited by Ann Snitow, Christine Stansell, and Sharon Thompson. New York: Monthly Review Press.

Ross, Ellen, and Rayna Rapp. 1983. "Sex and Society: A Research Note from Social History and Anthropology." Pp. 51–73 in *Powers of Desire: The Politics of Sexuality*, edited by Ann Snitow, Christine Stansell, and Sharon Thompson. New York: Monthly Review Press.

Sabo, Donald, and David Frederick Gordon. 1995. "Rethinking Men's Health and Illness." Pp. 1–19 in *Men's Health and Illness: Gender, Power, and the Body*, edited by Donald Sabo and David Frederick Gordon. Thousand Oaks, CA: Sage Publications.

Schneider, Beth E., and Meredith Gould. 1987. "Female Sexuality: Looking Back into the Future." Pp. 120–153 in *Analyzing Gender: A Handbook of Social Science Research,* edited by Beth B. Hess and Myra Marx Ferree. Thousand Oaks, CA: Sage Publications.

Staples, Robert. 1986. "Black Masculinity, Hypersexuality and Sexual Aggression." Pp. 57–63 in *The Black Family: Essays and Studies.* San Francisco: University of California Press.

Tiefer, Leonore. 1987. "In Pursuit of the Perfect Penis: The Medicalization of Male Sexuality." Pp. 165–184 in *Changing Men: New Directions in Research on Men and Masculinity,* edited by Michael S. Kimmel. Newbury Park, CA: Sage Publications.

Daring to Desire: Culture and the Bodies of Adolescent Girls

DEBORAH L. TOLMAN

This culture's story about adolescent girls and sexuality goes like this: Girls do not want sex; what girls really want is intimacy and a relationship. This concept of girls' sexuality, which permeates education and psychology, focuses on girls' emotional feelings and desire for intimacy and excludes their sexual feelings and their bodies. Statistics indicate that girls do in fact have sex (that is, sexual intercourse) and are beginning to have sex at younger and younger ages.[1] Keeping within the terms of the cultural story, the fact of girls' sexual activity is explained in terms of relationships: girls have sex in the service of relationships. However, the assumption that girls are having sex for the sake of relationships rather than in relation to their own desire has precluded empirical explorations of this aspect of girls' experiences of adolescence. The most striking feature of a review of the psychological research on adolescent girls' sexual desire is that there is virtually none. A search of *Psychological Abstracts* on the topic of adolescent girls' sexual desire retrieves only Michelle Fine's article on girls' sexuality in schools, subtitled "The Missing Discourse of Desire." Fine reports that in listening to how girls' sexuality was and was not talked about in a Northeastern urban school, she did not

hear any acknowledgement by adults that girls may experience sexual desire.[2] What she did hear was girls' sexuality spoken about in terms of violence, victimization, and individual morality; the possibility of desire as an aspect of their sexuality was named only on occasion, and only by girls themselves. It was, she writes, "a whisper, an interruption of the ongoing conversation."[3] The exclusion of the possibility that girls experience sexual feelings has also obscured the need for psychological or educational interventions that take girls' sexual feelings into account and might therefore enable girls to live healthier, happier, and safer lives.

Recent research in the psychology of women's development reveals that at adolescence girls come into a different and more problematic relation with themselves, with others, and with the culture(s) in which they are growing.[4] In essence, many girls appear to face a relational impasse or crisis. Carol Gilligan has characterized this crisis as a division between what girls know through experience and what is socially constructed as "reality." It is also at adolescence that girls come into relationship with their social contexts as sexual beings. As the unmistakable contours of a female body emerge, a girl's body becomes defined in cultural terms as an object of men's fantasies and desires.[5] When breasts grow and hips form, girls' bodies are rendered sexual, and the relationship between internal and external, the subjective experience of desire and the objective experience of finding oneself objectified, is essentially confusing and problematic for girls.[6] This psychologically difficult yet very real psychological challenge, coupled with the fact that adolescent girls are sexually active, makes the question of how adolescent girls experience sexual desire especially pressing.

In discussions of female adolescent sexuality among educators, psychologists, public policy and public health officials, and others who work with adolescents, the real dangers of AIDS and adolescent pregnancy and parenthood associated with sexual activity have obscured even the possibility that girls experience and must deal with their own sexual desire. If both desire and danger are real forces in girls' lives, adults' impulse to focus on and protect girls from danger and to discount girls' desire may in fact endanger rather than empower girls in their sexual choices. Therefore, adults concerned with the material and psychological welfare of adolescent girls should make knowing about and understanding girls' sexual desire central, rather than bury the possibility of girls' sexual desire and agency under relational wishes.

THE MISSING DISCOURSE OF DESIRE IN THE LITERATURE OF DEVELOPMENTAL PSYCHOLOGY

Adolescence is the moment when gender becomes entangled with sexuality in new ways. Although developmental psychologists state that the integration of sexuality is a critical task of adolescence,[7] there has been little research on girls' sexual experiences and none on their experiences of sexual desire. Developmentalists have focused on the desexualized aspects of "sexual" development—puberty,[8] sex-role development, and gender identity.[9] In other

places in the psychological literature "the adolescent" has meant the adolescent boy,[10] but in most research on adolescent sexual behavior "the adolescent" is the adolescent girl, and she is most often Black or Hispanic and economically disadvantaged.[11] The implication of this focus is that only the sexuality of girls, specifically girls who are poor and of color, is problematic and demands study. The focus on girls' sexual behavior in this research is a direct result of both the "moral panic"[12] over pregnancy and abortion among adolescent girls and the underlying agenda of identifying how sexual behavior that leads to pregnancy can be prevented.[13] The only difference among girls that is given credence in this literature is how often they are having sexual intercourse and at what age. Racial differences are often analyzed in these studies, but only in terms of outcome of sexual behavior; the possible differentials in experiences of sexuality along lines of race or ethnicity remain irrelevant and unexplored.[14]

In only one of scores of studies have researchers named or investigated female sexual desire as a predictor of sexual intercourse in girls, as a factor in sexual decision making, as an element in the development of adolescent sexual behavior, or as a variable to be controlled for in these inquiries.[15] This omission is particularly striking in light of the impressive array of predictors and correlates of sexual intercourse, sexual decision making, and contraceptive use among adolescent females studied by researchers.[16] In the studies that consider adolescent sexual behavior, girls are assumed not to have embodied sexual feelings. For instance, in scripting theory, sexual scripts mapping out appropriate sexual behavior are believed to be internalized as a process of socialization. Because the sexual script for girls reported by these authors speaks of desire in girls as an aberration, a departure from an appropriate sexual script, this theory reifies the belief that girls' wish is for a relationship exclusively.[17] In some studies girls are represented as and assumed to be sexual objects of boys' desire, incorporating an absence of girls' sexual desire into the very design.[18] Research on the sexual development of adolescent girls identifies girls' menarche as its subject and makes no reference to sexuality.[19] Lesbian girls do not appear to exist at all. Feminist psychologists who do address female adolescent sexuality assume that adolescent girls do not experience sexual desire and in fact often theorize this presumed gap in female experience without empirical evidence to support their assumption.[20] The obscuring of the adolescent girl's sexual desire and of her body in these extensive and notably disembodied bodies of theory and research suggests the power and the need in this culture to override girls' sexuality.

Why have psychologists maintained this silence on girls' sexual desire? Feminist analyses of patriarchal culture offer some insight. Feminist scholars have observed that the cultural context of women's lives denies female sexual desire or acknowledges it only to denigrate it, suppressing women's voices and bodies by making it socially, emotionally, and often physically dangerous for women to be in touch with or to speak openly about their own sexual feelings.[21] The absence of inquiry about girls' sexual desire occurs within this dominant culture that denigrates and suppresses female sexual desire. Yet even in feminist analyses of female sexual desire, a subject heavily theorized by feminist scholars outside of psychology, scant attention is paid to female adolescents. A handful of feminist researchers have studied female adolescent sexuality; since they did not inquire directly about girls' sexual desire, their occasional observations regarding girls' sexual desire are grounded in what girls do not say[22] or in sparse, vague quotes from girls that are difficult to interpret.[23] That few feminists have not explicitly identified adolescent girls' sexual desire as a domain of theory or research suggests the extent to which girls' own sexual feelings are resisted in the culture at large.

At best, psychologists seem to be colluding with the culture in simply assuming that adolescent girls do not experience sexual desire; at worst, by not using the power and authority conferred upon them to say what is important in human experience and growth, psychologists participate in the larger cultural resistance to this feature of female adolescence and thus reify and perpetuate this resistance. If desire is not theorized as a potentially relevant aspect of female experience or development, then what adolescent girls may know and feel about their desire and about the place of their bodies in their experiences of desire can and will remain unknown. The very existence of this silence about girls' sexual desire within the culture in which girls develop may have psychological, physical, and material consequences for girls and also for women. The aim of my study was to ask girls directly, in no uncertain terms, about their experiences of sexual desire and about the place of their bodies in those experiences.

THE STUDY

My study was framed by basic questions: Do adolescent girls speak of themselves as experiencing sexual desire? What do they say about it and about their bodies? In this study, I asked thirty girls—fourteen from an urban school, fourteen from a suburban school, and two from a gay and lesbian youth group—about their experiences of sexual desire. To "interrupt" the cultural story that denies girls their bodies, that says girls are interested solely in relationships and not in exploring or expressing their sexual feelings, I made a particular effort to include questions about if and how their bodies figure in these sexual experiences. The thirty young women who took part in my study brought many differences to my project—structural differences, such as class, culture, educational privilege, race, and religion, and individual differences in family situation, history of sexual abuse or violence, history of closeness and safety, physical appearance, and sexual experience. I interviewed each of these girls in a clinical interview between one and two hours long; in this explicitly relational approach to psychological inquiry the interviewer attends to the participant's experience as the guide for inquiring, using a flexible protocol.

The girls I interviewed said that no adult woman had ever talked to them before about sexual desire and pleasure "like this," that is, directly and in such depth; more than half of them said they had never spoken about sexual desire and pleasure with anyone. I was confronted with the problem of how to ask girls to speak about an aspect of their experience that has been rendered unspeakable, as well as how to do that across many lines of difference; I was especially attuned to differences between me and these girls in class and culture, differences that I had explicitly incorporated into this study because of the different ways that sexuality for girls may be constructed in different social contexts. For instance, one strategy I employed was to avoid asking the "usual" questions that girls, especially girls in the urban school, have come to expect of a white middle-class woman asking them about sex—for example, how often they have sex, their pregnancy and contraceptive histories and practices. Although I had to sacrifice useful information, I felt it was crucial to avoid these lines of questions if these girls were to take seriously my claim that I wanted to know about their experiences of sexual desire. For the purposes of this analysis, I selected one narrative told by each girl about a time when she experienced sexual desire; I supplemented these analyses with other information from the interviews when necessary. To analyze these narratives, I used an interpretive, hermeneutic approach to narrative analysis developed by members of the Harvard Project on Women's Psychology and Girls' Development, *The Listening Guide*.[24]

THREE VOICES OF DESIRE

While many of the girls in this study found it odd, uncomfortable, or unusual for an adult woman to want to know about their experiences of sexual desire, all of the girls who participated knew that sexual desire was something that adolescent girls could and did experience, even if they themselves said they did not feel sexual desire. Of the thirty girls I interviewed, eighteen said they did feel sexual desire; four of these eighteen girls said they felt desire but also said they were confused about their sexual feelings. Three of the thirty said they did not feel desire, and four said, "I don't know," when I asked them if they experienced sexual desire. For seven of the thirty girls who answered my questions, I could not tell by what they told me whether they felt sexual desire.[25] The distribution of these answers is remarkably similar across the race and class differences embedded in my study.[26] Although I realize that this is a small sample, this pattern suggests the ways girls speak about their sexual desire may be distributed consistently across some structural differences.[27]

When these girls spoke to me about their desire, they described their relationships with themselves—a relationship embedded in a web of other relationships, with other people, with the social world in which they lived. I discerned three distinct themes, or voices, in what they said: an erotic voice, a voice of the body, and a response voice.[28] For them, sexual desire is a feature of a relationship; the three voices of desire are relational voices. However, these girls make a key distinction between their sexual desire and their wish for a relationship. While their feelings of sexual desire most often arise in the context of relationships, they are not the same as or a substitute for wanting relationships. Rather, these girls say that sexual desire is a specific "feeling," a powerful feeling of wanting that the majority of these girls experience and describe as having to do with sex and with their bodies, a feeling to which they respond in the context of the many relationships that constitute their lives.

An Erotic Voice

In her essay, "Uses of the Erotic: The Erotic as Power," Audre Lorde has described what she calls the power of the erotic as "the *yes* within ourselves, our deepest cravings," and "how fully and acutely we can feel in the doing."[29] Lorde writes that in this culture, women have been systematically kept from this power in themselves because, she surmises, the power of the erotic makes women dangerous. She encourages women to reclaim and reconnect with this affirmative force that resides in them to enable them to glean pleasure in their work and in their existence. Lorde does not characterize the erotic as an explicitly sexual force but conceptualizes it more expansively; when she does speak of the connection between the sexual and the erotic, she observes how the erotic has often been reduced to the merely sexual in ways that have traditionally exploited and denigrated women, in ways, she says, that are in fact pornographic rather than sexual or erotic. In listening to the girls in my study, I was struck by the gap between how adolescent girls are portrayed, studied, and discussed and what they were saying. Out of sync with the cultural story about girls' sexuality, their words when speaking specifically about the sexual expressed the power, intensity, and urgency of their feeling and resonated with Lorde's description of the erotic. This resonance led me to call these ways that girls speak about their sexual desire an erotic voice.

What comes across powerfully in the narratives of the girls who say they feel sexual desire is that they experience it as having an unmistakable intensity. Inez knows she is feeling desire when "my body says yes yes yes yes." Lily calls feeling desire "amazing."

Rochelle feels it "so, so bad…I wanna have sex so bad, you know"; she explains, "you just have this feeling, you just have to get rid of it." Liz explains, "I just wanted to have sex with him really badly, and I just…and we just took off our bathing suits really fast [with laugh], and, um, it was almost like really rushed and really quick." For Barbara it is "very strong …an overwhelming longing" and "a wicked urge." Paulina's heart "would really beat fast"; she is "extremely aware of every, every touch and everything." Alexandra speaks of being "incredibly attracted" to her friend. Jane calls the power of her desire "demanding" and says "the feelings are so strong inside you that they're just like ready to burst." These direct acknowledgements of the power of sexual desire as these girls know it resonate across differences of class, race, and sexual orientation. These descriptions suggest a challenge to characterizations of "female" sexual desire as having an essence that is gentle, diffuse, and ephemeral.[30]

Some girls also convey the intensity of their desire by the strength of their voiced resistance to it; in response to her body's "yes yes yes yes," Inez explains that "my mind says no no no; you stop kissing him." Cassandra evidences the strength and the urgency of her feeling in narrating what she does not want to do, "stop": "He just like stopped all of a sudden, and I was like What are you doing? Cause I didn't want to stop at all." She says that for her, desire is "powerful." Lily contrasts not being "in the mood to do anything …because I just have all my clothes on… because it's just too inconvenient," with the power of her desire when she feels it "once in a while": "Even though it's inconvenient for me, sometimes I just have this feeling, Well I just don't care if I have to put my pantyhose on or not," the power of her desire overriding the usual paramount concern she has for maintaining a proper appearance. These girls, who express the intensity of their sexual feelings without speaking about them directly, use a kind of code; by not saying explicitly and directly that they have strong sexual feelings, perhaps they retain the power to deny being girls who desire, should they need to exercise that power for their own protection.

A Voice of the Body

I identified a voice of the body when the girls described bodily sensations or parts of their bodies as aspects of their sexual desire. A voice of the body is central in these narratives and often interacts with the erotic voice. Across class differences and also across differences in sexual orientation, the girls who said they did not feel sexual desire also spoke of voiceless, silent bodies, of an absence of feeling in their bodies. The girls who said they did not know if they experienced sexual desire, and the girls who said they felt desire but also voiced confusion about their desire, said they were confused about their bodies; it was unclear to them and to me what their bodily feelings signaled, or they were not sure if they felt feelings in their bodies. That is, the voices of their bodies were muffled, at best. The girls who said they experienced sexual desire also voiced their bodies. The girls whose experience of sexual desire remained uncertain voiced their bodies in ways that raised questions for me about the presence or absence of desire in their lives. For the girls in this group who said they did not feel desire, the voices of their bodies were audible, rendering their statements about the absence of their desire confusing to me. For those in this group who said they did feel desire, the silence or distress of their bodies made me wonder whether they did in fact feel sexual feelings.

Girls spoke about their bodies in two ways: they named the involvement of their bodies directly, or they signified their bodily feelings in veiled, subtle, and indirect ways. Megan spoke of knowing she was feeling sexual desire for boys because of what she felt in her body; as she said, "Kind of just this feeling, you know? Just this feeling inside my body." The voice of her body is explicitly sexual when she explains how she knows she is feeling desire for a boy: "Well, my vagina starts to kinda like act up, and it kinda like quivers and stuff, and, um, like I'll get like tingles, and you can just feel your hormones [laughing] doing something weird, and you just... you get happy, and you just get, you know, restimulated kind of, and it's just... and oh! Oh!" And "your nerves feel good." Although these girls spoke about feelings in their stomachs, shoulders, necks, and legs, as well as about all-over bodily sensations, Megan was one of the few girls who connected her desire to her "vagina," naming the sexual nature of her bodily feelings directly. Very few girls named the sexual parts of their bodies in these interviews. As Mary Calderone has observed, girls are not taught the names of the sexual parts of their bodies— "vagina," "labia," and "clitoris" are words that are not said to girls.[31]

Other girls spoke in less direct ways, revealing the embodied nature of their feelings through the logic of their stories rather than in explicit language. Trisha says of her feelings when she sees a boy to whom she is attracted, "And every time I see him, I just, like, just wanna go over and grab him and say, Let's go; I just... 'cause I just want him so bad; he just... I don't know... he just gives me a funny feeling; he's just like... you just wanna go over and grab him" even though "I know it's just gonna be one of those one-night stand type of things." Trisha's "want" is not for a relationship, since she is talking about a potential "one-night stand type of thing"; it is to be sexual in a way that is explicitly physical, to "grab" him. Although Trisha avoids overtly placing the "funny feeling" he gives her in her body, the facts of the story lead to no other conclusion but that this "feeling" is embodied. Not surprisingly, voicing their bodies was not easy for these girls. While many of them did speak about their bodies, they also spoke sparingly and said little. When they voiced their bodies in response to my direct questions, their reticence suggested their knowledge, which I shared, that in speaking about desire itself, we were breaking with culture, resisting a cultural taboo that renders the body, particularly a girl's body and the sexual parts of her body, unspeakable.

Voices of Response

The girls who said they felt sexual desire also described how they responded to their own embodied feelings of sexual desire when they told me narratives about their experiences. All of these girls voiced conflict in speaking of their responses to their sexual desire, conflict between the voices of their bodies and the realities of their lives. Whether they spoke of the reality of physical risk and vulnerability or the reality of getting a bad reputation or of cultural messages that silence or are silent about girls' sexual desire, these girls knew and spoke about, in explicit or more indirect ways, the pressure that they felt to silence the voices of their bodies, to disconnect from the bodies in which they inescapably live. When I asked these girls to speak specifically about their own experiences, a lot of these girls spoke about controlling their own sexual feelings rather than about controlling the sexual feelings of boys, raising the question to what or whom girls are being encouraged to "just

say no." When asked what they think and feel, they challenged the cultural story about their sexuality—which frames sexual feelings as male—by describing the conflict they experience between the feelings in their bodies and the cultural taboo on what they want. When they spoke of their responses to their sexual desire, they gave voice to an agency in which they are sexual subjects of their own feelings rather than simply objects of the desire of others. This agency is informed by their own embodied erotic voice and the voices of the social world in which they live.

Although an erotic voice and a voice of the body sounded similar across the differences of social context embedded in the study, I began to hear in these girls' descriptions differences between urban girls' and the suburban girls', heterosexual girls' and lesbian/bisexual girls', responses to sexual desire. These differences seemed to be connected to the real differences in the social contexts of these girls' lives that the design of this study highlighted.[32] I noticed distinct tones and characters in their voices that I think are related to the fact that some of these girls were bisexual and lesbian and some straight, that some of them lived in overtly dangerous urban areas, while others lived in the relatively safe environment of the suburbs. One way to characterize these differences is that some girls described an agency in the service of protection, whereas others told of an agency in the service of pleasure. . . .

NOTES

1. The national average age at first intercourse is 16.2 years for girls. See Melvin Zelnik and John Kantner, "Sexual and Contraceptive Experience of Young Unmarried Women in the United States, 1976 and 1978," in *Teenage Sexuality, Pregnancy, and Childbearing,* ed. Frank Furstenburg, Richard Lincoln, and Jane Menken (Philadelphia: University of Pennsylvania Press, 1981), 68–92. In addition, Lillian Rubin observes that recent studies show that girls are having sex at younger and younger

ages. See Lillian Rubin, *Erotic Wars* (New York: HarperCollins, 1990).

2. Michelle Fine, "Sexuality, Schooling, and Adolescent Females: The Missing Discourse of Desire," *Harvard Educational Review* 58, no. 1 (1988): 29–53.

3. Ibid., 33.

4. Carol Gilligan, "Joining the Resistance: Psychology, Politics, Girls, and Women," *Michigan Quarterly Review* 29, no. 4 (1990): 501–36. Lyn Mikel Brown, "Narratives of Relationship: Development

of a Care Voice in Girls Ages Seven to Sixteen" (Ed.D. diss., Harvard University, 1989); idem, "Telling a Girl's Life: Self-Authorization as a Form of Resistance," in *Women, Girls, and Psychotherapy: Reframing Resistance,* ed. Carol Gilligan, Annie Rogers, and Deborah L. Tolman (New York: Haworth Press, 1992), 71–86.

5. Susan Bordo, "The Body and the Reproduction of Femininity: A Feminist Appropriation of Foucault," in *Gender/Body/Knowledge,* ed. Alison Jaggar and Susan Bordo (New Brunswick, N.J.: Rutgers University Press, 1989), 13–33.

6. Carol Gilligan, "Joining the Resistance"; Elizabeth Debold and Lyn Brown, "Losing the Body of Knowledge: Conflicts Between Passion and Reason in the Intellectual Development of Adolescent Girls" (Paper presented at the annual meeting of the Association for Women in Psychology, March 1991); Deborah L. Tolman and Elizabeth Debold, "Conflicts of Body and Image: Female Adolescents, Desire, and the No-Body Body," in *Feminist Treatment and Therapy of Eating Disorders,* ed. Melanie Katzman, Pat Fallon, and Susan Wooley (New York: Guilford Press, in press).

7. Patricia Miller and William Simon, "The Development of Sexuality in Adolescence," in *Handbook of Adolescent Psychology,* ed. Joseph Adelson (New York: John Wiley and Sons, 1980).

8. See A. Peterson and B. Taylor, "The Biological Approach to Adolescence," and Richard Lerner and Terryl Foch, *Biological-Psychological Interactions in Early Adolescence* (Hillsdale, N.J.: Lawrence Erlbaum Associates, 1987).

9. L. Serbin and C. Sprafkin, "A Developmental Approach: Sexuality from Infancy Through Adolescence," in *Theories of Human Sexuality,* ed. James Geer and William O'Donohue (New York: Plenum Press, 1987), 163–96.

10. Carol Gilligan, *In a Different Voice: Psychological Theory and Women's Development* (Cambridge: Harvard University Press, 1982).

11. Karen Weddle, P. McHenry, and G. Leigh, "Adolescent Sexual Behavior: Trends and Issues in Research," *Journal of Adolescent Research* 3, nos. 3–4: 245–57; Catherine Chilman, *Adolescent Sexuality in a Changing American Society* (New York: John Wiley and Sons, 1983).

12. Michel Foucault, *The History of Sexuality,* vol. 1, *An Introduction* (New York: Vintage Press, 1966); Lisa Duggan, "From Instincts to Politics: Writing the History of Sexuality in the U.S.," *Journal of Sex Research* 27, no. 1 (1990): 95–112.

13. Jorgensen, "Beyond Adolescent Pregnancy: Research Frontiers for Early Adolescent Sexuality," *Journal of Early Adolescence* 3, nos. 1–2: 141–55; Weddle, McHenry, and Leigh, "Adolescent Sexual Behavior."

14. Janie Victoria Ward and Jill McLean Taylor, "Sexuality Education for Immigrant and Minority Students: Developing Culturally Appropriate Curriculum," Chapter 3, 51–68 in *Sexual Cultures and the Construction of Adolescent Identities* edited by Janice M. Irvine.

15. Deborah L. Tolman, "Discourses of Adolescent Girls' Sexual Desire in Developmental Psychology and Feminist Scholarship," (Unpublished manuscript, Harvard Graduate School of Education, 1990).

16. These predictors include age, race or ethnicity, gender, socioeconomic status, early maturation, religiosity, values and moral development, intelligence, academic achievement, pubertal development, frequency of sex, age at first intercourse, family characteristics, parental and peer-group influence, peer norms, nature of a relationship, sentiments of love and aspirations for marriage, lack of career goals, guilt about sexual intercourse, low self-esteem, risk-taking behavior, ecological factors, friends' attitudes, perception of narrow options, stage of dating, noncoital behaviors, sexual attitudes, number of years a girl has been sexually active, feminist sex roles, lack of heterosexual competence, problem behavior, ego development, cognitive style, cognitive development, use of interpersonal influence, internal controls, alcohol consumption, drug use, and assault. See Christine Hayes, ed., *Risking the Future: Adolescent Sexuality, Pregnancy, and Childbearing,* vol. 1 (Washington, D.C.: National Academy Press, 1987); J. Scott. "The Sentiments of Love and Aspirations for Marriage and Their Association with Teenage Sexual Activity and Pregnancy," *Adolescence* 18, no. 72: 889–97; Elizabeth Ortiz and B. Bassoff, "Adolescent Pregnancy Prevention: Strategies for the 80s" (Technical report, EDRS document no. ED 270 674, 1984); C. Aneshensel, E. Fielder, and R. Becerra, "Fertility and Fertility-Related Behavior Among Mexican-American and Non-Hispanic White Female Adolescents." *Journal of Health and Social Behavior* 30, no. 1 (1989): 56–75; Kristin Luker, *Taking Chances: Abortion and the Decision Not to Contracept*

(Berkeley and Los Angeles: University of California Press, 1975); Furstenberg et al., "Teenage Pregnancy"; J. Spain, "Psychological Aspects of Contraceptive Use in Teenage Girls," in *Psychological Aspects of Pregnancy, Birthing, and Bonding*, ed. Barbara Blum (New York: Human Sciences Press, 1980); R. Durant and J. Sanders, "Sexual Behavior and Contraceptive Risk Taking Among Sexually Active Adolescent Females," *Journal of Adolescent Health Care* 10, no. 1 (1989): 1–9; R. Durant, M. Jay, and C. Seymore, "Contraceptive and Sexual Behavior of Black Female Adolescents: A Test of a Social-Psychological Theoretical Model," *Journal of Adolescent Health Care* 11, no. 4 (1990): 430–39; M. Maskay and A. Juhasz, "The Decision-Making Process Model: Design and Use for Adolescent Sexual Decisions," *Family Relations* 32 (1983): 111–16; C. Robbins, H. Kaplan, and S. Martin, "Antecedents of Pregnancy Among Unmarried Adolescents," *Journal of Marriage and the Family* (August 1985): 567–83; P. Reicheit, "The Influence of Contraception on Adolescent Sexual Behavior" (Paper presented at the annual meeting of the American Association of Marriage and Family Counselors, October 1978); J. Roche, "Premarital Sex: Attitudes and Behavior by Dating Stage," *Adolescence* 21, no. 81 (1986): 443–51; J. DeLameter and M. MacCorquodale, *Premarital Sexuality: Attitudes, Relationships, Behaviors* (Madison: University of Wisconsin Press, 1979); C. Bingham, B. Miller, and G. Adams, "Correlates of Age at First Sexual Intercourse in a National Sample of Young Women," *Journal of Adolescent Research* 5, no. 1 (1990): 18–33; S. Jessor and R. Jessor, "Transition from Virginity to Nonvirginity Among Youth: A Social-Psychological Study over Time," *Developmental Psychology* 11 (1975): 473–84; M. Newcomb, G. Huba, and P. Bentler, "Determinants of Sexual and Dating Behaviors Among Adolescents," *Journal of Personality and Social Psychology* 50, no. 2 (1986): 428–38; Laurie Zabin, M. Hirsch, E. Smith, and J. Hardy, "Adolescent Sexual Attitudes and Behavior: Are They Consistent?" *Family Planning Perspectives* 16, no. 4 (1984): 181–85; E. Herold and J. McNamee, "An Explanatory Model of Contraceptive Use Among Young Single Women," *Journal of Sex Research* 18, no. 4 (1982): 289–304; T. Falbo and M. Eisen, "Interpersonal Influence Strategies Applied to Sexual Decision-Making of Adolescents" (Paper presented at the American Psychological Association, August 1984); L. Kastner, "Ecological Factors Predicting Adolescent Contraceptive Use: Implications for Intervention," *Journal of Adolescent Health Care* 5, no. 2 (1984): 79–86; A. Juhasz and M. Sonnenshein-Schneider, "Adolescent Sexuality: Values, Morality, and Decision-Making," *Adolescence* 22, no. 87 (1987): 579–90; Michael Resnick and Robert Blum, "Developmental and Personalogical Correlates of Adolescent Sexual Behavior and Outcome," *International Journal of Adolescent Medicine and Health* 1, nos. 3–4 (1985): 293–313; E. Smith and J. Udry, "Coital and Non-Coital Sexual Behaviors of White and Black Adolescents," *American Journal of Public Health* 75, no. 10 (1985): 1200–1203; G. Leigh, Karen Weddle, and I. Loewen, "Analysis of the Timing of Transition to Sexual Intercourse for Black Adolescent Females," *Journal of Adolescent Research* 3, nos. 3–4 (1988): 333–44; H. White and V. Johnson, "Risk Taking as a Predictor of Adolescent Sexual Activity and Use of Contraception," *Journal of Adolescent Research* 3, nos. 3–4 (1988): 317–31; F. Shah and Melvin Zelnik, "Parent and Peer Influence on Sexual Behavior, Contraceptive Use, and Pregnancy Experience of Young Women," *Journal of Marriage and the Family* (May 1981): 339–48; B. Flanigan, "The Social Context of Alcohol Consumption Prior to Female Sexual Intercourse," *Journal of Alcohol and Drug Education* 36, no. 1 (1990): 97–113; A. Handler, "The Correlates of the Initiation of Sexual Intercourse Among Young Urban Black Females," *Journal of Youth and Adolescence* 19, no. 2 (1990): 159–70; J. Billy and J. Udry, "The Influence of Male and Female Best Friends on Adolescent Sexual Behavior," *Adolescence* 20, no. 77 (1985): 21–32; L. Lister, *Human Sexuality, Ethnoculture, and Social Work* (New York: Haworth Press, 1986); V. Pestrak and D. Martin, "Cognitive Development and Aspects of Adolescent Sexuality," *Adolescence* 20, no. 80 (1985): 981–87; O. Westney, R. Jenkins, J. Butts, and I. Williams, "Sexual Development and Behavior in Black Preadolescents," *Adolescence* 19, no. 75 (1984): 557–68; D. de Anda, R. Becerra, and E. Fielder, "Sexuality, Pregnancy, and Motherhood Among Mexican-American Adolescents," *Journal of Adolescent Research* 3, nos. 3–4 (1988): 403–11; Robert Selverstone, "Adolescent Sexuality: Developing Self-Esteem and Mastering Developmental Tasks," *SIECUS Report*, nos. 1–3 (1989); D. Orr, "Reported Sexual Behaviors and Self-Esteem Among Young Adolescents," *American Journal of Diseases of Children* 143 (1989): 86–90; S. Jorgensen and J. Sonstegard, "Predicting Adolescent

Sexual and Contraceptive Behavior: An Application and Test of the Fishbein Model," *Journal of Marriage and the Family* 46, no. 1 (1984): 43–55; J. Gibson and J. Kempf, "Attitudinal Predictors of Sexual Activity in Hispanic Adolescent Females," *Journal of Adolescent Research* 5, no. 4 (1990): 414–30; V. Phinney, L. Jensen, J. Olsen, and B. Cundick, "The Relationship Between Early Development and Psychosexual Behaviors in Adolescent Females," *Adolescence* 25, no. 98 (1990): 321–32; D. Scott-Jones and S. Turner, "Sex Education, Contraceptive and Reproductive Knowledge, and Contraceptive Use Among Black Adolescent Females," *Journal of Adolescent Research* 3, no. 2 (1988): 171–87; M. Ensminger, "Sexual Activity and Problem Behaviors Among Black Urban Adolescents," *Child Development* 61 (1990): 2032–46.

17. Miller and Simon, "The Development of Sexuality in Adolescence."

18. Zella Luria, "Children's Constructions of Sexuality and Gender" (Paper presented at the American Psychological Association, August 1990); O. Westney, R. Jenkins, and C. Benjamin, "Sociosexual Development of Preadolescents," in *Girls at Puberty,* ed. Jeanne Brooks-Gunn and Anne Petersen (New York: Plenum Press, 1983), 273–300.

19. Elissa Koff, Jill Rierdan, and E. Silverstone, "Changes in Representation of Body Image as a Function of Menarcheal Status," *Developmental Psychology* 14, no. 6 (1978): 635–42; Jill Rierdan and Elissa Koff, "The Psychological Impact of Menarche: Integrative Versus Disruptive Changes," *Journal of Youth and Adolescence* 9, no. 1 (1979): 49–58; idem, "Representation of the Female Body by Early and Late Adolescent Girls," *Journal of Youth and Adolescence* 9, no. 4 (1980): 339–46; Sharon Golub, *Menarche: The Transition from Girl to Woman* (Lexington, Mass.: Lexington Books, 1983); Jeanne Brooks-Gunn, Michelle Warren, M. Samelson, and R. Fox, "Physical Similarity of and Disclosure of Menarcheal Status to Friends: Effects of Grade and Pubertal Status," *Journal of Early Adolescence* 6, no. 1 (1986): 3–14; Dale Blyth, Roberta Simmons, and D. Zakin, "Satisfaction with Body Image for Early Adolescent Females: The Impact of Pubertal Timing Within Different School Environments," *Journal of Youth and Adolescence* 14, no. 3 (1985): 207–25; Jeanne Brooks-Gunn and Diane Ruble, "The Experience of Menarche from a Developmental Perspective," in *Girls at Puberty,* ed. Brooks-Gunn and Petersen.

20. Jean Baker Miller, "The Development of Women's Sense of Self," *Work in Progress* (no. 12) (Wellesley, Mass.: Stone Center Working Papers Series, 1984); Jessica Benjamin, *The Bonds of Love* (New York: Pantheon Books, 1986). A discourse of desire is also missing from almost all of the research done by members of the Harvard Project in Women's Psychology and Girls' Development until very recently. However, adolescent girls in the studies that constitute the Harvard Project were not asked explicitly about their experiences of sexual desire; these researchers have thus only been able to hypothesize about the dynamic of desire in girls' development from scant evidence, examining closely the few times when girls have spoken spontaneously about their sexual desire (e.g., Carol Gilligan, "Joining the Resistance"; Gilligan, Rogers, and Tolman, *Women, Girls and Psychotherapy*; Deborah L. Tolman, "Just Say No to What" (Paper presented at the annual meeting of the American Orthopsychiatric Association, Miami, Fla., 1990); idem, "Adolescent Girls, Women and Sexuality: Discerning Dilemmas of Desire," in *Women, Girls, and Psychotherapy*; Deborah L. Tolman and Elizabeth Debold, "Conflicts of Body and Image"; Elizabeth Debold, "The Body at Play," in *Women, Girls, and Psychotherapy,* 169–84; idem, "The Flesh Becomes Word" (Paper presented at the Association for Women in Psychology, Western Massachusetts and Vermont Region, November 1990); idem, "Learning in the First Person: A Passion to Know" (Paper presented at the Laurel-Harvard Conference, April 1990).

21. See, for example, *Powers of Desire: The Politics of Sexuality,* ed. Ann Snitow, Christine Stansell, and Sharon Thompson (New York: Monthly Review Press, 1983); *Pleasure and Danger: Exploring Female Sexuality,* ed. Carole S. Vance (Boston: Routledge and Kegan Paul, 1984); and Janice Irvine, *Disorders of Desire: Sex and Gender in Modern American Sexology* (Philadelphia: Temple University Press, 1990).

22. Mica Nava, "'Everybody's Views Were Just Broadened': A Girls' Project and Some Responses to Lesbianism," *Feminist Review* 10 (1982): 37–59; Fine, "Sexuality, Schooling, and Adolescent Females"; Pat Macpherson and Michelle Fine, "Hungry for an Us: Adolescent Women Narrating Sex and Politics" (Unpublished manuscript, Philadelphia, 1991); Michelle Fine and Pat Macpherson, "Over Dinner: Feminism and Adolescent Female Bodies" (Unpublished manuscript, Philadelphia, 1991); Sharon

Thompson, "Search for Tomorrow: On Feminism and the Reconstruction of Teen Romance," in *Pleasure and Danger: Exploring Female Sexuality*, 350–84; idem, "'Drastic Entertainments': Teenage Mothers' Signifying Narratives," in *Uncertain Terms*, ed. Faye Ginsberg and A. Tsing (Boston: Beacon Press, 1991); Celia Cowie and Susan Lees, "Slags or Drags," in *Sexuality: A Reader*, ed. Feminist Review (London: Virago, 1987); Susan Lees, *Losing Out: Sexuality and Adolescent Girls*, (London: Hutchinson, 1986); idem, "Sexuality, Reputation, Morality, and the Social Control of Girls: A British Study," in *Aspects of School Culture and the Social Control of Girls* (European University Institute, no. 87/301), 1–20; Jane Ussher, *The Psychology of the Female Body* (London: Routledge and Kegan Paul, 1989).

23. Fine, "Sexuality, Schooling, and Adolescent Females," 1988.

24. This method allows me to reenter the relationships I have formed with the adolescent girls through interviewing them, using that information to support my effort to understand what the girls tell me about their experiences of sexual desire. Readers bring themselves knowingly into the process of listening, learning from their own thoughts and feelings, in response to what a girl is saying in her story, using clinical methods of empathy and listening to follow or make sense of what a girl is saying. Readers' attention to themselves also increases their ability to stay clear about what their own ideas and feelings are and how they do and do not line up with a girl's words. Thus, bringing themselves into the analytic relationship increases readers' ability to avoid "bias" or voicing over a girl's story with their own. The method involves four guided readings of a single narrative. For the purposes of my analyses, I integrated a grounded theory approach into developing appropriate readings. See Deborah L. Tolman, "Voicing the Body: A Psychological Study of Adolescent Girls' Sexual Desire" (Ph.D. diss., Harvard University, 1992), for a detailed description of this methodology and specific analyses of these data.

25. One of the bisexual girls said she felt desire for girls, but I could not tell whether she experienced sexual desire for boys.

26. Two urban girls and one suburban girl said they did not feel sexual desire; two urban girls and two suburban girls said, "I don't know," when I asked them about their desire; seven urban girls and nine suburban girls said they did feel desire; and I could not tell whether four urban girls and three suburban girls experienced sexual desire.

27. One question for further research, then, is why girls who live in different social contexts speak about their experiences of sexual desire in the same ways, in these ways.

28. For descriptions of these voices and how I articulated them, see Tolman, "Voicing the Body."

29. Audre Lorde, "Uses of the Erotic: The Erotic as Power," in *Sister Outsider* (Freedom, Calif.: Crossing Press, 1984), 54.

30. Susan Griffin, *Pornography and Silence: Culture's Revenge Against Nature* (New York: Harper Colophon Press, 1981); Jana Sawicki, "Identity Politics and Sexual Freedom: Foucault and Feminism," in *Feminism and Foucault: Reflections on Resistance*, ed. Irene Diamond and Lee Quinby (Boston: Northeastern University Press, 1988), 177–92.

31. Mary Calderone, "On the Possible Prevention of Sexual Problems in Adolescence," *Hospital and Community Psychiatry* 34, no. 6 (1983): 528–30.

32. I do not think that these are the only, or even necessarily the most important, differences among this group of girls regarding their experiences of sexual desire. My initial readings of these data suggest that other, more psychological differences, such as the presence or absence of a history of sexual abuse, or whether or not a girl has a critical perspective on messages about girls' sexuality, may also differentiate how these girls experience sexual desire.

The Sexual Dilemma

LILLIAN B. RUBIN

Some analysts of society point to the culture, to the ideologies that have defined the limits of male and female sexuality. Certainly there's truth in that. There's no gainsaying that, through the ages of Western society, women's sexuality has come under attack, that there have been sometimes extreme pressures to control and confine it—even to deny its existence. There's no doubt either that we have dealt with male sexuality with much more ambivalence. On the one hand, it too has been the object of efforts at containment; on the other, we have acknowledged its force and power—indeed, built myth and monument in homage to what we have taken to be its inherently uncontrollable nature.

Such social attitudes about male and female sexuality, and the behavioral ideals that have accompanied them, not only shape our sexual behavior but affect our experience of our own sexuality as well. For culture both clarifies and mystifies. A set of beliefs is at once a way of seeing the world more clearly while, at the same time, foreclosing an alternative vision. When it comes to sex—precisely because it's such a primitive, elemental force—all societies seek some control over it and, therefore, the mystification is greater than the clarification. Thus, for example, Victorian women often convinced themselves that they had no sexual feelings even when the messages their bodies sent would have told them otherwise if they had been able to listen. And, even now, men often engage in compulsive sexual behavior that brings them little, if any, pleasure without allowing themselves to notice the joylessness of it. Both behaviors a response to cultural mandates, both creating dissonance, if not outright conflict, when inner experience is at odds with behavioral expectations.

The blueprint to which our sexuality conforms, then, is drawn by the culture. But that's not yet the whole story. The dictates of any society are reinforced by its institutional arrangements and mediated by the personal experience of the people who must live within them. And it's in that confluence of social arrangement and psychological response that we'll come to understand the basis of the sexual differences that so often divide us from each other.

For a woman, there's no satisfactory sex without an emotional connection; for a man, the two are more easily separable. For her, the connection generally must precede the sexual encounter:

> For me to be excited about making love, I have to feel close to him—like we're sharing something, not just living together.

For him, emotional closeness can be born of the sexual contact.

> It's the one subject we never get anywhere on. It's a lot easier for me to tell her what she wants to hear

From *Intimate Strangers: Men and Women Together* by Lillian B. Rubin, pp. 100–104, published by Harper/Collins. Copyright © 1983 by Lillian B. Rubin. Permission granted by The Rhoda Weyr Agency, New York.

*when I feel close, and that's when I get closest—
when we're making love. It's kind of hard to explain
it, but [trying to find the words]...well, it's when
the emotions come roaring up.*

The issues that divide them around intimacy in the relationship are nowhere to be seen more clearly than here. When she speaks of connection, she usually means intimacy that's born of some verbal expression, some sharing of thought and feeling:

*I want to know what he's thinking—you know,
what's going on inside him—before we jump into
bed.*

For him, it's enough that they're in the same room.

*To me, it feels like there's a nice bond when we're to-
gether—just reading the paper or watching the
tube or something like that. Then, when we go to
bed, that's not enough for her.*

The problem, then, is not *how* we talk to each other but *whether* we do so. And it's connected to what words and the verbal expression of emotion mean to us, how sex and emotion come together for each of us, and the fact that we experience the balance between the two so differently—all of which takes us again to the separation and individuation experiences of childhood.

For both boys and girls, the earliest attachment and the identification that grows from it are much larger, deeper, and more all-embracing than anything we, who have successfully buried that primitive past in our unconscious, can easily grasp. Their root is pure eros—that vital, life-giving force with which all attachment begins. The infant bathes in it. But we are a society of people who have learned to look on eros with apprehension, if not outright fear. For us, it is associated with passion, with sex, with forces that threaten to be out of our control. And we teach our young very early, and in ways too numerous to count, about the need to limit the erotic, about our fears that eros imperils civilization.

In the beginning, it's the same for children of either sex. As the child grows past the early symbiotic union with mother, as the boundaries of self begin to develop, the social norms about sexuality begin to make themselves felt. In conformity with those norms, the erotic and emotional are split one from the other, and the erotic takes on a more specifically sexual meaning.

But here the developmental similarities end. For a boy at this stage, it's the emotional component of the attachment to mother that comes under attack as he seeks to repress his identification with her. The erotic—or sexualized—aspect of the attachment is left undisturbed, at least in heterosexual men. To be sure, the incest taboo assures that future sexual *behavior* will take place with a woman other than mother. But the issue here is not behavior but the emotional structure that underlies it.

For a girl, the developmental requirement is exactly the opposite. For her, it's the erotic component of the attachment to a woman that must be denied and shifted later to a man; the larger emotional involvement and the identification remain intact.

This split between the emotional and the erotic components of attachment in childhood has deep and lasting significance for the ways in which we respond to relationships—sexual and otherwise—in adulthood. For it means that, for men, the erotic aspect of any relationship remains forever the most compelling, while, for women, the emotional component will always be the more salient. It's here that we can come to understand the depth of women's emotional connection to each other—the reasons why nonsexual friendships between women remain so central in their lives, so important to their sense of themselves and to their well-being. And it's here also that we can see why nonsexual relationships hold such little emotional charge for men.

It's not, as folklore has held, that a woman's sexual response is more muted than a man's, or that she doesn't need or desire sexual release the way a man does. But, because it's the erotic aspect of her earliest attachment that has to be repressed in childhood if a girl is later to form a sexual bond with a man, the explicitly sexual retains little *independent* status in her inner life. A man may lust after *women,* but a woman lusts after *a man.* For a woman, sex usually has meaning only in a relational context—perhaps a clue to why so many girls never or rarely masturbate in adolescence or early adulthood.

We might argue that the social proscriptions against masturbation alone could account for its insignificance in girls and young women. But boys, too, hear exhortations against masturbation—indeed, even today, many still are told tales of the horrors that will befall them. Yet, except to encourage guilt and secrecy, such injunctions haven't made much difference in its incidence among them.

It would be reasonable to assume that this is a response to the mixed message this society sends to men about their sexuality. On the one hand, they're expected to exercise restraint; on the other, there's an implicit understanding that we can't really count on them to do so—that, at base, male sexuality cannot be controlled, that, after all, boys will be boys.

Surely such differences in the ways in which male and female sexuality are viewed could account for some of the differences between the sexes in their patterns and incidence of masturbation. But I believe there's something else that makes the social prohibitions take so well with women. For with them, an emotional connection in a relationship generally is a stimulus, if not a precondition, for the erotic.

If women depend on the emotional attachment to call up the sexual, men rely on the sexual to spark the emotional, as these words from a forty-one-year-old man, married fourteen years, show:

> *Having sex with her makes me feel much closer so it makes it easier to bridge the emotional gap, so to speak. It's like the physical sex opens up another door, and things and feelings can get expressed that I couldn't before.*

For women, emotional attachments without sex are maintained with little difficulty or discomfort; for men, they're much more problematic. It's not that they don't exist at all, but that they're less common and fraught with many more difficulties and reservations....

14

Sexuality and Sexual Identity

MICHAEL MESSNER

"Big Man on Campus." "Sexual Athlete." For many, these terms conjure up the dominant cultural image of the athlete on campus: He is extremely popular, self-assured, and (hetero)sexually active. Other boys and young men are envious of the ease with which he can "get women." My interviews at times revealed a grain of truth to this popular stereotype of the athlete. Chris H. said that even as a second-string professional basketball player, it was "just the good life." He laughed, "I mean, you could wave at one way up in the fifteenth row, and after the game, she's standing right there by the locker room…that's what makes it fun, you know." Similarly, when asked how he related to others when in school, Thomas M. said, "I liked to be the big man on campus, and sports was a highlight because it gave me that opportunity. *Everybody* knew who I was. Big Tom. *Everybody* knew who I was."

On the surface, these two statements affirm the stereotype of the athlete as a confident young man at ease with himself and with his sexuality among his peers. Interestingly though, when asked about their specific relationships with girls and women, a very different picture emerged. "Big Tom," for instance, stated that "girls, in high school, were really not prime in [his] life." He laughingly continued, "When I was in high school, I thought I was an ugly guy. You know, being under a lot

of pressure, and being so much bigger than everybody, and everybody's always looking at you. In high school, you don't know what looks *mean*—it could be good, it could be bad. At one time I felt I was a freak, so I was more or less into myself. I don't think I had one girlfriend." This youthful awkwardness and insecurity with respect to girls seemed almost universal among the men I interviewed. David P.'s shyness was compounded by his family's difficult economic situation, so for him, sport became an escape from dealing with girls: "No doubt I was shy, and I think it had to do with the fact that if I did make a date with a girl, how was I going to go? What was I going to spend? Because I had none of it. So I just used sports as an escape." Clarence T., who had no trouble paying for dates, nevertheless had similar problems with girls:

> In my senior year [of high school], I remember dating all these girls. It was real bizarre: I had this list I kept of all the girls I wanted to go out with, and it was like twenty-five people, and I went out with twenty of them. I was just going out with people. I wasn't sexually active—I hadn't had intercourse— I might have done a little petting, but never any genital stuff. I think I was popular, and was seen as an attractive boy, but I didn't have a sense of it. I just thought I was absolutely ugly as hell.

Several of the men I interviewed recalled hoping that being an athlete would give them the confidence to overcome their "lameness" with girls. Jon P. said that he had hoped that being on the basketball team would help him overcome his shyness "and make it easier to talk with girls. It didn't." But several of these men reported that they did eventually develop ways to talk to girls, despite their shyness. Eldon C., for instance:

> [In high school], I was lame, as they called it. So I didn't know how to do women so well. My stepmother threw a sixteenth birthday party for me and invited a lot of friends, and I remember that day, trying on a lot of the roles that I saw guys playing, and it kind of shocked me because the women took it seriously, you know. That was a big turning point for me. I didn't particularly like— some of the black modes of relating to women, I thought were stupid. Like: "you know, sugar, you know"—just nonsense—sweet nothings seemed silly to me. [But] anyway, I tried it, my version of it, and to my surprise some woman took it seriously. That meant it was possible [laughs].

Calvin H. describes a similar transformation from tortured shyness with girls in high school to a smooth "rap" with women in college:

> I was just scared, and bashful and shy. I did not know what to say or what to do. It was very uncomfortable. One of the things that were the rewards of being a good athlete, and you didn't really want it—I mean, you wanted it, but you didn't want it—you know, like, a girl likes you, but then, clamming up and not being able to communicate very effectively. This was a very bad time, because you're always around a lot of girls at parties. [I was] very uncomfortable in groups and with individuals. Finally [I went] off to college and went to the extreme of trying to attract a lot of girls, [and was] semisuccessful. You knew you had to have a date on Fridays, and knew you had to have one on Saturdays, and so you just walked through the student union, and you'd just have this rap you'd thought of, and you'd just put it on. It was peer pressure. I'm naturally a shy person. But somehow in college I was able to somehow fall into the right kinds of things to do and say.

We can see from these stories that developing a "rap" with women becomes an al-

most ritualized way that a young man helps himself overcome an otherwise paralyzing shyness, a sense of "lameness" when trying to relate to young women. This sort of verbal game involves a certain dramaturgy, a conscious self-manipulation ("you'd just put it on"), and one result is that girls and women become the objects of men's verbal manipulation. This kind of manipulation of women does not spring naturally or magically from men's shyness. Rather, it is socially learned through the male peer group. Notice that Eldon C. learned to "do women" by watching his friends. Calvin H., though somewhat mystified as to how he was able to overcome his shyness and "fall into the right things to say," also cites "peer pressure" as a motivating force. Clearly, an analysis of the development of men's sexual relationships with women must take into account the ways that male peer groups influence attitudes and feelings about sexuality and emotional commitment to women.

Peter Lyman, in his study of college fraternities, argues that there is an erotic basis to the fraternal bond in male groups.[1] In the past, the key to maintaining the male bond was the denial of the erotic. Organized sport, as it arose in the late nineteenth and early twentieth centuries, was based in part on a Victorian antisexual ethic. First, it was believed that homosocial institutions such as sport would masculinize young males in an otherwise feminized culture, thus preventing homosexuality.[2] Second, the popular (and "scientific") belief in the "spermatic economy" held that "the human male possessed a limited quantity of sperm, which could be invested in various enterprises, ranging from business through sport to copulation and procreation. In this context, the careful regulation of the body was the only path to the conservation of energy."[3] As sociologist Todd Crosset has pointed out, in a society in which it was held that young men's precious energies would be drained off should they expend too much sperm, sport was elevated as the key "to regenerate the male body and thus make efficient use of male energy."[4]

Some of the older men in this study went through adolescence and early adulthood when remnants of the ideology of the "spermatic economy" were still alive. Eldon C. reports that as a young runner, from the late 1940s through the mid-1950s, he had been "a bit cautious about sex, because [he] still had some old-fashioned notions about sexual energy [being] competitive with athletic stuff." Most of these men, though, came of age during the sexual revolution of the 1960s and early 1970s, when the dominant credo became, "if it feels good, do it."[5] As a result, the male peer group, within the athletic context, became a place where sexual activity and talk of sexual activity (real or imagined) was a key component of the status system.

But if the bond among men is erotic, and the culture is increasingly telling them, "if it feels good, do it," what is to prevent the development of sexual relations among young men who are playing, showering, dressing, and living in such close quarters? The answer is that the erotic bond between men is neutralized through overt homophobia and through the displacement of the erotic toward women as objects of sexual talk and practice. In boyhood, adolescent, and young adult male peer groups, "fag," "girl," and "woman" are insults that are used almost interchangeably. In this way, heterosexual masculinity is collectively constructed through the denigration of homosexuality and femininity as "not-male." Bill S. described nicely how his high school peer group helped to build his own public presentation of his sexuality: "I was shy [with girls]—I hung out more with guys. I never dated. I never was real intimate with anyone. It was just kind of scary because I thought I'd get teased by my peers." When I asked him whether he'd be teased for not being involved with women, he replied,

For being involved! But you've got to be involved to the point where you get 'em into bed, you know, *you fuck 'em, or something like that, yeah, that's real important* [laughs]—*but as far as being intimate, or close, I wasn't. And that wasn't real important. Just so I could prove my heterosexuality it was real important. But I always wanted to look good to females—because I didn't have the personality* [laughs]—*to get 'em into bed! So I wanted to be able to have the* body, *and the sort of friends around who admired me in some sort of way, to have that pull.*

This sort of use of women as objects of sexual conquest is important for gaining status in the male peer group, but it also impoverishes young males' relationships with females. As Bob G. put it, in high school, he and his friends would "tell a lot of stories about girls. I guess it was a way to show our masculinity. [But] I never got emotionally involved with any of the girls I went out with. I never got close to any of them." The link between young males' tendency to "tell [sexual] stories about girls" and their lack of intimacy with girls is an important one. As Peter Lyman points out, young males commonly use sexually aggressive stories and jokes as a means of "negotiating" the "latent tension and aggression they feel toward each other." They also are using this joking relationship to "negotiate the tension they [feel] between sexual interest in the girls and fear of commitment to them. [They use] hostile joking to negotiate their fear of the 'loss of control' implied by intimacy."[6] While talk of sex with females, then, bonds the males together, the specific forms of sexual talk (sexual objectification and conquest of women) helps them deal with their terror of intimacy with women (described, by many, as "shyness" or "lameness" etc.). Again, in the words of Lyman, "In dealing with women, the group separate[s] intimacy from sex, defining the male bond as intimate but not sexual (homosocial), and relationships with women as sexual but not intimate (heterosexual)."[7] In a very real sense, these young males' relationships with females—whether sexual or not—were constructed through (indeed, were often distorted by and subordinated to) their relationships with their male teammates. One logical result is the kind of attitude toward women that former pro football star Jim Brown describes in his book, *Out of Bounds.* When he played football for the Cleveland Browns, he explains, his male "partners started calling [him] the Hawk" because he was so successful in "chasing women." Now at age fifty-three, Brown continues to view women primarily as young, sexual bodies and as objects of consumption: "My lady right now is nineteen.... When I eat a peach, I don't want it overripe. I want that peach when it's peaking."[8] Clearly, this attitude tends to preclude Brown's developing a long-term intimate relationship with one woman. After all, every woman eventually ages, her body changes, and she can be discarded and replaced by what Brown sees as an endless supply of younger, firmer bodies.

Unlike Brown, many male athletes do yearn for, and manage to develop, more or less exclusive relationships with one woman. But this happens despite the fact that the male peer group tends to police its own members in terms of intimacy with females. Male peers might taunt boys and young men who start to spend too much time with a girlfriend, who are becoming too attached, telling them that they are "pussywhipped." Don Sabo, in writing about his own football career told this tale: "Once when I was a high school junior, the gang in the weight room accused me of being wrapped around my girlfriend's finger. Nothing could be further from the truth, I assured them, and in order to prove it, I broke up with her. I felt miserable about this at the time and I still feel bad about it."[9] Sociologist Timothy Curry found in his participant-observation study of two college male locker rooms that sexually aggressive talk about women usually takes the form of a loud public performance.[10] Curry also observed that any serious discussions between two men about actual relationships with girlfriends usually takes place in hushed tones, often at the edges of the locker room. If this sort of talk is discovered by the group, the speakers are often ridiculed and taunted to reveal details about the woman's body and whether or not she is sexually "putting out." The result of this locker room culture, according to Sabo, is that many men end up suffering a kind of "'sexual schizophrenia.' Their minds lead them toward eroticism while their hearts pull them toward emotional intimacy."[11] Some young men deal with this split by keeping their emotional attachments with women a secret, while continuing to participate in locker room discussions about sexuality with their male peers. Bob G. had one such relationship in high school: "We started sneaking around and going out late at night and no one else knew. I didn't tell any of my friends. We got along great, sexually and emotionally, though she said I didn't express my feelings enough."

At times, the male peer group's policing of its members' relationships with females took on a racial angle. Larry W., for instance, said that when he was in college "the biggest conflict we had was black males dating white girls. The white males would call up the white females and call them whores, bitches, and prostitutes—you know, insulting language, like 'If you ball him, you'll ball anybody, so come over here and ball me too.'" In this case, the peer group was not only policing intimacy with women, but also imposing controls on interracial sexuality.

The need to prove one's manhood through sexual conquests of women was experienced as a burden by many young heterosexual males, and was sometimes complicated by racial tensions, but it was especially oppressive for gay men. Mike T. threw himself into sport, rather than into dancing, largely because he was terrified that people might find out that he was gay. Sport allowed him to project a masculine public image. But this meant that he also had to project a heterosexual image:

I hated high school. I mean, I just didn't know who I was. I think I had quite a bit of negative self-esteem at that time, because I really felt different. I mean, I didn't drink, I didn't like to screw around, and this was what all my friends did, so I felt compelled to go along with this stuff, and all the time hating it. I dated some women, some that I loved because they were just really fine people—[but] physically, there was not a great deal of passion. For males, there was a passion. [But] homophobia was rampant, especially in athletics. You see, I think a lot of athletes go into athletics for the same reason I did. They need to prove their maleness. And I did, I readily admit it. I felt I've got to hide this thing—because I know what they were thinking: If I were gay, they would see me as less than a man, or not a man. So I'm going to be a man, because that's what I am.

Though his secret knowledge of his own homosexuality made this process a much more conscious one for Mike ("I was *clearly* aware of what I was doing"), his public construction of manhood-as-heterosexual was not all that different from what his nongay teammates were doing. Whether gay or heterosexual, the denial and denigration of gayness and femininity (in oneself and in others) were important to these young men's construction of masculine identities and status in their male peer group.[12] As Mike T. said,

> *Go into any locker room and watch and listen, and you'll hear the same kind of garbage—I call it garbage now, and I thought it was garbage then, but I felt compelled to go along with it, because I wanted that image. And I know others who did, too. I know a lot of athletes are gay. And I think a lot of athletes are attracted to athletics because they're fighting feelings of tenderness—not necessarily gay—but they're fighting feminine qualities. I know a lot of football players who very quietly and very secretly like to paint, or play piano, and they do it quietly because this to them is threatening if it's known by others.*

The pressure to be seen by one's peers as "a man"—indeed, the pressure to see oneself as "a man"—kept most young males in conformity (at least on the surface) with this homophobic and sexist locker room "garbage." Conformity with locker room culture was a way for both gay and heterosexual men to construct their public masculinity. But gay men were far more likely to see this process as a

strategy than were heterosexual men. As Arthur Brittan explains, "Gender identity…is a set of reflexive strategies which are brought into play whenever gender is put on the line. In everyday life most heterosexuals do not have to do too much identity work because they tend to function in contexts in which heterosexuality is taken for granted."[13] In the locker room, gay athletes must constantly engage in "identity work." Nearly every gay athlete that social scientist Brian Pronger interviewed agreed that being around all of those naked male bodies in the locker room "feed[s] the homoerotic imagination and provide[s] homoerotic contact." One gay athlete told Pronger, "[There is] a surprising amount of sexual cruising and activity in the university locker rooms and shower. I've certainly had sex there."[14] But since homosexual behavior—or even more subtle expressions of desire—violate the kind of masculinity that is common in the locker room, most gay men develop a strategy of identity construction that is "ironic": On the surface, they conform to the heterosexist masculine culture, while underneath, they view the locker room through their hidden knowledge of its highly charged eroticism.

Even for a few heterosexual men, the "garbage" of the locker room led them to question—even reject—the jock culture and the specific form of masculinity and sexuality that predominated there. Brent F., for instance, says that toward the end of high school, he "really got turned off to the way the guys were relating to the girls":

> *It was really ugly in certain ways, like just treating them like objects, totally judging them by their surface appearances, talking amongst themselves in really abusive language about girls, how they're going to do this or that to them. I thought it was wrong. I thought that people shouldn't be treated that way. I started to realize that the way I related to women was not the way these guys were relating to them, and therefore I didn't want to relate with them on that level. So I started to distance myself from the same activities, and started to feel really alienated from my buddies.*

This rejection of the sexist treatment of women was a rare exception to the rule. It is significant that this realization was made by a young athlete who several years earlier had decided that he was not a "career athlete." That he had already begun to disengage from his athletic career meant that he had less invested in the athletic male peer group. For young men who were fully committed to athletic careers, this sort of rejection of one of the key bonds of the group might have amounted to career suicide. So whether they liked it or not, most went along with it. Furthermore, when the "garbage" went beyond verbal sparring and to sexual behavior, peer group values encouraged these young men to treat females as objects of conquest. Eric M. described a night on the town with his male peers. He was in high school, a virgin, and terrified at his own lack of sexual experience. But when they hit the town, he said, "We were like wolves hunting down prey. Dave told me, 'If a girl doesn't give it up in sixty seconds, drop her!'"

It is this dynamic that is at the heart of what feminists have called "the rape culture."[15] One study of date rape revealed that college men who have experienced pressure from their current male friends to engage in sexual activity are more likely to commit acquaintance rape.[16] Similarly, a 1988 national study found that "involvement in peer groups that reinforce highly sexualized views of women" is an important predictor of "sexually aggressive behavior" by college males.[17] Robin Warshaw concluded from her research on date and acquaintance rape that "athletic teams are breeding grounds for rape [because they] are often populated by men who are steeped in sexist, rape-supportive beliefs."[18] Indeed, sportswriter Rich Hoffman reported in a story in the *Philadelphia Daily News* that between 1983 and 1986, a U.S. college athlete was reported for sexual assault an average of once every eighteen days.[19]

The sexual objectification of women among male athletes is probably, in most cases, a "rhetorical performance" that rarely translates into actual aggression against women."[20] But there is considerable evidence that men pay a price for these performances. As sociologist Miriam Johnson has argued,

> That the peer group's pressure to be heterosexual occurs in a context in which women are sex-objectified may well have the consequence of making it difficult for males to become sexually aroused in a relationship in which they do not feel dominant over the female. If one learns about sexuality in the context of being rewarded by other males for "scoring," for "getting pussy" or just "getting" it," then this does not augur well for egalitarian sex.[21]

Though this socially structured denigration of women truly does hurt young males, in terms of making the development of true intimacy with women more difficult to develop, ultimately, it is women—the "prey"—who pay the price for young men's fear of intimacy with each other.

Young men don't totally "go it alone" in constructing masculine identities and relationships. Athletic teams and organizations, after all, are organized and run by adult men....

NOTES

1. P. Lyman, "The Fraternal Bond as a Joking Relationship: A Case Study of Sexist Jokes in Male Group Bonding," in M. S. Kimmel, ed., *Changing Men: New Directions in Research on Men and Masculinity.* (Newbury Park, CA: Sage, 1987), pp. 148–63.

2. Here are some of the roots of the still-popular misconception that male homosexuality is connected to some essential "femininity," a confusion of sexual identity with gender identity. This confusion is clearly a cultural manifestation. See W. L. Williams, *The Spirit and the Flesh: Sexual Diversity in American Indian Culture* (Boston: Beacon Press, 1986).

3. D. J. Mrozek, *Sport and the American Mentality, 1880–1910* (Knoxville: University of Tennessee Press, 1983), p. 20.

4. T. Crosset, "Masculinity, Sexuality, and the Development of Early Modern Sport," in M. A. Messner and D. F. Sabo, eds., *Sport, Men, and the Gender Order: Critical Feminist Perspectives* (Champaign, Ill.: Human Kinetics Publishers, 1990), pp. 45–54.

5. I recall, though, that despite the fact that scientific "sexology" had long-since discredited the notion of the spermatic economy, and despite the fact that Joe Namath had exploded the myth in professional football by showing up for big games, even the Super Bowl, and making thinly veiled statements about whom he had slept with the previous night, I had a community college coach in 1971 who would routinely warn us before every weekend to "save [our] energies for the games...stay away from the split-tails" (which of course meant women).

6. Lyman, "The Fraternal Bond as a Joking Relationship," p. 151

7. Ibid., p. 156.

8. J. Brown, *Out of Bounds* (New York: Kensington, 1989), pp. 183–84, 190.

9. D. F. Sabo, "The Myth of the Sexual Athlete," in *Changing Men: Issues in Gender, Sex, and Politics* 20 (1989): 38–39.

10. T. J. Curry, "Fraternal Bonding in the Locker Room: A Profeminist Analysis of Talk about Competition and Women" *Sociology of Sport Journal* 8 (1991): 119–135.

11. Sabo, "The Myth of the Sexual Athlete," p. 39.

12. Christine Williams points out in her study of the construction of gender in the Marine Corps and in the nursing profession that homophobia and misogyny are a common part of basic training for male Marines. See C. L. Williams, *Gender Differences at Work: Women and Men in Nontraditional Occupations.* (Berkeley: University of California Press, 1989).

13. A. Brittan, *Masculinity and Power* (Oxford: Basil Blackwell, 1989), p. 41.

14. B. Pronger, *The Arena of Masculinity: Sports, Homosexuality, and the Meaning of Sex* (New York: St. Martin's Press, 1990), pp. 195, 199.

15. See, for instance, D. Herman, "The Rape Culture," in J. Freeman, ed., *Women: A Feminist Perspective*, 3d ed. (Mountain View, Cal.: Mayfield, 1984), pp. 20–38; T. Beneke, *Men on Rape* (New York: St. Martin's Press, 1982).

16. E. J. Kanin, "Date Rape: Differential Sexual Socialization and Relative Deprivation," *Victimology* 9 (1984): 95-108.

17. M. P. Koss, and T. E. Dinero, "Predictors of Sexual Aggression among a National Sample of Male College Students," in R. A. Prentky and V. Quinsey, eds., *Human Sexual Aggression: Current Perspectives, Annals of the New York Academy of Sciences* 528 (1988): 133–46. For a similar argument on how young male homosocial groups can promote rape, see P. Y. Martin and R. A. Hummer, "Fraternities and Rape on Campus," *Gender and Society* 3 (1989): 457–73.

18. Warshaw, R., *I Never Called It Rape* (New York: Harper and Row, 1988), p. 112.

19. Cited in ibid., p. 113.

20. An ethnographic study of a Texas high school football team revealed a lot of what anthropologist Douglas Foley called "rhetorical performance" about sex in the locker room. See D. E. Foley, "The Great American Football Ritual: Reproducing Race, Class, and Gender Inequality," *Sociology of Sport Journal* 7 (1990): 111–35.

21. M. M. Johnson, *Strong Mothers, Weak Wives* (Berkeley: University of California Press, 1988).

Social Class in Black Sexuality

BENJAMIN P. BOWSER

One of the most enduring sociological find-ings is that marriages tend to be more stable among well-educated, well-paid white-collar workers than among poorly educated, poorly paid blue-collar workers (Aborampah 1989). Does this explanation explain the higher levels of sexual activity among blacks in gen-eral and black men in particular? In a study of the 1976 and 1981 National Survey of Chil-dren, Furstenberg (1987) found that, when mother's education or family income were controlled, racial differences in sexual activ-ity were only partly accounted for. Social class made some differences. Middle-class blacks were less promiscuous than lower-class blacks, but they were still more sexually active than middle-class whites. In a second study by Weinberg and Williams (1988), ra-cial differences in sexual promiscuity were not found to be explainable by social class. The conclusion drawn by these and other investigators is that the uniformly higher lev-els of sexual activity among blacks, when compared to whites, were due to "cultural" differences.

An optimist would say that there is some progress in having exaggerated black sexual-ity explained through culture rather than through biology as it was in the prior century (Harris 1968). But to use only a cultural expla-nation leads back over old ground into what is now the classical and continuing bias in re-search on black Americans—to blame the vic-tim (Valentine 1968; Ryan 1976). To view black sexuality as cultural behaviors coming solely from black people requires the following as-sumptions: (1) that the larger society and cul-ture have no ongoing influence on black life and culture; (2) that black Americans are cul-turally and socially autonomous; (3) that the history of discrimination and poverty has had either little or no impact on black sexuality; (4) that the increasingly marginal position of black men in the economy does not impact their sexuality; (5) that there is one uniform black culture; and (6) that there is in fact little diversity among blacks, especially black men, with regard to sexuality.

Furthermore, the apparent inability of so-cial class to explain exaggerated black sexual-ity in comparison to whites is based on an erroneous understanding of social class. Black and white social classes are not directly com-parable. Students of race and social class have pointed out since the 1940s that objective measures of social class do not adequately ac-count for the variability among blacks in atti-tudes, beliefs, and values (Drake and Cayton 1944; Drake 1989). This means that even when blacks and whites have the same educational level, the same income, and the same occupa-tion, they are not necessarily in the same so-cial class. The might not even be in the same economic class.

Excerpted from *The American Black Male* edited by Richard G. Majors and Jacob U. Gordon, pp. 122–126. Copyright © 1994 by Nelson-Hall Inc. Reprinted with the permission of Nelson-Hall Publishers, Chicago.

Among black Americans, individuals who would be in the working class if they were white can identify with and be a part of the black middle class. In the same way, an individual who might appear to be in the middle class if white can identify with and be a part of the black working class. In each case, the basis of social class affiliation is group acceptance and identification with appropriate class-related attitudes, beliefs, and values. Social class among white Americans is much less conditional and more clearly bound. In contrast, because of the very narrow range in which black social classes are bound, objective measures of their social class do not necessarily correspond to subjective social class.

The research strategy of measuring black and white social classes by matching income, education, and occupation ignores major sources of intergenerational and intragenerational class differences—inherited wealth, savings, owning stocks and bonds, equity in property, the ability of relatives to give "gifts," access to financial information, number of generations in the middle class, percentage of one's extended family in the middle class, family as a mobility network, access to business, access to union crafts and professions based on family and ethnic membership, traditions of business ownership, and access to overseas investment. If just some of these factors were taken into account, we might very well find that the black middle class is actually more comparable to the white working class. In that case, "exaggerated" black sexuality might be social-class related after all, and the cultural explanation would be unwarranted.

AN ALTERNATIVE VIEW OF BLACK SEXUALITY

In order to understand the dimensions of attitude and behavior changes necessary to prevent the spread of AIDS, we have to fully appreciate sexuality's social context. Sexuality is an intrinsic part of a people's social experience. It is not isolated from their general experience or from the quality of their participation in the larger society. If black sexuality is in some way different than it is for whites, then there must be something different about the respective social conditions of each group. This point can be extended to the apparent exaggerated sexuality of black men. Are there some particular conditions common to black men that might affect their sexual attitudes and behaviors?

A contextual and conditional explanation might begin by looking at the extent to which black men are able and allowed to fully play out the male normative social and economic roles. I would propose that men in all social classes who experience frustrated instrumental and expressive roles place more emphasis on their sexuality. The degree of their frustration over time directly impacts the extent to which sexuality becomes emphasized. In addition to whether men are able to play normative roles, there is the concern of whether some traditional male roles can still be considered male roles. The broadening of the roles women can now play in the economy and in the community has reduced the roles that are clearly ascribed to men. Table 1 outlines the roles that men have traditionally played.

The traditional male economic and community roles are now partly shared by women in the general population. In most white American households the woman brings home a secondary income necessary to maintaining the quality of life and, optimally, shares in financial decision making. The man is still central to fulfilling the family's economic role. In households where the traditional male economic role is shared, the role has become transitional.

The sharing is of a very different nature among economically disadvantaged and middle-class blacks. Increasingly, black men in the working and lower classes are either underemployed or unemployed (Bluestone and Harrison 1982). They are far more economically

TABLE 1   Traditional Male Roles

ECONOMIC MALE ROLE	HUSBAND/ MANFRIEND ROLE	FATHER/ MALE ROLE	COMMUNITY MALE ROLE
Primary income	Companionship	Protection	Leadership
Economic security	Protection	Emotional support	Protection of quality of life
Financial decisions	Emotional support	Guidance	Physical upkeep
	Acceptance	Discipline	Mutual support
	Social status		

marginalized than black women and have no social welfare safety net (Center for the Study of Social Policy 1986). Black men in professional and skilled jobs may not be economically marginal, but they are more likely than black women to be socially marginal on the job and to be viewed as a threat by white men. Black men do not live or work in social contexts where they may play out male roles as fully as do white men in comparable circumstances. Among economically disadvantaged blacks, increasingly, black women are having to take on the full economic role—primary income and decision making. They are having to take on these responsibilities, not in order to maintain a high quality of life, but because they have to in order to survive due to the economic marginalization of black working-class and lower-class men.

For black men of all social classes who can no longer play the traditional male social and economic roles, tasks ordinarily assigned to men are not in transition. These roles have been reassigned either permanently or temporarily to black women. Social and economic role attrition for men sets into motion the attrition of other male roles as well. Many of these black men become less able to serve as husbands (manfriends), fathers, and community leaders.

Male role attrition has negative social-psychological consequences. The fewer the traditional male roles these black men are able to play, the less of "a man" they are perceived to be and the more they must struggle to see themselves as men. This is why it is now not unusual to hear black men and women refer in conversation to a man who is disappointing, a failure and unable to be a man, as a "bitch"—a term traditionally used to refer degradingly to a woman.

One way for men to compensate for this clearly unacceptable social identity as a failure and a "bitch" is to exaggerate all that is left. And that is sex. In sex a man has not been replaced, and he cannot be simply left out. He has to be included, and what is left of his manhood demands that he control this last frontier. The result is exaggerated sexuality; high energy and high emotional investment in competition with other black men; black-on-black violence; and, for some, chemical dependence as a way to escape the perception of threat to their self-identity as men. Figure 1 il-

FIGURE 1   Components and Process Leading to Exaggerated Male Sexuality

Economic and social marginality	→	Frustrated role fulfillment	→	Marginality as husband/ father/manfriend	→	Compensation in sexuality in male relations

lustrates the components and process that result in exaggerated black male sexuality.

One of the outcomes of economic marginality in the labor force and social marginality in larger society is the diminished opportunity to fulfill traditional and transitional male roles as manfriend, husband, father, and protector of the community. One way to compensate is to transfer frustrated motivation to competition with other black males and to exaggerated sexuality. A parallel and reinforcing process is the understandable unwillingness of black women, who have to assume the traditional male roles, to financially or emotionally support marginalized men or to defer to their diminished social manhood.

EFFECTIVE AIDS PREVENTION

Given the social and economic context of black male sexuality, it is going to require a lot more than information dissemination in order to get black men to practice AIDS-preventive behaviors. Since there is no way to immediately solve the problem of black male economic and social marginality, the prospects for changing black male sexual behaviors appear to be quite dim. But there are reasons for optimism.

There have been successes in the AIDS-prevention effort that can serve as models for how black males might be convinced to change their behaviors. Gay and bisexual men dramatically reduced their HIV-high-risk behaviors by first conducting AIDS education campaigns from within their communities (Coates 1990). This got the message out to everyone in their community. Then, through their own grass-roots discussions and persuasion, gay men developed a safe-sex social norm. HIV high-risk behaviors are now viewed as dangerous and as a reason for being cut off from the group. The most effective AIDS-prevention strategy has turned out to be for a group at high risk for AIDS to change its

social norms. We have also had success in persuading intravenous drug users to bleach their needles to prevent HIV infections (Biernacki 1986). An important key to this success was to enlist as community educators ex-addicts who know the IVDU community and culture. They influenced IVDUs to change their norms in order to get wide-scale group compliance.

There is a need for the same grass-roots AIDS education among black men, so that they will change their sense of what constitutes normative sexual behavior. The most effective way to develop such a new sexual norm would be to eliminate the motivation for exaggerated sexuality. To do so would require major structural changes in the position of black men in American society and in the way that they are perceived. Such a social transformation would also solve virtually all of the other major crises and problems facing black Americans. But short of a social transformation, black male sexual norms can still be altered in favor of AIDS prevention.

Social norms of exaggerated sexuality can be changed by redirecting the underlying motivation for this overcompensating behavior toward, not away from, safe-sex norms. AIDS prevention efforts need to be directed at helping black men (and women) to develop a new norm of what constitutes a black man. There are a number of proposed components to this redefinition (Aborampah 1989). Part of this new definition should include nonexploitative sexuality and safe-sex practices. This is not impossible: there are black men in the middle, working, and lower class who are already successfully practicing such behaviors, against current norms and perceptions. Change the sexual norms in favor of AIDS prevention, and these successful men will become the rule rather than the exception. But clearly, behavior and norm change has to come from within the world of black men and women who support new black sexuality and social norms.

REFERENCES

Aborampah, O. 1989. "Black Male-Female Relationships: Some Observations." *Journal of Black Studies* 19(3): 320–42.

Biernecki, P. 1986. *Pathways to Heroin Addiction.* Philadelphia, PA: Temple University Press.

Bluestone, B., and B. Harrison. 1982. *The Deindustrialization of America.* New York: Basic Books.

Center for the Study of Social Policy. 1986. "The Flip-Side of Black Families Headed by Women: The Economic Status of Black Men." In R. Staples (ed.), *The Black Family: Essays and Studies.* Belmont, CA.: Wadsworth.

Coates, T. 1990. "Strategies for Modifying Sexual Behavior for Primary and Secondary Prevention of HIV Disease." *Journal of Consulting and Clinical Psychology* 58(1): 57–69.

Drake, St. C. 1989. "Studies of African Diaspora: The Work and Reflections of St. Clair Drake." *Sage Race Relations Abstracts* 14(3): 1–15.

Drake, St. C., and H. Crayton. 1944. *Black Metropolis.* New York: Harper and Row.

Furstenberg, F., et al. 1987. "Race Differences in the Timing of Adolescent Intercourse." *American Sociological Review* 52: 511–18.

Harris, M. 1968. *The Rise of Anthropological Theory.* New York: T. Y. Crowell.

Ryan, W. 1976. *Blaming the Victim.* New York: Vintage Books.

Valentine, C. 1968. *Culture and Poverty.* Chicago: University of Chicago Press.

Weinberg, M., and C. Williams. 1988. "Black Sexuality: A Test of Two Theories." *Journal of Sex Research* 25(2): 197–218.

Childhood Lessons: Culture, Race, Class, and Sexuality

BECKY W. THOMPSON

If there is one story that is an integral part of the folklore of growing up female, it is the chronicle of the onset of menstruation. These accounts are often embarrassing—a thirteen-year-old girl has to ask her father to tell her what to do, another is sure that people can tell from her face what is going on in her body—and many, like that of the young teenager who gets a red cake with red candles from her mother to celebrate her first period, are funny. Usually told only in the company of other women, these stories of a rite of passage are often filled with pain, ingenuity, and humor—and sometimes joy.

Equally revealing stories about the development of female identity in the United States spring from lessons girls learn about their body sizes and appetites. Whether they are fat or thin, Latina or Jewish (or both), lesbian or heterosexual, girls are barraged by complicated messages about their bodies, skin, hair, and faces. Not surprisingly, girls who do not fit the standard mold—who look like tomboys, whose skin is dark, who have nappy hair, who are chubby or just plain big, who develop early or develop late—are most aware of negative assessments, and their stories are commonly filled with shame and confusion.

Although there is no single message to girls about weight and food that crosses regional, religious, and cultural lines in the United States, early lessons about weight and appetite often leave indelible marks on their lives. Growing up on a working farm may protect a girl from the pressure to diet, but she may learn elsewhere that a big appetite is not acceptable for girls and women. While being raised in the Dominican Republic may help a young girl value women of all sizes, if she emigrates to the United States, the pressures to assimilate culturally and linguistically may make her especially determined to be thin.

Increasingly, one of the few experiences common to growing girls in the United States is the pressure to diet. This pressure not only reveals strictures about body size, it also telegraphs complicated notions about race, culture, and class. A girl's body may become the battleground where parents and other relatives play out their own anxieties. Just as stories about a first menstruation tell us about a family's social traditions and the extent to which the girl's body is respected within them, lessons about weight and eating habits tell us an enormous amount about culture, race, religion, and gender. It is through these familial and cultural lenses that young girls make judgments about their bodies and their appetites. The nuances in the socialization of girls show why—across race, class, and religion—they may become vulnerable to eating problems and demonstrate how many girls begin to use food to cope with trauma.

GROWING UP LATINA

By the year 2020 the single largest minority group in the United States will be Latino people—including the descendants of people who were in what is now the United States before it was "discovered," people who fled El Salvador and Guatemala in the 1970s and 1980s, Puerto Rican people, and a host of others. Latinos share a history of struggling against colonialism and racism, and they share a common language. Other generalizations are often erroneous.

There is no single Latino ethic about body size and eating patterns. Even to profess that there is a common Puerto Rican expectation about women's body size would conflate significant generational and regional differences.[1] The notion that Latinas as a group are somehow protected from or ignorant of cultural pressure to be thin simply does not hold up in the face of their diversity. Nor can it be said that any particular group of women is isolated from the culture of thinness; the mass media have permeated even the most remote corners of the United States. The pressures of assimilation and racism may make some Latinas especially vulnerable to strictures about weight.

The task, then, is to identify both how ethnic, racial, and socioeconomic heterogeneity among Latinos and Latinas influences their socialization and how these factors may make Latinas susceptible to developing eating problems. One of the Latina women I interviewed, Elsa, was raised by German governesses in an upper-class family in Argentina. Another, Julianna, was cared for by her grandmother in a middle-class family in the Dominican Republic. The other three are Puerto Rican women who grew up in the United States and whose backgrounds ranged from working- to upper-middle-class; among these women, the degree of assimilation varied markedly depending on whether Spanish was their first language, the degree of contact with other Latinas, and the extent to which they identified as Puerto Ricans.

What the Latina women learned about weight and size was influenced by nationality. Julianna, who grew up in a small town in the Dominican Republic, was taught that

> *people don't think that fat is bad. You don't undermine fat people. You just don't.... The picture of a woman is not a woman who has a perfect body that you see on TV. A woman is beautiful because she is a virgin or because she is dedicated to her husband or because she takes care of her kids; because she works at home and does all the things that her husband and family want her to do. But not because she is skinny or fat.*

In the Dominican Republic, female beauty is closely linked to being a good wife and mother and obeying gendered expectations about virginity and monogamy. Thinness is not a necessary criterion for beauty, regardless of a woman's class. By contrast, the Argentinian woman, Elsa, said that a woman's weight was the primary criterion for judging her worth. The diets and exercise her father enforced among his wife and daughters were "oppressive and Nazi-like." But judgments about weight varied with class and degree of urbanization:

> *The only people who see being fat as a positive thing in Argentina are the very poor or the very rural people who still consider it a sign of wealth or health. But as soon as people move to the bigger cities and are exposed to the magazines and the media, dieting and figures become incredibly important.*

None of the Puerto Rican women I talked with benefited from the acceptance of size that the Dominican woman described. Laura, who lived in Puerto Rico with her family for four years when she was a child, recalls that "Latina women were almost expected to be more overweight. Latin women living in Puerto Rico were not uncomfortable with extra weight. To them it wasn't extra. It wasn't an issue." This didn't help Laura appreciate her own chunky size because her family's disdain for fat people was much more influential. Her father was British and her mother liked to "hang out with wealthy white women," both factors that impeded Laura's ability to adopt the Puerto Rican community's values.

Another Puerto Rican woman, Vera, who grew up in Chicago, was chunky as a child and learned that the people around her disapproved of her size. Vera remembers painful scenes at school and in clothing stores that taught her she should be embarrassed by her body size. Although she was an amazingly limber and energetic student in her ballet class, her mother took her out of it because Vera wasn't thin enough.

AFRICAN-AMERICAN GIRLS AND COMMUNITY LIFE

Rosalee grew up in Arkansas in a rural African-American community where, as she described it, "home grown and healthy" was the norm. She remembers that her uncles and other men liked a "healthy woman": as they used to say, "They didn't want a neck bone. They liked a picnic ham." Among the people in her community, skin color and hair were more important than weight in determining beauty. Unlike most of the other women I interviewed, Rosalee didn't think about dieting as a way to lose weight until she was a teenager. Because her family didn't always have money, "there were times when we hardly had food anyway so we tended to slim down. And then . . . when the money was rolling in . . . we celebrated. We ate and ate and ate." When poverty is a constant threat, Rosalee explained, "dieting just isn't a household word." This did not stop Rosalee from developing an eating problem when she was four years old as a response to sexual abuse and being a witness to beatings. Trauma, not size, was the primary factor.

Carolyn, a middle-class woman who grew up in an urban area, remembered that her African-American friends considered African-American women of varying weights to be desirable and beautiful. By contrast, among white people she knew, the only women who were considered pretty were petite. Both the white and the African-American men preferred white girls who were petite.

The women who went to schools in which there were only a few African-American students remember thinness as dominant. By contrast, those who went to racially mixed or predominantly African-American schools saw more acceptance of both big and thin women. One of the many hazards for black students who attend overwhelmingly white schools is pressure to adopt cultural values—including thinness—that may not reflect African-American values.[2]

The women who attended private, predominantly white schools were sent by parents who hoped to open up opportunities unavailable in public schools. As a consequence, both Nicole and Joselyn were isolated from other African-American children. Their parents discouraged them from socializing with neighborhood African-American children, who in turn labeled them arrogant, thus furthering their isolation. Both were teased by neighborhood children for being chubby and light-skinned. At school they were teased for being fat and were excluded by white people in ways both subtle and overt. Racist administrators and teachers granted the girls neither the attention nor the dignity they deserved. Joselyn, who attended Catholic schools, remembered both racial and religious intolerance: "Sister Margaret Anna told me that, basically, what a black person could aspire to at that time was to Christianize the cannibals in Africa." Neither Nicole nor Joselyn had a public context in which her racial identity was validated. As Nicole said, "By second or third grade I was saying I wished I was white because kids at school made fun of me. I remember...getting on the bus and a kid called me a brown cow." As the women were growing up, their weight and their race were used to ostracize them.

INTERSECTION OF RACE AND CLASS

Most of the African-American and Latina women were pressured to be thin by at least one and often all of their family members. For some, these pressures were particularly virulent because they were laced with racism. Rosalee, who grew up on a farm in the South, got contradictory messages about weight and size from her family. Like most of the African-Americans in her community, Rosalee's mother thought thin women were sickly and took her young daughters to the doctor because they weren't gaining enough weight. But her father told her she "had better not turn out fat like her mother." Rosalee and her mother often bore the brunt of his disdain as he routinely told them that African-American women were usually fatter and less beautiful than white women. Rosalee says:

> I can remember fantasizing that "I wish I was white."... It seemed to be the thing to be if you were going to be anything. You know, [white women] were considered beautiful. That was reinforced a lot by my father, who happened to have a strong liking for white women. Once he left the South and he got in the army and traveled around and had more freedom, he became very fond of them. In fact, he is married to one now. He just went really overboard. I found myself wanting to be like that.

Although she was not familiar with dieting as a child, she feared weight gain and her father's judgments. At puberty, she began to diet. Her father's sexism and prejudice against black women meant that she was raised with contradictory messages about weight. At the same time, she was learning about the dominant standard of beauty that emphasizes a fair complexion, blue eyes, and straight hair. About the lessons many black girls learn about straightening their hair and using lightening creams, Rosalee says:

> It was almost as if you were chasing after an impossible dream. I can remember stories about parents pinching their children's noses so they don't get too big. I laugh about it when I am talking about it with other people but on the inside I don't laugh at all. There is nothing there to reinforce who you are, and the body image gets really confused.

Some of the Latinas' and African-Americans' relatives projected their own frustrations and racial prejudices onto the girls' bodies. Joselyn, an African-American woman, remembers her white grandmother telling her she would never be as pretty as her cousins because they had lighter skin. Her grandmother often humiliated Joselyn in front of others, making fun of Joselyn's body while she was naked and telling her she was fat. As a young child Joselyn began to think that although she couldn't change her skin color, she could at least try to be thin.

When Joselyn was young, her grandmother was the only family member who objected to her weight. Then her father also began to encourage his wife and daughter to be thin as the family's social status began to change. When Joselyn was very young, her family was what she called "aspiring to be middle class." For people of Joselyn's parents' generation, having chubby, healthy children was a sign the family was doing well. But, as the family moved up the social ladder, Joselyn's father began to insist that Joselyn be thin:

> When my father's business began to bloom and my father was interacting more with white businessmen and seeing how they did business, suddenly thin became important. If you were a truly well-to-do family, then your family was slim and elegant.

Her grandmother's racism and her father's determined fight to be middle class converged, and Joselyn's body became the playing field for their conflicts. While Joselyn was pressured to diet, her father still served her large portions and bought treats for her and the neighborhood children. These contradictory messages confused her. Like many girls, Joselyn was told she was fat from the time she was very young, even though she wasn't. And, like many of the women I interviewed, Joselyn was put on diet pills and diets before puberty, beginning a cycle of dieting, compulsive eating, and bulimia. She remembers her father telling her, "You know you have a cute face, but from the body down, you are shot to hell. You are built just like your old lady."

Another African-American woman also linked contradictory messages about food to her parents' internalized racism. As Nicole explains it, her mother operated under the "house-nigger mentality," in which she saw herself and her family as separate from and better than other African-American people. Her father shared this attitude, saying that being Cherokee made him different. Her parents sent Nicole to private schools and a "very white Anglican upper-class church" in which she was one of a few black children. According to Nicole, both parents "passed on their internalized racism in terms of judgments around hair or skin color or how a person talks or what is correct or proper."

Their commandments about food and body size were played out on Nicole's body in powerful ways. Nicole's father was from a working-class rural Southern family. Her mother, by contrast, was from a "petit bourgeois family," only one of three black families in a small New Hampshire town. While Nicole's father approved of her being, as he said, "solid," her mother restricted her eating to ensure that Nicole would grow up thin. Each meal, however, was a multicourse event. Like Joselyn, Nicole was taught that eating a lot was a dangerous but integral part of the family tradition:

When I was growing up, I thought that breakfast was a four- or five-course meal the way you might think dinner is. I thought that breakfast involved fruit and maybe even juice and cereal and then the main course of breakfast, which was eggs and bacon and toast. On Sundays we had fancy breakfasts like fish and hominy grits and corn bread and muffins. So breakfast had at least three courses. That is how we are. Dinner was mostly meat and potatoes and vegetables and bread. Then my father would cajole my mother into making dessert. There were lots of rewards that all had to do with food, like going to Howard Johnson or Dunkin' Donuts.

At the same time, Nicole's mother put her on a diet when she was three and tortured her about her weight. Nicole became terrified of going to the doctor because she was weighed and lectured about her weight. Yet, after each appointment, her mother took her to Dunkin' Donuts for a powdered jelly doughnut. When her father did the grocery shopping, he bought Nicole treats, which her mother snatched and hid, accusing her father of trying to make her fat. When she was left alone, Nicole spent hours trying to find the food. In her mother's view, Nicole's weight and curly hair were what kept her from being perfect: her body became the contested territory onto which her parents' pain was projected.

The confusion about body size and class expectations that troubled some of the African-American women paralleled the experiences of two Puerto Rican women. Vera attributed her eating problems partly to the stress of assimilation as her family moved from poverty to the working class. When Vera was three, she was so thin that her mother took her to a doctor who prescribed appetite stimulants. By the time she was eight, though, she remembered her mother comparing her to other girls who stayed on diets or were thin. Vera attributed her mother's change of heart to pressure from family members:

Even though our family went from poverty to working class, there were members of my extended family who thought they were better than everyone else. As I grew up, the conversation was, "Who is going to college? Who has a job working for Diamonds?" It was always this one-upmanship about who was making it better than who. The one-upmanship centered on being white, being successful, being middle class...and it was always, "Ay, Bendito [Oh, God]! She is so fat! What happened?"

Vera's mother warned her that she would never make friends if she was fat. Her mother threatened to get a lock for the refrigerator door and left notes on it reminding Vera not to eat. While Vera's mother shamed her into dieting, she also felt ambivalent when Vera did not eat much. When Vera dieted, her mother would say, "You have to eat. You have to eat something. You can't starve yourself." The messages were always unclear.

Ruthie also remembers changes in the family ethic about size and eating that she attributes to assimilation with Anglo culture. In keeping with Puerto Rican tradition, Ruthie's mother considered chubby children a sign of health and well-being. According to Puerto Rican culture, Ruthie says, "if you are skinny, you are dying. What is wrong with you?" When Ruthie was ten to twelve years old, her mother made her take a food supplement and iron pills that were supposed to make her hungry. Ruthie did not like the supplement and felt fine about the size of her body. But how Ruthie looked was very important to her mother: "My mother used to get these dresses from Spain. She used to show everyone our closets. They were impeccable. Buster Brown shoes and dresses. She thought if I were skinny it would reflect badly on her." Ruthie questioned whether her mother cared about Ruthie or was actually worried about what the family and neighbors would say. When Ruthie became a teenager, her mother's attitude about weight changed:

When I was little, it was not okay to be skinny. But then, at a certain age, it was not okay to be fat. She would say, "Your sister would look great in a bikini and you wouldn't." I thought maybe this was because I felt fat.... Being thin had become something she valued. It was a roller coaster.

Ruthie attributed this change to her mother's acceptance of Anglo standards, which she tried to enforce on Ruthie's eating and body size.

The women's experiences dispel the notion that African-American and Latina women—as a group—are less exposed to or influenced by a culturally imposed thinness than white women. The African-American women who saw community acceptance of different sizes did not escape pressure to be thin from family members. While growing up in a rural area and attending predominantly black schools did protect two of the girls from pressures to diet, childhood traumas resulted in eating problems. For the women of color whose parents' internalized racism, an emphasis on thinness was particularly intense. Rosalee explains:

For a black woman dealing with issues of self-esteem, if you don't get it from your family, you [are punished] twice because you don't get self-esteem from society either. If you come from a dysfunctional or abusive family, there [are] just not a lot of places to go that will turn things around for you.

This reality underscores why some women of color may be more, rather than less, vulnerable than white women to eating problems....

NOTES

1. Iris Zavala Martinez explains that statistics and stereotypes often treat Puerto Rican women as if they were a homogeneous group. In her essay on the economic and "socio-emotional" struggles of Puerto Rican women, Martinez writes, "Such treatment fosters a myth that ignores class differences, racial variations, and differences in places of birth and cultural background, as well as in educational process or language preference." In response to this distorted picture Martinez cautions that "only when the portayals become richer, more sensitive to the multitude of such interacting characteristics,

will the dynamic, complex and changing world of Puerto Rican women come fully into view." See Iris Zavala Martinez, "En La Lucha: Economic and Socioemotional Struggles of Puerto Rican Women in the United States," in *For Crying Out Loud,* ed. Rochelle Lefkowitz and Ann Withorn, pp. 109–22 (Boston: Pilgrim, 1986), p. 112.

2. Elsie J. Smith, "The Black Female Adolescent: A Review of the Educational, Career and Psychological Literature," *Psychology of Women Quarterly* 6, no. 3. (Spring 1982).

Capitalism and Gay Identity

JOHN D'EMILIO

Although lesbians and gay men won significant victories in the 1970s and opened up some safe social space in which to exist, we can hardly claim to have dealt a fatal blow to heterosexism and homophobia. One could even argue that the enforcement of gay oppression has merely changed locales, shifting somewhat from the state to the arena of extra-legal violence in the form of increasingly open physical attacks on lesbians and gay men. And, as our movements have grown, they have generated a backlash that threatens to wipe out our gains. Significantly, this New Right opposition has taken shape as a "pro-family" movement. How is it that capitalism, whose structure made possible the emergence of a gay identity and the creation of urban gay communities, appears unable to accept gay men and lesbians in its midst? Why do heterosexism and homophobia appear so resistant to assault?

The answers, I think, can be found in the contradictory relationship of capitalism to the family. On the one hand, capitalism has gradually undermined the material basis of the nuclear family by taking away the economic functions that cemented the ties between family members. As more adults have been drawn into the free labor system, and as capital has expanded its sphere until it produces as commodities most goods and services we need for our survival, the forces that propelled men and women into families and kept them there have weakened. On the other hand, the ideology of capitalist society has enshrined the family as the source of love, affection, and emotional security, the place where our need for stable, intimate human relationships is satisfied.

This elevation of the nuclear family to preeminence in the sphere of personal life is not accidental. Every society needs structures for reproduction and childrearing, but the possibilities are not limited to the nuclear family. Yet the privatized family fits well with capitalist relations of production. Capitalism has socialized production while maintaining that the products of socialized labor belong to the owners of private property. In many ways, childrearing has also been progressively socialized over the last two centuries, with schools, the media, peer groups, and employers taking over functions that once belonged to parents. Nevertheless, capitalist society maintains that reproduction and childrearing are private tasks, that children "belong" to parents, who exercise the rights of ownership. Ideologically, capitalism drives people into heterosexual families: each generation comes of age having internalized a heterosexist model of intimacy and personal relationships. Materially, capitalism weakens the bonds that once kept families together so that their members experience a growing instability in the

From *Powers of Desire: The Politics of Sexuality* edited by Ann Snitow, Christine Stansell, and Sharon Thompson, pp. 108–111. Copyright © 1983, 1979 by the Monthly Review Press. Reprinted by permission of the Monthly Review Foundation.

place they have come to expect happiness—and emotional security. Thus, while capitalism has knocked the material foundation away from family life, lesbians, gay men, and heterosexual feminists have become the scapegoats for the social instability of the system.

This analysis, if persuasive, has implications for us today. It can affect our perception of our identity, our formulation of political goals, and our decisions about strategy.

I have argued that lesbians and gay identity and communities are historically created, the result of a process of capitalist development that has spanned many generations. A corollary of this argument is that we are *not* a fixed social minority composed for all time of a certain percentage of the population. *There are more of us* than one hundred years ago, more of us than forty years ago. And there may very well be more gay men and lesbians in the future. Claims made by gays and non-gays that sexual orientation is fixed at an early age, that large numbers of visible gay men and lesbians in society, the media, and the schools will have no influence on the sexual identities of the young, are wrong. Capitalism has created the material conditions for homosexual desire to express itself as a central component of some individuals' lives; now, our political movements are changing consciousness, creating the ideological conditions that make it easier for people to make that choice.

To be sure, this argument confirms the worst fears and most rabid rhetoric of our political opponents. But our response must be to challenge the underlying belief that homosexual relations are bad, a poor second choice. We must not slip into the opportunistic defense that society need not worry about tolerating us, since only homosexuals become homosexuals. At best, a minority group analysis and a civil rights strategy pertain to those of us who already are gay. It leaves today's youth—tomorrow's lesbians and gay men—to internalize heterosexist models that it can take a lifetime to expunge.

I have also argued that capitalism has led to the separation of sexuality from procreation. Human sexual desire need no longer be harnessed to reproductive imperatives, to procreation; its expression has increasingly entered the realm of choice. Lesbians and homosexuals most clearly embody the potential of this split, since our gay relationships stand entirely outside a procreative framework. The acceptance of our erotic choices ultimately depends on the degree to which society is willing to affirm sexual expression as a form of play, positive and life-enhancing. Our movement may have begun as the struggle of a "minority," but what we should now be trying to "liberate" is an aspect of the personal lives of all people—sexual expression.[1]

Finally, I have suggested that the relationship between capitalism and the family is fundamentally contradictory. On the one hand, capitalism continually weakens the material foundation of family life, making it possible for individuals to live outside the family, and for a lesbian and gay male identity to develop. On the other, it needs to push men and women into families, at least long enough to reproduce the next generation of workers. The elevation of the family to ideological preeminence guarantees that capitalist society will reproduce not just children, but heterosexism and homophobia. In the most profound sense, capitalism is the problem.[2]

How do we avoid remaining the scapegoats, the political victims of the social instability that capitalism generates? How can we take this contradictory relationship and use it to move toward liberation?

Gay men and lesbians exist on social terrain beyond the boundaries of the heterosexual nuclear family. Our communities have formed in that social space. Our survival and liberation depend on our ability to defend and expand that terrain, not just for ourselves but for everyone. That means, in part, support for issues that broaden the opportunities for living outside traditional heterosexual family units: issues like the availability of abortion and the ratification of the Equal Rights Amendment, affirmative action for people of color and for women, publicly funded day-care and other essential social services, decent welfare payments, full employment, the rights of young people—in other words, programs and issues that provide a material basis for personal autonomy.

The rights of young people are especially critical. The acceptance of children as dependents, as belonging to parents, is so deeply ingrained that we can scarcely imagine what it would mean to treat them as autonomous human beings, particularly in the realm of sexual expression and choice. Yet until that happens, gay liberation will remain out of our reach.

But personal autonomy is only half the story. The instability of families and the sense of impermanence and insecurity that people are now experiencing in their personal relationships are real social problems that need to be addressed. We need political solutions for these difficulties of personal life. These solutions should not come in the form of a radical version of the pro-family position, of some left-wing proposals to strengthen the family. Socialists do not generally respond to the exploitation and economic inequality of industrial capitalism by calling for a return to the family farm and handicraft production. We recognize that the vastly increased productivity that capitalism has made possible by so-cializing production is one of its progressive features. Similarly, we should not be trying to turn back the clock to some mythic age of the happy family.

We do need, however, structures and programs that will help to dissolve the boundaries that isolate the family, particularly those that privatize childrearing. We need community- or worker-controlled daycare, housing where privacy and community coexist, neighborhood institutions—from medical clinics to performance centers—that enlarge the social unit where each of us has a secure place. As we create structures beyond the nuclear family that provide a sense of belonging, the family will wane in significance. Less and less will it seem to make or break our emotional security.

In this respect gay men and lesbians are well situated to play a special role. Already excluded from families as most of us are, we have had to create, for our survival, networks of support that do not depend on the bonds of blood or the license of the state, but that are freely chosen and nurtured. The building of an "affectional community" must be as much a part of our political movement as are campaigns for civil rights. In this way we may prefigure the shape of personal relationships in a society grounded in equality and justice rather than exploitation and oppression, a society where autonomy and security do not preclude each other but coexist.

NOTES

1. This especially needs to be emphasized today. The 1980 annual conference of the National Organization for Women, for instance, passed a lesbian rights resolution that defined the issue as one of "discrimination based on affectional/sexual preference/orientation," and explicitly disassociated the issue from other questions of sexuality such as pornography, sadomasochism, public sex, and pederasty.

2. I do not mean to suggest that homophobia is "caused" by capitalism, or is to be found only in capitalist societies. Severe sanctions against homo-eroticism can be found in European feudal society and in contemporary socialist countries. But my focus in this essay has been the emergence of a gay identity under capitalism, and the mechanisms specific to capitalism that made this possible and that reproduce homophobia as well.

Difference, Desire, and the Self

ARLENE STEIN

The individual can only be what is possible within some specifically constructed historical world. But individuals, thus constrained, construct and reconstruct such historical worlds by exploiting the distinctive ambiguities of interaction. They bring with them to each of their interactions a unique and inner self.
—Dennis Wrong, "The Oversocialized Conception of Man in Modern Sociology," 1961

As we have seen, women who reached adolescence and young adulthood during the 1960s and 1970s—at a time when U.S. society was in a period of great social ferment, when gender and sexual norms were being publicly contested—confronted two different accounts of lesbianism. The medical model conceptualized lesbianism in terms of homosexual object choice or desires, which were fixed and immutable. This dominant explanation associated lesbianism with gender nonconformity, exemplified by the mannish woman. To become a lesbian was to reveal something that had before been hidden, to disclose something that occupied the very core of one's "being," and to build an identity on the basis of one's stigma.

In contrast, an emergent account, influenced by social constructionist thought, considered lesbianism to be a product of multiple influences rather than being traceable to a single cause, a lifestyle choice that entailed conscious self-reflection and identification. In the context of the feminist and gay liberation movements, to become a lesbian signified coming to self-knowledge, identifying with the collectivity of other lesbians, and making political commitments.[1]

The discourse of "coming out," as it was used by my interviewees, linked these two conceptions of homosexuality. It imagined the process of homosexual identification as a coming to terms with an "authentic" self, which implied the existence of a "core" sexual orientation, an internal "truth."[2] Yet it situated the development of a lesbian identity as a voluntaristic and reflexive act that challenged the pervasiveness of "compulsory heterosexuality" and was accessible to anyone who possessed the right political convictions. The women I interviewed shared a strong belief in the idea of "coming out," which they generally understood as two linked processes: the consolidation of a personal sense of self as lesbian and the development of a social identity as lesbian, the latter entailing a certain degree of public disclosure. When I began an interview by asking someone how she would describe her sexual identity, most interviewees promptly launched into their "coming out" story.

In one instance, I sat down with a forty-three-year-old woman, a carpenter in San Francisco, and asked her to tell me about her life. No sooner had I turned on the tape recorder than she proceeded to tell me her coming out story, beginning in early childhood and moving through time to the present. It seemed to me that she had told this story many times before. In the course of my research, this scene was repeated time after time. Immediately after I asked my subjects how they would define their sexual identities, they would embark upon their stories, carefully tracing their biographies in roughly chronological order.

Coming out as a lesbian typically took several years or more.[3] Like a fictional bildungsroman, in which a character achieves self-development by making a challenging journey, the process of coming out moved the individual from one state of being to another.[4] It guided her along a path that ended with the moment of resolution: the "final" achievement of a lesbian/gay identity. The relating of her coming out story was itself an important element of this process, in part because it was an act of disclosure. Though few disclosed their lesbianism to all whom they met, and at all times, the women I spoke with were "out" in many if not most aspects of their lives.

In telling me her story, each woman constructed a personal narrative of sexual identity development that helped to organize her autobiographical experience for herself and for me, the audience. In speaking with individuals, I was often struck both by the pervasiveness of the discourse of "coming out" and

by the great variety among the stories themselves.[5] Coming out was a narrative template that was expansive and adaptable enough to accommodate a diverse array of life experiences. Here are two of these stories.

BARB HERMAN: "JUST THE WAY I AM"

Forty-two-year-old Barb Herman was born to a lower-middle-class Italian family in New York. Barb experienced desires for other girls early in life and acted on these desires in isolation, often thinking that she was "the only one." She thinks of herself as having been a tomboy as a child. "I never played with dolls, and hardly ever played with girls. I wore boys' clothes at age eight or nine."

Barb remembers the 1950s and early 1960s as a time when she was "young and out of control, having all these feelings, and no place to go to talk about them." At fifteen, Barb had a first sexual experience with another girl. It was 1962. At the time, she had no words to describe her feelings, though she was vaguely aware of the existence of other lesbians. It was an experience that she describes as an epiphany, or defining moment. She felt a "mixture of fear and exhilaration. This is home after all these years. I knew that this was what I wanted, but I knew that it was a really bad thing."

Lesbian pulp novels—dimestore fiction sold during the 1950s and 1960s, featuring lurid covers and titles such as *Odd Girl Out* and *Strange Sisters*—told tales of lust, intrigue, and secrecy, of being young and confused, and of being a social misfit. These books remind Barb of her own adolescence, for she "faced the very same kind of struggles" as their characters. Once she had her first homosexual experience, she said, "I felt at peace with myself emotionally. This is home." Quoting the 1952 novel by Claire Morgan (Patricia Highsmith) called *The Price of Salt*, Barb recalled the line: "Nobody had to tell her that this was the way it was supposed to be."

Barb feels that she has always been a lesbian, that it was not at all a matter of choice. To become a lesbian, she simply "discovered" what was "already there." In contrast, she described her first girlfriend, who "turned straight" after a few years: "She flipped out. She became straight after a few years, got married, had kids, and seriously repressed that stuff: her sexual experience with me, her feelings for others. Maybe she had some doubts about really being gay. I couldn't repress it. I never did. I never had any doubts."

Yet it would be several years before Barb could actually name her lesbianism to others. Through her teens and early twenties, Barb had a series of relationships with women but never claimed a lesbian identity in the sense of affiliating with the lesbian subculture. She was seeing a psychiatrist at the time, who told her that she had "trouble relating to people" and prescribed tranquilizers. Several years after having had her first homosexual experience, Barb befriended Lore, the first "flesh and blood" lesbian she had ever met—the first woman she knew who identified as a lesbian. One day, Lore looked Barb in the eye and said: "You are a lesbian." At the time, Barb said, she scoffed at the allegation, "but it planted some sort of seed." Still, claiming a lesbian identity in a social sense, as a member of a stigmatized group, was not an easy task in the absence of any public lesbian visibility.

At the time the women's movement was just starting to struggle with lesbianism. I had no patience for it. I had no patience to struggle with them. Even if I said "I am not a lesbian," I think I always knew I was. But it's this funny thing. How you dissociate yourself from things that you're feeling, even if there is a label for what you're feeling in the English language. I always knew I was a lesbian, but I distanced myself from the word. It was too scary to consider…I remember looking at the rise of feminism, and thinking it was hopeful, and that things were moving in the right direction. But I remember thinking or sensing that they're not there yet. It's not all right to be a lesbian—yet.

There were all these strikes going on, and I still didn't quite get all the connections—with the war, with academic freedom, with general alternative education and feminism and black power. There were all these strikes all over campus. Kent State. Riots at Columbia. The world was going to pieces, but I was freaking out about being a lesbian. That was the most important thing to me.

But in 1970, a homophobic incident provided the catalyst for Barb's public coming out. While in college, she was living with a girlfriend and several other people in a communal house. One morning, she awoke to hear her housemates discussing whether the presence of Barb and her girlfriend was "warping the household." That was, she said, "the straw that broke the camel's back." Soon after this, Barb became involved with a radical lesbian political group that had just formed in town. She described attending a first meeting, in 1971: "It was like the messiah had come. There were all these people who were like me. They were all my age. They were lesbians. They were distributing mimeographed copies of 'The Woman Identified Woman.' I quickly realized I was a feminist as well as a lesbian."

Becoming a feminist lesbian meant that Barb could begin to think of her lesbianism in positive terms. It also meant that she could think of her femaleness and her lesbianism as compatible, rather than conflicting. She gained a sense that she could have a social as well as a personal identity as a lesbian.

The whole period from 1971 to 1973–74 was an incredible release. It was great. Because I had gone on marches—civil rights marches and other kinds of demonstrations—before, but none of it seemed to have much to do with my life. It was a thrill to be doing it for me instead of for everybody else. Getting involved in lesbian feminism was a very personal kind of thing. Things were happening very fast; every time you turned around there was more going on, more stuff being written, more things to read and talk about. We were up half the night talking. It was like the racetrack. For a while life was really exciting.

Barb says that she would be a lesbian regardless of these historical changes, but she imagines that she would have been forced to lead a far more secretive, far more unhappy life.

Barb's narrative exhibits many elements of the "dominant" account; she sees her lesbianism as an immutable orientation, fixed at birth or in early childhood. She talked about "knowing" she was a lesbian by age eight, even before she had words to describe her feelings. Adolescent girls vary in the extent to which they know their desires. Some are not at all aware of sexual feelings, heterosexual or homosexual, while others, like Barb, are deeply conscious of them. Girls with early awareness of their sexual feelings often experience their adolescence as a period in which their embodied sexual desire is simultaneously elicited and denigrated by the dominant culture.[6] One can imagine that girls with early lesbian desires rarely, if ever, receive reinforcement either in the dominant culture or within adolescent peer groups.

Barb identified desires for girls and women at a very early age, experiencing these desires as powerful and unwavering. In the context of the early to mid-1960s, Barb saw herself as virtually alone, having no one to discuss her feelings with. She compared her experiences with those of old dykes, who had come out as lesbians before feminism. "I was sort of an old lesbian. To be an old lesbian meant you were out before feminism. I wasn't out to anyone but myself." Being a lesbian in the mid-1960s was a "long stream of unfinished business." She thinks of herself as straddling the "old gay" and "new gay" worlds because she had same-sex experiences before the late 1960s, before the lesbian/gay movements expanded the social space open to lesbians and gay men. "But I knew when I was eight years old. I probably knew much earlier."

When I asked Barb why she is a lesbian, she replied, "It's just the way I am." Indeed, she found the question itself rather curious. Barb sees her adolescent experiences of differ-

ence and her eventual homosexuality as points on a continuum. Her personal identity as lesbian was never really in question. As she grew older and began to affiliate with the lesbian community, those connections gave her a social identity as well, a sense of direction and purpose that went beyond the self, and a way to counter some of the stigma she encountered. She spoke of the important role that the lesbian community played in allowing her to normalize her sexuality.

But the fact that she experienced her lesbian desires early in life has been crucial in shaping her sense of self and the meaning her lesbianism holds for her. Indeed, her identity account resembles the "old gay" account, insofar as secrecy looms large for those who have spent their formative years "managing" their stigma, carefully determining which parts of the self they would reveal to others. She feels that she has lived much of her life in the closet.

Perhaps because of these experiences, Barb tended to accentuate the differences between herself and heterosexual women, viewing lesbians and heterosexuals as two distinct categories, much as did women of an earlier prefeminist cohort. She thinks of lesbianism largely in essentialist terms. She believes that the only "real" lesbians are "born" lesbians—women like her, who have little choice in the matter of their sexuality.

MARGARET BERG: "COMING OUT THROUGH FEMINISM"

Margaret Berg grew up in New England; she was a red diaper baby, the daughter of Jewish leftist activists of mixed working-class and middle-class backgrounds. To be a woman in the 1950s and 1960s, she said, was to grow up with "the profound sense of oneself as a second-class citizen." Margaret spoke of her need to feign underachievement in school in order to catch a husband. She said that she experienced her heterosexual relationships as largely unsatisfying and her sexual interest in men as often conflicted, motivated more by accommodation to male needs and social expectations than by her own desires. "I had all the feelings about men that we all had; we thought they were like zombies. I felt that I took care of all the men I was involved with. I felt like I was much stronger than they were. I felt like I gave much more than I got." She recalled, "We were growing up in a world that was so invalidating of women. I straightened my hair, I was ambivalent about being smart, my physics teacher told my parents: she's doing fine for a girl."[7]

The women's movement emerged in the late 1960s to help her make sense of this alienation and situate it in the larger scheme of women's oppression. Margaret compared her exposure to feminism in 1969 to "coming out of a cave." Feminism, she said, was "the most exciting and validating thing that had happened in our lives." It allowed her and others to resolve the dissonance they felt between cultural codes and subjective experience. Within the context of the movement, Margaret developed an analysis and vocabulary for these feelings, seeing her problems in gendered terms for the first time. She began to believe that she had devalued herself as a woman and underestimated the importance of her female relationships.

Because of their growing idealization of other women—a change in attitude made possible by feminism—women like Margaret withdrew from primary relationships with men. This was less a conscious decision than the outcome of the growing separation between men's and women's social and political worlds, at least among the young, predominantly middle-class members of what became loosely called the "movement." At the time, she was romantically involved with a man, but as her women friends became more and more central, he became more peripheral. Eventually, "most of my friends were women, all of my friends were feminists, men were not

part of my life. It was all very seamless." Margaret had always thought of lesbianism as something that was involuntary; it was an orientation that one either did or did not "have." But when she was in her early twenties, she became aware of the possibility of constructing her own sexuality and of electing lesbianism. As she described it, she was one of those women who "came out through feminism."

When Margaret became involved in her first lesbian relationship, she said, "the only gay women I knew (and *we* wouldn't call ourselves gay) were my friend and myself." Her friend, Jennifer, eventually moved into her apartment. The world they traveled in was that of liberated sexuality and free use of drugs, and there was "a real sense of barriers breaking." She was drawn to Jennifer as a kindred spirit, an equal. "There was a certain reflection of myself I found in her." Margaret recalled that Jennifer had "much more self-consciously identified homoerotic feelings," while hers were more about sexual experimentation and rebellion.

In an effort to make sense of her feelings, and to find support for them, she began to attend a women's consciousness-raising group devoted to discussing questions of sexuality. Practically overnight, through the influence of gay liberation and lesbian feminism, the gathering transformed itself into a coming out group. There, Margaret was socialized into the lesbian world. She began to think of herself as a lesbian and call herself one.

There was a normative sense about discovering women and male domination and how disgusting men could be. Not to be a lesbian was stupid, masochistic . . . something called "lesbian consciousness" developed in our heads. It's hard to reconstruct just how the process occurred. We talked about "coming out" every four or five weeks. That term started having more and more ramifications as our lives changed. Not just making love with a woman for the first time—but every new situation where you experienced and/or revealed yourself as gay.

Within the context of a coming out group, Margaret carved out a place for herself in the lesbian subculture. Earlier, "coming out" had referred almost exclusively to the process of disclosure. But now women who had never experienced themselves as deeply and irrevocably different, but who shared a sense of alienation from gender and sexual norms, could also claim lesbian identities by developing "gay consciousness." The discourse of lesbian feminism conflated feminism and lesbianism. Lesbianism was reenvisioned to signify not simply a sexual preference but a way for women to gain strength and confidence, to bond with other women.

But the political strategy of coming out to others as a means of establishing unity often had the contradictory effect of heightening differences *among* women, and the tension between identity and difference within the coming out group soon became apparent. Margaret describes the "experiential gap" separating the women in the group who were "entering a first gay relationship" and those who were "coming out of the closet":

> One woman was quite involved with a man and left almost immediately—it was never clear exactly why she had joined the group, except that she felt good about women. Another woman pulled out because she felt there was a "bisexual" orientation to the group. . . . Her "coming out" was very different from the rest of ours. She wasn't entering a first gay relationship; rather, she was coming out of "the closet," entering a gay community and acquiring pride in an analysis of who she is . . . . There was a real experiential gap between her and the rest of the group. We had no understanding of the bar scene, of role-playing, of the whole range of experience of an "old gay." I'm sure a lot of this inexperience translated into moralistic arrogance—we were a good deal less than understanding when she called her lovers "girls."

In this clash of cultures we see two different visions of lesbianism: the old dyke world, which valorized gender roles, and the emergent lesbian feminist culture, which rejected gendered coupledom in favor of the communalized sensuality of the group circle dance.

> We all went to our first gay women's dance together. I was very scared by a number of older women dressed sort of mannishly. Not scared that they'd do anything to me, but wary of being identified with them. I was very relieved when a group of women . . . showed up and we all danced together in a big friendly circle. That was my first exposure to a kind of joyful sensuality that I've come to associate with women's dances. Looking around and seeing a lot of gay women enjoying themselves and each other helped me let go of a lot of my fears and validated the possibilities for growth and pleasure in the relationship with J.

The old gay world conceptualized lesbianism as desire; the new gay world reconceptualized it, more diffusely, as woman identification. Margaret saw differences in the group primarily in generational terms, evidencing the extent to which other distinctions may have been less salient at the time. For younger women, becoming a lesbian was a matter of developing lesbian consciousness, developing a personal sense of self as lesbian. For the second group, the issue was not really *being* a lesbian, a matter of personal identity, but *living* as one, developing a social identity. For Margaret, old dykes, particularly those who were very visibly butch, represented what she might become if she shunned heterosexuality. Gender inversion served as a symbolic marker of lesbianism, warning those who stepped out of their prescribed roles that the taint of lesbianism might soon follow them. But the older women also embodied a kind of protofeminism, a willingness to go against the social grain.

As she tried to figure out her place in the lesbian world, Margaret acknowledged that coming out is "an incredibly hard process." She alluded to the conflict between the dominant essentialist model and an emergent constructionist one. "Many women think there's some magic leap into gayness—that you suddenly lose all fears, doubts, heterosexual feelings. Others are afraid that they weren't 'born gay.' Come-out groups help women deal with all of those feelings. The existence of the Lesbian Mother's Group brought home to us that women are not born lesbians; that women who were both wives and mothers could decide to live with and love other women." After some initial doubts about whether or not she was "really" a lesbian, Margaret assured herself that even seemingly gender-conforming women, women who were once wives and mothers, can be lesbians. These "successful" women who had boyfriends and husbands could also become lesbians—thus, lesbians were not necessarily "failed women."

Her story suggests that some women used the discourse of "coming out" to claim authenticity and gain membership in the lesbian world. Clearly, this was a very different path to lesbianism than the one taken by women whose sense of self as lesbian was less in question, for whom coming out meant "coming out of the closet." While women such as Barb thought of their lesbianism pri-

marily as internally driven, for Margaret and other "elective" lesbians the adoption of lesbianism as a social identity tended to precede the consolidation of lesbianism as a personal identity.

Unlike Barb, Margaret did not trace her lesbianism to early childhood experiences or have the experience of being "not heterosexual" early on—even if she expressed alienation from heterosexual gender norms. Margaret also differs from Barb in her high degree of self-reflexivity, rooted at least in part in her more middle-class background. In general she framed her lesbianism within the development of "lesbian consciousness," viewing her involvement with women rather than men as a political rather than a sexual choice.[8] Because of her history, Margaret held the belief that any woman can choose to be a lesbian. However, she recognized that there were different "types" of lesbians, who exercised greater and lesser degrees of choice over their sexuality. . . .

NOTES

1. Plummer 1981 calls the dominant account the "orientation" model and the emergent account the "identity construct" model. They have also been referred to as "essentialist" and "constructionist" conceptions.

2. In its most radical form, the discourse of coming out suggested that all women were "naturally" lesbians who had become alienated from their authentic selves through a process of gender/sexual socialization that operated in the service of compulsory heterosexuality. A milder version suggested that many more women were "potential" lesbians, but that the taint of stigma kept the numbers of self-identified lesbians artificially low.

3. Many of my interviewees spoke about their lives in terms that sharply divided the period "before I came out" from that "after I came out," conveying the impression that coming out was a signal event. This event featured an epiphany or "defining moment" that altered the individual and allowed her to see the world differently,

changing the fundamental structures of meaning in her life. See Denzin 1989 for a discussion of the role of the "epiphany" in a self story.

4. On the coming out narrative in lesbian fiction, see Zimmerman 1990. For an examination of the notion of the closet, see Sedgwick 1990; for the foundational sociological study of stigma, deviance, and identity "management," see Goffman 1963.

5. I am certainly not the first to note variations among women who self-identify as lesbian. See Ponse 1978; Faderman 1991; B. Vance and Green 1984, Here I have refrained from labeling different "types" to avoid reifying them.

6. Zemsky 1991 cites studies indicating that the mean age at which women recognize and pronounce (at least to themselves) that this sense of difference and disquiet has something to do with lesbianism is approximately fourteen. See also Tolman 1991. Herdt and Boxer 1993 found a disparity between male and female homosexual experiences.

For males, first homoerotic sex typically preceded first heteroerotic sex. For girls, however, the average age of same-sex experience is later than the average age of first sex with a male.

7. For a sense of how dominant cultural norms shaped the lives of teenage girls in the 1950s, and how girls resisted these norms, see Breines 1992.

8. A. Rich 1980 and Kitzinger 1987 question whether lesbianism can ever really be a free "choice" or individual sexual "preference" under a system of normative heterosexuality.

REFERENCES

Breines, Wini. 1992. *Young, White, and Miserable: Growing Up Female in the 1950s.* Boston: Beacon.

Denzin, Norman. 1989. *Interpretive Biography.* Newbury Park, Calif.: Sage.

Faderman, Lillian. 1991. *Odd Girls and Twilight Lovers: A History of Lesbian Life in Twentieth-Century America.* New York: Columbia University Press.

Goffman, Erving. 1963. *Stigma: Notes on the Management of Spoiled Identity.* Englewood Cliffs, N.J.: Prentice Hall.

Herdt, Gilbert, and Andrew Boxer. 1993. *Children of Horizons: How Gay and Lesbian Youth Are Leading a New Way out of the Closet.* Boston: Beacon.

Kitzinger, Celia. 1987. *The Social Construction of Lesbianism.* Newbury Park, Calif.: Sage.

Plummer, Ken. 1981. "Homosexual Categories." In *The Making of the Modern Homosexual,* ed. Plummer. Totowa, N.J.: Barnes & Noble.

Ponse, Barbara. 1978. *Identities in the Lesbian World: The Social Construction of Self.* Westport, Conn.: Greenwood.

Rich, Adrienne. 1980. "Compulsory Heterosexuality and Lesbian Existence." *Signs* 5: 631–61.

Sedgwick, Eve Kosofsky. 1990. *Epistemology of the Closet.* Berkeley: University of California Press.

Tolman, Deborah L. 1991. "Adolescent Girls, Women, and Sexuality: Discerning Dilemmas of Desire," *Women & Therapy* 11(3–4): 55–69.

Vance, Brenda, and Vicki Green. 1984. "Lesbian Identities: An Examination of Sexual Behavior and Sex Role Attribution as Related to Age of Initial Same-Sex Sexual Encounter." *Psychology of Women Quarterly* 8(3): 293–307.

Wrong, Dennis. 1961. "The Oversocialized Conception of Man in Modern Sociology." *American Sociological Review* 26:183–93.

Zemsky, Beth. 1991. "Coming Out against All Odds: Resistance in the Life of a Young Lesbian." *Women & Therapy* 11(3–4): 185–200.

Zimmerman, Bonnie. 1990. *The Safe Sea of Women: Lesbian Fiction, 1969–1989.* Boston: Beacon.

PART FOUR

Gender and Education

Schools are a major institution of socialization and they also generally reflect the dominant cultural attitudes about gender (Sadker and Sadker 1994). Sociologists, psychologists, and educators interested in gender equity have focused on the way education reinforces gender inequity in the society. First, schools often structure policies that reinforce gender inequity. For example, traditionally, schools offered woodworking and drafting to boys and cooking and sewing to girls. Many schools have different sports programs for boys and girls, offering boys a wider variety of choices and funding them more generously. Ice hockey and football may be available as a boys' team only and girls are not allowed to try out. Another example is a school that dismisses classes early so that all students can attend the boys' football and basketball games, but does not do this for the girls' basketball and volleyball games. The school cheerleaders, all females, cheer for the boys' but not the girls' teams (Ayim and Houston, 1996).

A second way in which schools both reflect and reinforce gender inequity is through the sexism that is inherent in many teaching materials (Sadker and Sadker 1980). Although many of the most vulgar manifestations of racism and sexism have been muted, many of the dominant metaphors carry gender messages that are usually not decoded by the teacher. For example, Morgan (1996:110) points out that science is often presented in texts in a "domination-saturated rhetoric" that sends a message to scientifically talented girls that to achieve in the world of science, they have to be "one of the guys."

Schools are also settings in which the informal interactions between teachers and students as well as among students communicate, subtly or sometimes blatantly, that gender is a valid organizing principle and that boys are better than girls. Jane Butler Kahle, professor of science education at Miami University, studied the teaching methods of fourth- and fifth-grade teachers. With few exceptions, she found boys received more attention than girls in science classes. Girls tended to be praised for neatness or timeliness in completing experiments, while boys were recognized for the scientific content of their work (Travis 1993).

Teachers frequently use gender to organize activities for which gender is irrelevant, for instance, asking boys and girls to line up separately. This kind of unnecessary sex segregation constantly reminds children that they are boys or girls and that these categories make them different—even opposites. For example, an elementary school teacher punishes a male student for misbehavior by making him sit with the girls or a coach "puts down" a boy on the football team by calling him "a sissy" or "a pussy." Using "being like a girl" to embarrass and humiliate boys encourages a demeaning and contemptuous attitude toward girls (Ayim and Houston 1996).

Separate is not equal in a coeducational setting. Diane Hulse (1997) argues that both boys and girls benefit from being in separate schools precisely because gender is absent as an organizing principle. Based on her comparative study of a coeducational and an all-boys middle school, Hulse found that boys in the all-boys middle school were more egalitarian about sex roles than boys in the coed middle school. Thus, while Orenstein's (1994) discussion of the loss of self-esteem girls experience in coeducational middle schools supports the generally accepted notion that single-sex schools are useful for girls, Hulse argues that single-sex schools are also good for boys.

The two articles in this section are both reports of participant observation studies—one by a journalist, Peggy Orenstein (1994), and the other by a social scientist, Barrie Thorne (1986). Thorne observed two elementary schools, while Orenstein studied two middle schools. Thorne takes a microstructural approach, arguing that gender roles and boundaries are not fixed; that is, that situational variation heightens or lessens them. Thorne does not recommend single-sex schools, but implies that there's a lot that could be changed in coeducational schools. As a result of her study, Thorne concludes that sex segregation of children is largely the result of adult-organized activities. Relationships between boys and girls are not always marked by strong boundaries or heterosexual definitions; boys and girls often spontaneously interact in comfortable ways. She implies that teachers and administrators could increase that kind of interaction if they thought about it more.

The Orenstein selection is from her book *School Girls* (1994) which was written under American Association of University Women (AAUW) auspices as an adjunct to its nationwide poll of girls and boys, ages nine to fifteen, *Shortchanging Girls, Shortchanging America* (1991). For a girl, the passage into adolescence is marked by a loss of confidence in herself and her abilities, especially in math and science, and a scathingly critical attitude toward her body and a blossoming sense of personal inadequacy. The girl's loss of confidence in math and science usually *precedes* a drop in achievement rather than vice versa.

Thus, middle school, the beginning of adolescence, is the time of greatest self-esteem loss. African-American girls seem to retain more of their self-esteem than white or Hispanic girls, but it is related to personal and familial importance. They are *more* pessimistic than the others about their teachers and schoolwork. Hispanic girls experience the most profound loss of self-esteem when they enter adolescence and that seems to be related to the attitude toward women in Latino culture.

Why do girls lose their self-esteem when they go through puberty? Orenstein says the major reason is that they have a terrible time reconciling their traditional images of femininity (which are strongest when they are just becoming women) with their desires to be achievers and recognized as valuable people. Girls are caught between the stigmas of being a "schoolgirl" (i.e., smart) and a "slut" (i.e., sexual).

Not only are coeducational settings places where sex segregation and inequity are enforced, but they are all too frequently the setting for sexual terrorism through intimidation, threat, and even violence. Girls are sexually harassed by boys on the playground and in the corridors. They are frequently verbally abused and "put down" by boys, and much of this behavior is regarded by teachers and administrators as "boys being boys" (Morgan 1996).

Hostile Hallways: The AAUW Survey on Sexual Harassment in America's Schools (1993) presents the findings from a survey that was designed to profile the problem of sexual harassment in U.S. public schools and to answer many of the questions about school-based harassment. More than 1,600 public school students in seventy-nine schools across the continental United States in grades eight through eleven (female and male, African American, white, and Hispanic) were surveyed; students were instructed to answer only about their school-related experiences during school-related times (on the way to and from school, in classrooms and hallways, on school grounds during the day and after school, and on school trips). The study found 31 percent of girls said that they had experienced unwanted advances, gestures, touching, grabbing, and the like by teachers, other students, or other school employees as compared to 18 percent of the boys. Experiences of student-to-student harassment outnumbered all others.

Sexual discrimination in schools was not originally part of the Civil Rights Act of 1964; Title IX, which prohibits discrimination based on sex in institutions of higher education, was not signed into law until 1972. Its origin lies in a 1965 presidential executive order prohibiting federal contractors from discrimination in employment on the basis of race, color, religion, or national origin. That was amended by President Johnson in 1968, to include discrimination based on sex; since most universities and colleges have federal contracts, it was later extended to cover discrimination against women in higher education. By 1975, Title IX was expanded to include all school systems that receive federal funds as well as institutions of higher learning:

NO PERSON IN THE UNITED STATES SHALL, ON THE BASIS OF SEX, BE EXCLUDED FROM PARTICIPATION IN, BE DENIED THE BENEFITS OF, OR BE SUBJECTED TO DISCRIMINATION UNDER ANY EDUCATION PROGRAM OR ACTIVITY RECEIVING FEDERAL FINANCIAL ASSISTANCE.

Title IX applied only to sexual harassment by school personnel (i.e., administrators, teachers, and staff) until May 24, 1999, when the Supreme Court decided, by a narrow 5–4 decision, that schools are also liable for student-on-student sexual harassment. While the dissenting minority claimed that the decision represented an unwarranted intrusion into the day-to-day interaction of children, the majority claimed that the decision represented a weapon against behavior that is so severe that it impairs a victim's ability to learn (Greenhouse 1999).

Title IX led to the development of sexual harassment protocols as well as affirmative action in schools and universities. Another dramatic impact of Title IX has been in the area of interschool athletic programs. Since Title IX was started, the number of women participating in intercollegiate athletics increased 400 percent; the number of girls who played high school basketball increased 300 percent.

The increase in female participation in school sports has wide-ranging ramifications. Before Title IX, boys played team sports such as baseball and football while girls participated in one-on-one sports such as tennis, swimming, gymnastics, and skating. In 1977, Hennig and Jardim argued that part of the explanation for the "glass ceiling" that keeps women from reaching upper-level management positions in corporations was the result of women's lack of experience with team sports. They argued that women's lack of team experience was related to their focusing only on their own performance and being less likely than men to take the environment (i.e., other team positions) into account. They also contended that women were more vulnerable to criticism because they didn't have the experience of a coach criticizing them.

Title IX did a great deal to give girls and young women access to team sports. It seems to have had some of the effect that Hennig and Jardim would have predicted: Not only are girls who participate in team sports less likely to get pregnant, smoke, or drink, 80 percent of female managers of Fortune 500 companies have a sports background (Catalyst 1996).

Title IX has not only forced schools to change, but has pressed schools into the role of agents of social change. It has given women the opportunity to challenge gender inequities in the courts, forcing schools and universities to redistribute funding of athletics, change recruitment policies, and create protocols to deal with sexual harassment. As a result of these changes, the children and young adults attending these schools will develop a new consciousness about gender—they will be more likely to expect and demand equality.

REFERENCES

AAUW. 1991. *Shortchanging Girls, Shortchanging America.* Washington, D.C.: AAUW.

AAUW. 1993. *Hostile Hallways: The AAUW Survey on Sexual Harassment in America's Schools.* Washington, D.C.: AAUW.

Ayim, Maryann, and Barbara Houston. 1996. "A Conceptual Analysis of Sexism and Sexist Education." Pp. 9–30 in *The Gender Question in Education: Theory, Pedagogy, & Politics,* edited by A. Diller, B. Houston, K. P. Morgan, and M. Ayim. Boulder: Westview Press.

Catalyst. 1996. *Women in Corporate Leadership: Progress and Prospects.* New York: Catalyst.

Greenhouse, Linda. 1999. "Sex Harassment in Class is Ruled Schools' Liability." *New York Times,* May 25:A1, A24.

Hennig, Margaret, and Anne Jardim. 1977. *The Managerial Woman.* Garden City: Doubleday.

Hulse, Diane. 1997. *Brad and Cory: A Study of Middle School Boys.* Hunting Valley, OH: University School Press.

Morgan, Kathryn P. 1996. "Describing the Emperor's New Clothes: Three Myths of Educational (In-)Equity." Pp. 105–122 in *The Gender Question in Education: Theory, Pedagogy, & Politics,* edited by A. Diller, B. Houston, K. P. Morgan, and M. Ayim. Boulder: Westview Press.

Orenstein, Peggy. 1994. *School Girls: Young Women, Self-Esteem, and the Confidence Gap.* New York: Anchor Books.

Sadker, Myra, and David Sadker. 1980. "Sexism in Teacher Education Texts." *Harvard Educational Review* 50:36–45.

———. 1994. *How America's Schools Cheat Girls.* New York: Charles Scribners.

Thorne, Barrie. 1986. "Girls and Boys Together...But Mostly Apart: Gender Arrangements in Elementary School." Pp. 167–184 in *Relationships and Development,* edited by Willard W. Hartup and Zick Rubin. New York: Lawrence Erlbaum Associates.

Travis, John. 1993. "Making Room for Women in the Culture of Science." *Science* 260: 412–415.

Unbalanced Equations: Girls, Math, and the Confidence Gap

PEGGY ORENSTEIN

Although the skewed equations of voice and silence are not the exclusive province of math or science, they are arguably the most damaging in those classes, where the tradition of male dominance is most entrenched. *Shortchanging Girls, Shortchanging America* showed that girls and boys who like math and science have higher levels of self-esteem than other children (and, for that matter, that children with high self-esteem tend to like math and science). For girls in particular, those subjects are also tied to ambition: girls who like math and science—who are, perhaps, more resistant to traditional gender roles—are more likely to aspire to careers as professionals. As adults, women who have taken more than two math courses in college are the only ones who subsequently achieve pay equity and even earn more than their male counterparts.[1]

Unfortunately, girls are far less likely than boys to retain their affection for math and science. As they move through school, their confidence in their mathematical abilities falters and their competence soon follows suit.[2] It's important to note that the confidence drop often *precedes* the competence drop: even in early adolescence, girls who perform as well as boys often evaluate their skills as lesser. By their senior year, convinced of their ineptitude, they become less persistent in solving problems than their male peers and less likely than boys with poorer grades in the same class to believe they can pursue a math-related career.[3]

Amy is one of those girls who have little faith in her math skills, although her performance is well above average. "School is important to me," she says during lunch one day, when I catch her struggling with a homework assignment. "I want to do good in school and be proud of myself. I don't want to be a lazy bum. And I'll need math when I'm older. There's math in everything, no matter what, so it's important to learn. So I know I should have a better attitude, but I just want to give up. It's not that I don't try, it's just that I don't believe in myself and I don't get it. I'm just so *slow.*" She glares down at her paper.

Amy goes on to say that a person has to be smarter to do well at math than at English. She also believes that girls—herself included—have a natural bent toward English and boys toward math, which, by her logic, would make girls less intelligent than boys. When I point this out, she begins to backtrack, but then stops, leans forward, and drops her voice, continuing in a solemn, confidential tone. "Boys do better in math, believe me, they do. Girls, we have other things on our minds, I guess."

Yet in spite of this purported genetic disadvantage, during the same class in which Dawn receives her disappointing citizenship mark, Amy receives an A in math, which clinches her spot on the school honor roll. The news doesn't change her assumptions one whit.

"It's not hard to get an A in here," she says. "Basically you just have to show up. And I still think I've done it wrong every day. I'll probably be in, like, special ed. math next year."

From her vantage point in the front of the class, Mrs. Richter says she can see the girls' waning interest in her subject, and it frustrates her. She is especially disturbed by a trend she's recently noticed: the boys in her class tend to improve over the course of the school year—some even jump from D's to B's or A's—while girls stay exactly where they were in September: the good students remain good students, the poor students remain poor. She worries that, for the girls, the holding pattern is simply temporary. Next year, perhaps the year after, even the good students may begin to slide; they simply don't trust their ability.

"The boys see math as something that shows they're brainy and they like being able to show off that way," Mrs. Richter explains. "And they're more risk-taking than the girls, so they'll do better on tests every time, even if the girls turn in all their work and the boys don't. It's like the girls set themselves up to fail. They do the work. I see them practice one kind of problem over and over because I've told them it'll be on a test. But then the test comes and they miss it anyway. I've heard them say, 'Oh no, I got that kind of problem wrong last time.' So even though they practiced it, they go and get it wrong again. Amy does that. She'll look at a problem and say, 'There's no way I can do this,' and give up, even though I know she has the skills. But the

boys are different: they can get all the homework wrong, but they don't care as long as they tried. And then they figure out *why* it's wrong instead of being embarrassed about it. That makes them more confident."

Mrs. Richter considers parents, more than teachers, to be responsible for girls' confidence gap. Every year, she says, her female students tell her, "My mother said she couldn't do math either," as if math skills are genetic, which, the teacher hastens to add, they are not.[4] Still, she admits, the classroom culture can further undercut the girls. "I try to teach them the same; I try to call on them the same. But I know I don't always hold them accountable the same way. I let the girls off the hook because they get so embarrassed when they're wrong. And the boys want control of the class, so sometimes they get it..." She trails off, shaking her head. "I don't know," she says. "We try, but somehow we're still not getting to the girls, and we're going to lose them."

BAD CHEMISTRY: "GUYS LIKE IT WHEN YOU ACT ALL HELPLESS"

It is another late-fall morning under the oak tree at Weston. Amy, Becca, and Evie huddle together slightly apart from the other students, the intimate turn to their shoulders making it clear that they're exchanging the juiciest gossip. A squadron of seventh-grade boys on bicycles zips by and the girls look up, annoyed, sidling to the left to avoid being hit.

A few seconds later, Becca, usually the most reserved of her friends, shrieks.

"Get that away from me!"

The bikers are forgotten as the girls scatter, screaming, their faces flushed, revealing Carl Ross, a boy from Evie's math class, whose feet are firmly planted where the girls once stood. An uncapped jar labeled "Felicia" dangles from his left hand. Until a minute ago, it held a large spider he'd captured for extra credit in science class. Felicia is currently hanging from a dead pine needle in his other hand, her legs tucked in and body contracted in fear.

Becca runs about ten feet and turns around. When she smiles, she reveals a mouth full of braces. "I'm *deathly* afraid of spiders," she says, her eyes shining as she looks back at her tormentor.

The other two girls run up to her. "God, me too!" Amy says breathlessly, clutching her friend's arms. "When I saw *Arachnophobia* my dad had to go check my room for me. He had to look under the bed!"

Evie's cheeks are pink and her dark hair is falling from its bun. She tucks the wayward wisps back in place as a second boy lets the bug drop from his finger by a lengthening strand of web. "Yuck, how disgusting," she says, widening her eyes. "I hope he doesn't come near me with that."

As a woman standing among these girls, I wasn't sure how to react. I desperately wanted them to stand up to the boys who increasingly joined in the game. I wanted them to be brave, to marvel at the spider's jewel-green body, to ask for a turn at holding it and watching it try to spin its escape. But I felt the pressure too: a real girl, a girl who wants a boy to like her, runs screaming from spiders. The more she likes a boy, the more she allows him to terrorize her, and the more helpless she pretends to be. Showing any real interest in spiders would've been imprudent for the girls, a denial of their newly important femininity. During my year at Weston, I saw girls run from spiders innumerable times; with each flight toward traditional femininity, I thought about who has permission, who has the right in our culture, to explore the natural world, to get dirty and muddy, to think spiders and worms and frogs are neat, to bring them in for extra credit in science. In fact, to be engaged in science at all.

"I'm not *really* afraid of that stuff, except snakes and blood," Amy admits later, after the hoopla. "But guys like it if you act all helpless and girly, so you do." . . .

NOTES

1. Clifford Adelman, "Women at Thirtysomething: Paradoxes of Attainment," Washington, DC: Office of Educational Research and Improvement, 1991. Adelman tracked over 12,000 high school graduates from their high school graduation in 1972 until they were thirty-two. Although the women received higher grades, were awarded more scholarships, and completed their BAs faster, they subsequently received lower pay than their male counterparts, were awarded fewer promotions, and were more frequently unemployed. Women who had taken two or more math courses in college were the sole exception to this pattern.

2. Confidence is the variable most strongly correlated with achievement in math, particularly for girls. Yet even when they perform as well as boys, girls' confidence drops significantly during their middle school years, with girls who view the subject as "male" showing consistently poorer performance than girls who do not hold that view. The AAUW Educational Foundation, *The AAUW Report*, p. 28; Margaret R. Meyer and Mary Schatz Koehler, "Internal Influences on Gender Differences in Mathematics," in *Mathematics and Gender*, Elizabeth Fennema and Gilah C. Leder, eds., New York: Teachers College Press, 1990, pp. 91–92; Peter Kloosterman, "Attributions, Performance Following Failure, and Motivation in Mathematics," *Mathematics and Gender*, p. 119; Elizabeth Fennema and Julia Sherman, "Sex-Related Differences in Mathematics Achievement, Spatial Visualization and Affective Factors," *American Educational Research Journal*, 14, 1 (1977): pp. 51–71. American Association of University Women, *Shortchanging Girls, Shortchanging America: Executive Summary*, Washington, DC: American Association of University Women, 1991, p. 13, Graph G.

3. Heather Featherstone, "Girls' Math Achievement: What We Do and Don't Know," *The Harvard Education Letter*, January 1986, p. 3. Girls are also more likely than boys to lose heart after a failure in math and, subsequently, to achieve at a lower level. This may largely be due to a difference in what psychologists call "effort attribution." When girls do

well, they assume it is because they've worked hard or are lucky, while boys attribute success to ability. Meanwhile, girls blame failure on incompetence, while boys ascribe it to laziness or bad luck. Girls' relatively poorer performance on standardized tests may derive from this difference: since girls attribute success to hard work, they approach a test that purports to measure raw ability with less confidence than do boys. Unfortunately, standardized tests determine students' futures. In 1993, three out of five semifinalists for the National Merit Scholarship, which is based on Preliminary Scholastic Aptitude Test (PSAT) scores, were boys. That same year, a new federally funded college scholarship program intended to encourage students to enter math- and science-related fields used students' performance on the American College Testing Program Assessment (ACT) as its sole criterion, and conferred 75 percent of its awards on boys. Malcolm Gladwell, "Pythagorean Sexism," Washington *Post*, March 14, 1993, p. C3; "Boys Predominate in a Contest, Fueling Complaint of Test Bias," New York *Times*, May 26, 1993, p. B7; Michael Winerip, "Study Finds Boys Receive 75% of New Science Scholarships," New York *Times*, November 17, 1993, P. B7.

4. The "math gene" is a persistent, mythical explanation for girls' disinclination toward math. Yet Patricia B. Campbell points out that in studies conducted after 1974 (not, incidentally, coincident with the rise of the feminist movement in this country), gender differences in achievement have declined by 50 percent. Even the oft-cited gender difference in spatial ability declines dramatically when girls are exposed more frequently to spatial tasks. If math skills were biologically determined they would be impervious to changing political ideology. Nor can the "math gene" explain why girls' math achievement relative to boys' varies across ethnic lines: in a study of students in Hawaii, for instance, non-Caucasian girls both outperformed and outnumbered males in top math classes. Further, the studies that are most often used to support gender differences in math—conducted by Camilla Benbow and Julian Stanley of Johns Hopkins University—are flawed. Not only did they rely on the Scholastic Aptitude Test (SAT), which is considered by many to be biased against both girls and minority boys, but they assumed that, because the students were in the same classes, they had identical learning experiences. Finally, according to biologist Robert Sapolsky, the studies turned up enormous overlap between boys' and girls' scores, making it impossible to predict who would perform better in any randomly selected pair. Given these factors, a biologically driven achievement gap does not explain girls' reluctance to pursue math: a confidence gap, however, does. Patricia B. Campbell, "Math, Science and Too Few Girls: Enough Is Known for Action," documentation developed under the auspices of the Women's Educational Equity Act by Campbell-Kibler Associates, Groton, MA, 1991; Marcia C. Linn and Janet S. Hyde, "Gender, Mathematics, and Science," *Educational Researcher*, 18, 8, pp. 17–27; P. R. Brandon, B. J. Newton, and O. Hamond, "Children's Mathematics Achievement in Hawaii: Sex Differences Favoring Girls," *American Educational Research Journal*, 24, 3 (1987), pp. 437–61; Robert Sapolsky, "The Case of the Falling Nightwatchmen," *Discover*, July 1987, p. 44.

Girls and Boys Together . . . But Mostly Apart: Gender Arrangements in Elementary Schools

BARRIE THORNE

Throughout the years of elementary school, children's friendships and casual encounters are strongly separated by sex. Sex segregation among children, which starts in preschool and is well established by middle childhood, has been amply documented in studies of children's groups and friendships (e.g., Eder & Hallinan, 1978; Schofield, 1981) and is immediately visible in elementary school settings. When children choose seats in classrooms or the cafeteria, or get into line, they frequently arrange themselves in same-sex clusters. At lunchtime, they talk matter-of-factly about "girls' tables" and "boys' tables." Playgrounds have gendered turfs, with some areas and activities, such as large playing fields and basketball courts, controlled mainly by boys, and others—smaller enclaves like jungle-gym areas and concrete spaces for hopscotch or jumprope—more often controlled by girls. Sex segregation is so common in elementary schools that it is meaningful to speak of separate girls' and boys' worlds.

Studies of gender and children's social relations have mostly followed this "two worlds" model, separately describing and comparing the subcultures of girls and of boys (e.g., Lever, 1976; Maltz & Borker, 1983). In brief summary: Boys tend to interact in larger, more age-heterogeneous groups (Lever, 1976; Waldrop & Halverson, 1975; Eder & Hallinan, 1978). They engage in more rough and tumble play and physical fighting (Maccoby & Jacklin, 1974). Organized sports are both a central activity and a major metaphor in boys' subcultures; they use the language of "teams" even when not engaged in sports, and they often construct interaction in the form of contests. The shifting hierarchies of boys' groups (Savin-Williams, 1976) are evident in their more frequent use of direct commands, insults, and challenges (Goodwin, 1980).

Fewer studies have been done of girls' groups (Foot, Chapman, & Smith, 1980; McRobbie & Garber, 1975), and—perhaps because categories for description and analysis have come more from male than female experience—researchers have had difficulty seeing and analyzing girls' social relations. Recent work has begun to correct this skew. In middle childhood, girls' worlds are less public than those of boys; girls more often interact in private places and in smaller groups or friendship pairs (Eder & Hallinan, 1978; Waldrop & Halverson, 1975). Their play is more cooperative and turn-taking (Lever, 1976). Girls have

From *Relationships and Development* edited by Willard W. Hartup and Zick Rubin, pp. 167–184. Copyright © 1986 by Lawrence Erlbaum Associates. Reprinted by permission of Lawrence Erlbaum Associates, Inc.

more intense and exclusive friendships, which take shape around keeping and telling secrets, shifting alliances, and indirect ways of expressing disagreement (Goodwin, 1980; Lever, 1976; Maltz & Borker, 1983). Instead of direct commands, girls more often use directives which merge speaker and hearer, such as, "let's" or "we gotta" (Goodwin, 1980).

Although much can be learned by comparing the social organization and subcultures of boys' and of girls' groups, the separate worlds approach has eclipsed full, contextual understanding of gender and social relations among children. The separate worlds model essentially involves a search for group sex differences, and shares the limitations of individual sex difference research. Differences tend to be exaggerated and similarities ignored, with little theoretical attention to the integration of similarity and difference (Unger, 1979). Statistical findings of difference are often portrayed as dichotomous, neglecting the considerable individual variation that exists; for example, not all boys fight, and some have intense and exclusive friendships. The sex difference approach tends to abstract gender from its social context, to assume that males and females are qualitatively and permanently different (with differences perhaps unfolding through separate developmental lines). These assumptions mask the possibility that gender arrangements and patterns of similarity and difference may vary by situation, race, social class, region, or subculture.

Sex segregation is far from total, and is a more complex and dynamic process than the portrayal of separate worlds reveals. Erving Goffman (1977) has observed that sex segregation has a "with-then-apart" structure; the sexes segregate periodically, with separate spaces, rituals, groups, but they also come together and are, in crucial ways, part of the same world. This is certainly true in the social environment of elementary schools. Although girls and boys do interact as bound-aried collectivities—an image suggested by the separate worlds approach—there are other occasions when they work or play in relaxed and integrated ways. Gender is less central to the organization and meaning of some situations than others. In short, sex segregation is not static, but is a variable and complicated process.

To gain an understanding of gender which can encompass both the "with" and the "apart" of sex segregation, analysis should start not with the individual, nor with a search for sex differences, but with social relationships. Gender should be conceptualized as a system of relationships rather than as an immutable and dichotomous given. Taking this approach, I have organized my research on gender and children's social relations around questions like the following: How and when does gender enter into group formation? In a given situation, how is gender made more or less salient or infused with particular meanings? By what rituals, processes, and forms of social organization and conflict do "with-then-apart" rhythms get enacted? How are these processes affected by the organization of institutions (e.g., different types of schools, neighborhoods, or summer camps), varied settings (e.g., the constraints and possibilities governing interaction on playgrounds vs. classrooms), and particular encounters?

METHODS AND SOURCES OF DATA

This study is based on two periods of participant observation. In 1976–1977 I observed for 8 months in a largely working-class elementary school in California, a school with 8% Black and 12% Chicana/o students. In 1980 I did fieldwork for 3 months in a Michigan elementary school of similar size (around 400 students), social class, and racial composition. I observed in several classrooms—a kindergarten, a second grade, and a combined fourth-fifth grade—and in school hallways, cafeterias, and playgrounds. I set out to follow the round of the school day as children experience it, recording their interactions with one another, and with adults, in varied settings.

Participant observation involves gaining access to everyday, "naturalistic" settings and taking systematic notes over an extended period of time. Rather than starting with pre-set categories for recording, or with fixed hypotheses for testing, participant-observers record detail in ways which maximize opportunities for discovery. Through continuous interaction between observation and analysis, "grounded theory" is developed (Glaser & Strauss, 1967).

The distinctive logic and discipline of this mode of inquiry emerges from: (1) theoretical sampling—being relatively systematic in the choice of where and whom to observe in order to maximize knowledge relevant to categories and analysis which are being developed; and (2) comparing all relevant data on a given point in order to modify emerging propositions to take account of discrepant cases (Katz, 1983). Participant observation is a flexible, open-ended and inductive method, designed to understand behavior within, rather than stripped from, social context. It provides richly detailed information which is anchored in everyday meanings and experience.

DAILY PROCESSES OF SEX SEGREGATION

Sex segregation should be understood not as a given, but as the result of deliberate activity. The outcome is dramatically visible when there are separate girls' and boys' tables in school lunchrooms, or sex-separated groups on playgrounds. But in the same lunchroom one can also find tables where girls and boys eat and talk together, and in some playground activities the sexes mix. By what processes do girls and boys separate into gender-defined and relatively boundaried collectivities? And in what contexts, and through what processes, do boys and girls interact in less gender-divided ways?

In the school settings I observed, much segregation happened with no mention of gender. Gender was implicit in the contours of friendship, shared interest, and perceived risk which came into play when children chose companions—in their prior planning, invitations, seeking-of-access, saving-of-places, denials of entry, and allowing or protesting of "cuts" by those who violated the rules for lining up. Sometimes children formed mixed-sex groups for play, eating, talking, working on a classroom project, or moving through space. When adults or children explicitly invoked gender—and this was nearly always in ways which separated girls and boys—boundaries were heightened and mixed-sex interaction became an explicit arena of risk.

In the schools I studied, the physical space and curricula were not formally divided by sex, as they have been in the history of elementary schooling (a history evident in separate entrances to old school buildings, where the words "Boys" and "Girls" are permanently etched in concrete). Nevertheless, gender was a visible marker in the adult-organized school day. In both schools, when the public address system sounded, the principal inevitably opened with: "Boys and girls…," and in addressing clusters of children, teachers and aides regularly used gender terms ("Heads down, girls"; "The girls are ready and the boys aren't"). These forms of address made gender visible and salient, conveying an assumption that the sexes are separate social groups.

Teachers and aides sometimes drew upon gender as a basis for sorting children and organizing activities. Gender is an embodied and visual social category which roughly divides the population in half, and the separation of girls and boys permeates the history and lore of schools and playgrounds. In both schools—although through awareness of Title IX, many teachers had changed this practice—one could see separate girls' and boys' lines moving, like caterpillars, through the school halls. In the 4th–5th grade classroom the teacher frequently pitted girls against boys for spelling and math contests. On the playground in the Michigan school, aides regarded the space close to the building as girls' territory, and the playing fields "out there" as boys' territory. They sometimes shooed children of the other sex away from those spaces, especially boys who ventured near the girls' area and seemed to have teasing in mind.

In organizing their activities, both within and apart from the surveillance of adults, children also explicitly invoked gender. During my fieldwork in the Michigan school, I kept daily records of who sat where in the lunchroom. The amount of sex segregation varied: It was least at the first-grade tables and almost total among sixth graders. There was also variation from classroom to classroom within a given age, and from day to day. Actions like the following heightened the gender divide:

> In the lunchroom, when the two second-grade tables were filling, a high-status boy walked by the inside table, which had a scattering of both boys and girls, and said loudly, "Oooo, too many girls," as he headed for a seat at the far table. The boys at the inside table picked up their trays and moved, and no other boys sat at the inside table, which the pronouncement had effectively made taboo.

In the end, that day (which was not the case every day), girls and boys ate at separate tables.

Eating and walking are not sex-typed activities, yet in forming groups in lunchrooms and hallways children often separated by sex. Sex segregation assumed added dimensions on the playground, where spaces, equipment, and activities were infused with gender meanings. My inventories of activities and groupings on the playground showed similar patterns in both schools: Boys controlled the large fixed spaces designated for team sports (baseball diamonds, grassy fields used for football or soccer); girls more often played closer to the building, doing tricks on the monkey bars (which, for sixth graders, be-

came an area for sitting and talking) and using cement areas for jumprope, hopscotch, and group games like four-square. (Lever, 1976, provides a good analysis of sex-divided play.) Girls and boys most often played together in kickball, and in group (rather than team) games like four-square, dodgeball, and handball. When children used gender to exclude others from play, they often drew upon beliefs connecting boys to some activities and girls to others:

> A first-grade boy avidly watched an all-female game of jump rope. When the girls began to shift positions, he recognized a means of access to the play and he offered, "I'll swing it." A girl responded, "No way, you don't know how to do it, to swing it. You gotta be a girl." He left without protest.

Although children sometimes ignored pronouncements about what each sex could or could not do, I never heard them directly challenge such claims.

When children had explicitly defined an activity or a group as gendered, those who crossed the boundary—especially boys who moved into female-marked space—risked being teased. ("Look! Mike's in the girls' line!"; "'That's a girl over there,' a girl said loudly, pointing to a boy sitting at an otherwise all-female table in the lunchroom.") Children, and occasionally adults, used teasing—especially the tease of "liking" someone of the other sex, or of "being" that sex by virtue of being in their midst—to police gender boundaries. Much of the teasing drew upon heterosexual romantic definitions, making cross-sex interaction risky, and increasing social distance between boys and girls.

RELATIONSHIPS BETWEEN THE SEXES

Because I have emphasized the "apart" and ignored the occasions of "with," this analysis of sex segregation falsely implies that there is little contact between girls and boys in daily school life. In fact, relationships between girls and boys—which should be studied as fully as, and

in connection with, same-sex relationships—
are of several kinds:

1. "Borderwork," or forms of cross-sex interaction which are based upon and reaffirm
   boundaries and asymmetries between
   girls' and boys' groups;
2. Interactions which are infused with heterosexual meanings;
3. Occasions where individuals cross gender boundaries to participate in the world
   of the other sex; and
4. Situations where gender is muted in salience, with girls and boys interacting in
   more relaxed ways.

Borderwork

In elementary school settings boys' and girls'
groups are sometimes spatially set apart.
Same-sex groups sometimes claim fixed terri-
tories such as the basketball court, the bars, or
specific lunchroom tables. However, in the
crowded, multifocused, and adult-controlled
environment of the school, groups form and
disperse at a rapid rate and can never stay totally apart. Contact between girls and boys
sometimes lessens sex segregation, but gender-defined groups also come together in
ways which emphasize their boundaries.

"Borderwork" refers to interaction across,
yet based upon and even strengthening gender boundaries. I have drawn this notion
from Fredrik Barth's (1969) analysis of social
relations which are maintained across ethnic
boundaries without diminishing dichoto-
mized ethnic status.[1] His focus is on more
macro, ecological arrangements; mine is on
face-to-face behavior. But the insight is similar: Groups may interact in ways which
strengthen their borders, and the maintenance of ethnic (or gender) groups can best be
understood by examining the boundary that
defines the group, "not the cultural stuff that
it encloses" (Barth, 1969, p. 15). In elementary
schools there are several types of borderwork:
contests or games where gender-defined
teams compete; cross-sex rituals of chasing

and pollution; and group invasions. These interactions are asymmetrical, challenging the
separate-but-parallel model of "two worlds."

Contests.   Boys and girls are sometimes pitted against each other in classroom competitions and playground games. The 4th–5th
grade classroom had a boys' side and a girls'
side, an arrangement that re-emerged each
time the teacher asked children to choose their
own desks. Although there was some within-
sex shuffling, the result was always a spatial
moiety system—boys on the left, girls on the
right—with the exception of one girl (the
"tomboy" whom I'll describe later), who twice
chose a desk with the boys and once with the
girls. Drawing upon and reinforcing the children's self-segregation, the teacher often pitted the boys against the girls in spelling and
math competitions, events marked by cross-
sex antagonism and within-sex solidarity:

> The teacher introduced a math game; she would
> write addition and subtraction problems on the
> board, and a member of each team would race to be
> the first to write the correct answer. She wrote two
> score-keeping columns on the board: 'Beastly
> Boys'...'Gossipy Girls.' The boys yelled out, as
> several girls laughed, 'Noisy girls! Gruesome girls!'
> The girls sat in a row on top of their desks; some-
> times they moved collectively, pushing their hips or
> whispering 'pass it on.' The boys stood along the
> wall, some reclining against desks. When members
> of either group came back victorious from the front
> of the room, they would do the 'giving five' hand-
> slapping ritual with their team members.

On the playground a team of girls occasionally played against a team of boys,
usually in kickball or team two-square. Sometimes these games proceeded matter-of-factly,
but if gender became the explicit basis of team
solidarity, the interaction changed, becoming
more antagonistic and unstable:

> Two fifth-grade girls played against two fifth-grade
> boys in a team game of two-square. The game pro-
> ceeded at an even pace until an argument ensued
> about whether the ball was out or on the line.
> Karen, who had hit the ball, became annoyed,

flashed her middle finger at the other team, and called to a passing girl to join their side. The boys then called out to other boys, and cheered as several arrived to play. 'We got five and you got three!' Jack yelled. The game continued, with the girls yelling, 'Bratty boys! Sissy boys!' and the boys making noises—'weee haw' 'ha-ha-ha'—as they played.

Chasing.   Cross-sex chasing dramatically affirms boundaries between girls and boys. The basic elements of chase and elude, capture and rescue (Sutton-Smith, 1971) are found in various kinds of tag with formal rules, and in informal episodes of chasing which punctuate life on playgrounds. These episodes begin with a provocation (taunts like "You can't get me!" or "Slobber monster!"; bodily pokes or the grabbing of possessions). A provocation may be ignored, or responded to by chasing. Chaser and chased may then alternate roles. In an ethnographic study of chase sequences on a school playground, Christine Finnan (1982) observes that chases vary in number of chasers to chased (e.g., one chasing one, or five chasing two); form of provocation (a taunt or a poke); outcome (an episode may end when the chased outdistances the chaser, or with a brief touch, being wrestled to the ground, or the recapturing of a hat or a ball); and in use of space (there may or may not be safety zones).

Like Finnan (1982), and Sluckin (1981), who studied a playground in England, I found that chasing has a gendered structure. Boys frequently chase one another, an activity which often ends in wrestling and mock fights. When girls chase girls, they are usually less physically aggressive; they less often, for example, wrestle one another to the ground.

Cross-sex chasing is set apart by special names—"girls chase the boys"; "boys chase the girls"; "the chase"; "chasers"; "chase and kiss"; "kiss chase"; "kissers and chasers"; "kiss or kill"—and by children's animated talk about the activity. The names vary by region and school, but contain both gender and sexual meanings (this form of play is mentioned, but only briefly analyzed, in Finnan, 1981; Sluckin, 1981; Parrott, 1972; and Borman, 1979).

In "boys chase the girls" and "girls chase the boys" (the names most frequently used in both the California and Michigan schools) boys and girls become, by definition, separate teams. Gender terms override individual identities, especially for the other team ("Help, a girl's chasin' me!"; "C'mon Sarah, let's get that boy"; "Tony, help save me from the girls"). Individuals may call for help from, or offer help to, others of their sex. They may also grab someone of their sex and turn them over to the opposing team: "Ryan grabbed Billy from behind, wrestling him to the ground. 'Hey girls, get 'im,' Ryan called."

Boys more often mix episodes of cross-sex with same-sex chasing. Girls more often have safety zones, places like the girls' restroom or an area by the school wall, where they retreat to rest and talk (sometimes in animated postmortems) before new episodes of cross-sex chasing begin.

Early in the fall in the Michigan school, where chasing was especially prevalent, I watched a second-grade boy teach a kindergarten girl how to chase. He slowly ran backwards, beckoning her to pursue him, as he called, "Help, a girl's after me." In the early grades chasing mixes with fantasy play, for example, a first-grade boy who played "sea monster," his arms outflung and his voice growling, as he chased a group of girls. By third grade, stylized gestures—exaggerated stalking motions, screams (which only girls do), and karate kicks—accompany scenes of chasing.

Names like "chase and kiss" mark the sexual meanings of cross-sex chasing,... The threat of kissing—most often girls threatening to kiss boys—is a ritualized form of provocation. Cross-sex chasing among sixth graders involves elaborate patterns of touch and touch avoidance, which adults see as sexual. The principal told the sixth graders in the Michigan school that they were not to play "pom-pom," a complicated chasing game, because it entailed "inappropriate touch."

Rituals of Pollution. Cross-sex chasing is sometimes entwined with rituals of pollution, as in "cooties," where specific individuals or groups are treated as contaminating or carrying "germs." Children have rituals for transfering cooties (usually touching someone else and shouting "You've got cooties!"), for immunization (e.g., writing "CV" for "cootie vaccination" on their arms), and for eliminating cooties (e.g., saying "no gives" or using "cootie catchers" made of folded paper) (described in Knapp & Knapp, 1976). While girls may give cooties to girls, boys do not generally give cooties to one another (Samuelson, 1980).

In cross-sex play, either girls or boys may be defined as having cooties, which they transfer through chasing and touching. Girls give cooties to boys more often than vice versa. In Michigan, one version of cooties is called "girl stain"; the fourth graders whom Karkau, 1973, describes, used the phrase "girl touch." "Cootie queens," or "cootie girls" (there are no "kings" or "boys") are female pariahs, the ultimate school untouchables, seen as contaminating not only by virtue of gender, but also through some added stigma such as being overweight or poor.[2] That girls are seen as more polluting than boys is a significant asymmetry, which echoes cross-cultural patterns, although in other cultures female pollution is generally connected to menstruation, and not applied to prepubertal girls.

Invasions. Playground invasions are another asymmetric form of borderwork. On a few occasions I saw girls invade and disrupt an all-male game, most memorably a group of tall sixth-grade girls who ran onto the playing field and grabbed a football which was in play. The boys were surprised and frustrated, and, unusual for boys this old, finally tattled to the aide. But in the majority of cases, boys disrupt girls' activities rather than vice versa. Boys grab the ball from girls playing four-square, stick feet into a jumprope and stop an ongoing game, and dash through the area of the bars, where girls are taking turns performing, sending the rings flying. Sometimes boys ask to join a girls' game and then, after a short period of seemingly earnest play, disrupt the game:

> *Two second-grade boys begged to "twirl" the jumprope for a group of second-grade girls who had been jumping for some time. The girls agreed, and the boys began to twirl. Soon, without announcement, the boys changed from "seashells, cockle bells" to "hot peppers" (spinning the rope very fast), and tangled the jumper in the rope. The boys ran away laughing.*

Boys disrupt girls' play so often that girls have developed almost ritualized responses: They guard their ongoing play, chase boys away, and tattle to the aides. In a playground cycle which enhances sex segregation, aides who try to spot potential trouble before it occurs sometimes shoo boys away from areas where girls are playing. Aides do not anticipate trouble from girls who seek to join groups of boys, with the exception of girls intent on provoking a chase sequence. And indeed, if they seek access to a boys' game, girls usually play with boys in earnest rather than breaking up the game.

A close look at the organization of borderwork—or boundaried interactions between the sexes—shows that the worlds of boys and girls may be separate, but they are not parallel, nor are they equal. The worlds of girls and boys articulate in several asymmetric ways:

1. On the playground, boys control as much as ten times more space than girls, when one adds up the area of large playing fields and compares it with the much smaller areas where girls predominate. Girls, who play closer to the building, are more often watched over and protected by the adult aides.

2. Boys invade all-female games and scenes of play much more than girls invade boys. This, and boys' greater control of space, correspond with other findings about the organization of gender, and inequality, in our society: Compared with men and boys, women and girls take up less space, and their space, and talk, are more often violated and interrupted (Greif, 1980; Henley, 1977; West & Zimmerman, 1983).

3. Although individual boys are occasionally treated as contaminating (e.g., a third-grade boy who both boys and girls said was "stinky" and "smelled like pee"), girls are more often defined as polluting.... It is more taboo for a boy to play with (as opposed to invade) girls, and girls are more sexually defined than boys.

A look at the boundaries between the separated worlds of girls and boys illuminates within-sex hierarchies of status and control. For example, in the sex-divided seating in the 4th–5th grade classroom, several boys recurringly sat near "female space": Their desks were at the gender divide in the classroom, and they were more likely than other boys to sit at a predominantly female table in the lunchroom. These boys—two nonbilingual Chicanos and an overweight "loner" boy who was afraid of sports—were at the bottom of the male hierarchy. Gender is sometimes used as a metaphor for male hierarchies; the inferior status of boys at the bottom is conveyed by calling them "girls":

> Seven boys and one girl were playing basketball. Two younger boys came over and asked to play. While the girl silently stood, fully accepted in the company of players, one of the older boys disparagingly said to the younger boys, 'You girls can't play.'[3]

In contrast, the girls who more often travel in the boys' world, sitting with groups of boys in the lunchroom or playing basketball, soccer, and baseball with them, are not stigmatized. Some have fairly high status with other girls. The worlds of girls and boys are assymetrically arranged, and spatial patterns map out interacting forms of inequality.

Heterosexual Meanings

The organization and meanings of gender (the social categories "woman/man," "girl/boy") and of sexuality vary cross-culturally (Ortner & Whitehead, 1981)—and, in our society, across the life course. Harriet Whitehead (1981) observed that in our (Western) gender system, and that of many traditional North American Indian cultures, one's choice of a sexual object, occupation, and one's dress and demeanor are closely associated with gender. However, the "center of gravity" differs in the two gender systems. For Indians, occupational pursuits provide the primary imagery of gender; dress and demeanor are secondary, and sexuality is least important. In our system, at least for adults, the order is reversed: heterosexuality is central to our definitions of "man" and "woman" ("masculinity"/"femininity"), and the relationships that obtain between them, whereas occupation and dress/demeanor are secondary.

Whereas erotic orientation and gender are closely linked in our definitions of adults, we define children as relatively asexual. Activities and dress/demeanor are more important than sexuality in the cultural meanings of "girl" and "boy." Children are less heterosexually defined than adults, and we have nonsexual imagery for relations between girls and boys. However, both children and adults sometimes use heterosexual language—"crushes," "like," "goin' with," "girlfriends," and "boyfriends"—to define cross-sex relationships. This language increases through the years of elementary school; the shift to adolescence consolidates a gender system organized around the institution of heterosexuality.

In everyday life in the schools, heterosexual and romantic meanings infuse some ritualized forms of interaction between groups of boys and girls (e.g., "chase and kiss") and help maintain sex segregation. "Jimmy likes Beth" or "Beth likes Jimmy" is a major form of teasing, which a child risks in choosing to sit by or walk with someone of the other sex. The structure of teasing, and children's sparse vocabulary for relationships between girls and boys, are evident in the following conversation which I had with a group of third-grade girls in the lunchroom:

> Susan asked me what I was doing, and I said I was observing the things children do and play. Nicole volunteered, 'I like running, boys chase all the girls. See Tim over there? Judy chases him all around the school. She likes him.' Judy, sitting across the table, quickly responded, 'I hate him. I like him for a friend.' 'Tim loves Judy,' Nicole said in a loud, sing-song voice.

In the younger grades, the culture and lore of girls contains more heterosexual romantic themes than that of boys. In Michigan, the first-grade girls often jumped rope to a rhyme which began: "Down in the valley where the green grass grows, there sat Cindy (name of jumper), as sweet as a rose. She sat, she sat, she sat so sweet. Along came Jason, and kissed her on the cheek...first comes love, then comes marriage, then along comes Cindy with a baby carriage..." Before a girl took her turn at jumping, the chanters asked her "Who do you want to be your boyfriend?" The jumper always proffered a name, which was accepted matter-of-factly. In chasing, a girl's kiss carried greater threat than a boy's kiss; "girl touch," when defined as contaminating, had sexual connotations. In short, starting at an early age, girls are more sexually defined than boys.

Through the years of elementary school, and increasing with age, the idiom of heterosexuality helps maintain the gender divide. Cross-sex interactions, especially when children initiate them, are fraught with the risk of being teased about "liking" someone of the other sex. I learned of several close cross-sex friendships, formed and maintained in neighborhoods and church, which went underground during the school day.

By the fifth grade a few children began to affirm, rather than avoid, the charge of having a girlfriend or a boyfriend; they intro-

duced the heterosexual courtship rituals of adolescence:

> In the lunchroom in the Michigan school, as the tables were forming, a high-status fifth-grade boy called out from his seat at the table: 'I want Trish to sit by me.' Trish came over, and almost like a king and queen, they sat at the gender divide—a row of girls down the table on her side, a row of boys on his.

In this situation, which inverted earlier forms, it was not a loss, but a gain in status to publically choose a companion of the other sex. By affirming his choice, the boy became unteasable (note the familiar asymmetry of heterosexual courtship rituals: the male initiated). This incident signals a temporal shift in arrangements of sex and gender.

Traveling in the World of the Other Sex

Contests, invasions, chasing, and heterosexually defined encounters are based upon and reaffirm boundaries between girls and boys. In another type of cross-sex interaction, individuals (or sometimes pairs) cross gender boundaries, seeking acceptance in a group of the other sex. Nearly all the cases I saw of this were tomboys—girls who played organized sports and frequently sat with boys in the cafeteria or classroom. If these girls were skilled at activities central in the boys' world, especially games like soccer, baseball, and basketball, they were pretty much accepted as participants.

Being a tomboy is a matter of degree. Some girls seek access to boys' groups but are excluded; other girls limit their "crossing" to specific sports. Only a few—such as the tomboy I mentioned earlier, who chose a seat with the boys in the sex-divided 4th–5th grade—participate fully in the boys' world. That particular girl was skilled at the various organized sports which boys played in different seasons of the year. She was also adept at physical fighting and at using the forms of arguing, insult, teasing, naming, and sports-talk of the boys' subculture. She was the only Black child in her classroom, in a school with only 8%

Black students; overall that token status, along with unusual athletic and verbal skills, may have contributed to her ability to move back and forth across the gender divide. Her unique position in the children's world was widely recognized in the school. Several times, the teacher said to me, "She thinks she's a boy."

I observed only one boy in the upper grades (a fourth grader) who regularly played with all-female groups, as opposed to "playing at" girls' games and seeking to disrupt them. He frequently played jumprope and took turns with girls doing tricks on the bars, using the small gestures—for example, a helpful push on the heel of a girl who needed momentum to turn her body around the bar—which mark skillful and earnest participation. Although I never saw him play in other than an earnest spirit, the girls often chased him away from their games, and both girls and boys teased him. The fact that girls seek, and have more access to boys' worlds than vice versa, and the fact that girls who travel with the other sex are less stigmatized for it, are obvious asymmetries, tied to the asymmetries previously discussed.

Relaxed Cross-Sex Interactions

Relationships between boys and girls are not always marked by strong boundaries, heterosexual definitions, or by interacting on the terms and turfs of the other sex. On some occasions girls and boys interact in relatively comfortable ways. Gender is not strongly salient nor explicitly invoked, and girls and boys are not organized into boundaried collectivities. These "with" occasions have been neglected by those studying gender and children's relationships, who have emphasized either the model of separate worlds (with little attention to their articulation) or heterosexual forms of contact.

Occasions where boys and girls interact without strain, where gender wanes, rather than waxes in importance, frequently have one or more of the following characteristics:

1. The situations are organized around an absorbing task, such as a group art project or creating a radio show, which encourages cooperation and lessens attention to gender. This pattern accords with other studies finding that cooperative activities reduce group antagonism (e.g., Sherif & Sherif, 1953, who studied divisions between boys in a summer camp; and Aronson et al., 1978, who used cooperative activities to lessen racial divisions in a classroom).

2. Gender is less prominent when children are not responsible for the formation of the group. Mixed-sex play is less frequent in games like football, which require the choosing of teams, and more frequent in games like handball or dodgeball which individuals can join simply by getting into a line or a circle. When adults organize mixed-sex encounters—which they frequently do in the classroom and in physical education periods on the playground—they legitimize cross-sex contact. This removes the risk of being teased for choosing to be with the other sex.

3. There is more extensive and relaxed cross-sex interaction when principles of grouping other than gender are explicitly invoked—for example, counting off to form teams for spelling or kickball, dividing lines by hot lunch or cold lunch, or organizing a work group on the basis of interests or reading ability.

4. Girls and boys may interact more readily in less-public and crowded settings. Neighborhood play, depending on demography, is more often sex- and age-integrated than play at school, partly because with fewer numbers, one may have to resort to an array of social categories to find play partners or to constitute a game. And in less-crowded environments there are fewer potential witnesses to "make something of it" if girls and boys play together.

Relaxed interactions between girls and boys often depend on adults to set up and legitimize the contact.[4] Perhaps because of this contingency—and the other, distancing patterns which permeate relations between girls and boys—the easeful moments of inter-action rarely build to close friendship. Schofield (1981) makes a similar observation about gender and racial barriers to friendship in a junior high school.

IMPLICATIONS FOR DEVELOPMENT

I have located social relations within an essentially spatial framework, emphasizing the organization of children's play, work, and other activities within specific settings, and in one type of institution, the school. In contrast, frameworks of child development rely upon temporal metaphors, using images of growth and transformation over time. Taken alone, both spatial and temporal frameworks have shortcomings; fitted together, they may be mutually correcting.

Those interested in gender and development have relied upon conceptualizations of "sex role socialization" and "sex differences." Sexuality and gender, I have argued, are more situated and fluid than these individualist and intrinsic models imply. Sex and gender are differently organized and defined across situations, even within the same institution. This situational variation (e.g., in the extent to which an encounter heightens or lessens gender boundaries, or is infused with sexual meanings) shapes and constrains individual behavior. Features which a developmental perspective might attribute to individuals, and understand as relatively internal attributes unfolding over time, may, in fact, be highly dependent on context. For example, children's avoidance of cross-sex friendship may be attributed to individual gender development in middle-childhood. But attention to varied situations may show that this avoidance is contingent on group size, activity, adult behavior, collective meanings, and the risk of being teased.

A focus on social organization and situation draws attention to children's experiences in the present. This helps correct a model like "sex role socialization" which casts the present under the shadow of the future, or presumed "endpoints" (Speier, 1976). A situated analysis of arrangements of sex and gender among those of different ages may point to crucial disjunctions in the life course. In the fourth and fifth grades, culturally defined heterosexual rituals ("goin' with") begin to suppress the presence and visibility of other types of interaction between girls and boys, such as nonsexualized and comfortable interaction, and traveling in the world of the other sex. As "boyfriend/girlfriend" definitions spread, the fifth-grade tomboy I described had to work to sustain "buddy" relationships with boys. Adult women who were tomboys often speak of early adolescence as a painful time when they were pushed away from participation in boys' activities. Other adult women speak of the loss of intense, even erotic ties with other girls when they entered puberty and the rituals of dating, that is, when they became absorbed into the institution of heterosexuality (Rich, 1980). When Lever (1976) describes best-friend relationships among fifth-grade girls as preparation for dating, she imposes heterosexual ideologies onto a present which should be understood on its own terms.

As heterosexual encounters assume more importance, they may alter relations in same-sex groups. For example, Schofield (1981) reports that for sixth- and seventh-grade children in a middle school, the popularity of girls with other girls was affected by their popularity with boys, while boys' status with other boys did not depend on their relations with girls. This is an asymmetry familiar from the adult world; men's relationships with one another are defined through varied activities (occupations, sports), while relationships among women—and their public status—are more influenced by their connections to individual men.

A full understanding of gender and social relations should encompass cross-sex as well as within-sex interactions. "Border-work" helps maintain separate, gender-linked subcultures, which, as those interested in development have begun to suggest, may result in different milieux for learning. Daniel Maltz and Ruth Borker (1983) for example, argue that because of different interactions within girls' and boys' groups, the sexes learn different rules for creating and interpreting friendly conversation, rules which carry into adulthood and help account for miscommunication between men and women. Carol Gilligan (1982) fits research on the different worlds of girls and boys into a theory of sex differences in moral development. Girls develop a style of reasoning, she argues, which is more personal and relational; boys develop a style which is more positional, based on separateness. Eleanor Maccoby (1982), also following the insight that because of sex segregation, girls and boys grow up in different environments, suggests implications for gender-differentiated prosocial and antisocial behavior.

This separate worlds approach, as I have illustrated, also has limitations. The occasions when the sexes are together should also be studied, and understood as contexts for experience and learning. For example, assymmetries in cross-sex relationships convey a series of messages: that boys are more entitled to space and to the nonreciprocal right of interrupting or invading the activities of the other sex; that girls are more in need of adult protection, and are lower in status, more defined by sexuality, and may even be polluting. Different types of cross-sex interaction—relaxed, boundaried, sexualized, or taking place on the terms of the other sex—provide different contexts for development.

By mapping the array of relationships between and within the sexes, one adds complexity to the overly static and dichotomous imagery of separate worlds. Individual experiences vary, with implications for devel-opment. Some children prefer same-sex groupings; some are more likely to cross the gender boundary and participate in the world of the other sex; some children (e.g., girls and boys who frequently play "chase and kiss") invoke heterosexual meanings, while others avoid them.

Finally, after charting the terrain of relationships, one can trace their development over time. For example, age variation in the content and form of borderwork, or of cross- and same-sex touch, may be related to differing cognitive, social, emotional, or physical capacities, as well as to age-associated cultural forms. I earlier mentioned temporal shifts in the organization of cross-sex chasing, from mixing with fantasy play in the early grades to more elaborately ritualized and sexualized forms by the sixth grade. There also appear to be temporal changes in same- and cross-sex touch. In kindergarten, girls and boys touch one another more freely than in fourth grade, when children avoid relaxed cross-sex touch and instead use pokes, pushes, and other forms of mock violence, even when the touch clearly couches affection. This touch taboo is obviously related to the risk of seeming to *like* someone of the other sex. In fourth grade, same-sex touch begins to signal sexual meanings among boys, as well as between boys and girls. Younger boys touch one another freely in cuddling (arm around shoulder) as well as mock violence ways. By fourth grade, when homophobic taunts like "fag" become more common among boys, cuddling touch begins to disappear for boys, but less so for girls.

Overall, I am calling for more complexity in our conceptualizations of gender and of children's social relationships. Our challenge is to retain the temporal sweep, looking at individual and group lives as they unfold over time, while also attending to social structure and context, and to the full variety of experiences in the present.

NOTES

1. I am grateful to Frederick Erickson for suggesting the relevance of Barth's analysis.

2. Sue Samuelson (1980) reports that in a racially mixed playground in Fresno, California, Mexican-American, but not Anglo children gave cooties. Racial, as well as sexual inequality may be expressed through these forms.

3. This incident was recorded by Margaret Blume, who, for an undergraduate research project in 1982, observed in the California school where I earlier did fieldwork. Her observations and insights enhanced my own, and I would like to thank her for letting me cite this excerpt.

4. Note that in daily school life, depending on the individual and the situation, teachers and aides sometimes lessened and at other times heightened sex segregation.

REFERENCES

Aronson, E. et al. (1978). *The jigsaw classroom.* Beverly Hills, CA: Sage.

Barth, F. (Ed.). (1969). *Ethnic groups and boundaries.* Boston: Little, Brown.

Borman, K. M. (1979). Children's interactions in playgrounds. *Theory into Practice, 18,* 251–257.

Eder, D., & Hallinan, M. T. (1978). Sex differences in children's friendships. *American Sociological Review, 43,* 237–250.

Finnan, C. R. (1982). The ethnography of children's spontaneous play. In G. Spindler (Ed.), *Doing the ethnography of schooling* (pp. 358–380). New York: Holt, Rinehart & Winston.

Foot, H. C., Chapman, A. J., & Smith, J. R. (1980). Introduction. *Friendship and social relations in children* (pp. 1–14). New York: Wiley.

Gilligan, C. (1982). *In a different voice: Psychological theory and women's development.* Cambridge, MA: Harvard University Press.

Glaser, B. G., & Strauss, A. L. (1967). *The discovery of grounded theory.* Chicago: Aldine.

Goffman, E. (1977). The arrangement between the sexes. *Theory and Society, 4,* 301–336.

Goodwin, M. H. (1980). Directive-response speech sequences in girls' and boys' task activities. In S. McConnell-Ginet, R. Borker, & N. Furman (Eds.), *Women and language in literature and society* (pp. 157–173). New York: Praeger.

Greif, E. B. (1980). Sex differences in parent-child conversations. *Women's Studies International Quarterly, 3,* 253–258.

Henley, N. (1977). *Body politics: Power, sex, and nonverbal communication.* Englewood Cliffs, NJ: Prentice-Hall.

Karkau, K. (1973). *Sexism in the fourth grade.* Pittsburgh: KNOW, Inc. (pamphlet)

Katz, J. (1983). A theory of qualitative methodology: The social system of analytic fieldwork. In R. M. Emerson (Ed.), *Contemporary field research* (pp. 127–148). Boston: Little, Brown.

Knapp, M., & Knapp, H. (1976). *One potato, two potato: The secret education of American children.* New York: W. W. Norton.

Lever, J. (1976). Sex differences in the games children play. *Social Problems, 23,* 478–487.

Maccoby, E. (1982). *Social groupings in childhood: Their relationship to prosocial and antisocial behavior in boys and girls.* Paper presented at conference on The Development of Prosocial and Antisocial Behavior. Voss, Norway.

Maccoby, E., & Jacklin, C. (1974). *The psychology of sex differences.* CA: Stanford University Press.

Maltz, D. N., & Borker, R. A. (1983). A cultural approach to male-female miscommunication. In J. J. Gumperz (Ed.), *Language and social identity* (pp. 195–216). New York: Cambridge University Press.

McRobbie, A., & Garber, J. (1975). Girls and subcultures. In S. Hall and T. Jefferson (Eds.), *Resistance through rituals* (pp. 209–223). London: Hutchinson.

Ortner, S. B., & Whitehead, H. (1981). *Sexual meanings.* New York: Cambridge University Press.

Parrott, S. (1972). Games children play: Ethnography of a second-grade recess. In J. P. Spradley & D. W. McCurdy (Eds.), *The cultural experience* (pp. 206–219). Chicago: Science Research Associates.

Rich, A. (1980). Compulsory heterosexuality and lesbian existence. *Signs, 5,* 631–660.

Samuelson, S. (1980). The cooties complex. *Western Folklore, 39,* 108–210.

Savin-Williams, R. C. (1976). An ethological study of dominance formation and maintenance in a group of human adolescents. *Child Development, 47,* 972–979.

Schofield, J. W. (1981). Complementary and conflicting identities: Images and interaction in an interracial school. In S. R. Asher & J. M. Gottman (Eds.), *The development of children's friendships* (pp. 53–90). New York: Cambridge University Press.

Sherif, M., & Sherif, C. (1953). *Groups in harmony and tension.* New York: Harper.

Sluckin, A. (1981). *Growing up in the playground.* London: Routledge & Kegan Paul.

Speier, M. (1976). The adult ideological viewpoint in studies of childhood. In A. Skolnick (Ed.), *Rethinking childhood* (pp. 168–186). Boston: Little, Brown.

Sutton-Smith, B. (1971). A syntax for play and games. In R. E. Herron and B. Sutton-Smith (Eds.), *Child's Play* (pp. 298–307). New York: Wiley.

Unger, R. K. (1919). Toward a redefinition of sex and gender. *American Psychologist, 34,* 1085–1094.

Waldrop, M. F., & Halverson, C. F. (1975). Intensive and extensive peer behavior: Longitudinal and cross-sectional analysis. *Child Development, 46,* 19–26.

West, C., & Zimmerman, D. H. (1983). Small insults: A study of interruptions in cross-sex conversations between unacquainted persons. In B. Thorne, C. Kramarae, & N. Henley (Eds.), *Language, gender and society.* Rowley, MA: Newbury House.

Whitehead, H. (1981). The bow and the burden strap: A new look at institutionalized homosexuality in Native America. In S. B. Ortner & H. Whitehead (Eds.), *Sexual meanings* (pp. 80–115). New York: Cambridge University Press.

PART FIVE

Gender, Math, and Science

Although the words "scientist" and "mathematician" are not gendered, the culture of science and math is decidedly masculine. In fact, until 1989, the Oxford English Dictionary defined "scientist" as "a man of science"(Merton 1998). Math and science are male domains on a variety of levels: Women are still underrepresented as mathematicians and scientists; women are discouraged by teachers from developing confidence in their abilities in math and science; math and science are taught in ways that discourage women from pursuing careers in those areas; and many feminists argue that what scientists call "objective" is based on a masculine way of seeing the world.

In *Women Scientists in America,* Margaret Rossiter (1982) argues that before affirmative action women were not only discouraged from becoming scientists, but women who became scientists were largely invisible due to the systematic devaluation of their work and discrimination against them. Women make up 45 percent of the U.S. workforce, but even after thirty years of affirmative action, they account for 16 percent of computer science Ph.D.'s, 18 percent of mathematics Ph.D.'s, and 11 percent of physics Ph.D.'s. Sixteen percent of employed scientists and engineers are female (Alper 1993).

Some researchers argue that the gender gap among mathematicians and scientists is a result of the disparity in innate mathematical ability between males and females. They cite the gender gap in the math section of the Scholastic Assessment Test (SAT) as evidence (Alper 1993). Critics of the innate ability thesis fall into two camps. Some reject the innate ability thesis entirely, blaming the gender gap on methodology. For example, Linn and Hyde (1989) have challenged the objectivity of scores on the mathematics section of the SAT arguing that the test is gender biased. In addition, studies of sex differences across many areas accept the tradition of designing studies to test the null hypothesis of no sex differences and accepting the findings as significant only when the null hypothesis is rejected. The findings are only seen as publishable when the hypothesis of no sex differences is rejected at the 5 percent level. Therefore, we do not get to read many of the studies that found no sex differences and a "literature of differences" is created (Damarin 1995).

Other researchers argue that you cannot empirically demonstrate if there are innate differences in mathematical ability between the genders. However, there are social factors which discourage women because even among the most mathematically talented, far fewer women than men pursue science careers (Alper 1993). Therefore, some authors contend that the problem is not so much women's lack of mathematical ability, but rather the way they are taught (Carey, Fennema, Carpenter, and Franke 1995). For example, Mary Belenky and her colleagues found that women are not opposed to abstract concepts, but find them most useful when they are used to make sense of their experience. They do not relate to abstractions that precede or ignore their experience. Even the women who were adept at dealing with abstract concepts preferred to start from personal experience. Yet, math is most often taught in an experiential vacuum which is not conducive to motivating women. In addition, other researchers have found that women's confidence in their mathematical abilities is undermined by teachers who attribute female success in mathematics to hard work, whereas they attribute comparable male success to ability (Damarin 1995).

Criticisms of the sex bias of science are even more far-reaching. By and large the criticisms of mathematics posit that individual attitudes about the mathematical abilities of men and women are reinforced by teachers, testing, and the way research is done or reported. Feminist critics of science, on the other hand, focus on the epistemology—that is, way of knowing of science. Science, like every other area of knowledge, is a social product and therefore reflects the culture of its makers. Since science is controlled by men, if males have a distinctive way of seeing the world, this will color science. Science, from this point of view, is based on a masculine way of seeing the world called "objectivity." Sandra Harding (1986) points out that although scientists claim to be value-free and objective, science's claims to knowledge bear the fingerprints of its human producers—men. Indeed, Harding argues that science's discourse of value-neutrality is a powerful device for legitimating its own biases.

The equation between masculine and objective, more specifically masculine and scientific, is historically pervasive and yet flies in the face of our mythical image of science as emotionally and sexually neutral and value-free. The fact that the population of scientists is overwhelmingly male is not the cause of the attribution of masculinity to scientific thought, but a consequence of it. While it used to be common to hear scientists, teachers, and parents openly assert that women cannot and should not become scientists, the women's movement made such assertions unfashionable. However, we still dub the so-called "objective" sciences "hard," which is masculine as opposed to the "soft" social sciences which are feminine and more subjective. A woman thinking scientifically or objectively is thinking "like a man" (Keller 1985).

Indeed, women who have chosen science as a career tend to see themselves as "scientists," (i.e., thinking like men) and few women scientists are feminists or identify with the women's movement (Leavitt and Gordon 1988). Evelyn Fox Keller, on the other hand, is a mathematical biophysicist who began to question the laws of physics in the mid-1970s when she started to ponder how much the nature of science was bound up with the idea of masculinity. She argues that science bears the imprint of its masculinity in the description of reality it offers. Scientific ideology divides the world into the knower (mind) and the knowable (nature). The relation specified between the two is one of distance and separation; it is that between a subject and an object radically divided. The scientific mind is set apart from what is to be known. The characterization of both the scientific mind and its modes of access to knowledge as "objective" is masculine—it connotes autonomy, separation, and distance. While intuitive and empathic ways of knowing are characterized as "subjective" and feminine (Keller 1985).

Keller rejects the possibility that the associations between scientific and masculine reflect biological differences between male and female brains. Rather, Keller uses Chodorow's theory to explain why thinking that is characterized by a radical separation of self and object is masculine. Chodorow (1978) argues that female mothering leads to the development of boys who need to remain distant and separate so as not to regress to an undifferentiated state with their mother. She goes on to say that women have a sense of fluidity between self and object and are more intuitive, empathic, and nurturing. Thus, claims Keller, adherence to an objectivist epistemology, in which truth is measured by its distance from the subjective, has to be reexamined because "truth" itself is genderized as masculine.

This leads to a great divide among feminist critics of science. If men and women have different ways of knowing, even if they are based on gendered parenting rather than biology, we are left with the implication that there is a male science (in which the subject and object are radically separated) and a female science (in which the subject and object interact). However, most feminist critics of science, except for the most radical ones, do not try to substitute one set of gender loyalties for the other. They do not simply substitute "woman-centered" for "man-centered" hypotheses or, if they do, it is for the purpose of clarifying that the original one accepted as "objective" was actually "man-centered" (Harding 1986).

For example, Emily Martin (1996) argues that popular as well as scientific accounts of reproductive biology rely on stereotypes that imply female biological processes are less worthy than their male counterparts. She attempts to shine a bright light on the gender stereotypes hidden within the scientific language of biology. She points out that medical texts describe menstruation as the "debris" of the uterine lining implying that the system is producing wasted, scrap material. Yet, the male's vast production of sperm is not seen as wasteful despite the fact that a man produces millions of wasted sperm during his life.

Two selections in this section are written by scientists-turned-feminist critics—Ruth Hubbard and Ruth Bleier. Both of them point out that traditional scientific thought is subjective in its masculine bias. The first selection is by Ruth Hubbard—a professor of biology emeritus at Harvard. The reading in this section, "Fact Making and Feminism," is a chapter from her book *The Politics of Women's Biology* (1992). Hubbard believes that science has played a political role in legitimating the existing gendered distribution of power and division of labor. Hubbard views any claims of scientific neutrality as inherently ideological.

Bleier, the author of the second selection in this section, seems to take a similar position, but focuses on a specific example of fact making—the Man-the-Hunter theory. Bleier was a neurophysiologist recognized as a leading expert on the hypothalamus in animals. She wrote three definitive books on that topic, but is well known among feminist scholars for her other two books, *Science and Gender: A Critique of Biology and Its Theories on Women* (1984) and *Feminist Approaches to Science* (1986). Bleier was among the first scientists to examine critically the foundations of the modern biological sciences from a feminist perspective. She demonstrated the profound effect of gender on science: the gender of the investigators, of the subjects of investigations, and the assumptions about gender that underlie accepted research conclusions (Leavitt and Gordon 1988).

In this selection from *Science and Gender,* "Theories of Human Origins and Cultural Evolution: Man the Hunter," Bleier argues that implicit in bioevolutionary explanations of forms of social organization that we see in our Western industrialized countries is the notion that they have always been that way, are "natural," and hence unchangeable. The predominant theory relating gender and human cultural evolution is the Man-the-Hunter theory. This is the view of man as provider of food for his dependents; bonding with other males to hunt and defend his woman and children. Man-the-Hunter is also used to explain male aggression—it is the "killer" instinct of the hunter.

Bleier argues that despite much evidence against it, the Man-the-Hunter theory has been uncritically accepted because it neatly ties together a number of aspects of modern Western culture: women's economic dependence on men, the sexual division of labor, and male aggressivity. In an effort to explain the origins of present-day gender relations, the Man-the-Hunter explanation starts with the implicit assumption that these arrangements have a biological basis. Thus, Bleier clarifies how sociobiological views can form the ideological base for conservative or reactionary programs while appearing to be apolitical by carefully avoiding any recognition of the political, social, and cultural factors that could account for the presumably innate characteristics.

The third article in this section is a qualitative study by Henry Etzkowitz, Carol Kemelgor, Michael Neuschatz, and Brian Uzzi. They point out that women face barriers to entry and achievement at all steps of the academic ladder. The barriers begin very early, with the differential socialization of men and women, and continue with the taken-for-granted male model of doing science.

In sum, the examination of the relationship between gender, math, and science reveals the nature of a dominant ideology. Men have not simply dominated math and science by their numbers and their attitudes toward women who enter or might consider entering these fields, they have controlled the definition of what is "truth" and how one finds it.

REFERENCES——————————————————————————————

Alper, Joseph. 1993. "The Pipeline Is Leaking Women All the Way Along." *Science* 260:409–411.

Bleier, Ruth. 1984. "Theories of Human Origins and Cultural Evolution: Man the Hunter." Pp. 115–137 in *Science and Gender: A Critique of Biology and Its Theories on Women.* Elmsford: Pergamon Press.

Carey, Deborah A., Elizabeth Fennema, Thomas P. Carpenter, and Megan L. Franke. 1995. "Equity and Mathematics Education." Pp.93–125 in *New Directions for Equity in Mathematics Education,* edited by Walter G. Secada, Elizabeth Fennema, and Lisa Byrd Adajian. New York: Cambridge University Press.

Chodorow, Nancy. 1978. *The Reproduction of Mothering: Psychoanalysis and the Sociology of Gender.*Berkeley: University of California.

Damarin, Suzanne K. 1995. "Gender and Mathematics from a Feminist Standpoint." Pp. 242–257 in *New Directions for Equity in Mathematics Education,* edited by Walter G. Secada, Elizabeth Fennema, and Lisa Byrd Adajian. New York: Cambridge University Press.

Harding, Sandra. 1986. *The Science Question in Feminism.* Ithaca: Cornell University Press.

Hubbard, Ruth. 1992. *The Politics of Women's Biology.* New Brunswick: Rutgers University Press.

Keller, Evelyn Fox. 1985. *Reflections on Gender and Science.* New Haven: Yale University Press.

Leavitt, Judith Walzer, and Linda Gordon. 1988. "A Decade of Feminist Critiques in the Natural Sciences: An Address by Ruth Bleier." *Signs* 14:182–195.

Linn, M. C., and J. S. Hyde. 1989. "Gender, Mathematics and Science." *Educational Researcher* 18:22–27.

Martin, Emily. 1996. "The Egg and the Sperm: How Science Has Constructed a Romance Based on Stereotypical Male-Female Roles." Pp. 103–117 in *Feminism and Science,* edited by Evelyn Fox Keller and Helen E. Longino.New York: Oxford University Press.

Merton, Robert K. 1998. "De-Gendering 'Man of Science': A Venture in Sociological Semantics." The Ninth Charles R. Lawrence II Memorial Lecture.

Rossiter, Margaret. 1982. *Women Scientists in America: Struggles and Strategies to 1940.* Baltimore: Johns Hopkins University Press.

Travis, John. 1993. "Making Room for Women in the Culture of Science." *Science* 260:412–415.

Fact Making and Feminism

RUTH HUBBARD

Every fact has a factor, a maker. The Brazilian educator Paulo Freire (1985) has pointed out that people who want to understand the role of politics in shaping education must "see the reasons behind facts" (p. 2). So the interesting question is, As we move through the world, how do we sort those aspects of it that we permit to become facts from those that we relegate to being fiction—untrue or imagined— and from those that, worse yet, we do not even notice so that they do not become facts, fiction, or figments of the imagination? In other words, what criteria and mechanisms of selection do scientists use to make facts?

One thing is clear: Making facts is a social enterprise. People cannot just go off by themselves and dream up facts. When they do that, and the rest of us do not accept the facts they offer us, we consider them schizophrenic, crazy. If their facts sufficiently resemble ours or they have the power to force us to accept them and make us see the emperor's new clothes, the new facts become part of our shared reality, and their making, part of the fact-making enterprise.

Making science is such an enterprise. As scientists, our job is to generate facts that help people understand nature. In doing this job, we must follow the rules of the scientific community and go about our fact making in professionally sanctioned ways. We must submit new facts to review by colleagues and be willing to share them with qualified strangers by writing and speaking about them (unless we work for companies with proprietary interests, in which case we still must share our facts, but only with particular people). If we follow proper procedure, our facts come to be accepted on faith by large numbers of people who are in no position to say why what we put out are facts, not fiction. After all, a lot of scientific facts are counterintuitive, such as that the earth moves around the sun or that if you drop a pound of feathers and a pound of rocks, they will fall at the same rate. Recently some physicists have even hypothesized that a pound of feathers falls more rapidly than a pound of rocks, a fact even more counterintuitive than what I learned in physics.

What are the social or group characteristics of people who are allowed to make scientific facts? Above all, they must have a particular kind of education, which includes graduate and postgraduate training. With such an education, they not only learn scientific subject matter but also must familiarize themselves with that narrow slice of history and culture that deals primarily with the experiences of Western European and North American upper-class men during the past century or two. In addition, they must not deviate too far from accepted rules of individual and social behavior, and they are socialized to talk and think in ways that let them earn the academic degrees required of a scientist.

Until the 1960s, youngsters mainly from the upper-middle and upper classes, most of them male and white, had access to that kind of education. Since then, more white women and people of color (both women and men) have been able to gain access, but the class origins of scientists have not changed appreciably. The scientific professions still draw their members overwhelmingly from the upper-middle and upper classes. How about other kinds of people? Have they no part in making science? Quite the contrary. In the ivory (that is, white) towers in which science gets made, one can find lots of people from the working and lower-middle classes, but they are technicians, secretaries, and clean-up personnel.

Decisions about who gets to be a faculty-level fact maker are made by professors, deans, and university presidents, who call on scientists from other, similar institutions to recommend candidates they think will conform to the prescribed standards. At the larger, systemic level, decisions are made by governmental and private funding agencies, which operate by what is called peer review: Small groups of people with similar personal and academic backgrounds decide whether a particular fact-making proposal has enough merit to be financed. Scientists who work in the same, or related, fields sit on each other's decision-making panels, and although criteria are supposedly objective and meritocratic, orthodoxy and conformity count for a lot. Someone whose ideas or personality or both are out of line is likely not to succeed.

Thus, science is made, by and large, by a self-perpetuating group: by the chosen for the chosen. The assumption is that if the science is "good," in a professional sense, it will also be good for society. But no one or no group is responsible for looking at whether it is. Public accountability is not built into the system.

What are the alternatives? How could we have a science that is open and accessible, a science for the people? And to what extent could—or should—it also be a science by the people? After all, divisions of labor are not necessarily bad. There is no reason and, in a complicated society like ours, no possibility that everyone be able to do everything. Destructive inequalities arise not from the fact that different people do different things but from the fact that different tasks are valued differently and confer different amounts of prestige and power.

For example, this society values mental labor more highly than manual labor. We think mental labor requires more specifically human qualities and is superior. This assumption is wrong and especially so in laboratory work because it means that the laboratory chief—the person "with the ideas"—gets the credit, whereas the laboratory workers—the people who work with their hands (as well as, often, their imaginations)—are the ones who perform the operations and make the observations that generate new hypotheses and permit hunches, ideas, and hypotheses to become facts.

But it is not only because of the way natural science is done that head and hand, mental and manual work, tend to be linked. Natural science requires a conjunction of head and hand because it is an understanding of nature for use. Natural science and technology are inextricable because we can judge our interpretations of nature only by seeing to what extent they work. Scientific facts and laws are true only to the extent that they can be applied and used.

Because feminist methodology is grounded in women's experiences and practices, it offers a lens through which to examine the ways scientific facts are related to the ideological and social commitments of scientists—the people who have been able to make scientific facts. By juxtaposing women's lived realities with the scientific descriptions of them, we can try to judge to what extent the "facts" explain our experiences or whether they misrepresent and conceal them.

WOMAN'S NATURE: REALITIES VERSUS SCIENTIFIC MYTHS

As I said before, to be believed scientific facts must fit the worldview of the times. For this reason, since the social upheavals that started in the 1960s, some researchers have tried to "prove" that differences in the political, social, and economic status of women and men, blacks and whites, or poor people and rich people are the inevitable outcomes of people's inborn qualities. They have produced "scientific" evidence that blacks are innately less intelligent than whites, and that women are innately weaker, more nurturing, and less good at math than men.

This kind of science is specious and ideology-laden. Clearly the ideology of woman's nature differs drastically from the realities of women's lives and indeed is antithetical to them. The ideology that labels women as the natural reproducers of the species and men as producers of goods ignores the fact that women produce a large proportion of our goods and services. But this ideology can be used to shunt women out of higher-paying jobs, the professions, and other kinds of work that require continuity and provide a measure of power over their own and, at times, other people's lives. Most women who work for pay do so as secretaries or nurses or in other jobs that involve a great deal of responsibility but do not pay well. For this reason, insisting on equal pay within job categories will not remedy women's economic disadvantage as long as women's jobs are less well paid than men's jobs. Scientists underwrite this stratification when they produce specious research that "proves" that girls are not as good as boys at spatial perception, abstract reasoning, mathematics, and science.

Discriminatory practices are often justified by the claim that they follow from limits biology places on women's capacity to work. In the 1970s, a number of women employees in the American chemical and automotive in-dustries were forced to choose between working at relatively well-paying jobs that had previously been done by men or remaining fertile. In one instance, five women were required to submit to sterilization by hysterectomy in order to avoid being transferred from work in the lead-pigment department at the American Cyanamid plant in Willow Island, West Virginia, to janitorial work with considerably lower wages and benefits (Stellman and Henifin 1982). Even though none of these women was pregnant or planning a pregnancy in the near future (indeed, the husband of one had had a vasectomy), they were considered "potentially pregnant" unless they could prove they were sterile. Although exposure to lead can damage sperm as well as eggs, it is as though only women can expect to be parents. In addition, lead exposure can affect the health of male and female workers as well as a "potential fetus."

It is important to notice that this vicious choice has been forced only on women who have recently entered relatively well-paid and traditionally male jobs. Women who are exposed to reproductive hazards in traditionally female jobs, as nurses, x-ray technologists, laboratory technicians, or as cleaning women in surgical operating rooms, scientific laboratories, or the chemical and biotechnology industries, or as beauticians, secretaries, workers in the ceramics industry, and domestic workers, are not warned about the chemical and physical hazards of their work to their health or to that of a fetus should they be pregnant. In other words, scientific knowledge about fetal susceptibility to noxious chemicals and radiation is used to keep women out of better-paid jobs from which they were previously excluded by discriminatory employment practices, even though, in general, working women and men are not protected against occupational hazards to health.

The ideology of women's nature that is invoked in such cases posits that a woman's capacity to become pregnant leaves her always physically disabled in comparison with men. The scientific underpinnings for these ideas were produced in the nineteenth century by the white, university-educated, mainly upper-class men who made up the bulk of the new professions of obstetrics and gynecology, biology, psychology, sociology, and anthropology. These professionals realized that they might lose the kinds of personal attention they were accustomed to getting from their mothers, wives, and sisters if women of their own class gained access to the professions. They therefore used theories about women's innate frailty to disqualify girls and women of their own race and class who might compete with them for education and professional status. But they did not invoke women's weakness to protest the long hours poor women worked in the homes and factories belonging to members of their own class nor to protest the labor black slave women were forced to do.

Nineteenth-century biologists and physicians claimed that women's brains were smaller than men's and that women's ovaries and uteruses required much energy and rest in order to function properly. They "proved" that young girls should be kept away from schools and colleges once they began to menstruate and warned that without this kind of care women's uteruses and ovaries would shrivel and the human race would die out. But, once again, this analysis was not carried over to poor women, who not only were required to work hard but often were said to reproduce too much. Indeed, scientists interpreted the fact that poor women could work hard and yet bear many children as a sign that they were more animallike and less highly evolved than upper-class women.

REFERENCES

Freire, Paulo. 1985. *The Politics of Education.* South Hadley, Mass.: Bergin and Garvey.

Stellman, Jeanne M., and Mary Sue Henifin. 1982. "No Fertile Women Need Apply: Employment Discrimination and Reproductive Hazards in the Workplace." In Ruth Hubbard, Mary Sue Henifin, and Barbara Fried, eds., *Biological Woman—The Convenient Myth.* Cambridge, Mass.: Schenkman.

Theories of Human Origins and Cultural Evolution: Man the Hunter

RUTH BLEIER

The predominant theory relevant to human culture evolution for at least two decades has been the Man-the-Hunter theory. The theory that humanity originated in the club-wielding, man-ape, aggressive and masterful, is so widely accepted as scientific fact and vividly secure in our popular culture as to seem self-evident. This is the view of the male as provider of food for his dependents; bonding with other males to hunt and to defend; inventing, creating, speaking, and evolving.

> *In a very real sense our intellect, interests, emotions, and basic social life—all are evolutionary products of the success of the hunting adaptation. (Washburn and Lancaster, 1976, p. 293)*
>
> *To assert the biological unity of mankind is to affirm the importance of the hunting way of life.... The biology, psychology, and customs that separate us from the apes—all these we owe to the hunters of time past. (Ibid; p. 303)*

And, of course, "...it was the men who hunted the game, fought the enemies and made the decisions" (Fox, 1967). Where, we may wonder, were the women? Was their only role and destiny in our evolutionary history to be incubators, as is clearly implicit in Man-the-Hunter theories of human origins?

It may help in appreciating how pervasive and at the same time almost uncon-sciously implicit these theories about our human origins are in our minds if we stop here for a moment and allow whatever representation of prehistoric life we have to rise to consciousness. For most of us a cultural stereotype will appear. It will be a small band of fierce-looking, purposeful males carrying weapons and stalking game. If women appear at all, they are at the edge of the picture, placid-looking, holding babies, squatting by the fire, and stirring the contents of a pot. Scientific theory, in yet another form, has become a part of popular culture and of an ideology that finds modern social arrangements and gender relationships to be part of the natural order of things now and for millions of years past.

The Man-the-Hunter theory, in essence, describes the process whereby our increasingly upright bipedal (male) ancestors, from about 15 to 4 million years ago, used their freed hands to fashion tools and weapons for hunting (Washburn and Lancaster, 1968). Men banded together to hunt large animals and to share in the kill that they carried back to their female and young dependents. This primary sexual division led to an intensification of the sexual division of labor and of sexual differentiation in psychological and temperamental characteristics. The Man-the-Hunter theory thus explains female dependence upon males for survival and the evolution (among males) of cooperation and sharing, communication, and the invention of tools, weapons, equipment, *and* art. The origin of men as hunters is also linked with the origins and evolution of a presumed "killer" instinct in males that accounts for war, torture, homicide, and modern day hunting; and with the origins of male competitiveness, aggressivity, daring, and creativity that account for male dominance over women in all aspects of personal, social, political and economic life.

One is next led to wonder whether such a theory emerged from a mass of incontrovertible "facts" and just happens so felicitously to explain modern day social arrangements and inequalities, or instead represents a creation or construction argued back from the uncomfortable awareness that men's contributions to civilization have never been separate from their acts of violence, destruction, and domination. A theory that can show the positive contributions and the violences alike to be inevitable consequences of the same characteristics that ensured the survival and evolution of the species—the courage, strength, and aggressivity of man, the hunter—is a welcome addition indeed to social scientific theory and popular lore.

In this chapter I shall indicate some of the scientific roots of Man-the-Hunter theories of human cultural evolution and then show how available evidence from archaeology, primatology, and anthropology suggests that the social hunting of large animals is a relatively recent development and could not explain either human origins or the uniquely human aspects of our cultures. At the same time I shall present alternative interpretations of the same bodies of data and suggest that the nature of the evidence and of processes of change cannot support any Single Cause theory of human cultural evolution.

SOME SCIENTIFIC ROOTS OF CONTEMPORARY THEORIES OF HUMAN CULTURAL EVOLUTION

Studies and theories from a multitude of disciplines have converged in the efforts to explain the origins and evolution of the social and political organization of human "society" (in reality, of Western patriarchal, industrialized societies): primate anatomy and physiology, animal sociology (animal behaviors and social groups), physical anthropology and paleontology (the study of variations in structure and function and the correlations between them among humans, other primates, and fossil remains), comparative (across species) psychology or psychobiology, sexual and reproductive physiology and neuroendocrinology, population genetics, evolutionary and ecological field biology, and social or cultural anthropology. The major contributors to evolutionary speculations have usually synthesized theories and observations from a number of these disciplines.

In two recent essays, Donna Haraway (1978) has provided an analysis of the historical and philosophical development since the early 1900s of the ideas linking the human organism and animal sociology with a natural economy of the body politic and leading to contemporary theories and beliefs about human origins and human "nature." She describes the powerful ideological, linguistic, and metaphorical connections that have been made for many centuries between the political and the physiological. The perception of human society, of the social order or body politic, as an organism has permeated political theory since the time of the ancient Greeks. During the period of the Industrial Revolution, that link was especially evident in the concepts and terminologies ("survival of the fittest") shared by political theories of the marketplace and by biological theories as influential as those of Darwin. The significant element in that union of the political and physiological that Haraway considers to be critical for our understanding of the full social impact of science is that it

> ...has been a major source of ancient and modern justifications of domination, especially of domination based on differences seen as natural, given, inescapable, and therefore moral. (p. 22)

Haraway shows that the principle of domination is deeply imbedded in the theory and practice of contemporary natural sciences, especially those that seek to explain human behaviors and social organization. The particular field that has been important in this regard has been animal sociology, particularly primatology, where, Haraway documents, implicit political ideas of domination became an analytical principle; human social relations became embodied in the content and procedures of these presumably descriptive natural sciences. These sciences then served to reinforce a "vision of the natural and cultural necessity of domination" (p. 37). In particular, "animal sociology has been central in the development of the most thorough naturalization of patriarchal division of authority in the body politic and in reduction of the body politic to sexual physiology" (p. 26).

Haraway begins her historical analysis, which will be only briefly described here, with the work of Clarence R. Carpenter, who trained in the laboratories of Robert M. Yerkes, a pioneer in psychobiological studies of captive apes in the 1920s, 1930s, and 1940s, and was also a central figure linking science, government, foundations, intelligence testing, and "human engineering." Yerkes was influential in promoting sexuality as a subject for scientific investigation. Through his observations and interpretations linking female chimpanzee sexuality to male power and privilege (females trading sex for food and status), thus making an economic link between physiology and politics, he sought to establish sex, reproduction, and male dominance among primates as the bases for the emergence of human social relationships. These were assumptions that Carpenter automatically incorporated into his own pioneering observations of free-ranging Asian monkeys which he collected and transported to an island off Puerto Rico. Placing his findings within the framework of influential functionalist, evolutionary, biological, and social scientific theories between the two world wars, he based his work "on principles of hierarchical order of the body and body politic" (p. 31). Carpenter was convinced of the importance of male dominance and male hierarchies in intragroup organization. He perceived male dominance to be strongly correlated with successful sexual access to estrous females, and hence clearly evolutionarily significant and advantageous, since genes for "aggressivity" would be selectively transmitted. During this era covering approximately the first three decades of the twentieth century, Haraway concludes that the political principle of domination became transformed into the "legitimating scientific principle of dominance as a natural property with a physical-chemical base. Manipulations, concepts, organizing principles—the entire range of tools of the science—must be seen to be penetrated by the principle of domination" (p. 35).

An English physician and scientist, Solly Zuckerman, combined interests in paleontology, physical anthropology, reproductive physiology, and zoology to make significant theoretical contributions in the 1930s and later decades, when he also became a most influential figure in British science and administration. He held the conviction that "sexual physiology is the foundation of primate social order" and that hunting had crucial consequences for the sexual division of labor and the universality of the institution of the human family. Beginning in the early 1950s, Sherwood Washburn, a physical anthropologist and primatologist, made important contributions to evolutionary theory by formulating the possible relationships among bipedalism, upright posture, increased hand use, tool using, and the development of the brain and language. He is also the person primarily associated with the Man-the-Hunter theory of human cultural and psychological evolution as outlined briefly earlier in this chapter, further developing with collaborators the concept of the evolutionary importance of aggression and hierarchical ordering among monkeys, apes, and humans. Haraway presents the interesting parallel analysis of the primatologist Thelma Rowell, who, operating within the same theoretical framework as Zuckerman, rejected his theories of female passivity and male dominance and the association between male aggressivity and reproductive success; and of the anthropologists Nancy Tanner and Adrienne Zihlman, who, operating within Washburn's theoretical framework of social and evolutionary functionalism, rejected his Man-the-Hunter theory and provided a sociobiological account of human evolutionary descent from woman, the gatherer. Washburn himself, while providing an important theoretical context for use by Sociobiologists, has been a critic of the new Sociobiology and of uncritical extrapolations from apes to human behavior and, as Haraway points out, has also been an important influence and advisor for feminist and traditional investigators alike.

There are other important contributors within the Man-the-Hunter tradition who present interesting paradoxes that can be added to Haraway's account. Frank Beach, a comparative psychologist, has been a pioneering investigator over the past three decades in studies of the sexual and reproductive behavior of animals and the influences of hormones on that behavior. He had been careful to affirm the importance, however, of social context in understanding animal (or human) behaviors, as well as the principle that hormones cannot "cause" the occurrence of particular behavior patterns (Beach, 1974a). These convictions did not, however, interfere with Beach's writing a lengthy philosophical article on evolution, within the Yerkes-Zuckerman-Washburn tra-

dition that Haraway outlines, that would pass today as the production of a committed Wilsonian sociobiologist. Among other things, he wrote:

> *Male genotypes that were above average in promoting these characteristics specifically related to effective performance of the hunter role were especially adaptive from the point of view of group survival. (1974b, p. 351)*

Beach states in another paragraph that these genetic characteristics are "certain emotional tendencies such as less fearfulness and greater willingness to venture from the safety of the home base." He continues:

> *Within the female population, natural selection favored perpetuation and dissemination of those gene patterns which contributed most to behavior consonant with nonhunting, with gathering, with remaining near the home base. (Ibid; p. 351)*

The circumspection Beach advocates with respect to interpretations about the role of hormones on behavior, his own area of expertise, he casts aside in his speculations about the evolutionary origins of presumed gender differences and the function of genes in determining such dubiously biological characteristics as fearfulness, adventuresomeness, nonhunting, and remaining near home base.

But then within the context of a symposium (and subsequent book), Beach was clearly stung by the casual dismissal of comparative psychology, which is Beach's discipline, in E. O. Wilson's book, *Sociobiology* (1975). He reacted logically enough, as perhaps a feminist scholar might to the trivialization of her life's work by one of the eminent fathers in her field. Wilson had proclaimed that comparative psychology is "destined to be cannibalized by neurophysiology and sensory physiology from one end and sociobiology from the other" (p. 6). This is necessary because "the future, it seems clear, cannot be with the ad hoc terminology, crude models, and curve fitting that characterize most of contemporary ethology and comparative psychology." In response, Beach refers to Wilson as "the high priest of sociobiology" (1978, p. 116) and proceeds to dismember Sociobiological methodology with sarcasm:

> I recognize that in...sociobiology the postulates are sacrosanct by definition and need never be proved.... However, a distressing myopia impedes my labored search for reassuringly tangible connections between...the sociobiologist's formidable postulates and impeccable mathematical theoretical models and...the grubby raw material of empirical evidence with which a pedestrian comparative psychologist perforce must deal. (1978, p. 117)

This interchange perhaps suggests more poignantly than any theoretical formulation that I may offer the fragile and subjective nature of theory making and the influence than scientists' personalities, experiences, and beliefs have on the perspectives they incorporate into and express by their scientific writings.

With the advent of Sociobiology in the late 1970s, evolutionary reconstructions passed beyond speculation and hypotheses to become stated as fact:

> What we can conclude with some degree of confidence is that primitive men lived in small territorial groups, within which males were dominant over females. (E. O. Wilson, 1975, p. 567)

> ...sexual selection would tend to be linked with hunting, prowess, leadership, skill at tool making, and other visible attributes that contribute to the success of the family and the male band. (Ibid., p. 569)

But also during the 1970s, countercurrents were beginning to stir. In a landmark paper first appearing in 1971, Sally Slocum (1975) discussed the problem of male bias in anthropology, pointing out that the choice of asking certain questions *and not others* grows out of the cultural context in which anthropologists exist. While by 1971 Western anthropologists had begun to recognize their ethnic, racial, class, and academic biases, Slocum first demonstrated the *male* bias in the Man-the-Hunter theory of evolution. She described her alter-

nate version of evolution, which takes into account the participation of women as gatherers and mothers, and suggested the critical role such activities may have played in the evolution of food-sharing, cooperation, and the invention of containers and tools, all essential features for the evolution of the cooperative activity of large-scale social hunting. This line of investigation and writing has been carried forward by Nancy Tanner and Adrienne Zihlman (1976) and others.

During the past decade, it has become clear that there is a paucity of data either to support any theory of the signal importance of large-scale hunting as a driving force in evolution millions of years ago or to suggest that it even existed earlier than about 100,000 years ago. Furthermore, studies from a number of disciplines suggest a variety of interpretations of data bearing on our evolutionary history....

ARCHEOLOGICAL EVIDENCE BEARING ON HUNTING: HUNTING AS SYMBOL AND RITUAL

The archeological record indicates that the oldest known definite stone artifacts date back to about 2 to 2.5 million years ago. These are small hand-sized stones from which flakes were chipped leaving edges that may have been used for cutting or scraping (Isaac and Leakey, 1979; Leakey and Lewin, 1977). There is no reason to infer that these tools were weapons used to kill animals. The earliest association of cutting or scraping tools with the bones of large animals dates to the period between 1.5 and 0.5 million years ago. It is assumed by most anthropologists and archeologists that they were used to remove the flesh from animals found dead, sick, or mired and unable to flee (Isaac, 1978; Leakey, 1971; Tanner and Zihlman, 1976; Zihlman, 1978). The earliest evidence of actual systematic hunting dates to a site 500,000 years old in Spain, where elephants were regularly mired and butchered in a narrow pass (Crompton, 1980; Tanner and

Zihlman, 1976). It was not until the Neanderthal period, 100,000 to 35,000 years ago, that the first composite tools appeared; that is, attached flaked stone heads or points to wooden shafts to make hafted axes or spears that could be used as projectile weapons to kill large animals for the kind and scale of hunting that is postulated to be the signal force in human cultural evolution (Fagan, 1980). The earliest undisputed evidence for hunting large animals with weapons, an elephant with a spear between its ribs, was found in a site dating back about 100,000 years (Tanner and Zihlman, 1976), and bows and arrows appeared only about 15,000 years ago. In contrast to the sites in Africa, Europe, and northern Asia, no archeological collections of animal bones and stone tools have been found in southeast Asia, even though the fossil evidence for hominids is abundant. Zihlman (1978) concludes that *Homo erectus* in southeast Asia relied on plant foods, insects, and small animals rather than large game animals.

In short, the fossil evidence suggests that upright, bipedal humans evolved without benefit of the social hunting of large animals from the time of *Ramapithecus* about 15 million years ago or *Australopithecus* of 3 to 4 million years ago to the point between *Homo erectus* of 500,000 years ago and *Homo sapiens neanderthalensis* of about 100,000 years ago, a period constituting over 99 percent of hominid evolutionary time. During that same period of time, the brain increased dramatically from the estimated 300 cc. size of *Ramapithecus* or the 400 to 600 cc. of various australopithecine and *Homo habilis* brains to the neanderthal *Homo sapiens* brain of 100,000 to 35,000 years ago, which is approximately the size of the average modern *Homo sapiens'* brain (1450 cc.). Thus, the hominid brain experienced a growth spurt beginning around 3 million years ago and was already levelling off when large-game social hunting evidently developed. The dramatic enlargement of the brain tapered off around the period (100,000 to 35,000 years ago) during

which a dramatic forward leap occurred in cultural complexity: not only large-scale cooperative hunting with hafted weapons, but also rituals, symbolization, language, representational art, and increased sophistication of toolmaking. Rather than being a cause of the uniquely human aspects of hominid evolution and the human mind, cooperative hunting appears to have been one of the cultural developments made possible by an advanced technology and a brain close to the capacity of modern *Homo sapiens*.

There is no denying, however, that once established among various peoples, cooperative social hunting itself became a significant culture force in evolving hominid societies. But this is not necessarily because of the features obviously intrinsic to hunting itself, such as the obtaining of meat for the diet. Meat as a dietary supplement had probably always been available and eaten in the form of small game (where it existed), gathered as a part of regular foraging activities, as in contemporary foraging societies. Nor would its significance necessarily lie, as has been claimed in the Man-the-Hunter theory, in its being the prime force generating uniquely human characteristics, such as language, planning, advanced toolmaking, and cooperation. These capacities had probably largely developed by the time large-scale hunting appeared. Rather, during the period between 100,000 and 35,000 years ago (the period during which ritual and symbolic systems appear in the archeological record), large animal cooperative hunting, mainly by men, may have begun to attain greater significance in some cultures for ritual and symbolic reasons. These ritual and symbolic meanings could be quite separate from the meat-obtaining rewards of hunting and, in any particular society, would have particular significance within the context of that society's history, ecology, technology, and symbolic system. The symbolic meanings could be related, for example, to the significance of male networks of cooperation and exchange or to the establishment of a male sphere of authority separate from the women's spheres of production and reproduction.

More specifically, it is possible that the development of large-scale hunting with hafted weapons as a male activity symbolized, embodied, and perhaps even advanced an important aspect of gender differentiation in the division of labor. Emerging, as it appears to have done, during the period when a quantitative leap forward occurred in tool and weapon technology, hunting may have represented (in some places or times) differential access by women and men to tools and weapons and to tool and weapon technology. While the specifics vary from one culture to another, Tabet (1982) argues that it is a common feature of contemporary preindustrial cultures—hunting-gathering, fishing, horticulture, and agriculture—that women are underequipped and a technological gap exists between women and men. This general characteristic manifests itself in a number of ways. In foraging societies, even when the major contribution to the group's subsistence is produced through women's work in gathering, hunting, or fishing, as is usually the case, women's tools are rudimentary—sticks and nets or baskets—while the more advanced tools—harpoons, spears, spearthrowers, axes, knives, bows and arrows, and boats—are made, used by, and reserved for men. While both women and men can and do use rudimentary tools, women, in general, are prohibited the use of weapons or weapon-tools and the use of the more complex instruments of production. Usually woman's main tool is the primitive digging stick or her bare hands for the gathering of plants, animals, or fish. Tabet emphasizes the importance of the male monopoly of weapons in hunting-gathering societies (or their prohibition to women) to the relations between the sexes, both because of the significance of weapons in themselves and because weapons, such as the spearthrower, often are also privileged and more advanced tools of production.

In horticulture and agriculture, the work of soil preparation, seeding, weeding, and harvesting is done by digging sticks and hoes, usually by women, but it may be done by women or men; where the plow is introduced, it becomes a male tool. The work of clearing the fields and building fences requires stone or metal axes, knives, or machetes, and these are used almost exclusively by men. Further, when tools can be activated by wind, water, or animals, they are used by men, while women continue such operations by hand with tools like grinding and pounding stones and sticks and mortar and pestle. Tabet describes another area of gender differentiation with respect to tools and labor that results in male control over women's production. Hard materials, such as metals, stone, bone, wood, and shell are worked exclusively by men in 94 percent (horn and shell) to 99.8 percent (metal) of contemporary foraging and other nonindustrial societies. Soft or pliable materials can be worked by women or men, using bare hands or crude tools, whereas hard materials require more advanced tools. This means that all tools and weapons are also made almost exclusively by men, including the tools of women, such as the primitive digging stick and mortar and pestle. Tabet's argument is that the sexual division of labor is always a relationship of control and is the result not the cause of differential use of and access to tools.

While we do not yet know when or how gender differentiations developed, archeologists interested in the origins of language have dated the development of symbolization, abstraction, and ritualization to the same period in which evidence appears, from other archeological findings I have cited, for large-game social hunting and advanced tool- and weaponmaking. It seems likely that these are relative evolutionary phenomena. I am suggesting that large-scale social hunting was one of the many ritualized forms in which gender differentiations began to develop in the period between 100,000 and 35,000 years ago, when the human capacities for symbolization, language, and ritualization fully appeared and when tool and weapon technology was sufficiently advanced to make differential access a social possibility.

PRIMATOLOGICAL EVIDENCE BEARING ON HUNTING

In theorizing about early hominid evolution of hand use with bipedal posture, it is reasonable to assume that early hominids continued, with increasing skill, to do those same activities that were part of the selection forces that favored upright posture and bipedal locomotion. We assume these activities primarily comprised food gathering—foraging for seeds, nuts, fruits, plants, and insects; digging for roots; and catching small animals first in forests, then in savanna-woodland-fringe forest areas over the hundreds of thousands or millions of years when forests were receding. Among present-day chimps, it has been estimated that about 95 percent of the diet consists of fruits and plants; 5 percent consists of insects, eggs, and small animals (Zihlman, 1976). Gorillas appear to be strict vegetarians. Individual chimpanzees forage, find, and eat their own food on the spot. Occasionally they carry animal prey to a tree to eat or carry nuts a short distance in order to break them open. Chimpanzees have been observed to use tools: stripped twigs, bark, or grasses to fish for termites and ants; rocks to crack open nuts and fruits; sticks to knock down bananas; crumpled leaves to mop up water from hollows or brains from the skulls of dead animals (Goodall, 1968).

In addition to the fact that chimpanzees prepare and use tools, occasionally walk upright, share food, and communicate social and environmental information, they also are similar to humans anatomically and genetically. Comparative studies of proteins, DNA, and chromosomes have shown a virtual identity of many of these molecules, suggesting to some molecular biologists an evolutionary

divergence between the two species about 5 to 6 million years ago (Sarich and Wilson, 1967). For these reasons chimpanzees may be viewed, though cautiously, as indicating some features and behaviors that may have characterized some hominid populations ancestral to Australopithecines and other hominids millions of years ago (Tanner and Zihlman, 1976). (I am not suggesting that this is because such behaviors have been genetically transmitted but rather may have been within the biological and social capacity of our ancestors.)

In his detailed critique of Man-the-Hunter theories of hominization (i.e., of the divergence of humans from apes) and of human behavioral evolution, Geza Teleki (1975) refutes what he considers to be myths of human uniqueness in subsistence patterns and the false dichotomizations made of the diets and subsistence behaviors of apes and humans. He sees the basic erroneous assumption to be that hunting behavior originated within the primate evolutionary sequence as a uniquely human pattern, which in turn generated other unique human behaviors. The myths and false dichotomizations that follow the assumption include the following: that humans are carnivores and great apes are frugivors (fruit-eaters) and vegetarians; that men hunt and apes do not; that men hunt cooperatively but apes do not; that the pursuit and capture of game requires an advanced technological base; that language is necessary for cooperative hunting; that men share or exchange meat and apes do not; that men transport meat and apes do not. Teleki focuses his attention in this analysis on Sub-Saharan Africa, a region extending from South Africa to Ethiopia and including a range of ecological conditions from desert to savanna to forests, where he and others have extensively studied chimpanzee and baboon behaviors. Since this is also the region presently inhabited by three well-studied gatherer-hunter populations— the Mbuti Pygmies, the Hadsa, and the Kalahari Desert !Kung—and formerly inhabited by our hominid ancestors whose fossil remains provide the most complete archeological record presently available for one area, Teleki was able to impose some historical and geographic continuity upon his analysis.

The first important observation Teleki makes is that with the exception of the specialized leaf-eating colobine monkey, primates—monkeys, apes, and humans—are omnivorous, with the generalized primate diet including leaves, buds, fruits, berries, bark, nuts, seeds and grains, roots and bulbs, honey, eggs, insects, fish and molluscs, reptiles, birds, and mammals. Meat constitutes only about 20 to 30 percent of the diet of most gatherer-hunter peoples, most of it in the form of small game that is collected or trapped. And just as humans are not carnivores but omnivores, so are monkeys and apes not vegetarians but also omnivores, since they eat meat too. Chimpanzees and baboons not only opportunistically seize and eat immobilized prey they happen to come across, but actively engage in the seeking out, pursuit, and capture of prey.

The next dichotomy Teleki refutes concerns cooperative hunting. He points out that most, but not all, hunting by humans is a solitary or paired activity, so that while group cooperative hunting occurs, it is by no means diagnostic of humans or essential for success. On the other hand, Teleki and others have observed many cases of adult chimpanzees in groups of two to five stalking prey together, coordinating their movements over long periods with great precision (although without vocalizations or gestures) until they had isolated and cornered their prey or decided, in some fashion not discernible to the human observers, to give up the chase. Once the predators catch, kill, and divide up the prey, each attracts a cluster of chimpanzees who request a share by a variety of gestures and characteristic vocalizations. These efforts to procure a share are successful more often than not. Teleki notes that food-sharing is the only aspect of the hunting process that is character-

ized by communications through vocalization and gesture. After the sharing process and the initial eating, individual chimpanzees have been seen carrying some of the prey around with them during the day or to the nest to eat at night. The sharing of meat among human hunters is variable, ranging from nonexistent to persistent. In short, chimpanzees cooperate in hunting, communicate requests, share and transport food.

Bringing together the recent evidence on the subsistence activities of contemporary baboons, chimpanzees, and humans in Africa, Teleki shows both the similarities as well as the differences existing among primate species that coexist in the same habitat. He suggests that prior to the time that hominids and possibly the great apes evolved, there was an evolutionary development beginning with omnivorous forest-dwelling primates among whom predation on mammals arose in some species. He argues that predation would have emerged at many spatial and temporal loci, appearing and disappearing within various populations before becoming fixed as a species trait. He furthermore believes that while environmental factors are, and probably always were, important in molding dietary habits at particular habitats, the occurrence, extent of, and social relationships around predation or hunting have also been influenced by social factors among all primates. It is these social factors that account in part for the observed differences in subsistence behaviors among primate species that live in the same habitat.

Thus, Teleki sees few qualitative or exclusive differences in subsistence behaviors between humans and apes but rather suggests:

The nutritional as well as behavioral components of primate subsistence can be scaled along a single spectrum whereupon some species may occupy shorter or longer segments than do others, but most occupy overlapping and interlocking segments rather than discrete intervals. No species, in other words, exhibits exactly the same subsistence parameters as does another species on the spectrum, yet each species holds some features in common with all other species. For instance, the Gombe chimpanzees differ from the Kalahari bushmen in some specific patterns (e.g., weapon technology), but their collector-predator and gatherer-hunter lifestyles overlap on many broad patterns (e.g., cooperation in pursuit, distribution of meat). Our assumptions about man as the hunter of game and about ape as the collector of plants seem, as a result, to be no longer tenable, and since it was these assumptions which formed our current concepts of human origins and evolution, the concepts themselves may no longer be tenable. (p. 155)

His analysis and conclusion leave open the possibility, as I suggested previously, that the unique contribution that humans made to hunting, in some cultures at least, was not the technology advancement of a basic subsistence activity, but rather its elevation to an activity endowed with symbolic and ritual significance and meanings....

SUMMARY AND CONCLUSIONS

No single factor or event, such as hunting or gathering, carrying devices or campsites, tool-use, food-exchange, or language can in itself provide *the* key to human evolution. They all represent interdependent stages of hominid development, appearing variably in different populations of prehistoric hominids, and each is a product of many interrelated processes. The degree to which any behavioral complex became developed or significant for any society was (or is in today's gatherer-hunter societies) highly variable depending on that society's particular ecological, demographic, historic, social circumstances, and symbolic systems.

One has but to read accounts of our prehistory (see for example, Fagan, 1980) to begin to appreciate the diversity of subsistence patterns and social subsistence organization developing within the varied conditions of extreme ecological variations. Thus, within Africa, for example, economic specialization arose from environmental necessity. Foraging

bands on the shores of lakes and rivers lived by fishing; those in the open savanna captured game and gathered seasonally in woodlands; and those in rain forests relied on plant foods. Peoples in frigid zones live by the hunting of sea and land mammals. In addition, ecological diversity was drastically modified over many parts of the earth's surface, over time spans of tens or hundreds of thousands of years, with periods of glaciation and shifts in rainfall patterns that had significant effects on game populations and grasses (Fagan, 1980). Clearly in some areas and time periods, obtaining meat was and is essential to survival, just as vegetable foods or fish have been critical in others.

Subsistence activities within any particular habitat, whether hunting, gathering, or fishing, could have generated both the social communication and cooperativeness and the technological innovativeness that survival in particular circumstances might have required: digging sticks, stones pounders, choppers and grinders, and carrying receptacles for gathering; hooks, nets and eventually harpoons for fishing; clubs, rocks, stone flaked tools, and eventually spears and bows and arrows for hunting. Many of these innovations appeared only in the past 100,000 years, such as composite or hafted weapons, or as late as 15,000 years ago, such as bows and arrows. Nomadic foragers, with diverse subsistence techniques, constituted all the peoples of the earth until the period between 15,000 and 10,000 years ago when sedentarism and domestication of plants and animals began to develop in some parts of the world. By 2000 years ago, nomadic foragers had become a minority (Fagan, 1980) but still exist today in Africa, Australia, and elsewhere.

It is important to avoid single-cause theories of human evolution (or any other human phenomena), since they interfere with our ability to see and seek relevant data that could lead to some unforeseen and unpredetermined conclusions. They also impede our efforts to understand the complex processes and interrelationships and the non-uniform course that characterize human cultural evolution. The Man-the-Hunter theory has been such a conceptual framework, which straight-jackets observations, interpretations, and understanding. One reason for its attractiveness and uncritical acceptance may be that it neatly ties together a number of puzzling and disparate phenomena of modern social existence: women's economic dependence on men, the sexual division of labor, war, and male aggressivity. Yet therein lies its central flaw. In the effort to explain the *origins* of present-day gender-associated behaviors and social arrangements, popular theories of human evolution, such as Man-the-Hunter, start with implicit assumptions about the biological basis of such behaviors and characteristics and the existence of a woman's "nature" and a man's "nature." They then reconstruct earliest evolutionary history according to an idealized image of modern industrial societies. Their central actor is the fearless, aggressive, creative, and dominant male, who generated civilization and, through his bonding and hunting with other men, fed and protected the passive, dependent, subordinate female, who generated babies. They postulate for their prehistoric model the very conditions that they are presumably attempting to understand and explain—the sexual division of labor with women as economic dependents and men as providers and doers. However, the record, inadequate as it is, strongly suggests that someone besides man was also evolving, and that she, too, was very busy.

One also suspects that the origins and consequent popularity of the Man-the-Hunter theory of evolution reflect other common ethnocentric views. Since meat-eating is a central preoccupation and seems always to have been important in our recorded Western civilizations, it is assumed to have always been central to human diets everywhere if not to survival itself. Since hunting for sport or for sustenance has been primarily a male pursuit in written history and in today's world, it has been invested with much significance and is assumed to have always been a male accomplishment of central importance to the evolution of human civilization.

While foragers may always have gathered and eaten small animals, if they were available, along with plant food, the archeological record suggests that large-scale cooperative hunting with hafted weapons developed only about 100,000 years ago. This was at the beginning of the Neanderthal period and the Mousterian culture, during which rituals, complex symbolization, representational art, perhaps language, and complex tools also appeared. I have suggested that big game social hunting may have begun at that time to assume particular cultural significance for symbolic or ritual reasons, and that these may have been related to the emergence of differential access to tools and weapons and tool-weapon technology, sexual divisions of labor, and other gender asymmetries.

REFERENCES

Beach, F. Behavioral endocrinology and the study of reproduction. The fifth annual Carl G. Hartman Lecture. The society for the study of reproduction. 1974. (a)

Beach, F. Human sexuality and evolution. In W. Montagna and W. Sadler (Eds.), *Reproductive behavior.* New York: Plenum, 1974. (b)

Beach, F. Sociobiology and interspecific comparisons of behavior. In M. S. Gregory, A. Silvers, & D. Sutch (Eds.), *Sociobiology and human nature.* San Francisco: Jossey-Bass, 1978.

Crompton, R. Old bones shatter hunter myths. *Science for the people,* 1980, 12, 5–34.

Fagan, B. M. *People of the earth. An introduction to world prehistory.* New York: Little, Brown, 1980.

Fox, R. *Kinship and marriage.* Baltimore: Penguin, 1967.

Goodall, J. The behavior of free-living chimpanzees in the Gombe Stream Reserve. *Animal Behaviour Monographs*, 1968, *1*, 165–311.

Haraway, D. Animal sociology and a natural economy of the body politic, part I: a political physiology of dominance. *Signs*, 1978, *4*, 21–36.

Haraway, D. Animal sociology and a natural economy of the body politic, part II: The past is the contested zone: human nature and theories of production and reproduction in primate behavior studies. *Signs*, 1978, *4*, 37–60.

Hewes, G. Hominid bipedalism: independent evidence for the food-carrying theory. *Science*, 1964, *146*, 416–418.

Isaac, G. The food-sharing behavior of protohuman hominids. *Scientific American*, 1978, *238*, 90–108.

Isaac, G., and Leakey, R. *Human ancestors*. San Francisco: Freeman, 1979.

Leakey, M. *Olduvai gorge excavations in bed I and I, 1960–1963*. Cambridge: Cambridge University Press, 1971.

Leakey, R., and Lewin, R. *Origins*. New York: Dutton, 1971.

Lee, R., and DeVore, I. *Kalahari hunter-gatherers*. Cambridge: Harvard University Press, 1976.

Sarich, V., and Wilson, A. Immunological time scale for hominid evolution. *Science*, 1967, *158*, 1200–1203.

Slocum, S. Woman the gatherer: male bias in anthropology. In R. R. Reiter (Ed.), *Toward an anthropology of women*. New York: Monthly Review Press, 1975.

Tabet, P. Hands, tools, weapons. *Feminist Issues*, 1982, 2, 3–62.

Tanner, N. *On becoming human*. Cambridge: Cambridge University Press, 1981.

Tanner, N., and Zihlman, A. Women in evolution. Part I: Innovation and selection in human origins. *Signs*, 1976, *1*, 585–608.

Teleki, G. Primary subsistence patterns: Collector-predators and gatherer-hunters. *Journal of Human Evolution*, 1975, *4*, 125–184.

Washburn, S., and Lancaster, C. S. The evolution of hunting. In R. B. Lee and I. DeVore (Eds.), *Kalahari hunter-gatherers*. Cambridge: Harvard University Press, 1976.

Wilson, E. O. *Sociobiology: the new synthesis*. Cambridge, MA: Harvard University Press, 1975.

Zihlman, A. Sexual dimorphism and its behavioral implications in early hominids. In P. V. Tobias and Y. Coppens (Eds.), *Les plus anciens hominides*. Paris: C.N.R.S., 1976.

Zihlman, A. Women in evolution, part II: subsistence and social organization among early hominids. *Signs*, 1978, *4*, 4–20.

Athena Unbound: Barriers to Women in Academic Science and Engineering

HENRY ETZKOWITZ   *MICHAEL NEUSCHATZ*
CAROL KEMELGOR   *BRIAN UZZI*

The data traditionally relied upon to gauge the relative standing of women in science and engineering programs measures educational outcomes using simple attainment rates at different rungs on the academic ladder.[1] In absolute figures, the drop was from 230,000 women taking high school physics to less than 1,000 earning physics bachelors degrees to less than 100 earning physics PhDs in 1987. For men, the drop was from 390,000 men taking high school physics, to 4,400 earning bachelors degrees, to 1,000 earning PhDs. The kind of data that might help to explain why women disappear from one rung measurement to the next (such as tracking representative samples of women students over time to highlight critical points of attrition, evaluation of particular aspects of academic programs in terms of their impact on retention of women students, and so forth) and describe what happens to them beyond the simple fact of their disappearance (for example, specific reasons for leaving, and final academic and career destinations), have rarely been collected, due largely to an historical lack of interest and the need to conduct case studies, an unfashionable methodology (Mitchell, 1983).

The initial research site is classified as a Carnegie I research university (Boyer, 1987). Four science and engineering departments were selected for examination, including two basic sciences, physics and chemistry; an engineering discipline, electrical engineering; and a hybrid discipline, computer science,[2] to determine the receptivity of their cultures to women graduate students and faculty members.

Three hundred and fifty current students and 76 dropouts were identified in the four departments, along with 198 students who received their doctorates within the past five years. There are 117 faculty members including five women: two each in computer science and physics, and one in chemistry. At the time faculty data were collected, there was one tenured woman in the four departments. During the course of the study, another was granted tenure, she was apparently the first to be accorded permanent status in the engineering school.[3]

We collected data from departmental academic records on advisers and advisees and interviewed female and male faculty members, female graduate students and academic administrators. The quantitative data consists of a listing of current graduate students, along with PhD recipients over the last five years, paired with their main faculty advisers, although from one of the departments, Electrical Engineering, data on PhD recipients only spans the past two years.

Supplementing this, data were also gathered for students who dropped out of their programs prior to earning their doctorate. In the Computer Science and Physics departments, drop-out information was obtained for the previous five years, while in Chemistry it spans three years, and in Electrical Engineering only one. (However, since Physics students are not assigned a faculty adviser until after they have completed two years, adviser data were missing for those who dropped out of the program before this point. In Electrical Engineering, drop-out data were provided only for the prior year and it also did not include students who left after failing a qualifying exam administered after their first few months in the program.)

The qualitative data consists of 46 interviews with faculty, graduate student and administrator informants. Twenty five interviews were conducted with currently attending and recently graduated female PhD students within the physics, chemistry, electrical engineering and computer science departments. All five female faculty members were interviewed. Two recent former women faculty members, who are currently faculty members at other universities, were also interviewed.

Interviews were conducted with eight male faculty members who had been identified by chairs or graduate students as having either particularly good or poor relations with female graduate students. Chairs were interviewed to ascertain any special departmental policies concerning the recruitment of women (there were none). In addition, interviews were conducted with the administrators in the engineering and graduate schools.

Women's experience as faculty members and graduate students was studied in the same four disciplines at a public research university. A department of molecular biology with a critical mass of women faculty was studied at a third university to give a total of nine departments. This article primarily reports on the qualitative findings from the initial site.

BARRIERS TO ENTRY

Barriers against professional women have been framed in two different ways, emphasizing two stages at which obstacles might occur:

- A threshold 'beyond which gender no longer matters.' Women encounter difficulties advancing in a field but the obstacles fall away once a certain status is attained;
- A 'glass ceiling of gender-specific obstacles to advancement into top positions.' There is a particular career level women may attain at which point a blockage occurs to further advancement, for instance women are handicapped in attaining full professorship in science departments at leading universities (Sonnert, 1990).

The 'threshold effect' presumes that women only face barriers in the early stages of their career while the 'glass ceiling' presumes barriers only at the higher levels of careers.

We find that at all stages of the academic ladder women face barriers to entry and achievement. We have identified a series of mechanisms that mitigate against the progress of women in academic careers in science and engineering. First, the normal working of everyday features of academic science, such as advising patterns, have the unintended consequence of excluding women. Secondly, the negative effects of these academic norms are amplified by such extra-academic factors as the differential socialization of men and women. Thirdly, there are sources of subtle and not-so subtle bias derived from the taken-for-granted male model of doing science that also discourage women from full participation.

Needless to say these characteristics are often intertwined and a phenomenon discussed in one category of analysis will also overlap into another. We discuss examples of each of these three types of barriers to entry into scientific careers and offer suggestions as to how they can be eliminated or at least lowered.

Adviser–Advisee Relationships

In graduate school, students are expected to develop a close working relationship with their faculty adviser, a relationship that lasts several years and is crucial to the progress of the student through the program and out into the professional world. Previous researchers have identified negative interactional patterns in male advisers' relationships with their female graduate students that "...lessens their opportunity for advancement" (Frank-Fox, 1989, page 226). We also found a series of gender-related blockages to successful advisement. At best, there was an attempt at equal treatment based upon the faulty assumption that women had been socialized and educated the same as men. At worst, women graduate students were stereotyped as less capable, uncompetitive and were viewed as non-scientists. Such advisers simply could not take women seriously as graduate students.

Barriers to women deriving from the structure of the academic system are reinforced by 'cumulative disadvantage' factors that excluded other women from science but also carry over and affect the academic careers of women. These include the differential socialization of men and women, impaired self-confidence and expectations regarding the impact of children on women's academic careers.

The roots of this problem lie in the different gender experiences of boys and girls. As young girls and women, females are socialized to seek help and be help givers rather than be self-reliant, function autonomously or competitively, as are boys. Girls are encouraged to be good students in so far as they expect to be given a task, complete it well and then receive a reward from an authority figure. In graduate school, behavior is expected to be independent, strategic and void of interpersonal support.

These expectations are antithetical to traditional female socialization. In addition, the needs of women, based on socialization which encourages supportive interaction with teachers, is frowned upon by many male and some female faculty as indicative of inability. As a female graduate student put it: "The men have the attitude of why should people need their hands held?" Lack of a supportive environment exacerbates problems of an often already low level of self-confidence.

Many women come into graduate programs in science with a low degree of self-confidence. Women in physics, chemistry, and computer science reported that their graduate school experience further eroded their level of self-confidence. A female graduate student described the following symptoms: "Women couch their words with all these qualifiers [because they are so insecure] . . . 'I'm not sure, but maybe . . .'"

One female graduate student said: "I have the symptoms of the insecure woman. A comment from a professor can cripple me. I would be self-deprecating. My science is different because of my socialization, not my gender." Another woman reported that: "Women tend to measure themselves: 'Am I allowed to do this?' 'This I know and this I don't know.' 'This I should be ashamed I don't know.'"

If things are working out well, initial lack of self-confidence is not too important, but if problems arise then negative feelings come forth. For example, one woman had this to say, "It is much worse if a woman fails an exam because her self-confidence is so low. I got an A– on an exam and was upset. The man sitting next to me got a C and he said, 'so what.'" Another woman described the invidious comparisons that she began to make if things were not going well:

> If I'm not feeling good about myself, I start comparing myself to these brilliant people [highly qualified foreign students]. They are premier. It doesn't affect American males as much. Women have less confidence in certain abilities. [There are] certain things I've had no prior experience with, mechanical things which are no problem once you do them. But they are barriers.

Finally, if the barriers remain high, low self-confidence translates into an increased rate of attrition. A female graduate student said, "Women often have less confidence in their own ability. Then, if the environment seems hostile, they say, 'I can't function here,' and quit."

Such attrition can therefore be viewed as a result of an accumulative thwarting of the development of a viable professional identity. Even those who do not give up often reduce their professional aspirations.

Not surprisingly, low self-confidence in conjunction with lack of a viable professional identity produces reduced aspirations. A male faculty member said of his female students:

> Their job aspirations are so low, their self-confidence is so low, they tend not to apply for what they see as a very tough place. Quite good people can come in here and fail to get tenure. It takes a lot of self-confidence. Women carry less self-confidence than men, that's a problem.

Male faculty can exacerbate or mitigate the effects of traditional female socialization, depending upon their awareness, sensitivity and political stance on sex roles. There are two types of men in science with respect to women:

- Those who follow the male model with negative consequences for women;
- Those who are aware of the deleterious effect of the male model on women and who attempt to avert its worst consequences for their female advisees.

Female experiences with male advisers range from denigrative to supportive. On the negative side are interactions that leave women with doubt about their self-worth. Even though this adviser probably thought that he was allaying concerns, the effect was the reverse.

> He said to me, 'you don't have anything to worry about, they want women so you'll pass [the quals].' You have the feeling, 'Am I here because I'm a woman or because I am qualified?' It's like they take away all your achievements.

A woman graduate student reported that: "I never got close to any [faculty]. I felt I couldn't go to any of them." This alienation has been reported to impede women's progress (Frank-Fox, 1989, page 226). Women also discussed specific negative incidents of gender-related presumptions of lack of scientific ability. For example, a female student was talking to a professor about her problems and he said she was an 'emotional female.' "I couldn't believe he was thinking that. Maybe he was thinking I shouldn't be in physics. I always thought he was a nice guy. That's when I feel it: I'm out there on my own." In another instance:

> If I didn't know the answer to something, [my adviser said], 'Just do the experiment, don't do the theory.' Do this, do that, 'I can't believe you're so stupid.' It had a very bad effect on my self-confidence. You're a piece of shit. Go win one for the team. I think guys tend to respond to this, like being on a football team.

In another instance: "[My adviser] told me to pretend I was in my kitchen at my counter...'Listen, honey, you should be this, you should be that.'"

Attempts to find an analogy to the traditional female role for women in the laboratory are in accord with the thesis that academia is a 'male milieu' in which women's presence is viewed as disruptive and threatening. These 'degradation ceremonies' may be followed up by subtle and not-so-subtle attempts to eliminate the unwanted presence. For example, one woman commented:

> When I was trying to get something to work, [my adviser] would come up to me and say, 'did you see it yet? Did you see it yet?' Every day he would say, 'did you see it?' I should have stopped it, but sometimes it takes a long time to see what's going on. It was very humiliating.

In the following instance a presumption of failure was established at the outset:

> There was this woman who joined this group and [her adviser] sat her down and said, 'look, if you're going to join my group I don't want to know that you're going to leave in six months.' Of course this woman ended up leaving.

It is not only male advisers' treatment of female students that affects their situation but also how male advisers instruct their male students to act toward women. A female graduate student said:

> I hear rumors about myself...being involved with somebody. [I heard that] a faculty member was advising his students that it might be interesting to have an affair with me.

These frequent negative instances are complemented by occasions when men have served as successful advisers to women. A sensitive male adviser helped a student make future decisions based on the reality of being a woman within the field:

> His attitude toward women is very understanding, very supportive, without being condescending. He doesn't say 'I understand what's going on' which is offensive because it's hard for a man to understand what's going on. He doesn't bring these issues up, I bring them up. He is very politically aware. He'll say, 'don't talk to _____ because he's Greek.' Sometimes [his advice] was because of sexism and sometimes because this person was an arrogant son of a bitch and sometimes because this is a good person, but is just not comfortable with women.

Women report that the best advisers are encouraging, give you concrete directions and show you the ropes. As an older physics student said: "I enjoy being around people who can work the system because I don't understand the system." Women's relative lack of knowledge of how to negotiate the academic system was called into attention by a woman faculty member who explained that many women lacked a strategy to deal with the admissions process:

> What you're supposed to do is get a hold of the brochure and if you want to get in at least say that's what you want. The women don't seem to have grasped that...the men go down the list and say, I want to work with this professor for this reason, that professor for that reason...the females give me no indication that they have even looked at the brochure.

Without an adviser who is willing to encourage and be directive, women are often unable to puzzle out the strategies necessary to get through graduate school. Most women are not socialized to understand the political strategies necessary to advance within the academic system. As one woman put it:

> Part of the game of getting through graduate school is perceiving what the game rules are. One is not presented a list of the rules, it's up to one to divine the rules. The people from the same culture, background and sex seem to do better figuring out the rules.

These and other culture conflicts result in the discouragement of many women graduate students and young faculty members from pursuing careers at the highest academic levels.

Impact of Family

It is no surprise that pregnancy and childbearing still have negative consequences for women in the world of work in the United States (Gerson, 1985). However, the impacts appear to be especially strong in academic science, given its structural features that mandate virtually exclusive attention to research achievement during the years that coincide with fertility. Realization of what lies ahead sometimes deflects women from pursuing the PhD.

A woman engineer speaking to a colloquium at a private research university organized to encourage women students to pursue engineering careers advised them to seek jobs in industry after the BA. She said that once they were established in their group, industry would accommodate part-time work or work at home during child-bearing and early child-rearing years. She said that she had chosen not to pursue a PhD because she wanted to have her children before she was 30.

Marriage and children negatively impact women's careers in academic science at three key time periods: having a child during graduate school, marriage at the point of seeking a job, and pregnancy prior to tenure. In addition, we found some disparagement of marriage during the graduate student career. Women, but not men, are sometimes thought to be less than serious about their science if they do not stay single while in graduate school. As a female graduate student recalled:

> When I first interviewed to come here, I was single. On my first day of walking into this department I had an engagement ring on my finger. [My adviser's] attitude was 'families and graduate programs don't go together very well.' First he was worried I was going to blow my first year planning my wedding. I got a lot of flack about that and so did other women...teasing. 'So and so's not going to get much work done this semester because she'll be planning her wedding' [sarcastically]. The guys don't plan weddings.

Earlier in the century, marriage was grounds for a woman's expected retirement from a faculty position. The mutual exclusion of academic and family life has a long history. Until well into the 19th century, Oxbridge male academics were also expected to choose between academic career and marriage. Nevertheless, there have been few, if any, residual carryovers from the male academic celibate role. Even when a choice between academic career and family is no longer an official require-

ment, the presumption that each role requires a woman's total attention still survives. It next surfaces when children are contemplated or arrive.

Women graduate students expect that they will be penalized for having children. One informant visualized her adviser's and the department's reaction:

> If I had walked into _____'s office and said I was pregnant, they would have been happy for me as a woman, but in their list of priorities as to who to get out of the program and who to support I would have plummeted to the bottom of the list.

These concerns arise because the existing academic structure is ill equipped to deal with pregnancy. Pregnancy is discouraged and graduate women who have children are encouraged to take leaves of absence that tend to become permanent withdrawal. In one department an informant reported that: "The only one left is _____ [of the students who has a child]. Two women PhDs who got pregnant were strongly encouraged to take leaves of absence. One did and one did not come back." In another department a female graduate student reported that:

> One person took a leave of absence to get married and asked her adviser if she had a child would she be able to work part-time and he told her, 'Absolutely not. No way.' What if I should want to do something like that? Is it the end of my career in _____? Was it just the adviser? What am I going to do with my life? People say they're not going to have children until they're 40 and have tenure. I can't think like that. Thinking about [these] details is what scares me. That's when I think I should drop out.

Graduate student women were caught in a bind, wanting to have children and, while doing so, wanting to show that they could keep up with the pace of graduate work. A female faculty member reported that:

> I had one student who was having her child in the middle of the semester and was to take and pass her qualifiers at the end of the semester. She wanted to do it. I said, 'don't do it'...because of the emotional

state you are in and the physical state after having a baby. We discussed this at length at one of our meetings . . . she ended up not doing it.

One department had taken child-bearing into account to a limited extent:

During evaluations, if a PhD [student] has a child she will be given some leeway for that semester . . . I think that's pretty funny . . . it's such a small amount of time. I think the women should get more leeway, you're physically out of it. It should be longer . . . at least a year. What's the big deal. [In one case, a student] . . . had the baby in November and had until the end of the semester. It was partly her fault as well; she did not want to say she could do less. The faculty gave her a choice of doing a part-time thing or keeping up to pace. She chose to be put to the same standard as everyone else.

A peer had a somewhat different view of the faculty's action and described an unusual instance of solidarity among women graduate students:

She decided not to take a leave [when she had the child] and made the decision at the end of the semester when we are all evaluated. She got a particularly harsh letter, [the faculty] essentially threatened to cut her support. They gave her requirements that would not be achievable for anybody . . . even without a baby. Two people had left the department earlier in the semester. One was a new mother, the other was a man who was very involved with his family. We got the feeling this was being done to discourage her and tell her to go away. She was encouraged by her husband and a number of us to renegotiate this because it was clearly off base and came out of the blue.

The expectation that women students will succumb to the pressures of child-bearing and child-rearing makes some male and female faculty wary of taking on women students in the first place, especially since funding is tight and every place must be made to count. Another female faculty member stated that,

If a student had a baby with her, I wouldn't have her. Students who have babies here get no work done. It's not that I wouldn't take a woman with a child in the first place, but the first sign of trouble,

I would just tell them to go away. If my students fail it looks bad for me.

Women who survive the strain of lack of support for child-bearing and -rearing in academia and complete their degrees at the highest levels of achievement may nevertheless find that their career will not survive the next hurdle of the academic career path. Two shifts in work site: from PhD program to post-doctoral position in a different university and from post-doctoral to yet another work site are expected. The highest climbers on the academic ladder of success are able to accept the most promising and prestigious post-doctoral and faculty positions without regard to any other consideration. The rule of intellectual exogamy has disastrous career consequences for many women who are unable or unwilling to make individualistic locational decisions. As one observer put it (Rosenfeld, 1984, page 99):

The academic market is a national one. Those who do not accommodate their choice of geographical location and willingness to move to their careers may lose out.

The next impediment is at the point of the job search. When a married woman is about to attain the PhD, the 'two body' problem comes into play, typically deflecting women's careers from their highest potential. A male faculty member discussed the situation of:

Another woman I encouraged incredibly, she's a good example of where the problem can be. She was an NSF fellow. She married a male student here who was also an NSF fellow. The two of them went on the job market at the same time and they were around looking for jobs, but it turned out that most places liked one of them and not the other: it was not always the same one that they liked and nobody wanted to offer her a job and say well he can just take his chances. There was a place that offered him a job and said well she can just take her chances and they eventually decided to do that.
 . . . he took an academic job and she went into a company which is not a bad job but I think it's not as good a job as she should have had. But it was considered, both by the school that made the offer

and to some extent by them, [that] it was OK for her to make a compromise on the career but they would never have asked him to do it so she ended up the victim on this: a clear double standard.

Marriage and children are generally viewed by male faculty members as impediments to a scientific career for women. Even those most supportive of women note that:

I've had some disappointments with very good women who settled for jobs that are less than an equivalent man would do. You have some extremely good people you think are going to go out and make a mark and then somehow or other they marry somebody and spend their time in a bad career. For a man to decide not to take his career seriously is like admitting he takes drugs. For a woman to say she puts her family ahead of her career is considered a virtue; the pressures are all in that direction. The women are told, 'Isn't this wonderful. You are giving up your career to sacrifice for your husband.' The pressures come from society, relatives, to some extent the men involved, the parents of the husband.

On the other hand, a few women take a different tack. They are willing to break off personal relationships that interfere with accepting the best possible job. A male professor portrayed the situation of a woman, involved with a man, whom he said,

. . . could have gone either way. I asked her, 'to what extent is his career going to interact with what you do?' She said, 'Not at all, I want to find the best job I can and if it works out for him OK and if it doesn't well then that's the end of the relationship.' So she had decided that career is what really mattered. She's at [prestigious eastern university] and he's still out in California so that's the end of him. That was a decision she made. She took what I would say is a typically man's approach to things, that the career is the primary decision, but they don't all do that.

Even when a woman is willing to make the optimum locational decision based solely on career grounds; she may be constrained by the entanglements of the family circumstances of her mate. A woman faculty member in our sample contemplating marriage to a man with children from a previous marriage, who was required by a divorce agreement to limit his geographical mobility, found that she had to change her work site. In this instance, the site was an equally prestigious university so there was no loss in academic status.

Universities are seldom eager to hire both husband and wife in the same department. Given a situation in which the departmental work site tends to become a place where graduate students find marriage partners, disciplinary endogamy is not reflected in hiring practices. At the time of the study, a search for Chair was underway at one department in our sample. The leading candidate's wife was also seeking a position at a junior level. Even though she was regarded as eminently qualified for a line available in her area and the administration was willing to approve both hirings, faculty members' objections to bringing in both husband and wife overrode all other considerations.

Whenever one set of specific objections was taken into account such as removing the chair from oversight of review decisions concerning his wife by sending them directly to the Dean, new objections would be raised. The departmental culture was resistant to accommodating a dual career family. Department members believed that a married couple would bring a heightened level of personal relationships into the department and that this would be inevitably disruptive, beyond the usual friendship patterns and cliques of academic life.

Given the presumption of geographical mobility as a prerequisite for academic mobility, women typically suffer severe deleterious impacts to their career from the workings of this academic norm. Of course, there are no logical but only cultural reasons why the norm differentially impacts males and females. The requirements of intellectual exogamy illustrate how the genderization of society affects science and how presumed neutral requirements have a male bias built in.

As more men are married to women whose careers are important to them, male geographical mobility will also be slowed. As both men and women face geographical constraints on their job choices it can be predicted that the link between career success and ability to change work site will be weakened. Departments that made exceptions and hired their own female graduates, provided a significant, and at times essential, career boost for women who otherwise might have been shunted aside from research careers in academia due to locational constraints.

Finally, ... [after one attains] faculty status, children come into play again as a negative factor affecting the academic career, the 'three body' problem.... A faculty member [who has a child] is sometimes viewed as ...[having]...a lack of commitment to science, almost tantamount to declaring one's allegiance to a pseudoscience such as astrology or phrenology. During a pregnancy, while at another university, a woman faculty member felt that male colleagues were:

> ...jealous of my motherhood. They hoped I was going to stop. They made comments like, 'you should be at home resting, you are doing more than you can do.' They were astonished I was pregnant.

A faculty member's tenure review has caused an added measure of anxiety. She said:

> When it comes to the real facts that's when you feel discrimination. The pregnancy worries me. It's the wrong moment, always, the wrong moment. It puts you on a slower track. Maybe they do see it like that. Maybe I've ruined my chances. They want you to sacrifice something. If the baby hadn't shown up, I would have pushed for an early decision. Now I will wait.

Even under the best of circumstances the academic structure is resistant to accommodating family needs. A female faculty member in one department was able to arrange a modest reduced percentage of official time commitment involving a reduced teaching load. She reported that in her department: "The faculty

have been very supportive of me having children. After my review I've had people say, 'How can you do that and have children too?'" This professor adopted the strategy of reducing her work load and lengthening the time period before the tenure decision. She said that:

> The university policy allows you to work part-time to have children ... that part-time work stops the tenure clock for the percentage of time you are not working. Because of tenure, I didn't want to cut my [research] back by 50%, so I made an arrangement to work 70% and cut the teaching load. I could have done it [full time] with children, but I wouldn't have enjoyed it ... appreciated it. However, everybody assumed, including the chairman, that this time off would not count for tenure. A year before I was supposed to come up for tenure the chairman brought it up to the provost because [it was found that] the clock was still running. If it had stopped, I should have had an extra year before I was up for tenure so I would have more time to publish and get my research done. I decided not to fight it because I was concerned how going through a fight would affect the tenure decision. I was quite worried when the case went before the engineering school who are all older men who were looking at me not having worked full time.

In this instance, the outcome was favorable but the anxiety level, normally high about tenure prospects, had been raised even further by the difficulties that the academic structure had in recognizing the presence of children in her life. A few years later she was involved in an effort in the Senate of her university to make reduction in work load for women with children an official option. Some of the responses reported during the debate on the issue, that it should be among a list of limited choices in fringe benefits or equally available to men and therefore too costly to be made available at all, suggests that the academic system is still resistant to accommodating women's needs.

What is the response of women to the strictures of academic life? A majority of women graduate students in all departments studied, reported that they intended to pursue an industrial, rather than an academic, career since it was more compatible with family life. As an informant, comparing the two scenes, concluded:

> Women will go in to industry. It's 9 to 5. It's more flexible. They have day-care and child-care. There are federal rules they have to abide by in terms of maternity leave, whereas in academia you're on your own, and where there are rules to protect you, you are not protected by your peers who are saying, 'she hasn't been here in six months, she's not current with the literature.' The support systems exist [in industry] and it's the only way you can [have a family].

Of those who aspired to academia, most were interested in jobs in small teaching colleges rather than research universities because as one woman summed it up: "Science isn't everything." In recent years, two women had resigned their positions to take appointments at teaching colleges where they felt they could be respected as individuals and not have to confront a discriminatory environment. Given that the total number of women faculty in these departments was so small, even two women constitute a significant proportion of the total number.

Differential Treatment

As part of the cumulative thwarting of a female professional identity, devaluation of women's scientific contributions has been found to be widespread (Benjamin, 1991). It takes many forms including crediting the male partner in scientific collaborations and ignoring the work of women (Scott, 1990). At our primary research site, despite a formal and even at times a strongly stated commitment to non-discriminatory treatment of women, discrimination was manifested informally. For example, a female graduate student reported differential treatment of men's and women's contributions: "In group meetings I get the sense that if a woman says something, 'OK' and that's the end of that." On the other hand, male contributions were exaggerated:

> When I joined the group there was one man. When there were more men, it seemed that the women's statements weren't entirely ignored, but if a man said something, even completely off the wall and even stupid, [the professor] would find some way to twist it into something good. He would make this great effort for the men. Our immediate reaction was complete shock...and annoyance.

Sometimes women are devalued by not being included in events. A female graduate student reported that invisibility was imposed when: "If you have a visitor to the lab, the professor introduces the male students, but does not you." Another reported self-imposed invisibility in reaction to expectations that her contributions would not be valued:

> [In lab meetings] you feel very self-conscious saying what you think and I think it's because you are a woman. They would just as soon you would sit back and be quiet and when they ask you if it turned red or green, [you say] 'it turned red,' rather than saying 'it turned red and this is what we're going to do next.'

Women found it too difficult to be taken seriously as professionals outside the department as well. One said that: "If I go to conferences, if I ask a question, the answer gets addressed to a man in the room. It's worse in physics than in other fields." A female graduate student reported her response to being ignored: "It's always a thing where being invisible, you don't exist...It was a sense I didn't exist."

Other times, women are made to feel different by being given excessive visibility. A female graduate student reported that a professor was: "...addressing the class, 'Gentlemen'...and then made a big pause and looked at me and added, 'and lady.' I was different. Other people noticed it..."

Still other times women are patronized. A female graduate student told how: "I was sitting at this table and he kept referring to us as 'my girls.' In that context I didn't like it. He was thinking of us differently. He didn't say, 'my boys.'" At the public university, many graduate women felt that they were treated as 'one of the boys' but this was an unsatisfactory resolution as well, since differences between men and women with respect to childbearing were not taken into account.

ALTERNATIVE ROLE MODELS

Essentially, women are expected to follow a 'male model' of academic success involving a total time commitment to scientific work and aggressive competitive relations with peers. There are two contrasting 'ideal typical' responses to this situation by women graduate students and faculty members. We have identified two types of responses from women scientists to gender issues:

- Women who follow the male model and expect other women to also; and
- Women who attempt to delineate an alternative model, allowing for a balance between work and private spheres.

A relatively few women are willing to adapt to the male model of academic science, involving an aggressive, competitive stance and an unconditional devotion to work at least until tenure. Instead, most attempt to define a women's academic model, balancing work and non-work roles, with an emphasis by faculty members on co-operation at the work site among members of their research group (Kemelgor, 1989). This has resulted in two distinctive female scientist roles: 'instrumentals' and 'balancers.' Even when these models are in conflict with each other, they offer women students a range of possibilities to choose among.

Instrumentals are able to act independently and strategically. A female faculty member described her strategy for getting through graduate school:

When I went to grad school I specifically chose the chair as my adviser because I wanted to graduate …he had a reputation for graduating all his students. I knew I was doing well when I picked that

guy. [His research] didn't matter so much. The research I wanted to do, I could do after I graduated.

Instrumentals typically viewed the system as favorable to women and regard the status of women as a non-issue. A female graduate student who believed in doing "the politically right thing" said:

When you get to graduate school [physics is] incredibly biased in favor of women. They work much harder to keep the female students and there is good reason. Most of them don't come in with adequate preparation. There are women who talk themselves out of taking the qualifying exams.

Moreover, this individual was outwardly hostile toward women, favoring the men whom she emulated:

I worked all through my undergraduate career all by myself. I don't see the need to work with others. The women don't have enough intelligence to work things out for themselves.

However, she also noted the debilitating effects of traditional socialization on women:

The guys have more of an idea about mechanical things and are self-confident. Women end up getting help, and then they end up in graduate schools they wouldn't normally get into and they're stuck because it is built into them to get help, assistance.

Instrumentals were willing to put in night and weekend work hours, making the lab the center of their social as well as work life. One such woman faculty member said:

It never occurs to the males that they could come in at 9 and leave at 5, five days a week and get a PhD. They're here at 3 am, weekends. You never see a woman here off hours. You see all the males. The males are socialized that they have to do their work and it always pissed me off because I always worked as hard as the men and so did the women who went to school when I did.

Instrumentals were typically unmarried or divorced and without responsibilities for childrearing. An informant noted that:

A common pattern is that women who are successful are single or divorced and really dedicate most of their energy to their career.

They are often ambivalent toward women students who are not as directed as they are. A female faculty member said:

> *Males come to me immediately with a problem. Women muddle off. I try cajoling them, pleading with them, yelling at them. I would rather have men…I guess I don't really mean that.*

In contrast to the instrumentals who emulate the male model, balancers find the highly competitive nature of academic science to be problematic, since it conflicts with their own preference for co-operation as described by this student:

> *Given the competitiveness that goes on around here, it is a lot harder to be open, honest and supportive because you don't know if you are going to get turned on.*

Balancers are aware of their difficulties in functioning strategically. Anxiety and confusion over the desire to balance multiple roles, at times, overwhelmed students. One student expressed her fear of future strains:

> *I can't think like that [about how to balance]. Thinking about [these] details is what scares me.*

The current constrained funding climate further exacerbates women's unstable position, causing professors, fearful of productivity losses, to be less willing to tolerate deviation from the traditional male model of doing science.

Nevertheless, despite these obstacles a new scientific work role is emerging as women and men struggle to restructure traditional family and work roles (Gerson, 1985). To treat the lab strictly as a work site is a necessary strategy for women (and some men) who want both to be highly productive as scientists yet maintain an outside life. These faculty members had a commitment to raising children and interacting with their family that was of equal importance to their work commitment.

The balancers wished to pursue multiple roles, typically family and work, seeking a reasonable division between the two spheres. Perhaps ironically, multiple roles have recently become accepted for high-status males in science who wish to combine participation in entrepreneurial ventures with the professorial role (Etzkowitz, 1989). However, combining the professorial role with serious attention to family obligations is seldom an acceptable stance for a high-level career in academic science or other professions (Frank-Fox and Hesse-Bieber, 1984).

Informal activities outside of the department are also often linked to traditional sex role activities and venues. In one department in a related study, a regular pick-up basketball game was a site for exchange of informal comments on research activities along with visits to a male-oriented local bar. A female faculty member felt inevitably excluded from 'the club' (Kemelgor, 1989).

Some women were able to work out an accommodation with the demands of a career at a research university by strictly budgeting their work time and making every minute of it count. For these women the university was a work site, not a social environment as well. For many males the time put in in the lab is not all work related, but being in the lab extremely long hours is part of the accepted persona of the successful academic scientist. A single male professor in a related study (Etzkowitz, 1989) reported that:

> *A lab, in a sense, is a little bit like a country club. You have your friends here…I don't stay here because it's competitive. I stay here because who wants to go home…It's what I see most of the people here doing, too. They get the newspapers, they talk to their friends, this is the place. It's a club.*

Despite recognition of the non–work-related nature of some of this presence on the job, in the culture of academic science, time spent in the lab is still viewed as an independent indicator of strength of commitment to science.

The balancing stance is not solely a female response to academia. Some male faculty adopted this position to a limited extent but typically admitted that their participation in domestic life and child-rearing was less than their spouses'. Moreover, not all women who wished to balance the demands of an academic research career and family were able to achieve this goal. Graduate students who were encouraged to take leaves after a pregnancy often did not return.

PhDs interested in academic research careers often decided to accept industry positions, either to give their husband first preference in a job search and/or to have a work role that was explicitly limited to a 9 to 5 commitment. Some junior faculty members abandoned research careers to accept positions in teaching colleges.

Thus, at present, the strategy of balancing career and family is contrary to the culture of high-status research universities and is difficult to arrange and sustain. Nevertheless, this is the option that most women in our sample wished to pursue. Few had the support of their institutions or persons available whose example they could follow.

Relevant Role Models

Role modeling has been identified as an effective socialization mechanism in work life. Modeling oneself on an older person has been found to be a good way of creating a pathway into a career, making for likely early success. A younger person can take on the characteristics of an older person in a professional role while serving in a junior capacity. The closer the modeler is to the person modeled, the easier is it for the transformation process to occur. Conversely, the more differences that exist, whether in the behavior directly being modeled or in associated personal characteristics, the more difficult it is for the socialization process to work.

Previous research has indentified the characteristics of successful women role models who integrated, "…professional and personal concerns" (Mokros et al., 1980, page 11). Beyond strictly professional issues, women

mentees are concerned with the interpersonal quality of the relationship and seek a sympathetic mentor (Dowdall, 1978).

In the sciences, male senior researchers have traditionally served as role models for their junior colleagues. As women entered scientific careers they were expected to follow a male model, accept a distinctly subordinate status, the scientific equivalent of the traditional female role (research associate) or leave the profession.

More recently, some women have attempted to carve out a new status and professional identity for themselves in the world of academic science (Kemelgor, 1989). This involves a different relationship to work and students, in which work life is pared down to professional elements and limited in time so that a private life may be constructed and compartmentalized apart from the professional role. This is not dissimilar from a 9–5 job with little carry-over from work to home and vice-versa in terms of socializing, professional relationship and effect. Indeed it represents a formalization of the work role and an attempt to remove sexualizing and other personal elements that may interfere with work.

Women graduate students prefer to have a range of models of female behaviors in science available to emulate. At present, the numbers of female faculty are usually so small that there are often few, or even no, choices of role models to emulate. A junior female faculty member described her role model in graduate school:

> Another woman did quite well…many things I didn't like about her, but it showed it was possible. There were a number of women in my field who were well known as I was going through, most of them were single and remained single.

Most women graduate students made a sharp distinction between women faculty whom they viewed as relevant or irrelevant as role models. Women faculty who were perceived to be instrumentals, emulating an aggressive male scientist role and attempting to become 'one of the boys,' were often not viewed as viable models. As a female graduate student said:

> That's a real problem. There are no real good role models to follow. The women a generation ahead of us had it so difficult that they are by and large a very aggressive group. [They had to be so aggressive] and that's who got ahead. You have trouble looking at them and saying, 'I want to be like that.' You don't.

On the other hand, a woman faculty member who was successfully balancing career and family was looked to as a model by several women in her department, even though she was somewhat less available due to time constraints. A female graduate student said that:

> _____ is a role model precisely because she can balance the two. She definitely finds time for the things on both sides. It can be hard on her students. When you do find the time to finally meet with her, you do have her attention. Everyone feels the same way: Frustrated that it's tough to get her, but that they really have her when they do.

However, for most female students anxiety about the present and the future is exacerbated, because there is no model to demonstrate how to deal with problems or issues. "Women are dropping out because there are no role models to show you how 'you get there.'" This is related to the ability of men to identify culturally with male advisers and enhance their self-confidence, leaving women with no one to 'pave the way.'

The need for women faculty to show how professional and family responsibilities could both be met was expressed by a student who said:

> I think it would be interesting to see [the female professor] get pregnant, so we could see how someone else deals with the situation. I have no clue whatsoever. I don't know what it's like in academics. I'm scared about that.

Thus, for the most part, students are left to feel they must be pioneers. In some instances, this situation was resented. The few who felt they did have role models, identified them as being from high school, undergraduate school, from industry or were their mothers.

Most importantly, the role model women wanted was the woman who could concretely explain the necessary strategies and steps to be taken to succeed in graduate school. This conclusion derives from the reality that: (1) rules are made by men, (2) young men are socialized to those rules and further socialized in graduate school: they have learned the strategies, (3) most women have not been socialized to be autonomous, therefore are not strategists and have difficulty figuring out the rules, (4) because of bias or lack of sensitivity to women's situation, most male advisers do not concretely and directly teach women the strategies necessary to succeed.

Of course, this finding does not hold for those very few graduate women who excluded other interests in favor of their career. The absence of viable female role models in most of the departments studied creates anxiety among women graduate students and is believed by them to contribute to the rate of attrition. Nevertheless, women graduate students report successful and unsuccessful experiences with both men and women advisers. Men can be sensitive and women can be relevant role models, but few men and women faculty currently meet the needs of most women graduate students.[4] Women graduate students seek out women faculty members as advisers in hopes of finding a sympathetic mentor, while male graduate students sign up with a woman only after she has achieved a distinguished position in the field.

POLICY IMPLICATIONS

In response to these problems of women in science, the intersection of gender and science has become a focus of feminist theorizing, sociological investigation and human resource programs. Opening scientific careers to a broader range of women than those who are willing and able to adhere to the traditional male model is the key to solving the policy dilemma of women in science. To accomplish this end, the structure of the academic workplace must be changed.

Structural changes in academia going well beyond improved recruitment measures will be required to achieve universalism, viewed as a desired value or goal rather than as an existing norm or unwritten rule. Reforms proposed range from changes in the larger society to remove cultural barriers to young women thinking of mathematics and science as an appropriate activity, to changes within the structure of academic science to take account of women's needs rather than presuming that women must fit into an existing structure designed implicitly to meet male needs. Two basic strategies for changing the conditions of entry into academia have been identified:

- The provision of resources through offering fellowships or providing set up costs, such as the United States' National Science Foundation Visiting Professorships for Women and Presidential Young Investigator Awards programs; and
- Revising the academic structure, to eliminate gender-related obstacles to entry or retention, for example, the Israel Institute of Technology's extension of the time period before tenure review for women with children (Mannheim, 1990).

Without waiting for necessary changes in the larger society, we hold that significant steps can be taken to adapt the social structure of science to accommodate women, and improve their rate of participation and performance.

Creating Appropriate Academic Atmosphere

Administrative actions, engendered from above or below, even if they do not change attitudes, can affect behavior. A female gradu-

ate dean at another university reported on the efficacy at her institution of administrative leadership to remind people of gender and minority issues at every step of the academic process. "We had a graduate program director who took this issue up as a personal cause." She reported that it was most important to be stringent on sexual harassment so that everyone knew that it is morally and legally wrong, officially and unofficially.

The affirmative action officer at the primary research site, a female attorney, reported that she received virtually no complaints from women in the science and engineering departments, while there were many from the humanities and social sciences. She presumed that the universalistic spirit of science was responsible for the paucity of complaints rather than an environment that suppresses the expression of gender differences.

In one instance, a woman graduate student contemplated making a complaint against a male faculty member who was discussing pornographic images on a computer screen with his male graduate student. The incident took place in her presence in an office that she shared with the graduate student. She drew back from making an official complaint, fearful of endangering her degree. However, the matter attained sufficient visibility within the department that the chair sent out a strongly worded message condemning the practice as unacceptable and warning against its repetition.

One department studied had undergone significant change with respect to its treatment of women. Among its leadership were several middle-aged males who had simultaneously been in therapy in a community where the local culture had been strongly influenced by feminist values. In this context, one of them pointed out to the others that they were being unconsciously dismissive of the work of a female faculty member up for tenure. They accepted the validity of the charge, reviewed their behavior and decided to change their attitudes and practices.[5]

They also revised the departmental structure to emphasize collegiality and gender-blind decision making. For example, graduate student admission decisions are made by a committee with equal representation of faculty and students. Two students are elected each year to review and interview applicants. A male and a female had served in the previous year and two females in the current year. Applicants stay with other students when they come to campus to be interviewed. Once the incoming class has been picked, they are invited to a social event involving the entire department, with a picnic and sports.

All women students and faculty interviewed reported joining this department, rather than other prestigious institutions, based on their perception of a collaborative, co-operative and collegial milieu. They were attracted by the warm interpersonal interactions that they experienced when they interviewed and by a sense of personal concern by faculty and students for the candidate. They were also impressed by the happiness and well-being of members of the department. Most had been disturbed by the demoralization of students at other departments where they had interviewed, having heard stories of exploitative advisers and anonymity in large research groups.

Since almost all had previously worked in laboratories as undergraduates or as technicians in academia or industry, they had a clear idea of the laboratory environment that they wished to find as well as what they wanted to avoid. Several had suffered isolation in sexist, autocratically run, competitive laboratories in which their status as female technicians promoted loneliness and professional stagnation.

They had relocated to laboratories in which laboratory heads and post-doctoral fellows had enhanced their self-confidence through direct teaching, generosity in time for communication and responding to questions without derision. In each of these instances, the informant came away feeling capable and competent to undertake graduate work, having experienced empathy and understanding from a mentor figure, whether female or male.

While the science being done in the department or by a faculty member often initiated a candidate's interest in the school, the emotional gratification of the interview process together with a preference for a collegial research environment influenced the candidate's final decision. Thus, selecting this particular department was a means of recapturing a significant maturational experience that had promoted self-confidence and emergence of a scientific self-identity.

In this department a female academic model based on interpersonal relationships, affiliation and nurturance had become accepted as legitimate and had even become the departmental norm. This was in strong contrast to another research site where the expression by women of a need for these characteristics in the laboratory environment was derided as a desire for dependence and emotionality by the adherents of the patriarchal system that was in place.

It is not women or men in the position, by itself, but the ability to meet female relational needs that is essential for a successful mentor of women. Women professors who follow the male model, in fact, often heighten performance anxiety among their female students by expecting more of themselves and their women students than do males. Patriarchal institutional roles, whether enacted by men or women, result in female behaviors being misinterpreted as inferior rather than different, for example, when women express a preference for a collegial rather than a competitive working environment.

Moreover, most women students reject an academic lifestyle in which non-scientific relationships and activities, and the possibility of significant involvement in raising children are excluded. These conclusions necessitate additional changes in the academic system, beyond creating a supportive, non-sexist working environment.

Resolving Time Conflicts

There is an incompatibility between the seven-year race for tenure with the biological clock for child-bearing, with obvious negative consequences for women's participation in high-powered academic science. A female faculty member said of this conflict that:

> There is definitely the pressure to continue to produce and to show that you can do both. Sometimes I feel like I'm setting women back. The women who are having children don't want to say they can do less. But they haven't had one yet and they don't know. They feel they have to show they can do it [maintain productivity].

This professor has spoken up in faculty meetings, on behalf of extending the time before tenure review for women with children. However, she sees it as a double-edged sword. Pressure for reduced demands upon women with children might jeopardize their status by supporting the notion that women with children cannot be productive. Of course, the extension could be made gender-neutral, with the same provisions offered to men with extensive responsibilities for child-rearing. Nevertheless, in practice, it would likely be seen as a measure to accommodate women.

In addition, departmental and university-wide efforts to make workplace child-care facilities more widely available would help. An infant care center in a neighboring education school, discovered by a third-world female graduate student, made an important difference to the ability of several women with children, in one of the departments studied, to carry on their graduate work virtually without interruption.

A male faculty member told us that, if women would wait until after 35 to have children, there would be no problem. They would be able to pursue tenure single-mindedly without interference from other obligations. He recognized that most women were unwilling to delay having children that long and thus saw no answer to this dilemma. A graduate, now a professor at another university, reflected upon the relationship between the biological and tenure clocks. In discussing her plans for children she said:

> I take every day as it comes. It would be outrageously difficult. I would feel much more confidence if I had tenure but I would be 38 and I don't choose to have a child that late.

If the objective is to significantly increase the number of women pursuing high-powered scientific careers, institutional accommodations will have to be made for women who wish to combine family with career. To achieve equality it is not just a matter of opening up opportunities but of changing the structure of the academic system. Women who wish to pursue traditional female roles along with a scientific career must be accommodated by allowing a longer time span before the tenure decision. This had been promised to one faculty member in our sample, although in the end it was not allowed.

This is not a call for a 'mommy track,' with different and lower expectations of achievement and rewards, but a serious effort to accommodate the significant number of women who are not willing to forego family and children prior to tenure. It is unrealistic to expect significant numbers of women to follow the male model. If the goal is to substantially increase the participation of women in high-level academic science, a female model will have to be legitimated. Acceptance of an alternative career model is crucial both to placing more women in faculty slots in the immediate short term and to providing relevant role models for a broader range of female graduate students.

Conflicts of time will have to be accommodated for women faculty members with children. This currently happens for faculty members, typically men, who found firms or centers. However, these time conflicts usually occur after tenure while for women involved with family responsibilities they tend to occur earlier in their career trajectory, placing them at risk. While time conflicts at later career stages may affect colleagues' views of a department member, they seldom, if ever, have deleterious career consequences. Simply put, women are more vulnerable than men prior to tenure.

Overcoming Locational Immobility

The limited geographical mobility of many women restricts both their choice of graduate school and job. A highly successful female scientist interviewed in another study explained the impact of location on her career, given existing norms of hiring. As a research associate her advance in rank was limited, as was her exposure to students and the experience of raising her own funds. She felt that these consequences of having to accept a position of lesser status had delayed her professional maturation.

> I was married—I'm still married—and I didn't have the flexibility of moving around. That's one of the best ways to achieve a permanent position and to increase one's standing; to have the lever or the threat of saying, well, I'm going to leave. And to mean it. You can't do it as an empty threat. You have to be ready to leave, and people are. I was never in that position, so I could never use that threat (Dupree, 1991, page 117).

A typical scenario that has been identified is marrying a man in the same field who completes his graduate work before his wife. He finds the best job he can without geographical constraints. When the woman finishes, she finds what job she can in a circumscribed region (Max, 1982). Women who are already married often select their graduate school based on what is available in a region and choose a job with similar considerations in

mind. In many instances, second-rank research universities attract higher-quality candidates than they might otherwise, because of women's geographical restrictions.

The limited geographical mobility that many women face can be addressed in at least three ways:

- Making women's careers equal in importance to men's careers, allowing women a greater latitude in job choice; and
- Hiring both husband and wife, even in the same department, taking account of the fact that graduate students in the same discipline and department often marry;
- Relaxing formal and/or informal prohibitions against hiring one's own graduates.

The highest-achieving woman scientist in our sample was hired by her graduate department after a stint at a local college. This practice is especially significant for women who are geographically immobile in a region with few or even only one research university.

Achieving Critical Mass

The succession of impediments to the entry of women into scientific careers that narrows the stream to an extremely small flow at the stage of graduate training has been conceptualized as cumulative disadvantage. However, even given these disadvantages a significant number of women receive degrees in science at the BA and even the PhD levels. Nevertheless, fewer pursue careers in science and there are few senior women professors (Moen, 1988).

The disadvantages that cumulate to narrow the flow into the science career pipeline are supplemented by additional disadvantages, at the margin, that discourage even the most highly motivated women who have taken steps to pursue scientific and engineering careers at the doctoral level. It is expected that removal of some or all of these barriers at the doctoral, junior and senior faculty levels could have an effect, in the short term, in increasing women's participation in science and engineering.

Taking such steps could also provide a critical increment of role models to assist in long-term efforts to lower barriers at the early stages of the life course, thereby increasing the flow into the science career pipeline. Thus, the importance of focusing policy intervention at the later stages is two-fold:

- To encourage the creation of a critical mass of women faculty in academic science and engineering departments that, in and of itself, has an effect in changing academic cultures and, by implication, lowering barriers for future generations; and
- To revise the image of high-level careers in science and engineering for women from an anomalous to a 'normal' role thereby providing the incentive of widespread examples of achievement to encourage younger women to break through the barriers prevalent at early stages of the life course.

These graduate students and professors, after successfully negotiating the numerous barriers to entry that exclude so many other women, often pursue less-demanding careers than their male peers. These are not women lost to science. Rather they are women who, with a few exceptions, are excluded from positions in the top academic departments in their field. Many pursue research careers in industry. Others have taken appointments down the academic ladder in teaching colleges.

Whether these scientists are excluded from high-level academic careers, through discrimination by academic departments unwilling to accept women as equals, or confer upon them an authentic professional identify or by choice, through their unwillingness to conform to an academic system that makes little accommodation for non-work roles and obligations, the result is the same. There is a pool of women scientists working in industry and lower down the academic ladder whom their advisers, usually men, agree are the equal of their male peers who are pursuing research careers at the highest academic levels.

If lines were made available, qualified women scientists could be recruited to create a critical mass of at least three women in each leading academic department. This would provide the range of female role models necessary to bring forth an enlarged next generation of women scientists.

Women who have avoided the effects of cumulative disadvantage, even accumulating some advantages that should propel their career forward, nevertheless suffer a marginal disadvantage at the graduate and junior faculty stages that significantly reduces the entry of women into research careers in academic science. While the causes of cumulative disadvantage are largely beyond the control of academic departments, the causes of marginal disadvantage such as advisement, role modeling and hiring practices are part of the academic enterprise, and departments can influence how they take place.

While culture is generally believed to be highly resistant to change we believe that our findings suggest a few key points of intervention. Specific steps could be undertaken to mitigate the negative effects of the male scientific ethos on the recruitment of women to science and engineering. The rigidity of the existing academic structure and male faculty misperceptions of women scientists constitute formidable barriers to the entry and retention of women at the highest levels of academic science. However, the fact that qualified women who would be interested in academic research careers are now in industry or teaching colleges suggests that, should these final barriers be lowered or removed, a pool of women scientists already exists that is available to pursue careers at the highest levels of academic science.

CONCLUSION

What can be done to implement these proposals? A first step is to become more self-conscious about the social organization of human scientific endeavors and that is, after all, a practical contribution that the social studies of science is expected to make to the conduct of the natural sciences. Deconstructing the taken-for-granted gendered dimensions of science allows science to be expanded in at least as many ways as it is currently limited. By accepting as universal various parochial ways of conceptualizing, investigating and organizing the conduct of science, significant sectors of the population have been excluded from full participation and alternative cognitive perspectives and organizational styles have been repressed.

As we become aware of such factors as masculine models of gender as the basis for many modes of doing science, a policy space is opened up where change can take place. Social movements and support groups organized by excluded groups, changes in departmental practices and university policies taken at the initiative of faculty and administrators, and governmental affirmative action policies and funding programs are all part of the emerging picture of science open to all talent in fact as well as by precept.

Science policy for women in science (Abir-Am, 1991) is the second step toward transcending masculine and feminine scientific roles and practices—the de-genderization of science and society. In self-exemplifying fashion the sociology of gender and science itself has moved beyond comparing men and women scientists according to implicitly masculine criteria such as number of publications, with article counts accepted as a primary indicator of productivity and achievement. On the other hand, women publish less, but their publications are more highly cited (Long, 1990). This finding may indicate different gender styles of scientific work. Perhaps women work more intensively on a subject before making their work public while men are more willing to go into print and try out their ideas with less evidence.

There is much to be said for and against each of these styles of scientific work. By viewing scientific practices from a perspective that relativizes both traditional male and female gendered perspectives and integrates them into a broader non-sexist framework in which alternative modes of doing science would be acceptable for both men and women, experimentation and verification of knowledge would be freed from the exclusionary oppositions in which that which is defined as feminine is automatically perceived as antithetical to 'good science' (Keller, 1980). Under these conditions universalism would be realized as a normative, as well as an ideological, component of the social structure of science. Then Athena, as well as Prometheus, will realize her full potential.

NOTES

1. In physics, for example, the sharp decline in the proportion of women as the educational level rises has been reported for years (see following discussion).

2. At this university the Computer Science Department is located jointly in the Engineering School and the Faculty of Arts and Sciences.

3. The physics department previously had two tenured women, one now emeritus and the other deceased.

4. 22% of the female students in the four departments at private research university, as against only 4% of the male students, have female faculty advisers. While the proportion of female and male students entering subfields where female faculty advisers are available is fairly similar (32% and 24%, respectively), the proportion actually signing up with those female professors differs by a factor of four (68% to 17%).

5. In another instance the change did not come voluntarily but only after a female faculty member threatened to resign when a sexist male faculty member was about to be named permanent chair. This action received nationwide publicity, forcing

university officials to do something about the sexist environment of the department. They prescribed a year of gender sensitivity training for the acting chair who resigned the position. See *Chronicle of Higher Education*, 1 April 1992, page A14.

REFERENCES

Pnina Abir-Am (1991), "Science policy for women in science: from historical case studies to an agenda for the 1990's," History of Science Meetings, Madison, Wisconsin, 2 November.

Marina Benjamin (1991), *Science and Sensibility: Gender and Scientific Enquiry; 1780–1945* (Basil Blackwell, London).

Ernest Boyer (1987), *Classification of Institutes of Higher Education* (Carnegie Foundation for the Advancement of Teaching, Princeton).

Jean Dowdall (1978), "Mentors in academe: the perceptions of protégés," American Sociological Association Annual Meeting, Boston, Massachusetts.

Andrea Dupree (1991), "Interview with Andrea Dupree," in Zuckerman *et al*, *The Outer Circle* (Norton, New York).

Henry Etzkowitz (1989), "Entrepreneurial science in the academy: a case of the transformation of norms," *Social Problems*, 36(1), February.

Mary Frank-Fox (1989), "Women in higher education: gender differences in the status of students and scholars," in Jo Freeman (editor), *Women: a Feminine Perspective* (Mayfield Publishing Co, Mountain View, Ca).

Mary Frank-Fox and Sharlene Hesse-Bieber (1984), *Women at Work* (Mayfield Publishing Company, Palo Alto, Ca).

Kathleen Gerson (1985), *Hard Choices: How Women Decide about Work, Career and Motherhood* (University of California Press, Berkeley).

Evelyn Fox Keller (1980), "How gender matters, or, why it's so hard for us to count past two" in Jan Harding (editor) (1986), *Perspectives on Gender and Science* (Falmer Press, London).

Carol Kemelgor (1989), *Research Groups in Molecular Biology: A Study of Normative Change in Academic Science*, BA Thesis, SUNY Purchase.

Scott Long (1990), "The origins of sex differences in science," *Social Forces*.

Bilha Mannheim (1990), Personal communication, August.

Karl Mannheim (1936), *Ideology and Utopia* (Harvest, New York).

Claire Max (1982), "Career paths for women in physics," in Shiela Humphreys (editor), *Women and Minorities in Science: Strategies for Increasing Participation* (Westview, Boulder).

Clyde Mitchell (1983), "Case and situation analysis," *Sociological Review*, 31(2), pages 187–211.

Phyllis Moen (1988), "Women as a human resource," National Science Foundation, Sociology Program, Washington DC, Division of Social and Economic Science.

Janice R. Mokros *et al* (1980), "A new role for professors," *College Board Review*, Winter, pages 2–5.

Rachel Rosenfeld (1984), "Academic career mobility for psychologists," in Haas and Perrucci (editors) (1986), *Women in Scientific and Engineering Professions* (University of Michigan Press, Ann Arbor).

Joan Scott (1990), "Disadvantage of women by the ordinary processes of science: the case of informal collaboration," in Marianne Ainley, *Despite the Odds: Essays on Canadian Women and Science* (Vehicule Press, Montreal).

Gerhart Sonnert (1990), "Careers of women and men postdoctoral fellows in the sciences," American Sociological Association Meetings, August.

PART SIX

Gender and Religion

Religion makes attitudes about gender "sacred" and less open to question than in other areas of social life. Religion provides most of us with powerful symbols and conceptions that shape our view of the world around us—it is a powerful source of collective identity and social control. Religious belief influences a variety of social attitudes and behaviors—particularly those involving sexuality and gender roles (Andersen 1997). Recently, the Southern Baptist Convention, which is the nation's largest Protestant denomination with 16 million members, passed a resolution restating that the attitude of a Christian wife should be submissiveness to her husband, and Pope Paul II has reiterated the Catholic Church's view that birth control is a sin and women cannot be priests (Bragg 1998; Stanley 1998).

The feminist critique of religion has taken several different directions—for example, feminists are split about the representation of women in biblical stories. Some feminists argue that we should pay more attention to biblical stories where women are presented in a positive light (Ruether and McLaughlin 1979); others emphasize the dearth of women in the Bible or claim that they are usually represented as either nonsexual or evil (Stockard and Johnson 1992); and others argue that there *are* strong women in the Bible, such as Sarah and Rebekah in Genesis, but the bottom line is that it is not the women who receive the covenant from God or pass on its lineage (Biale 1984).

Feminists also focus on the male-centered view of theology, distinguishing between the seemingly patriarchal aspects of religion which are inherent in the fundamental teachings (which are supposedly given by God) as opposed to those which reflect an interpretation which is used to bolster men's power. They argue that cultures emphasize different aspects of religious teaching at different times and under different conditions and feel that traditional religions can be reformed, for instance, the emphasis on Mary's virginal versus motherly characteristics has varied greatly in different historical periods. For a good part of the Middle Ages, Mary's virginity was celebrated over her child-rearing capacity, reflecting male Catholic theologians association of women's sexuality with the devil (Thurer 1994; Harris 1978). In Judaism, the evolution of the laws of divorce, over the course of ten centuries, reflects changing attitudes about the fundamental imbalance of power between men and women which characterizes biblical law (Biale 1984).

The most radical feminists believe that traditional religions should be discarded entirely because the patriarchal elements are *inherent* in the canons of the religion—God's word is used to justify men's power. Imagining God as a man has a profound effect on how we relate to God, as well as our willing-ness to give men higher religious status than women.

The articles in this section are by women who do not want to reject their religions. Rather, they want women to play an equal part in their religious in-stitutions and are searching for a way to prevent the power of religion from being used against women. Susan Farrell wants radical reform within the Ro-man Catholic Church. She challenges the Roman Catholic Church's patriar-chal discourse, which bases the understanding of women and sexuality on biologically determined or God-given roles. In a similar vein, Judith Plaskow and Fatima Mernissi are critical of their religions' patriarchal traditions. Like Farrell, Plaskow and Mernissi are concerned about the exclusion of women from shaping religious doctrine. Plaskow believes that Jewish feminism de-mands creating a Torah that is new.

While religions generally recognize and include both masculine and femi-nine images, the depictions, and which depictions are emphasized, reflect and reinforce the dominant gender relations. In some religions, women are por-trayed as being responsible for sin and the fall of man and are relegated to con-ception and obedience in everyday life. In other religions, it is men who are associated with the beginning of evil and women who bring the first people into the world (Sanday 1981). Figures of full-breasted women have been found in ar-cheological excavations of preagricultural hunting societies dating from 2000 to 4000 B.C., suggesting feminine deities who symbolized birth and renewal in pre-Greek society (Stockard and Johnson 1972). Classical Greek mythology indi-cates that before Zeus there were goddesses. However, beginning with Zeus, a patriarchy was introduced to Mt. Olympus. Zeus brought moral order and cul-ture by fathering the Hours, the Fates, the Muses, and the Graces. He denied power to women including the power to give birth—Zeus gave birth to Athena through his head and to Dionysus from his thigh (Pomeroy 1975).

Pandora, who was the first woman in Greek mythology, can be compared to the first Judeo-Christian temptress, Eve. She opened the box, which can be viewed as a metaphor for carnal knowledge—the source of evil to men. The poet Hesiod attributes the woes of *man*kind to Pandora, calling her "a pain to hard-toiling men" (Pomeroy 1975:3).

In modern religions, male images predominate. The founders of the ma-jor Western religious systems were male—Moses, Jesus, and Mohammed. In Christianity, the image of Jesus, the son of a male God, brings rebirth and ev-erlasting life to the faithful—the son is more powerful than the mother, Mary. Biale (1984) points out that Jacob had a daughter, but only his sons became the twelve tribes of Israel.

The biblical story of Adam and Eve is the classic example of a creation myth in which female sexuality is viewed as powerful and dangerous, which is reflective of a culture of male dominance (Sanday 1981). Although there are different versions of the story, the most common version of the Fall places major guilt on Eve—merging her with the Greek Pandora (Thurer 1994). Eve is depicted as persuading Adam to eat the apple, dooming them to live in a world of sin.

While most religions try to control sexuality, they vary in terms of the attitude toward sexual pleasure—particularly within marriage. In Judaism, for example, marriage is for procreation, but sexual pleasure is seen as part of marriage. In the eyes of the Catholic Church, on the other hand, because of the high value put on celibacy, marriage is for the purpose of procreation, not sexual pleasure. In the early Middle Ages, the Church prohibited sexual intercourse on Sundays, Wednesdays, Fridays, and many other days—and warned against husbands loving their wives too much (Thurer 1994).

The Church fathers consistently combined their praise of virgins with their hatred of women in general; the celibate ideal was connected with hostility and fear of women (Harris 1978). Shari Thurer (1994) argues that during the witch craze, which began in the late Middle Ages, witches were viewed as women who were sexually insatiable and instruments of Satan. She claims that the witch and the virgin mother are inversions of each other—the witch was the anti-mom. The Malleus Maleficarum issued by the Catholic Church in 1484 defined the Church's position on witches, saying that witchcraft stemmed from women's carnal lust. Men's fear of women was reflected in beliefs that witches collected penises for use in satanic rituals; stole semen from sleeping men; and cast spells over men that would make their sex organs disappear. Many women were tortured or killed as witches, with estimates varying from thousands to millions (Thurer 1994).

Both Catholics and Protestants participated in the witch craze. However, the Protestant attitude toward female literacy, the rejection of the celibate ideal, and the elimination of the monastery created a different set of attitudes toward marriage. With the end of the monastery, home and school were the places for cultivating Christian virtues formerly associated with the members of religious orders. Given their views about the family, Protestants considered marriage a positive good, rather than a necessary evil to perpetuate the race. In contrast to the medieval Catholic view, for the past 150 years, the largely Protestant Anglo-American culture has defined women as less sexual and more moral than men. Indeed, by the end of the nineteenth century, male medical experts said most women had sexual anesthesia (Harris 1978).

In addition to shaping our views about sexuality, religions also have different official roles for men and women. Men usually have the closest ceremonial ties to the deities. Most modern religions have power structures that are patriarchal—in the Roman Catholic Church, for example, men are priests and women are nuns. Nuns teach and nurse, but they cannot celebrate Mass; only priests may perform the ceremony that links the faithful directly with God. Similarly, among orthodox Jews, only men may be rabbis (Stockard and Johnson 1992).

Feminists have challenged the internal authority structure of religious institutions arguing that it is inconsistent with the reality of women's involvement in religion. Women's church attendance and participation in volunteer activities is greater than men's. In addition, in 1990, 210 parishes in the United States were administered by nonpriests because of the shortage of priests—over 60 percent of the parishes were headed by nuns (Wallace 1992).

Furthermore, the areas in which Christian churches act as moral custodians, such as marriage, family, and sexuality, are vital to women's interests. Some religious organizations deny the concept of female ordination in principle—that is, Orthodox Judaism and Roman Catholicism. Other religious organizations did not have theological justifications for opposing women's ordination, but since it ran counter to the practice in their church, it was denied until the 1970s (Briggs 1987).

The debates surrounding women's ordination in Reform Judaism exemplify the ambivalence of liberal religious bodies toward women's participation in religious authority. Reform Judaism has a history of acknowledging the religious equality of women with men. In late-nineteenth-century America, women attended the rabbinical seminary of Reform Judaism in Cincinnati at a time when access to ministerial studies for Christian women was rare. Yet, the actual ordination of women lagged far behind the acceptability of women rabbis in principle. The willingness of mainline Protestant churches and Reform Judaism to ordain women in increasing numbers since the 1970s reflects the impact of feminism on the perception of appropriate professional roles for women (Briggs 1987).

While Farrell and Plaskow focus on Roman Catholicism and Judaism, Mernissi is one of a group of Muslim thinkers who have a common concern with the empowerment of women within a rethought Islam. They are concerned with the question of what is intrinsically Islamic (i.e., in the Koran) with respect to ideas about women and gender as opposed to what is related to a patriarchal culture. In order to disentangle the two, the Muslim feminists have looked at religious texts and historical documents with a critical eye. However, there is great divisiveness among them—some believe that women's position is more a result of social practices than the principles of Islam, while others locate women's inferior status in the religion itself (Yamani 1996). Mernissi is one of the more radical Muslim feminist thinkers because she locates the secondary status of Muslim women in the Koran. For example, she views polygamy and repudiation (the unconditional right of the male to break the marriage bond without any justification) as principles of Islam that are humiliating to women.

In societies in which there is no separation between church and state, women's civil rights are often obliterated. Women and what they do or wear are at the heart of fundamentalist policies in Afghanistan, Iran, and Algeria. For example, Algerian women have suffered considerably more than men at the hands of Islamic fundamentalists; many women have been murdered and their homes set on fire for the "crime" of living on their own (Karmi 1996). Fatima Mernissi points out that in Morocco while many institutions have been put outside the control of religious law (business contracts, for example), the family remains bound by it. Women are kept subjugated by a system of family laws based on male authority (Karmi 1996). A Moroccan woman needs permission from a male relative to marry, to name her children, or to work. She can be forced into marriage or polygamy and can be beaten by her husband without recourse. Men also have a unilateral right to divorce their wives (Simons 1998).

The practice of mutilating female genitals between birth and puberty is a more extreme method of controlling women's sexuality than simply covering their bodies. Genital mutilation is a ritualized custom, not in the Koran. It is practiced in many Muslim countries in Africa and Southwest Asia, effecting an estimated 90 million women. The three most prevalent forms of female genital mutilation are as follows: the labia minor and the tip of the clitoris are removed; clitoridectomy, in which the entire labia and entire clitoris are removed; and infibulation after clitoridectomy, in which the vagina is completely sealed with only a small opening left for menstrual flow. The vagina can only be opened again by the husband's penis or his knife—men control female sexuality (Lax 1992).

The Mernissi selection in this section comes from her book *Beyond the Veil: Male-Female Dynamics in Modern Muslim Society*. Mernissi points out that, in general, religions fall into two groups with respect to the way they regulate sexual behavior. One group enforces respect of sexual rules by a strong internalization of sexual prohibitions during the socialization process. The other enforces respect of sexual rules by external precautions and safeguards such as avoidance rules in Orthodox Judaism and Islam. The difference between these two types of societies is their concept of female sexuality.

Freud believed that girls become feminine when they give up their active sexuality (which he calls "masculine") and replace it with a passive, receptive sexuality. Mernissi takes this idea and turns it on its head. She argues that Muslim society is characterized by a contradiction between what can be called an "explicit theory" of female sexuality and an "implicit theory." The explicit theory is the prevailing contemporary belief that men are aggressive in their interaction with women and women are passive. Women must be protected from men. The implicit theory of female sexuality, on the other hand, is that women have sexual power over men and men must subjugate women's power and neutralize its disruptive effects; men must be protected from women. The most potentially dangerous woman is one who has experienced sexual intercourse because she will be more active in her desire. Thus, unmarried women must be kept virgins and married women must be veiled.

In religions in which seclusion and surveillance of women prevail, Mernissi claims, the implicit concept of female sexuality is active. For example, the seclusion and veiling of women in the Muslim religion is a device to keep men from losing control over themselves. Similarly, Orthodox Jewish women cover their elbows and knees in public and do not touch men to whom they are not related. In religions in which there are no such methods of surveillance and coercion of women's dress and behavior, the concept of female sexuality is passive—only men are seen as actively sexual.

One key to whether religious believers accept transformed religious roles for women hinges on whether they believe that religious texts, including the Bible, the Torah, and the Koran, are cultural and historical documents that are subject to interpretation or are the literal word of God. Those that view religious texts as open to changing interpretations argue, for example, that Christianity was used to justify both slavery and emancipation. Arguing that slaves were heathens, slave traders and owners justified their exploitation of

Africans. On the other hand, abolitionists used Christianity as their justification for fighting against slavery (Andersen 1997). Mernissi, Farrell, and Plaskow believe that religious texts and hierarchies that reflect and reinforce gender inequality are not God's will, but men's.

REFERENCES

Andersen, Margaret L. 1997. *Thinking About Women: Sociological Perspectives on Sex and Gender.* Boston: Allyn and Bacon.

Biale, Rachel. 1984. *Women and Jewish Law: An Exploration of Women's Issues in Halakhic Sources.* New York: Schocken Books.

Bragg, Rick. 1998. "Old Baptist Church, Women and All, Is Set to Leave Fold." *New York Times,* July 25: A1, A11.

Briggs, Sheila. 1987. "Women and Religion." Pp. 408–437 in *Analyzing Gender: A Handbook of Social Science Research,* edited by Beth B. Hess and Myra Marx Ferree. Newbury Park, CA: Sage Publications.

Harris, Barbara J. 1978. *Beyond Her Sphere: Women and the Professions in American History.* Westport, CT: Greenwood Press.

Karmi, Ghada. 1996. "Women, Islam and Patriarchalism." Pp. 69–85 in *Feminism and Islam: Legal and Literary Perspectives,* edited by Mai Yamani. Washington Square: New York University Press.

Lax, Ruth. 1992. "A Tribute to Alice Walker, Who Spoke Out Loud." *The Round Robin* newsletter of Section I, Psychologist-Psychoanalyst Practitioners, Division of Psychoanalysis (39), American Psychological Association. Volume 8, No. 3.

Pomeroy, Sarah B. 1975. *Goddesses, Whores, Wives, and Slaves: Women in Classical Antiquity.* New York: Schocken Books.

Reuther, Rosemary, and Eleanor McLaughlin, eds. 1979. *Women of Spirit: Female Leadership in the Jewish and Christian Traditions.* New York: Simon and Schuster.

Sanday, Peggy Reeves. 1981. *Female Power and Male Dominance: On the Origins of Sexual Inequality.* New York: Cambridge University Press.

Simons, Marlise. 1998. "Cry of Muslim Women for Equal Rights is Rising." *New York Times,* March 9: A1, A6.

Stanley, Alessandra. 1998. "Pope Tightens Grip by Rome on Its Bishops." *New York Times,* July 24: A1, A2.

Stockard, Jean, and Miriam M. Johnson. 1992. *Sex and Gender in Society.* Englewood Cliffs, NJ: Prentice Hall.

Thurer, Shari L. 1994. *The Myths of Motherhood: How Culture Reinvents the Good Mother.* New York: Penguin Books.

Wallace, Ruth. 1992. *They Call Her Pastor: A New Role for Catholic Women.* Albany: State University of New York Press.

Yamani, Mai. 1996. *Feminism and Islam: Legal and Literary Perspectives.* Washington Square: New York University Press.

The Muslim Concept of Active Female Sexuality

FATIMA MERNISSI

According to George Murdock, societies fall into two groups with respect to the manner in which they regulate the sexual instinct. One group enforces respect of sexual rules by a 'strong internalization of sexual prohibitions during the socialization process', the other enforces that respect by 'external precautionary safeguards such as avoidance rules', because these societies fail to internalize sexual prohibitions in their members.[1] According to Murdock, Western society belongs to the first group while societies where veiling exists belong to the second.

> Our own society clearly belongs to the former category, so thoroughly do we instil our sex mores in the consciences of individuals that we feel quite safe in trusting our internalized sanctions.... We accord women a maximum of personal freedom, knowing that the internalized ethics of premarital chastity and post-marital fidelity will ordinarily suffice to prevent abuse of their liberty through fornication or adultery whenever a favourable opportunity presents itself. Societies of the other type...attempt to preserve premarital chastity by secluding their unmarried girls or providing them with duennas or other such external devices as veiling, seclusion in harems or constant surveillance.[2]

However, I think that the difference between these two kinds of societies resides not so much in their mechanisms of internalization as in their concept of female sexuality. In societies in which seclusion and surveillance of women prevail, the implicit concept of female sexuality is active; in societies in which there are no such methods of surveillance and coercion of women's behaviour, the concept of female sexuality is passive.

In his attempt to grasp the logic of the seclusion and veiling of women and the basis of sexual segregation, the Muslim feminist Qasim Amin came to the conclusion that women are better able to control their sexual impulses than men and that consequently sexual segregation is a device to protect men, not women.[3]

He started by asking who fears what in such societies. Observing that women do not appreciate seclusion very much and conform to it only because they are compelled to, he concluded that what is feared is *fitna*: disorder or chaos. (*Fitna* also means a beautiful woman—the connotation of a *femme fatale* who makes men lose their self-control. In the way Qasim Amin used it *fitna* could be translated as chaos provoked by sexual disorder and initiated by women.) He then asked who is protected by seclusion.

> If what men fear is that women might succumb to their masculine attraction, why did they not institute veils for themselves? Did men think that their

From *Beyond the Veil: Male-Female Dynamics in Modern Muslim Society* by Fatima Mernissi, pp. 30–45. Copyright © 1987 by Fatima Mernissi. Reprinted by permission of Indiana University Press.

ability to fight temptation was weaker than women's? Are men considered less able than women to control themselves and resist their sexual impulse? . . . Preventing women from showing themselves unveiled expresses men's fear of losing control over their minds, falling prey to fitna *whenever they are confronted with a non-veiled woman. The implications of such an institution lead us to think that women are believed to be better equipped in this respect than men.*[4]

Amin stopped his inquiry here and, probably thinking that his findings were absurd, concluded jokingly that if men are the weaker sex, they are the ones who need protection and therefore the ones who should veil themselves.

Why does Islam fear *fitna*? Why does Islam fear the power of female sexual attraction over men? Does Islam assume that the male cannot cope sexually with an uncontrolled female? Does Islam assume that women's sexual capacity is greater than men's?

Muslim society is characterized by a contradiction between what can be called 'an explicit theory' and 'an implicit theory' of female sexuality, and therefore a double theory of sexual dynamics. The explicit theory is the prevailing contemporary belief that men are aggressive in their interaction with women, and women are passive. The implicit theory, driven far further into the Muslim unconscious, is epitomized in Imam Ghazali's classical work.[5] He sees civilization as struggling to contain women's destructive, all-absorbing power. Women must be controlled to prevent men from being distracted from their social and religious duties. Society can survive only by creating institutions that foster male dominance through sexual segregation and polygamy for believers.

The explicit theory, with its antagonistic, machismo vision of relations between the sexes is epitomized by Abbas Mahmud al-Aqqad.[6] In *Women in the Koran* Aqqad attempted to describe male-female dynamics as they appear through the Holy Book. Aqqad

opened his book with the quotation from the Koran establishing the fact of male supremacy ('the men are superior to them by a degree') and hastily concludes that 'the message of the Koran, which makes men superior to women is the manifest message of human history, the history of Adam's descendants before and after civilization.'[7]

What Aqqad finds in the Koran and in human civilization is a complementarity between the sexes based on their antagonistic natures. The characteristic of the male is the will to power, the will to conquer. The characteristic of the female is a negative will to power. All her energies are vested in seeking to be conquered, in wanting to be overpowered and subjugated. Therefore, 'She can only expose herself and wait while the man wants and seeks.'[8]

Although Aqqad has neither the depth nor the brilliant systematic deductive approach of Freud, his ideas on the male-female dynamic are very similar to Freud's emphasis on the 'law of the jungle' aspect of sexuality. The complementarity of the sexes, according to Aqqad, resides in their antagonistic wills and desires and aspirations.

> *Males in all kinds of animals are given the power—embodied in their biological structure—to compel females to yield to the demands of the instinct (that is, sex). . . . There is no situation where that power to compel is given to women over men.*[9]

Like Freud, Aqqad endows women with a hearty appetite for suffering. Women enjoy surrender.[10] More than that, for Aqqad women experience pleasure and happiness only in their subjugation, their defeat by males. The ability to experience pleasure in suffering and subjugation is the kernel of femininity, which is masochistic by its very nature. 'The woman's submission to the man's conquest is one of the strongest sources of women's pleasure.'[11] The machismo theory casts the man as the hunter and the woman as his prey. This vision is widely shared and deeply ingrained in both men's and women's vision of themselves.

The implicit theory of female sexuality, as seen in Imam Ghazali's interpretation of the Koran, casts the woman as the hunter and the man as the passive victim. The two theories have one component in common, the woman's *qaid* power ('the power to deceive and defeat men, not by force, but by cunning and intrigue'). But while Aqqad tries to link the female's *qaid* power to her weak constitution, the symbol of her divinely decreed inferiority, Imam Ghazali sees her power as the most destructive element in the Muslim social order, in which the feminine is regarded as synonymous with the satanic.

The whole Muslim organization of social interaction and spacial configuration can be understood in terms of women's *qaid* power. The social order then appears as an attempt to subjugate her power and neutralize its disruptive effects. The opposition between the implicit and the explicit theories in Muslim society would appear clearly if I could contrast Aqqad and Imam Ghazali. But whereas the implicit theory is brilliantly articulated in Imam Ghazali's systematic work on the institution of marriage in Islam, the explicit theory has an unfortunate advocate in Aqqad, whose work is an amateurish mixture of history, religion and his own brand of biology and anthropology. I shall therefore contrast Imam Ghazali's conception of sexual dynamics not with Aqqad's but with that of another theoretician, one who is not a Muslim but who has the advantage of possessing a machismo theory that is systematic in the elaboration of its premisses—Sigmund Freud.

IMAM GHAZALI VERSUS FREUD: ACTIVE VERSUS PASSIVE

In contrasting Freud and Imam Ghazali we are faced with a methodological obstacle, or rather what seems to be one. When Imam Ghazali was writing the chapter on marriage in his book *The Revivification of Religious Sciences*, in the eleventh century, he was endeavouring to reveal the true Muslim belief on the subject. But Freud was endeavouring to build a scientific theory, with all that the word 'scientific' implies of objectivity and universality. Freud did not think that he was elaborating a European theory of female sexuality; he thought he was elaborating a universal explanation of the human female. But this methodological obstacle is easily overcome if we are 'conscious of the historicity of culture.'[12] We can view Freud's theory as a 'historically defined' product of his culture. Linton noted that anthropological data [have] shown that it is culture that determines the perception of biological differences and not the other way around.

> *All societies prescribe different attitudes and activities to men and to women. Most of them try to rationalize these prescriptions in terms of the physiological differences between the sexes or their different roles in reproduction. However, a comparative study of the statuses ascribed to women and men in different cultures seems to show that while such factors may have served as a starting point for the development of a division, the actual prescriptions are almost entirely determined by culture. Even the psychological characteristics ascribed to men and to women in different societies vary so much that they can have little physiological basis.*[13]

A social scientist works in a biographically determined situation in which he finds himself 'in a physical and sociocultural environment as defined by him, within which he has his position, not merely his position in terms of physical space and outer time or of his status and role within the social system but also his moral and ideological position.'[14] We can therefore consider Freud's theory of sexuality in general, and of female sexuality in particular, as a reflection of his society's beliefs and not as a scientific (objective and ahistorical) theory. In comparing Freud and Imam Ghazali's theories we will be comparing the two different cultures' different conceptions of sexuality, one based on a model in which the female is passive, the other on one in which the female is active. The purpose of the comparison is to highlight the particular character of the Muslim theory of male-female dynamics, and not to compare the condition of women in the Judeo-Christian West and the Muslim East.

The novelty of Freud's contribution to Western contemporary culture was his acknowledgement of sex (sublimated, of course) as the source of civilization itself. The rehabilitation of sex as the foundation of civilized creativity led him to the reexamination of sex differences. This reassessment of the differences and of the consequent contributions of the sexes to the social order yielded the concept of female sexuality in Freudian theory.

In analysing the differences between the sexes, Freud was struck by a peculiar phenomenon—bisexuality—which is rather confusing to anyone trying to assess sex differences rather than similarities:

Science next tells you something that runs counter to your expectations and is probably calculated to confuse your feelings. It draws your attention to the fact that portions of the male sexual apparatus also appear in women's bodies, though in an atrophied state, and vice versa in the alternative case. It regards their occurrence as indications of bisexuality as though an individual is not a man or a woman but always both—merely a certain amount more one than the other.[15]

The deduction one expects from bisexuality is that anatomy cannot be accepted as the basis for sex differences. Freud made this deduction:

You will then be asked to make yourself familiar with the idea that the proportion in which masculine and feminine are mixed in an individual is subject to quite considerable fluctuations. Since, however, apart from the very rarest cases, only one kind of sexual product, ova or semen, is nevertheless present in one person, you are bound then to have doubts as to the decisive significance of those elements and must conclude that what constitutes masculinity or femininity is an unknown characteristic which anatomy cannot lay hold of.[16]

Where then did Freud get the basis for his polarization of human sexuality into a masculine and a feminine sexuality, if he affirms that anatomy cannot be the basis of such a difference? He explains this in a footnote, apparently considering it a secondary point:

It is necessary to make clear that the conceptions 'masculine' and 'feminine', whose content seems so unequivocal to the ordinary meaning, belong to the most confused terms in science and can be cut up into at least three paths. One uses masculinity and femininity at times in the sense of activity and passivity, again in the biological sense and then also in the sociological sense. The first of these three meanings is the essential one and the only one utilizable in psychoanalysis.[17]

The polarization of human sexuality into two kinds, feminine and masculine, and their equation with passivity and activity in Freudian theory helps us to understand Imam Ghazali's theory, which is characterized precisely by the absence of such a polarization. It conceives of both male and female sexuality partaking of and belonging to the same kind of sexuality.

For Freud, the sex cells' functioning is symbolic of the male-female relation during intercourse. He views it as an antagonistic encounter between aggression and submission.

The male sex cell is actively mobile and searches out the female and the latter, the ovum, is immobile and waits passively.... This behaviour of the elementary sexual organism is indeed a model for the conduct of sexual individuals during intercourse. The male pursues the female for the purpose of sex union, seizes hold of her and penetrates into her.[18]

For Imam Ghazali, both the male and female have an identical cell. The word sperm (ma', 'water drop') is used for the female as well as for the male cell. Imam Ghazali referred to the anatomic differences between the sexes when clarifying Islam's position on coitus interruptus ('azl), a traditional method of birth control practised in pre-Islamic times. In trying to establish the Prophet's position on 'azl, Imam Ghazali presented the Muslim theory of procreation and the sexes' contribution to it and respective roles in it.

The child is not created from the man's sperm alone, but from the union of a sperm from the male with a sperm from the female . . . and in any case the sperm of the female is a determinant factor in the process of coagulation.[19]

The puzzling question is not why Imam Ghazali failed to see the difference between the male and female cells, but why Freud, who was more than knowledgeable about biological facts, saw the ovum as a passive cell whose contribution to procreation was minor compared to the sperm's. In spite of their technical advancement, European theories clung for centuries to the idea that the sperm was the only determining factor in the procreation process; babies were prefabricated in the sperm[20] and the uterus was just a cozy place where they developed.

Imam Ghazali's emphasis on the identity between male and female sexuality appears clearly in his granting the female the most uncontested expression of phallic sexuality, ejaculation. This reduces the differences between the sexes to a simple difference of pattern of ejaculation, the female's being much slower than the male's.

The difference in the pattern of ejaculation between the sexes is a source of hostility whenever the man reaches his ejaculation before the woman. . . . The woman's ejaculation is a much slower process and during that process her sexual desire grows stronger and to withdraw from her before she reaches her pleasure is harmful to her.[21]

Here we are very far from the bedroom scenes of Aqqad and Freud, which resemble battlefields more than shelters of pleasure. For Imam Ghazali there is neither aggressor nor victim, just two people cooperating to give each other pleasure.

The recognition of female sexuality as active is an explosive acknowledgement for the social order with far-reaching implications for its structure as a whole. But to deny that male and female sexuality are identical is also an explosive and decisive choice. For example, Freud recognizes that the clitoris is an evident phallic appendage and that the female is consequently more bisexual than the male.

There can be no doubt that the bisexual disposition which we maintain to be characteristic of human beings manifests itself much more plainly in the female than in the male. The latter has only one principal sexual zone—only one sexual organ—whereas the former has two: the vagina, the true female organ, and the clitoris, which is analogous to the male organ.[22]

Instead of elaborating a theory which integrates and elaborates the richness of both sexes' particularities, however, Freud elaborates a theory of female sexuality based on reduction: the castration of the phallic features of the female. A female child, bisexual in infancy, develops into a mature female only if she succeeds in renouncing the clitoris, the phallic appendage: 'The elimination of the clitoral sexuality is a necessary pre-condition for the development of femininity.'[23] The pubertal development process brings atrophy to the female body while it enhances the phallic potential of the male's, thus creating a wide discrepancy in the sexual potential of humans, depending on their sex:

Puberty, which brings to the boy a great advance of libido, distinguishes itself in the girl by a new wave of repression which especially concerns the clitoral sexuality. It is a part of the male sexual life that sinks into repression. The reinforcement of the inhibitions produced in the woman by the repression of puberty causes a stimulus in the libido of the man and forces it to increase its capacity; with the height of the libido, there is a rise in the overestimation of the sexual, which can be present in its full force only when the woman refuses and denies her sexuality.[24]

The female child becomes a woman when her clitoris 'acts like a chip of pinewood which is utilized to set fire to the harder wood.'[25] Freud adds that this process takes some time, during which the 'young wife remains anesthetic.'[26] This anesthesia may become permanent if the clitoris refuses to relinquish its excitability. The Freudian woman, faced with her phallic partner, is therefore predisposed to frigidity.

> *The sexual frigidity of women, the frequency of which appears to confirm this disregard (the disregard of nature for the female function) is a phenomenon that is still insufficiently understood. Sometimes it is psychogenic and in that case accessible to influence; but in other cases it suggests the hypothesis of its being constitutionally determined and even of being a contributory anatomical factor.*[27]

By contrast with the passive, frigid Freudian female, the sexual demands of Imam Ghazali's female appear truly overwhelming, and the necessity for the male to satisfy them becomes a compelling social duty: 'The virtue of the woman is a man's duty. And the man should increase or decrease sexual intercourse with the woman according to her needs so as to secure her virtue.'[28] The Ghazalian theory directly links the security of the social order to that of the woman's virtue, and thus to the satisfaction of her sexual needs. Social order is secured when the woman limits herself to her husband and does not create *fitna*, or chaos, by enticing other men to illicit intercourse. Imam Ghazali's awe of the overpowering sexual demands of the active female appears when he admits how difficult it is for a man to satisfy a woman.

> *If the prerequisite amount of sexual intercourse needed by the woman in order to guarantee her virtue is not assessed with precision, it is because such an assessment is difficult to make and difficult to satisfy.*[29]

He cautiously ventures that the man should have intercourse with the woman as often as he can, once every four nights if he has four wives. He suggests this as a limit, otherwise the woman's sexual needs might not be met.

> *It is just for the husband to have sexual intercourse with his wife every four nights if he has four wives. It is possible for him to extend the limit to this extreme. Indeed, he should increase or decrease sexual intercourse according to her own needs.*[30]

Freud's and Ghazali's stands on foreplay are directly influenced by their visions of female sexuality. For Freud, the emphasis should be on the coital act, which is primarily 'the union of the genitals',[31] and he deemphasizes foreplay as lying between normal (genital) union and perversion, which consists '…in either an anatomical transgression of the bodily regions destined for sexual union or a lingering at the intermediary relations to the sexual object which should normally be rapidly passed on the way to definite sexual union.'[32]

In contrast, Imam Ghazali recommends foreplay, primarily in the interest of the woman, as a duty for the believer. Since the woman's pleasure necessitates a lingering at the intermediary stages, the believer should strive to subordinate his own pleasure, which is served mainly by the genital union.

> *The Prophet said, 'No one among you should throw himself on his wife like beasts do. There should be, prior to coitus, a messenger between you and her.' People asked him, 'What sort of messenger?' The Prophet answered, 'Kisses and words.'*[33]

The Prophet indicated that one of the weaknesses in a man's character would be that

> *…he will approach his concubine-slave or his wife and that he will have intercourse with her without having prior to that been caressing, been tender with her in words and gestures and laid down beside her for a while, so that he does not harm her, by using her for his own satisfaction, without letting her get her satisfaction from him.*[34]

THE FEAR OF FEMALE SEXUALITY

The perception of female aggression is directly influenced by the theory of women's sexuality. For Freud the female's aggression, in accordance with her sexual passivity, is turned inward. She is masochistic.

> *The suppression of woman's aggressiveness which is prescribed for them constitutionally and imposed on them socially favours the development of power-*

ful masochistic impulses, which succeed, as we know, in binding erotically the destructive trends which have been diverted inwards. Thus masochism, as people say, is truly feminine. But if, as happens so often, you meet with masochism in men, what is left for you but to say that these men exhibit very plainly feminine traits.[35]

The absence of active sexuality moulds the woman into a masochistic passive being. It is therefore no surprise that in the actively sexual Muslim female aggressiveness is seen as turned outward. The nature of her aggression is precisely sexual. The Muslim woman is endowed with a fatal attraction which erodes the male's will to resist her and reduces him to a passive acquiescent role. He has no choice; he can only give in to her attraction, whence her identification with *fitna*, chaos, and with the anti-divine and anti-social forces of the universe.

The Prophet saw a woman. He hurried to his house and had intercourse with his wife Zaynab, then left the house and said, 'When the woman comes towards you, it is Satan who is approaching you. When one of you sees a woman and he feels attracted to her, he should hurry to his wife. With her, it would be the same as with the other one.'[36]

Commenting on this quotation, Imam Muslim, an established voice of Muslim tradition, reports that the Prophet was referring to the

...fascination, to the irresistible attraction to women God instilled in man's soul, and he was referring to the pleasure man experiences when he looks at the woman, and the pleasure he experiences with anything related to her. She resembles Satan in his irresistible power over the individual.[37]

This attraction is a natural link between the sexes. Whenever a man is faced with a woman, *fitna* might occur: 'When a man and a woman are isolated in the presence of each other, Satan is bound to be their third companion.'[38]

The most potentially dangerous woman is one who has experienced sexual inter-course. It is the married woman who will have more difficulties in bearing sexual frustration. The married woman whose husband is absent is a particular threat to men: 'Do not go to the women whose husbands are absent. Because Satan will get in your bodies as blood rushes through your flesh.'[39]

In Moroccan folk culture this threat is epitomized by the belief in Aisha Kandisha, a repugnant female demon. She is repugnant precisely because she is libidinous. She has pendulous breasts and lips and her favourite pastime is to assault men in the streets and in dark places, to induce them to have sexual intercourse with her, and ultimately to penetrate their bodies and stay with them for ever.[40] They are then said to be inhabited. The fear of Aisha Kandisha is more than ever present in Morocco's daily life. Fear of the castrating female is a legacy of tradition and is seen in many forms in popular beliefs and practices and in both religious and mundane literature, particularly novels.

Moroccan folk culture is permeated with a negative attitude towards femininity. Loving a woman is popularly described as a form of mental illness, a self-destructive state of mind. A Moroccan proverb says

Love is a complicated matter
If it does not drive you crazy, it kills you.[41]

The best example of this distrust of women is the sixteenth-century poet Sidi Abderahman al-Majdoub. His rhymes are so popular that they have become proverbs.

Women are fleeting wooden vessels
Whose passengers are doomed to destruction.

Or

Don't trust them [women], so you would not be betrayed
Don't believe in their promises, so you would not be deceived
To be able to swim, fish need water
Women are the only creatures who can swim without it.[42]

And finally

Women's intrigues are mighty
To protect myself I run endlessly
Women are belted with serpents
And bejewelled with scorpions.[43]

The Muslim order faces two threats: the infidel without and the woman within.

The Prophet said, 'After my disappearance there will be no greater source of chaos and disorder for my nation than women.'[44]

The irony is that Muslim and European theories come to the same conclusion: women are destructive to the social order—for Imam Ghazali because they are active, for Freud because they are not.

Different social orders have integrated the tensions between religion and sexuality in different ways. In the Western Christian experience sexuality itself was attacked, degraded as animality and condemned as anti-civilization. The individual was split into two antithetical selves: the spirit and the flesh, the ego and the id. The triumph of civilization implied the triumph of soul over flesh, of ego over id, of the controlled over the uncontrolled, of spirit over sex.

Islam took a substantially different path. What is attacked and debased is not sexuality but women, as the embodiment of destruction, the symbol of disorder. The woman is *fitna*, the epitome of the uncontrollable, a living representative of the dangers of sexuality and its rampant disruptive potential. We have seen that Muslim theory considers raw instinct as energy which is likely to be used constructively for the benefit of Allah and His society if people live according to His laws. Sexuality *per se* is not a danger. On the contrary, it has three positive, vital functions. It allows the believers to perpetuate themselves on earth, an indispensable condition if the social order is to exist at all. It serves as a 'foretaste of the delights secured for men in Paradise',[45] thus encouraging men to strive for paradise and to obey Allah's rule on earth. Finally, sexual satisfaction is necessary to intellectual effort.

The Muslim theory of sublimation is entirely different from the Western Christian tradition as represented by Freudian psychoanalytic theory. Freud viewed civilization as a war against sexuality.[46] Civilization is sexual energy 'turned aside from its sexual goal and diverted towards other ends, no longer sexual and socially more valuable'.[47] The Muslim theory views civilization as the outcome of satisfied sexual energy. Work is the result not of sexual frustration but of a contented and harmoniously lived sexuality.

The soul is usually reluctant to carry out its duty because duty [work] is against its nature. If one puts pressures on the soul in order to make it do what it loathes, the soul rebels. But if the soul is allowed to relax for some moments by the means of some pleasures, it fortifies itself and becomes after that alert and ready for work again. And in the woman's company, this relaxation drives out sadness and pacifies the heart. It is advisable for pious souls to divert themselves by means which are religiously lawful.[48]

According to Ghazali, the most precious gift God gave humans is reason. Its best use is the search for knowledge. To know the human environment, to know the earth and galaxies, is to know God. Knowledge (science) is the best form of prayer for a Muslim believer. But to be able to devote his energies to knowledge, man has to reduce the tensions within and without his body, avoid being distracted by external elements, and avoid indulging in earthly pleasures. Women are a dangerous distraction that must be used for the specific purpose of providing the Muslim nation with offspring and quenching the tensions of the sexual instinct. But in no way should women be an object of emotional investment or the focus of attention, which should be devoted to Allah alone in the form of knowledge-seeking, meditation, and prayer.

Ghazali's conception of the individual's task on earth is illuminating in that it reveals that the Muslim message, in spite of its beauty, considers humanity to be constituted by males only. Women are considered not only outside of humanity but a threat to it as well. Muslim wariness of heterosexual involvement is embodied in sexual segregation and its corollaries: arranged marriage, the important role of the mother in the son's life, and the fragility of the marital bond (as revealed by the institutions of repudiation and polygamy). The entire Muslim social structure can be seen as an attack on, and a defence against, the disruptive power of female sexuality.

NOTES

1. George Peter Murdock, *Social Structure* (New York: Macmillan & Co. Free Press), 1965, p. 273.

2. *Ibid.*

3. Kacem Amin, *The Liberation of the Woman.* (Cairo: 'Umum al-Makatib Bimisr Wa-Iharij, 1928) p. 64.

4. *Ibid.*, p. 65.

5. al-Ghazali, *The Revivification of Religious Sciences*, Vol. II, chapter on marriage; and Mizan al-'Amal ("Criteria for Action") (Cairo: Dar al-Ma'arif, 1964).

6. 'Abbas Mahmud al-Aqquad, *The Women in the Koran* (Cairo: Dar al-Hilal, n.d.)

7. *Ibid.*, p. 7; the verse he refers to is verse 228 of Surah II which is striking by its inconsistency. The whole verse reads as follows:

> And they [women] have rights similar to those [of men] over them in kindness, and men are a degree above them.
> tempted to interpret the first part of the sentence as a simple stylistic device to bring out the hierarchical content of the second part.
> translation of the Quran used throughout is that of Mohammed Marmaduke Pickthall, The Meaning of the Glorious Koran. (New York: New American Library, A Mentor Religious Book, 13th printing, n.d.)

8. *Ibid.*, p. 24.

9. *Ibid.*, p. 25. The biological assumptions behind Aqquad's sweeping generalizations are obviously fallacious.

10. *Ibid.*, p. 18.

11. *Ibid.*, p. 26.

12. A. Schutz, "The Problem of Social Reality" *Collected Papers*, Vol. I (The Hague: Martinus Nijhoff, n.d.) p. 101.

13. Ralph Linton, *The Study of Man.* (London: Appleton-Century Co., 1936), p. 116.

14. A. Schultz, *Collected Papers*, p. 9.

15. Sigmund Freud, *New Introductory Lectures on Psychoanalysis.* College Edition. (New York: Norton and Co., 1965), p. 114.

16. *Ibid.*

17. Sigmund Freud, *Three Contributions to the Theory of Sex*, 2nd ed. (New York: Dutton and Co., 1909) p. 77.

18. Sigmund Freud, *New Introductory Lectures*, p. 114.

19. al-Ghazali, *Revivification of Religious Sciences*, p. 51.

20. Una Stannard, "Adam's Rib or the Woman Within," *Transaction*. November-December 1970, Vol. 8, Special Issue on the American Woman, pp. 24–36.

21. al Ghazali, *Revivification*, p. 50. Not only is the woman granted ejaculation, she is also granted the capacity to have nocturnal ejaculation and "see what the man sees in sleep." (Ibn Saad, *Kitab al-Tabaqat Al Kubra*, Dar Beyrouth 1958). (Beirut: Vol. 8, "On Women" p. 858.)

22. Sigmund Freud, *Sexuality and the Psychology of Love* (New York: Collier Books, 1963 pp. 196–197.

23. *Ibid.*, p. 190.

24. Sigmund Freud, *Three Contributions*, p. 78.

25. *Ibid.*

26. *Ibid.*

27. Sigmund Freud, *New Introductory Lectures*, p. 132.

28. al-Ghazali, *Revivification*, p. 50.

29. *Ibid.*

30. *Ibid.*

31. Sigmund Freud, *Three Contributions*, p. 14.

32. *Ibid.*, p. 15.

33. al-Ghazali, *Revivification*, p. 50.

34. *Ibid.*

35. Sigmund Freud, *New Introductory Lectures*, p. 116.

36. Abbi 'Issa at-Tarmidi, *Sunan at-Tarmidi* (Medina: al-Maktaba as Salafiya, n.d.) Vol. II, p. 413. Bab: 9, Hadith: 1167. (Hereinafter Bab will be indicated by the letter B, and Hadith by the letter H.)

37. Abu al-Hassan Muslim, *al-Jami' as-Sahih* (Beirut: al-Maktaba at-Tijariya, n.d.) Vol. III. Book of Marriage, p. 130.

38. at-Tarmidi, *Sunan at-Tarmidi.* p. 419, B:16, H:1181. See also al-Bukhari, *Kitab al-Jami' as-Sahih* (Leyden, Holland: Ludolph Krehl, 1868) Vol. III. Kitab 67, B:11. (Hereinafter Kitab will be indicated by the letter K.)

39. at-Tarmidi, *Sunan at-Tarmidi*, p. 419, B:17, H:1172.

40. Edward Westermarck, *The Belief in Spirits in Morocco,* (Abo, Finland: Abo-Akademi, 1920).

41. Edward Westermarck, *Wit and Wisdom in Morocco: A Study of Native Proverbs* (London: MacMillan and Co., 1926) p. 330.

42. Sidi Abderahaman al-Majdoub. *Les Quatrains du Mejdoub le Sarcastique, Poete Magrebin du XVIieme Siecle,* collected and translated by J. Scelles-Millie and B. Khelifa (Paris: G. P. Maisonneuver and Larose, 1966) p. 161.

43. *Ibid.,* p. 160.

44. Abu Abd Allah Muhammad Ibn Ismail al-Bukhari, *Kitab al-Jami' as-Sahih* (Leyden, Holland: Ludolph Krehl, 1868) p. 419, K:67, B:18.

45. al Ghazali, *Revivification,* p. 28.

46. Sigmund Freud, *Civilization and Its Discontents* (New York: Norton and Co., Inc., 1962).

47. Sigmund Freud, *A General Introduction to Psychoanalysis* (New York: Pocket Books, 1952), p. 27.

48. al-Ghazali, *Revivification,* p. 32.

"It's Our Church, Too!": Women's Position in the Catholic Church Today

SUSAN A. FARRELL

How do women go about living in an institution that many find patriarchal, clericalist, bureaucratic, and oppressive? This chapter examines some of the issues facing women in the contemporary Roman Catholic Church. The women discussed in this chapter do not want to, and have no intention of, leaving the church. Contrary to prior reform movements these women are asserting that they are the church, too, and have invested much of their lives in living out what to them is the gospel message. Living and working in great tension between what the institution is, and what they envision it could and should be, Catholic feminists are searching for alternative models of church while maintaining their identity as Roman Catholics. These women, theologians, ethicists, sisters, and laywomen, have taken to heart and are trying to bring to fulfillment the message of the church itself, declared in the "Pastoral Constitution on the Church in the Modern World" (*Gaudium at Spes*):

> *Where they have not yet won it, women claim for themselves an equity with men before the law and in fact.... With respect to the fundamental rights of the person, every type of discrimination, whether social or cultural, whether based on sex, race, color, social condition, language, or religion, is to be overcome and eradicated as contrary to God's intent. For in truth it must still be regretted that funda-*

mental personal rights are not yet being universally honored. Such is the case of a woman who is denied the right and freedom to choose a husband, to embrace a state of life, or to acquire an education or cultural benefits equal to those recognized for men. (Abbott 1966, pp. 207, 227–28)

The task that these women see for themselves is radical reform from within the church, without being coopted or so marginalized that they have no impact on the institution.

WOMEN'S POSITION IN THE CATHOLIC CHURCH TODAY

According to Wallace (1988), Roman Catholic women are creating a new social reality which "represents a shift from their passive and subservient roles vis-á-vis the clergy to a more active participation in the life of the Church" (p. 25). Influenced by the secular women's movement in which many are active, Roman Catholic women want and are demanding more participation at higher levels of the organizational church. More and more women, both lay and religious, are filling administrative positions, jobs that only ordained clergymen used to do. Although these opportunities for women in some measure come from the current shortage of priests, women have also been encouraged by the Second

Vatican Council's call in the early 1960s for greater involvement of the laity in the day-to-day life of the church (Abbott 1966).

However, women's continued advancement and increased participation at higher organizational levels is blocked by church practice and discipline that does not allow the ordination of women to the priesthood. All top-level positions of authority and decision-making in the Roman Catholic Church are held by ordained celibate men, which also effectively removes married men from these positions. In essence, as the *Declaration on the Question of the Admission of Women to the Ministerial Priesthood* (Sacred Congregation for the Doctrine of the Faith 1976) states and has been repeated by Pope John Paul II, women cannot be ordained because they cannot act *in persona Christi* (in the person of Christ) because they are not biological men (1988, pp. 89–90). Thus, the hierarchical structure of the church and its division of labor is based very clearly on a biologized concept of sex and gender.

The organizational structure of Roman Catholicism reveals what Acker (1991) states is often hidden in modern bureaucratic organizations, a negative view of sexuality that is linked to misogyny and heterosexism. According to Acker, organizations are "gendered processes in which both gender and sexuality have been obscured through a gender-neutral, asexual discourse" (p. 163). The ideology underlying the Roman Catholic organizational structure that denies ordination to women and also represses men's sexuality becomes the example par excellence of Acker's point that "gender is a constitutive element in organizational logic" (p. 168). Obscuring sexuality also hides human procreation and "helps to reproduce the underlying gender relations" (p. 172).

FEMINIST SCHOLARS' CHALLENGE

Feminist scholars in Christianity and Roman Catholicism have illustrated the origins and results of the patriarchal religious ideology upon which the hierarchy of Roman Catholicism is constructed. According to Schüssler Fiorenza (1984):

> Much feminist theological writing accepts a two-fold pre-supposition: that the root of women's oppression is dualistic thought or patriarchalism as a mind set or projection, and that monotheistic religions of Judaism and Christianity constitute the bedrock of Western patriarchalism. This hierarchical pattern of Western society, culture, and religion is characterized by the split between subject-object, superior-inferior, spirituality-carnality, life-death, mind-body, men-women.... They have fashioned an absolute transcendent God in the image of men and declared women "the other" who cannot image or represent God. (pp. 296–7)

Schüssler Fiorenza is summarizing the work done by many Jewish, Christian, and post-Christian feminist theologians and philosophers who have uncovered the patriarchal roots of Judeo-Christianity and the Judeo-Christian roots of patriarchy.[1] In this androcentric ethical discourse, as it has been institutionalized in Christianity and the Roman Catholic church, women have not been acknowledged as full moral agents by men. This view is based on a patriarchal interpretation of the creation stories in Genesis.

Post-Christian feminist Mary Daly insists that since genesis stories were written by men and their conception of God is irrevocably androcentric, they cannot be useable for and by women (1973, 1978, 1984). Based on this conclusion, Daly herself left the Roman Catholic Church believing the Judeo-Christian tradition to be intrinsically patriarchal and beyond redemption. Other Christian and Roman Catholic feminists, however, are trying to reclaim the past, arguing that religious mythology has been subverted by men to serve their interests. It is a feminist project to deconstruct and then reconstruct a past to make it into a useable present and to transform it for a liberated future for women in the church (Fiorenza 1983, pp. 28–32).

Trible (1978) gives an intriguing alternate interpretation of Genesis. According to Trible, the creation stories are hierarchically told, going from the simplest to the most complex creatures. Woman, being the last created, is the pinnacle of creation. She also makes note of wrongly translated names and genders. "Adam" actually means "humankind," not "man." The full quote is "Let us make humankind in our image, after our likeness; and let *them* have dominion (Genesis 1:26) (her emphasis, 1978, p. 18). Jewish midrash (a collection of interpretations of and commentaries on Biblical texts, especially those written during the first ten centuries C.E.) offers a variety of creation stories that provide feminists with an alternative to the patriarchally accused and condemned Eve. Called Lilith stories, Plaskow (1974) retells one version that has Adam complaining to God that Lilith, his first wife, does not obey him, she is an "uppity woman" (p. 341). He wants another more tractable woman. God complies. He gives Adam Eve and Lilith leaves the garden. She roams outside the garden wall, calling to Eve. When Eve climbs the garden wall and meets her, Lilith recounts her story: "They taught each other many things, and told each other stories, and laughed together, and cried, over and over, till the bond of sisterhood grew between them.... And God and Adam were expectant and afraid the day Eve and Lilith returned to the garden, bursting with possibilities, ready to rebuild it together" (pp. 342–3).

These scholars are transforming theological discourse using a well-honed feminist method: the experience of oppression discovered through the sharing of life stories. Welch (1985) describes this method as being simultaneously a way of doing research and an act of resistance:

> This politicization gives women the courage to persist in resistance, recognizing that their difficulties have not only an individual basis but a social and political basis as well. (pp. 41–2)

Using Daly's vision of a community of sisterhood as a locus of "creative resistance," Welch says that this experience of sisterhood is

> an experience of resistance and liberation, an affirmation of an identity that is different from that imposed by the dominant patriarchal social structures. The experience of resistance is itself a denial of the necessity of patriarchy; it is a moment of freedom, the power to embody momentarily an alternative identity. This affirmation serves as the ground for political resistance to social structures. (1985, pp. 41–2)

Linking this experience of oppression with a critique of mainstream religion offered by liberation theology, Welch goes on to describe the task of the feminist theologian in the church:

> The philosopher or theologian of resistance then brings the skills of his or her training in analysis and synthesis to bear on the power relations manifest in oppression...an analysis of the concrete mechanisms of exclusion and domination.... In theology, commitment and reflection have led to... works that describe specific historics of oppression, criticize the role of the church and theology in that oppression, and offer alternative interpretations of the gospel and ecclesia [church]. (1985, pp. 42–3)

It is this understanding of their role as resisters, subversives, and, ultimately, transformers of a patriarchal church that sustains feminists who choose to remain in the institution.

FEMINIST ETHICISTS

One group that has maintained this embattled position of working from within are Roman Catholic feminist ethicists. Choosing to focus on sexual ethics, they highlight the sense of struggle and conflict between official church discourse and feminist discourse. Even in the larger society, sexuality is a "contested zone" (Weeks [1985] 1989, p. 4), but it is especially so in Roman Catholicism. Feminist ethicists are engaging in a struggle for meaning in a discourse that men have dominated for centuries.

The first task of Christian feminist theologians and ethicists was the critique of ethics and moral theology that revealed its androcentric and patriarchal bias (see especially Andolsen, Gudorf, and Pellauer 1985; Daly 1978; Fiorenza 1983; Harrison 1985; Heyward 1989; Ruether 1975, 1983). Using Foucault's (1979) insight that sexuality is also a locus of power,

Christian feminist ethicists have linked the institutional church's sexual repressiveness and misogyny with the question of women's ordination.[2] The Roman Catholic Church has also made sexual issues, particularly abortion, a litmus test for orthodoxy and evidence of loyalty to Rome. Outstanding male theologians such as Charles Curran, Matthew Fox, Hans Küng, and Edward Schillebeeckx have been censured, had teaching licenses revoked, and been silenced (a Vatican discipline that prohibits the person in question from speaking or writing about a particular subject, usually because the theologian has disagreed with, or is challenging, the official Vatican position). These sanctions have usually been invoked over areas of disagreement concerning either sexual ethics or perceived support for increased participation by women in the ministry, especially ordination.

Understanding the nature of the church as a complex social organization can help contextualize the ethical discourse and why it is perceived as a threat to the hierarchy. The Roman Catholic Church fits Weber's (1978) model of a hierocracy:

> A "hierocratic organization" is an organization which enforces its order through psychic coercion by distributing or denying religious benefits.... A compulsory hierocratic organization will be called "church" insofar as its administrative staff claims a monopoly of the legitimate use of hierocratic coercion. (p. 54)

In the Roman Catholic Church, religious benefits, for example, grace, mainly come through the sacraments. Except for baptism, only ordained priests can administer the sacraments. Technically, in matrimony, the couple administers the sacrament to each other, but a priest must be present to witness it and bless the couple, which is really the distribution of a special grace. Despite some relaxation of administration because of the shortage of priests, an ordained minister is preferred for administering the sacraments.

Because all women and most men are excluded, a small minority of Roman Catholic men do indeed possess a monopoly over the dispensation of the sacraments and the graces that accompany them and, ultimately, the salvation that all Catholics desire.

Using their own judgment, priests can also deny the sacraments. For example, in California, a Catholic woman running for public office was denied communion because of her pro-choice stand on abortion. A few years ago, a young woman was denied confirmation because her mother worked in a women's health clinic where abortions were performed. Excommunication is the ultimate sanction that can be brought to bear against Roman Catholics who disobey. There is only one case where excommunication is automatic. According to the new code of canon law, "A person who procures a successful abortion incurs an automatic excommunication" (Canon 1398, Canon Law Society 1983).

Clearly, punishment is more likely to be meted out for "sins" related to sexual than other practices because no other act incurs automatic excommunication. Women, and men who support them, are also more likely to be targets of sanctions and reprimands. The signers of the *New York Times* (October 7, 1984) advertisement advocating discussion and a "diversity of opinions regarding abortion" in the Roman Catholic community, especially members of religious orders directly under Vatican authority, were special targets of a campaign of harassment. Those priests, sisters, and brothers of religious communities who did not formally retract, or whose religious communities did not do so for them, "were penalized by segments of the institutional church" (*Declaration of Solidarity*, 1986, p. 21).

Laypersons not associated with an official Roman Catholic institution were not so hardpressed, because it was difficult for the hierarchy either to locate them or to sanction them. A number of laywomen I interviewed felt that their "lowly status" has a positive side in that it allows them to teach or function as ethical practitioners in a way not readily observable by the institutional church. They therefore believe they have a more subversive role. Women who have no official standing in the institutional church, in contrast to nuns and sisters, are outside many of the watchdog agencies of the Vatican, such as the Sacred Congregation for Religious Communities. Although their lives may be irrelevant to the church except for their so-called biological function of procreation, their usefulness as teachers, pastoral assistants, counselors, and the myriad voluntary positions they fill makes them necessary to the functioning of the church. From these positions, they can quietly subvert the dominant discourse with little fear of incurring sanctions.

Canon law is like the U.S. Constitution; it is the core of the laws and regulations that govern the life of the institutional church. However, because the ruling body of the church is the Curia, which is made up only of celibate clergymen, women and laymen have no input into creating, changing, or maintaining these laws. The monopoly is not simply one of an elite class based on economics or education. It is also clearly based on gender and sexual practices. Laws relating to sexual behavior are rooted largely in the "naturalness" of heterosexuality. Heterosexual intercourse is regulated by limiting its practice to the confines of the social institution of marriage and mainly for the purposes of procreation and regulation of concupiscence (strong sexual desire). Women, and men associated with women in sexual relationships, i.e., heterosexual marriage (which for the institutional church is the only acceptable sexual relationship), are barred from ordination and therefore from the ruling class of the institution.

The roots linking authority and power with sexist and heterosexist ideology go back to struggles with Gnosticism and Manicheism in the early history of Christianity, the influence of stoicism on the early church fathers,

especially Augustine, and the consolidation of church power in the Holy Roman Empire (Katchadourian 1989). According to Heyward (1989)

> The Council of Elvira (Spain), at which for the first time an explicitly antisexual code was made law for western christians, was held in 309 C.E. . . . [T]he christian church still operates on the basis of this same antisexual dualism, which is in effect, an antifemale dualism. From the second century on, the church had portrayed sex as something pertaining to women and as evil, "the devil's gateway." This attitude, for the first time, is canonized at the dawn of the era in which the church's social, political, and economic power is inaugurated. (pp. 42, 44)

Based on the image of Eve as seductive temptress, Christian theologians have associated women with sexuality and viewed both with deep suspicion and fear. Throughout the history of Christianity and Roman Catholicism, theologians, moralists, and ethicists have inveighed against women as corrupt, weak, lustful, evil "daughters of Eve" and to be avoided at all costs. Debates raged over whether women were fully human, possessed of rational souls, or capable of redemption. In Augustine's view, women were unfortunately needed for procreation, which seemed to be the only reason for their existence (Prusak 1977, p. 8). Thomas Aquinas concurred, and Roman Catholic theology and ethics has had to try to redeem women by concentrating on their biological function (Daly [1968] 1975, 1973, 1978; Osiek 1977; Tavard 1977; Quistlund 1977). Using Mary, Jesus' mother, as a counterpoint, the church fathers and scholastics resolved women into dualistic images: virgin-mother or whore—the latter a negative image, the former an improbable achievement.

Feminist ethicists seeking to transform the discourse are up against an ideological authoritarianism wherein sexual ethics are based in biological determinism and constructed on a belief in "natural law." In addition, as illustrated in anti-choice rhetoric, the discourse is deontological: it is more concerned with duties, the minimal threshold for conformity, absolute values, and universalization of standards, laws, and guidelines than with consequences of actions, extenuating circumstances, and social contexts. According to its major proponent, Immanual Kant, *deontological ethics* consists of the will to do one's duty for duty's sake, which...is the essence of human morality (Lake 1986, p. 480 and footnote 6, p. 480). A concrete example of deontological behavior is conformity to moral rules, for example, the Ten Commandments. According to Lake, "In a deontological ethical system, it is by definition right to obey the rules and wrong to disobey them" (p. 482). Rules and laws are stripped of their historical and social context and universalized. It is an abstract and absolute ethic which does not ask about consequences (Weber 1946, p. 120). There are no people, no contextualized lived experience, nothing that takes into account the "average deficiencies of people" (p. 121).

FEMINIST ETHICAL DISCOURSE

Since issues of sexuality have become the testing sites of sin and error, feminist ethical discourse presents a major challenge to traditional religious institutions, especially the Catholic Church. In an ironic way, women have been and continue to be the "objects" of both sides of this discourse. For traditional male theologians, it is women's sexuality that must be controlled, restrained, constrained, regulated, and harnessed for procreative reasons. Men's sexuality gets out of hand only because of women: Either they tempt men or they fail to satisfy them and thus are responsible when men lose control (Weeks [1986] 1989, p. 32, 38–9). Encyclicals, Vatican declarations, and official instructions concerning sexuality have been directed primarily toward women's sexual behavior and their responsibilities in marriage and child-rearing. Frequently addressed to bishops, theologians, pastors, and other official churchmen, they exhort them to keep "the faithful" faithful. In matters of sexuality, the burden of conformity is on women, who fail as wives and mothers when they do not conform to the church's teachings.

John Paul II's recent (1988) encyclical, *On the Dignity and Vocation of Women*, is a prime example of patriarchal institutional discourse that bases the official church's understanding of women and sexuality on a socially constructed belief in biologically determined gender roles, especially surrounding parenthood:

> *Scientific analysis fully confirms that the very physical constitution of women is naturally disposed to motherhood—conception, pregnancy and giving birth—which is a consequence of the marriage union with the man. At the same time this corresponds to the psychophysical structure of women.... Motherhood as a* human *fact and phenomenon is fully explained on the basis of the truth about the person. Motherhood* is linked to the personal structure of the woman and to the personal dimension of the gift: *"I have brought a man into being with the help of the Lord"* (Genesis 4:1). (pp. 64–5, his emphasis)

John Paul's underlying belief is that mothers are more important in raising children than fathers are and that there is no connection between men's procreative role in conception and their social role as fathers; only mothers are socially defined by their procreative role:

> *Although both of them together are parents of their child,* the woman's motherhood constitutes a special "part" in this shared parenthood, *the most demanding part. Parenthood—even though it belongs to both—is realized much more fully in the woman, especially in the prenatal period. It is the woman who "pays" directly for this shared generation, which literally absorbs the energies of her body and soul. It is therefore necessary that* the man *be fully aware that in their shared parenthood he owes* a special debt to the woman. *No program of "equal rights" between women and men is valid unless it takes this fact fully into account.* (1998, p. 65, his emphasis)

Schüssler Fiorenza, in an effort to refute this essentialist notion of women, agrees with feminist social theorists such as Katz Rothman (1989) about the social construction of motherhood. She quotes Judith Plaskow:

> nature and motherhood are human constructs and institutions, on the one hand, and ... women's physicality is a "resource rather than a destiny," and the ground "of all we make ourselves to be" on the other hand. (Fiorenza 1984, pp. 297–8)

The ideology expressed by John Paul II is also the basis for church laws prohibiting contraception, abortion, new reproductive technologies, and homosexuality, as well as "camouflage (for) the issue of power" (Quistlund 1977, p. 265). It is an ideology that, despite reference to "scientific analysis" and "anthropological truths," still remains androcentric. This official discourse refers to "eternal truths" taught by the male *magisterium* to whom they have been revealed. It is not open to discussion nor can a diversity of opinion be tolerated. Challenge would upset the natural order of creation—two complementary "sexes" with God-given roles. Woman-centered theology and ethics would threaten the power structure because questioning the "natural order" also questions man's superior place in the social order, and thereby the ownership of truth and authority by celibate clergymen.

It is precisely this ideology that the discourse of feminist ethicists *does* challenge. In their alternative view of women and men, gender identities and roles and sexual identities and practices are constituted out of the centrality of women's lived experience. Analysis of women's experiences brings to light a crucial component of the social construction of feminist ethics: women's experiences are not homogeneous:

> Women's lives are very different. Among differences that seem most significant are the following: Some women are mothers; others are not. Some women come from upper-class backgrounds; others from the middle class; still others from the working class or from poverty. Some are lesbian; some, heterosexual. Women are Black, White, Native American, Asian-American, or Latina. Women are Jewish, Catholic, Protestant, adherents to other traditional world religions, followers of the Goddess, or nonreligious. Women have very different work experiences as homemakers, clerical workers, service workers, factory operatives, managers, or professionals. If feminist ethics is to be based on the experience of all women, then such differences in experience must be acknowledged and incorporated into feminist theory. (Andolsen, Gudorf, and Pellauer 1985, p. xv)

This statement summarizes the quality of feminist ethics: constant re-creation in the crucible of the diversity of women's experiences. Unlike the institutional church, feminist ethics recognizes women as moral agents who are capable of making their own choices—even if they are not the best ones, even if they make mistakes. It also understands those choices as made in reference to a particular community: family, neighborhood, workplace.

Carol Robb, a feminist ethicist of "resistance," lays out a framework for a feminist ethics that starts with "reflection upon very concrete situations" (1985, p. 213). She notes that defining the problem is a political act. Like Gilligan (1982) she believes that women's morality and ethics cannot be tested with prefabricated, androcentric dilemmas, since women reconstruct these dilemmas for themselves and create inventive ways to solve them. Robb goes on to enumerate the guidelines she believes are important for "doing ethics." Ethicists must gather data about the historical situation and context; they must analyze the roots of oppression; they must uncover loyalties—community ties as well as political ones; and finally a theory of values has to be clarified.

A FEMINIST THEORY OF VALUES

The issue of variance has become problematic for feminists. Various models for a value system have been proposed, creating heated debates not only within the feminist community but within the ethical community at large.[3] Robb (1985), for example, asks if "feminists have claim to any values independent of either a theory that biology is determinative, or a commitment to social justice shared with others" (p. 215), e.g., commitments to racial or economic justice.

Ethics generally recognizes three modes: teleological, deontological (discussed earlier), and situation-response. The *teleological mode* identifies "goals toward which people should aspire," acknowledging "*gradations* of right and wrong." Contingencies and consequences may mitigate an act that is formally proscribed by "interjecting subjective interpretations in uncertain circumstances" (Lake 1986, pp. 480–1, 486). Robb (1985) claims that "feminist ethics is done largely in the teleological mode, when the understanding of teleology allows for inclusion of the relational mode" (1985, p. 216). The *situation-response mode* "holds that there are no a priori right or wrong actions. Rather, moral value is determined only as a result of human choice in concrete situations.... [S]ituationism is highly individualistic, emphasizing the constitutive role of human choice in ethical determinations." (Lake 1986, p. 486).[4]

Referring to Daly, Robb agrees that feminist ethics is "metaethical." Setting it up as opposed to conventional ethics, Daly states that:

> *radical feminist metaethics is of a deeper intuitive type than "ethics." The latter, generally written from one of several (but basically the same) patriarchal perspectives, works out of hidden agendas concealed in the texture of language, buried in mythic reversals which control "logic" most powerfully because unacknowledged. Thus for theologians and philosophers, Eastern and Western, and particularly for ethicists, woman-identified women do not exist. The metaethics of radical feminism seeks to uncover the background of such logic.... [I]t is, of course, a new discipline that "deals critically" with nature, structure, and the behavior of ethics and ethicists. (Daly 1978, p. 13)*

With Daly, Robb reminds us that feminist ethics is critical and a discourse of resistance, but she maintains that its teleology, or relational mode, must be inclusive, which distinguishes it from simple utilitarianism (1985, p. 217) and situation ethics, both of which emphasize the individual, leaving out the community and social context of the moral agents. Robb emphasizes the importance of inclusive relationality, while *"granting the complexities* of this method" (1985, p. 217, my emphasis), "making the connections" among the family, the community, and the workplace. Inclusive relationality means taking into account the social and cultural differences among women and includes the economic dimension in moral decision-making, especially the way it often constrains women's choices (Harrison 1984, 1985). Gilligan has characterized women's morality as an "ethic of responsibility" (1982); Noddings (1984) calls it an "ethic of caring."

Feminist ethics criticizes the notion of "the moral agent as dispassionate and disengaged...for its failure to recognize the social foundation of self" (Robb 1985, p. 217). Building on Gilligan's critique of Kohlberg's moral dilemmas and moral decision-making, Robb and other feminists (Harding, 1986; Parlee, 1979) reject what they see as an androcentric notion of moral agent who stands outside a social context. The construction of an idealized human moral agent has been shown to actually mean "man" in its particular sense and not the so-called inclusive sense which male ethicists, theologians, and philosophers maintain is what they "really mean" (Andolsen, Gudorf, and Pellauer 1985, p. xxii).

The detached moral agent ignores, hides, and makes invisible the inequality between men and women (Robb 1985). Ignoring social context and relations within a family, community, or workplace limits women's moral agency:

> *In this sense, the economic dependency of women in the family, the inequality of pay and promotion in the labor force tied to women's role as childbearer and child-rearer, the possibility of sexual harassment or physical abuse from a stranger or an intimate, and further, in psychological terms, the*

tendency toward lack of ego differentiation in women's personality formation, are all factors impinging upon women's sense of self which can be autonomous confronting or defining ethical situations. (Robb 1985, p. 218)

Nevertheless, according to Robb, motivation will make us know the right thing and gets us to do it. This willingness to "do the right thing" begins "when women become engaged in collective efforts of self-definition. . . . [they create] an energy which overcomes or at least mitigates against alienation between the will and the right" (Robb 1985, p. 218).

A DISCOURSE OF RESISTANCE

Repeatedly, feminist ethicists return to community and relationships as the grounding for both resistance and revisioning. Roman Catholic feminists understand church to be a community of believers for whom "there are no more distinctions between Jew and Greek, slave and free, male and female" (Galatians 3:28). They see their role within the institutional church as prophetic: calling the church to a more faithful living out of the gospel message which they see as nonhierarchical and inclusive, not exclusive and hierarchically bureaucratic. Schüssler Fiorenza (1979) articulates a feminist model of church based on Jesus' exhortation to his followers "to call no man 'father'. . . nor should you be called 'leader'" (Matthew 23:9–11). Initiated by a lay Catholic organization, "Call to Action," and supported by the Women's Ordination Conference, a recent advertisement, "A Call for Reform in the Catholic Church," linked abuse of authority and power with sexism, clericalism, racism, ethnocentrism, heterosexism, and classism (Call to Action 1990). Lernoux (1989) sees various reform movements as aligned with liberation theology as does Welch (1995). Lernoux sees all, as the subtitle of her last book put it, as "the struggle for world Catholicism."

Roman Catholic feminists refuse to leave or be put out of the church. Instead, they are fighting from within, creating resistance and

alternative voices. Feminist ethicist Mary Hunt (1990) envisions a coalition of the disenfranchised groups who are attempting to reform the institution. The most active are what she calls "the women-church groups" (p. 3). *Women-church* is a term used to describe a movement rather than a single organization. Comprised of several national organizations like the Women's Ordination Conference, Conference for Catholic Lesbians, Women's Alliance for Theology, Ethics, and Ritual (WATER—Mary Hunt is a codirector), and Catholics for a Free Choice, Women-church is also made up of local feminist base communities which function as alternatives to parish churches.

Women-church is a loose women-centered alliance, a way of saying that "we are religious while not institutionally affiliated" (Hunt 1990, p. 3). Although eclectic enough to include other religious traditions, many remain Christian in their orientation and spirituality. What they have rejected is not the basic Christian message but its present institutional embodiment. According to Hunt, of all the lay-led groups in the coalition, Women-church groups, though far from perfect, "show the greatest promise in terms of new models of leadership. . . . [S]uch women-led groups are accomplishing goals and developing organizations that embody a commitment to women's empowerment." (1990, p. 3–4)

For Mary Hunt and other Roman Catholic feminists, the revisioning of the church is the creation of a new moral community which is inclusive yet diverse. In their attempt to deconstruct the institution and reconstruct a new community, they feel that they are also part of the larger feminist project of human liberation. Schüssler Fiorenza (1983) sees Women-church, or what she calls the *ekklesia of women*, as

overcoming all the structural-patriarchal dualisms between Jewish and Christian women, lay-women and nun-women, homemakers and career women, between active and contemplative, between Protestant and Roman Catholic women, between married and

*single women, between physical and spiritual moth-
ers, between heterosexual and lesbian women, between church and the world, the sacral and the
secular. However, we will overcome these dualisms
only through and in solidarity with all women and
in a catholic sisterhood that transcends all patriarchal ecclesiastical divisions. . . . It must be lived in a
prophetic commitment, compassionate solidarity,
consistent resistance, affirmative celebration, and in
grassroots organizations of ekklesia of women.
(p. 349)*

CONCLUSION

Creating a moral community that is viable for
both women and men is an important aspect
of feminist ethics. It is also a growing concern
for social scientists trying to find moral consensus in an increasingly pluralistic world. Sociologist Alan Wolfe sees the moral order
being created in the actual discourse and process of attempting to arrive at a consensus. The
ethical and moral community and its norms

are created by and within the struggle for
shared meanings; they are socially constructed
by the challenge of marginalized groups: "for
society as a whole moral questions are raised
whenever an outcast group seeks entry, no
matter what the reasons for its liminal status—
social class, gender, sexual preference, geography, or color" (Wolfe 1989, p. 216).

Liminality, uniting at the threshold, is certainly what women have experienced in the
Roman Catholic Church as well as in the
larger society. Their moral and ethical discourse has taken place at the edge of the dominant ideological discourse. These women
perceive themselves as challenging the institutional discourse in order to transform not
only the discourse but the institution itself.
They are in the midst of creating the "new social reality" (Wallace 1988) so that a new ethical vision can emerge, an ethical vision that
will transform the institution of which they
are an integral part.

NOTES

1. See Buckley 1978; Christ and Plaskow 1979;
Daly [1968], 1975, 1973, 1978, 1984; Fiorenza 1983,
1984; Plaskow and Christ 1989; Ruether 1974, 1975,
1983, 1986; Swidler and Swidler 1977 and the *Journal of Feminist Studies in Religion* are a few examples of the ever-increasing amount of scholarship
in this field.
2. See Swidler and Swidler (1977) for an extensive
and scholarly commentary by the leading theologians and scholars in the U.S. Roman Catholic
Church.

3. See works by Cooey, Farmer, and Ross 1987;
Gilligan, 1982; Habermas 1984, 1987: Harrison 1985,
Hoagland 1988, Kittay and Meyers 1987; MacIntyre
1984; Noddings 1984; Ruddick 1984; Whitbeck
1984; Wolfe 1989.
4. See Lake (1986) for a discussion of the teleological mode versus the deontological with regard to
the abortion debate.

REFERENCES

Abbott, W. M. 1966. *The Documents of Vatican II.*
New York: America Press.
Acker, J. 1991. "Hierarchies, Jobs, Bodies: A Theory
of Gendered Organizations." Pp. 162–179 in
The Social Construction of Gender, edited by J.
Lorber and S. H. Farrell. Newbury Park, CA:
Sage Publications, Inc.

Andolsen, B. Hilkert, C. E. Gudorf, and M. D. Pellauer
(eds.). 1985. *Women's Consciousness, Women's Conscience.* San Francisco: Harper & Row.
Buckley. M. I. 1978. "Jesus, Representative of Humanity: What Is Not Assumed Is Not Re-
deemed." Mimeo. Theology in the Americas
and Women's Ordination Conference.

Call to Action. 1990. "Call for Reform in the Catholic Church." *New York Times* (February 28).

Canon Law Society of America. 1983. *Code of Canon Law,* (Latin-English edition). Washington, DC: author.

"Catholic Statement on Pluralism and Abortion." 1984. *New York Times* (October 7).

Christ, C., and J. Plaskow. (eds.). 1979. *Womanspirit Rising: A Reader in Feminist Religion.* New York: Harper & Row.

Cooey, P. M., S. A. Farmer, and M. E. Ross. 1987. *Embodied Love: Sensuality and Relationship as Feminist Values.* San Francisco: Harper & Row.

Daly, M. [1968]. 1975. *The Church and the Second Sex.* Boston: Beacon.

———. 1973. *Beyond God the Father.* Boston: Beacon.

———. 1978. *Gyn/Ecology: The Metaethics of Radical Feminism.* Boston: Beacon.

———. 1984. *Pure Lust.* Boston: Beacon.

"Declaration of Solidarity." 1986. *Conscience* VII:21.

Fiorenza, E. Schüssler. 1979. "You Are Not to Be Called Father." *Cross Currents* Fall: 301–23.

———. 1983. *In Memory of Her: A Feminist Theological Reconstruction of Christian Origins.* New York: Crossroad.

———. 1984. "Claiming the Center: A Critical Feminist Theology of Liberation." Pp. 293–317 in *Women's Spirit Bonding.* edited by J. Kalven and M. I. Buckley. New York: Pilgrim Press.

Foucault, M. 1979. *The History of Sexuality,* vol. I. New York: Vintage Books.

Gilligan, C. 1982. *In a Different Voice.* Cambridge, MA: Harvard University Press.

Habermas, J. 1984, 1987. *Theory of Communicative Action* vols. 1 & 2. Boston: Beacon.

Harding, S. 1986. *The Science Question in Feminism.* Ithaca, NY: Cornell University Press.

Harrison, B. 1984. *Our Right to Choose.* Boston: Beacon.

———. 1995. *Making the Connections: Essays in Feminist Social Ethics.* Boston: Beacon.

Heyward, C. 1989. *Touching Our Strength: The Erotic as Power and the Love of God.* New York: Harper & Row.

Hoagland, S. L. 1988. *Lesbian Ethics: Toward New Values.* Palo Alto, CA: Institute for Lesbian Studies.

Hunt, M. 1990. "New Coalitions Replacing Church as Faith-Proprietor." *NCR* (February 2).

John Paul II. 1988. *On the Dignity and Vocation of Women.* Boston: St. Paul Books and Media.

Katchadourian, H. A. 1989. *Fundamentals of Human Sexuality,* 5th ed. Fort Worth: Holt, Rinehart, & Winston.

Kittay, E. Feder, and D. T. Meyers. 1987. *Women and Moral Theory.* Savage, MD: Rowman & Littlefield.

Lake, R. 1986. "The Metaethical Framework of Anti-Abortion Rhetoric." *Signs: Journal of Women in Culture and Society* 11:478–99.

Lernoux, P. 1989. *People of God: The Struggle for World Catholicism.* New York: Viking Press.

MacIntyre, A. 1984. *After Virtue.* Notre Dame, IN: Notre Dame University Press.

Noddings, N. 1984. *Caring: A Feminine Approach to Ethics and Moral Education.* Berkeley, CA: University of California Press.

Osiek, C. 1977. "The Church Fathers and the Ministry of Women." Pp. 78–80 in *Women Priests: A Catholic Commentary on the Vatican Declaration,* edited by L. Swidler and A. Swidler. New York: Paulist Press.

Parlee, M. 1979. "Psychology and Women." *Signs: Journal of Women in Culture and Society* 5:121–33.

Plaskow, J. 1974, "The Coming of Lilith." Pp. 341–3 in *Religion and Sexism: Images of Woman in the Jewish and Christian Traditions* edited by R. Radford Ruether. New York: Simon & Schuster.

Plaskow, J., and C. P. Christ (eds.). 1989. *Weaving the Visions: New Patterns in Feminist Spirituality.* San Francisco: Harper & Row.

Prusak, B. P. 1977. "Use the Other Door; Stand at the End of the Line." Pp. 81–4 in *Women Priests: A Catholic Commentary on the Vatican Declaration,* edited by L. Swidler and A. Swidler. New York: Paulist Press.

Quistlund, S. A. 1977. "In the Image of Christ." Pp. 260–70 in *Women Priests: A Catholic Commentary on the Vatican Declaration,* edited by L. Swidler and A. Swidler. New York: Paulist Press.

Robb, C. 1985. "A Framework for Feminist Ethics." Pp. 211–33 in *Women's Consciousness, Women's Conscience,* edited by B. Hilkert Andolsen, C. E. Gudorf, and M. D. Pellauer. San Francisco: Harper & Row.

Rothman, B. Katz. 1989. *Recreating Motherhood.* New York: W. W. Norton.

Ruddick, S. 1984. "Maternal Thinking." Pp. 213–30 in *Mothering: Essays in Feminist Theory* edited by J. Trebilcot. Totowa, NJ: Rowman & Allanheld.

Ruether, R. Radford (ed.). 1974. *Religion and Sexism.* New York: Simon & Schuster.

———. 1975. *New Woman New Earth.* New York: Crossroad.

———. 1983. *Sexism and God-Talk: Toward a Feminist Theology.* Boston: Beacon.

———. 1986. *Woman-Church: Theology & Practice.* San Francisco: Harper & Row.

Sacred Congregation for the Doctrine of the Faith. 1976. *Declaration on the Question of the Admission of Women to the Ministerial Priesthood.* Vatican Translation, *L'osservatore Romano.* Boston: The Daughters of St. Paul.

Swidler, L., and A. Swidler (eds.). 1977. *Women Priests: A Catholic Commentary on the Vatican Declaration.* New York: Paulist Press.

Tavard, G. H. 1977. "The Scholastic Doctrine." Pp. 99–106 in *Women Priests: A Catholic Commentary on the Vatican Declaration,* edited by L. Swidler and A. Swidler. New York: Paulist Press.

Trible, P. 1978. *God and the Rhetoric of Sexuality.* Philadelphia: Fortress Press.

Wallace, R. A. 1988. "Catholic Women and the Creation of a New Social Reality." *Gender & Society* 2:24–38.

Weber, M. 1946. "Politics as a Vocation." Pp. 77–128 in *From Max Weber: Essays in Sociology,* edited by H. H. Gerth and C. Wright Mills. New York: Oxford University Press.

———. 1978. *Economy and Society,* Vol. 1. Edited and translated by G. Roth and C. Wittich. Berkeley, CA: University of California Press.

Weeks, J. [1985] 1989. *Sexuality and Its Discontents.* London: Routledge.

———. [1986] 1989. *Sexuality.* London: Routledge.

Welch, S. D. 1985. *Communities of Resistance and Solidarity.* Maryknoll, NY: Orbis.

Whitbeck, C. 1984. "The Maternal Instinct." Pp. 185–98 in *Mothering: Essays in Feminist Theory,* edited by J. Trebilcot. Totowa, NJ: Rowman & Allanheld.

Wolfe, A. 1989. *Whose Keeper?* Berkeley, CA: University of California Press.

Setting the Problem, Laying the Ground

JUDITH PLASKOW

The need for a feminist Judaism begins with hearing silence. It begins with noting the absence of women's history and experiences as shaping forces in the Jewish tradition. Half of Jews have been women, but men have been defined as normative Jews, while women's voices and experiences are largely invisible in the record of Jewish belief and experience that has come down to us. Women have lived Jewish history and carried its burdens, but women's perceptions and questions have not given form to scripture, shaped the direction of Jewish law, or found expression in liturgy. Confronting this silence raises disturbing questions and stirs the impulse toward far-reaching change. What in the tradition is ours? What can we claim that has not also wounded us? What would have been different had the great silence been filled?

Hearing silence is not easy. A silence so vast tends to fade into the natural order; it is easy to identify with reality. To ourselves, women are not Other. We take the Jewish tradition as it has been passed down to us, as ours to appropriate or ignore. Over time, we learn to insert ourselves into silences.[1] Speaking about Abraham, telling of the great events at Sinai, we do not look for ourselves in the narratives but assume our presence, peopling the gaps in the text with women's shadowy forms. It is far easier to read ourselves into male stories than to ask how the foundational stories within which we live have been distorted by our absence. Yet it is not possible to speak into silence, to recover our history or reclaim our power to name without first confronting the extent of exclusion of women's experience. Silence can become an invitation to experiment and explore—but only after we have examined its terrain and begun to face its implications.

This chapter has two purposes: to chart the domain of silence that lies at the root of Jewish feminism and to take up the methodological presuppositions that inform my thinking. While it is not my primary intention to set out an indictment of Judaism as a patriarchal tradition, criticism is an ongoing and essential part of the Jewish feminist project. Not only is criticism a precondition for imagining a transformed Judaism; without a clear critique of Judaism that precedes and accompanies reconstruction, the process of reconstruction easily can be misconstrued as a form of apologetics. In exploring the territory of silence and describing my methodology, I mean to prevent this misunderstanding by clarifying the stance and intent that underlie my constructive thinking.

EXPLORING THE TERRAIN OF SILENCE

In her classic work *The Second Sex*, Simone de Beauvoir argues that men have established an absolute human type—the male—against which women are measured as Other. Otherness, she says, is a pervasive and generally fluid category of human thought; I perceive and am perceived as Other depending on a particular situation. In the case of males and females, however, Otherness is not reciprocal: men are always the definers, women the defined.[2] While women's self-experience is an experience of selfhood, it is not women's experience that is enshrined in language or that has shaped our cultural forms. As women appear in male texts, they are not the subjects and molders of their own experiences but the objects of male purposes, designs, and desires. Women do not name reality, but rather are named as part of a reality that is male-constructed. Where women are Other, they can be present and silent simultaneously; for the language and thought-forms of culture do not express their meanings.

De Beauvoir's analysis provides a key to women's silence within Judaism, for, like women in many cultures, Jewish women have been projected as Other. Named by a male community that perceives itself as normative, women are part of the Jewish tradition without its sources and structures reflecting our experience. Women are Jews, but we do not define Jewishness. We live, work, and struggle, but our experiences are not recorded, and what is recorded formulates our experiences in male terms. The central Jewish categories of Torah, Israel, and God all are constructed from male perspectives. Torah is revelation as men perceived it, the story of Israel told from their standpoint, the law unfolded according to their needs. Israel is the male collectivity, the children of a Jacob who had a daughter, but whose sons became the twelve tribes.[3] God is named in the male image, a father and warrior much like his male offspring, who confirms and sanctifies the silence of his daughters. Exploring these categories, we explore the parameters of women's silence.[4]

In Torah, Jewish teaching, women are not absent, but they are cast in stories told by men. As characters in narrative, women may be vividly characterized, as objects of legislation, singled out for attention. But women's presence in Torah does not negate their silence, for women do not decide the questions with which Jewish sources deal. When the law treats of women, it is often because their "abnormality" demands it. If women are central to plot, the plots are not about them. Women's interests and intentions must be unearthed from texts with other purposes, for both law and narrative serve to obscure them.

The most striking examples of women's silence come from texts in which women are most central, for there the normative character of maleness is especially jarring. In the family narratives of Genesis, for example, women figure prominently. The matriarchs of Genesis are all strong women. As independent personalities, fiercely concerned for their children, they often seem to have an intuitive knowledge of God's plans for their sons. Indeed, it appears from the stories of Sarah and Rebekah that they understand God better than their husbands. God defends Sarah when she casts out Hagar, telling Abraham to obey his wife (Gen. 21:12).[5] Rebekah, knowing it is God's intent, helps deceive Isaac into accepting Jacob as his heir (Gen. 25:23; 27:5–17). Yet despite their intuitions, and despite their wiliness and resourcefulness, it is not the women who receive the covenant or who pass on its lineage. The establishment of patrilineal descent and the patriarchal family takes precedence over the matriarch's stories.[6] Their relationship to God, in some way presupposed by the text, remains an undigested element in the narrative. What was the full theophany to Rebekah, and how is it related to the covenant with Isaac? The writer does not tell us; it is not sufficiently important. And so the covenant remains the covenant with Isaac, while Rebekah's experience floats at the margin of the story.

The establishment of patrilineal descent and patriarchal control, a subtext in Genesis, is an important theme in the legislation associated with Sinai. Here again, women figure prominently, but only as objects of male concerns. The laws pertaining to women place them firmly under the control of first fathers, then husbands, so that men can have male heirs they know are theirs. Legislation concerning adultery (Deut. 22:22, also Num. 5:11–31) and virginity (Deut. 22:13–21) speaks of women, but only to control female sexuality to male advantage. The *crime* of adultery is sleeping with another man's wife, and a man can bring his wife to trial even on suspicion of adultery, a right that is not reciprocal. Sleeping with a betrothed virgin constitutes adultery. A man who sleeps with a virgin who is not betrothed must simply marry her. A girl whose lack of virginity shames her father on her wedding night can be stoned to death for harlotry. A virgin who is raped must marry her assailant. The subject of these laws is women, but the interest behind them is the purity of the male line.

The process of projecting and defining women as objects of male concerns is expressed most fully not in the Bible, however, but in the Mishnah, an important second-century legal code. Part of the Mishnah's Order of Women (one of its six divisions) develops laws discussed in the Torah concerning certain problematic aspects of female sexuality. The subject of the division is the transfer of women—the regulation of women who are in states of transition, whose uncertain status threatens the stasis of the community. The woman who is about to enter into a marriage or who has just left one requires close attention. The law must regularize her irregularity, facilitate her transition to the normal state of wife and motherhood, at which point she no longer poses a problem.[7] But it is not even the contents of the order, male-defined as they are, that trumpet most loudly women's silence. In a system in which a divi-

sion of Men would be unthinkable nonsense, the fact of a division of Women is sufficient evidence of who names the world, who defines whom, in "normative" Jewish sources.

Thus Torah—"Jewish" sources, "Jewish" teaching—puts itself forward as *Jewish* teaching but speaks in the voice of only half the Jewish people. This scandal is compounded by another: The omission is neither mourned nor regretted; it is not even noticed. True, the rabbis were aware of the harshness of certain laws pertaining to women and sought to mitigate their effects. They tried to find ways to force a recalcitrant husband to divorce his wife, for example. But the framework that necessitated such mitigations went unquestioned. Women's Otherness was left intact. The Jewish passion for justice did not extend to Jewish women. As Cynthia Ozick puts it, one great "Thou shalt not"—"Thou shalt not lessen the humanity of women"—is missing from the Torah.[8]

For this great omission, there is no historical redress. Indeed, where one might expect redress, the problem is compounded. The prophets, those great champions of justice, couch their pleas for justice in the language of patriarchal marriage. Israel in her youth is a devoted bride, subordinate and obedient to her husband/God (for example, Jer. 2:2). Idolatrous Israel is a harlot and adulteress, a faithless woman whoring after false gods (for example, Hos. 2:3). Transferring the hierarchy of male and female to God and his people, the prophets enshrine in metaphor the legal subordination of women.[9] Those who might have named and challenged women's marginalization thus ignore and extend it.

The prophetic metaphors mark an end and a beginning. They confront us with the injustice of Torah; they link that injustice to other central Jewish ideas. If exploring Torah means exploring a terrain of women's silence, this is no less true of the categories of Israel or God.

Israel, the bride, the harlot, the people that is female (that is, subordinate) in relation to God is nonetheless male in communal self-perception. The covenant community is the community of the circumcised (Gen. 17:10), the community defined as male heads of household. Women are named through a filter of male experience: that is the essence of their silence. But women's experiences are not recorded or taken seriously because women are not perceived as normative Jews. They are part of but do not define the community of Israel.

The same evidence that speaks to women's silence in the tradition, to the partiality of Torah, also reflects an understanding of Israel as a community of males. In the narratives of Genesis, for example, the covenant moves from father to son, from Abraham to Isaac to Jacob to Joseph. The matriarchs' relation to their husbands' God is sometimes assumed, sometimes passed over, but the women do not constitute the covenant people. Women's relation to the community is also ambiguous and unclear in biblical legislation. The law is couched in male grammatical forms, and its content too presupposes a male nation. "You shall not covet your neighbor's wife" (Ex. 20:17). Probably we cannot deduce from this verse that women are free to covet! Yet the injunction assumes that women's obedience is owed to fathers and husbands, who are the primary group addressed.

The silence of women goes deeper, however, than who defines Torah or Israel. It also finds its way into language about God. Our language about divinity is first of all male language; it is selective and partial. The God who supposedly transcends sexuality, who is presumably one and whole, comes to us through language that is incomplete and narrow. The images we use to describe God, the qualities we attribute to God, draw on male pronouns and experience and convey a sense of power and authority that is clearly male. The God at the surface of Jewish consciousness is a God with a voice of thunder, a God who as lord and king rules his people and leads them into

battle, a God who forgives like a father when we turn to him. The female images that exist in the Bible and (particularly the mystical) tradition form an underground stream that occasionally reminds us of the inadequacy of our imagery without transforming its overwhelmingly male nature.

This male imagery is comforting and familiar—comforting because familiar—but it is an integral part of a system that consigns women to the margins. Since the experience of God cannot be directly conveyed in language, imagery for God is a vehicle that suggests what is actually impossible to describe. Religious experiences are expressed in a vocabulary drawn from the significant and valuable in a particular culture. To speak of God is to speak of what we most value. In attributing certain qualities to God, we both attempt to point to God and offer God's qualities to be emulated and admired. To say that God is just, for example, is to say both that God acts justly and that God demands justice. Justice belongs to God but is also ours to pursue. Similarly with maleness, to image God as male is to value the quality and those who have it. It is to define God in the image of the normative community and to bless men—but not women—with a central attribute of God.

But our images of God are not simply male images; they are images of a certain kind. The prophetic metaphors for the relation between God and Israel are metaphors borrowed from the patriarchal family—images of dominance softened by affection. God as husband and father of Israel demands obedience and monogamous love. He repays faithfulness with mercy and loving-kindness, but punishes waywardness, just as the wayward daughter can be stoned at her father's door Deut. 22:21). When these family images are combined with political images of king and warrior, they reinforce a particular model of power and dominance. God is the power over us, the One out there over against us, the sovereign warrior with righteousness on his side.

Family and political models of dominance and submission are recapitulated and rendered plausible by the dominance and submission of God and Israel. The silence and submission of women becomes part of a greater pattern that makes it appear fitting and right.

What emerges then is a "fit," a tragic coherence between the role of women in Jewish life, and law, teaching, and symbols. Women's experiences have not been recorded or shaped the contours of Jewish teaching because women do not define the normative community; but of course, women remain Other when we are always seen through the filter of male interpretation without ever speaking for ourselves. The maleness of God calls for the silence of women as shapers of the holy, but our silence in turn enforces our Otherness and a communal sense of the "rightness" of the male image of God. Moreover, if God is male, and we are in God's image, how can maleness *not* be the norm of Jewish humanity? If maleness is normative, how can women not be Other? And if women are Other, how can we not speak of God in a language of Otherness and dominance, a language drawn from male experience?

Confronting these interconnections is not easy. But it is only as we hear women's silence as part of the texture of Jewish existence that we can place our specific disabilities in the context in which they belong. Women's exclusion from public religious life, women's powerlessness in marriage and divorce are not accidental; nor are they individual problems. They are pieces of a system in which men have defined the interests and the rules, including the rules concerning women. Manipulating the system to change certain rules—even excision of many of them—will not of itself restore women's voices or women's power of naming. On the contrary, without awareness of the broader context of women's silence, attempts to redress concrete grievances may perpetuate the system of which they are part. Thus, as feminists demand that women be allowed to

lead public prayer, the issue of language is often set aside. Traditional modes of liturgical expression are assumed to be adequate; the only issue is who has access to them. But women's leadership in synagogue ritual then leaves untouched the deeper contradictions between formal equality and the fundamental symbols of the service, contradictions that can be addressed only through the transformation of religious language. Similarly, attempts to solve particular legal (*halakhic*) problems often assume the continued centrality and religious meaningfulness of *halakhah* (law). But halakhah is part of the system that women did not have a hand in creating. How can we presume that if women add our voices to tradition, law will be our medium of expression and repair? To settle on halakhah as the source of justice for women is to foreclose the question of women's experience when it has scarcely begun to be raised.

Clearly, the implications of Jewish feminism reach beyond the goal of equality to transform the bases of Jewish life. Feminism demands a new understanding of Torah, Israel, and God. It demands an understanding of Torah that begins by acknowledging the injustice of Torah and then goes on to create a Torah that is whole. The silence of women reverberates through the tradition, distorting the shape of narrative and skewing the content of the law. Only the deliberate recovery of women's hidden voices, the unearthing and invention of women's Torah, can give us Jewish teachings that are the product of the whole Jewish people and that reflect more fully its experiences of God.

Feminism demands an understanding of Israel that includes the whole of Israel and thus allows women to speak and name our experience for ourselves. It demands we replace a normative male voice with a chorus of divergent voices, describing Jewish reality in different accents and tones. Feminism impels us to rethink issues of community and diversity, to explore the ways in which one people can acknowledge and celebrate the varied experiences of its members. What would it mean for women *as women* to be equal participants in the Jewish community? How can we talk about difference without creating Others?

Feminism demands new ways of talking about God that reflect and grow out of the redefinition of Jewish humanity. The exclusively male naming of God supported and was rendered meaningful by a cultural and religious situation that is passing away. The emergence of women allows and necessitates that the long-suppressed femaleness of God be recovered and explored and reintegrated into the Godhead. But feminism presses us beyond the issue of gender to examine the nature of the God with male names. How can we move beyond images of domination to a God present *in* community rather than over it? How can we forge a God-language that expresses women's experience?...

NOTES

1. Carol P. Christ, "Spiritual Quest and Women's Experience," in *Womanspirit Rising: A Feminist Reader in Religion,* edited by Carol P. Christ and Judith Plaskow (San Francisco: Harper & Row, 1979), 229.

2. Simone de Beauvoir, *The Second Sex,* translated by H. M. Parshley (New York: Bantam Books, 1961), xv–xvii.

3. Dina's birth is mentioned in Gen. 30:21; her story is found in Gen. 34. In naming their anthology of Jewish feminist writing *The Tribe of Dina: A Jewish Woman's Anthology* (1986; reprint ed., Boston: Beacon Press, 1989), Melanie Kaye/Kantrowitz and Irena Klepfisz restore Dina to her rightful place.

4. The following discussion is based on my article, "The Right Question is Theological," in *On Being a Jewish Feminist: A Reader,* edited by Susannah Heschel (New York: Schocken Books, 1983), 223–33.

5. The fact that God takes Sarah's side does not alter the problematic nature of the relationship between Sarah and Hagar, which has been explored especially powerfully by black women. See, for example, Delores Williams, "Womanist Theological Perspectives on the Hagar–Sarah Story" (paper delivered at Princeton University, May 17, 1988).

6. See Savina Teubal, *Sarah the Priestess: The First Matriarch of Genesis* (Athens, OH: Swallow Press, 1984) and "Sarah and Hagar: Power in Ritual" (paper delivered at the 1985 Annual Meeting of the American Academy of Religion).

7. Jacob Neusner, *A History of the Mishnaic Law of Women,* 5 vols. (Leiden: E. J. Brill, 1980), 5: 13f., 271f.

8. Cynthia Ozick, "Notes Toward Finding the Right Question," in *Lilith* 6 (1979): 19–29; reprinted in Heschel, *On Being a Jewish Feminist,* 120–51; quotation, 149.

9. See T. Drorah Setel, "Prophets and Pornography: Female Sexual Imagery in Hosea," in *Feminist Interpretation of the Bible,* edited by Letty M. Russell (Philadelphia: Westminster Press, 1985), 86–95.

PART SEVEN

Gender, Health, and Illness

Until the 1960s, thinking about gender and health issues was grounded in the biomedical model. However, male physicians traditionally viewed the female as a kind of imperfect male (Sagan 1998). Using men's bodies as a model led to a variety of negative results: Normal female processes such a menstruation or menopause were defined as "diseases"; physicians did not realize that differences that exist between men and women often necessitate developing distinct therapeutic treatments; and female symptoms were sometimes disregarded (Sagan 1998; Lorber 1997).

Since the 1960s, the sociocultural model began to challenge the overemphasis on biological processes and feminists challenged the male model arguing that "illness" is a social experience. At first, sex was simply added to other demographic variables such as race and income, which was useful in epidemiological research. Descriptive findings revealed that men die younger than women; women have higher rates of depression; and women see doctors more frequently than men.

During the 1970s and 1980s, the women's health movement and feminist scholarship led to more comprehensive theoretical approaches to understanding the linkages between gender and health issues. Researchers studied the ways that differential gender socialization influenced perceptions of illness; they documented gender discrimination in the health care delivery system and gender stratification in the health professions (Sabo and Gordon 1995).

We now know that gender affects the physician-patient relationship, the labeling of disease, the risk of disease, and coping strategies. For example, many investigators have noted the discrepancy between the large number of women who come to health care settings with symptoms indicating abusive relationships and the low rate of detection. In one study, health care providers in a large public hospital which serves a low-income, predominantly black and Hispanic population were unreceptive to battered women. Although women came in with clear symptoms indicative of abuse, neither nurses nor doctors were willing to directly address the issues a battered woman brings to the emergency room. They did not ask for information about the relationship or make any attempt to intervene. However, nurses reported cases to the police, while physicians simply prescribed painkillers. Race and class, in addition to gender, increased the distance in the health care worker–patient relationship and made getting access to treatment for battering more difficult (Warshaw 1989).

While it is clear that the interactions between health care workers and patients are social, it is important to recognize that a social process is also involved in labeling an experience as "mental illness" or "illness." Sometimes the problem is that processes that are a normal part of a woman's life, such as menopause, get labeled as a "disease." In other instances, women's physical symptoms are viewed as psychological. For example, premenstrual syndrome (PMS) was classified in the American Psychiatric Association's *Diagnostic and Statistical Manual of Mental Disorders (DSM IV)* in 1994 (Markens 1996).

Sometimes thinking in terms of a male body model leaves women's symptoms undefined and lacking legitimacy. For example, there were numerous medical reports that the opportunistic infections that were symptoms of women with AIDS were different than those of men. However, it took years of protests at AIDS conferences and a lawsuit against the Social Security Administration before the Centers for Disease Control (CDC) changed the list of diagnostic signs for AIDS to include those that affect women. Before that change, women who did not fit the CDC's male pattern were denied AIDS-targeted disability and medical benefits (Lorber 1997). Thinking in terms of the male body model can also be dangerous for women. For example, most major studies of heart disease have confined their observations to men, therefore the application of most cardiovascular drug therapies for women is based on data derived predominantly or exclusively from young and middle-aged men (Julian and Wenger 1997).

Structural or institutional context also produces social situations that have different effects on the health of men and women. For example, the fact that men are more likely than women to be miners means that they are more likely to develop black lung disease. In addition, pressure to conform to gender role expectations result in men and women engaging in different kinds of risky behavior that can have detrimental effects on health. For example, in Western culture, dieting, breast reduction and enhancement, and face-lifts are ways that white girls and women engage in risky behavior in order to change their bodies to fit an ideal of feminine beauty (Lorber 1997). Boys and men who are bodybuilders and athletes, on the other hand, put themselves at risk by using steroids and engaging in extreme weight loss or gain practices (Sabo and Gordon 1995).

Men and women also have different risk factors for the transmission of HIV. In developed or Westernized countries, the main sources of transmission are unprotected anal intercourse and the use of unsterile needles to inject drugs. In this pattern, most of those with HIV infection and AIDS are men. In the United States, among white males, transmission of HIV is primarily through unprotected anal intercourse, while the prime risk for black and Latino men is from contaminated needles. Among women between the ages of 25 and 44, AIDS lags behind cancer and heart disease, but 1995 estimates are that it will be the second leading cause of death for women of that age group in a year or two (Lorber 1997).

The second pattern of transmission is found in developing countries in Africa, India, and Asia where the main source of transmission is heterosexual intercourse. As a result, almost half of those with HIV infection or AIDS are women. According to the United Nations in June 1996, about 42 percent of the estimated 21 to 22 million adults throughout the world who are HIV-positive are women. In sub-Saharan African countries where HIV-positive people account for 64 percent of the worldwide total, more women than men are infected (Lorber 1997).

In general, the recipient of semen is more likely to become infected. As Lorber (1997) points out, the powerlessness of the penetrated is the essence of vulnerability to HIV infection. The risk is not in the nature of the sexual behavior so much as the sexual relationship. Condoms offer the best protection against HIV whatever the gender composition of the couple. However, the closer the relationship of the couple, the less likely they are to use a condom (Lorber 1997).

The division between having safe sex with casual partners and unprotected sex with intimate partners has considerable risk due to overconfidence about the partner's fidelity. The paradox is that casual sex is less likely to be penetrative, yet people are more likely to use condoms—while sex between intimates is more likely to be penetrative and people are less likely to use a condom. In response to the rising incidence of HIV infection among heterosexual women and the problem of the lack of cooperation of male partners, the World Health Organization has called for the development of a vaginal microbicide—a virus-killing cream or foam (Lorber 1997).

In addition to men and women having different risks for illnesses, they also use different coping strategies to deal with illness. Gordon (1995) studied men who survived testicular cancer in order to understand how men cope with the loss of one or both testicles. He found that the men defined the cancer as something they could "fight," and they were therefore able to view the experience as increasing their masculinity. The men avoided confronting their feelings by trying not to think about it, joking, and returning to previous activities as soon as possible. They used a task-oriented approach, while women who have breast cancer tend to focus on altering their emotions and mobilizing family support.

Two articles in this section focus on diseases that are increasing among women—heart disease and AIDS. Heart disease has traditionally been seen as a "man's disease." While it is true that men are more frequently affected in middle age, at older ages, heart disease is just as common in women as in men. As the population ages there will be a greater number of elderly women and an increase in the prevalence of heart disease in women (Julian and Wenger 1997).

Vicki Helgeson's article in this section argues that traditional masculinity not only places men at greater risk of developing heart disease in middle age, but also shapes men's subsequent adjustment to it. For example, men's unwillingness to ask for help and inability to express emotions may pose obstacles to successful adjustment to heart disease.

Hortensia Amaro's article is also about the relationship between gender and risk factors for disease. She points out that the fastest growing group of women who will die of AIDS are black or Hispanic—and heterosexual intercourse has surpassed drug injections as the most common route of transmission. Amaro claims that Latinas find it very difficult to talk about sex and to get their male sexual partners to use condoms. She is interested in how the power relationship between minority men and women puts black and Latina women more at risk than white women.

Both Helgesen and Amaro look at illness as an objective phenomenon and focus on how gender roles create different risk factors and coping abilities for men and women. Roberta Satow, on the other hand, is interested in "hysteria" as a label for a variety of female behaviors, the supposed causes of which reflect male fantasies about women's bodies and sexuality. Indeed, the word *hysteria* comes from *hystera*, which means uterus. While Helgeson and Amaro are interested in the relationship between gender and illness in contemporary America, Satow takes an historical approach, tracing *hysteria* back to antiquity.

REFERENCES

Amaro, Hortensia. 1995. "Love, Sex and Power: Considering Women's Realities in HIV Prevention." *American Psychologist* 50:437–447.

Gordon, David Frederick. 1995. "Testicular Cancer and Masculinity." Pp. 246–265 in *Men's Health and Illness: Gender, Power, and the Body,* edited by Donald Sabo and David Frederick Gordon. Thousand Oaks, CA: Sage Publications.

Helgeson, Vicki S. 1995. "Masculinity, Men's Roles, and Coronary Heart Disease." Pp. 68–104 in *Men's Health and Illness: Gender, Power, and the Body,* edited by Donald Sabo and David Frederick Gordon. Thousand Oaks, CA: Sage Publications.

Julian, Desmond G., and Nanette Kass Wenger, editors. 1997. *Women and Heart Disease.* London: Martin Dunitz Ltd.

Lorber, Judith. 1997. *Gender and the Social Construction of Illness.* Thousand Oaks, CA: Sage Publications.

Markens, Susan. 1996. "The Problematic of 'Experience': A Political and Cultural Critique of PMS." *Gender & Society* 10:42–58.

Sabo, Donald, and David Frederick Gordon. 1995. "Rethinking Men's Health and Illness." Pp. 1–19 in *Men's Health and Illness: Gender, Power, and the Body,* edited by Donald Sabo and David Frederick Gordon. Thousand Oaks, CA: Sage Publications.

Sagan, Dorion. 1998. "Gender Specifics: Why Women Aren't Men." *New York Times,* Section 15, June 21:1, 20.

Satow, Roberta. 1979. "Where Has All the Hysteria Gone?" *Psychoanalytic Review* 66:465–477.

Stolberg, Sheryl Gay. 1998. "Eyes Shut, Black America Is Being Ravaged by AIDS." *New York Times,* June 29:A1, A12.

Warshaw, Carole. 1989. "Limitations of the Medical Model in the Care of Battered Women." *Gender & Society* 3:506–517.

Masculinity, Men's Roles, and Coronary Heart Disease

VICKI S. HELGESON

As the leading causes of death in the United States shifted from infectious disease during the first half of the 20th century to chronic disease (e.g., cancer, heart disease) during the last half of the 20th century, the sex differential in mortality widened. In 1920, men lived to be 54 and women lived to be 56. In 1990, men lived to be 72 and women lived to be 79. It is unlikely that the increase in the sex differential in mortality can be attributed to changes in biology (Johnson, 1977). Men are more likely than women to die of the four leading causes of death in the United States: (a) heart disease, (b) cancer, (c) cerebrovascular disease, and (d) accidents (Verbrugge, 1985). As Ingrid Waldron (1995) and Judith Stillion (1995) have demonstrated, these leading causes of death are ones in which psychological, social, and behavioral factors contribute to men's substantially higher mortality rates compared to women. They argue that a sizable portion of men's excess mortality over women is linked to masculine identity, men's roles, and gendered patterns of socialization.

There is emerging evidence that aspects of masculine identity and male socialization are related to men's risk for coronary heart disease. Strickland (1988) suggests that men cope with stress by independent and aggressive behavior, which results in a higher rate of male-to-female heart disease. For example, traditionally masculine behaviors such as smoking and drinking have been linked to heart disease. Aspects of masculinity also overlap with the Type A behavior pattern, which has been linked to coronary heart disease (CHD). Traditional masculinity not only may place men at greater risk for disease but also may shape men's personal reactions and subsequent adjustment to heart disease. Specifically, men's unwillingness to rely on others for assistance and inability to express emotions may pose obstacles for successful adjustment to heart disease....

Research has ruled out the possibility that sex differences in the primary CHD risk factors (e.g., hypertension, high cholesterol) explain sex differences in CHD mortality (Johnson, 1977; Wingard, Suarez, & Barrett-Connor, 1983). Social scientists have suggested that cultural and economic pressures related to the role of men in our society account for men's shorter life expectancy, in general (Harrison, 1978), and encourage the development of coronary prone behavior, in particular, resulting in excess mortality from CHD (Waldron, 1976). In fact, in a study of life expectancy on a kibbutz where men's and women's roles are more similar than they are in the United States, gender differences in

Excerpted from *Men's Health and Illness* edited by Donald Sabo and David Frederick Gordon, pp. 68–89. Copyright © 1995 by Sage Publications, Inc. Reprinted by permission of Sage Publications, Inc.

life expectancy were reduced (Leviatan & Cohen, 1995).

THEORETICAL LINKS OF MASCULINITY TO CHD

The aspect of the male gender role that I examined in studies of coronary heart disease was trait masculinity. I suggest that trait masculinity consists of a set of psychosocial characteristics that place men at risk for heart disease. A model of how masculinity might be related to CHD is displayed in Figure 1. First, there is a set of traditional coronary risk factors, including smoking, hypertension, diabetes, alcohol abuse, and high cholesterol, that place one at risk for CHD. Some of these risk factors may be related to masculinity, for example, smoking. Second, independent of this biological pathway, masculinity may place one at risk for heart disease by leading to the development of (a) impaired social networks, (b) Type A behavior, and (c) poor health care. All three of these psychosocial characteristics place one at risk for CHD.

Type A Behavior

Extensive research, mostly with men, has shown a relation between the Type A behavior pattern and CHD (see Matthews & Haynes, 1986, for a review), but researchers have failed to recognize that characteristics of the traditional masculine role overlap with characteristics of Type A behavior. The Type A behavior pattern includes extreme aggressiveness, easily aroused hostility, sense of time urgency, and competitive achievement striving (Friedman & Rosenman, 1974). It also is characterized by an intense focus on central rather than peripheral information. This full allocation to central events or tasks (such as job-related activities) has been suggested to decrease awareness of symptoms (Carver & Humphries, 1982; Jennings, 1983). Research has shown that Type As report fewer symptoms than Type Bs (Hart, 1983), particularly symptoms associated with fatigue (Carver, Coleman, & Glass, 1976; Weidner & Matthews, 1978). And fatigue is one of the warning signs of an impending heart attack (Carver &

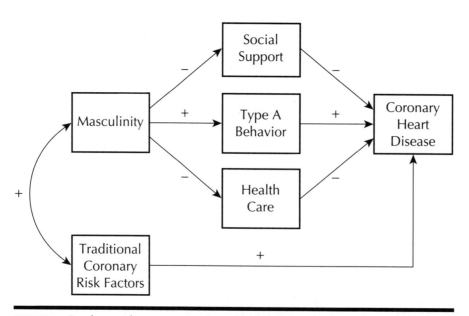

FIGURE 1   Psychosocial components of men's risk for coronary heart disease

Humphries, 1982; Greene, Moss, & Goldstein, 1974).

Interestingly, many of these components—competitiveness, hostility, symptom suppression, and attentional style—are similar to trait masculinity as defined by personality theorists and social psychologists (Bem, 1974; Spence et al., 1974). The BSRI (Bem Sex Role Inventory) (Bem, 1974) and the PAQ (Personal Attributes Questionnaire) (Spence et al. 1974) include traits such as aggressive, competitive, never gives up, hostile, dictatorial, arrogant, not being excitable in a major crisis, not crying, standing up well under pressure, and looking out for oneself. Research has shown that both males and females who score high on masculinity also score higher on measures of Type A behavior (Batlis & Small, 1982; DeGregorio & Carver, 1980; Nix & Lohr, 1981; Payne, 1987). Those who endorse the traditional male gender role (as measured by the Brannon Masculinity Scale) also endorse Type A behavior (Thompson et al., 1985). All of these studies were conducted, however, with college students—who are unlikely to show symptoms of CHD.

The characteristics of the coronary-prone individual described by List (1967) are strikingly similar to the characteristics of the traditional male gender role. List suggests that coronary-prone persons hide weaknesses, inhibit emotional expression, lack empathy, fear homosexuality, and fail to reveal their true selves partly from a lack of self-knowledge and partly from a desire to conform to others' expectations. The overlap between trait masculinity and coronary-prone behavior, or Type A behavior, is shown in Table 1.

Social Support

The lack of an adequate social support network is associated with mortality (Berkman & Syme, 1979; Blazer, 1982; House, Robbins, & Metzner, 1982), including mortality from CHD (Berkman & Syme, 1979; Ruberman,

TABLE 1 Comparison of Coronary Prone Behavior and Trait Masculinity

CHARACTERISTICS OF THE CORONARY-PRONE INDIVIDUAL	SAMPLE OF TRAIT MASCULINITY FEATURES
Fails to attend to others' feelings[a]	
Lacks self-knowledge	*Independent*
Isolated	*Active*
Hides weaknesses	*Never cries*
Rigid performance at work	Never gives up
Self-control	*Self-confident*
Inhibited expression	*Hostile*
Fears homosexuality	*Not excitable in a major crisis*
Lacks empathy[a]	*Competitive*
	Arrogant, egotistical
	Looks out for self
	Greedy
	Dictatorial
Impatient	Cynical
Hostile	
Preoccupied with self	
Guilty if relaxed	
Achievement-oriented	*Ambitious*
Appears *self-confident*	Athletic
Active	Assertive
Independent	Willingness to take risks
Competitive drive	*Dominant*
Hyperaggressiveness	*Aggressive*
Dominant	Leader

Source: Bem (1974); Friedman & Rosenman (1974); Friedman & Ulmer (1984); List (1967); Spence, Helmreich, & Stapp (1974); and Spence, Helmreich, & Holahan (1979).

Note: Italicized words are those that are common to both columns.

[a]The counterpart of these characteristics are features of trait femininity.

Weinblatt, Goldberg, & Chaudhary, 1984). The social networks of coronary-prone persons are impoverished (see Jennings, 1983, for a review), and men, in general, are at a support disadvantage compared to women

(Belle, 1987; Burda, Vaux, & Schill, 1984; Hirsch, 1979; Roos & Cohen, 1987, see Shumaker & Hill, 1991, for a review). Men provide and receive less social support than women (Belle, 1987; Burda et al., 1984; Roos & Cohen, 1987; Stokes & Wilson, 1984). Men also are less likely than women to seek social support (Butler, Giordano, & Neren, 1985), presumably because asking for help implies weakness and dependence. Social support may act as a buffer against stress and an aid to recovery, and masculinity plays a role in the nature of a person's social supports.

One study demonstrated that sex differences in social support (women greater than men) were reduced when gender role (trait femininity) was statistically controlled (Burda et al., 1984). This finding suggests that men's support disadvantage is partly due to a lack of feminine traits. The characteristics of the traditional male gender role are inconsistent with the provision, activation, and receipt of social support, particularly emotional support (i.e., comfort, caring, understanding, reassurance). The provision and receipt of support is more likely to occur in a relationship characterized by emotional expressiveness, mutual self-disclosure, and empathy. The traditional male gender role poses difficulties for enacting each of these behaviors.

First, men experience and express less *emotion* than women in close relationships (Sprecher & Sedikides, 1993). The male emphasis on self-control, toughness, and autonomy prevents the expression of emotions and feelings (Kilmartin, 1994). Men are socialized to believe that expressiveness is inconsistent with masculinity (Balswick & Peek, 1971), and, in fact, trait masculinity has been related to less emotional expression (Ganong & Coleman, 1984). O'Neil and colleagues (1986) believe that men's fears of appearing feminine underlie their inability to express emotion. In a study in which college men were asked to role play different emotions, subjects high in masculine gender-role stress were rated by

observers as less verbally and nonverbally expressive (Saurer & Eisler, 1990). Men's inability to express emotions may make them uncomfortable asking for support and less capable of eliciting it nonverbally (Saurer & Eisler, 1990).

Men's cool detachment, which is intended to convey strength and objectivity, unfortunately, may inhibit the development of close relationships and lead to misunderstandings (Nichols, 1975). One reason that men's relationships suffer is because they are more concerned with maintaining objectivity and proving themselves than with being expressive (Keith, 1974). According to Naifeh and Smith (1984), the more a man becomes confused about his emotions, the more he will retreat into the safer realm of rationality and objectivity. Unfortunately, avoiding feelings may result in the inability to feel (Nichols, 1975). Rubin (1983) has said that some men simply do not know how to respond to the question, How do you feel?, and that feelings consciously available to women are not always available to men who have learned to repress them.

Research has indirectly substantiated the belief that repression of emotions has adverse health consequences. Pennebaker, Kiecolt-Glaser, and Glaser (1988) randomly assigned college students to write about either a traumatic event or a superficial event that they had experienced. A comparison of the two groups revealed that those who wrote about traumatic experiences had better immune function and visited the heath center less frequently than those who wrote about superficial events. The conclusion drawn from this study is that expressing emotions is good for one's health.

Second, a way to develop close relationships and a support network is through revealing personal information about oneself, *self-disclosure*. According to Jourard (1971), men are difficult to love because they do not disclose their needs. Men do not self-disclose to the extent that women do (Notarius & John-son, 1982) for three reasons. First, men's "re-stricted emotionality" inhibits self-disclosure (Snell, 1986). Second, self-disclosure implies revealing weaknesses or vulnerabilities which is inconsistent with the masculine image of strength and control. Third, revealing vulner-abilities provides the recipient with a source of power over the discloser. Self-disclosure is inversely related to trait masculinity (Win-stead, Derlega, & Wong, 1984) and endorse-ment of the traditional male gender role (Thompson et al., 1985). In a study of college students who were asked to become ac-quainted by discussing intimate topics, half of the males in this study refused to initiate this type of discussion (Walker & Wright, 1976).

Third, *empathy*, a useful skill used to maintain a support network, is not as avail-able to men as it is to women (see Hoffman, 1977, for a review). Empathy is inversely re-lated to trait masculinity (Hansson, Jones, & Carpenter, 1984). A recent study of empathy and social support showed that sex differ-ences in social support can be accounted for by women's greater empathy compared to men (Trobst, Collins, & Embree, 1994). A lack of empathy also has been described as a fea-ture of the coronary-prone individual. The coronary-prone individual has been de-scribed as paying less attention to the feelings and emotions of others (List, 1967) and failing to notice important social cues.

Each of these features of the male gender role—restricted emotionality, unwillingness to self-disclose, and lack of empathy—appears to influence men's relationships. Friendships among men are often restricted by competi-tiveness (Garfinkel, 1985; Goldberg, 1976; Ko-marovsky, 1974, 1976; Lewis, 1978; Tognoli, 1980) and homophobia (Garfinkel, 1985; Lewis, 1978; McGill, 1985; Tognoli, 1980). Competition inhibits the disclosure of vulner-abilities, and fear of being labeled a homosex-ual keeps men from showing affection to one another (Naifeh & Smith, 1984; Nichols, 1975).

Our culture promotes negative affect and in-hibits positive affect among men (Lewis, 1978).

Men's relationships with other men are often activity focused rather than emotion focused—"doing" instead of "being" (Rubin, 1985; Wright, 1982). Men emphasize same sex friends who do the same things, whereas women emphasize same sex friends who feel the same about things (Caldwell & Peplau, 1982). Men tend to compartmentalize their relationships with other men, having differ-ent friends for different functions, whereas women tend to have friends with whom they share all aspects of their lives (McGill, 1985; Wright, 1982).

The limits on male-male friendships may cause men to rely too heavily on women for in-timacy and emotional support (Pleck, 1976; Rubin, 1983). Men often find it easier to show emotion and self-disclose to women than to other men. Komarovsky's male college stu-dents revealed that their primary confidant was their closest female, rather than male, friend. In a study of college students, Wheeler, Reis, and Nezlek (1983) found that the amount of time men spent with men was associated with more loneliness and the amount of time men spent with women was associated with less loneliness. The authors also showed that male-male interactions were less intimate than any interaction involving a female. Further ev-idence for the positive effects of relationships with women on men's psychological well-being comes from a recent study of college stu-dent long-distance romantic relationships (Helgeson, 1994). Men whose relationships had dissolved were more distressed than men whose relationships remained intact, whereas the converse occurred for women (i.e., women whose relationships had dissolved were less distressed than women whose relationships remained intact). This finding among dating couples parallels that found among married couples. Most studies find that men benefit more psychologically and physically from marriage compared to women (Belle, 1987; Berkman & Syme, 1979; Gove, 1973), and suffer more upon divorce and widowhood compared to women (Bloom, White, & Asher, 1979; Stroebe & Stroebe, 1983; Umberson, Wortman, & Kessler, 1992; Wallerstein & Kelly, 1980). One reason for these findings is that men rely almost solely on their wives for support, whereas wives retain family and friends as members of their network (Fischer & Phillips, 1982; Lowenthal & Haven, 1968; Veroff, Douvan, & Kukla, 1981).

Just because men are at a support disadvantage compared to women does not mean that the presence of support will not have a positive effect on men's health. There is some evidence that support has a stronger impact on men's health than women's health. Seeman and Syme (1987) studied men and women undergoing coronary angiography and found that social support was related to less severe disease among men but not women. In a study of heart attack survivors, inability to disclose to one's spouse was associated with a cardiac-related rehospitalization during the next year for men but not women (Helgeson, 1991).

Jourard (1971) suggests that being loved and loving gives value to a man's life. If this is true, he concludes that the male handicap in love is lethal for men. Men are prone to what Jourard (1971) calls *dispiritation;* that is, the loss of a sense of meaning in life. Instead of investing in intimate relationships, men depend on their jobs, status, and sexual potency for their identities, none of which are immutable. When all of these things are gone—for example, when men retire or become chronically ill—much of life's meaning is lost. Thus, Jourard (1971) suggests that men become susceptible to illness and Naifeh and Smith (1984) conclude that men die earlier.

Having outlined the features of the male gender role that leave men vulnerable to a lack of support, it must be noted that there are some aspects of the male gender role they are quite consistent with social support. The kind of social support described above was more of an emotional nature. Among the kinds of support, researchers consider emotional support to be the primary function (Cohen & Hoberman, 1983; House, 1981; Schaefer, Coyne, & Lazarus, 1981). There are other kinds of support, however, such as instrumental support and informational support that may be more consistent with masculinity. Men who have an instrumental orientation may find it easier to provide advice or guidance (informational support) and tangible assistance (instrumental support).

Health Care

A third way that the male gender role may be linked to CHD is through health practices. Men have shown a greater failure to follow standard health practices, report symptoms, and visit physicians compared to women (Lewis & Lewis, 1977; Nathanson, 1977; Verbrugge, 1985; Waldron, 1976). In a survey of Dayton residents, redivorced men cited depression twice as often as redivorced women, but did not seek therapy for it to the extent that women did (Balk, 1985).

Men's lack of desire to seek help for problems may be due, in part, to society's response to men with problems. For example, other people view depressed men more negatively than depressed women (Hammen & Peters, 1977, 1978). Others may encourage men to solve their own problems or to overcome symptoms of illness (Goldberg, 1976). The extent to which other people adhere to or endorse the male gender role is likely to influence the kind of support given to men. For example, a study of male counselors showed that counselors who held traditional attitudes toward men emphasized vocational concerns (rather than emotional or psychological concerns) among their clients (Thoreson, Shaughnessy, Cook, & Moore, 1993).

Researchers have suggested that sex differences in illness behavior are due to differences between male and female role expectations (Nathanson, 1975; Verbrugge, 1985). The male gender role, and people who endorse it, discourages men from admitting vulnerabilities and from seeking help when they first realize they may need it. These beliefs are instilled during men's childhood (Lewis & Lewis, 1977). Men learn to avoid or refuse to admit pain, to not ask for help, and to try to appear strong. It is even possible that socialization has taught men not to experience feelings and symptoms that they perceive as signs of weakness (Rubin, 1983). The individual who adheres to the male gender role may practice poor health care and fail to respond to symptoms because he or she either believes help is not warranted or it is inappropriate to seek help. Seeking help is inconsistent with self-reliance and restricting emotions, and it may signify weakness. Traditional attitudes toward men and male gender-role conflict have been related to negative attitudes toward seeking psychological help and to a history of not having sought help for personal or vocational problems (Good, Dell, & Mintz, 1989).

The potential harmfulness of this component of the male gender role becomes especially clear when considering the consequences of a delay in seeking treatment for an acute myocardial infarction (MI). Failure to notice symptoms and respond to them will affect health behavior that may be critical to survival from an MI (e.g., seeking needed rest, altering eating and smoking habits, seeking medical attention; Jennings, 1983). Sixty percent of those who die from myocardial infarction do so before reaching the hospital (Wright, 1980). Noticing and reporting symptoms at an early stage of the disease might reduce the 55% to 80% of deaths that occur within 4 hours of the onset of symptoms (Hackett & Rosenbaum, 1980). The recent development of thrombolytic agents (e.g., streptokinase, tissue plasminogen activator) to halt heart damage during a heart attack makes a timely response to symptoms even more critical.

A 1991 episode of "20/20" illustrated the association of traditional masculinity with the failure to seek help for symptoms of a heart attack in one instance and colon cancer in the other instance. The man who had the heart attack said he had felt symptoms but refused to admit or report them because symptoms signified weakness that contradicted the masculine role. He also refused to seek help for symptoms because it would have interfered with his business, which was his primary route to affirming his masculine identity. Ironically, his failure to adhere to good health behavior after the first MI led to a second, more debilitating, MI that resulted in the loss of the business he was striving to maintain.

SUMMARY

I have suggested three pathways by which the male gender role, specifically trait masculinity, might be linked to coronary heart disease: Type A behavior, impoverished social networks, and poor health care. Trait masculinity may have positive as well as negative implications for each of the three pathways. For example, the overlap between the features of trait masculinity and Type A behavior might be responsible for a high-achievement orientation and a successful career as well as a risk factor for heart disease. Some features of the trait masculinity (e.g., restricted emotionality) may inhibit the availability of social support, whereas other features of trait masculinity (e.g., self-confidence) may attract potential supporters. Finally, trait masculinity has been linked with both good health habits (e.g., exercise) and poor health behaviors (e.g., smoking).

The male gender role is a multifaceted construct, and even trait masculinity has been found to have different components. An important distinction has been made between positive trait masculinity (nonextreme version) and negative trait masculinity (extreme version) or between agency and unmitigated agency. Nonextreme masculinity (positive masculinity) consists of characteristics such as self-confident, independent, and stands up well under pressure; whereas extreme masculinity (negative masculinity) consists of characteristics such as hostile, arrogant, and selfish. There is a common dimension underlying these two constructs, as evidenced by their positive correlation. Yet the two scales have divergent effects on well-being and mediators of well-being. The distinction between positive masculinity and negative masculinity, therefore, may account for some of the paradoxical findings relating trait masculinity to health or risk factors for health.

REFERENCES

Balk, D. M. (1985, March 30). Divorced males' plight cited in study. *Denver Post.*

Balswick, J., & Peek, C. (1971). The inexpressive male: A tragedy of American society. *The Family Coordinator, 20*, 363–368.

Batlis, N., & Small, A. (1982). Sex roles and Type A behavior. *Journal of Clinical Psychology, 38*(2), 315–316.

Belle, D. (1987). Gender differences in the social moderators of stress. In R. C. Barnett, L. Biener, & G. K. Baruch (Eds.), *Gender and stress* (pp. 257–277). New York: Free Press.

Bem, S. L. (1974). The measurement of psychological androgyny. *Journal of Consulting and Clinical Psychology, 42*, 155–162.

Berkman, L. F., & Syme, S. L. (1979). Social networks, host resistance, and mortality: A nine-year follow-up of Alameda County residents. *American Journal of Epidemiology, 109*, 186–204.

Blazer, D. (1982). Social support and mortality in an elderly community population. *American Journal of Epidemiology, 115*, 684–694.

Bloom, B. L., White, S. W., & Asher, S. J. (1979). Marital disruption as a stressful life event. In G. Levinger & O. C. Moles (Eds.), *Divorce and separation* (pp. 184–200). New York: Basic Books.

Burda, P. C., Vaux, A., & Schill, T. (1984). Social support resources: Variation across sex and sex role. *Personality and Social Psychology Bulletin, 10*, 119–126.

Butler, T., Giordano, S., & Neren, S. (1985). Gender and sex-role attributes as predictors of utilization of natural support systems during personal stress events. *Sex Roles, 13*, 515–524.

Caldwell, M. A., & Peplau, L. A. (1982). Sex differences in same-sex friendship. *Sex Roles, 8*, 721–732.

Carver, C. S., Coleman, A. E., & Glass, D. C. (1976). The coronary-prone behavior pattern and the suppression of fatigue on a treadmill test. *Journal of Personality and Social Psychology, 33*, 460–466.

Carver, C. S., & Humphries, C. (1982). Social psychology of the Type A coronary-prone behavior pattern. In G. S. Sanders & J. Suls (Eds.), *Social psychology of health and illness.* Hillsdale, NJ: Lawrence Erlbaum.

Cohen, S., & Hoberman, H. M. (1983). Positive events and social supports as buffers of life change stress. *Journal of Applied Social Psychology, 13*(2), 99–125.

DeGregorio, E., & Carver, C. S. (1980). Type A behavior pattern, sex role orientation, and psychological adjustment. *Journal of Personality and Social Psychology, 39*, 286–293.

Fischer, C. S., & Phillips, S. L. (1982). Who is alone? Social characteristics of people with small networks. In L. A. Peplau & D. Perlman (Eds.), *Loneliness: A sourcebook of current theory, research and therapy.* New York: John Wiley.

Friedman M., & Rosenman, R. H. (1974). *Type A behavior and your heart.* New York: Knopf.

Friedman, M., & Ulmer, D. (1984). *Treating Type A behavior and your heart.* New York: Fawcett Crest.

Ganong, L. H., & Coleman, M. (1984). Sex, sex roles, and emotional expressiveness. *Journal of Genetic Psychology, 146*(3), 405–411.

Garfinkel, P. (1985). *In a man's world. Father, son, brother, friend, and other roles men play.* New York: New American Library.

Goldberg, H. (1976). *The hazards of being male.* New York: New American Library.

Good, G. E., Dell, D. M., & Mintz, L. B. (1989). Male role and gender role conflict: Relations to help seeking in men. *Journal of Counseling Psychology, 36*(3), 295–300.

Gove, W. R. (1973). Sex, marital status, and mortality. *American Journal of Sociology, 79*, 45–67.

Greene, W. A., Moss, A. J., & Goldstein, S. (1974). Delay, denial, and death in coronary heart disease. In R. S. Eliot (Ed.), *Stress and the heart*. New York: Futura.

Hackett, T. P., & Rosenbaum, J. F. (1980). Emotion, psychiatric disorders, and the heart. In E. Braunwald (Ed.), *Heart disease: A textbook of cardiovascular medicine*. Philadelphia: W. B. Saunders.

Hammen, C. L., & Peters, S. D. (1977). Differential responses to male and female depressive reactions. *Journal of Consulting and Clinical Psychology, 45*, 994–1001.

Hammen, C. L., & Peters, S. D. (1978). Interpersonal consequences of depression: Responses to men and women enacting a depressed role. *Journal of Abnormal Psychology, 87*, 322–332.

Hansson, R. O., Jones, W. H., & Carpenter, B. N. (1984). Relationship competence and social support. In P. Shaver (Ed.), *Review of personality and social psychology* (Vol. 5). Beverly Hills, CA: Sage.

Harrison, J. (1978). Warning: The male sex role may be dangerous to your health. *Journal of Social Issues, 34*(1), 65–86.

Hart, K. E. (1983). Physical symptom reporting and health perception among Type A and B college males. *Journal of Human Stress, 9*(4), 17–22.

Helgeson, V. S. (1991). The effects of masculinity and social support on recovery from myocardial infarction. *Psychosomatic Medicine, 53*, 621–633.

Helgeson, V. S. (1994). Long-distance romantic relationships: Sex differences in adjustment and breakup. *Personality and Social Psychology Bulletin, 20*, 254–265.

Hirsch, B. J. (1979). Psychological dimensions of social networks: A multimethod analysis. *American Journal of Community Psychology, 7*, 263–277.

Hoffman, M. L. (1977). Sex differences in empathy and related behaviors. *Psychological Bulletin, 84*, 712–722.

House, J. S. (1981). *Work stress and social support*. Reading, MA: Addison-Wesley.

House, J. S., Robbins, C., & Metzner, H. L. (1982). The association of social relationships and activities with mortality: Prospective evidence from the Tecumseh Community Health Study. *American Journal of Epidemiology, 116*, 123–140.

Jennings, J. R. (1983). Attention and coronary heart disease. In D. S. Krantz, A. Baum & J. E. Singer (Eds.), *Handbook of psychology and health* (Vol. 3). Hillsdale, NJ: Lawrence Erlbaum.

Johnson, A. (1977). Sex differentials in coronary heart disease: The explanatory role of primary risk factors. *Journal of Health and Social Behavior 18*, 46–54.

Jourard, S. M. (1971). *The transparent self* (Rev. ed.). New York: Van Nostrand Reinhold.

Keith, J. (1974). My own men's liberation. In J. H. Pleck & J. Sawyer (Eds.), *Men and masculinity* (pp. 81–88). Englewood, NJ: Prentice Hall.

Kilmartin, C. T. (1994). *The masculine self*. New York: Macmillan.

Komarovsky, M. (1974). Patterns of self-disclosure of male undergraduates. *Journal of Marriage and Family, 36*, 677–686.

Komarovsky, M. (1976). *Dilemmas of masculinity: A study of college youth*. New York: Norton.

Leviatan, U., & Cohen, J. (1985). Gender differences in life expectancy among kibbutz members. *Social Science and Medicine, 21*, 545–551.

Lewis, C. E., & Lewis, M. A. (1977). The potential impact of sexual equality on health. *New England Journal of Medicine, 297*, 863–868.

Lewis, R. A. (1978). Emotional intimacy among men. *Journal of Social Issues, 34*(1), 108–121.

List, J. S. (1967). *A Psychological Approach to Heart Disease*. New York: Institute of Applied Psychology.

Lowenthal, M. F., & Haven, C. (1968). Interaction and adaptation: Intimacy as a critical variable. *American Sociological Review, 33*, 20–30.

Matthews, K. A., & Haynes, S. G. (1986). Type A behavior pattern and coronary disease risk: Update and critical evaluation. *American Journal of Epidemiology, 123*, 923–960.

McGill, M. E. (1985). *The McGill report*. New York: Holt, Rinehart & Winston.

Naifeh, S., & Smith, G. (1984). *Why can't men open up? Overcoming men's fear of intimacy*. New York: Clarkson N. Potter.

Nathanson, C. (1975). Illness and the feminine role: A theoretical review. *Social Science and Medicine, 9*, 57–62.

Nathanson, C. A. (1977). Sex, illness and medical care: A review of data, theory, and method. *Social Science and Medicine, 11*, 13–25.

Nichols, J. (1975). *Men's liberation: A new definition of masculinity*. New York: Penguin.

Nix, J., & Lohr, J. M. (1981). Relationship between sex, sex-role characteristics and coronary-prone behavior in college students. *Psychological Reports, 48,* 739–744.

Notarius, C., & Johnson, J. (1982). Emotional expression in husbands and wives. *Journal of Marriage and the Family, 44,* 483–489.

O'Neil, J. M., Helms, B. J., Gable, R. K., David, L., & Wrightsman, L. S. (1986). Gender-Role Conflict Scale: College men's fear of femininity. *Sex Roles, 14,* 335–350.

Payne, F. D. (1987). "Masculinity," "femininity," and the complex construct of adjustment. *Sex Roles, 17,* 359–374.

Pennebaker, J. W., Kiecolt-Glaser, J. K., & Glaser, R. (1988). Disclosure of traumas and immune function: Health implications for psychotherapy. *Journal of Consulting and Clinical Psychology, 56,* 239–245.

Pleck, J. H. (1976). The male sex role: Definitions, problems and sources of change. *Journal of Social Issues, 32*(3), 155–164.

Roos, P. E., & Cohen, L. H. (1987). Sex roles and social support as moderators of life stress adjustment. *Journal of Personality and Social Psychology, 52,* 576–585.

Ruberman, W., Weinblatt, E., Goldberg, J. D., & Chaudhary, B. S. (1984). Psychosocial influences on mortality after myocardial infarction. *New England Journal of Medicine, 311,* 552–559.

Rubin, L. B. (1983). *Intimate strangers.* New York: Harper & Row.

Rubin, L. B. (1985). *Just friends.* New York: Harper & Row.

Saurer, M. K., & Eisler, R. M. (1990). The role of masculine gender role stress in expressivity and social support network factors. *Sex Roles, 23*(5/6), 261–271.

Schaefer, C., Coyne, J. C., & Lazarus, R. S. (1981). The health-related functions of social support. *Journal of Behavioral Medicine, 4,* 381–407.

Seeman, T. E., & Syme, S. L. (1987). Social networks and coronary artery disease: A comparison of the structure and function of social relationships as predictors of disease. *Psychosomatic Medicine, 49,* 340–353.

Shumaker, S. A., & Hill, D. R. (1991). Gender differences in social support and physical health. *Health Psychology, 10*(2), 102–111.

Snell, W. E. (1986). The masculine role inventory: Components and correlates. *Sex Roles, 15*(7/8), 443–455.

Spence, J. T., Helmreich, R. L., & Holahan, C. K. (1979). Negative and positive components of psychological masculinity and femininity and their relationship to self-reports of neurotic and acting out behaviors. *Journal of Personality and Social Psychology, 37,* 1673–1682.

Spence, J. T., Helmreich, R. L., & Stapp, J. (1974). The Personal Attributes Questionnaire: A measure of sex-role stereotypes and masculinity-femininity. *JSAS Catalog of Selected Documents in Psychology, 4,* 127.

Sprecher, S., & Sedikides, C. (1993). Gender differences in perceptions of emotionality: The case of close, heterosexual relationships. *Sex Roles, 28*(9/10), 511–530.

Stillion, J. (1995). Premature death among males. In D. Sabo & D. F. Gordon (Eds.), *Men's Health and Illness* (pp. 46–67). Thousand Oaks, CA: Sage Publications, Inc.

Stokes, J. P., & Wilson, D. G. (1984). The inventory of socially supportive behaviors: Dimensionality, prediction, and gender differences. *American Journal of Community Psychology, 12*(1), 53–69.

Strickland, B. R. (1988). Sex-related differences in health and illness. *Psychology of Women Quarterly, 12,* 381–399.

Stroebe, M. S., & Stroebe, W. (1983). Who suffers more? Sex differences in health risks of the widowed. *Psychological Bulletin, 93,* 279–301.

Thompson, Jr., E. H., Grisanti, C., & Pleck, J. H. (1985). Attitudes toward the male role and their correlates. *Sex Roles, 13*(7/8), 413–427.

Thoreson, R. W., Shaughnessy, P., Cook, S. W., & Moore, D. (1993). Behavioral and attitudinal correlates of masculinity: A national survey of male counselors. *Journal of Counseling and Development, 71,* 337–342.

Tognoli, J. (1980). Male friendship and intimacy across the life span. *Family Relations, 29,* 273–279.

Trobst, K., Collins, R. L., & Embree, J. M. (1994). The role of emotion in social support provision: Gender, empathy and expressions of distress. *Journal of Social and Personal Relationships, 11,* 45–62.

Umberson, D., Wortman, C. B., & Kessler, R. C. (1992). Widowhood and depression: Explaining long-term gender differences in vulnerability. *Journal of Health and Social Behavior, 33,* 10–24.

Verbrugge, L. M. (1985). Gender and health: An update on hypotheses and evidence. *Journal of Health and Social Behavior, 26,* 156–182.

Veroff, J., Douvan, E., & Kukla, R. (1981). *The inner American: A self-portrait from 1957–1976.* New York: Basic Books.

Waldron, I. (1995). "Contributions of changing gender differences in behavior and social roles to changing gender differences in mortality." In D. Sabo and D. F. Gordon (Eds.), *Men's Health and Illness* (pp. 22–45). Thousand Oaks, CA: Sage Publications, Inc.

Waldron, I. (1976). Why do women live longer than men? *Social Science and Medicine, 10,* 349–362.

Walker, L. S., & Wright, P. H. (1976). Self-disclosure in friendship. *Perceptual and Motor Skills, 42,* 735–742.

Wallerstein, J. S., & Kelly, J. B. (1980). *Surviving the breakup: How children and parents cope with divorce.* New York: Ticknor and Fields.

Weidner, G., & Matthews, K. A. (1978). Reported physical symptoms elicited by unpredictable events and the Type A coronary-prone behavior pattern. *Journal of Personality and Social Psychology, 36*(11), 1213–1220.

Wheeler, L., Reis, H., & Nezlek, J. (1983). Loneliness, social interaction, and sex roles. *Journal of Personality and Social Psychology, 45,* 765–778.

Wingard, D. I., Suarez, I., & Barrett-Connor, E. (1983). The sex differential in mortality from all causes and ischemic heart disease. *American Journal of Epidemiology, 117,* 165–172.

Winstead, B. A., Derlega, V. J., & Wong, P. T. P. (1984). Effect of sex-role orientation on behavioral self-disclosure. *Journal of Research in Personality, 18,* 541–553.

Wright, I. S. (1980). Care of the severely ill cardiovascular patient. In J. Reiffel, R. DeBellis, L. C. Mark, A. H. Kutscher, P. R. Patterson, & B. Schoenberg (Eds.), *Psychosocial aspects of cardiovascular disease.* New York: Columbia University Press.

Wright, P. H. (1982). Men's friendships, women's friendships, and the alleged inferiority of the latter. *Sex Roles, 8,* 1–20.

Love, Sex, and Power
Considering Women's Realities
In HIV Prevention

HORTENSIA AMARO

On June 19, 1991, ACT UP and over 200 supporters placed a full-page advertisement in the *New York Times* ("Women Don't Get AIDS, They Just Die From It") to highlight ways in which women have been ignored in the United States' response to the HIV/AIDS epidemic. The advertisement referred to the then-current Centers for Disease Control (CDC) definition of AIDS, which did not include infections and disease manifestations characteristic of women with HIV—many of whom had died without ever meeting the criteria for an AIDS diagnosis. Whereas internationally the impact of AIDS on women has received attention, in the United States the nature of the first wave of the epidemic left many with the false impression that women were not affected by this disease.[1] The actions by ACT UP and later by the Congressional Women's Caucus helped focus attention both on the unique medical and service needs of women with HIV/AIDS and to the necessity to conduct research on the natural history of HIV in women and the effectiveness of medical therapies for women with HIV/AIDS.

However, there continues to be a relative dearth of attention to the needs of women in behavioral and prevention research in HIV/AIDS (Institute of Medicine, 1994). The major prevention method available today to reduce sexual transmission of HIV is a traditional condom, which requires male cooperation and, thus, places women at a disadvantage for determining their exposure to risky sexual behaviors. The recently developed female condom may be a promising method for some populations; however, its broad-based access, acceptability, and effectiveness in populations at high risk is not established (Institute of Medicine, 1994). For this reason, there has been a growing call for the development of an effective and safe method that is under the woman's control and can be used without the knowledge of her sexual partner (Potts, 1994; Stein, 1990). However, until the development of a female-controlled method, the tool relied on by most prevention programs for reducing risk is condom use. Because health psychologists' task continues to be to find behavioral interventions that are effective in reducing risk for women, knowledge about human behavior, and gender relations in particular, is critical to developing HIV prevention programs for women.

This article examines how existing models of behavioral risk reduction used in understanding sexual risk behaviors have been hampered by the lack of attention to gender.

We propose that behavioral models of HIV risk reduction have failed to consider a host of contextual social factors that shape the reality of sexual behaviors and the potential for sexual risk reduction among women. In an effort to understand women's sexual behaviors and risk of infection in a more contextual manner, we suggest additional factors that need to be considered in the behavioral theories that guide HIV/AIDS prevention programs.

EPIDEMIOLOGY OF HIV/AIDS IN WOMEN

By the end of June 1994, 401,749 cases of AIDS, 51,235 of which were in women, had been reported to the CDC (CDC, 1994). The number of AIDS cases in women is growing more rapidly than in men, with the proportion of cases changing from approximately 4% in 1981–1982 to 16.7% between July 1993 and July 1994 (CDC, 1994). In some areas of the United States (e.g., New York, New Jersey, and Puerto Rico), women represent an even larger percentage of persons with AIDS, and in those areas AIDS is the leading cause of death among women (Chu, Buehler, & Berkelman, 1990; Guinan, 1992; Guinan & Hardy, 1987).

Compared with their representation in the population (Bureau of the Census, 1993a, 1993b), Blacks (12%) and Latinos (9%) are overrepresented among persons diagnosed with AIDS (32.5% and 17.2%, respectively) (CDC, 1994). This trend is even more pronounced in women. The majority of women diagnosed with AIDS are Black (54%) or Latina (20.5%).

There are important general differences in the modes of transmission for women and for men (CDC, 1994). Women are primarily infected through injection drug use (48%) or heterosexual transmission from an infected partner (36%), who is often a drug user himself (54.8%). Alternatively, among men the major mode of transmission has been sexual contact between gay men. Heterosexual trans-

mission represents a small proportion of cases in men (3%).

A major contributing factor to the difference in heterosexual transmission among women is that male-to-female transmission of HIV is more probable than female-to-male transmission. Padian, Shiboski, and Jewell (1990) found that the odds of male-to-female transmission are 12 times greater than of female-to-male transmission. Heterosexual transmission of HIV is clearly the fastest growing mode for infection among women (Holmes, Karon, & Kreiss, 1990).

The growing importance of heterosexual transmission among women is also evident in the increasing number of adolescent girls diagnosed with AIDS who were infected by a male sexual partner. Girls represent the majority (91.5%) AIDS cases known to have occurred through heterosexual transmission among adolescents (CDC, 1994).

It is also important to note that drug use plays a major role in women's risk of infection. In addition to the risks associated with injection drug use, which represents the major route of transmission for 67.6% of AIDS cases among women (CDC, 1994), female drug users are also at risk from having unprotected sex with their male partners, many of whom are injection drug users at high risk for HIV infection. Furthermore, although many women with partners who are injection drug users are not themselves injection drug users, they are often users of other drugs, including crack (Chitwood et al., 1991; Corby, Wolitski, Thornton-Johnson, & Tanner, 1991). Addiction to crack among women is associated with high-risk sexual behaviors, such as the exchange of sex for drugs or money with concomitant increased risk for HIV infection and other sexually transmitted diseases (Booth, Watters, & Chitwood, 1993; Chiasson et al., 1991).

In summary, heterosexual intercourse is a significant and growing route of transmission among women. Yet, HIV infection prevention efforts have, at best, been only modestly effective in changing risky sexual behaviors among heterosexuals—especially those at highest risk (Institute of Medicine, 1994). There is a pressing need to develop prevention programs that are effective in reducing the risky sexual behaviors that increasingly place women at high risk for infection (Hankins & Handley, 1992; Tortu, Beardsley, Deren, & Davis, 1994; Weissman, 1991)....

LIMITATIONS OF EXISTING MODELS OF SEXUAL RISK BEHAVIOR

Current models of HIV risk behaviors are based on a series of assumptions that limit their usefulness in understanding risk behaviors of a sexual nature. First, most models are based on an individualistic conceptualization of behavior and fail to consider the broader cultural and social context of sexuality. These approaches ignore the way in which distal cultural forces and expectations as well as more immediate social norms and patterns in the individual's network and specific situational factors affect sexuality and sexual behaviors. Second, the models are based on the assumption that sexual behaviors and encounters are controlled totally by the individual and that these encounters are always initiated under the individual's control. However, sexual behavior is often impulsive and motivated physiologically. Moreover, under certain circumstances (and more often for women than for men), sexual encounters are imposed and not voluntary (e.g., in the extreme cases, encounters that lead to rape). Third, gender roles as well as cultural values and norms at least influence, and sometimes define, the behavior of men and women and the interpersonal relationships in which sexual behavior occurs (Ehrhardt & Wasserheit, 1991). Developmental research has documented how society separates and labels infants on the basis of gender and that, as a result, by age 3 or 4, gender identity is solidified and becomes part of an individual's personality (Ehrhardt & Wasserheit, 1991). Gender identity is strongly dependent on learning and social reinforcement, and it is reflected in gender-role behavior (masculine or feminine). One outcome of gender roles is a difference, first seen in childhood, in communication and conflict resolution styles, wherein boys are more likely to use physical dominance and girls to use verbal persuasion; this can place girls at a disadvantage in such encounters with boys (Charlesworth & Dzur, 1987; Jacklin & Maccoby, 1978; Maccoby, 1988). Ehrhardt and Wasserheit (1991), experts in the fields of gender role and sexual behavior, noted that "Gender roles obviously are important modifiers in how sexual encounters are negotiated and who determines which sexual practices will prevail" (p. 99).

For women, this often means that sexual behavior occurs in the context of unequal power and in a context that socializes women to be passive sexually and in other ways. Yet, none of the behavior models used to study HIV risk behaviors explicitly includes gender dynamics (e.g., power in relationships, as well as attitudes and values regarding gender roles) as factors that affect sexual behavior directly. Sex (female vs. male), in contrast to gender, can be built into the models as a predictor of their components. For example, in all of the noted models it is possible to investigate sex differences in the various components that predict behavior. However, testing for sex differences in the fit of these models is largely absent in the literature. Even more surprising is that in most studies, sexual risk behaviors (e.g., not using a condom) in both women and men are seen as the same behavior. In fact, these are distinctly different behaviors. For men, the behavior is wearing the condom: for women, the behavior is persuading the male partner to wear a condom or, in some cases, deciding not to have sex when the male partner refuses to wear a condom.

Some components of the currently popular theories could be used to investigate the role of gender. For example, a central concept of the theory of reasoned action, perceived social norms, could be used to better understand the role of norms for gender appropriate behaviors. Simliarly, in the health belief model, the consideration of costs for implementing a new health behavior could be used to explore gender-specific costs. To date, the application of these theories to HIV prevention has not included work that systematically investigates gender issues. There is a need for work that examines how these theories can include gender issues relevant to HIV risk behaviors and behavior change.

The most important point is that although current theoretical models could be adapted to investigate gendered behavior (e.g., the relative importance of each of the components for women and men in predicting sexual risk behaviors), their basic conceptualization is devoid of gender as a central determinant of sexual behavior. This is a significant omission because condom use is a sexual behavior that is clearly under the control of men and is embedded in a socially sanctioned inequality between partners. This fact is not captured by these models.

Therefore, these models fail to consider a host of contextual social factors relating to gender that shape the reality of risk and potential for risk reduction among women. Overall, this has led to a lack of research on the way that gender roles are related to HIV risk in both women and men.

GROWING EVIDENCE OF THE IMPORTANCE OF GENDER

A number of studies have investigated features of HIV risk behaviors among adolescent girls and women, including the following aspects: factors for risk behaviors (Grinstead, Kegeles, Binson, & Eversley, 1993), successful interventions for women (El-Bassel & Schilling, 1992; Feucht, Stevens, & Gibbs, 1991; Jemmot & Jemmot, 1992; Rhodes, Wolitski, &

Thornton-Johnson, 1992; Schilling, El-Bassel, Schinke, Gordon, & Nichols, 1991), and which women should be targeted for behavior change interventions, given differential levels of knowledge about HIV and prevention methods (Hobfoll, Jackson, Lavin, Britton, & Shepherd, 1993; Weinstock, Lindan, Bolan, Kegeles, & Hearst, 1993.) These researchers and others point to the need for future research to consider issues specific to particular groups of women (e.g., substance abusers, women of various racial or ethnic groups, and adolescent girls).

In these mostly psychosocial studies there is an absence of discussion about gender roles, and only occasionally is there an explanation of why the authors believe women may behave or respond to an intervention differently than men (Hobfoll et al., 1993; Weinstock et al., 1993). Some researchers consider women's issues by looking at the contexts of women's lives, including family and primary relationships; the factors that affect decision making; and economic concerns. They acknowledge that women may have distinct circumstances and needs vis-à-vis health education and behavior change strategies. However, the same researchers do not provide a theoretical framework for understanding gender differences or the social factors that may be uniquely important for risk reduction in women. One study, for example, tested couples' counseling intervention among HIV discordant couples but did not address aspects of the nature of male-female relationships, such as the imbalance in power, that may differentially affect behavior in male and female partners (Padian, O'Brien, Chang, Glass, & Francis 1993).

Some researchers have attempted to integrate theoretical issues of gender roles and cultural definition (Fullilove, Fullilove, Haynes, & Gross, 1990; Kline, Kline, & Oken, 1992; Simon, Morse, Balson, Osofsky, & Gaumer, 1993). For example, one small focus group study with African American and Latina women sought information on women's power in their relationships with men by investigating the extent to which disempowerment and economic dependence on men was evident and, if so, whether it affected sexual decision making (Kline et al., 1992).

A growing number of investigators have recognized that gender differences influence HIV risk behaviors and barriers to behavior change (Fullilove et al., 1990; Gomez & Marin, 1993; Grinstead, Kegeles, Binson, & Eversley, 1993; Icovics & Rodin, 1992; Mondanaro, 1991; Schilling, El-Bassel, & Gilbert, 1993; Seidman, Mosher, & Aral, 1992; Soskolne, Aral, Magder, Reed, & Bowen, 1991; Weinstock et al., 1993). However, these studies have been based on theoretical models that do not provide an explanation for the expected and observed gender differences. Their results suggest a need to look closer at values, beliefs, and practices related to the roles of women and men and their sexuality, as well as the implications of these for HIV risk behaviors and behavior change strategies. The work of Pleck, Sonestein, and Ku (1993) on the relationship of masculine ideology and sexual behavior among White, Black, and Latino young men demonstrates how gender roles are of major importance in understanding sexuality and HIV risk behaviors.

Pleck et al.'s (1993) analysis of the 1988 National Survey of Adolescent Males included a representative sample of 1,717 Black, Latino, and non-Latino White adolescent boys aged 15–19. Pleck et al. reported that even when controlling for socioeconomic status and personal background characteristics, boys who held traditional attitudes toward masculinity indicated that they had more sexual partners in the past year, a less intimate relationship at the time of their last intercourse with their current partner, a greater belief that relationships between women and men are adversarial, more negative attitudes toward condom use, less current use of condoms, less belief in males' responsibility to prevent pregnancy, and a greater belief that pregnancy validates masculinity. Pleck et al. concluded that traditional masculinity ideology is associated with characteristics that limit the quality of adolescent males' close heterosexual relationships and increase the risk of unintended pregnancy and sexually transmitted diseases among their female partners.

The impact of gender roles on communication regarding sexuality and the negotiation of safer sex has been largely ignored, yet there is evidence that this may be one of the most important variables in predicting condom use among heterosexual women and men. A study of a multiethnic population-based sample of San Francisco neighborhoods revealed that the more important predictor of condom use among women and men was the Sexual Communication Scale, which measured perceptions and verbal interactions with new sexual partners concerning safe sex and sexual histories (Catania, Coates, Kegeles, et al., 1992). Women who scored high on this scale were six times more likely to report that their partners always used condoms, and men who scored high on sexual communication were seven times more likely to report condom use than were those with low scores on sexual communication. It is also noteworthy that self-efficacy beliefs and perceived susceptibility, two components of most traditional HIV/AIDS education models, were not significantly associated with frequency of condom use for either heterosexual women or men. Self-efficacy beliefs were associated with condom use only among gay or bisexual men. On the basis of their findings, Catania, Coates, Kegeles, et al. concluded that "interventions for minority women that focus only on condom enjoyment and social skills training may not be sufficient to increase condom use without taking into account other facets of their sexual relationships" (p. 286).

Other researchers have also demonstrated gender and cultural differences in sexual behavior. For example, work by Marin and colleagues (Marin, Gomez, & Hearst, 1993;

Marin, Gomez, & Tschann, 1993; Marin, Tschann, et al., 1993) indicates that (a) important gender differences exist in sexual behavior, (b) acculturation is associated with different changes in sexual behavior for Latinas and Latinos, (c) important differences exist between Latinos and non-Latinos in sexual behavior among married men, and (d) important differences exist across Latino groups in sexual behaviors. This work credits not only the relevance of gender for understanding sexual behavior but also the role of acculturation and cultural influences on gender differences.

Evidence on the importance of gender roles in sexual behavior and risk reduction among Latina women also comes from a focus group study that asked 2,527 participants living in communities throughout the Northeast to discuss barriers to HIV risk reduction (Amaro & Gornemann, 1992). In nearly 75% of 69 women-only focus groups, the issue of power and gender roles emerged as a central barrier to risk reduction. Women talked about this in many ways. For example, they referred to men's stubbornness and unwillingness to use condoms and expressed feelings of powerlessness, low self-esteem, isolation, lack of voice, and inability to affect risk reduction decisions or behaviors with their partners. In contrast, in mixed gender groups these issues were not discussed as frequently, perhaps suggesting that issues of gender roles and power differentials in relationships are generally difficult for women to discuss openly with men.

RETHINKING SEXUAL RISK AMONG WOMEN: CONSTRUCTS TO CONSIDER A GENDERED CONTEXT

As psychologists rethink theoretical models for understanding HIV risk behavior among women, it would be useful to incorporate concepts from gender studies and the psychology of women into a new formulation of which factors affect risk for women. There are at least four central assumptions that should underlie any theoretical model for understanding women's sexual risk behaviors: (a) women's social status as a central feature in women's risk, (b) connection and the relational self in women's development and the fear of disconnection due to conflict as critical features in women's risk, (c) male partners as key role players in women's risk, and (d) experience and fear of physical and sexual abuse as an important barrier to risk reduction among some women.

Women's Social Status Is a Central Feature in Women's Risk

The central premise of a gender-specific approach to prevention is that risk of HIV infection among all women, and especially among poor and addicted women, must be viewed in relation to the broader social context of women's "permanent inequality" in status and power (Miller, 1986, p. 6). Framing women's risk behaviors in this context is especially relevant because for most women, sexual risk of HIV infection occurs within the context of their relationships with men.

In her book, *Toward a New Psychology of Women,* Jean Baker Miller (1986) explored the meaning of the permanent inequality in relationships in which one member is defined as unequal by society on the basis of criteria such as sex, race, class, or another characteristic ascribed at birth. Miller argued that women's permanent inequality has a powerful and pervasive impact on women's life experiences, including the nature of male-female relationships. One of the consequences of such permanent inequality is that subordinates are "described in terms of, and encouraged to develop, personal psychological characteristics that are pleasing to the dominant group. These characteristics form a certain familiar cluster: submissiveness, passivity, docility, dependency, lack of initiative, inability to act, to decide, to think" (Miller, 1986, p. 7).

The impact of women's unequal social status on their risk of becoming infected with HIV has been noted by experts worldwide. For example, experts at an international meeting on HIV stated, "The unequal status of women puts them at severe disadvantage in negotiating sexual encounters and in seeking and utilizing educational and health services" (Chen, Sepulveda Amor, & Segal, 1991, p. 199). One of the conference recommendations called for frameworks in HIV programs that take into account both the complex factors that determine women's sexual and health behaviors and the range of information and services required to empower women to protect and maintain their health (p. 199).

However, women's unequal social status has been generally ignored in prevention programs, which, as a key aspect of HIV prevention, should serve to increase women's skills and assertiveness in negotiating safer sex. In many ways, this strategy is in direct conflict with socialized "female" characteristics such as submissiveness, passivity, and lack of initiative. The tasks of safer sex negotiation for women require them to act in conflict with their traditional socialization as unequals and subordinates to men: thus, negotiating safer sex is a much more complex and conflict-laden task than it would be in a relationship between individuals with equal social status (e.g., between two men). Prevention approaches must be based on an understanding of how much this negotiating task requires of women; approaches should be designed to help women understand the social context of such actions and to provide women with adequate support to carry them out.

The need to develop a model of sexual risk behaviors that considers women's social status has led psychologists to investigate the variables that reflect a woman's power in a specific relationship and her adherence to traditional roles. Such measures might include (a) a woman's attitudes, values, and beliefs regarding the role of women, (b) a woman's level of comfort with behaviors that contradict traditional gender norms, and (c) a woman's power in the relationship relative to that of her partner.

Importance of Connection for Women

Jean Baker Miller and others have provided a critique of psychoanalytic and developmental theories that stresses the value of individuation, autonomy, and separation (Jordan, Kaplan, Miller, Stiver, & Surrey, 1991; Miller, 1986). They have argued that traditional theories of development are based on the notion that a feature of healthy development is disconnecting from relationships. From this perspective, relationships are viewed as a means to individual achievement. It seems clear that traditional theories of healthy growth and development have influenced theories of behavior to focus on the individual as autonomous and separate from his or her relationships and the general context of living.

Miller (1986), who proposed a connection-based theory of women's development, the self-in-relation theory, suggested that the relational self is the core of self-structure in women and the basis for their growth and development. She claims that women's sense of personhood is grounded in the motivation to make and enhance relationships to others (Miller, 1986). Although this provides women with the potential for more advanced development—the ability to "encompass others' needs and to do this with ease" (p. 62), women's social status as subordinates also encompasses the denial of their own needs "to serve others—first men, and later, children" (p. 62). Because of women's basic orientation to others, their relationships and the maintenance of relationships have highly charged meaning. Miller stated that "eventually, for many women the threat of disruption of connections is perceived not just as a loss of a relationship but as something closer to total loss of self" (p. 83).

Thus, changes in such relationships, including changes related to infection risk reduction, necessitate that women take great personal risks. Viewed from a relational perspective, the great threat for women is the fear of loss stemming from a disconnection caused by conflict. The difficulty of the choices (e.g., staying in relationships in which they are exposed to the risk of infection or in which they face the threat of loss of self), as well as the anger that is generated in a subordinate position, may promote a real fear of loss that is likely to undermine women's intentions and attempts to reduce sexual risk.

If giving to others is a central aspect of women's identity, what are the implications for their sexuality? Miller (1986) argued that within women's ascribed roles as unequals, sex is something that women give to men in which there is little room for women's acceptance of their own sexuality. From this perspective, stepping out of the traditional role, as required by safer sex negotiation, places women in direct conflict and challenge with men (Miller, 1986). This presents women with a very difficult situation because

> Since women have had to live trying to please men, they have been conditioned to prevent men from feeling even uncomfortable. Moreover, when women suspect that they have caused men to feel unhappy or angry, they have a strong tendency to assume that they themselves are wrong. (Miller, 1986, p. 58)

On the basis of the self-in-relation theory, change in such situations necessitates that women examine the quality of their connections rather than thinking first of pleasing the male partner and conforming to his desires and expectations (Miller, 1986). When this orientation is structured into women's experience and their acquired sense of self, risk reduction can present a formidable challenge.

Furthermore, gender roles that stress the value of motherhood for women as another form of connection to their male partners can also represent an obstacle to the adoption of HIV sexual risk reduction through condom use. This may be a particularly strong barrier to risk reduction among Latinas because of the strong cultural value placed on motherhood and childbearing (Ramirez & Arce, 1981; Sabogal, Marin, Otero-Sabogal, Marin, & Perez-Stable, 1987).

A new model of HIV sexual risk reduction that recognizes connection as a central feature in women's lives suggests that to better understand risk behavior and risk reduction, psychologists must examine factors such as the following: (a) the centrality of connection to others as a core aspect of self, (b) the degree to which conflict in relationships (especially conflict related to safer sex negotiation) and fear of disconnection is threatening to women, (c) the degree of mutuality in the relationship with the male partner, (d) skills and comfort in dealing with conflict, and (e) the degree to which pregnancy and childbearing are perceived as avenues for further connecting with male partners.

Male Partners Play a Key Role in Women's Risk

Astounding as it may seem, the central role of male partners and male gender roles in women's ability to reduce their risk of injection has not received serious consideration in HIV prevention. This is evident in the preponderance of HIV sexual risk reduction efforts targeted solely at women (e.g., commercial sex workers and pregnant women). As in previous efforts targeted at contraception, women rather than men have been asked to take the responsibility for sexual risk reduction.

The work of Pleck et al. (1993) with adolescent boys indicates that attitudes, beliefs, and behaviors related to male gender roles have a major impact on sexual behaviors and the risk posed for their female partners. The research indicates that masculinity ideology guides young men's sexual behaviors and attitudes toward their female partners. This ideology, together with a gender role socialization that implores boys to be sexually aggressive, results in risky behaviors among boys, which in turn place girls at risk. Furthermore, this research suggests that traditional masculinity ideology does not promote the sexual communication and negotiation associated with condom use (Catania, Coates, Kegeles, et al., 1992).

In addition, the pertinent literature has documented that male partners often play a critical role in the initiation of drug use among girls and women (Amaro, Zuckerman, & Cabral, 1989; Anglin, Hser, & McGlothlin, 1987; Hser, Anglin, & McGlothlin, 1987; Rosenbaum, 1981; Worth & Rodriguez, 1987). For girls and women, more often than for boys and men, the initiation and progression of drug use occurs within the context of a love or sexual relationship, which can make it more difficult for them to disengage from drug use, to insist on safer sex practices, or both.

On the basis of work such as that previously described, any model of HIV risk behaviors that places gender roles central to understanding such behavior must consider the role of male partners in women's risk, leading to the investigation of factors such as (a) men's attitudes, beliefs, values, and norms regarding male and female roles, (b) men's attitudes toward women and their roles, (c) the degree to which men adhere to traditional male sexual and other behaviors, (d) the degree of power of the male partner in the relationship, and (e) drug use by male partners and its role in women's use of drugs.

Women's Experience of Fear and Abuse

The last assumption in a model of HIV sexual risk behavior that places gender central to the analysis of women's risk is that fear of or the experience of abuse (emotional, sexual, or physical) are important factors in women's ability to carry out risk reduction measures.

As a group, women have been defined by society as subservient to men, and their lower status is reflected in many dimensions, such as their historically disadvantaged legal status, inequities in compensation for women's work outside the home, lack of recognition and compensation for women's work in the home, and generally lower access to equitable employment opportunities and positions of power in social institutions.

Women's generally disempowered status as a group has direct ramifications for their exposure to violence, especially within relationships with men. Miller (1986) and Freire (1970, 1990) both argued that violence and the threat of violence are tools used by socially defined dominant groups to control socially defined subservient groups. In their recent book on violence toward women, *No Safe Haven*, Koss et al. (1994) noted that "Male-perpetrated violence is a major cause of fear, distress, injury, and even death for women in this country" (p. ix). Data on violence toward women indicate that women's greatest risk of assault is from male partners, with women more likely to be injured, raped, or killed by a male partner than by any other type of assailant (Koss et al., 1994).

The work of Gomez and Marin (1993) suggests that fear of a partner's anger in response to requests to use condoms is an important predictor of condom use among a significant group of Latinas in the general population. Among women at highest risk for HIV infection (e.g., those who use injection drugs and those whose partners do), the experience of violence and abuse are part and parcel of everyday life. Negotiating condom use in this context is likely to become only another opportunity for conflict and potential abuse.

A study of 430 female undergraduates at the University of Rhode Island found that intrapsychic factors do not determine a woman's ability to engage in safer sex or to choose a risky sexual partner. Rather, behavioral factors (e.g., sexual experience and substance abuse)

and interpersonal factors (e.g., sexual assertiveness and victimization) were most important in predicting risk behaviors (Harlow,
Grimle, Quina, & Morokoff, 1992). This study
provides support for the contextual importance among women of sexual abuse and victimization and the relational nature of sex
(Gallant, Coons, & Morokoff, 1994).

Among female drug users and women
whose partners use drugs, the experience of
violence is even more common than among
those who are not affected by drugs (Amaro,
Fried, Cabral, & Zuckerman, 1990; Fullilove,
Fullilove, Kennedy, et al., 1992; Koss et al.,
1994). In addition, a large proportion of alcoholic and drug-dependent women report
childhood or adult sexual abuse, including

rape and incest (Benward & Densen-Gerber,
1975; Schaefer & Evans, 1987; Walker et al.,
1992; Wilsnack, 1984). Such traumatic events
are likely to affect women's current ability to
negotiate sexual behaviors.

Given the facts of violence toward
women, a model that considers how gender
roles affect women's HIV sexual risk behaviors and behavior reduction would lead to the
investigation of (a) women's history and their
current experience with the presence of threats
and violence in relationships, (b) women's
fear—including fear occurring in response to
condom negotiation, (c) male attitudes regarding violence and abusive behaviors toward women, and (d) male history of threats
or violence against women....

NOTE

1. Although many of the arguments presented in
this article could be applied to women in other
countries, this article focuses on women in the
United States. Although an examination of the cultural factors that affect gender relations in other
countries is important, it is beyond the scope of this
article.

REFERENCES

Amaro, H., Fried, L., Cabral, H., & Zuckerman, B.
(1990). Violence during pregnancy: The relationship to drug use among women and
their partners. *American Journal of Public
Health, 80*, 575–579.

Amaro, H., & Gornemann, I. (1992). *HIV/AIDS related knowledge, attitudes, beliefs, and behaviors
among Hispanics: Report of findings and recommendations.* Boston: Boston University School
of Public Health and Northeast Hispanic AIDS
Consortium.

Amaro, H., Zuckerman, B., & Cabral, H. (1989).
Drug use among adolescent mothers: A profile
of risk. *Pediatrics, 84*, 144–151.

Anglin, D., Hser, Y., & McGlothlin, W. (1987). Sex
differences in addict careers II: Becoming addicted. *American Journal of Drug and Alcohol
Abuse, 13*, 59–71.

Benward, J., & Densen-Gerber, J. (1975). Incest as a
causative factor in anti-social behavior: An ex-
ploratory study. *Contemporary Drug Problems,
4*, 323–340.

Booth, R. E., Watters, J. K, & Chitwood, D. D. (1993).
HIV risk-related sex behaviors among injection drug users, crack smokers, and injection
drug users who smoke crack. *American Journal
of Public Health, 83*, 1144–1148.

Bureau of the Census. (1993a). *We, the American
Blacks.* Washington, DC: U.S. Department of
Commerce, Economics and Statistics Admin-
istration.

Bureau of the Census. (1993b). *We, the American
Hispanics.* Washington, DC: U.S. Department
of Commerce, Economics and Statistics Administration.

Catania, J. A., Coates, T. J., Kegeles, S., Thompson-
Fullilove, M., Peterson, J., Marin, B., Siegel, D.,
& Hulley, S. (1992). Condom use in multi-
ethnic neighborhoods of San Francisco: The
population-based AMEN (AIDS in multi-ethnic

neighborhoods) study. *American Journal of Public Health, 82,* 284–287.

Centers for Disease Control and Prevention. (1994). *HIV/AIDS Surveillance Report, 6,* 8–12.

Charlesworth, W. R., & Dzur, C. (1987). Gender comparisons of preschoolers' behavior and resource utilization in group problem-solving. *Child Development, 58,* 191–200.

Chen, L. C., Sepulveda Amor, J., Segal, S. I. (Eds.). (1991). *AIDS and women's reproductive health.* New York: Plenum Press.

Chiasson, M. A., Stoneburner, R., Hildebrandt, D., Ewing, W., Telzak, E., & Jaffe, H. (1991). Heterosexual transmission of HIV-1 associated with use of smokeable freebase cocaine (crack). *AIDS, 5,* 1121–1126.

Chitwood, D. D., Inciardi, J. A., McBride, D. C., McCoy, C. B., McCoy, H. V., & Trapido, E. (1991). *A Community Approach to AIDS Intervention.* Westport, CT: Greenwood Press.

Chu, S. Y., Buehler, J. W., & Berkelman, R. L. (1990). Impact of the human immunodeficiency virus epidemic on mortality in women of reproductive age, United States. *Journal of the American Medical Association, 264,* 225–229.

Corby, N., Wolitski, R., Thornton-Johnson, S., & Tanner, W. (1991). AIDS knowledge, perception of risk, and behaviors among female sex partners of injection drug users. *AIDS Education and Prevention, 3,* 353–366.

Ehrhardt, A. A., & Wasserheit, J. N. (1991). Age, gender, and sexual risk behaviors for sexually transmitted diseases in the United States. In J. N. Wasserheit, S. O. Aral, K. K. Holmes, & P. J. Hitchcock (Eds.), *Research issues in human behavior and sexually transmitted diseases in the AIDS era* (pp. 97–121). Washington, DC: American Society for Microbiology.

El-Bassel, N., & Schilling, R. (1992). Fifteen-month followup of women methadone patients taught skills to reduce heterosexual HIV transmission. *Public Health Reports, 107,* 500–504.

Feucht, T., Stephens, R., & Gibbs, B. (1991). Knowledge about AIDS among intravenous drug users: An evaluation of an education program. *AIDS Education and Prevention, 3,* 10–20.

Freire, P. (1970). *Pedagogy of the Oppressed.* New York: Seabury Press.

Freire, P. (1990). *Education for critical consciousness.* New York: Continuum.

Fullilove, M. T, Fullilove, R. E., Haynes, K., & Gross, S., (1990). Black women and AIDS prevention: A view towards understanding the gender roles. *The Journal of Sex Research, 27,* 47–64.

Fullilove, M., Fullilove, R., Kennedy, G., & Smith, M. (1992, July). *Trauma, crack and HIV risk.* Paper presented at the meeting of the Eighth International Conference on AIDS, Amsterdam.

Gallant, S., Coons, H. L., & Morokoff, P. H. (1994). Psychology and women's health: Some reflections and future directions. In V. J. Adesso, D. M. Reddy, & R. Flemming (Eds.), *Psychological perspectives on women's health* (pp. 315–346). Washington, DC: Taylor & Francis.

Gomez, C., & Marin, B. (1993, June). *Can women demand condom use? Gender and power in safer sex.* Paper presented at the meeting of the Ninth International Conference on AIDS, Berlin, Germany.

Grinstead, O. A., Kegeles, B., Binson, E., & Eversley, R. (1993). Women's sexual risk for HIV: The National AIDS Behavioral Surveys. *Family Planning Perspectives, 6,* 252–257.

Guinan, M. E. (1992). Finding HIV-infected women: The clinician's role. *Journal of the American Medical Women's Association, 47,* 92–93.

Guinan, M. E., & Hardy, A. (1987). Epidemiology of women and AIDS in the United States. *Journal of the American Medical Association, 257,* 2039–2042.

Hankins, C. A., & Handley, M. A. (1992). HIV disease and AIDS in women: Current knowledge and a research agenda. *Journal of AIDS, 5,* 957–971.

Harlow, L., Grimle, D., Quina, K., & Morokoff, P. (1992, March). *Behavioral, interpersonal, and psycho-situational predictors of HIV-risk in women.* Paper presented at the meeting of the Society of Behavioral Medicine, New York.

Hobfoll, S., Jackson, A., Lavin, J., Britton, P. J., & Shepherd, J. B. (1993). Safer sex knowledge, behavior, and attitudes of inner-city women. *Health Psychology, 12,* 481–488.

Holmes, K., Karon, J., & Kreiss, J. (1990). The increasing frequency of heterosexually acquired AIDS in the United States, 1983–1988. *American Journal of Public Health, 80,* 858–863.

Hser, Y., Anglin, D., & McGlothlin, W. (1987). Sex differences in addict career, I: Initiation of use. *American Journal of Drug and Alcohol Abuse, 13,* 33–57.

Icovics, J., & Rodin, J. (1992). Women and AIDS in the United States: Epidemiology, natural history, and mediation mechanisms. *Health Psychology, 11*, 1–16.

Institute of Medicine. (1994). J. D. Auerbach, C. Wypijewska, & H. K. Brodie. (Eds.). (1994). *AIDS and behavior: An integrated approach.* Washington, DC: National Academy Press.

Jacklin, C. N., & Maccoby, E. E. (1978). Social behavior at 33 months in same-sex and mixed-sex dyads. *Child Development, 49*, 557–569.

Jemmot, L., & Jemmot, J. (1992). Increasing condom-use intentions among sexually active black adolescent women. *Nursing Research, 41*, 273–279.

Jordan, J. D., Kaplan, A. G., Miller, J. B., Stiver, I. P., & Surrey, J. L. (Eds.). (1991). *Women's growth in connection.* New York: Guilford Press.

Kline, A., Kline, E., & Oken, E. (1992). Minority women and sexual choice in the age of AIDS. *Social Science and Medicine, 34*, 447–457.

Koss, M. P., Goodman, L. A., Browne, A., Fitzgerald, L. F., Puryear-Keita, G., & Russo, N. F. (1994). *No safe haven: Male violence against women at home, at work, and in the community.* Washington, DC: American Psychological Association.

Maccoby, E. E. (1988). Gender as a social category. *Developmental Psychology, 24*, 755–765.

Marin, B. V., Gomez, C. A., & Hearst, N. H. (1993). Multiple heterosexual partners and condom use among Hispanics and non-Hispanic whites. *Family Planning Perspectives, 25*, 170–174.

Marin, B. V., Gomez, C. A., & Tschann, J. M. (1993). Condom use among Hispanic men with secondary female sexual partners. *Public Health Reports, 108*, 742–750.

Marin, B. V., Tschann, J. M., Gomez, C. A., & Kegeles, S. (1993). Acculturation and gender differences in sexual attitudes and behaviors: Hispanic vs. non-Hispanic white unmarried adults. *American Journal of Public Health, 83*, 1759–1761.

Miller, J. B. (1986). *Toward a new psychology of women.* Boston: Beacon Press.

Mondanaro, J. (1991). Community-based AIDS prevention interventions: Special issues for women intravenous drug users. In C. G. Leukefeld, R. J. Battjes, & Z. Amsel (Eds.), *AIDS and intravenous drug use, community intervention and prevention* (pp. 68–82). New York: Hemisphere.

Padian, N. S., O'Brien, T. R., Chang, Y., Glass, S., & Francis, D. P. (1993). Prevention of heterosexual transmission of human immunodeficiency virus through couple counseling. *Journal of Acquired Immune Deficiency Syndromes, 6*, 1043–1048.

Padian, N. S., Shiboski, S., & Jewell, N. (1990). The effect of the number of exposures on the risk of heterosexual HIV transmission. *Journal of Infectious Diseases, 161*, 883–887.

Pleck, J. H., Sonestein, F. L., & Ku, L. (1993). Masculinity ideology: Its impact on adolescent males' heterosexual relationships. *Journal of Social Issues, 49(3)*, 11–19.

Potts, M. (1994). The urgent need for a vaginal microbicide in the prevention of HIV transmission. *American Journal of Public Health, 86*, 890–891.

Ramirez, O., & Arce, C. (1981). The contemporary Chicano family: An empirically-based review. In A. Baron (Ed.), *Explorations in Chicano psychology* (pp. 3–28). New York: Praeger.

Rhodes, R., Wolitski, R., & Thornton-Johnson, S. (1992). An experimental program to reduce AIDS risk among female sex partners of injection-drug users. *Health and Social Work, 17*, 261–272.

Rosenbaum, M. (1981). *Women on heroin.* New Brunswick, NJ: Rutgers University Press.

Sabogal, F., Marin, G., Otero-Sabogal, R., Marin, B. V., & Perez-Stable, E. J. (1987). Hispanic familism and acculturation: What changes and what doesn't? *Hispanic Journal of Behavioral Sciences, 9*, 397–412.

Schaefer, S., & Evans, S. (1987). Women, sexuality, and the process of recovery. *Journal of Chemical Dependency Treatment, 1*, 91–120.

Schilling, R. F., El-Bassel, N., & Gilbert, L. (1993). Predictors of changes in sexual behavior among women on methadone. *American Journal of Drug and Alcohol Abuse, 19*, 409–422.

Schilling, R. F., El-Bassel, N., Schinke, S., Gordon, K., & Nichols, S. (1991). Building skills of recovering women drug users to reduce heterosexual AIDS transmission. *Public Health Reports, 106*, 297–304.

Seidman, S., Mosher, W., & Aral, S. (1992). Women with multiple sexual partners: United States, 1988. *American Journal of Public Health, 82*, 1388.

Simon, P. M., Morse, E. V., Balson, P. M., Osofsky, H. J., & Gaumer, H. R. (1993). Barriers to human immunodeficiency virus related risk reeducation among male street prostitutes. *Health Education Quarterly, 20*, 261–273.

Soskolne, V., Aral, S., Magder, L., Reed, D., & Bowen, G. (1991). Condom use with regular and casual partners among women attending family planning clinics. *Family Planning Perspectives, 23,* 223.

Stein, Z. (1990). HIV prevention: The need for methods women can use. *American Journal of Public Health, 80,* 460–462.

Tortu, S., Beardsley, M., Deren, S., & Davis, W. R. (1994). The risk of HIV infection in a national sample of women with injection drug-using partners. *American Journal of Public Health, 84,* 1243–1249.

Walker, E. D., Katon, W. J., Hansom, J., Harrop-Grifiths, J., Homs, L., Jones, M. L., Hickok, L., & Jemelka, R. P. (1992). Medical and psychiatric symptoms in women with childhood sexual abuse. *Psychosomatic Medicine, 54,* 658–664.

Weinstock, H. S., Lindan, C., Bolan, G., Kegeles, S., & Hearst, N. (1993). Factors associated with condom use in a high-risk heterosexual population. *Sexually Transmitted Diseases, 20,* 14–20.

Weissman, G. (1991). National AIDS Research Consortium. AIDS prevention for women at risk: Experience from a national demonstration research project. *Journal of Primary Prevention, 12,* 49–63.

Wilsnack, S. (1984). Drinking, sexuality, and sexual dysfunction in women. In S. C. Wilsnack & L. J. Beckamn (Eds.), *Alcohol problems in women* (pp. 189–227). New York: Guildford Press.

Worth, D., & Rodriguez, R. (1987). Latina women and AIDS. *Radical America, 20,* 63–67.

Where Has All the Hysteria Gone?

ROBERTA SATOW

Although hysteria in its various forms accounts today for only a small percentage of the reported mental illnesses among women, it is not clear why, because "hysteria" has been a label used for a potpourri of female ailments and nonailments alike since antiquity. In reading about the history of hysteria, one is struck by the fact that it has been a common syndrome for so long. The Greeks and Romans called almost all female complaints hysteria and believed the cause of all these female maladies to be a wandering uterus. In the Middle Ages women exhibiting the symptoms that would have earlier been called hysteria were viewed as witches possessed by the devil. In eighteenth- and nineteenth-century Europe behavior that would have been labeled hysteria in ancient times and "witchcraft" in medieval society was once again viewed as hysteria; however, sexual lasciviousness was seen as the cause. At the turn of the century, Freud wrote his famous case studies in which he attributed hysterical manifestations to unconscious processes and conflicts and also changed the concept of hysteria by distinguishing between conversion (similar to the ancient syndrome called hysteria) and anxiety hysteria (phobias).

Despite the fact that hysteria has historically been a common malady, it is not a common diagnosis today. For example, in a British survey of general practitioners covering a million patients, the diagnosis of hysteria was made in only 5.5 percent of the cases referred to psychiatrists.[1] And in the United States hysteria is not ranked as one of three most frequently made diagnoses of males or females admitted to psychiatric facilities.[2] One explanation of this is that the diagnosis of hysteria has declined, but not the *behavioral syndrome* traditionally called hysteria.

Szasz[3] argues that so-called "hysterical" patients have not disappeared, but that they go to general practitioners and are loath to admit that their problem is psychiatric and not physical.[4] Gardner[5] estimates that 30 percent of all patient visits to general medical practitioners involve patients with emotional stress. Therefore it is very difficult to know what the actual *rate of prevalence* of the syndrome is, because the *reported rate* is limited to psychiatric facilities. Slater[6] claims there is much more of a problem because the diagnosis of hysteria is so general it is a disguise for ignorance, and the more sophisticated we become, the more useless that diagnostic category becomes. Attempting to discern why hysteria has declined, or *if* it has, is an extremely difficult task because, in different historical periods, the labels attached to the original syndrome and the assumed causes of the syndrome have changed. This article traces those changes and makes explicit the kinds of complex methodological problems involved in trying to

From "Where Has All the Hysteria Gone?" by Roberta Satow. *The Psychoanalytic Review* 66: 465–477, 1979. Reprinted by permission of *The Psychoanalytic Review* published by The National Psychological Association for Psychoanalysis, Inc., volume 66, pages 465–477.

answer what originally seemed to be a simple question: "Where has all the hysteria gone?"

In various Hippocratic texts the term hysteria, derived from the Greek work *hystera*, which means uterus, is applied to a large variety of female complaints such as: respiratory conditions (i.e., difficulty in breathing or choking sensations); pains in various parts of the body; sensory loss (i.e., taste, voice, vision, hearing, or feeling); violent, epileptic-like seizures; diuresis; inability to eat; fatigue; and headaches. The Greeks and Egyptians believed that the disorder was caused by a displaced uterus and that the symptoms differed according to the organ to which the wandering uterus attached itself. If it attached itself to the liver, for example, the patient lost her voice and gritted her teeth; if it moved up to the heart, it would cause feelings of anxiety, oppression, and vomiting.[7] Fumigation of the uterus was a well-known treatment in Egypt as well as Greece, where it was believed that fumigation would lure the wandering uterus back to its natural position.[8]

Toward the end of Antiquity, Galen of Pergamon denied that the womb could move around and argued that "seminal retention" due to sexual abstinence was the cause of hysteria. Galen explained that women have a secretion produced by the uterus that is similar to the semen of the male. Retention of this substance, he argued, leads to its spoiling and corrupting the blood, eventually resulting in hysteria. The only way this "female semen" could be released was through orgasm; Galen therefore advocated masturbation as a solution to hysteria if intercourse was not possible.[9] Galen's theory was the culmination of the increasing emphasis put on sexual factors in the etiology of hysteria.

In the Greek period the emphasis had been on the search for natural causes for events; hysterical symptoms were regarded as tangible, logical reactions to temporary imbalances in the body. But this concept of sex as a natural function without social stigma encountered great opposition when Christianity took hold. Ecclesiastic writers viewed sexual pleasure as sin and abstinence as virtue. The early ascetic Christians translated into church doctrine their condemnation of the sexual impulse. Marriage was viewed, at best, as a sop to animal passions; since the temptation of man lay in the direction of woman, woman became *ipso facto* evil. Sexual activity was considered a complete evil, and the absence of sexual activity came to be thought of as a complete good.[10] Hence, to attribute deleterious effects (i.e., hysterical attacks) to sexual abstinence was unthinkable (pp. 37–43).[7]

The first Christian theological explanation for hysterical manifestations was that they were caused by a person's alliance with the devil. Except for the few who were fortunate enough to fall into the hands of physicians who still believed in the ancient uterine theory or Galen's dictum about seminal retention, women who would have earlier been defined as hysterics became prime victims of the witch craze. Between 1100 and 1700 European concern with witches became a major intellectual and juridical preoccupation. Witch beliefs, of course, long antedated this period, but from 1100 on these indistinct strains of belief were systematized into a uniform ideology.[11] Thus there was a transition from a medical to a moral metaphor as the syndrome earlier labeled as hysteria was redefined as evidence of witchcraft.

One of the tests for witches was to prick their skin for areas of anesthesia (loss of sensation is a classic symptom of hysteria). Anesthetic areas were considered satanic stigmata confirming bewitchment.[12] In England and Scotland detection of witches became a lucrative occupation. The "common pricker" traveled about testing suspects for anesthetic regions. If the suspect did not feel the pin, she was judged to be a witch. However, not everyone who was possessed by demons was defined as a witch. People could be temporarily bewitched if a witch cast a spell on them.

By the eighteenth century the witch craze was over in Europe, and French physician Phillippe Pinel reintroduced sex as a major factor in the etiology of hysteria. He identified nymphomania as well as sexual abstinence as hysterical manifestations. In the nineteenth century many physicians assumed that hysteria was the result of immoderate sexual needs and demands. The Victorian physicians' contempt for female hysterics and, by implication, female sexuality was reflected in the common cures. Neurologist Nikolaus Friedrich (1825–1882) cauterized the clitoris of hysterical patients and gynecologist Alfred Hegar (1830–1924) performed ovariectomies. Jules Falret, a psychiatrist at Salpêtrière Hospital in Paris, said:[7]

> The life of the hysteric is nothing but one perpetual falsehood; they affect airs of piety and devotion ... while secretly abandoning themselves to the most shameful actions. ... (p. 211)

In the United States in 1846 Dixon reported that masturbation caused hysteria and other physicians concurred, pointing out that the naturally harsh public and medical reactions to hysterical women were due to their understanding that masturbation was the cause. Another American physician reported that hysteria was commonly found among lower-class women because of their base sensuality.[13] In general, nineteenth-century physicians seemed to maintain a delicate balance in their view of the sexual etiology of hysteria; anything that deviated from moderation could cause hysteria—whether it was prostitution or extended virginity.

A relatively unknown British psychiatrist, Robert Brunell Carter (1828–1918), first offered a theory of repression as a main factor in the etiology of hysteria.[7] In his book, *On the Pathology and Treatment of Hysteria* (1853), Carter said that an event or situation triggered off the first hysterical attack, and the extent to which the person felt compelled to conceal or "repress" the exciting cause, because of social convention, determined whether or not she would have an hysterical attack and the intensity of it. He said that since women are more sensitive in their emotional structure than men and more compelled by convention to repress their sexual needs, they were more susceptible to hysteria (p. 201). Carter's insights were never widely disseminated, and it was left to Jean Martin Charcot (1825-1893) and Freud to convince the medical and psychiatric establishments that the etiology of hysteria was purely emotional.

In 1862 Charcot became the physician at Salpêtrière Hospital, which housed about 5000 indigents, epileptics, and insane patients. Charcot separated the hysterics and epileptics from the psychotics and found that the hysterics imitated the epileptic seizures and hallucinations. At first he did not realize that the seizures were due to imitation and assumed it was a new disease, which he dubbed "hystero-epilepsy"; however, he later pointed to this kind of mimicking as the basis for the hysterical contagion that results in mass hysteria. Charcot induced hysterical attacks of paralysis in patients under hypnosis to show that the emotional element plays a significant role in the etiology of the disorder. He viewed psychic trauma as a primary precipitant of hysterical attacks and suggested that patients be separated from their psychogenic environment.

Freud's interest in the psychological aspects of medicine began in 1886, when he went to Paris to study with Charcot. Freud was very impressed with Charcot's willingness to stand in opposition to the medical establishment. For example, Charcot took hysterical symptoms as real despite the common attitude at that time, which considered them merely imagined. He also insisted that men could be hysterics, which opposed the traditional idea that it was an exclusively female disorder.[14]

By the time Freud returned to Vienna he was a champion of Charcot's ideas, and Josef

Breuer was sympathetic to his ideas. In 1880 Breuer had treated a young girl who had classical hysterical symptoms: paralysis of the limbs, anesthesias, and disturbances of vision and speech. Breuer hypnotized her and encouraged her to speak about the experiences that coincided with her symptoms. The memories that Anna O. recalled were accompanied by the experience of the strong emotions she had felt during the original experience that led to the development of the symptoms. The situation that had set off the hysterical manifestations was the illness of Anna's father. Breuer attempted to trace back each of her conversion symptoms to feelings or experiences she had during her father's illness.

This case became the basis for Freud's collaboration with Breuer. The concept of the unconscious and of the repression of unacceptable ideas began taking shape. In 1895 Freud and Breuer published *Studies in Hysteria*, in which they discussed the idea that hysteria is caused by the repression of a memory of a traumatic event.[15] By maintaining that the key to curing the hysterical symptom was to give these blocked, repressed memories and the feelings attached to them free expression, Freud and Breuer freed the concept of "hysteria" from the ancient concept of the wandering uterus and from the medieval concept of possession by devils. In addition, the Freudian view that hysteria resulted from sexual repression was a reversal of medieval and Puritanical attitudes about sexual restraint.

Soon Freud realized that hypnosis was gravely limited because the unconscious material remembered under hypnosis was quickly forgotten again; it had not been integrated into the person's conscious mind. Therefore any improvements were transient. To replace hypnosis, Freud developed the technique of "free association" by which the unconscious material becomes conscious. It can then be "worked through"; the patient's ego integrates the previously repressed material.

Freud's emphasis on unconscious processes in the etiology of hysteria isolated it as a specific clinical entity. Previously hysteria had encompassed a vast variety of physical symptoms and also personality characteristics resembling the modern concept of "hysterical personality" and the popular epithet "hysterical woman"[16] Freud devised a very specific definition of hysteria, focusing on its intrapsychic causes. He described two types of hysterical neurosis: conversion hysteria and anxiety hysteria. Conversion hysteria is similar to what the Greeks and Egyptians identified as hysteria. In this type of hysteria a psychical conflict is expressed symbolically in varied somatic symptoms, such as hysterical paralyses, lumps in the throat, and anesthesias.

Anxiety hysteria is quite different from the syndrome known to the ancients as hysteria. It results, according to Freud, from the ego's defending itself against some incompatible idea by attaching anxiety to an external object. As long as the person avoids the phobic object, he or she avoids the anxiety attached to the idea that the object symbolically represents.

The similarity between anxiety hysteria and conversion hysteria is that in both cases repression separates painful affects from ideas. In anxiety hysteria the anxiety is controlled by focusing it on an external object; in conversion hysteria the affect is separated from the idea by being converted into a somatic symbolization. According to Freud, both forms of hysteria are neurotic for two reasons. First, the dominant mechanism of defense against the idea or feeling that causes anxiety is repression rather than some more primitive mechanism. Second, the ideas or feelings that are repressed are related to the oedipal conflict, not to preoedipal conflicts.

Although Freud considered conversion symptoms and phobias as symptomatic of hysterical neuroses, psychoanalysts no longer base diagnosis solely on symptoms.[17] They now believe that in order to diagnose a patient accurately, it is also necessary to ascertain the patient's level of object relations, ego functioning, and anxiety. In other words, symptoms and level of psychic organization are independent. For example, Rangell[18] has pointed out that conversion symptoms can occur on a continuum from the most primitive to the most highly developed levels of psychic organization. Patients with conversion symptoms therefore may be neurotic, borderline, or psychotic. Conversion symptoms do not necessarily mean, as Freud believed, that the patient is hysterical (i.e., neurotic).

Similarly, Greenson[19] argues that although Freud believed that phobias are attempts to defend against castration anxiety produced by oedipal conflict, phobias can actually be defenses against any type of anxiety. According to Greenson, on the phallic level, as Freud had also realized, castration anxiety dominates; however, on the anal level, fear of loss of control dominates and, in the oral phase, fear of being devoured dominates. Consequently, the presence of a phobia does not necessarily mean that the person has reached the oedipal level and is hysterical. Kernberg[20] agrees, pointing out that borderline personalities often present multiple phobias. Thus current psychoanalytic theory holds that the presence of phobias does not mean, as Freud believed, that the person is necessarily neurotic (i.e., has anxiety hysteria).[21]

In contrast to Freud's focus on the oedipal period, current psychoanalytic literature increasingly emphasizes preoedipal conflicts. If therapists view conflicts in the patient as predominantly preoedipal, their diagnoses are more likely to be "borderline" than "neurotic" (unless the patient is psychotic). However, if the conflicts are viewed as predominantly oedipal, the patient would most likely be diagnosed "neurotic." In fact, the expanding interest in the preoedipal period may be the reason that many therapists today claim they are getting more and more borderline patients and fewer and fewer neurotics (i.e., hysterics). But it is difficult to know whether this claim is a function of a "sicker" society, a broader range of patients because of the community mental health movement and the prolifera-

tion of low-cost clinics, or an increased theoretical emphasis on preoedipal conflicts. In addition, although changes in diagnostic classifications are important for understanding the seeming decline in hysteria, it is also essential to analyze the objective changes in sex roles that might have contributed to changes in the symptomatology of women.

Many feminist writers have criticized Freud for not realizing that what he called "symptoms" were actually the reaction of Victorian women to their oppressive life circumstances.[22–24] They argue that Freud generalized his description of Victorian women to all women and, therefore, one cannot validly apply his theories to women today because women's position has changed so drastically. These writers claim that hysterical symptoms reflected not only sexual repression but also enabled women to express anger in a socially acceptable manner.[22] Historian Smith-Rosenberg,[13] in her discussion of hysteria in nineteenth-century America, also claims that female hysteria was the expression of rage and that the hysteric was playing a social role resulting from the structured regression that was reinforced in women. It was feminine to faint, just as it was feminine to nibble at your food. Hysterical symptoms, she argues, were really a caricature of the stereotypical female personality and were developed unconsciously by women to express dissatisfaction with their lives. From this point of view, the decline of hysteria as a "classic disease" is not simply due to changes in diagnostic classifications; it is the result of an objective change in the position of women. Hollender[25] argues that hysterical symptoms tend to erupt when a person who is relatively powerless and dependent cannot cope with someone who is powerful and unassailable. Thus he claims it is not at all surprising, considering the inferior position of women, that they were more prone than men to react with hysterical behavior. On the other hand, Gove and Tudor[26] claim that women today are frustrated by low prestige and boredom, are anxious because of the ambiguous expectations confronting them, and suffer from feelings of meaninglessness because of the decline of the importance of the family. This indicates that sex roles may have changed but not necessarily *improved* since the nineteenth century (as reflected by a change from hysterical symptoms to depression).

Hysteria was a way of dealing with sexual and aggressive feelings that were not allowed direct expression. However, as the position of women has changed, so have the child-rearing methods and the view of what it means to be a woman. Zola[27] points out that in the United States nausea is a common and widespread symptom of early pregnancy, yet Margaret Mead reports that there is no morning sickness among Arapesh women. Nor do Arapesh women report any pain during menstruation as American women do. Therefore it seems that whatever the prevailing notion of what it means to be a woman will determine what women expect to feel; and what they expect to feel will be *experienced* because it will be *recognized*. Since the concept of hysteria comes from the Greek word for uterus, hysterical seizures were seemingly regarded as part of what it meant to be a woman. Of course, not every woman had these seizures, but they were common enough so that there were many role models for young girls. Since current research shows that lower-class women are more likely to come to the attention of psychiatric personnel because of somatic complaints than because of directly psychological ones, and since lower-class women may be expected to have less psychological sophistication, it makes sense that a lack of sophistication about psychological matters is related to a higher incidence in somatic complaints. In the pre-Freudian era no one was "sophisticated" about psychological matters; it is therefore logical that there was a greater amount of somatization. Perhaps since more women are college educated and since sexual mores are more liberal for women as compared to the nineteenth century, there is an increased tendency toward intellectualization and other modes of defense and a declining tendency toward repression as a dominant mechanism of defense. In other words, as the population becomes more sophisticated, "vocabularies of discomfort" change.[4]...

REFERENCES

1. n.a. Eclipse of Hysteria. *British Medical Journal,* Vol. J, 1965, pp. 1387–1390.
2. U.S. Dept. of Health, Education and Welfare 1973 Statistical Note 81: Differential Utilization of Psychiatric Facilities by Men and Women, United States, 1970. Rockville, Md.: National Institute of Mental Health.
3. Szasz, T. *The Myth of Mental Illness.* New York: Harper & Row, 1974, p. 71.
4. Bart, P. Social Structure and Vocabularies of Discomfort: What Happened to Female Hysteria. *Journal of Health and Social Behavior,* Vol. 9, 1968, pp. 188–193.
5. Gardner, E. Emotional Disorders in Medical Practice. *Annuals of Internal Medicine,* Vol. 73, 1970, pp. 651–653.
6. Slater, E. Diagnosis of "Hysteria." *British Medical Journal,* Vol. I, 1965, pp. 1395–2451.
7. Veith, I. *Hysteria: The History of a Disease.* Chicago, Ill.: University of Chicago Press, 1965, pp. 37–43, 211, 201.
8. Alexander, F., and S. Selesnick. *The History of Psychiatry.* New York: Harper & Row, 1966, p. 21.
9. Bullough, V. Medieval Medical and Scientific Views of Women. *Viator,* Vol. 4, 1973, pp. 485–501.
10. May, G. *Social Control of Sex Expression.* New York: William Morrow, 1930, pp. 35–56.
11. Kors, A. C. and E. Peters (Eds.). *Witchcraft in Europe, 1100–1700.* Philadelphia: University of Pennsylvania Press, 1972.
12. Russell, J. *Witchcraft in the Middle Ages.* Ithaca, N.Y.: Cornell University Press, 1972, p. 136.
13. Smith-Rosenberg, C. The Hysterical Woman: Sex Roles in 19th Century America. *Social Research,* Vol. 39, 1972, pp. 652–678.

14. Veith, I. Hysteria. *Modern Medicine.* Vol. 28, 1960, pp. 178–183.

15. Breuer, J., and S. Freud. *Studies in Hysteria.* New York: Basic Books, 1957.

16. Chodoff, P. and H. Lyons. Hysteria. The Hysterical Personality and "Hysterical Conversion." *American Journal of Psychiatry,* Vol. 114, 1958.

17. Zetzel, E. The So-Called Good Hysteric. *International Journal of Psycho-Analysis,* Vol. 49, 1968, pp. 256–260.

18. Rangell, L. The Nature of Conversion. *Journal of the American Psychoanalytic Association,* Vol. 7, 1959, pp. 632–661.

19. Greenson, R. Phobia, Anxiety and Depression. *Journal of the American Psychoanalytic Association,* Vol. 7, 1959, pp. 663–673.

20. Kernberg, O. *Borderline Conditions and Pathological Narcissism.* New York: Jason Aronson, 1975.

21. Wangh, M. Psychoanalytical Thought on Phobia: Its Evolution and its Relevance for Therapy. *American Journal of Psychiatry,* Vol. 123, 1967, pp. 1075–1081.

22. Chesler, P. *Women and Madness.* New York: Avon, 1972, p. 108.

23. Firestone, S. *The Dialectic of Sex: The Case for Feminist Revolution.* New York: William Morrow, 1970.

24. Friedan, B. *The Feminine Mystique.* Baltimore: Penguin Books, 1963.

25. Hollender, M. Conversion Hysteria: A Post-Freudian Reinterpretation of 19th Century Psychosocial Data. *Archives of General Psychiatry,* Vol. 26, 1972, pp. 311–314.

26. Gove, W. R., and J. F. Tudor. Adult Sex Roles and Mental Illness. *American Journal of Sociology,* Vol. 78, 1973, pp. 812–835.

27. Zola, I. K. Culture and Symptoms—An Analysis of Patients' Presenting Complaints. *American Sociological Review,* Vol. 31, 1966, pp. 615–630.

PART EIGHT

Gender and Reproductive Technology

Much of the sociological analysis of technology has been focused on production, paid labor, and the public sphere—that is, for the most part, men's relationship to technology. As a result, reproductive technology, a vital aspect of women's relationship to technology has been ignored (McNeil 1990). Yet, there were great advances in reproductive technology, particularly birth control in the nineteenth century. For example, in 1837 Charles Goodyear succeeded in vulcanizing rubber by combining raw latex with sulfur at high temperature and by the 1850s the first inexpensive condoms and diaphragms were produced. By 1865, the middle class knew about the withdrawal method, spermicidal douches, the vaginal diaphragm, rubber condoms, and the rhythm method. After the passage of the Comstock Act in 1873, birth control information could not be sent through the mail, but knowledge of these methods was already widespread (Reed 1978).

From that time until the development of the birth control pill in 1960, there was not very much progress in the field of reproductive technology. However, there have been great advances in technologies related to reproduction since then. The new technologies are widely varied—genetic screening, amniocentesis, sonograms, fetal monitors, birth control implants, ICSI (intracytoplasmic sperm injection), morning after pills, *in vitro* fertilization (IVF), surrogacy, ovary-stimulating hormones, and many more.

The first successful *in vitro* fertilization was done in England in 1978. *In vitro* fertilization means fertilization in a glass Petri dish. A woman is given large doses of various hormones in order to increase the number of eggs ovulated. The eggs are then removed from the woman and fertilized in a Petri dish. The fertilized eggs are then implanted in the woman's uterus (Steinberg 1990). More recently, reproductive scientists have perfected the use of donor eggs; the first baby conceived with donated eggs was born in 1984. In 1989 there were less than 100 live births from donated eggs and in 1995 there were 1,200 (Stolberg 1998).

Demand for egg donation exploded around 1990 amid news reports that it had become available for postmenopausal women. Until then the technology was only offered to women thirty-five and younger. However, in the early 1990s it was also offered to women in their late thirties or early forties. Egg donation was a ground-breaking advancement because a forty-four-year old woman attempting IVF with her own eggs at Pacific Fertility Clinic (one of the largest) has a 3.5 percent chance of giving birth. If that same woman uses the donor eggs of a younger woman, her chances of giving birth are 50 percent (Belken 1997).

Most recently, women are carrying embryos that bear no relation to them or their partners. Clinics are selling embryos; they can be bought ready-made or custom-made. If you buy them ready-made, they cost about $2,750, while custom-made embryos, with sperm and egg from donors the couple has selected costs about $16,000 (Kolata 1997).

These new forms of reproductive technology are generally viewed as progressive—increasing procreative freedom and offering women more choices. However, national health policies related to reproductive technologies reflect societal values about social inequality. Policies vary enormously in the extent to which they perpetuate or seek to reduce inequities that vary by social class, race, and ethnicity. For example, in countries with socialized health care systems designed to reduce social inequality, access to and equity in birth-related services is the norm. In the United States, on the other hand, where many Americans are uninsured or the insurance does not cover many reproductive technologies, many critics argue that social policies in the reproductive technology area have increased social inequality (Ruzek 1991).

Marxist feminist critics argue that the emphasis on individual rights is a liberal, individualistic approach to issues of reproduction. It ignores the question of how race and class influence the possibility of choice. The language of individual choice makes it easier to regard reproductive rights and technology as consumer goods (McNeil 1990).

The language of consumerism and individual rights implies that individuals who can afford the cost of the product have a "right" to it and those who cannot afford it do not have the same right. In the case of the new reproductive technologies, then, many feminists have supported the "right" of white, upper-middle-class and upper-class women to have children, while ignoring minorities and those who cannot afford them.

One of the most striking features of the new reproductive technologies is that when they have been directed toward whites they are used to increase procreation, but when they are directed toward blacks they have been used to restrict procreation. Procedures such as IVF are used almost entirely by upper-middle-class white couples because few black couples can afford it. The median cost of one IVF cycle is about $8,000 and patients usually try it several times before either succeeding or giving up. Using donor eggs makes the procedure even more costly—$10,000 to $20,000 for each attempt. Most medical insurance plans, including Medicaid, do not cover the full cost of infertility services. Even liberal Senator Ted Kennedy voted to rescind government aid for fertility drugs (Roberts 1997).

High-tech approaches to infertility are not only expensive, but require a privileged lifestyle that permits devotion to the rigorous process of daily hormone shots, ultrasound examinations, blood tests, egg extraction and implantation, and travel to and from a fertility clinic (Roberts 1997). Women who work for hourly wages or don't have flexibility in their work schedules find it impossible to go through the process and maintain their employment.

However, the issue is not simply that the cost and time commitment is prohibitive for many minority couples. There is a different attitude toward increasing white and minority procreation. For example, Linden and Jacqueline Thompson were the first black family in the United States to have sextuplets on May 8, 1997. Yet, hardly anyone noticed—there was no media coverage. But, when the McCaugheys, a white couple, had septuplets six months later on November 19, it was considered a national event and they were on every television news program. Their children received college scholarships, a van, a lifetime supply of free diapers from Procter and Gamble, car seats, strollers, groceries, and an invitation to the White House (Seelye 1998).

The muted public response to the Thompsons seems to be a racial matter since black multiple births are much less common than white ones. The major reason for this is that most multiple births are the result of new reproductive technologies which are less likely to be used by blacks despite the fact that blacks have an infertility rate one and one-half times higher than whites. The latest national survey found only 12.8 percent of black women as compared to 27.2 percent of white women used specialized infertility services such as fertility drugs, artificial insemination, tubal surgery, or IVF (Roberts 1997).

An example of the technology that *is* made available to blacks is the sickle-cell anemia screening test (Roberts 1997). Around 1970, proposals for sickle-cell screening programs gained support in both the medical establishment and the black community. But what began as a strategy to improve the health of blacks soon turned into an instrument of medical abuse. Fourteen states made the tests mandatory for blacks enrolling in school or applying for a marriage license. Screening programs often offered no counseling, so many people who had the sickle cell trait believed, mistakenly, they had the disease. Carriers who did receive counseling were often counseled not to have children or to be sterilized regardless of whether their mate was a carrier (Roberts 1997).

Roberts (1997) is not only concerned about women not having the same access to reproductive technology that increases procreation, she is also concerned about sterilization abuse. Sterilization abuse became a focus of the reproductive rights movement in the early 1970s as the result of publicity about several horrifying cases: two young black girls sterilized without their knowledge in Alabama; the patterned sterilization abuse of Native American women by the U.S. Indian Health Service; the series of abuses in Los Angeles of Mexican American women; and the extensive abuse of women in Puerto Rico (Clarke 1989). These well-publicized cases were blatant abuses, but subtle abuse is much more common. For example, unnecessary hysterectomies are often performed by professionals who feel they should be the ultimate arbiters of poor women's fertility. Historically, hysterectomies and sterilization have been a common medical practice for institutionalized mentally retarded girls and women. Even when the girls and women are not mentally retarded, several studies have documented situations in which the women were told that their tubes would be tied and they mistakenly thought that their tubes could be untied; in one study, 40 percent of the women who had been sterilized believed they could become pregnant again (Clarke 1989).

Most feminists have not focused their critique of the medical-scientific establishment on the restrictions to procreation, but rather on technological procedures that interfere with the life choices of women in order to protect the "rights" of the fetus (Strickler 1992; Ruzek 1991; Steinberg 1990; Crowe 1990). Ruzek (1991), for example, is concerned that advances in neonatal care and prenatal diagnosis have created a new focus on the legal rights of the unborn—pitting birthing women against their babies. The "individual rights" model has led to a "competing individual rights" model in which the concept of the "fetus as patient," results in doctors, hospitals, and lawyers demanding that the rights of the woman should be secondary to the rights of the fetus. This has resulted in women being subjected to physical regulation, forced surgery, detention, and to criminal and civil punishment for behavior deemed dangerous to the fetus (Ruzek 1991). Taking drugs or drinking alcohol while pregnant is being redefined as "child abuse."

However, technological innovations that allow premature babies to survive earlier and earlier, sometimes against the will of the parents because they may have severe physical and mental damage, are very costly to society. Ruzek (1991) argues that it would be more equitable to provide basic care to pregnant women who do not have access to basic health services rather than trying to improve birth outcomes with expensive machines and procedures.

In this section of the reader, Strickler (1992) deals with reproductive technology as a social issue like temperance, abortion, or the Equal Rights Amendment; different groups have different positions on the issue depending on how they understand their own interests. She examines the position of three interest groups: physicians, infertile consumers, and feminists. She contrasts the way each group defines the problem, views technological solutions, and weighs psychological and social factors.

As Strickler points out, many feminists consider the new reproductive technologies harmful and threatening to women's reproductive rights as a group even though it may increase some individual women's choices. For example, Crowe (1990) believes that the ideology surrounding IVF reinforces the notion that women are supposed to have children and that it should occur in a heterosexual, nuclear family context.

In the second article in this section, Woliver (1995) discusses some other negative aspects of the new reproductive technologies for women from a feminist perspective. She focuses on the exploitation of lower-class and lower-middle-class women for surrogacy, the undermining impact of neonatal technology on abortion rights, and the dehumanization of women involved in the technological procedures.

We can see that sociological discussions of the new reproductive technologies fall into two main groups. The first group focuses on doctors' control of women's access to these technologies as well as how class, race, and sexual orientation play a large part in determining which women get access to them and to which ones they get access. On the other hand, there is a growing literature that emphasizes the negative impact these technologies have had on the reproductive rights of women as a group.

REFERENCES

Belken, Lisa. 1997. "How Old Is Too Old?" *New York Times Magazine,* October 26, pp. 36-39, 48, 49.

Clarke, Adele. 1989. "Subtle Forms of Sterilization Abuse: A Reproductive Rights Analysis." Pp. 188–205 in *Test-Tube Women: What Future for Motherhood.* London: Pandora Press.

Crowe, Christine. 1990. "Whose Mind over Matter? Women, *In Vitro* Fertilization and the Development of Scientific Knowledge." Pp. 27–57 in *The New Reproductive Technologies,* edited by Maureen McNeil, Ian Varcoe, and Steven Yearly. New York: St. Martin's Press.

Kolata, Gina. 1997. "Clinics Selling Embryos Made for 'Adoption'." *New York Times,* November 25:1, 34.

McNeil, Maureen. 1990. "Reproductive Technologies: A New Terrain for the Sociology of Technology." pp. 1–25 in *The New Reproductive Technologies,* edited by Maureen McNeil, Ian Varcoe, and Steven Yearly. New York: St. Martin's Press.

Reed, James. 1978. *The Birth Control Movement and American Society.* Princeton: Princeton University Press.

Roberts, Dorothy. 1997. *Killing the Black Body: Race, Reproduction, and the Meaning of Liberty.* New York: Pantheon.

Rothman, Barbara Katz. 1989. "The Meanings of Choice in Reproductive Technology." Pp. 23–33 in *Test-Tube Women: What Future for Motherhood.* London: Pandora Press.

Ruzek, Sheryl. 1991. "Women's Reproductive Rights: The Impact of Technology." Pp. 65–86 in *Women and New Reproductive Technologies: Medical, Psychosocial, Legal and Ethical Dilemmas,* edited by Judith Rodin and Aila Collins. Hillsdale: Lawrence Erlbaum Associates.

Seelye, Katharine Q. 1998. "First Black Sextuplet Belatedly Win Public Notice." *New York Times,* January 8: A12.

Steinberg, Deborah Lynn. 1990. "The Depersonalisation of Women through the Administration of *In Vitro* Fertilisation." Pp. 1–25 in *The New Reproductive Technologies* edited by Maureen McNeil, Ian Varcoe, and Steven Yearly. New York: St. Martin's Press.

Stolberg, Sheryl Gay. 1998. "Quandary on Donor Eggs: What to Tell the Children." *New York Times,* January 18: A1, A20.

Strickler, Jennifer. 1992. "The New Reproductive Technology: Problem or Solution?" *Sociology of Health & Illness* 14:111–132.

Woliver, Laura R. 1995. "Reproductive Technologies, Surrogacy Arrangements, and the Politics of Motherhood." Pp. 346–359 in *Mothers in Law: Feminist Theory and the Legal Regulation of Motherhood,* edited by Martha Albertson Fineman and Isabel Karpin. New York: Columbia University Press.

The New Reproductive Technology:
Problem or Solution?

JENNIFER STRICKLER

INTRODUCTION

Infertility, a condition which is estimated to affect 15 per cent of American couples[1], is generally acknowledged to be a 'major life crisis'. Emotionally devastated, many infertile couples pursue fertility drugs, surgery and new technologies in their desperate attempts to have children. Physicians have intensified research in this area and have recently developed several new options for the treatment of infertility. In vitro fertilisation (IVF) and other high technology methods, where conception takes place in a laboratory, have become a recent focus of medical research and practice and are now routinely recommended to infertile couples.

Expansions of the medical profession into new areas of women's health have been treated with suspicion by feminist scholars in recent years (Ruzek 1979, Gordon 1977, Ehrenreich and English 1978), and many feminists have been alarmed by the new reproductive technologies. To Gena Corea, member of the Feminist International Network Resisting Reproductive and Genetic Engineering (FINRRAGE), 'the issue is not fertility. The issue is the exploitation of women' (1985:7). Many feminist sociologists, biologists and philosophers consider IVF, embryo freezing,

egg donation and other new developments in infertility treatment harmful and threatening to women's right to control their reproduction. In fact, the degree of consensus among feminists on the issue of reproductive technologies is rarely found on other topics. Internal dissent on the underlying theoretical issue of the centrality of motherhood in women's lives has not created conflict over the acceptability of IVF, but instead has led to disagreement over the principal reasons for criticising these technologies.

The literature on the social construction of social problems (McCrea 1984, Emerson and Messinger 1977, Spector and Kitsuse 1977) helps to put the contradictory discourse on the new reproductive technologies into sociological perspective. Clearly, the way the infertility problem has been defined has shaped the alternative solutions which are considered, and groups have organised and advocated for their particular position on the problem. Previous research has traced the natural history of other social problems, and this paper does not describe the claims-making that IVF proponents and opponents have engaged in to lobby for their desired end.

However, an interesting issue which has not been adequately addressed in the social problems literature is what are the roots of the different constructions of the problem. An analysis of the rhetoric used by those concerned about missing children argues that values are tools of the claims maker, rather than the underlying motivation for a particular position (Best 1987). Similarly, Hilgartner and Bosk (1987) discount the role of 'compassion', suggesting that the level of one's concern about a given social problem is first and foremost determined by one's 'master status' and consequent personal stake in the issue.

This essay suggests that one's position on reproductive technology is imbedded in vested interests, and mediated by an associated intersubjective meaning of reproduction. By 'interest', I mean the extent to which one has 'something to gain or lose over and above the way everyone else in society might be affected' (Spector and Kitsuse 1977:87). Thus, interests can be concrete (for example, making money or obtaining a baby) or more abstract (enhancing one's professional prestige or the status of motherhood). In this context, 'meaning of reproduction' refers to the way in which procreation helps a person make sense of his/her life (Wuthnow 1987:35). Interests and values are not competing (or even separate) influences in one's understanding of reproductive technologies, but mutually reinforcing factors which determine how the problem of infertility will be defined, and consequently, how the solution will be constructed[2].

Analyses of other social issues such as temperance (Gusfield 1963), abortion (Luker 1984), and the Equal Rights Amendment (Ehrenreich 1983, Mansbridge 1986) conclude that debates which appear to deal with a single moral problem can represent more general social issues. Just as the struggle for temperance laws in the 1920s symbolised political power to reformers (Gusfield 1963), and abortion activism (both pro and con) reflected the centrality of motherhood for women's sense of fulfilment (Luker 1984), disagreement about the consequences of reproductive tech-

nology may also symbolise a broader struggle over the meaning of reproduction.

For obstetricians, reproduction is an area of professional specialisation, defined in terms of pregnancy and childbirth. Reproductive technology offers these physicians a means of entry into the high-pay, cutting-edge circle of high-technology medicine, therefore enhancing their professional prestige. To patients, reproduction means the ability to procreate—to create a new life in their bodies; they focus exclusively on the biological aspects of the reproductive process. Feminists see reproduction as a potential source of women's power, since it is a uniquely female ability, and also as the historical justification for the limitation of women's power. Thus, each group's attitude toward the issue of procreative technology is imbedded in a world view which gives reproduction a distinct meaning, and in each case, the meaning attributed to the reproductive process is central to the group members' self-definition.

This paper examines the literature of three groups involved in the debate: physicians who specialise in reproductive technologies, their infertile patients, and the feminists who are alarmed by the increase in physicians' control over reproduction. The first three sections describe how these groups define the problem of infertility, the potential for a technological solution and the psychological and social effects of infertility, in order to clarify basic differences in how the issue is framed. The last section discusses the meaning of reproduction implicit in the interpretation of reproductive technology and the underlying interest that each group has in its own particular construction of the issue.

1: PHYSICIANS

Reproduction has become increasingly defined as a medical process. While contraception, childbirth and other aspects of women's reproductive health were once the domain of the midwife and/or female relatives, they have come within the realm of professional medicine (Ehrenreich and English 1978). Pregnancy, menopause and premenstrual syndrome are treated as diseases, which lend themselves to medical cures. Infertility is a relatively new area of interest to physicians, emerging as a certifiable subspecialty of the American College of Obstetrics and Gynaecology in 1974 (Office of Technology Assessment 1988). The following discussion of the medical perspective on infertility and reproductive technologies draws on medical textbooks, journal articles and laypersons' guides to infertility services.

Definition of the Problem

The medical literature frames the problem of infertility in a narrow and clinical manner. The causes of infertility are defined as the proximate causes: pelvic scarring, endometriosis, low sperm count and the like. To the extent that the epidemiology is discussed, infertility is attributed to the postponement of childbearing until the thirties and to sexually transmitted diseases, which cause pelvic scarring (Khatamee 1988). From a historical perspective it is interesting that until the 1970s, infertility was most often seen as a psychosomatic problem, not amenable to medical intervention (Sandelowski 1990). The change in approach could be attributed to technological advances which have made medical treatment possible, or to demographic pressures which have forced obstetricians to seek out new markets for their service (Scritchfield 1989).

The response to infertility is medical intervention with the goal of pregnancy. With the exception of references to psychological disturbance and stress (Keye 1984), medical literature rarely discusses the nonbiological context of infertility: the impact on a marriage, family relationships, career, or other aspects of everyday life. The goal of infertility specialists is to enable couples to have their own biological children.

Technological Solutions

Physicians' response to infertility has become increasingly technological. Psychological factors are considered of minimal importance, and surgical intervention is emphasised. Surgery has not only become more common, but the nature of the surgery has changed. While earlier treatment for infertility involved trying to cure the immediate cause of the problem (for example, removing adhesions), more recent medical advances have focused on the use of IVF. This procedure entails removing one or more eggs from a woman's ovary, fertilising them in a test-tube and inserting the embryo(s) into the woman's uterus.

Physicians, not surprisingly, welcome technological advances which permit new forms of medical intervention. Dr. John Stangel writes in his layperson's guide to infertility treatments:

> The results of current research will mean conception for those couples who are untreatable today ... The question is only 'how soon?'. The only thing more exciting than imagining what the future will bring is working in an area of medical research that will actually produce those advances, and being able to tell a couple once thought to be untreatable, 'Congratulations, the pregnancy test is positive. You're pregnant!' (1988:210–11).

Many physicians expect IVF to become the treatment of choice for various causes of infertility (Laufer and Navot 1986, Edwards 1984). According to one article:

> Currently, the indications for IVF-ET include not only tubal disease, but also male factor infertility as well as idiopathic or unexplained infertility. Although IVF has not replaced conventional forms of therapy for infertility, ... it is expected that in the future, as pregnancy success increases, IVF-ET will replace many of the conventional surgical therapies ... (Marrs and Vargyas 1986:565).

The potential for improving pregnancy rates in infertile couples is welcomed; clinicians find failures frustrating and disappointing (Greenfield and Hazeltine 1986, Lasker and Borg 1987). In fact, physicians seem to encourage couples to pursue whatever treatment is available, to the extent of repeating procedures which have been tried without success. Rarely are the costs (financial, emotional or physical) of treatment considered or discussed in the medical literature.

Psychological and Social Factors

The inability to have a child is seen as profoundly disturbing; in interviews, several physicians refer to the fact that the infertile are 'desperate', 'driven' and suffering from depression and grief. It is also recognised that the infertility workup itself, consisting of scheduled sexual intercourse, surgery, physician visits and monthly cycles of hope and despair, is quite stressful. Physicians tend to interpret this stress as evidence of the couple's desperation, and consequently search for new and alternative therapies for treating infertility (Lasker and Borg 1987).

Some physicians recognise the impact of infertility on their patients' psychological well-being, and there is now an awareness of the importance of psychological counselling for infertility patients (Greenfield and Hazeltine 1986, Keye 1984, Mazor 1984). As one infertility specialist describes, the patients' desire for children, combined with the physicians' desire for success can lead to prolonged emotional suffering for the couple:

> When pregnancy is not achieved despite long and thorough investigation and intensive treatment, a frustrating situation for both gynecologist and patient is again created ... Women are operated on over and over again, and couples travel from one doctor to the other unnecessarily prolonging their own torment. Although I know how difficult it is to resist such pressures, it should also be said that it is the doctor who, unwilling to accept his or her failure to perform, keeps the couple on a string (Van Hall 1983:364).

2: CONSUMERS

The infertile consumers of these procedures play a part in defining the infertility problem.

The most vocal voice of the infertile is RESOLVE, a referral and support organisation founded in 1973 by Barbara Eck Menning, an infertile woman. There are also several recent books on the experience of infertility and its medical treatment (Pfeffer and Woollett 1983, Glazer and Cooper 1988, Frank and Vogel 1988, Lasker and Borg 1987). I draw on the words of the infertile patients as a group with a strong interest in mobilising empathy, understanding and resources toward meeting the medical and psychological needs of the infertile.

It should be noted, however, that this discussion pertains specifically to *consumers*, that is, couples who pursue medical treatment. I expect that the experience of people who are infertile but do not undergo medical or surgical treatment (whether because of cost or inclination) is very different.[3]

Definition of the Problem

For patients, the problem is not 'blocked tubes' or 'endometriosis', but the inability to have children 'of their own'. The perspective of the infertile is individualistic—their overwhelming concern is their own childlessness, which can become an obsession. For these people, infertility carries with it a feeling of loss of control over their bodies and their lives. The intensity of their emotions speaks to the *centrality* of biological parenthood for IVF patients. Raising a child is not enough; they endure financial, emotional and physical hardship for the possibility of having a child which carries their genes.

Most literature by and about the infertile presents the feelings and opinions of women, leaving one to infer that women are the primary agents in defining the problem of infertility and its solutions. However, this inference ignores the dynamics of gender and power within marital relationships. Anecdotal evidence suggests that men are less willing to consider adoption than women, and it may be the foreclosure of this option that leads women to focus exclusively on biological parenthood. While this paper treats the couple as a unit making joint decisions, there is certainly a strong theoretical and empirical foundation for questioning this assumption of consensus (see, for example, Hartmann 1981, Lorber 1989).

Technological Solutions

Infertile couples who pursue treatment seem to have a love-hate relationship with reproductive technology. These technologies offer their only hope of becoming pregnant, but at the same time lead to more tests, expenses, operations and prolonged uncertainty. In a conference on reproductive technology in 1979, Menning stated:

> The couples who are infertile owing to hopeless tubal damage run a 100 per cent risk of remaining childless if they are not allowed access to in vitro fertilization as a technology...Let those of us who are infertile decide whether we are willing to subject ourselves to the instrumentation and intervention necessary...(1981:264).

Previous to IVF, most couples attempted drug and surgical therapies in order to induce ovulation, repair fallopian tubes or treat endometriosis. These therapies can be unpleasant or dangerous, but again they offer hope:

> The next step was a big one—Pergonal. I had heard of the rigors and the side effects of this treatment—as well as the multiple births—and was frightened to try it. But we were at the end of the line, so there wasn't much choice (Horlitz 1988:15).

According to two surveys of IVF patients (Bonnicksen 1986; Mao and Wood 1984), most women are satisfied with their experience, even if they did not conceive. There is a recurring theme of control; patients seem to feel that they are exerting as much control as possible over their lives by pursuing all options rather than passively accepting their fate of infertility:

> Those who became pregnant were relieved that their struggle to conceive was over. Those who did

not conceive still tried to find benefits from their experience. These included the satisfaction of having left no stone unturned..., added knowledge about their own infertility that came from trying IVF..., and information that helped them close one stage of life and move to another (Bonnicksen 1986:203).

However, not all patients consider their treatment a positive experience. Alexis Brown, who suffers from endometriosis, writes:

> To further maximize my chances to conceive, I took a six-month course of Danocrine, a male hormone that suppresses the monthly cycle...The problem is that there are side effects: weight gain, mood changes, headaches. Worse yet, it meant six months with no chance of conception. Had the surgeries and the Danocrine led to a pregnancy, I surely would look back and say that it was all worth it. But they did not. I am thirty and childless, trying to hold on to hope, as it grows dim (1988:14).

Infertility requires continual decision-making about whether to continue treatment, try a new drug or procedure, or accept one's infertility and go on with other things in life. The development of new technologies offers at once both new hope and more difficult decisions. One woman quoted in Lasker and Borg (1987:28) expresses her frustration:

> It wouldn't be so difficult if I had an answer. I could cope, I could come to terms with myself. Now I can't decide whether I should go another two months for the inseminations or another six months...If I knew, I think I could resign myself to the fact that that's the way things are and look for another option, maybe adoption or childfree living.

Psychological and Social Factors

The common thread of the literature on infertility patients is that it is a devastating experience, and interferes with almost all aspects of a couple's life: relations with family and friends, their sexual relationship, careers and other major decisions.

Many infertile people find it difficult to be around pregnant women and small children, and thus avoid friends and relatives. In the words of one infertile woman, 'I felt the fertile world was callous, cruel, stupid...I had no interest in seeing a pregnant woman, friend or no friend. I didn't want to have someone else's success flaunted in my face' (Liebmann-Smith 1987:72–3).

Infertility often produces a sense of isolation, resentment and anger which can lead to a vicious circle of cutting oneself off from social support networks:

> Infertile couples experience a difficult dilemma, particularly around holiday time or important family events...The infertile couple is caught in an emotional bind. They already feel isolated from most of the world. They want to be with their families, yet their pain is even greater when they are among pregnant siblings or with very young nieces and nephews (Glazer and Cooper 1988:53).

Couples often put off other decisions while they are involved in an infertility investigation, which can take several years. Women undergoing treatment often turn down promotions or postpone job-hunting, since they 'could be pregnant at any minute' (Santiesteban 1988). They also postpone decisions about buying a house, returning to school or pursuing other options such as surrogate motherhood or adoption. The lives of many infertile people revolve around basal thermometers, semen analyses, hormone injections and 'monthly cycles of anxiety, uncertainty and despair' (Glazer and Cooper 1988:146).

One woman describes the emotional toll that infertility has taken on her:

> It's excruciating to go through this month after month, having to put your life on such a clinical, systematic chart. It's terrible having raised expectations and having them dashed. It's always with me. I wake up with it, I go to sleep with it and I think about it literally fifty times a day. I dream about it. It's night and day, day and night, seven days a week ever since this began (Liebmann-Smith 1987:97).

As is apparent from the discussion above, infertile patients find it very difficult to accept their inability to bear children, and it seems very important to most couples that they pursue all available options before accepting their infertility (Bonnicksen 1986, Frank and Vogel 1988, Glazer and Cooper 1988). For these couples, biological parenthood seems to be a crucial factor in their sense of control and fulfilment in their lives.

3: THE FEMINIST RESPONSE

Feminist literature in the last two decades has criticised the increasing medicalisation of reproduction (Ehrenreich and English 1978, Gordon 1977, Petchesky 1980, Ruzek 1979). To many feminist scholars, reproductive technologies are just a new form of medical interference with women's bodies. In this section, I examine the arguments of a variety of books and articles which present the feminist analysis of technology and procreation. In addition, I draw on the proceedings of several conferences which have dealt with the impact of reproductive technologies on the lives of women.

Definition of the Problem

While infertile women see IVF as one of the many medical treatments for infertility, most feminists who write on the topic see a qualitative difference between infertility treatment, which 'needs to be recognized as an issue of self-determination' (Rothman 1989:140), and the new procreative technologies, which threaten women's role in procreation (Corea 1985, Rothman 1989). One of the best-known feminist health books, Our Bodies, Ourselves (Boston Women's Health Book Collective 1984), has one chapter on infertility which encourages treatment, and another, fairly critical, chapter on reproductive technology.

While few feminists come out in support of procreative technology, there is extensive debate among feminist scholars about similar issues such as parental leave, surrogate motherhood and women's participation in the military, where privileging motherhood is posed in opposition to equality with men. In fact, these policy debates can be seen as real-world applications of two threads of feminist theory: the 'essentialist' view which sees women as inherently different from men; and the 'structuralist' view which sees male-female differences as products of social interaction and/or social structure[4].

These two lines of feminist analysis translate into two separate critiques of IVF and similar technologies. First, the investment in and emphasis on new technologies which facilitate biological parenthood reinforce the idea that women need to be mothers in order to feel fulfilled. Since motherhood has historically been an important justification for limiting women's opportunities in society, many feminists are very apprehensive about technological developments which place motherhood at the centre of women's lives.

Second, technological conception transfers reproductive control from women to physicians. While recognising that some women who are unable to conceive may benefit from IVF, the feminist literature asserts that on a societal level this technology harms women as a collective group more than it helps them. From this perspective, feminists who put a high value on motherhood find the technologies threatening, since women lose control over conception, as well as gestation. IVF pregnancies are very closely monitored by physicians, and in fact are more likely to be delivered by Caesarian section (Cohen, Mayaux and Guihard-Moscato 1988). While the individual women who undergo the procedure may appreciate the availability of medical resources, the concern is that such involvement will legitimate increasing medical involvement in 'natural' pregnancies.

Robyn Rowland writes:

For feminists, these new techniques mean rethinking our attitudes toward motherhood, pregnancy, and most important, the relationship between an individual's right to exercise choice with respect to motherhood and the necessity for women to ensure that those individual choices do not disadvantage women as a social group . . . Increased technological

intervention into the processes by which women conceive is increasing the male-dominated medical profession's control of procreation and will lead inevitably to greater social control of women by men (1987: 513, 524).

To feminists, the problem is not a woman's inability to bear children (which is seen as an individual, not social, problem) but the structure and institutions of society which reinforce the necessity of childbearing for women's fulfilment on one hand, and physicians' increasing power in managing procreation on the other.

Technological Solutions

This literature treats medical technology as a development which decreases women's control over reproduction and exploits the vulnerability of the infertile:

Control over one's body is perhaps the central feminist credo. It is what is now feared will be lost through the new reproductive technologies. It was perhaps inevitable in our technological age that conception, the last of the cottage industries, will be taken out of the home and placed in the antiseptic factory of the lab. The fear is that all reproduction will become artificial, given the technical means for it . . . (Baruch 1988:136).

Gena Corea states:

Reproductive technology is a product of the male reality. The values expressed in the technology— objectification, domination—are typical of the male culture. The technology is male-generated and buttresses male power over women (1985:4).

There is expressed concern about the potential routinisation of in vitro fertilisation, following the examples of Caesarean section, ultrasound and foetal monitoring, all of which started out as responses to particular conditions and have become routine procedures (Rothman 1984). A striking example of this pattern is the use of IVF in cases where the male has a fertility impairment (Lorber 1989). The least invasive procedure to solve this problem is artificial insemination, which involves nonsurgical insemination with sperm from a donor. However, it is becoming more common to use IVF (which involves surgery, drugs and a much higher financial cost) in these cases, in spite of the fact that the woman's reproductive system is unimpaired (Cohen *et al* 1988).

A related concern of the feminist literature is the extent of iatrogenic (physician-induced) infertility. Caesarian section, the IUD and DES (an anti-abortifacient prescribed from 1940 to 1970) are all associated with increased risk of infertility (Overall 1987, Poff 1987). Pregnancies from IVF are more likely than naturally conceived pregnancies to result in ectopic pregnancy, a condition which is potentially life-threatening and further damages the reproductive tract (Cohen *et al* 1988). In these situations, physicians themselves are responsible for the very condition which they are treating. In light of the fact that several studies (Collins *et al* 1983, Correy *et al* 1988) estimate the incidence of spontaneous pregnancy among infertility patients at approximately 40 per cent, feminists question the benefit of technological intervention.

The possibility of using reproductive technologies for selection of the sex or other characteristics of a child also concerns many feminists (Overall 1987, Corea 1985, Powledge 1981). IVF could be used for sex preselection through the implantation of embryos of the desired sex. Gena Corea describes this procedure as gynaecidal:

> If many women in the Third World are eliminated through sex predetermination, if fewer firstborn females exist throughout the world, if the percentages of poor women and richer men rise in the overdeveloped nations, then it is indeed gynecide we are discussing (1985:206).

Thus, new procreative technology is attacked on four principal grounds: 1) it takes reproductive control away from women and gives it to (mostly male) physicians; 2) it is

physically and emotionally harmful to women; 3) it reinforces the importance of motherhood in women's lives; and 4) it carries with it the potential for eugenic uses.

Psychological and Social Factors

To structural feminists, the psychic pain of infertility comes from two sources: the inability to fulfil their socially constructed desire to have children, and the stress of going through infertility treatment. They point out that women are trained from childhood to be mothers and have few alternatives for fulfilling lives (Chodorow 1978, Overall 1987). The importance of genetic ties to children is culturally and historically specific (Stanworth 1987, Zelizer 1985), and to assert otherwise 'is a remnant of biological deterministic thinking (akin to "mother-right") that should have no place in feminist thought' (Petchesky 1980)[5].

While recognising that the infertile do suffer emotionally, feminists deny that medical intervention is the appropriate response:

> *The suffering infertility causes women is enormous and deserves to be treated seriously. I do not think that those who respond to the suffering by offering to probe, scan, puncture, suction and cut women in repeated experiments are taking that suffering more seriously than I. They are not asking how much of women's suffering has been socially structured and inflicted and is therefore not inevitable (Corea 1985:6).*

In many cases medical treatment only exacerbates the suffering of infertile women, since treatment is lengthy, painful and generally ineffective. Furthermore, by offering increasingly extreme technologies, physicians make it more difficult to choose non-motherhood, thus reinforcing the status quo (the idea that women need to be mothers to feel fulfilled). As the feminist philosopher Deborah Poff explains:

> *A precondition for choice is a meaningful alternative. This requires that men and women cease to*

believe that childbearing is essential to the defini-
tion and nature of being a woman. It also requires
that women have equal access to education, equal
career or job choices, equal pay for the same jobs
and equal pay for work of equal value (1987:113).

4: THE MEANING OF REPRODUCTION

The above discussion of the perspectives of
physicians, consumers and feminists on reproductive technology clearly illustrates that
each group defines a different problem, although there is some overlap between the
doctors and their patients. In order to understand the roots of this disagreement, it is necessary to look at both the vested interest that
each group has in its definition of the problem
and the intersubjective meaning that procreation holds for members of each group. While
it would be a mistake to assume that each
group is homogeneous (debate among feminist scholars has already been mentioned),
there are common structural and cultural factors, as well as organisations[6], which give
members of a group a common understanding of the role of reproduction in their lives.

The cohesiveness of each group becomes
more apparent if one asks which issues are addressed in the literature and which are brack-
eted from discussion. In fact, physicians rarely
write about guidelines for discontinuing treatment for infertility, their patients do not question the source of their desire to reproduce,
and feminists are reluctant to discuss the issue
of individual self-determination. Thus, the
reason that each group defines a different
problem is that they ask different questions;
each drawing on its own framework of meaning to define issues and concerns.

Physicians

With few exceptions, the medical literature on
reproduction and infertility is limited to a discussion of the biological aspects of reproduction and possible interventions to facilitate
the process. This may seem like an obvious

point, but it is an important one, since physicians have a great deal or influence in shaping
how problems are seen by their patients and
by society (see Conrad and Schneider 1980,
Friedson 1970).

The meaning of reproduction for physicians is commensurate to their level of intervention. If reproduction were a biological
process which required no medical involvement, then it would mean nothing to physicians as a group. Intervention which facilitates
reproduction (prenatal care, medical assistance at childbirth) gives reproduction meaning for physicians, and interventions which
make reproduction possible enhance this
meaning.

Reproductive technologies not only increase the meaning of reproduction for physicians, but also increase the professional
prestige of those medical specialties which
control the new technologies. Obstetrics and
gynaecology have traditionally been a low-
status area of medicine (Pfeffer and Woollett
1983, Summey and Hurst 1986), and the
world-wide coverage of 'miracle' babies has
given ob/gyns a function more complex and
prestigious than just 'baby-catching'.

In addition to enhancing the status of ob/
gyns as a profession, technological innovations in reproduction give individual physicians the opportunity to pursue pathbreaking
research, thus making a name for themselves
which would be impossible doing routine gynaecology and obstetrics. In the words of one
infertility specialist quoted in Lasker and
Borg (1987:124):

> *My thing in life is not just to be in the front run-*
> *ning: I want to be right out there in the very front.*
> *The grant money in my area dried up, so I became*
> *interested in infertility. Personally, it is important*
> *to me that the work I do helps women. But by far*
> *the most exciting part professionally is the re-*
> *search and the new data we get.*

Although it is almost never discussed in
the medical literature (one exception is Soules

1985), another field of meaning for physicians is economic. Some demographers (Menken *et al* 1986, Aral and Cates 1983) and several feminists (Powledge 1988, Corea 1985) have alluded to the fact that physicians have a financial interest in reproductive technology. As birth rates decline in the more developed countries, ob/gyns need to expand their repertoire of services in order to maintain patient demand. While it is unclear whether the supply of infertility services preceded or followed the demand for such services, it is not surprising that more and more physicians are becoming infertility specialists (Office of Technology Assessment 1988).

The relationship between the meaning of reproduction and technology for physicians and medical involvement in the development of reproductive technologies is never explicitly stated, since technological innovations are always described in purely medical terminology. However, in order to understand the phenomenon, we must look at how this technological development fits into broader sociological patterns, rather than as an isolated technical innovation.

Previous research has found similar patterns in the medicalisation of other aspects of every day life, such as criminal behaviour, eating disorders and depression. Friedson (1970) argues that the expansion of medicine is rooted in desire for professional control, rather than scientific logic. Medical expansion into areas such as sports, personal appearance (diet, cosmetic surgery), and substance abuse is consistent with this analysis. As with infertility, the fact that obesity, drug use and facial wrinkles have medical 'cures' may reflect physicians' interest in expanding their sphere of influence, rather than any inherently medical characteristic of the problem. In fact, some argue that diseases are not 'inherently' medical problems, but have been defined as such through a process of social construction or 'framing' (see Foucault 1973 and Rosenberg 1989 for further elaboration of this argument).

The Infertile Consumers

The meaning of reproduction for infertile patients appears to be connected to a sense of control over their lives. The desire for children is not simply a desire to raise children, because adoption would be less expensive and physically traumatic. The important aspects of reproduction for these people are the productive aspects—creating a child of their own genetic material. This is consistent with several characteristics of upper-middle class culture in the United States; a focus on individuality and an expectation of being able to achieve one's goals with enough hard work. Many of these women planned to have children after establishing a career, and they expected that with the proper planning they would be able to have professional and financial success, as well as raise a family. In the words of one infertility counsellor quoted in Lasker and Borg:

> These women . . . have essentially lived with the belief that if you plan, if you're achievement oriented, think ahead, and try to do things right, having a baby is something that should simply happen when you decide, just as a (college) degree should (1987:206).

Since they have come to expect success in their endeavours and control over their lives, their sense of self is shaken by the failure to become pregnant. 'At this time in my life, I wanted a house, I wanted a career. I wanted the kids and everything . . . Instead I feel that there's nothing left in my life' (quoted in Lasker and Borg 1987:24).

One alternative for infertile couples is adoption. However, this may be a less satisfactory solution for the upper-middle class than for less wealthy people. Most children available for adoption are nonwhite and from poor families, in other words 'lower quality' children. Again, the issue of control is raised: couples who have control over many aspects of their lives (for example work, housing, education) are probably less willing to relinquish control over the race, genetic make-up and prenatal care of their children. One man stated his feelings quite bluntly: 'If we can't have our own children, I don't want anybody else's children. And besides, there are no healthy, normal, intellectually curious caucasian babies up for adoption' (Liebmann-Smith 1987:150).

As with each group discussed, the perspective of consumers is part of a coherent world view, or set of meanings. People tend to frame their desire for genetic offspring in terms of individualism and personal rights. They wonder what they did to deserve their suffering, and feel that their infertility is 'unfair' and abrogates their 'right to reproduce'. While patients claim to have a strong, even overpowering, desire for a baby, they often express hostility and resentment toward friends and relatives who have small children. Thus, the desire for a child appears to be a desire for *their own* child rather than a desire to interact with children or even play a central part of the lives of young nephews and nieces. Consistent with the reluctance to adopt 'imperfect' children is an emphasis on children as products or possessions rather than children as desired companions.

The recent practice of surrogate motherhood, where a woman is chosen by a couple to be impregnated with the husband's sperm is also indicative of the concern about the quality of one's child; as Viviana Zelizer puts it, 'Surrogacy is not just a sentimental search for any child to love, but the deliberate manufacture of a particular, suitable child' (1988:28). In fact, many surrogacy contracts specify that the pregnant woman must have an abortion if amneocentesis shows 'unacceptable' results (Zelizer 1988).

Feminists

To feminist critics of reproductive technologies, reproduction is the first step in the experience of child-raising. What gives reproduction (in the biological, not social, sense) special significance to this group is that it is a process unique to women. While there has been a great deal of debate among feminist scholars in the last several decades over whether women's childbearing role is a source of fulfilment or oppression (for example Hewlett 1986, Raymond 1986), most feminists agree that increasing medicalisation of childbirth and pregnancy is harmful to women. Thus, reproduction is a locus of struggle between women and those physicians who are trying to increase their control over the reproductive process.

As advocates for women's autonomy, feminists have an interest in maintaining female control over the procreative process and affirming women's experience of reproduction. There are two separate arguments which need to be sorted out: 1) the desire for children is socially constructed and has been used to keep women in a domestic role (Hubbard 1981, Overall 1987); and 2) pregnancy, childbirth and motherhood are special experiences and unique to women (Rothman 1989, O'Brien 1981). These two threads of the feminist discourse are loosely tied to the 'structuralist' and 'essentialist' branches of feminism, respectively.

The justification of IVF because women 'need' or have a 'right' to bear children reinforces the attitude that motherhood is central to womanhood, and assumes biological determinism: the 'drive' to have children is seen as deeper than other desires. Structural feminists argue that this 'drive' is the product of a social structure that gives women few alternative routes to fulfilment and of a socialisation process that teaches young girls to grow up to be mothers (see Tuchman, Daniels and Benet [1978] for an account of the social forces which reinforce the importance of motherhood for women). In fact, women who are successful in their careers are more likely to be childless than other women (Hewlett 1986) and the proportion of women who are voluntarily childless has increased in recent years (Veevers 1979); these figures suggest that achievement in other realms may substitute for motherhood.

Focusing on the importance of motherhood makes it more difficult for women to choose childlessness and causes even more misery for the infertile (Robertson 1988).

At the same time, other feminists, who consider motherhood an essential aspect of women's lives, claim that use of these technologies usurps women's procreative power. The technological focus on children as 'products' inherently denigrates women's experience, reducing women to 'mother machines' or 'test-tube women'. The emphasis on genetic ties, rather than nurturance, as the basis of parenthood defines reproduction in a male-centred way, since men's usual contribution to their children is genetic, unlike women, who nurture their children in pregnancy and later (Rothman 1989). While not explicitly offering solutions for women who are unable to conceive, these authors suggest that the desires of individual women must be balanced against the well-being of women as a group (Rowland 1987, Rothman 1984).

Feminists evaluate the impact of these technologies in a social context, rather than simply as medical procedures. They consider the fact that physicians can legally force women to undergo Caesarean section (Daniels 1990), the involuntary sterilisation of poor and minority women, and the thousands of women who have become infertile because of exposure to DES, IUD use, or unnecessary pelvic surgery (Corea 1985). In light of these occurrences, the new technologies seem to serve as the latest in a series of mechanisms for enhancing male control over procreation rather than tools to increase women's reproductive choices.

In the case of feminists, the world view with which they evaluate reproductive technologies is more overt than in the case of physicians or infertile patients. The feminist perspective advocates enhancing women's control over their lives and broadening their choices of autonomy. While feminists may disagree about the centrality of motherhood (as discussed in section 3), there is general agree-

ment that technologies which emphasise the importance of motherhood, define it very narrowly (genetic/gestational), and transfer control over the procreative process from the mother to the physician, are antithetical to feminist interests.

CONCLUSION

In this examination of the feminist, medical and consumer literature on reproductive technology, differences in the construction of the problem are clarified. I suggest that these alternative perspectives are rooted in vested interests as well as differences in the meaning of reproduction among the groups. Physicians see reproduction as a medical problem, for which IVF and related procedures are appropriate interventions. They gain professional prestige, expand their market and sphere of intervention, and derive emotional satisfaction from the advent of these technologies. The infertile patients see the inability to bear a child as the problem, and like the physicians, they look to technology for the answer. Their interest is in continuing a pattern of individual success and achievement which is disrupted by the inability to have a child who is genetically related to them. Feminists see male exploitation of women, which includes the use of IVF, as problematic. Although not discussed specifically in the literature reviewed here, the proposed solution is a health care system (in fact, an entire political system) which is responsive to women's needs and experiences. The goal of feminism is to expand women's choices and control over their lives; to the extent that this aim is threatened by reproductive technology, feminists have a vested interest in the topic.

Only by understanding the differences in the meaning of reproduction and, consequently, related technologies can we make sense of the rhetoric used in the literatures examined here. Both feminists and consumers authentically feel that they are defending 'reproductive rights'; all groups *are* concerned with the emotional stress of infertility. These different positions cannot be resolved by facts alone: we need to understand the differences in perspectives which cause facts to be interpreted differently by each group. The interpretation of virtually any statistic or 'objective' fact will be shaped by assumptions about the meaning of reproduction.

Value-laden rhetoric is not just a resource which is mobilised to garner support for a particular definition of a social problem as claimed by some (Spector and Kitsuse 1977, Best 1987), but a reflection of real differences in the meaning of the problem. The underlying debate is not *whether* reproduction is important, but *which aspects* of parenthood are important. Emphasis on genetic and gestational factors reflect the professional interests of physicians and the goal of the wealthy and professional infertile to have a 'high quality' child. On the other hand, the feminist literature emphasizes the nurturant aspects of parenthood, as well as the importance of women's control over the reproductive process. These concerns reflect an analysis which focuses on reproduction as a process of interaction, rather than an attainment process.

As with other debates on women's rights, such as abortion and the ERA, it is difficult for each group to understand the countervailing viewpoint. To concede validity to the opposing perspective would be threatening to each group's values and unarticulated interests. Physicians would be conceding that medical intervention cannot solve all physical problems. IVF patients would be recognising that the desire for biological offspring does not warrant expensive and controversial technology. Feminists would have to concede that the desire for biological children is a powerful force in many people's lives. To give ground on this issue would call into question the meanings which are central to group members' self-definition and their understanding of how the world works.

NOTES

1. The prevalence of infertility varies cross-nationally, as well as among subgroups within a country. In some parts of Africa, approximately 30 per cent of couples are believed to be infertile (World Health Organisation 1975), while in England, the figure is 10 percent (Pfeffer and Woollett 1983). Infertility generally increases with age and tends to be higher among those of low socio-economic status (Henshaw and Orr 1987). These patterns indicate that infertility is to some extent determined by social factors such as sexually transmitted disease, general level of health and age patterns of child-bearing.

2. In her book on the roots of the conflict over abortion rights, Luker (1984) develops this framework in greater detail.

3. One suggestive fact is that blacks and people with less than college education are more likely to be infertile, but less likely to use infertility services (Anonymous 1987).

4. Offen (1988) offers an historical overview of these theoretical perspectives. Also, see Elshtain (1981) for a representative view of the essentialist view, and Epstein (1988) for a structuralist perspective.

5. It should be noted that this is not a universally agreed-upon position on motherhood. Many feminists embrace motherhood as a source of power and pleasure. See, for example, Rossi (1985) and O'Brien (1981).

6. Each of the groups discussed has at least one organisation which facilitates within-group communication: the American Fertility Society for physicians; RESOLVE for infertile couples; and FINNRAGE for feminists.

REFERENCES

Anonymous (1987) To have or have not. *American Demographics*. June:20.

Aral, S. and Cates, W. (1983) The increasing concern with infertility: why now? *Journal of the American Medical Association*, 250, 2327–31.

Baruch, E.H. (1988) A womb of his own. In E. H. Baruch *et al* (eds.) *Embryos, Ethics, and Women's Rights* New York: Harrington Press.

Best, J. (1987) Rhetoric in claims-making: constructing the missing children problem. *Social Problems*, 34, 101–21.

Bonnicksen, A. (1986) In vitro fertilization and public policy: turning to the consumer. *Population Research and Policy Review*, 5, 197–215.

Boston Women's Health Book Collective. (1984) *The New Our Bodies, Ourselves*, 3rd ed. New York: Simon and Schuster.

Brown, A. (1988) Endometriosis. In E. Glazer and S. Cooper (eds.) *Without Child* Lexington, MA: Lexington Books.

Chodorow, N. (1978) *The Reproduction of Mothering* Berkeley: University of California Press.

Cohen, J., Feehill, C. B., Fishel, S. B., Hewitt, J., Purdy, J., Rowland, G. F., Steptoe, P. C. and Webster, J. (1985) In vitro fertilization: a treatment for male infertility. *Fertility and Sterility*, 43, 3:422–32.

Cohen, J., Mayaux, M. J. and Guihard-Moscato, M. L. (1988) Pregnancy outcomes after in vitro fertilization. *Annals of the New York Academy of Sciences*, 541, 1–6.

Collins, J. A., Wrixon, W., Janes, L. B. *et al* (1983) Treatment-independent pregnancy among infertile couples. *New England Journal of Medicine*, 309, 1201–206.

Conrad, P. and Schneider, J. (1980) *Deviance and Medicalization* St. Louis: Mosby.

Corea, G. (1985) *The Mother Machine* New York: Harper and Row.

Correy, J., Watkins, R. A., *et al* (1988) Spontaneous pregnancies and pregnancies as a result of treatment in an *in vitro* fertilization program terminating in ectopic pregnancies or spontaneous abortions. *Fertility and Sterility*, 50, 85–8.

Daniels, J. (1990) Court-ordered Caesareans: a growing concern for indigent women. In M. Fried (ed.) *From Abortion to Reproductive Freedom* Boston: South End Press.

DeCherney, A. (1983) Doctored babies. *Fertility and Sterility*, 40, 724–27.

Edwards, R. G. (1984) Current status of human in vitro fertilization. In R. F. Harrison, J. Bonnar and W. Thompson (eds.) *Fertility and Sterility* Boston: MTP Press.

Ehrenreich, B. and English D. (1978) *For Her Own Good* New York: Anchor.

Ehrenreich, B. (1983) *The Hearts of Men* New York: Anchor.

Elshtain, J. (1981) *Public Man, Private Woman* Princeton, NJ: Princeton University Press.

Emerson, R. and Messinger, S. (1977) The micropolitics of trouble. *Social Problems*, 25, 121–34.

Epstein, C. F. (1988) *Deceptive Distinctions* New Haven: Yale University Press.

Foucault, M. (1973) *The Birth of the Clinic: An Archaeology of Medical Perception* New York: Pantheon.

Frank, D. and Vogel, M. (1988) *The Baby Makers* New York: Carroll and Graf.

Freidson, E. (1970) *Profession of Medicine* New York: Dodd Mead and Company.

Glazer, E. and Cooper, S. (eds.) (1988) *Without Child* Lexington, MA: Lexington Books.

Gordon, L. (1977) *Woman's Body, Woman's Right* London: Penguin Books.

Greenfeld, D. and Haseltine, F. (1986) Candidate selection and psychosocial considerations of in-vitro fertilization procedures. *Clinical Obstetrics and Gynecology*, 29, 119–26.

Gusfield, J. (1963) *Symbolic Crusade* Urbana: University of Illinois Press.

Hartmann, H. (1981) The family as the locus of gender class and political struggles: the example of housework. *Signs*, 6, 366–94.

Henshaw, S. and Orr, M. (1987) The need and unmet need for infertility services in the United States. *Family Planning Perspectives*, 19, 4, 10–186.

Hewlett, S. (1986) *A Lesser Life* New York: Warner.

Hilgartner, S. and Bosk, C. (1988) The rise and fall of social problems: a public arenas model. *American Journal of Sociology*, 94, 1, 53–78.

Horlitz, C. (1988) Pergonal: the final step. In E. Glazer and S. Cooper (eds.) *Without Child* Lexington, MA: Lexington Books.

Hubbard, R. (1981) The case against in vitro fertilization and implementation. In H. B. Holmes, B. B. Hoskin and M. Gross (eds.) *The Custom-Made Child? Women-Centered Perspectives* Clifton, NJ: Humana Press.

Hubbard, R. (1988) Eugenics: new tools, old ideas. In E. H. Baruch, A. F. D'Amadeo and J. Seager (eds.) *Embryos, Ethics and Women's Rights* New York: Harrington.

Khatamee, M. (1988) Infertility: a preventable epidemic? *International Journal of Fertility*, 33, 246–51.

Keye, W. (1984) Psychosexual responses to infertility. *Clinical Obstetrics and Gynecology, 27*, 760–6.

Lasker, J. and Borg, S. (1987) *In Search of Parenthood* Boston: Beacon Press.

Laufer, N. and Navot, D. (1986) Human in vitro fertilization. In A. DeCherney (ed.) *Reproductive Failure* New York: Churchill Livingstone.

Liebmann-Smith, J. (1987) *In Pursuit of Pregnancy* New York: Newmarket Press.

Lorber, J. (1989) Choice, gift or patriarchal bargain? Women's consent to *in vitro* fertilization in male infertility. *Hypatia, 4*, 23–36.

Luker, K. (1984) *Abortion and the Politics of Motherhood* Berkeley: University of California Press.

Mansbridge, J. (1986) *Why We Lost the ERA* Chicago: University of Chicago Press.

Mao, K. and Wood, C. (1984) Barriers to treatment of infertility by in-vitro fertilization and embryo transfer. *The Medical Journal of Australia*, 140:532–3.

Marrs, R. and Vargyas, J. (1986) Human in vitro fertilization: state of the art. In D. Mishell and V. Davajan (eds.) *Infertility, Contraception and Reproductive Endocrinology* Oradell, New Jersey: Medical Economics Books.

Mazor, M. (1984) Emotional reactions to infertility. In M. Mazor and H. Simons (eds.) *Infertility: Medical, Emotional and Social Considerations* New York: Human Sciences Press.

McCrea, F. (1984) The politics of menopause: the 'discovery' of a deficiency disease. *Social Problems, 31*, 111–23.

Menken, J., Trussell, J. and Larsen, U. (1986) Age and infertility. *Science, 233*, 1389–94.

Menning, B. E. (1981) In defense of in vitro fertilization. In H. B. Holmes, B. B. Hoskins and M. Gross, (eds.) *The Custom-Made Child? Women-Centered Perspectives* Clifton, NJ: Humana Press.

O'Brien. M. (1981) *The Politics of Reproduction* London: Routledge and Kegan Paul.

Offen, K. (1988) Defining feminism: A comparative historical approach. *Signs, 14*, 119–57.

Office of Technology Assessment (1988) *Infertility: Medical and Social Choices* Washington, DC: U.S. Government Printing Office.

Overall, C. (1987) *Ethics and Human Reproduction* Boston: Allen and Unwin.

Petchesky, R. P. (1980) Reproductive freedom: beyond 'a woman's right to choose.' *Signs, 5*, 661-85.

Pfeffer, N. and Woollett, A. (1983) *The Experience of Infertility* London: Virago.

Poff, D. (1987) Content, intent and consequences: life production and reproductive technology. *Atlantis, 13*, 111–15.

Powledge, T. (1981) Unnatural selection: on choosing children's sex. In H. B. Holmes, B. B. Hoskins and M. Gross (eds.) *The Custom-made Child?* Clifton, NJ: Humana Press.

Powledge, T. (1988) Reproductive technologies and the bottom line. In E. H. Baruch, A. F. D'Amadeo and J. Seager (eds.) *Embryos, Ethics and Women's Rights* New York: Harrington Park Press.

Raymond, J. (1986) *A Passion for Friends: Toward a Philosophy of Female Friendship* Boston: Beacon.

Robertson, J. (1988) Procreative liberty, embryos, and collaborative reproduction: a legal perspective. In E. H. Baruch, A. F. D'Amadeo and J. Seager (eds.) *Embryos, Ethics and Women's Rights* New York: Harrington Park Press.

Rosenberg, C. (1989) Disease in history: frames and framers. *The Milbank Quarterly, 67* (Supplement 1). 1–15.

Rossi, A. (1985) Gender and parenthood. In A. Rossi (ed.) *Gender and the Lifecourse* New York: Aldine.

Rothman, B. K. (1984) The meanings of choice in reproductive technology. In R. Arditti, R. D. Klein and S. Minden (eds.) *Test-tube Women* London: Pandora Press.

Rothman, B. K. (1989) *Recreating Motherhood* New York: W. W. Norton and Company.

Rowland, R. (1987) Technology and motherhood: reproductive choice reconsidered. *Signs, 12*, 512–29.

Ruzek, S. B. (1979) The *Women's Health Movement* New York: Praeger.

Sandelowski, M. (1990) Failures of volition: female agency and infertility in historical perspective. *Signs, 15*, 475–99.

Santiesteban, M. (1988) But I could be pregnant any minute. In E. Glazer and S. Cooper (eds.) *Without Child* Lexington, MA: Lexington Books.

Scritchfield, S. (1989) The infertility enterprise: IVF and the technological construction of reproductive impairments. In D. Wertz (ed.) *Research in the Sociology of Health Care* Greenwich, Connecticut: JAI Press.

Soules, M. (1985) The in vitro fertilization pregnancy rate: let's be honest with one another. *Fertility and Sterility, 43*, 511–13.

Spector, M. and Kitsuse, J. (1977) *Constructing Social Problems* Menlo Park, CA: Cummings.

Stangel, J. (1988) *The New Fertility and Conception* New York: New American Library.

Stanworth, M. (1987) Reproductive technologies and the deconstruction of motherhood. In M. Stanworth (ed.) *Reproductive Technologies* Minneapolis: University of Minnesota Press.

Summey, P. and Hurst, M. (1986) Ob/gyn on the rise: the evolution of professional ideology in the twentieth century—Part II. *Women and Health*, 11, 103–23.

Tuchman, G., Daniels, A. K. and Benet, J. (1978) *Hearth and Home* New York: Oxford University Press.

Van Hall, E. V. (1983) The infertile couple and the gynaecologist: psychosocial and emotional aspects. In R. F. Harrison, J. Bonnar and W. Thompson (eds.) *Fertility and Sterility* Boston: MTP Press.

Veevers, J. (1979) Voluntary childlessness: a review of the issues and evidence *Marriage and Family Review*, 2, 2–26.

World Health Organization (1975). *The Epidemiology of Infertility* Geneva: World Health Organization.

Wuthnow, R. (1987) *Meaning and Moral Order* Berkeley: University of California Press.

Zelizer, V. (1985) *Pricing the Priceless Child* New York: Basic.

Zelizer, V. (1988) From baby farms to Baby M. *Society*, March/April, 23–8.

Reproductive Technologies, Surrogacy Arrangements, and the Politics of Motherhood

LAURA R. WOLIVER

New reproductive technologies add at least three new issues to political debates about abortion in the United States. First, new reproductive technologies are predicated on the availability of legal abortion, which is constantly under threat in this country. Amniocentesis, ultrasound, genetic screening, embryo transfer, test-tube babies, to name but a few, are procedures in which the option of abortion or destruction of excess embryos are inherent. Any changes in abortion laws will directly affect the use of these technologies. These technologies bring into abortion debates a new group of potential abortion users, who desire the abortion option for slightly different reasons than the original position on reproductive choice taken by the early women's movements. In addition, new medical knowledge is beginning to blur the boundaries between contraception and abortion. The controversy over introducing the French "abortion pill," RU-486, into the United States is one current example (Richard 1989:947–48).

Second, reproductive technologies such as ultrasound and fetal medicine are playing a significant, if subtle, role in the efforts to restrict abortion rights by furthering the construction of the image of the fetus as an entity distinct from the woman who carries and delivers it. These images are powerful symbols in United States prolife, antiabortion politics. "The idea that knowledge of fetal life, and especially confrontation with the visual image of the fetus, will 'convert' a woman to the pro-life position has been a central theme in both local and national right-to-life activism," Ginsburg found. "A popular quip summarizes this position: 'If there were a window on a pregnant woman's stomach, there would be no more abortions'" (1989:104). Images of the fetus used by antiabortion activists in the United States, it should be emphasized, usually exclude visualization of the woman the fetus is within (Petchesky 1984:353; Ginsburg 1989:107–9; Condit 1990:79–95; Duden 1993). These carefully constructed fetal images are powerful aspects of the antiabortion discourse,

> When pro-Life rhetors talk about why they believe as they do, the role of the photographs and films becomes quite clear. Without these pictures, pro-Life advocates would have only an abstract argument about the importance of chromosomes in determining human life or a religious argument about the "soul"... neither of those options could sustain the righteous fire of the public movement. (Condit 1990:80)

Fetal images, combined with artful political commentary and voice-overs by antiabortion spokespeople, help the antichoice movement in its attempt to define the fetus as a human person (Petchesky 1987; Condit 1990:86–89). In ultrasound images, or microscopic views of zygotes, the viewer's eye must be trained to "see" the "life," since it is not clear to the uninitiated (Duden 1993:73–78; see also Rowland 1992); this training, as well as the viewing of women's innards, is an integral part of the politics and the cultural shift of re-visioning (Duden 1993). Technologies, therefore, that allow viewing, studying, and possibly treating fetuses medically "are likely to elevate the moral status of the fetus" (Blank 1988:148).

Fetal medicine and the technologies that allow the visualization of the fetus push women out of the center of medical attention in gestation and birth, except for efforts to control female behavior for the well-being of the fetus. Discussions and lawsuits about what pregnant women eat and drink (alcohol, tobacco, drugs) or how they live (working in unsafe occupations, engaging in unsafe sex, or practicing risky sports) have troubling implications in the United States for controlling women's behavior. Much of the emphasis in these discussions is on what the women do, not what the men in their lives are doing, or on the socioeconomic conditions that might influence women's habits, employment patterns, and prenatal care. Particularly chilling is the fact that some earlier medically recommended treatments and advice for pregnant women have subsequently proved very harmful (the use of X-rays in prenatal care is just one example). How do we know that the prevailing medical wisdoms of today will not be proven unsafe in the future? The inadequate, short-term testing of ultrasound is a troubling case in point (Oakley 1984:155–86; 1987:44–48).

Envisioning the fetus as a separate patient, combined with more detailed and heightened monitoring of the behavior of pregnant women, might have an impact on abortion choice. After all, if society oversees the nutrition and lifestyle of pregnant women in order to ensure the health of the fetal "patient," how would the women be allowed to abort this "patient"? The elevation of the fetus as a patient in medicine and politics, though, marginalizes the women involved. As Gallagher reminds us, "given the very geography of pregnancy, questions as to the status of the fetus must follow, not precede, an examination of the rights of the woman within whose body and life the fetus exists" (1989:187–98; see also Wingerter 1987).

Third, neonatal technologies are altering perceptions of fetal viability, and thus undermining one of the premises of *Roe v. Wade* (the 1973 U.S. precedent for legal abortion, based partly on the viability of fetuses). As U.S. Supreme Court Justice Sandra Day O'Connor noted, *Roe* is on "a collision course with itself" because of these changes (O'Connor, quoted from *City of Akron v. Akron Center for Reproductive Health, Inc.*:458). Neonatal technologies are pushing back the gestational age when fetuses might be viable outside the womb (Blank 1984b:584–602; Blank 1988:64–65). The result might be to pit the woman's rights against those of her fetus. Indeed, recent U.S. cases indicate that "when maternal actions are judged detrimental to the health or life of the potential child, the court has shown little hesitancy to constrain the liberty of the mother" (Blank 1984a:150). In reality only a very small number of women and babies have access to these neonatal technologies, but the experience of a privileged few is being generalized into the abortion debate as a whole. In addition to the attack by conservatives and antiabortion activists on abortion choice (see, for example, Steiner 1983; Luker 1984; Cohan 1986; Glendon 1987; Ginsburg 1989; Condit 1990; Himmelstein 1990:89–90; to name but a few), feminists now must respond to the pressure the new technologies exert on abortion politics.

INCREASED MARGINALIZATION OF WOMEN

The values inherent in these technologies are making women, as Rothman states it, "transparent" (1986). A cultural shift has occurred where women have been "skinned" and authorities are permitted to examine and monitor their innards (Duden 1993:7). The role of the woman is becoming secondary to that of the medical profession and those who can broker surrogacy and adoption contracts.

When they are used for contraception, sex-selective abortions, and sterilization, reproductive technologies have already seriously violated the rights, dignity, and indigenous cultures of poor women the world over while failing to address the underlying poverty and inequalities in these women's societies (Shapiro 1985; Hartmann 1987; Tobin 1989). The coercive "choices" presented to impoverished third-world women to "select" sterilization or dangerous contraceptives such as Depo-Provera in exchange for food, clothing, or other benefits show how professional medical technologies can be used to harm women, yet be justified with the language of individual choice (see, for example, Bunkle 1984; Clarke 1984; Akhta 1987; Hartmann 1987; Kamal 1987). "We will have to lift our eyes from the choices of the individual woman," writes Rothman, "and focus on the control of the social system that structures her choices, which rewards some choices and punishes others, which distributes the rewards and punishments for reproductive choices along class and race lines" (1984:33; see also Dworkin 1983:182; Corea 1985b:2–3, 27; Rowland 1987:84; Gordon 1976, especially chap. 15; Rhode 1993–94).

In population control politics, the desires of women are largely ignored, their reproductive choices are narrowed, their knowledge of their own bodies is belittled, and traditional female and community-based healers are driven out of business. Contraceptive technologies emphasized by international aid agencies for less-developed countries, for example, sacrifice "women's health and safety in the indiscriminate promotion of hormonal contraception, the IUD, and sterilization, at the same time as they have neglected barrier methods and natural family planning" (Hartmann 1987:xv). The problem with barrier methods, from the point of view of many population planners, is that they are not effective enough, since they are under women's control and discretion. Hartmann found: "The thrust of contraceptive research in fact has been to remove control of contraception from women, in the same way that women are being increasingly alienated from the birth process itself" (1987:32).

Similarly, studies of the United States show that minority and poor women receive less quality health care, are subject to more intrusive medical procedures, and have limited "choice" to use expensive reproductive technologies (Martin 1987; Nsiah-Jefferson 1989; Davis 1990:53–65). Medical advice to poor and minority women is often uninformed regarding the language skills, cultural background, and desires of these patients. In these settings, therefore, "the graph she is asked to look at during her visit to the clinic only serves to mystify her experience. In ways that she cannot fathom, expert professionals claim to know something about her future child, much more, in fact, than she could ever find out by herself. Long before she actually becomes a mother she is habituated to the idea that others know better and that she is dependent on being told" (Duden 1993:29).

The marginalization of women in these new reproductive arrangements is shockingly clear in the language that is used to describe the women involved. Women are discussed in the new reproductive literature by bodily parts: "maternal environment" replaces a woman's womb, a pregnant woman becomes "an embryo carrier" (see, for example, Klein 1987:66). Surrogate mothers are likened to reproductive machines and are described as inanimate objects: "rented wombs," "incubators," "receptacles," "a kind of hatchery," "gestators," "a uterine hostess," or a "surrogate uterus" (see, for example, Ince 1984:99–116; Corea 1985b:222; Hollinger 1985:901, 903). Fetal well-being appears more important than "invasions" of mother's bodies (Laborie 1987; Burfoot 1988:108, 110).

In vitro fertilization is sometimes described without once intimating that a human woman is involved. No woman, for example, is mentioned in the following overview of the 1978 birth of Louise Brown, the first "test-tube" baby:

> *After many years of frustrating research, Drs. Edwards and Steptoe had succeeded in removing an egg from an ovarian follicle, fertilizing it in a dish, and transferring the developing zygote to a uterus where it implanted and was brought to term. (Robertson 1986:943)*

The women involved in these procedures are truly marginal. It is important to recall that "test-tube" babies are born from mothers who carried them during pregnancy. In addition, these women were sometimes experimented on without their full consent, or they participated based on misleading information concerning the probability of actually having a baby (Corea 1985b:112–17, 166–85; Corea and Ince 1987; Lasker and Borg 1987:53–55).

The future role of mothers in a medical system oriented toward technological intervention and control in conception, gestation, and birth, where life itself is just another commodity and women's bodies producers of quality products, is very troubling. "To use the law for these complicated moral decisions," writes Rothman, "is to lose the nuances, the idiosyncrasies, and the individuality that protect us from fundamentally untrustworthy political institutions" (1989:87). In addition to the marginalization of women in these reproductive arrangements, these technologies deflect pressures for social reforms by promising technological fixes for reproductive difficulties. Some women delay motherhood and possibly increase reproductive risks, for example, to conform to male career timetables (such as the tenure system in universities or the partner process in law firms, to name but two). The new reproductive technologies allow this to continue by implying to women that they will suffer few consequences by delaying motherhood. Women's delay of motherhood is also used to justify the "demands" for the technologies by women. Potential pressures to change corporations, universities, and other employers, then, are blunted by this technological turn (Woliver 1989a:39; see also Woliver 1989b and 1990). New reproductive technologies and surrogacy arrangements are increasingly making women marginal in the new politics of motherhood.

REFERENCES

Akhtar, Farida. 1987. "Wheat for Statistics: A Case Study of Relief Wheat for Attaining Sterilization Target in Bangladesh." In Patricia Spallone and Deborah Lynn Steinberg, eds., *Made to Order: The Myth of Reproductive and Genetic Progress*, pp. 154–60. New York: Pergamon.

Blank, Robert H. 1984a. *Redefining Human Life: Reproductive Technologies and Social Policy*. Boulder: Westview.

———. 1984b. "Judicial Decision Making and Biological Fact: *Roe v. Wade* and the Unresolved Question of Fetal Viability." *Western Political Quarterly* 37:584–602.

———. 1988. *Rationing Medicine*. New York: Columbia University Press.

Bunkle, Phillida. 1984. "Calling the Shots? The International Politics of Depo-Provera." In Arditti, Klein, and Minden, eds., *Test-Tube Women: What*

Future for Motherhood?, pp. 165–87. London: Pandora.

Burfoot, Annette. 1988. "A Review of the Third Annual Meeting of the European Society of Human Reproduction and Embryology." *Reproductive and Genetic Engineering: Journal of International Feminist Analysis* 1, no. 1: 107–11.

Clarke, Adele. 1984. "Subtle Forms of Sterilization Abuse: A Reproductive Rights Analysis." In Arditti, Klein, and Minden, eds., *Test-Tube Women: What Future for Motherhood?,* pp. 188–212.

Cohan, Alvin. 1986. "Abortion as a Marginal Issue: The Use of Peripheral Mechanisms in Britain and the United States." In Joni Lovenduski and Joyce Ourshoorn, eds., *The New Politics of Abortion,* pp. 27–48. Newbury Park, Calif.: Sage.

Condit, Celeste M. 1990. *Decoding Abortion Rhetoric: The Communication of Social Change.* Urbana: University of Illinois Press.

Corea, Gena. 1985a, Updated Edition. *The Hidden Malpractice: How American Medicine Mistreats Women.* New York: Harper Colophon.

———. 1985b. *The Mother Machine: Reproductive Technologies from Artificial Insemination to Artificial Wombs.* New York: Harper and Row.

Corea, Gena and Susan Ince. 1987. "Report of a Survey of IVF Clinics in the USA." In Patricia Spallone and Deborah Lynn Steinberg, eds., *Made to Order: The Myth of Reproductive and Genetic Progress,* pp. 133–45. New York: Pergamon.

Davis, Angela Y. 1990. *Women, Culture, and Politics.* New York: Vintage.

Davis, Peggy. 1989. "Law as Microaggression." *Yale Law Journal* 98:1559.

Duden, Barbara. 1993. *Disembodying Women: Perspectives on Pregnancy and the Unborn.* Cambridge: Harvard University Press.

Dworkin, Andrea. 1983. *Right-Wing Women.* New York: Perigee.

Gallagher, Janet. 1989. "Fetus as Patient." In Nadine Taub and Sherrill Cohen, eds., *Reproductive Laws for the 1990s,* pp. 185–235. Clifton, N.J.: Humana.

Ginsburg, Faye D. 1989. *Contested Lives: The Abortion Debate in an American Community.* Berkeley: University of California Press.

Glendon, Mary Ann. 1987. *Abortion and Divorce in Western Law.* Cambridge: Harvard University Press.

Gordon, Linda. 1976. *Woman's Body, Woman's Right: A Social History of Birth Control in America.* New York: Grossman.

Hartmann, Betsy. 1987. *Reproductive Rights and Wrongs: The Global Politics of Population Control and Contraceptive Choice.* New York: Harper and Row.

Himmelstein, Jerome L. 1990. *To the Right: The Transformation of American Conservatism.* Berkeley: University of California Press.

Hollinger, J. H. 1985. "From Coitus to Commerce: Legal and Social Consequences of Noncoital Reproduction." *University of Michigan Journal of Law Reform* 18 (Summer): 865–932.

Ince, Susan. 1984. "Inside the Surrogate Industry." In Arditti, Klein, and Minden, eds., *Test-Tube Women: What Future for Motherhood?,* pp. 99–116.

Kamal, Sultana. 1987. "Seizure of Reproductive Rights? A Discussion on Population Control in the Third World and the Emergence of the New Reproductive Technologies in the West." In Patricia Spallone and Deborah Lynn Steinberg, eds., *Made to Order: The Myth of Reproductive and Genetic Progress,* pp. 146–53. New York: Pergamon.

Klein, Renate D. 1987. "What's 'New' About the 'New' Reproductive Technologies." In Gena Corea et al., eds., *Man-Made Women: How New Reproductive Technologies Affect Women,* pp. 64–73. Bloomington: Indiana University Press.

Laborie, Françoise. 1987. "Looking for Mothers, You Only Find Fetuses." In Patricia Spallone and Deborah Lynn Steinberg, eds., *Made to Order: The Myth of Reproductive and Genetic Progress.* New York: Pergamon.

Lasker, Judith and Susan Borg. 1987. *In Search of Parenthood: Coping with Infertility and High-Tech Conception.* Boston: Beacon.

Luker, Kristin. 1984. *Abortion and the Politics of Motherhood.* Berkeley: University of California Press.

Martin, Emily. 1987. *The Woman in the Body: A Cultural Analysis of Reproduction.* Boston: Beacon.

Nsiah-Jefferson, Laurie. 1989. "Reproductive Laws, Women of Color, and Low-Income Women." In Nadine Taub and Sherrill Cohen, eds., *Reproductive Laws for the 1990s,* pp. 23–67. Clifton, N.J.: Humana.

Oakley, Ann. 1984. *The Captured Womb: A History of the Medical Care of Pregnant Women.* Oxford: Basil Blackwell.

Oakley, Ann. 1987. "From Walking Wombs to Test-Tube Babies." In Michelle Stanworth, ed., *Reproductive Technologies: Gender, Motherhood, and Medicine*, pp. 36–56. Minneapolis: University of Minnesota Press.

Petchesky, Rosalind. 1984. *Abortion and Woman's Choice: The State, Sexuality, and Reproductive Freedom*. New York: Longman and Boston: Northeastern University Press.

———. 1987. "Fetal Images: The Power of Visual Culture in the Politics of Reproduction." *Feminist Studies* 13:263–92. Also published in M. Stanworth, ed., *Reproductive Technologies: Gender, Motherhood, and Medicine*, pp. 57–80. Minneapolis: University of Minnesota Press.

Rhode, Deborah L. 1993–1994. "Adolescent Pregnancy and Public Policy." *Political Science Quarterly* 108, no. 4:635–69.

Richard, Patricia Bayer. 1989. "Alternative Abortion Policies: What Are the Health Consequences?" *Social Science Quarterly* 70, no. 4: 941–55.

Robertson, John A. 1986. "Embryos, Families, and Procreative Liberty: The Legal Structure of the New Reproduction." *Southern California Law Review* 59: 939–1041.

Rothman, Barbara. 1984. *Giving Birth: Alternatives in Childbirth*. New York: Penguin.

Rothman, Barbara Katz. 1986. *The Tentative Pregnancy: Prenatal Diagnosis and the Future of Motherhood*. New York: Viking.

———. 1989. *Recreating Motherhood: Ideology and Technology in a Patriarchal Society*. New York: Norton.

Rowland, Robyn. 1987. "Technology and Motherhood: Reproductive Choice Reconsidered," *Signs* 12:512–28.

———. 1992. *Living Laboratories: Women and Reproductive Technologies*. Bloomington: Indiana University Press.

Shapiro, Thomas. 1985. *Population Control Politics: Women, Sterilization, and Reproductive Choice*. Philadelphia: Temple University Press.

Steiner, Gilbert Y., ed. 1983. *The Abortion Dispute and the American System*. Washington, D.C.: The Brookings Institution.

Wingerter, Rex B. 1987. "Fetal Protection Becomes Assault on Motherhood." *In These Times* (June 10–23): 3, 8.

Woliver, Laura R. 1989a. "The Deflective Power of Reproductive Technologies: The Impact on Women." *Women & Politics* 9, no. 3 (November): 17–47.

———. 1989b. "New Reproductive Technologies: Challenges to Women's Control of Gestation and Birth." In Robert Blank and Miriam K. Mills, eds., *Biomedical Technology and Public Policy*, pp. 43–56. Westport, Conn.: Greenwood.

———. 1990. "Reproductive Technologies and Surrogacy: Policy Concerns for Women." *Politics and the Life Sciences* 8, no. 2 (February): 185–93.

PART NINE

Gender and Politics

Sociological discussions of gender and politics have taken several different directions: empirical studies of male/female political participation; studies of the effect of U.S. welfare state policies on women; studies of social movements that have been supported by women or used to control them; and studies of the intervention of the state in organizing family life and sexuality (Ackelsberg and Diamond 1987). In this section the readings deal with two of these issues—the article by Linda Gordon is about the evolution of the birth control movement and its influence in giving male doctors legal control over women's reproduction, and the reading by Sally Avery Bermanzohn focuses on the effect of U.S. welfare state policies on women.

Gordon discusses how Margaret Sanger's original goal of giving working-class women more control over their lives evolved into a movement to control the population of immigrants and minorities. Margaret Sanger (1879–1966) was the founder of the birth control movement in the United States. She understood that although the criminalization of abortion in the 1860s and 1870s was intended as an antidote to the declining fertility rate of native white married women, it affected all women. Indeed, the impact was greatest on working-class women. Although many of them were desperate to limit the size of their families, they were less likely to know about methods of contraception or be able to afford illegal abortions than middle-class women.

Sanger's mother had eleven children and Margaret helped deliver a fourteen-and-a-half pound brother when she was eight. She remembered that her mother always had a cough, but she kept on having babies until she died of tuberculosis in her forties. Margaret's father, in contrast, lived to be eighty-four (Reed 1978).

Sanger started out as a labor radical but was increasingly angered by the callousness of her fellow radicals toward the concerns of working women. She was appalled by the misery of the wives and children of strikers and at the indifference of male labor leaders to the special needs of women. She said that, indeed, many of the labor leaders were tyrants in their own homes. Sex was one of the few pleasures these men had and they refused to limit their own enjoyment by using condoms or withdrawing (Reed 1978).

She realized that wages would never be adequate if family size was not controlled, but male socialists insisted that if the problem of wages was solved, the question of women and children would take care of itself. Sanger rejected that idea and insisted that the revolution had to begin at home. Too many children meant crowding, lack of nurturing, and more poverty. Yet these women did not use birth control—either they didn't know about it or their husbands refused to cooperate. Desperate women resorted to back-alley or self-induced abortions and many of them died as a result (Reed 1978).

Sanger, a trained nurse, claimed that the death of one of her patients from a second self-induced abortion was the traumatic event that led her to open her clinic. In 1916, Sanger and her sister opened the first center for contraceptive instruction in the United States. The clinic, in Brownsville, Brooklyn, showed women how to use diaphragms which were available in any drug store. However, Sanger and her sister were soon arrested under a state law which made it a misdemeanor to give away or sell any information about contraception (Reed 1978).

Gordon argues that while Sanger was originally motivated by her concern with working-class women's rights and autonomy, male physicians and eugenicists who took over the birth control movement in the 1920s were motivated by the wish to expand their own influence and control the reproduction of the masses. Most physicians (who happened to be male) were opposed to birth control just as they were opposed to legal abortions. For the most part, their position was based on nineteenth-century "separate spheres" ideology: The major function of women was having children and caring for them; the male sex drive is naturally greater than the female; and female chastity is protected by the fear of pregnancy. Lack of birth control information and access to abortion kept the fear of pregnancy a strong method of social control over women.

In the 1920s, only a few physicians supported birth control. Gordon blames Sanger for her conciliatory, even humble attitude toward doctors and her support for "doctors-only" type of birth control legislation which gave male doctors control over women's reproduction. Sanger saw the "doctors-only" legislation as a way of legitimizing birth control. She hoped that she could counteract the powerful anti–birth control role of the Catholic Church and defuse the impact of her own radical political background by cloaking birth control as a "medical" problem.

The eugenicists, in contrast to the physicians, supported birth control right from the beginning. Nineteenth-century eugenics was based on the idea that acquired characteristics could be inherited. By the 1920s that idea had long been discredited and the new eugenics was based on the concept of selective breeding. The eugenics movement supported immigration restrictions, miscegenation laws in the South, and birth control.

Black feminists argue that throughout this century, there has been a systematic, institutionalized denial of reproductive freedom to black women. Some focus on the attempt to limit the reproduction of blacks. They contend that the collusion of feminists and birth control advocates with the eugenicists is at the heart of black women's distrust of both the feminist and birth control movements (Roberts 1997; Davis 1983).

Gordon points out that the feminist birth controllers did, indeed, accept the racist and ethnocentric attitudes of the eugenics movement. She claims they were not attracted to eugenics because they were racists, but they had no strong tradition of antiracism on which to base a critique of eugenics. Sanger's rhetoric gradually shifted from proclaiming the rights of the masses to advocating mass sterilization. While eugenics ideology was eclipsed by the rise of the Nazis, the politics of population control is certainly evident in current debates about welfare reform.

Roberts (1997) argues that welfare reform policies are based on the notion that Aid to Families with Dependent Children (AFDC) encourages poor black women to bear children and that black illegitimacy is a major social problem. It assumes a clientele that needs state incentives or punishments to reproduce responsibly. Thus, black feminists are concerned about the state interfering with the reproductive rights of poor women by trying to limit procreation in families collecting AFDC.

Most scholarship about the welfare state does not use gender as a category of analysis. Researchers have focused on the dynamics of the labor markets, capitalist economics, and class struggle. However, a feminist critique of the welfare system begun in the 1970s, argues that the traditional studies of the welfare state—covering AFDC as well as Social Security, unemployment insurance, and most other social programs—failed to consider the ways in which social welfare programs enforced the doctrine of separate spheres as well as the work ethic and treated men and women differently. The welfare state also reproduces gender inequality. For example, Social Security and unemployment insurance benefits are wage-based. Because women generally are paid less than men, women receive lower benefits than men. Ignoring the gender wage gap reproduces inequality (Abramovitz 1996; Rose 1995).

Barbara Nelson (1990) and Diana Pearce (1990) have argued that there is a double standard in welfare provisions for men and women that is rooted in the assumption that women, especially mothers, are supported by men. The lack of gender analysis has hidden the fact that even identical welfare programs have different effects on men and women—especially mothers who already do the vast majority of parenting and housework. Since so many women's major work is taking care of children, defining whether AFDC recipients are working or malingering is highly controversial (Gordon 1990).

Rose (1995) points out that the United States has a tradition of two types of welfare programs—workfare and fair work. Workfare is based on the view that relief recipients must be forced to work; fair work is founded on the assumption that its participants want to work. Workfare is highly stigmatized and ignores the value of work in the home—it requires participants to work for low pay or no pay. Fair work programs tend to base payments on local wages and be aimed at men, whereas workfare is usually aimed at women (Rose 1995).

Bermanzohn's article in this section claims that the 1996 welfare reform bill is an example of workfare and that welfare policies in the 1980s and 1990s ignored the structural causes of poverty. She maintains that the economic transformation from an industrial-based economy to one centered on service and information, which has been going on in the United States for the past twenty years, has hit single-parent (female-headed) families particularly hard. The rhetoric, however, blames AFDC recipients for their own situations. Berman-zohn points out that the 1996 welfare reform bill is called the "Personal Responsibility and Work Opportunity Reconciliation Act of 1996." The law ends AFDC as an entitlement, replacing it with a program called "Temporary Assistance to Needy Families (TANF)," which insists that single mothers work and limits how long they can receive TANF even if they do not get a job.

We can see that state policies about birth control and AFDC are political issues and attitudes toward them change depending on economic conditions and the balance of power between pressure groups and political parties. It is important to keep in mind that these are political issues that affect men and women differently, but in both cases, men are in control of the policy-making apparatus on both state and federal levels.

REFERENCES

Abramovitz, Mimi. 1996. *Under Attack, Fighting Back: Women and Welfare in the United States.* New York: Monthly Review Press.

Ackelsberg, Martha, and Irene Diamond. 1987. "Gender and Political Life: New Directions in Political Science." Pp. 504–525 in *Analyzing Gender: A Handbook of Social Science Research,* edited by Beth Hess and Myra Marx Ferree. Newbury Park, CA: Sage Publications.

Davis, Angela. 1983. *Women, Race, and Class.* New York: Vintage.

Gordon, Linda. 1990. "The New Feminist Scholarship on the Welfare State." Pp. 9–35 in *Women, the State, and Welfare,* edited by Linda Gordon. Madison: University of Wisconsin Press.

Nelson, Barbara J. 1990. "The Origins of the Two-Channel Welfare State: Workmen's Compensation and Mothers' Aid." Pp. 123–151 in *Women, the State, and Welfare,* edited by Linda Gordon. Madison: University of Wisconsin Press.

Pearce, Diana. 1990. "Welfare is Not for Women: Why the War on Poverty Cannot Conquer the Feminization of Poverty." Pp. 265–279 in *Women, the State, and Welfare,* edited by Linda Gordon. Madison: University of Wisconsin Press.

Reed, James. 1978. *The Birth Control Movement and American Society: From Private Vice to Public Virtue.* Princeton: Princeton University Press.

Roberts, Dorothy. 1997. *Killing the Black Body: Race, Reproduction, and the Meaning of Liberty.* New York: Pantheon.

Rose, Nancy E. 1995. *Workfare or Fair Work: Women, Welfare and Government Work Programs.* New Brunswick: Rutgers University Press.

The Politics of Birth Control, 1920–1940: The Impact of Professionals

LINDA GORDON

Birth control can have three major social purposes: to increase the individual freedom of women; to control overall population trends; and to improve and protect health. When the modern birth control movement began in the early twentieth century, the first was its dominant motive. Organizations demanding the legalization of birth control were formed by feminists and other radical political activists concerned with women's rights. The medical and population control motivations for supporting birth control came primarily from other sources which entered the birth control movement later but ended by dominating it.

Beginning in the 1920s birth control as a cause was taken over by male professionals, many of them physicians, in a "planned parenthood" campaign that made women's equality and autonomy a secondary issue. In the 1970s a revived feminist movement reentered the birth control cause, mainly through campaigns for legal abortion. The existence once more of an approach to birth control primarily concerned with individual human rights has created an historical context in which it is appropriate to reexamine the historical legacies behind birth control.

In this article I argue that the influx of professionals into the cause changed the goals of the birth control movement from a campaign to increase the area of self-determination for women and all working-class people to a campaign infused with elitist values and operated in an elitist manner. These professionals were mainly of two groups: doctors and eugenists. The latter group was not, of course, a professional occupation in itself, but was mainly composed of university professors and researchers. However, professional eugenics organizations brought them together and gave them a collective consciousness as strong as that among doctors. Despite important differences, the two groups had an ultimately similar influence on birth control.

The need to identify and analyze the influence of doctors and eugenists is not merely a question of setting the historical record straight. Their impact on birth control has left serious problems today for anyone concerned with that issue. The identification of the birth control movement with the demographic theories of the population controllers and the small-family ideal of white, prosperous Americans has created antagonism to birth control among many poor people, and especially the nonwhite poor, in the United States and abroad. They often perceive population control programs as coercive, imposing alien cultural values. That antagonism to birth control is sometimes associated with an

Excerpted from "The Politics of Birth Control, 1920–1940: The Impact of Professionals" by Linda Gordon. *International Journal of Health Services* 5(2):253–277. Copyright © 1975 by the Baywood Publishing Company, Inc. Reprinted with the permission of the Baywood Publishing antagonism to feminism, especially since feminism until recently has been primarily a movement of educated and prosperous women. I would argue, on the contrary, that birth control has failed to cross class lines because it has not been feminist enough. A feminist birth control movement would struggle to expand women's options, to extend their right to choose, not to impose a certain economic or political theory upon them. For example, in the first agitation for birth control, feminists argued for the legitimacy of having children, in or out of marriage, and for mothers' and children's rights to a decent standard of living, as well as for women's rights not to have children.

After a brief survey of the state of the birth control movement in the early twentieth century, I will discuss first the general meaning of professionalization and then the roles of doctors and eugenists separately. There will not be space here for an evaluation of the new birth control movement that those groups created, mainly associated with Planned Parenthood, but I will offer some tentative conclusions.

THE BIRTH CONTROL MOVEMENT IN THE EARLY TWENTIETH CENTURY

In 1915 the issue of birth control came out into the public rather suddenly, as radicals like Emma Goldman and Margaret Sanger deliberately defied obscenity laws by distributing information on contraception. By late 1916 there was a nationwide campaign of agitation and direct action for birth control. By 1917 there were national and local organizations, run almost entirely by women, devoted to the legalization of contraception. Most of these groups considered themselves within the feminist tradition, concerned with women's right to reproductive self-determination. In many instances these organizations were connected to the Socialist Party or to local socialist and anarchist groups.

Nineteenth-century feminists had argued that involuntary childbearing and childrearing were an important cause of women's subjection. Their agitation for "voluntary motherhood,"[1] beginning in the 1870s, was limited by the prudish sexual fears and moralities that pervaded capitalist society at that time.[2] In the first decades of the twentieth century a loosening in acceptable standards of sexual conduct, particularly in the cities, made public advocacy of mechanical contraceptive devices politically possible.

Still, birth control did not immediately become respectable. Not only was it illegal, but its militant advocates were occasionally arrested on obscenity charges, though none were heavily sentenced. By the outbreak of the First World War Margaret Sanger had become the chief spokesperson for the cause. In her regular column in the *New York Call*, a Socialist Party paper, she began in 1911 to write about birth control, venereal disease, and other previously unmentionable topics. In 1914 she published seven issues of a revolutionary feminist paper, *The Woman Rebel*, which advocated birth control, printed the views of Emma Goldman, and attacked the suffrage movement for its irrelevance to working-class women. Sanger wrote that she saw birth control primarily as a means to alleviate the suffering of working-class and poor women from unwanted pregnancies, and in the long run she identified the demand for birth control as an important weapon in the class struggle.

Rejecting the path of lobbying and winning over influential people, Sanger chose direct action. In October 1916 she, her sister, and a few other women opened a birth control clinic in Brownsville, Brooklyn. She and her sister were arrested, and the publicity around their trial and imprisonment gave them a public platform from which to present their ideas. Largely through their influence, direct action became a part of the tactics of the large network of local birth control organizations that existed by 1917.

World War I, however, brought with it a sharp and effective attack on the American Left. One of the fatalities of the rightward political swing of this period was the feminist movement. Although the woman suffrage organizations went on to victory after the war, they lost their left wing—those whose analysis of women's oppression led them to demand social change more fundamental than extension of the franchise. In 1916 the birth control activists had been politically connected to the left wing of the feminists and to profeminist groups of socialists and anarchists. When these political groupings were broken up, the birth control advocates—mostly educated women and some even upper-class—floundered politically. Losing confidence in the legitimacy of the rebellion of women of their own class, they fell back into an orientation as social workers, in the tradition of the settlement houses. Their own class position often led them to isolate the birth control issue from other social and economic pressures working-class people faced; this separation made their appeals unconvincing to the working-class women they hoped to win over. The continued existence of organized feminism might have reinforced their inclination to fight for *themselves* (as the abortion movement of the 1960s and 1970s has been powerful because it has been essentially a movement of women fighting in their own interests). Without it, the birth controllers remained social workers, with the tendency to think that they knew best what was good for their "clients." Given this orientation, it was not unnatural that the birth controllers, despite their feminism, welcomed the aid of professional experts and, in many cases, sought them out.

Of those among the original birth controllers who resisted the rightward swing of the war and postwar era, many deserted the birth control movement. For most socialists, the war itself, and then the Russian Revolution and the defense of the American Left against repression, seemed the most pressing issues after 1918. They were able to change causes because most of them had seen birth control as a reform issue rather than a revolutionary demand, something requiring less than fundamental change in the society. The tendency to distinguish between fundamental and superficial change, between revolution and reform, was characteristic of those influenced by a Marxist analysis of society. Historical and material determinism argued that certain aspects of social reality determined others, and the traditional Marxist interpretation had placed matters of sexual and reproductive relations in the "superstructure," among other cultural phenomena determined ultimately by the "substructure" which was economic relations. Liberal reformers, however, did not share this view, and several groups of professionals perceived birth control as especially fundamental. Doctors saw it as a health measure, and increasingly a preventive health measure; and naturally doctors viewed human health as a fundamental, not a superficial, condition of social progress. Eugenists saw it as a race health measure; their hereditarian views led them to consider reproduction the fundamental condition of social progress. Both groups considered reproduction fundamental, and once converted, could devote themselves to the birth control cause with passion and perseverance.

PROFESSIONALISM

Professionals entering the birth control movement brought with them a unique self-image and consciousness that made their reform work an integral part of their careers. They believed, by and and large, that they worked not only to earn a living but simultaneously to help humanity, to improve society. Since they saw the content of their work as important, not merely its function in earning wages, they saw unity between their paid work and their volunteer activities. Clearly, this view is produced by the opportunity professionals have to do creative, self-directed work. There is no mystery about the relative absence of this consciousness among working-class people or businessmen. The professional attitude toward work is largely dependent on not being paid by the hour and, for higher professionals, on the opportunity to determine their own work schedules. Furthermore, many of the professionals active in birth control, particularly doctors, were not wage workers at all, but self-employed. For both kinds of professionals—employed and self-employed—participation in reform activities if respectable enough could add to their prestige in their vocation and among their colleagues.

The desire to make a contribution to civilization led many professionals to go beyond their places of employment to seek wider social influence. For many professionals, seeking political influence seemed a contribution, not an indulgence, because they believed society needed them. Especially in the early twentieth century, many professionals believed that their superior intelligence and education entitled them to a larger share of political leadership than their numbers in the population would automatically create in a true democracy. Their review of democracy was meritocratic. Edward L. Thorndike, a eugenist educator, wrote in 1920: "The argument for democracy is not that it gives power to men without distinction, but that it gives greater freedom for ability and character to attain power!"[3] Henry Goddard, who introduced the intelligence test in the United States, thought that democracy was "a method for arriving at a truly benevolent aristocracy."[4]

Behind these politics was, first of all, the assumption that superior intelligence and education were coincident with superior political virtue. Hereditarian analyses of the causes of crime supported this view—from the theory that feeble-mindedness was a major cause of crime, to the more general attitude that if crime flowed from poverty, poverty in turn was caused by lesser ability or laziness. Professional psychologists in the 1920s were engaged in developing intelligence tests, and the bias of these tests was consistently hereditarian and meritocratic: they measured ability to solve the kinds of problems urban professionals met with the kinds of solutions urban professionals would approve. Indeed, the Stanford-Binet test—for years the standard—classified intelligence in terms of what was "required" for five occupational groupings, the professions considered the highest. (The remaining were semiprofessional work, skilled labor, semiskilled labor, and unskilled labor, in descending order.)[5]

Professionals did not assume that their intellectual superiority came entirely from innate ability. On the contrary, they perceived that rigorous training in intellectual discipline, general knowledge, and tested methodologies had given them skills unavailable to the masses. They did not see their monopolization of this expertise and knowledge as special privilege because they were committed to equal opportunity. They did not usually perceive the effective social and economic barriers that kept most people from these opportunities. But they never doubted that their expertise and knowledge were useful guides for social policy. They did not hesitate to build professional organizations, institutions, and programs of self-licensing which excluded others from their privileges and influence, because they had confidence in the universality, objectivity, and social value of the expertise they possessed. Conscious, many of them, of having rejected aristocratic and plutocratic values, they did not think that their meritocratic values were antisocial or unjust. Their basic assumption was that greater intellectual ability, learned and innate, should be rewarded and entrusted with public power.

In the birth control movement, professionals behaved much as they did throughout the society. They sought to solve what had previously been ethical and political questions by objective study. In order to lend their support or even their names to the cause, they needed to be satisfied that it was honest, its strategies careful, and its tactics appropriate to their dignity. Even inside of voluntary associations, therefore, they distrusted leaders who did not share their own values, skills, and social status. Inevitably, their influence transformed birth control leagues from participatory membership associations into staff organizations.

Had the professionals merely changed the structure and methods of the birth control movement, their influence could not have worked. Structure and methods in social movements cannot be separated from goals. Despite their posture as reformers who sought changes for the benefit of the whole society, or for the less fortunate in it, in fact professional men brought to the birth control movement their own political beliefs and social needs. Molded by professional training and practice but also by class origin and individual experiences, these beliefs were by no means identical among professionals and even within one profession. But leading professionals shared a common set of values, with meritocracy at its root. The professionals of the 1920s believed that some individuals were more valuable to society than others. Whether environmentalists or hereditarians or both, they doubted that superior individuals were equally distributed within all classes and ethnic groups, and believed that scientific study could determine where talent was most likely to be born. Birth control appealed to them as a means of lowering birth rates *selectively* among those groups less likely to produce babies of great merit.

Professionals also perceived themselves as social benefactors, eager not just to legalize birth control for themselves and their wives, but anxious also to install it as social policy. Their commitment to individual liberty was tempered by their recognition that some people were wiser than others, and that good social policy would not necessarily result from allowing each individual to make private decisions about such matters as birth control. Furthermore, many professionals were placed by their jobs in positions of influencing people—doctors, social workers, educators, and psychologists, for example. Accepting meritocratic political views, they naturally taught them to others. They not only disapproved of but feared a democracy that meant that all individuals, despite their educational or intellectual qualifications, would have equal power in the society; they genuinely feared the unfortunate political decisions that might result. Goddard wrote in 1920: "The disturbing fear is that the masses—the seventy or even eighty-six million—will take matters into their own hands." Rather, he argues, they should be directed by the four million of superior intelligence.[6] This self-conscious elitism reflected not only fear but also an effort to reassure themselves of their differences from the "masses."

DOCTORS

Most physicians remained opposed to contraception in the early 1920s. The predominant position among prestigious doctors was not merely disapproval, but revulsion so hysterical that it prevented them from accepting facts. As late as 1925 Morris Fishbein, editor of the *Journal of the American Medical Association*, asserted that there were no safe and effective birth control methods.[7]

In 1926 Frederick McCann wrote that birth control had an insidious influence on the female, causing many ailments previously regarded as obscure in their origins; and that while "biology teaches" that the primary purpose of the sexual act is to reproduce, the seminal fluid also has a necessary and healthful local and general effect on the female.[8] Many doctors believed that they had a social and moral responsibility to fight the social degeneration that birth control represented. George Kosmak, a prominent gynecologist, asked rhetorically: "Is this movement to be ascribed to an honest intent to better the world, is it another expression of the spread of feministic doctrines…or is it merely another instance of one of those hysterical waves with which our civilization is so frequently assailed?"[9] The social values underlying Kosmak's opposition were extremely conservative:

> Fear of conception has been an important factor in the virtue of many unmarried girls, and ... many boys are likewise kept straight by this means ... the freedom with which this matter is now discussed ... must have an unfortunate effect on the morals of our young people. It is particularly important ... to keep such knowledge from our girls and boys, whose minds and bodies are not in a receptive frame for such information.

Running throughout Kosmak's attack was an expression of strong elitism:

> Those classes of our social system who are placed in a certain position by wealth or mental attainments, require for their upkeep and regeneration the influx of individuals from the strata which are ordinarily regarded as of a lower plane ... it is necessary for the general welfare and the maintenance of an economic balance that we have a class of the population that shall be characterized by "quantity" rather than by "quality." In other words, we need the "hewers of wood and the drawers of water" and I can only repeat the question that I have already proposed to our good friends who believe in small families, that if the "quantity" factor in our population were diminished as the result of their efforts, would they be willing to perform certain laborious tasks themselves which they now relegate to their supposed inferiors? Might I ask whether the estimable lady who considered it an honor to be arrested as a martyr to the principles advocated by Mrs. Sanger, would be willing to dispose of her own garbage at the river front rather than have one of the "quantity" delegated to this task for her?[10]

Kosmak's concern to guard accustomed privilege also applied to the particular prerogatives of his profession, and reflected the professional ideology that expertise should decide social values:

> The pamphlets which have received the stamp of authority by this self-constituted band of reformers ... are a mixture of arrant nonsense, misinformation, false reports, and in addition, in some cases,

seditious libels on the medical profession. These publications are not scientific and in most instances have been compiled by non-scientific persons.... Efforts to impress the public with their scientific character need hardly be dignified by further professional comment, and yet they are a source of such potential danger that as physicians we must lend our assistance in doing away with what is essentially indecent and obscene.... Shall we permit the prescribing of contraceptive measures and drugs, many of which are potentially dangerous, by non-medical persons, when we have so jealously guarded our legal rights as physicians against Christian Scientists, osteopaths, chiropractors, naturopaths and others who have attempted to invade the field of medical practice by a short cut without sufficient preliminary training such as is considered essential for the equipment of every medical man? Will we not by mere acquiescence favor the establishment of another school of practice, the "contraceptionists," ... if as physicians we do not raise our voices against the propaganda which is spreading like a slimy monster into our homes, our firesides, and among our young people?"[11]

In protecting his profession Kosmak was very like a craft unionist. But in his sense of responsibility for morality, his point of view was uniquely professional. The sexual values that the anti-birth-control doctors cherished were not so different from nineteenth-century conservative values: that the major function of women and sexual intercourse both was reproduction of the species; that the male sex drive is naturally greater than the female, an imbalance unfortunately but probably inevitably absorbed by prostitution; that female chastity is necessary to protect the family and its descent; and that female chastity must be enforced with severe social and legal sanctions, among which fear of pregnancy functioned effectively and naturally.

Toward Medical Birth Control

A significant minority of physicians, however, did not share these conservative values. Arguments for a higher valuation of human sexuality as an activity in itself, separate from reproduction, were expressed not only by radicals such as Dr. William Josephus Robinson but by liberal physicians as well in the early 1920s. A leading spokesman of this point of view among prestigious physicians was gynecologist Robert Latou Dickinson. He had applied his medical expertise to social problems for several decades already. He believed that mutual sexual satisfaction was essential to happy marriage. He shared the view of Kosmak and the anti-birth-controllers that doctors ought to assert moral leadership, but chose a more flexible approach. Dickinson encouraged his Ob-Gyn colleagues to take greater initiatives as marriage and sex counsellors. In his 1920 address as President of the American Gynecological Society he recommended that the group take an interest in sociological problems. He, too, disliked the radical and unscientific associations of the birth control movement. But unlike Kosmak he preferred to respond not by ignoring the movement but by taking it over, and he urged his colleagues to that strategy as early as 1916.[12]

Sensitive to the difficulties of pulling his recalcitrant colleagues into a more liberal view of contraception, Dickinson began his campaign with a typical professional gambit. In 1923 he organized a medical group to *study* contraception, with the aim of producing the first scientific and objective evaluation of its effectiveness and safety. He consciously used antiradicalism to win support for the plan. "May I ask you...whether you will lend a hand toward removing the Birth Control Clinic from the propaganda influence of the American Birth Control League...," he wrote to a potential supporter in 1925.[13] So firm was Dickinson's insistence that the group would merely study, without preformed opinion, that he was able to get Kosmak himself to serve on the committee. He got financial support from wealthy Gertrude Minturn Pinchot and a qualified endorsement from the New York Obstetrical Society.

Dickinson did not merely *use* antiradicalism; it was in part his genuine purpose. His Committee on Maternal Health (CMH), as his "study" project was called, was a reaction to Margaret Sanger's efforts to open and maintain a birth control clinic.[14] Continuing her search for medical acceptance, when she planned a second clinic beginning in 1921 she projected it primarily as a center for the medical study of contraception; the women who would receive contraception would be its research subjects. When it opened in January 1923, she called it the Clinical Research Bureau. It had a physician as its supervisor, but she was a woman, not a gynecologist but formerly employed as a public health officer by the state of Georgia—in other words, she did not have professionally impressive credentials. Furthermore, Sanger had insisted on considering social and economic problems as sufficient indications for prescribing contraception. Thus because of Sanger's alternative, many doctors, while remaining suspicious of birth control, supported Dickinson's endeavor as a lesser evil.

At first Dickinson's group was hostile to the Sanger clinic. They tried to get Sanger and Dr. Bocker, head of the Clinical Research Bureau, to accept the supervision of a panel of medical men, but failed. In 1925 Dickinson wrote a report scathingly critical of the value of Bocker's scientific work.[15] But several factors intervened to lessen this hostility and even bridge the gap between Sanger and the Committee on Maternal Health. One was the fact that the CMH clinic found it difficult to get enough patients with medical indications for contraception. The CMH insistence on avoiding publicity and open endorsement of birth control made women reluctant to try the clinic, anticipating rejection and/or moralistic condemnation of their desire for birth control. Furthermore, it was still extremely difficult to obtain diaphragms, which had to be smuggled into the country. By 1926, three years of work had produced only 124 incomplete case histories. Meanwhile, Sanger's clinic saw 1655 patients in 1925 alone, with an average of three visits each.[16]

Another factor leading toward unity between the two clinics was Sanger's conciliatory, even humble, attitude toward Dickinson and other influential doctors. The American Birth Control League (ABCL), which united some of the local birth control leagues into a national propaganda and lobbying staff organization, primarily under Sanger's control throughout the 1920s, had been courting medical endorsement since its establishment in 1921. The League accumulated massive medical mailing lists, for example, and sent out reprints of pro-birth-control articles from medical journals.[17] Sanger got her millionaire husband to pay a $10,000 yearly salary to a doctor, James F. Cooper, to tour the country speaking to medical groups for the ABCL.[18] Although even he was not immune from attacks as a quack,[19] he commanded the attention of male physicians as no woman agitator could ever have done. And Cooper's prestige was enhanced by sharing the speakers' platform with prestigious European physicians at the International Birth Control Conference held in New York in 1925 under ABCL auspices. Indeed, the prestige of the Europeans—whose medical establishment was far more enlightened on the birth control question than was the American—was sufficient to entice the president of the American Medical Association, William A. Pusey, to offer a lukewarm endorsement of birth control at that conference.[20] The ABCL kept exhaustive files, not only of letters but also from their clipping service, on every physician who appeared even mildly favorable to birth control. By 1927 they had 5484 names.[21] Sanger's standard procedure in response to letters asking for information on contraceptives was to send the writer the names of nearby sympathetic doctors. In response to criticism of her clinic from the Dickinson group in 1925, Sanger, avoiding any defensive reaction, asked the Committee on

Maternal Health to take over and run the clinic, hoping in return to be able to get licensing from the New York State Board of Charities. Dickinson demanded in return the removal of all propagandistic literature and posters, to which Sanger agreed. The scheme failed anyway, because Sanger's radical reputation, and opposition from the Catholic Church, led the State Board to refuse a license.[22] Dickinson, on the other hand, made his professional influence clear and useful to Sanger by procuring for her a $10,000 grant from the Rockefeller-backed Bureau of Social Hygiene.

Undoubtedly the largest single factor drawing doctors into the birth control movement, however, was Sanger's support for a "doctors only" type of birth control legislation, legislation that would simply strike out all restrictions on doctors' rights to prescribe contraception, giving them unlimited discretion. A corollary to Sanger's support for federal and state "doctors only" bills was her work on birth control conferences at which nonmedical personnel were excluded from the sessions which discussed the technique of contraception. At birth control conferences in 1921 and 1925 organized by the ABCL, sessions on contraception were for physicians only and by invitation only.

Meanwhile, other birth control groups, such as the Voluntary Parenthood League, continued to campaign for open bills, exempting discussion of contraception from all restrictions for anyone. These groups had substantial objections to the "doctors only" bill. In a letter to members of the Voluntary Parenthood League, President Myra Gallert wrote:

> *Yes, of course we believe in medical advice for the individual, but again how about the large mass of women who cannot reach even a clinic?...Mrs. Sanger's own pamphlet on methods finds its way through the American mails...and it is not a physician's compilation...Mrs. Sanger herself testified "that the Clinical Research Department of the American Birth Control League teaches methods so*

simple that once learned, any mother who is intelligent enough to keep a nursing bottle clean, can use them."[23]

Furthermore, the "doctors only" bills left "the whole subject"...still in the category of crime and indecency.[24] Not only did they accept the definition of sexuality without reproduction as obscene, but they also removed the technique of birth control from a woman's own control. If women could not have direct access to birth control information, they would have to get their information from doctors, accompanied by censorship at worst and moral guidance at best.

Tactically, the "doctors only" bill also had serious repercussions. As Dr. Antoinette Konikow wrote, the very advantage that its supporters liked—that it would make birth control seem safely controlled—was its worst feature "because it emasculates enthusiasm. To the uninformed the exemption seems hardly worth fighting for."[25] The very substance of the politics doctors brought to the birth control movement tended to squash widespread participation in the movement.

Many doctors, of course, believed that they had weighty reasons to oppose an "open bill." Sharing the views expressed by Kosmak in 1917, their sense of professional responsibility and importance led them to anticipate all sorts of moral and physiologic disasters should contraceptive information and devices be generally available.

A Local Birth Control League: The Massachusetts Case

The effect of concentration on a "doctors only" bill can be seen by examining the work of a local birth control league. While there were of course many differences in the histories of the local leagues, we are emphasizing here certain developments that were common to most of them while illustrating them with specifics from the Massachusetts case. A birth control group had emerged in Boston in 1916

with the arrest of a young male agitator, a Fabian socialist, for giving a police agent a pamphlet entitled "Why and How the Poor Should Not Have Many Children." Supporters of the accused, Van Kleeck Allison, organized a defense committee which later became the Birth Control League of Massachusetts (BCLM). The League members were from the beginning a coalition of radicals (Allison's fellow Fabians and members of local Socialist Party groups) and liberals (social workers and eugenics reformers in particular). As elsewhere, no doctors—with the exception of the revolutionary socialist Dr. Antoinette Konikow—were conspicuous in the movement in its first years.[26]

The BCLM members agreed in 1916 and 1917 on tactics designed to make birth control a public issue and a popular cause. They tried and often succeeded in getting publicity in the popular press, they held mass meetings and public debates, and they contacted 900 women's clubs around the state in efforts to recruit supporters. They accepted support from all quarters, and featured speakers identified as radicals. From the beginning, however, some of the socialists in the BCLM encountered a tension between offering a genuinely radical social alternative and using the support of conservative but powerful people to win immediate gains. Cerise Carman Jack, a Harvard faculty wife of radical leanings, expressed her conflicts about the tension between her radical ideas and her desire to win:

It is the same old and fundamental question that everyone who has any independence of mind encounters as soon as he tries to support a really radical movement by the contributions of the conservative.... The Settlements have...found it out and have become...crystallized around activities of a noncreative sort; the politician has found it out and is for the most part content to lose his soul in the game.... [But] half-baked radicals...[tend to] have nothing to do with any movement that savors of popularity and...think that all reforms must be approached by the narrow path of martyrdom.[27]

Cerise Jack was typical of many women of similar views when she decided in 1918 that the most important and strategic direction for her political efforts should be defense work against political repression. Birth control could wait; it would come anyway after the revolution, would "come so spontaneously wherever the radicals get control of the government, just as the war has brought suffrage...now is the time to work for the fundamentals and not for reform measures."[28]

In Massachusetts, as in many places, the immediate effect of the defection of radicals and the entrance of professionals into the Birth Control League was a period of inactivity. In 1918, birth control supporters among high professionals were still the minority. Most doctors, lawyers, ministers, and professors found birth control too radical and improper a subject for public discussion. Besides, they feared "race suicide" among their own class. But throughout the 1920s quiet but steady concentration on a "doctors only" bill by remaining birth control activists transformed medical opinion. Despite Massachusetts' special problem of strong Catholic pressure against birth control, the League got 1200 doctors to endorse its bill.[29] The principle of doctors' rights even led the by now exclusively liberal and conservative Massachusetts Birth Control League to defend radical Dr. Antoinette Konikow. She regularly lectured on sex hygiene to women, demonstrating contraceptives as she discussed birth control, and was arrested for this on February 9, 1928. She appealed to the now defunct League and her defense in fact rehabilitated the League under its old president, Blanche Ames Ames. Konikow was a difficult test case for the League to accept: a Bolshevik and a regular contributor to revolutionary socialist periodicals, she lacked a refined personal style and was rumored to be an abortionist. Nevertheless, the principle at stake was too important for the doctors to ignore: the prosecution of any physician under the obscenity statutes would have set a dangerous precedent for all physicians. The Emergency Defense Committee formed for Konikow worked out an extremely narrow line of defense: that she was not exhibiting contraceptive devices within the meaning of the law but was using them to illustrate a scientific lecture and warn against possible injuries to health.[30] This line worked and Konikow was acquitted.

The verdict stimulated renewed birth control activity and a new BCLM nucleus drew together with the goal of persuading doctors to support birth control and passing a "doctors only" bill in Massachusetts. A new board for the BCLM was chosen, and ten of the sixteen new members were physicians. The lobbying activities took all the League's time, and there was virtually no public visibility in this period. Konikow herself was extremely critical of this policy. She saw that commitment to it required maintaining a low profile and specifically meant giving up the project of a clinic. She argued, in fact, that opening a clinic would in the long run do more to bring the medical profession around than a long, slow legislative lobbying campaign.[31] Konikow's criticisms angered the League people. Possibly in retaliation, they refused to lend her the League mailing list of 1500 names to publicize her new book, *The Physicians' Manual of Birth Control*. Konikow's angry protests condemned what she saw as a new kind of organization quite different from that of the original local birth control leagues: "the relations between the Executive Board and the membership are so distant that the members do not know what the official policy of the organization is..."[32]

As Konikow had predicted, one of the consequences of this new kind of organization was failure. While the BCLM had become narrow and elitist, the opposition from the Catholic Church was based on mass support. The Birth Control League, meanwhile, had become less an organization than a professionals' lobbying group. Furthermore, no matter how decorous and conservative the League's arguments for birth control, they could not escape red-baiting and other forms of scurrilous attack. Cardinal O'Connell said that the bill was a "direct threat...towards increasing impurity and unchastity not only in our married life but...among our unmarried people..." The chief of obstetrics at a Catholic hospital said that the bill was "the essence and odor that comes from that putrid and diseased river that has its headquarters in Russia." Another opponent made the direct charge that this was a campaign supported by Moscow gold.[33] A broad opposition defeated the doctors' bill. Even non-Catholic attackers recognized the radical potential of birth control: separation of sex from reproduction, and removal of one of the main sanctions for marital chastity—involuntary pregnancy. Even had birth control never had its reputation "damaged" by association with socialists, anarchists, and Free Lovers, its content could not be disguised. This was the weak point in the conservative strategy of the BCLM, even measured against its own goals. If birth control was inherently radical, subversive of conventional morality in its *substance*, no form of persuasion could bring around those who needed and benefited from the conventional morality. The meaning of birth control could not be disguised by coating it as a medical tool.

While the Catholic Church played a particularly large role in Massachusetts, "doctors only" bills were defeated in every state in which they were proposed, even in states without large Catholic populations.[34] Indeed, the whole pattern of development of the BCLM was echoed in many local birth control leagues. After the radical originators of the movements left because of the War and other causes that seemed to them more pressing (or, in a few instances, were pushed out by professionals and conservatives), the birth control leagues fell into much lower levels of activity and energy. The impact of professionals— particularly doctors—on birth control as a social movement was to depress it, to take it out of the mass consciousness as a social issue,

even as information on contraceptives continued to be disseminated. Furthermore, the doctors did not prove successful in the 1920s even in winning the legislative and legal gains they had defined as their goals. While some birth control organizers, such as Cerise Jack of the BCLM, felt that they were torn between radical demands and effectiveness, in fact there is reason to question whether the surrender of radical demands produced any greater effectiveness at all.

The Problem of Clinics

The Massachusetts example, while typical of the national struggle for legislation legalizing birth control, was not representative of the development of birth control clinics. By 1930 there were fifty-five clinics in twenty-three cities in twelve states. In Chicago in 1923 a birth control clinic was denied a license by the City Health Commissioner, but the League secured a court order overruling him and granting a license. Judge Fisher's decision in this case marked out important legal precedents. His opinion held that the project was a clinic under the meaning of the law; that there existed contraceptive methods not injurious to health; that the actions of the Health Commissioner (who had cited Biblical passages in his letter of refusal to license!) amounted to enforcing religious doctrines, an illegal use of power; that the obscenity statutes only sought to repress "promiscuous" distribution of contraceptive information; and that "where reasonable minds differ courts should hesitate to condemn."[35]

As the clinic movement mushroomed around the country, however, conflict raged about how and by whom the clinics should be controlled. Margaret Sanger still resisted relinquishing personal control of her New York clinic to the medical profession. No doubt part of her resistance came from a desire to control things herself, especially since she had lost control of the American Birth Control League and its publication, the *Birth Control Review,* by

1929. (Sanger was undoubtedly a difficult person who did not thrive on cooperative work. Her personal struggles within the birth control movement are well described in Kennedy.)[36] But part of her resistance, too, came from disagreement with the doctors' insistence on requiring medical indications for the prescription of contraceptive devices. Her Clinical Research Bureau had consistently stretched the definition of appropriate indications; and if an appropriate medical problem that justified contraception could not be found, a patient was often referred to private doctors whose prescriptions would be less dangerous.[37] Sanger was willing to avoid an open challenge to the law on the question of indications, but she was not willing to allow close medical supervision to deprive physically healthy women of access to contraception.

She still wanted a license to guarantee the safety and stability of her clinic. When she withdrew the clinic from the auspices of the ABCL in 1928, Sanger once again approached Dickinson, requesting that he find her a medical director whose prestige might help obtain a license. Dickinson in reply demanded that the clinic be entirely turned over to a medical authority, suggesting New York Hospital. Sanger was convinced that such an affiliation would hamstring her work and refused it. Then, in April 1929, the clinic was raided by the police. A plainclothes policewoman asked for and was supplied with a contraceptive device. She even came for her second checkup to make sure her diaphragm was fitting her well, and then returned five days later with a detachment of police who arrested three nurses and two physicians, and confiscated the medical records. The last action was a mistake on the part of the police, for it could not help but unite the medical profession behind Sanger, in defense of confidential medical records. Furthermore, the policewoman had been a poor choice because the clinic doctors had indeed found pelvic abnormalities that provided a proper medical indication for giving her a diaphragm. The case was thrown out of court. (Some time later the policewoman returned to the clinic, off duty, to seek treatment for her pelvic disorders!)[38]

This episode produced good feelings between Sanger and the doctors who supported her, and Dickinson followed it up with a last attempt to persuade her to give up the clinic—this time into the hands of the New York Academy of Medicine rather than a hospital. Sanger was probably closer to acceding now than she had ever been and might have done so had it not been for countervailing pressure she was getting from another group of professionals—the eugenists. Though easily as conservative as the doctors in terms of the feminist or sexual freedom implications of birth control, they were solidly in Sanger's camp on the issue of indications. They could not be content with a medical interpretation of contraception, i.e., that its function was to prevent pathologies in mothers. The eugenists sought the kind of impact birth control might have when disseminated on a mass basis; they wanted to improve the quality of the whole population, not just protect the health of women. They also felt a certain amount of professional rivalry with the physicians. Eugenists had been among the earliest of the nonradicals to support birth control, and some of them had spoken out for it publicly even before the War. They perceived the doctors as joining the cause after it was safe, and trying to take it over from its originators.[39] Though politically conservative, their intensity of commitment to their reform panacea—selective breeding—allowed them to accept Sanger's militant rhetoric and her willingness to challenge and stretch the law. At the same time the eugenists had a great influence not only on Sanger but on the whole birth control movement.

EUGENISTS

Eugenics attitudes had attracted reformers of all varieties for nearly a century. Lacking a correct genetics, nineteenth-century eugenics was largely utopian speculations based on the assumption that acquired characteristics could be inherited. This assumption meant that there was no necessary opposition between environmentalism and heredity. The scientific discrediting of the theory of the inheritance of acquired characteristics changed the political implications of eugenics, and more narrow applications of it became dominant. Margaret Sanger described the development of eugenics succinctly: "Eugenics, which had started long before my time, had once been defined as including free love and prevention of conception.... Recently it had cropped up again in the form of selective breeding."[40] The new eugenics, "selective breeding," was rigidly elitist, intended to reproduce the entire American population in the image of those who dominated it politically and economically. The "new" eugenics was not a reform program but a justification for the status quo. Its essential argument—that the "unfit," the criminal, and the pauper were the products of congenital formations—suited the desire of its upper-class supporters to justify their own monopoly on power, privilege, and wealth.

Eugenics Ideology

New genetic theories provided reliable methods of prediction, and therefore control, of the transmittal of some identifiable physical traits, and they stimulated a great deal of scientific research into human genetics. The first eugenics organizations were research centers, such as the Eugenics Record Office and the Station for Experimental Evolution. As eugenics enthusiasts developed specific political and social proposals for action, they established organizations to spread the gospel generally and do legislative lobbying specifically. The first of these was the Eugenics Section of the American Breeders Association, set up in 1910, in 1913 human breeding became the main focus of the Association which changed its name to the American Genetic Association.

Several other organizations were established in the next decade....

The eugenics movement strongly supported immigration restriction,[41] and contributed to the development of racist fears and hatreds among many Americans. In 1928, the Committee on Selective Immigration of the American Eugenics Society recommended that future immigration be restricted to white people.[42] The movement also supported the enactment of antimiscegenation laws throughout the South,[43] and Southern racists used the respectability of eugenics to further the development of segregation. For example, the Virginia State Board of Health distributed a pamphlet among schoolchildren entitled "Eugenics in Relation to the New Family and the Law on Racial Integrity," published in 1924. It explained in eugenic terms the valiant and lonely effort of Virginia to preserve the race from the subversion fostered by the nineteen states plus the District of Columbia which permitted miscegenation. It concluded, "Let us turn a deaf ear to those who would interpret Christian brotherhood to mean racial equality."

Toward Eugenical Birth Control

When they turned their attention to "positive eugenics," most eugenists were antagonistic toward birth control. To appreciate this conflict fully, one must remember that the eugenists were concerned not only with the inadequate reproduction of the "superior," but also with a declining birth rate in general. As late as 1940, demographers worried that the net reproduction rate of the United States was below the replacement level.[44] Many eugenists clung to the mercantilist notion that a healthy economy should have a steadily growing population. In addition, they adopted the "race suicide" analyses that birth control was being practiced in a particularly dysgenic way, the best "stock" producing the fewest children. In the area of "negative" eugenics, they approved of birth limitation, of course, but preferred to see it enforced more permanently—through sterilization and the prohibition of dysgenic marriages.

The feminist content of birth control practice and propaganda was especially obnoxious to the eugenists. They feared the growing "independence" of women. Eugenists were frequently involved in propaganda for the protection of the family, and in antidivorce campaigning. The most common eugenics position was virulently antifeminist, viewing women primarily as breeders. One typical eugenist wrote in 1917: "In my view, women exist primarily for racial ends. The tendency to exempt the more refined of them from the pains and anxieties of childbearing and motherhood, although arising out of a very attractive feeling of consideration for the weaker individuals of the race, is not, admirable as it seems, in essence a moral one."[45]

While most eugenists were opposed to birth control, some were not, and all saw that they had certain common interests with the birth controllers. Some believed that while sterilization would be necessary in extreme cases, birth control could be taught to and practiced by the masses. Especially the younger eugenists and the demographer-sociologists (demography was not at this time a distinct discipline) were convinced that the trend toward smaller families was irrevocable, and that the only thing to do to counteract its dysgenic tendency was to make it universal. Finally, they shared with birth controllers an interest in sex education and freedom of speech on sexual issues.

If these factors contributed to close the gap between eugenists and birth controllers, the attitudes of the birth controllers contributed even more. While eugenists by and large opposed birth control, birth controllers did not make the reverse judgment. On the contrary, almost all birth control supporters, both leaders and followers, agreed with eugenics goals and felt that they could gain from the popularity of eugenics.

Identification with eugenics goals was, for many birth controllers, based on familiarity with the nineteenth-century radical eugenics tradition. Most of them did not immediately apprehend the transformation of eugenics by the adoption of exclusively hereditarian assumptions. Some radicals were critical of the class basis of eugenics programs, as was socialist Henry Bergen in 1920:

> *Unfortunately eugenists are impelled by their education and their associations and by the unconscious but not less potent influences of the material and social interests of their class to look upon our present environment ... as a constant factor, which not only cannot be changed but ought not to be changed.*[46]

But most socialists accepted the fundamental eugenics belief in the importance of congenital characteristics. Thus British birth controller and socialist Eden Paul wrote in 1917 that the "socialist tendency is to overrate the importance of environment, great as this undoubtedly is..."[47] Furthermore, on issues of race or ethnic differences the Left shared with the Right deep prejudices. In the same article in which Bergen identified the class function of eugenics, he endorsed the goal of using eugenics programs to improve the white race.[48] In a socialist collection of essays on birth control published in 1917 we find passages such as this:

> *Taking the coloured population in 1910 as ten millions; it would in 1930 be twenty millions; in 1950 forty millions; in 1970, eighty millions; and 1990, one hundred and sixty millions. A general prohibition of white immigration would thus, within the space of about eighty years, suffice to transform the Union into a negro realm. Now, although individual members of the Afro-American race have been able, when educated by whites, to attain the highest levels of European civilisation, negroes as a whole have not hitherto proved competent to maintain a lofty civilisation. The condition of affairs in the black republic of Haiti gives some justification for the fear that negro dominance would be disastrous.*[49]

Like the rest of the Left, the feminist birth controllers tended to accept racist and ethnocentric attitudes. As did most middle-class reformers, the feminists also had a reservoir of anti-working-class attitudes. The American feminist movement had its own traditions of elitism, in the style of Elizabeth Cady Stanton's proposal for suffrage for the educated.[50] Many feminists had been active in the temperance movement, and saw immigrants and working-class men as drunken undesirables. Anti-Catholicism particularly had been an undercurrent in the women's rights movement for decades, stimulated by Catholic opposition to prohibition and women's rights. Southern feminists used the fear of the black vote as an argument for suffrage, and were supported by the national women's suffrage organizations in doing so.[51] Birth control reformers were not attracted to eugenics *because* they were racists; rather, they had interests in common with eugenists and had no strong tradition of antiracism on which to base a critique of eugenics.

Sanger, too, had always argued the "racial" values of birth control, but as time progressed she gave less attention to feminist arguments and more to eugenical ones. "More children from the fit, less from the unfit—that is the chief issue of birth control," she wrote in 1919.[52] In *Woman and the New Race*,[53] published in 1920, she put together statistics about immigrants, their high birth rates, and low literacy rates in a manner certain to stimulate racist fears. In *The Pivot of Civilization*,[54] published in 1922, she urged applying stockbreeding techniques to society in order to avoid giving aid to "good-for-nothings" at the expense of the "good." She warned that the masses of the illiterate and "degenerate" might well destroy "our way of life." She developed favorite eugenical subthemes as well, such as the cost to the society of supporting the "unfit" in public institutions, and the waste of funds on charities that merely were putting Bandaids on sores rather than curing diseases. Society is divided into three demographic groups, she argued: the wealthy who already practiced birth control; the intelligent and responsible who wanted birth control; and the reckless and irresponsible, including "the pauper element dependent entirely upon the normal and fit members of society."[55] She shifted her imagery about such social divisions, for later in the 1920s she cited a "Princeton University authority" who had classified the United States population as twenty million intellectual, twenty-five million mediocre, forty-five million subnormal, and fifteen million feebleminded.[56] The racism and virulence of her eugenical rhetoric grew most extreme in the early 1930s. In 1932 she recommended the sterilization or segregation by sex of "the whole dysgenic population."[57] She complained that the government, which was so correctly concerned with the quality of immigrants, lacked concern for the quality of its native-born....[58]

The Decline of a People's Birth Control Movement

It is important to understand correctly the birth controllers' conversion to eugenics and their desertion of feminism. They did not disavow their earlier feminism so much as find it not useful because of the more general change in the country's political climate. Had they had deeper feminist or antiracist convictions, they might have found eugenics ideas more uncomfortable. But feeling no discomfort, they found eugenics ideas useful. They could get from the eugenists a support that they never got from the Left. The men who dominated the socialist movement did not perceive birth control as fundamental to their own interests, and their theory categorized it as a reform peripheral to the struggle of the working class. Eugenists, on the other hand, once they caught on to the idea of urging birth control upon the poor rather than condemning it among the rich, were prepared to offer active and powerful support.

Nevertheless, the professionalization of the birth control movement was identical with its takeover by men. Although women remained the majority of the membership of the large birth control organizations, the officers and the clinic directors more and more frequently became men. By 1940 Margaret Sanger had been kicked upstairs to being "honorary chairman." Men came to occupy the positions of president, general director, and all the five vice-presidents. Two of them were noted eugenists and authors of explicitly racist tracts—anti-immigrant and anti-black.[59] The only remaining woman on the board was Mrs. Mary Woodard Reinhardt, secretary....

In the 1930s eugenics went into eclipse as a mass cause. Nazi eugenic policies tarnished the image of the movement, and scientific criticisms of Galtonian genetics stripped away much of the academic respectability that had clothed eugenical racism. On the other hand, the success of birth control also contributed to the decline of eugenics....

CONCLUSION

Birth control emerged as a movement in the second decade of the century among radicals, especially feminists, who sought basic social change in sexual and class relations. By the end of the 1930s birth control was no longer a popular movement but had become a staff organization of experts lobbying for reforms on behalf of a larger constituency. I have argued that this transformation was accomplished by the large-scale entrance of professionals into the birth control cause; in this article I have singled out doctors and academic eugenists, but in the book from which this is an excerpt I have also discussed the important role of social workers....[60]

The struggle for birth control today offers opportunities for those concerned with the welfare of women and of the poor—for those concerned with social equality in general—to change its previously elitist direction. The history of the birth control movement suggests that it is possible to make of it a popular cause that reaches people of all classes if its basic principle is self-determination through increasing the real choices that people have. Legalized abortion that remains out of the price range of most women does not, for example, represent real self-determination. Offering women contraceptives without thorough, female-centered sex education does not represent self-determination. Offering women inadequately tested pills, and testing those pills on poor and nonwhite women as has been the custom of the drug companies, does not represent self-determination, nor is it likely to make poor people favorably inclined toward birth control as a reform. Similarly, it makes no sense to offer advice or contraceptives without adequate general medical care, or to offer it through disrespectful and condescending doctors. Self-determination must mean a birth control program that is part of an overall program of good medical care, education, respect, and equal opportunity for all women.

NOTES

1. L. Gordon, "Voluntary Motherhood," *Feminist Studies* 1, nos. 3–4 (1972–73): 5–22.

2. This does not mean that contraception was not practiced in the nineteenth century. In fact, there was widespread use of douches, male withdrawal, abortion, and vaginal pessaries to prevent or interrupt pregnancy.

3. C. J. Karier, "Testing for Order and Control," in *Roots of Crisis: American Education in the Twentieth Century*, ed. C. J. Karier, P. Violas, and J. Spring (Chicago: Rand-McNally, 1973), p. 122.

4. H. Goddard, *Psychology of the Normal and Subnormal* (New York: Dodd, Mead, 1919).

5. Karier, "Testing for Order and Control," p. 121.

6. Ibid., p. 122.

7. M. Fishbein, *Medical Follies* (New York: Boni & Liveright, 1925), p. 142.

8. F. McCann, "Presidential Address to League of National Life," *Medical Press and Circular,* November 3, 1926, p. 359.

9. G. Kosmak, in *Bulletin, Lying-In Hospital of the City of New York* (August 1917): 181–92.

10. Ibid.

11. Ibid.

12. D. Kennedy, *Birth Control in America: The Career of Margaret Sanger* (New Haven: Yale University Press, 1970), p. 179.

13. R. L. Dickinson, letter to J. Bentley Squier, November 10, 1925. Dickinson Manuscripts, Countway Library, Harvard University Medical School, Boston.

14. Ibid.

15. Kennedy, *Birth Control in America*, p. 191.

16. Ibid., p. 190; J. Reed, "Birth Control and the Americans: 1830–1970, Part III: Robert L. Dickinson and the Committee on Maternal Health" (Ph.D. diss., Harvard University, 1974), pp. 77–82; L. Lader, *The Margaret Sanger Story* (Garden City, N.Y.: Doubleday, 1955), p. 216.

17. F. M. Vreeland, American Birth Control League files. In "The Process of Reform with Especial Reference to Reform Groups in the Field of Population" (Ph.D. diss., University of Michigan, 1929), p. 280.

18. M. Sanger, letter to J. Noah Slee, February 22, 1925. Sanger Manuscripts, Library of Congress, Washington, D.C.

19. W. N. Wishard, Sr., "Contraception: Are Our County Societies Being Used for the American Birth Control League Propaganda?" *J. Indiana State Med. Assoc.* (May 1929): 187–89.

20. *Proceedings, Sixth International Birth Control Conference,* vol. III (New York: American Birth Control League, 1925), pp. 19–30, 49–60.

21. Vreeland, American Birth Control League files. In "The Process of Reform," p. 280.

22. Kennedy, *Birth Control in America*, pp. 193–96.

23. Mimeographed letter to Voluntary Parenthood League members from President Myra P. Gallert, December 2, 1925. Alice Park Manuscripts, Stanford University Library, Stanford, Cal.

24. M. W. Dennett, *Birth Control Laws* (New York: Frederick H. Hitchcock, 1926), pp. 72–93.

25. A. F. Konikow, "The Doctor's Dilemma in Massachusetts," *Birth Control Review* 15, no. 1 (1931): 21–22.

26. C. C. Jack, in *Birth Control Review* 2, no. 3 (1918): 7–8.

27. C. C. Jack, letter to Charles Birtwell, June 17, 1917. Ames Manuscripts, Sophia Smith Collection, Smith College Library, Northampton, Mass.

28. C. C. Jack, letter to Blanche Ames Ames, January 7, 1918. Ames Manuscripts, Sophia Smith Collection, Smith College Library, Northampton, Mass.

29. Birth Control League of Massachusetts Records, Schlesinger Library, Radcliffe College, Cambridge, Mass.

30. Ibid.

31. Konikow, "The Doctor's Dilemma."

32. Birth Control League of Massachusetts Records, Schlesinger Library, Radcliffe College, Cambridge, Mass.

33. *Boston Post*, July 25, 1916. Quoted in D. McCarrick Geig, "The Birth Control League of Massachusetts" (B.A. thesis, Simmons College, 1973), p. 21.

34. Dennett, *Birth Control Laws*, pp. 72–93.

35. Birth Control and Public Policy, Decision of Judge Harry M. Fisher of the Circuit Court of Cook County, November 23, 1929. Illinois Birth Control League, 1924 (pamphlet).

36. Kennedy, *Birth Control in America*.

37. Ibid., p. 197.

38. M. Sanger, *Autobiography* (New York: W. W. Norton, 1938), pp. 374, 402–8.

39. C. C. Little, letter to Robert L. Dickinson, October 28, 1925. Sanger Manuscripts, Library of Congress, Washington, D.C.

40. Sanger, *Autobiography*, p. 374.

41. M. Haller, *Eugenics: Hereditarian Attitudes in American Thought* (New Brunswick, N.J.: Rutgers University Press, 1963), p. 55.

42. Fourth Report, Committee on Selective Immigration, American Eugenics Society, June 30, 1928, p. 16. Anita Newcomb McGee Manuscripts, Library of Congress, Washington, D.C.

43. P. Popenoe and R. H. Johnson, *Applied Eugenics* (New York: Macmillan, 1918), pp. 294–97.

44. F. Lorimer, E. Winston, and L. K. Kiser, *Foundations of American Population Policy* (New York: Harper and Brothers, 1940), pp. 12–15.

45. S. H. Halford, "Dysgenic Tendencies of Birth-Control and of the Feminist Movement," in *Population and Birth Control,* ed. Eden and Cedar Paul (New York: Critic and Guide, 1917), p. 238.

46. H. Bergen, "Eugenics and the Social Problem," *Birth Control Review* 4, no. 4 (1920): 5–6, 15–17.

47. E. Paul. "Eugenics and Birth-Control," in *Population and Birth Control*, p. 134.

48. Bergen, "Eugenics and the Social Problem."

49. L. Quessel, "Race Suicide in the United States," in *Population and Birth Control.*

50. Letter of December 20, 1865, from Elizabeth Stanton to Martha Wright, in *Elizabeth Cady Stanton as Revealed in Her Letters, Diary and Reminiscences,* ed. T. Stanton and H. Stanton Blatch (New York: Harper and Brothers, 1922).

51. A. Kraditor, *Ideas of the Woman Suffrage Movement 1890–1920* (New York: Columbia University Press, 1965), ch. 7.

52. M. Sanger, "Why Not Birth Control Clinics in America?" *Birth Control Review* 3, no. 5 (1919): 10–11.

53. M. Sanger, *Woman and the New Race* (New York: Brentano's, 1920), p. 34.

54. M. Sanger, *The Pivot of Civilization* (New York: Brentano's, 1922), pp. 177–78.

55. Stenographic Record of the Proceedings of the First American Birth Control Conference, 1921 (New York: American Birth Control League, 1921), p. 24.

56. "The Necessity for Birth Control." Speech by Margaret Sanger in Oakland, Cal., December 19, 1928. Stenographic record in Sanger Manuscripts, Library of Congress, Washington, D.C.

57. "My Way to Peace." Speech by Margaret Sanger to New History Society, January 17, 1932. Margaret Sanger Manuscripts, Smith College Library, Northampton, Mass.

58. "The Necessity for Birth Control." Speech by Margaret Sanger.

59. Dr. Richard N. Pierson, president; Dr. Woodbridge E. Morris, general director; vice-presidents were Dr. Robert Latou Dickinson, Henry Pratt Fairchild, Frederick C. Holden, Clarence C. Little, and Charles Edward Amory Winslow. Little and Fairchild were eugenists. Winslow was closely associated with Rockefeller family enterprises.

60. Linda Gordon, *Woman's Body, Woman's Rights* (New York: Grossman/Viking, 1976).

The 1996 Welfare Law: Dismantling Aid to Families with Dependent Children

SALLY AVERY BERMANZOHN

On August 12, 1996, President Clinton stated, "today we are ending welfare as we know it," as he signed into law the "Personal Responsibility and Work Opportunity Reconciliation Act." The law dismantled Aid to Families with Dependent Children (AFDC), a federal entitlement that had served poor families for 60 years, replacing it with more limited and temporary assistance to families that could last no longer than five years in any individual's lifetime.

Why did lawmakers end a program that had served our nation's poorest families for six decades? The 1996 law reflects the ascent of conservative over liberal social policy. The assumption underlying the law is that single mothers with young children should be able to find jobs that pay enough to raise their families. This article challenges that assumption and critiques the law by analyzing recent economic and political trends and their impact on poverty. During the past two decades, the United States has been going through an economic transition that has hurt low-income people while benefiting the wealthy. A conservative political trend has intensified the problems for poor single mothers, and the 1996 welfare law is an important part of this trend.

ECONOMIC CHANGES SINCE LATE 1970s HAVE HURT POOR FAMILIES

Over the past two decades the United States has been undergoing a postindustrial transformation often called "globalization" or the "information revolution" that has dislocated many. The American economy has been changing from industrial-based to one centered on service and information. Blue-collar employees used to be the majority of workers, but by 1990 they comprised less than 30 percent of the labor force. Service and information occupations grew to account for two out of three workers. The industrial base of many urban areas declined; New York City, for example, lost 500,000 manufacturing jobs in the 1970s through the 1980s.[1] The number of unionized workers has fallen significantly. New jobs have opened in the service and information sector at lower pay than the blue-collar jobs they replaced. Many companies have been "streamlining" or "downsizing," which means firing people. Many jobs have moved overseas.

The postindustrial transformation has benefited the wealthy while it has intensified poverty among the poor. Figures 1 and 2 illustrate this trend. Since the 1980s, the rich have been getting a growing share of the country's total annual income; by 1995 the top fifth of the population received almost half of the nation's aggregate household income (see Figure 1). Poor families have lost 9 percent of their aggregate income during the eighties and early nineties (see Figure 2).

The economic transition squeezed the middle class. From the 1980s to the 1990s, the value of both the average wage and the minimum wage fell (see Figures 3 and 4). Many families

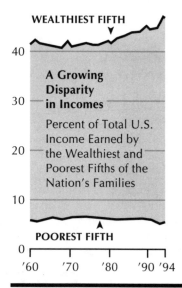

FIGURE 1 Disparity of income: the wealthiest 20 percent and the poorest 20 percent, 1960–1994

Source: U.S. Census Bureau. Graph from *New York Times,* 6/20/96.

maintained their standard of living only by increasing the number of workers in the household. Married women with young children entered the work force in large numbers. Many adult children remained in or returned to their parents' households because their low wages made it impossible for them to live independently.

To make it in today's marketplace, specialized skills and higher education are needed more than ever. Poor people with little education are most vulnerable to these economic changes, and children have fared worst. Figure 5 reveals how the percentage of children under six in poverty has increased over the past two decades. By the mid-1990s, 25 percent of young children were poor, and another 20 percent of young children were only a little better off. Thus, close to half of our children—our country's future—were growing up in or near poverty.[2] The Urban Institute predicted that the implementation of the 1996 welfare legislation would throw an additional 1.1 million children into poverty.[3]

MINIMUM WAGE DOES NOT PAY ENOUGH FOR A SINGLE PARENT TO SUPPORT A FAMILY

Proponents of the 1996 welfare law argue that work is the solution for poor women. But pushing poor mothers into the labor market does not bring them out of poverty. If a person works full time every week of the year at minimum wage, she gets an annual income of $10,712. This is calculated by multiplying $5.15 (minimum wage in 1997) by 40 hours a week times 52 weeks a year. In 1997, $893 a month is not enough to pay for shelter, food,

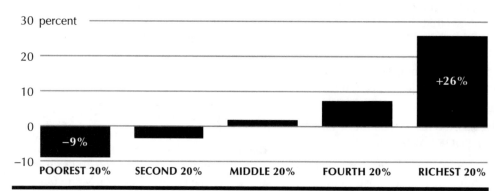

FIGURE 2 Increase or decrease in family income from 1979–1995

Source: U.S. Census Bureau. Graph from *New York Times,* 1/9/97.

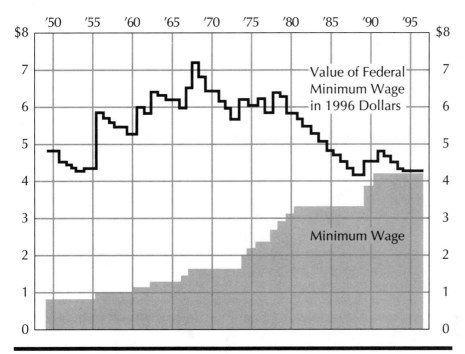

FIGURE 3   Minimum wage and value of minimum wage in inflation-adjusted 1996 dollars, 1950–1996

Source: Bureau of Labor Statistics. Graph from *New York Times,* 10/97.

clothing, transportation, and child care. In many places it barely pays the rent.

The value of minimum wage has fallen since the late 1960s, illustrated in Figure 3. Congress first legislated a minimum wage of $0.90 almost four decades ago, but has never indexed it for inflation. Over the years, Congress periodically raised minimum wage, up to $5.15 in 1997. But the cost of living has grown faster. As Figure 3 reveals, the value of minimum wage in the 1990s is lower than it was in the late 1950s. In 1998, minimum wage would need to be $7.33/hour for it to have the same purchasing power it had in 1968.[4]

SOCIAL WELFARE LEGISLATION CAN HELP OR HURT POOR PEOPLE

Aid to Families with Dependent Children (AFDC) served poor families for six decades.[5] Established in 1935 as part of the Social Secu-

rity Act, it provided federal funds for assistance to poor women raising children alone, whether the father had died, deserted the family, or never married the mother of his children. AFDC was run by the states as a "means-tested" program, meaning that to receive aid an individual had to prove poverty repeatedly through documentation. Each state government determined the amount for the grant and most of the guidelines, and the federal government provided approximately half of the funding. As a result, welfare eligibility and payments varied widely from state to state and never provided more than the bare minimum for survival. Despite its meager payments, AFDC allowed many women to raise their children. Initially the rules did not require recipients to work outside the home because society's expectation of women in those times was that they stay home and raise their children.

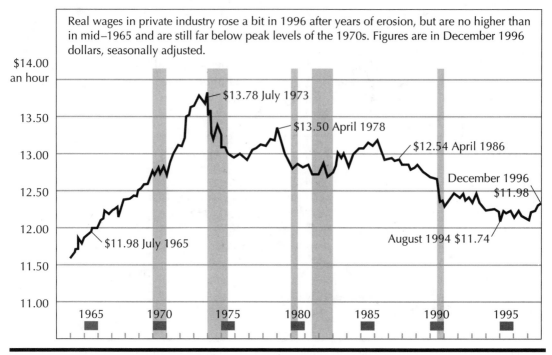

Real wages in private industry rose a bit in 1996 after years of erosion, but are no higher than in mid–1965 and are still far below peak levels of the 1970s. Figures are in December 1996 dollars, seasonally adjusted.

FIGURE 4 Value of average wage in inflation-adjusted 1996 dollars, 1965–1996
Shaded areas represent recessions.
Source: Haver Analytics. Graph from *New York Times,* 2/13/97.

Public assistance for women and children never developed widespread public popularity. The structure of AFDC meant that the program depended on state governments for funding and policies. Powerful interests in many states wanted to keep welfare payments very low and the eligibility strict to discourage applications, and so ensure that women would work at very low wages instead of getting welfare.[6] State legislatures debated welfare budgets and policies endlessly, often characterizing recipients in negative ways to keep the allocations low. Whether recipients were "moral" became a public issue, and moral directives were written into the legislation, such as prohibiting AFDC families from taking in other adults or accepting gifts. Sometimes officials made midnight raids to see if there were any men in the house. As a result of such humiliation, many women who qualified did not apply for help.

In the 1960s, social movements pushed mainstream America in a liberal direction, and Congress drafted significant new federal programs. Food stamps increased the ability of the poor to buy food, Medicare provided health care for the elderly, and Medicaid provided health care for the poor. The conditions of both the poor and middle class improved during the sixties and seventies. The percentage of people living below the poverty level in the United States declined, as illustrated in Figure 6. Congress raised the minimum wage ten times between 1960 and 1980, increasing its value relative to inflation to its highest ever in 1968 (see Figure 3). The middle class also made steady gains as their pay scales in-

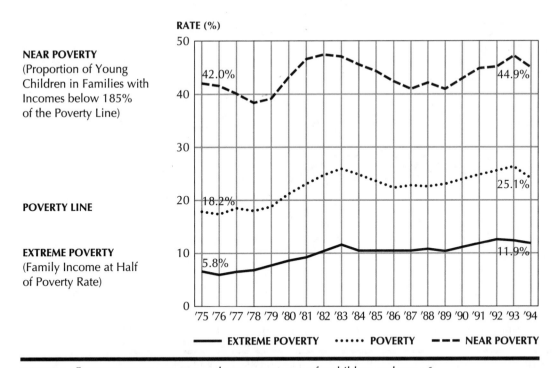

RATE (%)

NEAR POVERTY (Proportion of Young Children in Families with Incomes below 185% of the Poverty Line)

42.0%

44.9%

POVERTY LINE

18.2%

25.1%

EXTREME POVERTY (Family Income at Half of Poverty Rate)

5.8%

11.9%

'75 '76 '77 '78 '79 '80 '81 '82 '83 '84 '85 '86 '87 '88 '89 '90 '91 '92 '93 '94

—— **EXTREME POVERTY**   ⋯⋯ **POVERTY**   ——— **NEAR POVERTY**

FIGURE 5   Extreme poverty, poverty, and near poverty rates for children under age 6, 1975–1994

Source: U.S. Census Bureau. Graph from *One in Four: America's Youngest Poor,* National Center for Children in Poverty, Columbia School of Public Health, N.Y., 1996.

creased; the average wage climbed steadily, peaking in 1973 (see Figure 4).

By the mid-1970s, inflation ran into the double digits year after year, cutting the gains made in workers' salaries. Social Security payments and food stamps automatically kept up with inflation as required by law. But the only way to raise AFDC was through state legislation. States balked at increasing payments, and the value of AFDC checks declined rapidly as inflation rose. By the end of the 1970s, the real value of the average welfare check had fallen by 25 percent. Figure 6 illustrates how poverty increased among those under eighteen, while poverty diminished among older individuals, whose Social Security checks automatically grew with cost-of-living increases.

The Reagan Revolution of the 1980s ushered in a conservative trend in American pol-

itics that redistributed earnings upward, from the poor and middle classes to the wealthy. As American politics shifted to the right, Reagan cut taxes (benefiting primarily the wealthy), increased defense spending, and cut social programs. One legacy of the Reagan Revolution was the growth of income disparity between rich and poor. Figure 4 illustrates the downward trend of the value of the average wage.

The needs of poor women and the rising percentage of children in poverty pointed to increasing assistance. But since the 1980s, the trend in social policy has been in the opposite direction, with the attempt to cut back and even eliminate help to recipients. Conservative political leaders advocated tax cuts and criticized the public spending on welfare as the source of high taxes. In fact, government

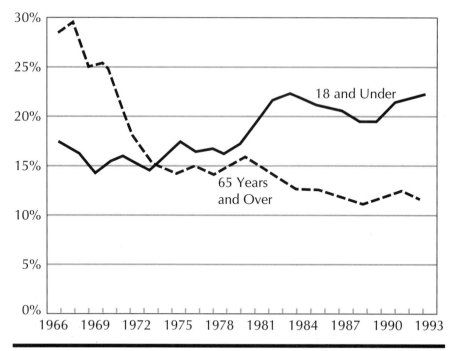

FIGURE 6   Poverty rate for persons 18 years and under and 65 years and older, 1966–1993

Source: U.S. Census Bureau. Graph from Randy Albelda and Nancy Folbre, *The War on the Poor* (New York: New Press, 1996).

spending on poverty programs has never been a large part of the federal budget. In the early 1990s, AFDC comprised only 1 percent of the federal budget.[7]

Politicians scapegoated welfare recipients in ways that distorted reality. The public image of an AFDC mother was a black woman with many children whose family has been on welfare for several generations. Although there are recipients who fit this description, the average welfare family has two children and leaves the rolls in under two years, and there are as many white recipients as black.[8] Despite the facts, politicians accused "welfare queens" of dragging down the economy. The Reagan administration embraced the right-wing policy analysis of Charles Murray. Murray rationalized the Reagan welfare cuts and

called for eliminating welfare entirely by saying that the increased federal spending of the 1970s *hurt* poor people. Murray advocated

> ... *scrapping the entire federal welfare and income-support structure for working-age persons, including AFDC, Medicaid, Food Stamps, Unemployment Insurance, Worker's Compensation, subsidized housing, disability insurance, and the rest. It would leave the working-aged person with no recourse whatsoever except the job market, family members, friends, and public or private locally funded services.*[9]

Under the Republican administrations of Reagan and Bush, AFDC was cut back but not eliminated, because the program had the support of the Democratic majorities in both houses of Congress. Senator Daniel Patrick Moynihan (Democrat from New York) spearheaded welfare reform, sponsoring the Family Support Act of 1988, a compromise between Democrats and Republicans, liberals and conservatives. Conservatives got the requirement that welfare recipients had to work or be involved in training for work. But the Family Support Act also contained money for child care, transportation, education and training programs, and provided continued Medicaid coverage for a period of time after the recipient left the welfare rolls. Under it, some states established educational opportunities and training programs, and welfare recipients flocked to them. In California, 125,000 welfare recipients enrolled in the community college system to get education and training. In New York State, thousands of students on public assistance attended City University of New York. A study of welfare recipients who graduated from four-year senior colleges in New York State found over 90 percent of them were off welfare and in the labor market or in graduate school.[10]

Meanwhile in the early 1990s, a recession hit. AFDC rolls increased, as they always do during economic downturns, and states cut back funding to implement Moynihan's welfare reform law.

1996: BILL CLINTON ENDS WELFARE AS WE KNOW IT

In his 1992 campaign, Clinton spoke eloquently about welfare reform and promised to "end welfare as we know it," but he left his meaning vague. Liberals believed he meant giving mothers more training and child care to be better able to cope in the labor market. Conservatives thought he meant simply ending welfare programs. In 1994, Republicans won majorities in both houses of Congress and passed legislation abolishing AFDC as an entitlement. Twice Clinton vetoed the legislation, but in August 1996, during the height of his reelection campaign, he signed the welfare bill into law.

The legislation's title, "Personal Responsibility and Work Opportunity Reconciliation Act of 1996," implied that poverty was due to "personal responsibility." Clinton's speech at the signing made this legislation sound like a step forward. He stated, "Today we are ending welfare as we know it.... We are taking a historic chance to make welfare what it was meant to be: a second chance, not a way of life...." The new law would restore "America's basic bargain of providing opportunity and demanding in return responsibility." He continued:

> I hope this day will be remembered not for what it ended but for what it began: a new day that offers hope, honors responsibility, rewards work and changes the terms of the debate so that no one in America ever feels again the need to criticize people who are poor or on welfare.[11]

Clinton's rhetoric is an example of how misleading words can be. Echoing Charles Murray, Clinton sounded concerned about recipients' well-being, while cutting their benefits. The law ends AFDC as an entitlement, replacing it with a program called Temporary Assistance to Needy Families (TANF). TANF is not an entitlement; if funds run out (as they did for many localities in the Great Depression), people will be denied assistance. Each state government organizes its own TANF, using federal government block grants. But the federal money will decline over time: $5.5 billion is slated to be *cut* from the federal budget to TANF over the next six years. Moreover, an individual can receive TANF for no more than five years in her lifetime, even if she cannot find a job or support her family.

Welfare rolls fell across the country as the new law went into effect. During the first half of 1997, the number of recipients fell by 750,000, or 18 percent.[12] Politicians pointed to this decline as a great success. But did leaving welfare mean these families were no longer poor? Jobs were available in many parts of the country, thanks to the continuing economic expansion of the 1990s, but most did not pay enough to bring poor families out of poverty. Single mothers leaving welfare for jobs are often worse off, not only because wages are low, but also because health benefits are rare. Moreover, the jobs are often seasonal or unstable. Surveys of former recipients in several states found that only about half had jobs.[13]

For those who continued to receive public assistance, the clock started ticking toward the five-year time limit. Under TANF, recipients must work twenty to twenty-five hours a week (thirty hours a week by the year 2000) just to receive benefits. In "workfare" programs in New York City and other places, welfare mothers work side by side with employees receiving higher compensation for the same work.[14] States have the option of allowing education and training programs to fulfill the requirements. But many states, including New York, do *not* allow enrollment in a four-year college to substitute for work, even though going to college is considered by many to be the best way to prepare for the labor force.[15] College students on public assistance in New York City have been forced out of college to participate in the city's welfare program.

Several problems loom in the future: When the economy sours and unemployment grows, what will happen to poor families? What will happen after single mothers on welfare reach the five-year lifetime limit? The 1996 welfare law blames poor people for being poor. It does nothing to alter the fact that full-time work at minimum wage leaves a single-parent family in poverty. Over the past two decades, the poor have been hit hard by both economic changes and political decisions. The new welfare law continues this trend and will result in even greater income disparity, as the poor get even poorer and the rich get richer. Debates over welfare policy has persisted for decades. The problems inherent in the 1996 welfare legislation indicate that this debate is far from over.

NOTES

1. John Mollenkopf and Manuel Castells, eds. *Dual City: The Restructuring of New York City* (New York: Russell Sage Foundation, 1991).

2. *One in Four: America's Youngest Poor,* National Center for Children in Poverty, Columbia School of Public Health, N.Y., 1996, pp. 22–24.

3. Urban Institute Report, Washington, D.C., 1996.

4. *New York Times,* 2/11/98, p. A16.

5. Originally the program was called Aid to Dependent Children (ADC), but in 1950, the name changed to Aid to Families with Dependent Children (AFDC). For a brief history of social welfare policy, see S. A. Bermanzohn, "What Is Welfare?" in *People Power and Politics,* 8th edition, Brooklyn College Departments of Political Science and Sociology (N.Y.: Simon and Schuster, 1998) pp. 131–151.

6. Mimi Abramovitz, *Regulating the Lives of Women: Social Welfare Policy from Colonial Times to the Present* (Boston: South End Press, 1988).

7. The 1994 federal budget totaled $1.6 trillion of which $16 billion (or 1 percent) was allocated for AFDC, and $25 billion (1.8 percent) for Food Stamps. *New York Times,* 11/20/94, section IV, p. 5.

8. Randy Albelda and Nancy Folbre, *The War on the Poor* (New York: New Press, 1996); *New York Times,* 12/30/97, p. 1.

9. Charles Murray, *Losing Ground: American Social Policy 1950–1980* (New York: Basic Books, 1984), pp. 227–228. See also the critiques of Murray: Robert Greenstein, "Losing Faith in 'Losing Ground,'" *New Republic,* March 25, 1985; and Christopher Jencks, *Poor Support* (New York: Basic Books, 1988).

10. Marilyn Gittell, "The Window of Opportunity," *Women's Review of Books,* Feb. 1997, p. 18.

11. *New York Times,* 8/23/96, p. A1

12. *New York Times,* 12/30/97, p. A1.

13. Ibid.

14. *New York Times,* 4/13/98, p. A1.

15. Marilyn Gittell, "Creating Social Capital at CUNY," Howard Samuels State Policy Center, New York, 1996, p. 16.

PART TEN

Gender and the Law

Many feminist sociologists and legal theorists have focused on how the secondary status of women has been reinforced by the content and interpretation of the law. Traditionally, women's secondary status in both the public and private spheres was bolstered by legal disadvantages—but women have also looked to the law to improve their political, social, and economic positions. Early feminists fought for women's suffrage, property rights, right to divorce and child custody, protection against male violence, and rights to reproductive control—with varying degrees of success (Baron 1987).

In this section the three articles are about the relationship between gender and law. Rosemarie Skaine views the law as a tool to remedy gender inequality, whereas Rosalind Pollack Petchesky argues that the Supreme Court legitimates whatever is the dominant view in national politics. In the case of women's right to abortion, Petchesky sees the Court moving to the right. The third article, "Nora," focuses on the effects of illegal abortion and is a personal memoir of a woman who had three abortions before the Supreme Court legalized it in 1973.

Skaine points out that sexual harassment is about power—and men are more likely to have power over women than vice versa. Boys and men have gender-based social power based on greater physical strength and the general cultural pattern of male dominance. Men have straightforward economic power on the job—women earn less and often depend on men for promotions or better jobs. Men also have more status or role-based social power over women generally because men monopolize the highest-status positions in so many fields—even female-dominated ones such as librarianship, teaching and nursing. Sexual harassment behavior is the use of power derived from a nonsexual sphere used to gain benefits in the sexual sphere. Thus, economic and sexual inequality reinforce each other to undercut women's potential for social and economic equality (Martin 1989).

Sexual harassment is not new to women. What is relatively new is that sexual pressure imposed on someone who is not in a position to refuse it became illegal. Catherine MacKinnon (1979) is the feminist legal scholar who first argued that sexual harassment was sex discrimination in employment and therefore should be covered by Title VII. During the late 1970s and early 1980s MacKinnon's argument was increasingly accepted—in 1980, the Equal Employment Opportunity Commission issued the first comprehensive guidelines on sexual harassment. However, it was not until 1986 that the Supreme Court ruled on a sexual harassment case and confirmed that sexual harassment is prohibited by Title VII—Catharine MacKinnon was co-counsel for the plaintiff.

Sexual harassment is part of women's lives in school as well as work, but Title VII did not cover schools. Yet, the American Association of University Women's survey on sexual harassment in America's schools found that 33 percent of girls (as compared to 18 percent of boys) of 1,600 public school students said that they had experienced unwanted advances, gestures, touching, grabbing, and so forth by teachers, other students, or other school employees (AAUW 1993). In 1972, Congress passed Title IX as part of the Education Amendments to the Civil Rights Act of 1964. Title IX stipulated that school systems create grievance procedures for sexual harassment complaints and ensures legal protection against discrimination against students and employees in educational institutions receiving federal financial assistance—which is most public and private schools.

In contrast to sexual harassment law, which did not exist before Title VII of the Civil Rights Act, the Supreme Court decision making abortion legal was a reversal of an earlier law. In 1973, in *Roe v. Wade,* the Supreme Court held that prior to viability (the point at which a fetus is able to live outside the womb) states may not interfere with a woman's right to have an abortion. The Court based women's right to abortion on the constitutional right to privacy. Under *Roe,* states could not regulate abortion during the first trimester of pregnancy. However, *Roe* was not a new position on abortion—it was the formal legalization of a position that was traditionally accepted in the United States until the 1860s.

Before the 1860s there were no laws on abortion. Abortion practice was governed by common law, inherited from England, which did not formally recognize the existence of a fetus as a life until "quickening." Quickening was the mother's experience of the baby moving, usually between the fifteenth and the eighteenth week. An unmarried or married woman who wanted to end the pregnancy could approach her family doctor and ask to be treated for a menstrual blockage. There was knowledge of various drugs and techniques to end a pregnancy and it was not considered morally or legally wrong before quickening (Petchesky 1984).

This attitude started to change around the middle of the nineteenth century. The nation's birthrate started to plummet and abortion was more frequently used by married women rather than single ones in trouble (Petchesky 1984). In 1880, only France among the nations of Western Europe had a lower ratio of children to women of childbearing age (Reed 1978). Abortion became more visible and frequently practiced among the white Protestant wives of the middle and upper class. The total white fertility rate in the United States decreased by half between 1800 and 1900, primarily because the number of children born per married woman fell from 7.04 to 3.56. The decline was due to the widespread practice of abstinence, availability of contraception, and acceptability of abortion in the decades before the Civil War (Petchesky 1984).

The two groups that were most active in making abortion illegal were the feminists and male doctors. You might find it surprising that feminists have historically been ambivalent about reproductive rights. Many early feminists supported antiabortion legislation in the 1860s and 1870s. Ironically, they opposed legalized abortion because they thought the need for it was the result of women being used for the sexual pleasure of their husbands. Elizabeth Cady Stanton said that if the husbands didn't "degrade" them with their sexual needs, the abortions wouldn't be necessary.

Physicians, on the other hand, were outspokenly against abortions for two reasons. First, the procedures became so common that nonphysicians were doing them and competing with physicians. Second, they argued that abortions allowed women to be as sexual as they wanted and that was viewed as dangerous.

If Petchesky is correct about the Supreme Court, feminists have good reason to be concerned about keeping abortion legal. She argues that the Supreme Court plays a predominantly ideological role, using legal language and techniques to resolve the tension between liberal and conservative elements—it swings in whichever way it perceives the dominant trends in national politics. We may soon see *Roe v. Wade* overthrown by the Supreme Court because a national poll reported that since 1989, supporters of generally available legal abortion have declined from 40 percent to 32 percent (Goldberg and Elder 1998). Public opinion in the United States seems to be moving in the direction of limiting access to abortion. In addition, physicians are increasingly loathe to perform abortions. The majority of the 1.5 million abortions performed each year are done by a diminishing group of doctors who are old enough to remember what it was like when abortions were not legal (Hitt 1998). Thus, access to abortions is becoming increasingly limited both because of the small number of doctors willing and able to perform them and the increasing stipulations about when and under what conditions they may be performed. Not all women are affected in the same way. Ross (1998) points out that when contraceptives were unavailable and abortion was illegal, 80 percent of deaths caused by illegal abortions in New York in the 1960s involved black and Puerto Rican women.

Antiabortion activists have been increasingly successful in electing abortion rights opponents to Congress and state legislatures. They are making inroads on the state level by getting states to enact measures that hinder access to abortion; in 1997, 31 states enacted 55 such laws as compared to 9 states passing only 14 laws in 1996. Congress is also increasingly antiabortion. The National Abortion and Reproductive Action League reported that only 33 out of 100 senators and only 131 out of 435 members of the House of Representatives were reliable supporters of abortion rights. The increasing power of the antiabortion rights forces is reflected in the fact that Congress has held 81 votes on abortion measures since the Republicans took control in 1995 and abortion opponents won all but 10 of them (Seelye 1998).

Abortion and sexual harassment laws are examples of the importance of law in reinforcing gender inequality or remedying it. Skaine seems hopeful that we are moving toward greater use of the law as a remedy for gender inequality. On the other hand, if Petchesky is correct, the law is eminently political, subject to the ebb and flow of politics, and the right to legal abortion is in jeopardy.

REFERENCES

AAUW. 1993. *Hostile Hallways: The AAUW Survey on Sexual Harassment in America's Schools.* Washington, D.C.: AAUW.

Baron, Ava. 1987. "Feminist Legal Strategies: The Powers of Difference." Pp. 474–503 in *Analyzing Gender: A Handbook of Social Science Research,* edited by Beth B. Hess and Myra Marx Ferree. Thousand Oaks, CA: Sage Publications.

Goldberg, Carey, and Janet Elder. 1998. "Public Still Backs Abortion, But Wants Limits, Poll Says." *New York Times,* January 16: A1, A16.

Hitt, Jack. 1998. "Who Will Do Abortions Here?" *New York Times Magazine,* January 18; 20–27, 42, 45, 46, 54, 55.

MacKinnon, Catharine. 1979. *Sexual Harassment of Working Women: A Case of Sex Discrimination.* New Haven: Yale University Press.

Martin, Susan Ehrlich. 1989. "Sexual Harassment: The Link Joining Gender Stratification, Sexuality, and Women's Economic Status." Pp. 57–73 in *Women: A Feminist Perspective, Fourth Edition,* edited by Jo Freeman. Mountain Valley, CA: Mayfield Publishers.

Petchesky, Rosalind Pollack. 1984. *Abortion and Woman's Choice: The State, Sexuality and Reproductive Freedom.* New York: Longman.

Reed, James. 1978. *The Birth Control Movement and American Society: From Private Vice to Public Virtue.* Princeton: Princeton University Press.

Ross, Loretta. 1998. "African-American Women and Abortion." Pp. 161–207 in *Abortion Wars: A Half Century of Struggle, 1950–2000,* edited by Rickie Solinger. Berkeley: University of California Press.

Seelye, Katharine Q. 1998. "Advocates of Abortion Rights Report a Rise in Restrictions." *New York Times,* January 15: A16.

Defining Sexual Harassment

ROSEMARIE SKAINE

Know thyself.
—Socrates

Defining sexual harassment is both simple and complex. It is simple because it is defined as unwelcome sexual behavior by one person against another person; if it is unwelcome, it is sexual harassment. It is complex because it can involve behaviors that in other contexts are considered positive and reaffirming.

OPERATIONAL DEFINITION

By law, sexual harassment is a form of sex discrimination. Operationally, the definition that has the widest acceptance and greatest force is that formulated by the U.S. Equal Employment Opportunity Commission (EEOC) and upheld by the U.S. Supreme Court. The EEOC defines sexual harassment thus: "Unwelcome sexual advances, requests for sexual favors, and other verbal or physical conduct of a sexual nature constitute sexual harassment when submission or rejection of this conduct explicitly or implicitly affects an individual's employment, unreasonably interferes with an individual's work performance or creates an intimidating, hostile or offensive work envi-

ronment."[1] Federal and state courts have applied this definition to work and educational settings. An early study reported 49 percent of the institutional definitions received derived their content from the guidelines on sexual harassment issued by the Equal Employment Opportunity Commission. The other 51 percent of the definitions received were a mixture.[2]

SOCIOLOGICAL DEFINITION

While sexual harassment affects both women and men, it is not gender neutral: the victim is usually a woman and the harasser is usually a man.[3] Like rape, sexual harassment is not about love or romance, it is about social control. It is often a power bid. When Anita Hill's sexual harassment charges against Clarence Thomas surfaced during the confirmation hearings for Thomas as a nominee for the U.S. Supreme Court, Gibbs says that the outpouring of testimony from women who had been harassed helped lawyers explain that sexual harassment is not about civility, not about a man making an unwelcome pass, telling a dirty joke, or commenting on someone's appearance: "rather it is an abuse of power in which a worker who depends for her livelihood and professional survival on the goodwill of a supervisor is made to feel vulnerable."[4]

TYPES

The two types of sexual harassment are *quid pro quo* and hostile environment. *Quid pro quo* harassment exists when an employee's supervisor or a person of higher employment rank demands sexual favors from a subordinate in exchange for tangible job benefits. Hostile environment or environmental harassment is a pattern of intimidating, hostile, or offensive behaviors that affect the person being harassed.

FORMS

Sexual harassment takes many forms. The forms range from easy-to-identify sexual behaviors to subtle and not so subtle nonsexual behaviors. Easy-to-identify sexual forms are: an open invitation for sexual intercourse in exchange for a favor, stroking, squeezing, assaultive hugs, pinching, grabbing, offensive sexual comments, rape, and attempted rape. Subtle nonsexual forms are: staring, intimidating through silence, and innuendo. Not-so-subtle nonsexual forms are: isolating, altering a person's job responsibility, and terminating a person's job. The prevalent form of harassment varies with the type of occupation. For example, women in menial jobs are more commonly the target of physical violence.

In her book *Backlash: The Undeclared War Against American Women*, Susan Faludi explains that sexual harassment is more than a woman being grabbed and being told she will be fired if she does not go along. It is the more subtle form of making a woman uncomfortable by saying, "What's the matter, you can't

handle it? You wanted equality: I'm going to give it to you with a vengeance." Faludi expands: "It's a slow, relentless accumulation of slights and insults that add up to the same thing—the message that we don't want you here and we are going to make your hours here uncomfortable."[5]

So what is sexual harassment anyway? It is a continuum running from gestures to assault. It is fused to an ideology that places all behavior in the context of male power. Flirting and jokes are fine, rape is bad, but increasingly sociologists say they all send the same disempowering message to women.[6] Male dominance brings with it its counterpart, female compliance. If women act powerless at work, they will almost certainly be taken advantage of.

SETTINGS

Sexual harassment occurs almost everywhere in our society: on the job, in educational settings, in the home, in social settings, in the streets, in churches, in housing....

SOCIOECONOMIC DIMENSIONS

Sexual harassment has socioeconomic dimensions. Wendy Reid Crisp, director of the National Association for Female Executives, the largest women's professional association, says, "We define this issue as economic intimidation."[7] Economic intimidation is a factor we should not underestimate. We are talking about survival, whether we discuss sexual harassment as a single instance of a severe form or as a pattern of harassing behaviors over time.

The first victims of sexual harassment through economic intimidation were female slaves in American colonial times. Later, during the Industrial Revolution, women who were forced to enter the workforce and were a cheap labor source were victimized. In the post–World War II era, as more women entered the workplace, women across the economic and social spectra were affected. Ironically, as women became more free and were empowered by the sexual revolution, the women's liberation movement, and the Civil Rights Act of 1964, more of them became victims of sexual harassment.

LEGAL DIMENSIONS

Federal Laws Governing Sexual Harassment

Federal laws treating sexual harassment are Title VII of the Civil Rights Act of 1964, Title IX of the 1972 Education Amendments, and Titles I, II, and III of the Civil Rights Act of 1991. Title VII of the 1964 Civil Rights Act prohibits sex discrimination in employment. The victim must prove that harassment is a form of sex discrimination.[8] Title IX of the 1972 Education Amendments prohibits sex discrimination in education. Title I of the 1991 Civil Rights Act expands the rights of sexual harassment victims to enable them to collect monetary damages.[9] Title II, commonly referred to as the "Glass Ceiling Act of 1991," encourages corporate practices and policies that promote opportunities for, and eliminate artificial barriers to, the advancement of women and minorities into higher-level positions.[10] Title III establishes fair employment practices for government employees who were previously not covered. Now covered are employees of the House of Representatives, the Senate, and the Executive Office of the President. Protection is also extended to other employees of the executive branch and to some state and local employees not covered by current federal laws, such as political appointees.[11]

Enforcement of Title VII harassment cases is within the jurisdiction of the Equal Employment Opportunity Commission (EEOC). Enforcement of Title IX rests with the Department of Education, Office for Civil Rights. Title III of the 1991 Civil Rights is enforced through internal mechanisms of the Congress and the Executive Office of the President.

State Laws Governing Sexual Harassment

The states that have laws on sexual harassment vary in their approach. At one end of the continuum are states with very detailed laws that define sexual harassment extensively and explicitly, and include sexual harassment policies for state employees; at the opposite end are states that have only clauses within laws and these clauses are subject to legal interpretation. In the middle of the continuum are states that have a brief section on sexual harassment or have clauses on discrimination only.

State laws also vary as to how sexual harassment is to be litigated. An individual who seeks to file a complaint within the state's legal system should be aware of the laws of that state. A victim should also be aware that enforcement of these laws varies from state to state. Each state assigns enforcement to a particular state agency or agencies, such as the state civil rights commission or even the office of the state's attorney general.

EEOC Guidelines

In 1980 the EEOC issued guidelines to define sexual harassment. These guidelines were updated in 1988.

They have been important for all people involved with the issue of sexual harassment. They have figured in numerous court decisions. These guidelines are just that, guidelines, and it has been the evolving case law that has defined sexual harassment ever more precisely and resolved key issues, such as employer liability.

Case Law

Court cases help define and determine the meaning of the law and, as such, constitute case law.[12] The first court cases dealt with charges of *quid pro quo* harassment. Initially, district courts ruled that sexual harassment was not sex discrimination under the law. Four of the first five early cases were decided that way.[13] The first decision finding that sexual harassment violated Title VII was in the case of *Williams v. Saxbe* in the District Court of the District of Columbia in 1976.[14] On appeal, the decisions in all four cases determining that sexual harassment was not sex discrimination were reversed.[15] *Quid pro quo* sexual harassment reached the U.S. Supreme Court in 1986 in the *Meritor Savings Bank v. Vinson* case. The Supreme Court affirmed that *quid pro quo* sexual harassment was a form of sex discrimination under Title VII.[16]

Environmental harassment is more commonly called hostile environment. The criteria for hostile environment harassment were set down in 1982 by the U.S. 11th Circuit Court of Appeals in the *Henson v. City of Dundee*.[17] The Henson hostile environment criteria were later confirmed by the Supreme Court in the Meritor case.[18] In the Meritor case, the Supreme Court affirmed that a victim may comply voluntarily with a sexually harassing behavior but may not welcome it. If it is *unwelcome*, it is sexual harassment. The Meritor case was precedent setting also because it established employer liability for acts of sexual harassment committed by its employees. The Court ruled that *quid pro quo* and environmental harassment are two distinct claims, but that they can and often do occur at the same time. It is necessary to distinguish between them when employer liability is being determined; the employer is always liable in *quid pro quo* harassment but may not always be liable in hostile environment cases.

Recent court decisions have greatly expanded the victim's rights in sexual harassment cases. In January 1991 a Florida court extended hostile environment to include photographs and language. The case, *Robinson v. Jacksonville Shipyards*, involved a female ship-

yard worker. The court ruled the nude pinups in a workplace constitute illegal harassment.[19] About a week later, in *Ellison v. Brady,* a three-judge federal appeals court panel in San Francisco ruled that in cases where men and women might see a pattern of behavior differently, the deciding factor should be whether "a reasonable woman" might feel threatened. The court concluded that the "perspective of a reasonable woman rather than that of reasonable person, is adopted primarily because of belief that sex-blind reasonable person standard tends to be male-biased and tends systematically to ignore experiences of women."[20]

On February 26, 1992, the U.S. Supreme Court significantly expanded protection for student victims. For the first time, students have the right to win monetary damages from schools that receive federal funds. The case involved a Georgia high school student, Christine Franklin. The law at issue in this case was Title IX, which prohibits schools that receive federal funds from discrimination but does not give alleged victims the explicit right to file lawsuits. This decision provides strong motivation for schools to engage in a proactive strategy to prevent sexual harassment.[21]

The U.S. Supreme Court on November 9, 1993, in *Harris v. Forklift Systems,* ruled that to be actionable as abusive work environment harassment conduct need not seriously affect an employee's psychological well-being or lead the plaintiff to suffer injury.[22] Thus, the Court reaffirmed the *Meritor Savings Bank v. Vinson,* 477 U.S. 57, Title VII, and hostile environment. "This standard requires an objectively hostile or abusive environment—one that a reasonable person would find hostile or abusive—as well as the victim's subjective perception that the environment is abusive."[23]

Federal and state laws that govern sexual harassment are being changed. Case law is still evolving. It will be years before laws and case law become settled, because we as a society are still exploring the dimensions of sexual harassment. Gibbs writes that the Hill-

Thomas hearings were a "crash course" making it clear that most women and men, especially most senators, had only the barest understanding of the power of the law. She maintains that the courts have worked out the law, but most Americans have not. Debates are heated when people try to decide what constitutes a "hostile working envirnoment." Charles Looney, regional director of the EEOC, New England office in Boston, believes the courts are more concerned with the woman's reaction than the man's intent. "If I run a stop sign," he says, "I have broken the law even if I did not intend to.... People can create hostile environments without knowing that it would be considered sexual harassment, but they are still liable."[24]

SEXISM AND SEXUAL HARASSMENT

Sexism and sexual harassment are related. Sexism is the pattern of institutional and societal responses that determines an individual's roles and status on the basis of gender. It sets up artificial patterns to which a person is pressured to conform. Sexism produces sexual harassment when a person, usually a woman, is harassed for behaving contrary to the expectations of society or of particular individuals. Susan Rubenstein, an attorney in San Francisco who specializes in sexual harassment cases, says, "A secretary will get harassed before a lawyer, a paralegal will get harassed before an associate."[25] Gibbs adds, "Particularly in male bastions, women find that feminism becomes, ironically, a weapon in the attack."

GENDER HARASSMENT AND SEXUAL HARASSMENT

In the abstract, gender harassment or intimidation has no sexual aspect, although it is directed solely against one sex.[26] I have concluded that, in practice, a vital relationship exists between gender harassment and sexual harassment. Sexual harassment is interpreted in the context of women's work and sex roles. Because women as a group are seen to occupy a structurally inferior and distinct place, sexual harassment is a reminder of a woman's lower status. Her sexuality is used to reinforce her status as a worker. Sexual harassment is used to perpetuate her status as a subordinate, particularly when she is fearful that her job will be altered or that she will be fired. Thus a subtle and unfortunate employment consequence of sexual harassment is the curtailment of women's ambitions."[27] The "glass ceiling" provisions of the Civil Rights Act of 1991 are intended to correct some of these consequences; they incorporate measures designed to enable women to realize their potential. These provisions are designed primarily to enable women on the upper end of the corporate ladder to advance. The Glass Ceiling Commission studies corporate practices, rather than actual employees who are affected by such practices.

The term *glass ceiling* was popularized in "The Corporate Woman" report in the March 24, 1986, edition of *The Wall Street Journal*. It "refers to artificial barriers based on attitudinal or organizational bias that prevent qualified minorities and women from advancing into mid- and senior-level management positions."[28] The U.S. Department of Labor collected evidence from its routine compliance reviews of federal contractors. This research showed that while minorities and women have made significant gains in entering the workforce, there are still relatively few minorities and women in mid- and senior-level management positions. The department then initiated a pilot project to investigate the glass ceiling in corporate America. This effort involved corporate management reviews of nine *Fortune* 500 companies, evaluation of independent research, and lengthy discussions with representatives from business, labor, women's, and civil rights organizations. Each of the nine companies reviewed had a level beyond which minorities and women had not advanced. In addition, this ceiling was at a much lower management level than first thought, and minorities plateaued at lower levels of the workforce than women. The Labor Department also found that companies needed to improve monitoring of minorities and women for equal access and opportunity for promotion, and monitoring of compensation policies that determine salary, bonuses, incentives, and perquisites for minorities and women in staff positions. The department also found that the companies had inadequate record keeping in recruitment, employment, and developmental activities for management-type positions.

At the same time, the department identified some barriers. Recruitment practices relied on networking and word-of-mouth and did not make known affirmative action and equal employment opportunity (EEO) requirements. Management development and training programs and career-enhancing assignments often were not available to minorities and women. Corporate accountability for EEO responsibilities did not reach the senior-level executives and decision makers. From the beginning, the Labor Department's aim was "to encourage industry that it is in its own best interest to provide equal career advancement opportunities to minorities and so as to develop all of their human resources—to identify and voluntarily resolve any impediments to equal opportunity which may exist."[29]

Secretary of Labor Lynn Martin announced the program to "dismantle the glass ceiling—barriers that keep qualified minorities and women from moving up in corporate America." Martin contends that we have to unleash the full potential of the American workforce if we are to compete successfully in today's global market. Unleashing the potential means to her that "the time has come to tear down, to dismantle, to remove and to shatter—the 'Glass Ceiling.'" Martin concludes that the department could not generalize about corporate practices because every

company is different. It found a number of companies on the cutting edge of promoting diversity in the workforce. Most of the companies truly believed they were fulfilling their obligations in developing individuals, but they did not make these opportunities as available to minorities and women. A number of corporations are taking a hard look at themselves. Forcefully, Martin concludes, "We must do everything in our power to ensure that each and every individual counts. When the litmus test for success is ability, and ability alone, only then can we become a color and sex blind society." Over the next decade, white males will make up only 15 percent of the net growth in our workforce; therefore, American businesses are beginning to understand that their bottom-line success may well depend on recruiting, training, and retraining the best possible workforce. Given today's demographics, that means recruiting minorities including the physically handicapped and women.[30] About three months after the publication of this study, the U.S. Congress included glass ceiling provisions in the Civil Rights Act of 1991.

The "Glass Ceiling" part of the Civil Rights Act of 1991 does not create new legal protections for women workers, although the findings and recommendations of the Glass Ceiling Commission's study should help employers design more inclusive management development policies.[31] The Department of Labor is beginning the effort to dismantle the glass ceiling. Perhaps the glass ceiling efforts will have a trickle-down effect for qualified women in positions on the lower rungs on the socioeconomic ladder. Can the study reduce or eliminate the artificial barriers in institutions of higher learning which keep qualified women and minorities in the secretarial and other nonacademic professions from advancing to faculty and administrative positions? In my opinion, little is being done to address "women's" jobs. Faley agrees that, despite statutes and presidential orders forbidding policies and procedures that foster a sex-segregated work climate, nearly 75 percent of working women are still employed in "women's" jobs or in job categories or workplaces that are segregated on the basis of sex yet controlled by men.[32] Faley considers the potential of such environments and concludes that it is no surprise that surveys in the late 1970s and early 1980s have reported the incidence of sexual harassment to be quite high. Faley, Gutek, and others agree that most attention has been and is being given to women in highly prestigious positions and in academia. This lack of attention to the majority of American women may be perhaps one of the reasons why the Civil Rights Act of 1991 could prove to be a small victory for women.

The Department of Labor wasted no time in evaluating the effects of the glass ceiling legislation. In August 1992 it published "Pipelines of Progress," which examines what has occurred and is occurring in the United States to ensure that artificial barriers are broken so that merit can determine the career advancement of talented minorities and women.[33] This report is a good news–bad news document. The good news is that, in just a year, the participation rates of minorities and women in corporate management have improved. The bad news is that surveys in the corporate world do not point to an optimistic future unless commitments to positive change are sustained and enhanced. The report also underscores the fact that the challenge to shatter the glass ceiling takes far more time and effort than even the strongest of commitments produced in one year.

Another ceiling for women is the "stained-glass ceiling." Women are often excluded from the highest ranks of some religious denominations and are also excluded from the priesthood in the Roman Catholic Church. According to one editor, "At a time when women are increasingly accepted on an equal footing with men in society at large, they have yet to break into the hierarchy of the Roman Catholic Church. The men who lead the church say that will never change."[34]

Two years after the *Pipelines* progress report, in 1994, the Women's Bureau of the U.S. Department of Labor issued a report, *Working Women Count,* which reflected the concerns and experiences of over a quarter of a million women.[35] Women make up nearly half of the workforce. Although 79 percent of women respondents said they loved or liked their jobs, there was a powerful consensus about what is wrong with their jobs. Work women do, whether in the home or on the work site, continues to be devalued, and thus frustration with the signs of inequality both visible and invisible also continues. Women are compensated less than men even though they are often the sole support of their households, hold a like level of responsibility on the job, and make a societal contribution. Problems with child care affect families of all economic classes. Benefits such as health, pension, vacation, and sick leave are in need of change. More than half (61 percent) say they have little or no ability to advance. The figure increases to 69 percent for blue-collar workers and 70 percent for technical workers. Women with families, women who work part-time, older women, and women of color find themselves more economically disadvantaged in the world of work. Yet some women with more education find their work is not rewarded as much as a male's.

These results are indeed a challenge to build high-performance workplaces that will value women as equal partners in American life, the report adds. Although the Clinton administration has much to its credit, perhaps government cannot do it all. According to this report, we must build a national consensus for change. To me, when women are valued as equal, women will be paid fairly and treated fairly. I think it is very hard for males acculturated with traditional values to let go and empower women to advance. Part of the reluctance may be economic, but when the older, established white male who finds he cannot let go and empower, it is more likely due to his traditional values rather than to an economic threat. Yet some of those same males most likely realize that change is on the horizon, for they can permit educated, professional, and sometimes younger women to advance. The real question is whether the educated, professional women also get pay commensurate with that of their male counterparts. And those very few females who are promoted from entry-level or other lower hierarchical—do they also get the responsibility and authority that go with the title and the higher pay? Or are they given the trappings but not the job? Societal change takes place slowly, but I think it has begun. The change is central to eradicating sexual harassment.

MISCONCEPTIONS

What the misconceptions are about sexual harassment may depend on where you work or go to school, or where you find yourself at a given point in time, on a bus, for example, somewhere other than your hometown. Some frequent misconceptions about sexual harassment I have heard are (1) it is only physical in nature; (2) it occurs only because the harasser wants "sex"; (3) only certain types of people are harassed; (4) the person harassed is usually at fault; (5) only women are harassed; and (6) only men are sexual harassers.

Sexual Harassment Is Only Physical in Nature

For a time, many people thought sexual harassment was only physical in nature. Some employers or supervisors would use the phrase "There is no loaded gun." In fact, most incidences of sexual harassment are not physical, they are verbal. The next most frequent is nonverbal behavior. The third most frequent is the physical. It is true, however, that the physical is considered the most serious by the courts, because it can qualify as assault.[36]

Sexual Harassment Occurs Only Because the Harasser Wants "Sex"

A person who harasses may want a sexual relationship with the person being harassed, but often the harassment occurs as a power bid or to punish a person occupying a nontraditional role—for example, a woman in construction work, which is considered a male occupation.

Only Certain Types of People Are Sexually Harassed

Although all types of persons are sexually harassed—rich or poor, young or old, attractive or unattractive, female or male—usually women are the targets of harassment.

The Person Being Sexually Harassed Is Usually at Fault

The evidence demonstrates that the person who harasses usually is at fault. The determination of fault, however, is decided on a case-by-case basis. "In determining whether alleged conduct constitutes sexual harassment, the [Equal Employment Opportunity] Commission will look at the record as a whole and at the totality of the circumstances, such as the nature of the sexual advances and the context in which the alleged incidents occurred. The determination of the legality of a particular action will be made from the facts, on a case by case basis."[37] Some contend that if actual intercourse takes place without the exercise of force, the woman has given her permission. The *Meritor Savings Bank v. Vinson* case clearly spells out that a woman can voluntarily comply but still not welcome a sexual act. In my experience, the "voluntary-unwelcome" aspect is a woefully misunderstood part of the law surrounding sexual harassment. Marcia Mullikin clarifies the point: "Many women particularly feel they have no recourse for claiming sexual harassment if they've had a sexual relationship with their boss at some point, [but] consent can't be given when one person has something to lose and the other doesn't."[38] Even if someone has had a consensual sexual relationship in the past, that person may not wish to continue it. If it becomes unwelcome, then it is sexual harassment.

Only Women Are Sexually Harassed

Studies reveal that both men and women are harassed. The U.S. Merit Systems Protection Board reported that 42 percent of the women in both its 1980 and 1988 surveys of federal merit system employees responded that they had been harassed. A surprising 15 percent of the men in 1980 and 14 percent in 1988 said they had been sexually harassed. Maypole and Skaine reported that 8 percent of the men responding in their study of blue-collar workers said they had been harassed.[39] Most studies reflect these percentages.

Only Men Are Sexual Harassers

Usually men are the harassers, but women have also been reported to have harassed others. The Merit Systems Protection Board statistics show that 60 percent of the male victims were harassed by a woman and that 12 percent of the men were harassed by two or more females. Three percent of the women were harassed by another woman. Twenty-two percent of the men were sexually harassed by one or more men.[40] Most studies reflect similar percentages.

An Iowa district court rejected a man's contention that he was sexually harassed by his female boss. The evidence clearly showed that the female boss sat on the male victim's lap during breaks, touched him on the buttocks, and engaged in similar physical acts and conduct with him and other male employees, yet the judge did not find in favor of the male complainant. He ruled, that "the conduct was more in the nature of friendly horseplay in an atmosphere of camaraderie and did not create a continuous pervasively sexually hostile work environment affecting the conditions of his employment."[41] The judge was in error in this case, but it does illustrate that women do harass men. This male victim was no more believed than his counterpart, the female victim. It will not help anyone, woman or man, if there are many bad decisions like this one....

NOTES

1. EEOC, *Facts About Sexual Harassment* (Washington, D.C.: n.d.) Equal Employment Opportunity Commission.

2. Claire Robertson, Constance E. Dyer, and D'Ann Campbell, "Campus Harassment: Sexual Harassment Policies and Procedures at Institutions of Higher Learning," *Signs* 13:4 (Summer 1988), 805.

3. Studies conducted over the last 18 years have shown the percentage of women who have been sexually harassed ranges from 30 to 70. The percentage of men ranges from 3 to 15. The same studies show that the clear majority of harassers are men.

4. Nancy Gibbs, "Office Crimes," *Time*, Oct. 21, 1991, 53.

5. Susan Faludi, *Backlash: The Undeclared War Against American Women*, 1st ed. (New York: Crown, 1991) quoted in Nancy Gibbs, "Office Crimes," 53–54.

6. Frances Grossman, in Gibbs.

7. Wendy Reid Crisp, in Gibbs.

8. Alliance Against Sexual Coercion, *Sexual Harassment at the Workplace* (Cambridge, Mass.: AASC, 1977).

9. *Civil Rights Act of 1991* (§ 1745), "Title I—Federal Civil Rights Remedies," § 102, § 1977a,(b).

10. *Civil Rights Act of 1991* (§ 1745), "Title II—Glass Ceiling," § 201, 202.

11. *Civil Rights Act of 1991* (§ 1745-18), "Title III—Government Employee Rights," § 301, (b), 318, and 320.

12. R. J. Murray, "Employer: Beware of 'Hostile Environment' Sexual Harassment," *Duquesne Law Review* 26 (1988), 461–84.

13. *Barnes v. Train* Civil Action No. 1828-73 (D.D.C. 1974); *Corne v. Bausch and Lomb, Inc.,* 390 F. Supp. 161 (D. Ariz. 1975); *Miller v. Bank of America,* 418 F. Supp. 233 (N.D. Cal. 1976); *Tompkins v. Public Service Electric & Gas Co.,* 422 F. Supp. 553 (D.N.J. 1976).

14. *Williams v. Saxbe,* 413 F. Supp. 654 (D.D.C. 1976).

15. *Barnes v. Costle (Barnes v. Train* at D.C.), 561 F.2d 983 (D.C. Cir. 1977); *Corne v. Bausch and Lomb, Inc.,* 562 F.2d 55 (9th Cir. 1977); *Miller v. Bank of America,* 600 F.2d 211 (9th Cir. 1979); *Tompkins v. Public Service Electric & Gas Co.,* 568 F.2d 1044 (3d Cir. 1977).

16. *Meritor Savings Bank v. Vinron,* S. Ct. 106, 2399.

17. *Henson v. City of Dundee,* case (U.S. Court of Appeals, 11th Circuit) cited 26 EPD Article 32, 993 on page 26,707 of *CCH Employment Practices Decisions,* 1982; *Meritor Savings Bank FSB v. Vinson,* 106 S. Ct. 2399, 2405 (1986).

18. Equal Employment Opportunity Commission, *Policy Guidance on Current Issues of Sexual Harassment,* N-915-050 (Washington, D.C.: EEOC, March 19, 1990), 3, 3n.

19. *Robinson v. Jacksonville Shipyards, Fair Employment Practice Cases,* Bureau of National Affairs, Inc. (BNA), Washington, D.C. 1991, v 54, cited 54 FEP Cases, 83–88.

20. *Ellison v. Brady, Fair Employment Practice Cases,* BNA, Washington, D.C. 1991, v 54, cited 54 FEP Cases, 1346, 1353.

21. *Christine Franklin, Petitioner v. Gwinnett County Public Schools and William Prescott,* no. 90-918, BNA, Washington, D.C., 1992, extra ed. no. 2 Supreme Court Opinions, v 60, n 33, 4172.

22. Supreme Court of the United States, On writ of Certiorari to the United States Court of Appeals for the Sixth Circuit, *Teresa Harris v. Forklift Systems, Inc.,* 1993, WL 453611, *1 (U.S.).

23. *Harris v. Forklift Systems, Inc.*

24. Charles Looney, in Gibbs.

25. Susan Rubenstein, in Gibbs.

26. Alan Goldberg, "Comment: Employment Discrimination—Sexual Harassment and Title VII."

New York University Law Review 51 (April 1976), 148–49.

27. Mary Bularzik, "Sexual Harassment at the Workplace: Historical Notes," in F. Brodhead, et al. (eds.), *Radical America* 12:4 (June–Aug. 1978), 25–43; Jill Laurie Goodman, "Sexual Demands on the Job," *Civil Liberties Review* 4 (March–April 1978), 57–58; Lisa Kraymer, "Work: The Intimate Environment," *Alternative Lifestyles* 2 (Feb. 1979), 11–12; Catherine A. MacKinnon, *Sexual Harassment of Working Women: A Case of Sex Discrimination* (New Haven, Conn.: Yale Univ. Press, 1979), 158.

28. U.S. Department of Labor, Office of the Secretary, Office of Information and Public Affairs, *The Glass Ceiling Initiative—Q & A,* Washington, D.C., 1991, 1–24.

29. U.S. Dept. of Labor, *A Report on the Glass Ceiling Initiative,* 24.

30. U.S. Dept. of Labor, Office of Information, *News,* 2–3.

31. Elsie Vartanian, Director, Women's Bureau, U.S. Dept. of Labor, letter to author, Jan. 14, 1992.

32. Women's Bureau, U.S. Dept. of Labor, *Handbook of Women Workers,* Bulletin no. 197, 1975, 91.

33. Lynn Martin. *Pipelines of Progress: A Status Report on the Glass Ceiling,* U.S. Dept. of Labor, Aug. 1992, 1–41.

34. Editorial, "The Stained-Glass Ceiling," *Des Moines Register,* Nov. 27, 1992, 6A.

35. Women's Bureau, U.S. Dept. of Labor, *Working Women Count! A Report to the Nation,* 1994, 1–44.

36. James E. Gruber, "Sexual Harassment Research: Problems and Proposals," paper presented at the annual meetings of the American Sociological Association, Aug. 1989, table 3.

37. EEOC, *Guidelines on Sexual Harassment,* Federal Register vol. 45, no. 219, Nov. 10, 1980, Rules and Regulations 74676–74677, (b).

38. Marcia Mullikin, Executive Director, Family Service League, and a therapist, Waterloo, Iowa, *Waterloo Courier,* Oct. 21, 1991, A7.

39. U.S. Merit Systems Protection Board, *Summary of Preliminary Findings on Sexual Harassment in the Federal Workplace Given Before the Subcommittee on Investigations Committee on Post Office and Civil Service, U.S. House of Representatives,* rpt., Sept. 25 1980; U.S. Merit Systems Protection Board, *Sexual Harassment in the Federal Government: An Update, a Report to the President and the Congress of the United States by the*

U.S. Merit Systems Protection Board, June 1988, 16; Donald E. Maypole, and Rosemarie Skaine, "Sexual Harassment of Blue Collar Workers," *Journal of Sociology and Social Welfare* 9:4 (Dec. 1982), 682–95.
40. U.S. Merit Systems Protection Board, *Sexual Harassment in the Federal Government: An Update,* 21.

41. Nancy Raffensperger, "Sexual Harassment Ruling Here May Break New Ground," *Waterloo Courier,* Aug. 2, 1991, A5.

Protecting Family Integrity:
The Rightward Drift in the Courts

ROSALIND POLLACK PETCHESKY

This right of privacy...is broad enough to encompass a woman's decision whether or not to terminate her pregnancy.
—Justice Blackmun, *Roe* v. *Wade,* Jan. 1973

I fear for the liberty and equality of the millions of women who have lived and come of age in the 16 years since Roe was decided.
—Justice Blackmun, dissent, *Webster* v. *Reproductive Health Services,* July 1989

Antiabortion forces consider January 22, 1973, the date on which *Roe* v. *Wade* was decided, to be a day of infamy. They see the Supreme Court and other federal courts as bastions of liberalism in regard not only to abortion but to policies such as affirmative action, racial integration, and the prohibition of school prayer. In reality, the role of the federal courts, including the Supreme Court, in mediating and interpreting public policy is much more complex than any conspiracy theory would suggest. On the broadest level, the courts more often *follow* than initiate political trends. Within that framework, the courts play a specific part in constructing the ideology that legitimates the policy. In particular, they pro-vide legal and conceptual tools that *accommodate conservative cultural and political tendencies to a prevailing tradition of liberal institutions and liberal procedures.*

Liberal tradition is not static but changes as historical conditions change. At the moment, there are several principles in the ideology of the liberal state that have been incorporated into popular understanding and that New Right and neoconservative politicians find it difficult to dislodge even from their own rhetoric. They include (1) deference to medical authority and medical rationales for policy; (2) the legitimacy of state intervention in matters affecting population, reproduction, and sexuality; and (3) voluntary

Excerpted from *Abortion and Woman's Choice: The State, Sexuality, and Reproductive Freedom, Revised Edition* by Rosalind Pollack Petchesky, pp. 286–304, 322–325. Copyright © 1990 by Rosalind Pollack Petchesky. Reprinted with the permission of Rosalind Pollack Petchesky.

consent and freedom of choice. In reproductive rights litigation, the courts have functioned to accommodate an increasingly conservative social content to these formal liberal principles.

This is not to deny that the courts are essentially arenas where political struggles are fought and, sometimes even on progressive terms, are won. Radical groups and feminists sometimes win victories in the courts because the courts reflect political currents, and at certain moments progressive movements are strong. In the long run, however, the courts play a predominantly ideological role, using legal language and techniques to resolve the tension between liberal and conservative elements in the capitalist state. This tension has existed throughout the history of capitalism, regardless of political parties, and persists today in a climate of right-wing resurgence. An image of New Right policies suddenly superimposed on the capitalist state is false. It obscures both the process of accommodation through which conservative revisions of the dominant liberal ideology get hammered out and the conservative values and practices contained within the liberal state all along. No president, we should recall, has ever publicly supported legal abortion; and the state-sponsored attack on abortion rights was initiated under a Democratic-controlled Congress and a Democratic administration. (President Carter's refusal to support Medicaid-funded abortions was premised on the sanctimonious observation that "some things in life are just unfair."[1])

Similarly, the Supreme Court began its backtracking from *Roe* v. *Wade* well before a conservative administration was in office. In fact, liberal principles, those applied by the courts in rationalizing their decisions, contain conservative as well as radical potentialities. "Medical necessity" or "health reasons" may be used to expand women's access to necessary reproductive health services or to restrict women's sphere of action in favor of parents'

or physicians' authority. "Privacy" may be invoked to defend a woman's right to decide about abortion and the state's obligation to provide access to abortion, or it may be invoked in the name of abandoning public services to the private sector. Even "consent" may be turned around so that the "freedom to choose" is subordinated to the *"capacity to choose."* The *social content* of well-being or freedom is never determined by liberal principles. Politics determine that content, and the courts use legal doctrine and procedures to legitimate it.

The recent history of abortion decisions underscores this political role of the Supreme Court and demonstrates a "pendulum" theory: The Court's views swing whichever way it perceives the dominant trends in national politics to be going, and it functions largely as a barometer of those trends.[2] From *Roe* v. *Wade* onward, Supreme Court pronouncements on abortion may be read as a series of knots and fences, drawn increasingly tighter, hedging in the "right" to abortion with qualifications and exceptions that limit its practical availability among the women most in need of it: poor women and teenagers. Even in periods of heightened liberalism and attention to social welfare, the feminist concept of abortion as rooted in women's right/need to control their bodies was never accorded legitimacy by the state.

This skeptical interpretation of recent state policy making regarding abortion and the Supreme Court's role in it is very different from the view that "with the advent of a new national administration and a new Congress, the abortion debate shifted from the courts to Congress."[3] The implication here is that the courts were the "liberal" force in national abortion politics and that the conservative trend was inaugurated with the Reagan administration in its ties with the New Right, whose stronghold since the 1980 elections has been the Senate. In fact, Congress began engaging in "the abortion debate" in 1977 with its passage of the first of an increasingly restrictive series of amendments to limit Medicaid funds for abortion. During the congressional debates on the Hyde Amendment and when the right-wing, antifeminist current was in full swing, *no one* in Congress stood up and defended a woman's right to decide about abortion *because* it is her body and she is the one who will bear the consequences of pregnancy and childbearing. On the contrary, the most liberal congressmen scrambled to assure their constituents that they were opposed to "abortion for convenience."[4] The Supreme Court responded with characteristic deference, anxious to smooth over rather than accentuate the more liberal dimensions of *Roe* v. *Wade.*

Thus the reactive shifts in abortion politics must be seen in terms not of a constitutional balance of powers but of the totality of political forces that by the late 1970s had come to determine reproductive issues. The reasons for a backsliding so rapid, so "bipartisan," and so massive ... were not constitutional but social and sexual. They expressed a reaction in all the "centers of power" to abortion, not as an antidote to unwanted pregnancies, but as a condition and a signifier of women's social and sexual autonomy. Any analysis of the legal definitions of abortion policy has to be situated in this larger setting.

Roe v. *Wade* was certainly the most expansive and libertarian of the Court's decisions concerning privacy. That "landmark" decision was the product, not of judicial invention or fiat, but of a groundswell of popular feeling and practice that was given powerful political expression by the feminist movement, liberal professionals and politicians, and the population control establishment. It was the product of a social and political moment, which was transformed all too quickly. Soon after the *Roe* decision, policy makers and courts began to chip away at the formal legalization of abortion under the Constitution, reducing it through one restriction after another. This process, even before the rise of a nationally powerful antiabortion movement, reflects the fact that public policy to liberalize abortion was *nowhere framed in feminist terms*—declaring access to abortion a *social right and need of all women*. Rather, it was framed in terms either of a concept of "medical necessity" or medical prerogative or of an abstract "right of privacy" that, in practice, has often excluded those too poor or too young to exercise their rights without public support. These terms left legalization open to a welter of exceptions: "conscience clause" statutes that exempted medical professionals with religious objections from the obligation to provide abortions, parental and spousal consent or notification requirements, compulsory waiting periods, and retraction of public funds and abortion-related services. Through the courts and through bureaucratic maneuvers, a "counterrevolution" is occurring that is attempting to re-create the austere conditions of pre-*Roe* days when a woman's judgment was considered suspect, and she had to pass medical and bureaucratic hurdles for her abortion to be deemed "necessary."

The following guidelines, fundamentally at odds with abortion as a "woman's right," have surfaced in post-*Roe* revisionist case law: (1) women should not get abortions unless they are "medically necessary"; (2) even when abortions are "medically necessary," the state has no obligation to pay for them (i.e., they do not qualify as a "welfare right"); (3) abortion is not generally a medical or health issue but a "religious" and "moral" issue; (4) women, particularly if they are unmarried teenagers, may be incompetent to choose between abortion and childbirth. With this increasingly prevalent line of reasoning, the Supreme Court has moved ever closer to the right-wing position on abortion.

"MEDICAL NECESSITY" VERSUS WOMEN'S AUTONOMY: *ROE* v. *WADE*

The concept of "medical necessity," or "therapeutic abortion," defines nonmedical abortions as "elective," meaning they are somehow frivolous, unnecessary.[5] This bifurcated view distorts reality; it denies that familial, economic, and sexual conditions, as well as those of physical health, create genuine needs that justify abortion. It also reduces the meaning of health, ignoring the extent to which medical problems are related to social, economic, and family-sexual conditions, a point made by Judge Dooling in *McRae* when he argued that "poverty is itself, persistently, a medically relevant factor."[6]

Above all, "medical necessity" makes the physician the final arbiter of the abortion decision. Within this framework, it contains the old eugenic idea of childbearing as a "scientific" undertaking for which only certain women are "fit." Thus it can allow abortions in some cases because women are seen as too poor, too young, or too mentally or physically incompetent to bear children. Abortion and contraception become not a *right* of women to self-determination but a *duty* (to the nation, the "race," the family, or even the self). In this way, therapeutic-eugenic discourse about fertility control, including abortion, allows the liberal state to accommodate without legitimating feminist demands. *Roe* v. *Wade* granted women the "right" to choose abortion in a spirit that was imbued with the "medical necessity" concept. Indeed, how the court defined the "private choice" of abortion hinged very much on the role of medical authority.

The most important legal doctrine invoked to support women's "right to choose" abortion is that of a "right of privacy." Though not granted explicitly in the Constitution, the right of privacy has been found by the courts to reside inherently in various amendments and the "penumbras of the Bill of Rights," particularly with regard to activities related to sexuality and, reproduction (marriage, contraception, procreation, homosexuality, childrearing).[7] It was given its most far-reaching expression in Justice Brennan's opinion in *Eisenstadt* v. *Baird* (1972), which involved a ban on the sale of nonhazardous contraceptives to unmarried persons:

> If the right of privacy means anything, it is the right of the individual, *married or single, to be free from unwarranted governmental intrusion into matters so fundamentally affecting a person as the decision whether to bear or beget a child.*[8]

This was not a majority opinion, and so it carried no precedential weight. Moreover, the qualifying term "unwarranted" implied that there might be situations in which "governmental intrusion" into the privacy of reproductive decisions would be justified. In 1973, what the Supreme Court was doing was not so much securing the privacy of a woman's right to choose abortion as defining the scope and limits of the state's authority to intervene.

Roe v. *Wade* and *Doe* v. *Bolton* were very clear in stating that the "privacy right" involved in abortion decisions was not "absolute." In its most positive formulation, the Court held that "this right of privacy…is broad enough to encompass a woman's decision whether or not to terminate her pregnancy" and went on to enumerate—in terms it would lay aside in 1980—the serious health consequences that may result for women if this right is denied, including "a distressful life and future," "psychological harm," and harm to "mental and physical health."[9] Nevertheless, it also concluded that the constitutional right of privacy does not entail "an unlimited right to do with one's body as one pleases," or "abortion on demand"; the abortion decision may be limited by certain "important state interests in regulation."[10] These interests include that of "preserving and protecting the health of the pregnant woman," on the one hand, and "protecting the potentiality of human life," on the other. According to the Court's complicated formula—in actuality, the heart of *Roe* v. *Wade*—these two state interests are "separate and distinct," each becoming "compelling" at a different *stage* of pregnancy. Thus the Court implied that during the first trimester, state regulation of abortion was unconstitutional; during the second trimester, the state might intervene for reasons of "protecting the woman's health"; and in the final trimester, which the Court associated with fetal "viability," the state's "interest in potential life" could justify a *prohibition* of abortion "except when it is necessary to preserve the life *or health* of the mother."[11]

May we nonetheless presume that women were being granted an unqualified "right to choose" abortion in the first stage of pregnancy? Here is how the Supreme Court clarified it in *Roe*:

> The decision vindicates the right of the physician *to administer medical treatment* according to his professional judgment *up to the points where important state interests provide compelling justifications for intervention. Up to those points,* the abortion decision in all its aspects is inherently, and primarily, a medical decision, and basic responsibility for it must rest with the physician.[12]

Thus the Court "was not upholding a *woman's* right to determine whether to bear a child, as abortion proponents and feminists had argued. Instead, it was upholding a *doctor's* right to make a medical decision!"[13] This was even clearer in *Doe* v. *Bolton*. There the Court's opinion seemed to reject the "medical model" by invalidating statutory requirements that abortions be performed only in accredited hospitals with the approval of the hospital abortion committee and two outside physicians. Although the Court was paring away some of the more cumbersome medical restrictions on abortion maintained by AMA policy and past medical practice, it did so explicitly on behalf of *"licensed physicians."* Nurses, counselors, paramedicals, and other potential providers were denied standing to sue in the case, since they "are in no position to render medical advice."[14] The bureaucratic restrictions were struck down by the Court because they were held to infringe on *"the woman's right to receive medical care in accordance with her licensed physician's best judgment and the physician's right to administer it"*—*"the physician's right to practice."*[15]

Roe v. *Wade* and *Doe* v. *Bolton* therefore simply confirmed the model of abortion decisions being made within a private, confidential doctor-patient relationship—a model that already prevailed in clinical practice for white middle-class women. But the Court was not saying anything about a woman's right to *have* this kind of medical care. If anything, it was upholding the traditional professional autonomy of private practicing physicians over determinations of when (and for whom) medical care is warranted. It was explicitly fitting abortion within the market-oriented medical paradigm. Moreover, it was reserving the legitimacy of state interference with this professional autonomy in the interests of "protecting women's health" or "preserving potential life." With regard to this last point, while the Court in *Roe* v. *Wade* is widely read as dismissing the notion of "fetal personhood" or "fetal rights" as constitutionally relevant (which essentially it does), still another carefully veiled hedge foreshadows *Harris* v. *McRae*. Acknowledging that abortion is covered by the constitutionally protected right of privacy, the Court nevertheless suggests in an ominous aside that abortion may not be a right to the same degree as other rights:

> The pregnant woman cannot be isolated in her privacy. She carries an embryo, and, later, a fetus.... The situation is thus inherently different *from marital intimacy, or bedroom possession of obscene material, or marriage, or procreation, or education....*[16]

Why, then, was the 1973 abortion decision so widely interpreted as a victory for women's right of privacy and the language about "medical judgment" and "inherent difference" from other privacy rights overlooked? Again, we have to look at the political and social context in which the decision was rendered. The strength of the women's liberation movement and the broad approval in the society for liberal feminist ideas about equality and self-determination meant that *Roe* would be interpreted by the lower courts and policy makers, as well as by the general public, as giving women a "fundamental right" to abortion. I would also argue that, despite its limitations, *Roe* v. *Wade* genuinely reflected this liberal climate. It established the legality and legitimacy of abortion, and it did so within a normative framework that emphasized women's health, very broadly defined, rather than abstract moralism or "fetal rights." In this sense, it was progressive, and its immediate impact was to expand women's access to abortion significantly.[17]

In fact, the concept of "medical necessity" or "protecting women's health" cuts in different ways. It may be interpreted as, simply, whatever doctors decide is necessary; this outcome is reinforced by the absence, in a private, profit-oriented medical system, of any socialized, uniform processes for determining standards of need. But it may also refer to the standards themselves, their material content, as Judge Dooling did when he enumerated with great sympathy and detail the array of physical and psychological difficulties that unwanted pregnancy may provoke. These two criteria, *medical authority* and *health needs*, may come into conflict (e.g., in the passage of "conscience clause" statutes that allow doctors to refuse to perform abortions on grounds unrelated to women's health). Understood expensively, however, "health reasons" for abortion may provide the broadest *practical* basis for abortion services *within the health-care system as it is currently structured*. This is

why the medical emphasis in *Roe* v. *Wade* may have been, at a particular moment, relatively progressive for women. In the broad language of the Court, the injuries to *health* that women suffer from being denied access to abortion may even include "a distressful life and future," and at *no* time during a pregnancy is the state justified in withholding legal abortion if such injuries to health would result.[18]

While feminist thinking sees the medical necessity criterion as restrictive of women's rights in principle, increasingly since *Roe* v. *Wade* the opposite is true in practice. It has been a hard fight to get abortion recognized as a legitimate health concern at all. Within the health-care system, only conditions defined as "disease" usually receive insurance coverage, even though many nonpathological conditions (i.e., much of reproductive health and all preventive services) require the same costly medical facilities and personnel. If abortion was clearly understood as health related, it would be much more difficult politically to exclude it from Medicaid coverage. (The Supreme Court was able to rationalize denial of Medicaid funding for abortion in 1980 only by choosing to ignore its own strong language about health consequences in 1973.)

The pressure that the health-care system exerts to define abortion in medical terms was spelled out in a memorandum by the late Frederick S. Jaffe, director of Planned Parenthood's Center for Family Planning Program Development, shortly after *Roe* v. *Wade*.[19] He argued for the "need to develop rapidly a viable concept of 'medical necessity' or 'medical indications' for fertility control (and particularly abortion)—and that we have to find a way to have such a concept adopted by the medical profession and the insurance industry." The alternative was that abortion would "be shut out of U.S. health financing mechanisms." Jaffe was aware of the problems in urging "medical indications" as the basis for abortion services for institutional and funding purposes. He acknowledged that it was "repugnant" to the idea of women's "constitutional *right* to avoid involuntary pregnancy ...for her own reasons, without the need for any external justifications." But to define most abortions as "elective" (i.e., a question of individual choice) is *ipso facto* to disqualify them "from public or private financing," thus to "win the battle and lose the war."[20] The contradiction between abstract, formal "right" and practical access to services is structured into the existing health-care system.

In 1976, Congress began the interminable Hyde Amendment debates that marked the escalation of the "right-to-life" movement's antiabortion crusade to the national level. Low-income women watched grimly as what they thought was their court-approved constitutional right to choose abortion was systematically whittled down by a legislative body composed almost entirely of men: first to "medically necessary" abortions; then to those indicated by a risk of "severe and long-lasting *physical* health damage," as certified by two physicians, or to those precipitated by (duly reported) rape or incest; and finally, to those necessitated by actual danger to the woman's life. These restrictions were subsequently adopted by all but 14 states and the District of Columbia, which provided 92 percent of the public funds used to finance abortions for poor women in 1981.[22] At the federal level, funds are restricted not only to Medicaid-dependent women but to military dependents, Peace Corps volunteers, and working women dependent on employment-related pregnancy disability benefits.[23]

From the beginning of this massive legislative assault on abortion funding, the posture of liberals in Congress and the courts was to retreat into a defense of "medical necessity." A review of early legislative debates on the Hyde Amendment suggests that feminists' apprehensions about the limits of this framework as a way of thinking about abor-

tion, even in a period of repression, are well founded. Throughout the debates, liberal senators who were most outspoken against the "right-to-life" proposals and in favor of retaining Medicaid funding based their arguments on a strict notion of medical autonomy. Senator Brooke, who introduced an amendment that would have attached the phrase "where medically necessary" to the provisions, clarified the concept thus: "The only alternative was to allow the doctors to make the decisions that only they were qualified to make, and that [the principle of medical necessity] would leave the medical decisions where they so clearly belonged...[he] made clear that the doctor would have to make a medical determination, however, and not take the word of the pregnant woman."[24] Brooke's position, considered the most liberal in Congress at the time, is immediately recognizable as the official AMA policy since 1967 on abortion. Similarly, other liberal senators, such as Javits, Bayh, and Kennedy, declared their support for federal funding for abortions where *doctors* determine there are "sound medical reasons" (Javits) or "in cases of genuine medical necessity" (Kennedy), but decidedly *not* for "abortion on demand" or "as a method of family planning or for emotional or social convenience."[25] Even opponents of the Hyde Amendment in the Senate were infected by the rapidly mounting anti-feminist backlash, the view that abortion rates were a reflection of women's "selfishness."

On the other hand, "right-to-lifers" in Congress were resolutely opposed to any reference to "medical necessity" or even medical approval as part of the Hyde Amendment exceptions, arguing that this would open the door to "abortion on demand." By 1979, they had succeeded in eliminating all medical criteria from the amendment, reducing Medicaid-funded abortions to those where a woman's life is threatened and thereby virtually wiping out publicly financed abortions for most poor women. In this new political context the defense of "health reasons" for abortion seemed not only vital but relatively progressive.

PRIVACY RIGHTS VERSUS SOCIAL JUSTICE: MEDICAID FUNDING

By defining abortion as an individual privacy right under the liberty clause of the Fourteenth Amendment, the Supreme Court in *Roe* v. *Wade* managed to evade the more complicated social realities that may prevent women from securing safe abortions, regardless of their formal "rights." ("Pro-choice" advocates effect the same evasion when they define "abortion rights" as an individual matter, one of "conscience" rather than socially determined need.) The right of privacy is a "shaky" constitutional basis for women's abortion rights insofar as it lends itself to interpretations favoring the professional and proprietary claims of doctors.[26] Another reason why the right of privacy is a dubious principle for asserting women's need for reproductive freedom is that the principle asserts the *personal* and *individual* character of pregnancy and childbearing; it provides no basis for demanding that women, as a "class," are entitled to abortion services and that denial of access to those services is prejudicial to the legitimate interests and needs of women collectively.[27] In turn, the denial of a collective or social basis of women's need and right of access to abortion, its portrayal as a "private choice" rather than a condition of a decent life, serves to perpetuate class divisions *among* women. In a class-divided society, leaving individuals to their own private resources to secure a right means inevitably to exclude those who lack the resources.

The constitutional doctrine used to show that some group, or "class," has been treated unfairly is the equal protection clause of the Fifth and Fourteenth Amendments. But, incredibly, the Supreme Court, in its spate of decisions affecting women's rights, has not seen fit to consider women a "suspect class" for

purposes of "equal protection"—for purposes of showing that a law or policy discriminates against women without any "compelling state interest" that would justify such discrimination. (Racial groups and illegitimate children have been accorded such status, but not women nor, for that matter, the poor.[28]) Yet, logically, it would seem that an "equal protection" argument would be necessary, within the framework of American constitutional law, to make the case that abortion rights must be made available to *all* women equally and not simply to "individuals" abstractly.

By early 1977, the political pendulum had swing to the right. The women's movement was fragmented and on the defensive; the "right-to-life" movement was engaged in a well-funded and well-organized political offensive; and Congress was embroiled in debate over provisions of the Hyde Amendment, which would curtail federal financing of abortions. The Supreme Court responded accordingly. In June it issued three decisions related to state Medicaid programs to reimburse abortions: *Beal* v. *Doe*, *Maher* v. *Roe*, and *Poelker* v. *Doe*.[29] Essentially, it set the stage for *Harris* v. *McRae* and the denial of an "equal protection" basis for guaranteeing that poor women would have the same access to abortion services as middle-class women. The linchpin of its rulings was the distinction—"revived with a vengeance," as Willis put it—between "medically necessary" and "nontherapeutic" abortions. Pennsylvania was justified, said the Court, in excluding "nontherapeutic abortions from Medicaid coverage"; this did not constitute a denial of equal protection to Medicaid-dependent women because of the state's "valid and important interest in encouraging childbirth" and in "protecting the potentiality of human life."

What, then, had happened to the woman's "fundamental right," in consultation with her doctor, to choose abortion for any reason without state interference, at least in the first trimester of pregnancy? By 1977 the Court was apparently denying the existence of such a right, instead incanting the state's "valid and important interest," its "significant" interest, its "unquestionably strong and legitimate interest" in childbirth[30] in a litany that all but drowned out the woman's and the physician's right of decision as laid down in *Roe*.

The Court distinguished its 1977 rulings from *Roe* v. *Wade* by an extraordinary piece of verbal agility. The right to choose became, instead, the "freedom to decide whether to terminate her pregnancy" free from "unduly burdensome interference" by the state. There is no such "interference," the Court held in *Maher*, when the state refuses to allocate public funds to support abortions for poor women or implements policy "favoring childbirth over abortion." Such policy is different from statutes that impose "obstacles," such as criminal penalties; the state is under no obligation to provide women with the means necessary to realize their constitutionally protected rights, only to refrain from putting any "obstacles" in their "path":

> An indigent woman who desires an abortion suffers no disadvantage as a consequence of Connecticut's decision to fund childbirth; she continues as before to be dependent on private sources for the service she desires. The State may have made childbirth a more attractive alternative, thereby influencing the woman's decision, but it has imposed no restriction on access to abortions that was not already there. The indigency that may make it difficult—and in some cases, perhaps, impossible—for some women to have abortions is neither created nor in any way affected by the Connecticut regulations.[31]

Of course, the Court's reasoning here is built on a pile of misconceptions: that state policy "favors childbirth" for indigent women, when in fact it favors sterilization (for which Medicaid funds 90 percent of the costs); that there is "no discrimination" because neither poor women nor poverty in general constitutes a "suspect class... so recognized by our

cases";[32] and that "an indigent woman who desires an abortion" could always obtain "private sources for the services she desires." The legalistic burden/benefit distinction distorts reality, conditioning a woman's right in a way that virtually dissolves it for poor women. Although "medical necessity" still seemed to be the cutting edge of abortion politics, the profound class bias exhibited in the 1977 decisions demonstrates that the Supreme Court was merely keeping pace with the regressive currents that were sweeping the country....

SEXUAL FREEDOM VERSUS "AUTHORITY IN THEIR OWN HOUSEHOLD": THE RIGHTS OF MINORS

> *... every human being of adult years and sound mind has a right to determine what shall be done with his own body.*
>
> —Judge Cardozo, *Schloendorff* v. *The Society of New York Hospital*, 1914

> *Many minors, like appellant, oppose parental notice and seek instead to preserve the fundamental, personal right to privacy.... Involving the minor's parents against her wishes effectively cancels her right to avoid disclosure of her personal choice.*
>
> —Justice Marshall, *H.L.* v. *Matheson*, 1981, dissenting

The desire to engage freely and comfortably in heterosexual sex is a major reason why women seek reliable birth control and abortion. But the language of medical necessity, individual privacy, and "procreative rights" favored by the courts deliberately avoids acknowledging this fact. They avoid it because they do not wish to seem approving of behavior that the state has never publicly endorsed: sex outside marriage. As a result, legal abortion and birth control were from the start burdened with an ambiguity reflected in various public statements, including judicial opinions, that extended rights in the name of reproductive "privacy" and then restricted them in the name of moral "protection." This pattern was most intense with regard to unmarried minors. The legalization of contraception and abortion contributed to the image of a wave of sexual permissiveness, particularly among young unmarried people; this visibility called forth overt political responses from policy makers and judges. As teenage sexuality and pregnancy became the major focus of the abortion debate, so the regulation of teenage sexuality, through the requirement of parental consent or notification for abortion and contraception, became a major focus in the courts.

In *Roe* v. *Wade* and *Doe* v. *Bolton,* the Supreme Court left undecided whether "unemancipated" (legally dependent) minors could be prohibited from obtaining an abortion without their parents' knowledge or consent.[33] In subsequent cases, however, the Court came up against the conflict between its liberal principles in *Roe* and the "understood" policy of discouraging nonmarital sex. This conflict was always embedded in government-funded family planning programs, particularly for adolescents and unwed welfare recipients, since the prevention of unwanted pregnancies and the prevention of "promiscuous sex" seemed at odds. But through much of the 1970s, state policy leaned toward pregnancy prevention. Title X legislation, enacted in 1970 to make "comprehensive voluntary family planning services readily available to all persons desiring such services," was amended in 1978 by the Adolescent Health, Services, and Pregnancy Prevention and Care Act, through which Congress mandated the executive to provide special services for adolescents—encouraging consultation with parents, but by no means requiring it.[34] Almost simultaneously, the predictable sexual control backlash emerged, through an array of state and federal court cases and local ordinances challenging the right of women under eighteen to obtain an abortion or contraceptive services. Couched in terms of parental rights (to know about and administer their children's "health") and "family integrity," these challenges were brought by the same forces whose stated goals are to recriminalize abortion and legislate "teenage chastity." Their clear purpose is to make abortions harder to get and heterosexual activity penalty-ridden for unmarried teenage girls. Yet the means they use often involve an accommodation of liberal rhetoric about "health reasons" and "consent."

The response of the Supreme Court to this onslaught was cautious at first but gradually has become more receptive. The balance between its position "that minors have rights …to access to sex-related health care"[35] and its position that the state should protect "parental consent to or involvement in important decisions by minors"[36] increasingly tends toward the latter. In fact, what the Court has done is attempt to accommodate both principles, in a doctrine freighted with ambiguity.

On the one hand, its decisions cast the issue of whether minors ought to decide for themselves about abortion and contraception within the standard legal framework of "informed consent" to medical treatment. Thus, the Court has evolved the notion that, as with any other treatment, informed consent requires that a person be "sufficiently intelligent and mature to understand the situation and the explanation" and that "mature minors" be distinguished, in this regard, from "immature" ones.[37] Its recent case law has exempted "mature minors" from statutory requirements of parental consent or notification regarding abortion and has required a speedy judicial or administrative process to determine maturity if it is in question.[38] But the emphasis on "informed consent" to abortion contains all the inadequacies of the medical, or therapeutic, model from which it derives. It ignores that the decision whether to get an abortion or have a baby is not only a health issue and that the competence of a teenage girl to make that decision is altogether different from her competence to decide whether to undergo major surgery.

On the other hand, the Court's increasing deference to "family integrity" and the authority of parents over their children[39] cuts in a different direction from the therapeutic model, which implies that children's interests (health and well-being) supersede parental discretion and may be protected by the state. The "parental authority" principle derives from a *moral* model of abortion and assumes that abortion is a matter that "raises profound moral and religious concerns" more than medical ones,[40] concerns that parents rather than doctors or judges should oversee. In this part of its reasoning, the Court ignores the reality that access to abortion affects women's health and well-being dramatically, particularly so for younger women. But neither the therapeutic nor the moral model contains much space for the notion that the abortion decision ought to belong to the young woman herself, as a fundamental right "nearly allied to her right to be." What the two approaches have in common is their assumption that dependent minors must, like the mentally incompetent, be protected at any cost....

NOTES

1. Press conference, 12 July 1977, quoted in Jaffe, Lindheim, and Lee, *Abortion Politics*, p. 132.

2. This is also the sense of Kristin Booth Glen, "Abortion in the Courts: A Laywoman's Historical Guide to the New Disaster Area," *Feminist Studies* 4 (February 1978): 1–26. Much of my analysis of Supreme Court decisions regarding abortion from 1973 to 1977 is based on Glen's incisive work.

3. Mary C. Segers, "Can Congress Settle the Abortion Issue?" *Hastings Center Report*, June 1982, p. 20.

4. See *Congressional Record* 123 (1977): S11051–53. The debates are also summarized in an appendix in *McRae* v. *Harris*, 491 F. Supp. 630 (1980), pp. 787–95.

5. See my summary of the feminist critique of this concept in Chapter 3 of Petchesky, Rosalind Pollack, *Abortion and Women's Choice: The State, Sexuality, and Reproductive Freedom, Revised Edition*. Boston: Northeastern University Press. 1990.

6. *McRae* v. *Califano*, 491 F.Supp. 630 (1980), pp. 689–90.

7. See *Roe* v. *Wade*, 410 U.S. 142 (1973), pp. 152–56 and cases cited. The most famous case was *Griswold* v. *Connecticut*, 381 U.S. 479 (1965), where the Court denied the constitutionality of state laws prohibiting the sale of contraceptives to married couples.

8. *Eisenstadt* v. *Baird*, 405 U.S. 438 (1972), p. 453; Glen, p. 8.

9. *Roe* v. *Wade*, p. 153.

10. Ibid.; and *Doe* v. *Bolton*, 410 U.S. 179 (1973), p. 189, where the Court says outright: "a pregnant woman does not have an absolute constitutional right to an abortion on her demand."

11. *Roe* v. *Wade*, pp. 162–63. This formulation is ambiguous on the question of "viability." While the Court associates viability with the third trimester, its language leaves open the possibility that, should viability be pushed forward as technology for sustaining a fetus outside the uterus "advances," then the "state's important and legitimate interest in potential life" may become operative at a point earlier than the third trimester.

12. Ibid., p. 166; emphasis added.

13. Glen, p. 9.

14. *Doe* v. *Bolton*, p. 189.

15. Ibid., pp. 197–98; emphasis added.

16. *Roe* v. *Wade*, p. 159; emphasis added.

17. See Forrest, Tietze, and Sullivan (1978); Lindheim (1979); and Jaffe, Lindheim, and Lee. They give precise accounts of the expansion of abortion services after *Roe* v. *Wade* and the important geographic and demographic variations in availability of services.

18. 410 U.S. 142, pp. 162–163.

19. Frederick S. Jaffe, memorandum, 4 January 1974, Center for Family Planning Program Development, Planned Parenthood–World Population, New York. My thanks to Rhonda Copelon for this valuable document.

20. Ibid., p. 6.

21. Ibid., p. 8.

22. Beginning in FY 1977, the Hyde Amendment (named for Rep. Henry Hyde, R. Ill., its original sponsor) has been attached to the annual appropriations bill for the Departments of Health and Hu-

man Services (formerly Health, Education and Welfare) and Labor. Except for its first year, when a court order enjoined its enforcement, and a 7-month period in FY 1980, when the *McRae* court ordered the federal government to fund all medically necessary abortions, the amendment has become increasingly restrictive; by 1981, the only criterion left was life endangerment. At this writing, medically necessary abortions are being funded by 10 states and the District of Columbia voluntarily (Alaska, Col., D.C., Hawaii, Md., Mich., N.Y., N. Car., Ore., Wash.); and 5 states under court order (Cal., Ga., N.J., Pa., W. Va.). See Rachel Benson Gold, "Publicly Funded Abortions in FY 1980 and FY 1981," *Family Planning Perspectives* 14 (July/August 1982): 204–7 and Tables 1–2.

23. These restrictions are embodied in amendments to the Defense Appropriations Acts of 1978 and 1979; the Foreign Assistance Program regarding Peace Corps volunteers; and the Civil Rights Act of 1964, as amended in 1978, which excludes abortion coverage from pregnancy disability benefits (the "Beard Amendment").

24. *Congressional Record* 123 (1977): S11050.

25. Ibid., pp. S11052–53.

26. Glen, pp. 9–10.

27. Ann Corinne Hill makes this point forcefully in "Protection of Women Workers and the Courts: A Legal History," *Feminist Studies* 5 (Summer 1979): 266–67. Commenting on the Supreme Court's 1974 decision, which struck down forced maternity leave policies as an unjustifiable interference in a woman's "freedom of personal choice in matters of marriage and family life," Hill notes that this emphasis on pregnancy as a "personal matter" totally ignored the fact "that the forced leave policy was sex discriminatory."

28. See ibid., p. 267, and Glen, pp. 10–11. Glen provides a clear explanation of the equal protection clause and the various rules applied by the courts to determine when laws discriminatory in their effect may nevertheless be valid. The ultimate absurdity of the Court's position that refuses to treat women as a "suspect class" became clear in two decisions, *Gedulig* v. *Aiello*, 417 U.S. 484 (1974), and *Gilbert* v. *General Electric*, 429 U.S. 125 (1976). The Court declined to find any violation of the equal protection clause in employment health and disability insurance plans that do not cover pregnancy and childbirth, on the ground that "pregnant persons," not

women per se, were the object of discrimination in the statute!

29. *Beal* v. *Doe*, 432 U.S. 438; *Maher* v. *Roe*, 432 U.S. 464; and *Poelker* v. *Doe*, 432 U.S. 519. All are 1977 cases.

30. See *Beal* v. *Doe*, p. 466; and Glen, pp. 12–13. The Court's determination that this "significant state interest" exists "throughout the course of the woman's pregnancy" clearly contradicts its sharp distinction in *Roe* between the first and second trimesters.

31. *Maher* v. *Roe*, 432 U.S. 464, p. 474; emphasis added.

32. Ibid., pp. 470–71.

33. The first case to deal with this issue directly was *Planned Parenthood of Missouri* v. *Danforth*, 428 U.S. 52 (1976), in which the Court approached the question of parental consent and notification requirements still very much in the spirit of *Roe*. The state may not impose a "blanket requirement of parental consent" on unmarried, unemancipated women under eighteen who wish to get an abortion or use contraception, since *"the right to privacy in connection with decisions affecting procreation extends to minors as well as adults"* (p. 74; emphasis added). It was notably "procreative" rights, however, not sexual rights, that the Court was endorsing.

34. Asta M. Kenney, Jacqueline D. Forrest, and Aida Torres, "Storm Over Washington: The Parental Notification Proposal," *Family Planning Perspectives* 14 (July/August 1982): 187. Recommendations of the House Select Committee on Population, whose hearings in 1978 paved the way for the act, were liberal to the point of including a proposal for mass distribution of condoms and foam through vending machines. See U.S. House of Representatives, Select Committee on Population, 95th Cong., 2d sess., *Final Report* (Washington, D.C.: Government Printing Office, 1978), p. 19.

35. Eve W. Paul and Harriet E. Pilpel, "Teenagers and Pregnancy: The Law in 1979," *Family Planning Perspectives* 11 (September/October 1979): 297.

36. *Bellotti* v. *Baird*, 443 U.S. 622 (1979), p. 637.

37. Paul and Pilpel, p. 300.

38. These were the two major holdings in *Bellotti* v. *Baird*.

39. Ibid., pp. 637–38.

40. *H. L.* v. *Matheson*, 450 U.S. 398 (1981). 101 S.Ct. 1164. p. 1171.

Nora

THE AUTHOR IS A FEMINIST HISTORIAN AND EDUCATOR

There was a doctor who did surgical abortions in Virginia, in the early fifties. He was ultimately arrested and, I believe, sent to prison. I remember reading about his arrest in the *Daily News.*

I went to him, to that place in Virginia, in the spring of '52. He was recommended by a doctor in Washington, D.C., who I think may have gotten a cut of the money. (He maintained that he didn't, but he talked about it so much that I think he probably did.)

Preparations for doing this were very complicated and anxiety-filled. I had to stand on a street corner in Washington, D.C., holding a copy of *Time* magazine. A woman was supposed to approach me and ask me if I had a problem, and I said, "Yes, I have a problem," and, "Can we discuss it?" She said, "No, this is only the first stage." Then I had to make a phone call and this time I was told to be in a hotel lobby with a copy of the *Washington Post,* which I thought was kind of funny, since *most* people carried the *Washington Post.* The next stage happened a week later. I was picked up by a car, on still another street corner, by someone who took me to a place where there was a long black limousine waiting. I think there were three or four other young women in the limousine when I got in. I can remember that the radio was on, and Rockefeller was trying to get the Presidential nomination, in preparation for the '52 election. By the time I got in the car, I think I figured everything was okay. In the earliest stages I was afraid of being turned down. I had some idea that I had to be the right kind of person for them to accept. It's a little weird to have thought that....

All right, then we left Washington, and the car stopped, and the driver said, "And now, for fun, we're going to put these little goggles over your eyes." And so we all wore masks. But the limousine had opaque windows, so no one could see that these people were sitting there wearing masks. And then we arrived at a farmhouse. I know you'll be able to find information about this operation, but I can't tell you his name, because I never knew. When we got to the farmhouse, it was very well staffed. There were a lot of guards, strong, tough-looking men. The limousine was put in a garage and we walked from there into the house. There were guards standing around with guns, three or four nurses, and a staff of maybe ten. The procedure itself was a D&C with local anesthesia, which meant that there was not too much pain, but it was scary as hell. The woman who had met me on the corner was there as a kind of social worker, I guess, to say pleasant things. I remember she asked me who my favorite movie stars were,

From *Back Rooms: Voices from the Illegal Abortion Era* edited by Ellen Messer and Kathryn E. May, pp. 147–153. Copyright © 1988, 1994 by Ellen Messer and Kathryn E. May. Reprinted by permission of Ellen Messer and Kathryn E. May.

and I said, "Oh, Christ, leave me alone." [Laughing.] That was supposed to be...help!

And the doctor. I couldn't see the doctor because he was all done up for surgery. He talked as he worked, because I think he sensed that I didn't want the routine: "Who are your favorite movie stars?" So he said, "You know, the things people talk about are interesting. I have had movie stars on this table, I've had doctors, lawyers, etc.... etc...." The doctor did have a somewhat reassuring quality. I had heard stories about people on the table being called whores and sluts by the doctors, but this man was really trying to let me know that I was being well taken care of. And then later someone said that there was a landing field there, and that they brought in helicopters and private planes.

This cost four hundred dollars. It was well done. I had volunteered to be first, not wanting to see or hear anything else, but I found out later that I wouldn't have seen or heard anything because there were television sets all over the house, playing very loudly, and in addition, the toilets were calibrated to flush every half-minute or so, so there was a lot of noise. If anyone had freaked out and yelled, I don't think you would have heard it. My guess was there was also a lot of soundproofing.

I just remember being terrified. When it was over, I was taken into a bedroom and laid down with white sheets. The nurses had white uniforms, so it was all this sterile kind of thing, and then we were taken back to Washington—the same routine.

The driver took each person back to where he picked them up, and I said, "For four hundred dollars I think I should be taken home," and he said, "But then I will know where you live!" and I said, "And I can identify you more carefully, so let's call it a trade." But he kept saying, "But I've never done that before!" And I kept saying, "For four hundred dollars...." Finally he took me home, and that was the end of that.

I was given antibiotics and pills for breast milk. As far as I could see, it was done very well. The whole operation must have involved a great deal of money.

I never knew anyone else who went there. At that time I was nineteen, and I had learned about all this in secret, and carried it out in secret, and didn't discuss it with anyone. The only person who knew where I was was a woman in my office. The man I was dating did not know I was having the abortion. He knew I was pregnant, and had wanted to get married. I was very relieved that I had managed to get out of this mess. I had no feelings of being guilty or having been a murderer, or ...I had none of that.

No later than the mid-fifties, the doctor was arrested. He must have been involved with so many payoffs that one of them didn't go through. There were so many people involved. Well, four hundred dollars. I made fifty dollars a week, but I managed it on my own. I had some savings. And I said, well, that would never happen again. Unfortunately, that wasn't true. The next time was with Dr. Spencer. You already know about him.

And the third time was a Dr. Abelove in Brooklyn. At that point I was married, and my husband was insistent that we were not ready to have a child. Abelove was a G.P., I think, with a private practice in the basement of a building in a residential area. I don't remember who had told me about him, but I know several people who had gone to him, and he seemed pleasant enough. However, there was a great problem that developed. He told me that if I could be hypnotized, he could do the abortion without using any injections or medication, and it would be a lot easier. And so when I went to him for the preliminary interview, he tried hypnosis, and it worked like a charm. I couldn't raise my arm, I couldn't blink my eye, so, terrific, that's what it was going to be. Well, what had worked for the practice session did not work for the real thing...and it was quite horrendous. He was very...I can remember the sweat pouring down his face, and him saying, "Holy shit, what am I going to do?" I was in terrible pain, and I just...I...He kept saying he couldn't stop, and I called him a fuckin' butcher, and we exchanged a few words there, and he kept saying, "I'm so sorry I let you do it"...he didn't know I had ambivalence about it, which I certainly did.

Everything seemed okay. He talked to my husband when he was finished, and he gave us the whole thing about if there are cramps or hemorrhaging, I was to come back to him. But he kept wiping his brow, as if I had caused him terrible problems, you see, and saying, "I'll never do this again unless I'm really sure."

Well, what I discovered during the next three or four years, when I tried to have a baby, was that during that process, my cervix was lacerated, and I consequently had two late miscarriages, and ultimately I had to have a corrective operation. I gather that the chance of lacerating the cervix are nine out of ten when you're dealing with a moving body. I doubt that he knew he'd done that, because the doctors who examined me afterward saw nothing wrong. It was only empirically, when I later became pregnant and the fetus reached the fifth month the first time, and the fourth month the second time—when the fetus reached a certain size—the cervix was too elastic, and I went into labor. It took some time to discover that.

I'm resentful about the whole experience, but I don't know who to be angry at: Abelove, my husband, me for being too passive. In the meantime, I helped quite a number of other women to locate help, and I heard about many others.

I took someone to a doctor on Long Island named Lothringer. Does that sound familiar? It was in *The New York Times*. Remember that? This was the one who did an abortion on someone who was five and a half months pregnant and she died on the operating table,

he chopped her up into little pieces and flushed her down his toilet. Let's see. He was arrested in the summer of 1961. He came to trial during the great newspaper strike in New York which lasted for nine months. There was no real coverage. I looked at *Time* and *Life* and in the Long Island papers, and they had a file on him, but it wasn't as much as there would have been.

My friend wanted me to go with her because she was very frightened. She had gotten his name from someplace and she wanted me to check out whether he was reliable and competent. He had an office on a boulevard in Queens and he was a G.P. I remember he had NO SMOKING signs all over, which was very unusual in the sixties, and while I was waiting, a child rushed in from the street with a bloody finger and was yelling, "Doctor, Doctor, help me," and the doctor was very sweet and put him on his lap and put a Band-Aid on.

Anyway, then I went in to find out what he did, and in retrospect, I should never have let my friend go there, but...He wanted to show me his tools, his equipment. He'd gotten his instruments from West Germany, he said, and they were the only instruments that were safe to use. I still think of it as tools—and he started talking about the price.

I had been told it was four hundred dollars. Somehow there was this magic figure of four hundred dollars. I had been told that this guy charged four hundred dollars so I had four hundred dollars in cash. He asked me how much I had brought. I said, "What do you mean how much did I bring?" I said, "What is the price?" and he said, "What did you bring?" We did that for a while, and then he took out a piece of paper and said, "Let's play a game. You write on your piece of paper what you have and I'll write on my piece of paper what I want," and I got up and said, "This is beginning to sound very ugly. I think we'd better forget the whole thing." At that point he said, "Are you willing to pay four hundred dollars?" and I said, "Yes."

Well, look, everything seemed very clean, and he had all the medical degrees on the wall, but his showing me the instruments was weird. So he told me to go away, and to come back and get my friend later, she would be fine, and she was. She didn't like him. She said he made a comment—he told her to pull her slip up, and when she hesitated he said, "Well, you've done that many times in the past," or some such innuendo. She didn't like him, but she had no problem. He had used a local anesthetic so she didn't have much pain and she was fine.

It was maybe two weeks to a month later, she phoned me at work. She started to scream; I thought she'd had some kind of breakdown. She said, "Go get the newspaper!" So indeed I went out, and the newsstand people were yelling, "Dismembered body found on Long Island," and I knew in a minute that was Dr. Lothringer. Later at his trial, friends, neighbors, patients came in and said what a wonderful man he was and that he'd been a bulwark in the community, and if he had done this they thought it was just a fluke. They seemed to want to excuse him. What he had done was—the parents of a very young girl, a convent student, had come to him, and he had said that she was too advanced. And then they came back and offered more money and he had said okay. Well, as I understand it, you can't do an abortion at that stage, so she

died, and he did what I said—chopped her up and put her in the toilet. Then—get this—he decided that his goose was cooked, so he and his nurse, who was apparently his mistress, took off for Switzerland. He'd had these plans—Swiss accounts and all kinds of arrangements in case this happened. They went to the airport, and he made a phone call to some kind of company—what we call it is Roto-Rooter—the folks that clean out drains. He called and told them he was leaving the country, but that he had noticed that his toilet seemed to be clogged, and would they mind pumping it out and that he would send them a check. So he got on the plane, and they came, but someone noticed a—you can imagine—something surfacing.

Now, question: Was that his way of confessing, or did he really imagine their equipment was such that they could get rid of it? I suppose we'll never know that, right? It sort of looked like a confession. So that's what he did, and then the parents came forward and said their daughter was missing—well, they found her, right?

He then was "on the lam" till they found him the next spring. They found him in Switzerland and he was extradited and brought back. I do not know what kind of sentence he got, because I only saw one little thing from— maybe it was *Newsday*. . . .

PART ELEVEN

Gender and Violence

Many people assume violent behavior is individual and can happen to anyone—but women live with a fear of male violence that is not individual at all. Some feminists argue that violence and the threat of violence are crucial elements in the ongoing process of female subordination. A major method by which men exert control over women is by frightening them. Sheffield (1987) claims that "sexual terrorism" is the foundation for and the means of maintaining the subordination of women in all other spheres of society. Ewing (1993) argues that in the United States there is a continuing cultural advocacy of violence against women—violence is presented as an appropriate and necessary behavior of power and control. Other theorists argue that there are two hierarchical systems in society: one in which men dominate women and the other, a system in which men compete for dominance. These two hierarchical systems reflect and feed one another. For example, male violence in one sector (e.g., training for aggression in the male worlds of football, the military, or street gangs) fuels violence in the other sector (e.g., assaults by men on women in the form of date rape or wife battering) (Sabo and Gordon 1995; Messner and Sabo 1994; Messner 1992). The Marxist perspective claims that when men feel powerless because of their position in the class system, they compensate for it by violence against women.

In this section, Patricia Yancey Martin and Robert A. Hummer suggest that fraternities create a sociocultural context in which the use of coercion in sexual relations with women is a way of attaining status among men. Kimberly A. Huisman takes a cultural perspective on wife battering, focusing on the patriarchal values that Asian women share with the men that beat them. Alan Soble takes a Marxist perspective on pornography—arguing that men who feel powerless in their productive lives are attracted to it because it makes them feel powerful in their fantasies.

Many feminists believe pornography promotes violence toward women and that any discussion of violence and gender has to include pornography. MacKinnon (1987) argues that pornography promotes and legitimizes violence toward women by eroticizing the dominance and submission dynamic. She contends that the debate about pornography has been dominated by the male point of view that pornography is not a power, but a moral, issue related to the public display of sexually explicit material. On the other hand, MacKinnon's view is that pornography has to do with gender-based power versus powerlessness. She believes that pornography should *not* be covered

by the First Amendment as free speech, just as yelling "fire" in a movie the-
ater is not. However, the male interpretation of the First Amendment treats
yelling "fire" as an incitement to action, while pornography is considered
speech.

Sheffield (1987) agrees with MacKinnon, arguing that pornography articulates a male fantasy in which women are typically depicted as appropriate
objects for rape, bondage, mutation, and even murder. But there is a great
deal of controversy (even among feminists) about what is most appealing
about pornography, the effects of it, the distinction between pornography
and eroticism, and the wisdom of antiobscenity campaigns.

Soble argues that the use of pornography is an attempt to recoup, in the
domain of sexual fantasy, what is denied to men in production and politics—
it is a form of substitute gratification. When men feel demeaned and degraded at work they want to feel able to fantasize demeaning and degrading
someone else—a woman.

Female socialization imparts both the fear of sexual violence and the message that women bring it on themselves. Girls are warned not to wear skirts
too short, blouses too open, walk on the street too late, go in the park at night,
and so on. All these warnings implicitly blame the victim—and imply that it is
men who are strangers that women must take care not to tempt (Herman
1989). Yet, ironically, two-thirds of all the violent crimes against women were
committed by someone the woman knew, including approximately 500,000
rapes and sexual assaults each year. Approximately 28 percent of female homicide victims were killed by intimates (i.e., husbands, former husbands, boyfriends, or former boyfriends) as opposed to 3 percent of male homicide
victims. Strangers were responsible for only one out of every five rapes or sexual assaults on women; men are more than twice as likely as women to experience acts of violence by strangers (Bachman and Saltzman 1995).

Despite the fact that a substantial amount of violence against women occurs within the family, concern about family violence over the last century
has not been at all consistent. The periods of silence about family violence do
not reflect a lull in actual violence as much as a need to deny and suppress evidence of it. The women's rights movement has always been the most influential force in confronting family violence and demanding action against it.
Thus, concern with family violence usually grows when feminism is strong
and ebbs when it is weak (Gordon 1988).

The first social agencies devoted to family violence problems arose in the
1870s; they were called Societies for the Prevention of Cruelty to Children.
The anti-cruelty-to-children movement was an extension of the temperance
movement because drinking was considered the cause of most violence toward children—but *family violence* did not include wife beating.

One of the roots of women's status in U.S. law is the common law concept
of women as property which was adopted in the colonies. From the time of
the Norman Conquest of England in 1066, the common law developed a complex body of theory based on the presumption that the husband and wife

were one person "in the eyes of the law"—and the one person was the husband. Upon marriage, the woman assumed her husband's name and rank and she came under his protective cover—a condition designated as "coverture." When a free woman married, her legal existence was suspended—she was incapable of making contracts or wills, owning property, retaining control of her separate inherited estate, retaining her own name, or testifying against her husband in court. She also lost control of her body—her husband had disciplinary authority over it and the right to sexual intercourse on demand (Bartlett 1993).

Coverture imposed serious procedural and substantive disabilities on the wife. The principle of the sanctity of the home was invoked to reduce married women's rights, while spousal immunity clauses exempted husbands from the criminal and civil liabilities that applied to others (Baron 1987). In other words, the government would not protect married women from their husbands, nor could women enter the public sphere to bear witness against their husbands (Bartlett 1993). In addition, all of the wife's personal property as well as management of her property went to her husband—but men who did not support their families were not held legally accountable. Furthermore, according to common law, a man could not be convicted of raping his wife by forcing her to engage in sexual intercourse because *rape* was defined at the time as a male having sexual intercourse with a female who was *not* his wife (Bartlett 1993). The traditional explanation for this was that rape involves a lack of consent—but the marriage contract was viewed as blanket consent to sexual intimacy. The recognition of wife assault as a social problem was primarily a product of the women's movement which began in the 1960s—the first battered women's shelters in the United States opened in 1973–1974 (Gordon 1988).

Battered women of color are in a particularly vulnerable situation because they have to balance the often conflicting needs and expectations of their batterers, their communities, and the larger society. These conflicting loyalties often compromise the strategies available to women of color to liberate themselves from violent relationships. They are also concerned about how the batterer will be treated by the police and the judicial system. Seeking help for the abuse they are suffering requires balancing loyalty to themselves, their batterers, and their communities (Richie and Kanuha 1997).

Asian Indian women, for example, feel pressured to present an unblemished image of the community to American outsiders (Dasgupta 1996). Their community and their sense of responsibility for the family honor discourages them from attempting to secure services. The Huisman article included in this section deals with Asian women's particular difficulties in getting help when they are physically abused by their husbands. Huisman points out that Asian women are underrepresented in prevalence studies on wife battering because of language barriers, cultural misunderstandings, and the stereotyped belief that Asians are a "model minority." She argues that another reason for the underestimates of wife battering in Asian communities is that

Asian women are less likely than women from other racial and ethnic minorities to report the abuse—those who do usually wait until the battering is at a crisis level. Huisman attributes the reluctance to report abuse, particularly among recently arrived immigrants and refugees, to the women's internalization of patriarchal attitudes which sanction the abuse of women.

The three articles in this section are quite different. Martin and Hummer begin with a case study of an alleged gang rape of an eighteen-year-old student and go on to do open-ended interviews with a variety of fraternity members, nonfraternity members, and informants knowledgeable about such sexual assaults. Soble, on the other hand, offers a theoretical explanation of men's interest in pornography, while Huisman focuses on practical ways of offering better services to Asian women who are battered. Martin and Hummer point to the organizational context of fraternities in promoting male violence toward women; Soble points to men's class position and resulting powerlessness leading to fantasies of sexually dominating women; and Huisman sees patriarchal cultural values as the source of Asian men's violence toward women.

REFERENCES

Bachman, Ronet, and Linda E. Saltzman. 1995. "Violence against Women: Estimates from the Redesigned Survey." *National Crime Victimization Survey.* Washington, D.C.: Bureau of Justice Statistics.

Baron, Ava. 1987. "Feminist Legal Strategies: The Powers of Difference." Pp. 474–503 in *Analyzing Gender: A Handbook of Social Science Research,* edited by Beth B. Hess and Myra Marx Ferree. Thousand Oaks, CA: Sage Publications.

Bartlett, Katharine T. 1993. *Gender and Law: Theory, Doctrine, Commentary.* Boston: Little, Brown and Company.

Dasgupta, Shamita Das. 1996. "In the Footsteps of Arundhati" *Violence against Women* 2:238–259.

Ewing, Wayne. 1993. "The Civic Advocacy of Violence." Pp. 200–205 in *Gender Basics: Feminist Perspectives on Women and Men,* edited by Anne Minas. Belmont, CA: Wadsworth Publishing Company.

Gordon, Linda. 1988. *Heroes of Their Own Lives: The Politics and History of Family Violence.* New York: Viking.

Herman, Dianne. 1989. "The Rape Culture." Pp. 20–44 in *Women: A Feminist Perspective, Fourth Edition,* edited by Jo Freeman. Mountain View, CA: Mayfield Publishers.

MacKinnon, Catharine. 1987. "Not a Moral Issue." Pp. 146–162 in *Feminism Unmodified: Discourses on Life, and Law.* Cambridge: Harvard University Press.

Messner, Michael A. 1992. *Power at Play: Sports and the Problem of Masculinity.* Boston: Beacon Press.

Messner, Michael A., and Donald Sabo. 1994. *Sex, Violence and Power in Sports: Rethinking Masculinity.* Freedom, CA: Crossing Press.

Richie, Beth E., and Valli Kanuha. 1997. "Battered Women of Color in Public Health Care Systems: Racism, Sexism and Violence." Pp. 121–129 in *Through the Prism of Difference: Readings on Sex and Gender,* edited by Maxine Baca Zinn, Pierrette Hondagneu-Sotelo, and Michael A. Messner. Boston: Allyn and Bacon.

Sabo, Donald, and David Frederick Gordon (Eds.). 1995. *Men's Health and Illness.* Thousand Oaks, CA: Sage Publications.

Sheffield, Carole J. 1987. "Sexual Terrorism: The Social Control of Women." Pp. 171–189 in *Analyzing Gender: A Handbook of Social Science Research,* edited by Beth B. Hess and Myra Marx Ferree. Thousand Oaks, CA: Sage Publications.

Fraternities and Rape on Campus

PATRICIA YANCEY MARTIN
ROBERT A. HUMMER

Rapes are perpetrated on dates, at parties, in chance encounters, and in specially planned circumstances. That group structure and processes, rather than individual values or characteristics, are the impetus for many rape episodes was documented by Blanchard (1959) 30 years ago (also see Geis 1971), yet sociologists have failed to pursue this theme (for an exception, see Chancer 1987). A recent review of research (Muehlenhard and Linton 1987) on sexual violence, or rape, devotes only a few pages to the situational context of rape events, and these are conceptualized as potential risk factors for individuals rather than qualities of rape-prone social contexts.

Many rapes, far more than come to the public's attention, occur in fraternity houses on college and university campuses, yet little research has analyzed fraternities at American colleges and universities as rape-prone contexts (cf. Ehrhart and Sandler 1985). Most of the research on fraternities reports on samples of individual fraternity men. One group of studies compares the values, attitudes, perceptions, family socioeconomic status, psychological traits (aggressiveness, dependence), and so on, of fraternity and nonfraternity men (Bohrnstedt 1969; Fox, Hodge, and Ward 1987; Kanin 1967; Lemire 1979; Miller 1973). A second group attempts to identify the effects of fraternity membership over time

on the values, attitudes, beliefs, or moral precepts of members (Hughes and Winston 1987; Marlowe and Auvenshine 1982; Miller 1973; Wilder, Hoyt, Doren, Hauck, and Zettle 1978; Wilder, Hoyt, Surbeck, Wilder, and Carney 1986). With minor exceptions, little research addresses the group and organizational context of fraternities or the social construction of fraternity life (for exceptions, see Letchworth 1969; Longino and Kart 1973; Smith 1964).

Gary Tash, writing as an alumnus and trial attorney in his fraternity's magazine, claims that over 90 percent of all gang rapes on college campuses involve fraternity men (1988, p. 2). Tash provides no evidence to substantiate this claim, but students of violence against women have been concerned with fraternity men's frequently reported involvement in rape episodes (Adams and Abarbanel 1988). Ehrhart and Sandler (1985) identify over 50 cases of gang rapes on campus perpetrated by fraternity men, and their analysis points to many of the conditions that we discuss here. Their analysis is unique in focusing on conditions in fraternities that make gang rapes of women by fraternity men both feasible and probable. They identify excessive alcohol use, isolation from external monitoring, treatment of women as prey, use of pornography, approval of violence, and excessive concern with competition as precipitating conditions to gang rape (also see Merton 1985; Roark 1987).

The study reported here confirmed and complemented these findings by focusing on both conditions and processes. We examined dynamics associated with the social construction of fraternity life, with a focus on processes that foster the use of coercion, including rape, in fraternity men's relations with women. Our examination of men's social fraternities on college and university campuses as groups and organizations led us to conclude that fraternities are a physical and sociocultural context that encourages the sexual coercion of women. We make no claims that all fraternities are "bad" or that all fraternity men are rapists. Our observations indicated, however, that rape is especially probable in fraternities because of the kinds of organizations they are, the kinds of members they have, the practices their members engage in, and a virtual absence of university or community oversight. Analyses that lay blame for rapes by fraternity men on "peer pressure" are, we feel, overly simplistic (cf. Burkhart 1989; Walsh 1989). We suggest, rather, that fraternities create a sociocultural context in which the use of coercion in sexual relations with women is normative and in which the mechanisms to keep this pattern of behavior in check are minimal at best and absent at worst. We conclude that unless fraternities change in fundamental ways, little improvement can be expected.

METHODOLOGY

Our goal was to analyze the group and organizational practices and conditions that create in fraternities an abusive social context for women. We developed a conceptual framework from an initial case study of an alleged gang rape at Florida State University that involved four fraternity men and an 18-year-old coed. The group rape took place on the third floor of a fraternity house and ended

with the "dumping" of the woman in the hallway of a neighboring fraternity house. According to newspaper accounts, the victim's blood-alcohol concentration, when she was discovered, was .349 percent, more than three times the legal limit for automobile driving and an almost lethal amount. One law enforcement officer reported that sexual intercourse occurred during the time the victim was unconscious: "She was in a life-threatening situation" (*Tallahassee Democrat*, 1988b). When the victim was found, she was comatose and had suffered multiple scratches and abrasions. Crude words and a fraternity symbol had been written on her thighs (*Tampa Tribune*, 1988). When law enforcement officials tried to investigate the case, fraternity members refused to cooperate. This led, eventually, to a five-year ban of the fraternity from campus by the university and by the fraternity's national organization.

In trying to understand how such an event could have occurred, and how a group of over 150 members (exact figures are unknown because the fraternity refused to provide a membership roster) could hold rank, deny knowledge of the event, and allegedly lie to a grand jury, we analyzed newspaper articles about the case and conducted open-ended interviews with a variety of respondents about the case and about fraternities, rapes, alcohol use, gender relations, and sexual activities on campus. Our data included over 100 newspaper articles on the initial gang rape case; open-ended interviews with Greek (social fraternity and sorority) and non-Greek (independent) students (N = 20); university administrators (N = 8, five men, three women); and alumni advisers to Greek organizations (N = 6). Open-ended interviews were held also with judges, public and private defense attorneys, victim advocates, and state prosecutors regarding the processing of sexual assault cases. Data were analyzed using the grounded theory method (Glaser 1978; Martin and Turner 1986). In the following analysis, concepts generated from the data analysis are integrated with the literature on men's social fraternities, sexual coercion, and related issues.

FRATERNITIES AND THE SOCIAL CONSTRUCTION OF MEN AND MASCULINITY

Our research indicated that fraternities are vitally concerned—more than with anything else—with masculinity (cf. Kanin 1967). They work hard to create a macho image and context and try to avoid any suggestion of "wimpishness," effeminacy, and homosexuality. Valued members display, or are willing to go along with, a narrow conception of masculinity that stresses competition, athleticism, dominance, winning, conflict, wealth, material possessions, willingness to drink alcohol, and sexual prowess vis-à-vis women.

Valued Qualities of Members

When fraternity members talked about the kind of pledges they prefer, a litany of stereotypical and narrowly masculine attributes and behaviors was recited and feminine or woman-associated qualities and behaviors were expressly denounced (cf. Merton 1985). Fraternities seek men who are "athletic," "big guys," good in intramural competition, "who can talk college sports." Males "who are willing to drink alcohol," "who drink socially," or "who can hold their liquor" are sought. Alcohol and activities associated with the recreational use of alcohol are cornerstones of fraternity social life. Nondrinkers are viewed with skepticism and rarely selected for membership.[1]

Fraternities try to avoid "geeks," nerds, and men said to give the fraternity a "wimpy" or "gay" reputation. Art, music, and humanities majors, majors in traditional women's fields (nursing, home economics, social work, education), men with long hair, and those whose appearance or dress violate current

norms are rejected. Clean-cut, handsome men who dress well (are clean, neat, conforming, fashionable) are preferred. One sorority woman commented that "the top ranking fraternities have the best looking guys."

One fraternity man, a senior, said his fraternity recruited "some big guys, very athletic" over a two-year period to help overcome its image of wimpiness. His fraternity had won the interfraternity competition for highest grade-point average several years running but was looked down on as "wimpy, dancy, even gay." With their bigger, more athletic recruits, "our reputation improved; we're a much more recognized fraternity now." Thus a fraternity's reputation and status depends on members' possession of stereotypically masculine qualities. Good grades, campus leadership, and community service are "nice" but masculinity dominance—for example, in athletic events, physical size of members, athleticism of members—counts most.

Certain social skills are valued. Men are sought who "have good personalities," are friendly, and "have the ability to relate to girls" (cf. Longino and Kart 1973). One fraternity man, a junior, said: "We watch a guy [a potential pledge] talk to women...we want guys who can relate to girls." Assessing a pledge's ability to talk to women is, in part, a preoccupation with homosexuality and a conscious avoidance of men who seem to have effeminate manners or qualities. If a member is suspected of being gay, he is ostracized and informally drummed out of the fraternity. A fraternity with a reputation as wimpy or tolerant of gays is ridiculed and shunned by other fraternities. Militant heterosexuality is frequently used by men as a strategy to keep each other in line (Kimmel 1987).

Financial affluence or wealth, a male-associated value in American culture, is highly valued by fraternities. In accounting for why the fraternity involved in the gang rape that precipitated our research project had been recognized recently as "the best fraternity chapter in the United States," a university official said: "They were good-looking, a big fraternity, had lots of BMWs [expensive, German-made automobiles]." After the rape, newspaper stories described the fraternity members' affluence, noting the high number of members who owned expensive cars (*St. Petersburg Times*, 1988).

The Status and Norms of Pledgeship

A pledge (sometimes called an associate member) is a new recruit who occupies a trial membership status for a specific period of time. The pledge period (typically ranging from 10 to 15 weeks) gives fraternity brothers an opportunity to assess and socialize new recruits. Pledges evaluate the fraternity also and decide if they want to become brothers. The socialization experience is structured partly through assignment of a Big Brother to each pledge. Big Brothers are expected to teach pledges how to become a brother and to support them as they progress through the trial membership period. Some pledges are repelled by the pledging experience, which can entail physical abuse; harsh discipline; and demands to be subordinate, follow orders, and engage in demeaning routines and activities, similar to those used by the military to "make men out of boys" during boot camp.

Characteristics of the pledge experience are rationalized by fraternity members as necessary to help pledges unite into a group, rely on each other, and join together against outsiders. The process is highly masculinist in execution as well as conception. A willingness to submit to authority, follow orders, and do as one is told is viewed as a sign of loyalty, togetherness, and unity. Fraternity pledges who find the pledge process offensive often drop out. Some do this by openly quitting, which can subject them to ridicule by brothers and other pledges, or they may deliberately fail to make the grades necessary for initiation or transfer schools and decline to reaffiliate with

the fraternity on the new campus. One fraternity pledge who quit the fraternity he had pledged described an experience during pledgeship as follows:

> *This one guy was always picking on me. No matter what I did, I was wrong. One night after dinner, he and two other guys called me and two other pledges into the chapter room. He said, "Here, X, hold this 25 pound bag of ice at arms' length 'til I tell you to stop." I did it even though my arms and hands were killing me. When I asked if I could stop, he grabbed me around the throat and lifted me off the floor. I thought he would choke me to death. He cussed me and called me all kinds of names. He took one of my fingers and twisted it until it nearly broke.... I stayed in the fraternity for a few more days, but then I decided to quit. I hated it. Those guys are sick. They like seeing you suffer.*

Fraternities' emphasis on toughness, withstanding pain and humiliation, obedience to superiors, and using physical force to obtain compliance contributes to an interpersonal style that de-emphasizes caring and sensitivity but fosters intragroup trust and loyalty. If the least macho or most critical pledges drop out, those who remain may be more receptive to, and influenced by, masculinist values and practices that encourage the use of force in sexual relations with women and the covering up of such behavior (cf. Kanin 1967).

Norms and Dynamics of Brotherhood

Brother is the status occupied by fraternity men to indicate their relations to each other and their membership in a particular fraternity organization or group. Brother is a male-specific status; only males can become brothers, although women can become "Little Sisters," a form of pseudomembership. "Becoming a brother" is a rite of passage that follows the consistent and often lengthy display by pledges of appropriately masculine qualities and behaviors. Brothers have a quasi-familial relationship with each other, are normatively said to share bonds of closeness and support, and are sharply set off from nonmembers. Brotherhood is a loosely defined term used to represent the bonds that develop among fraternity members and the obligations and expectations incumbent upon them (cf. Marlowe and Auvenshine [1982] on fraternities' failure to encourage "moral development" in freshman pledges).

Some of our respondents talked about brotherhood in almost reverential terms, viewing it as the most valuable benefit of fraternity membership. One senior, a business-school major who had been affiliated with a fairly high-status fraternity throughout four years on campus, said:

> Brotherhood spurs friendship for life, which I consider its best aspect, although I didn't see it that way when I joined. Brotherhood bonds and unites. It instills values of caring about one another, caring about community, caring about ourselves. The values and bonds [of brotherhood] continually develop over the four years [in college] while normal friendships come and go.

Despite this idealization, most aspects of fraternity practice and conception are more mundane. Brotherhood often plays itself out as an overriding concern with masculinity and, by extension, femininity. As a consequence, fraternities comprise collectivities of highly masculinized men with attitudinal qualities and behavioral norms that predispose them to sexual coercion of women (cf. Kanin 1967; Merton 1985; Rapaport and Burkhart 1984). The norms of masculinity are complemented by conceptions of women and femininity that are equally distorted and stereotyped and that may enhance the probability of women's exploitation (cf. Ehrhart and Sandler 1985; Sanday 1981, 1986).

Practices of Brotherhood

Practices associated with fraternity brotherhood that contribute to the sexual coercion of women include a preoccupation with loyalty, group protection and secrecy, use of alcohol as a weapon, involvement in violence and physical force, and an emphasis on competition and superiority.

Loyalty, Group Protection, and Secrecy. Loyalty is a fraternity preoccupation. Members are reminded constantly to be loyal to the fraternity and to their brothers. Among other ways, loyalty is played out in the practices of group protection and secrecy. The fraternity must be shielded from criticism. Members are admonished to avoid getting the fraternity in trouble and to bring all problems "to the chapter" (local branch of a national social fraternity) rather than to outsiders. Fraternities try to protect themselves from close scrutiny and criticism by the Interfraternity Council (a quasi-governing body composed of representatives from all social fraternities on campus), their fraternity's national office, university officials, law enforcement, the media, and the public. Protection of the fraternity often takes precedence over what is procedurally, ethically, or legally correct. Numerous examples were related to us of fraternity brothers' lying to outsiders to "protect the fraternity."

Group protection was observed in the alleged gang rape case with which we began our study. Except for one brother, a rapist who turned state's evidence, the entire remaining fraternity membership was accused by university and criminal justice officials of lying to protect the fraternity. Members consistently failed to cooperate even though the alleged crimes were felonies, involved only four men (two of whom were not even members of the local chapter), and the victim of the crime nearly died. According to a grand jury's findings, fraternity officers repeatedly broke appointments with law enforcement officials, refused to provide police with a list of members, and refused to cooperate with police and prosecutors investigating the case (*Florida Flambeau*, 1988).

Secrecy is a priority value and practice in fraternities, partly because full-fledged membership is premised on it (for confirmation, see Ehrhart and Sandler 1985; Longino and Kart 1973; Roark 1987). Secrecy is also a boundary-maintaining mechanism, demarcating in-group from out-group, us from them. Secret rituals, handshakes, and mottoes are revealed to pledge brothers as they are initiated into full brotherhood. Since only brothers are supposed to know a fraternity's secrets, such knowledge affirms membership in the fraternity and separates a brother from others. Extending secrecy tactics from protection of private knowledge to protection of the fraternity from criticism is a predictable development. Our interviews indicated that individual members knew the difference between right and wrong, but fraternity norms that emphasize loyalty, group protection, and secrecy often overrode standards of ethical correctness.

Alcohol as Weapon.   Alcohol use by fraternity men is normative. They use it on weekdays to relax after class and on weekends to "get drunk," "get crazy," and "get laid." The use of alcohol to obtain sex from women is pervasive—in other words, it is used as a weapon against sexual reluctance. According to several fraternity men whom we interviewed, alcohol is the major tool used to gain sexual mastery over women (cf. Adams and Abarbanel 1988; Ehrhart and Sandler 1985). One fraternity man, a 21-year-old senior, described alcohol use to gain sex as follows: "There are girls that you know will fuck, then some you have to put some effort into it…. You have to buy them drinks or find out if she's drunk enough…."

A similar strategy is used collectively. A fraternity man said that at parties with Little Sisters: "We provide them with 'hunch punch' and things get wild. We get them drunk and most of the guys end up with one." "'Hunch punch,'" he said, "is a girls' drink made up of overproof alcohol and powdered Kool-Aid, no water or anything, just ice. It's very strong. Two cups will do a number on a female." He

had plans in the next academic term to surreptitiously give hunch punch to women in a "prim and proper" sorority because "having sex with prim and proper sorority girls is definitely a goal." These women are a challenge because they "won't openly consume alcohol and won't get openly drunk as hell." Their sororities have "standards committees" that forbid heavy drinking and easy sex.

In the gang rape case, our sources said that many fraternity men on campus believed the victim had a drinking problem and was thus an "easy make." According to newspaper accounts, she had been drinking alcohol on the evening she was raped; the lead assailant is alleged to have given her a bottle of wine after she arrived at his fraternity house. Portions of the rape occurred in a shower, and the victim was reportedly so drunk that her assailants had difficulty holding her in a standing position (*Tallahassee Democrat*, 1988a). While raping her, her assailants repeatedly told her they were members of another fraternity under the apparent belief that she was too drunk to know the difference. Of course, if she was too drunk to know who they were, she was too drunk to consent to sex (cf. Allgeier 1986; Tash 1988).

One respondent told us that gang rapes are wrong and can get one expelled, but he seemed to see nothing wrong in sexual coercion one-on-one. He seemed unaware that the use of alcohol to obtain sex from a woman is grounds for a claim that a rape occurred (cf. Tash 1988). Few women on campus (who also may not know these grounds) report date rapes, however; so the odds of detection and punishment are slim for fraternity men who use alcohol for "seduction" purposes (cf. Byington and Keeter 1988; Merton 1985).

Violence and Physical Force.   Fraternity men have a history of violence (Ehrhart and Sandler 1985; Roark 1987). Their record of hazing, fighting, property destruction, and rape has caused them problems with insurance companies (Bradford 1986; Pressley 1987). Two university officials told us that fraternities "are the third riskiest property to insure behind toxic waste dumps and amusement parks." Fraternities are increasingly defendants in legal actions brought by pledges subjected to hazing (Meyer 1986; Pressley 1987) and by women who were raped by one or more members. In a recent alleged gang rape incident at another Florida university, prosecutors failed to file charges but the victim filed a civil suit against the fraternity nevertheless (*Tallahassee Democrat*, 1989).

Competition and Superiority. Interfraternity rivalry fosters in-group identification and out-group hostility. Fraternities stress pride of membership and superiority over other fraternities as major goals. Interfraternity rivalries take many forms, including competition for desirable pledges, size of pledge class, size of membership, size and appearance of fraternity house, superiority in intramural sports, highest grade-point averages, giving the best parties, gaining the best or most campus leadership roles, and, of great importance, attracting and displaying "good looking women." Rivalry is particularly intense over members, intramural sports, and women (cf. Messner 1989).

FRATERNITIES' COMMODIFICATION OF WOMEN

In claiming that women are treated by fraternities as commodities, we mean that fraternities knowingly, and intentionally, *use* women for their benefit. Fraternities use women as bait for new members, as servers of brothers' needs, and as sexual prey.

Women as Bait

Fashionably attractive women help a fraternity attract new members. As one fraternity man, a junior, said, "They are good bait." Beautiful, sociable women are believed to impress the right kind of pledges and give the impression that the fraternity can deliver this type of woman to its members. Photographs of shapely, attractive coeds are printed in fraternity brochures and videotapes that are distributed and shown to potential pledges. The women pictured are often dressed in bikinis, at the beach, and are pictured hugging the brothers of the fraternity. One university official says such recruitment materials give the message: "Hey, they're here for you, you can have whatever you want," and, "we have the best looking women. Join us and you can have them too." Another commented: "Something's wrong when males join an all-male organization as the best place to meet women. It's so illogical."

Fraternities compete in promising access to beautiful women. One fraternity man, a senior, commented that "the attraction of girls [i.e., a fraternity's success in attracting women] is a big status symbol for fraternities." One university official commented that the use of women as a recruiting tool is so well entrenched that fraternities that might be willing to forgo it say they cannot afford to unless other fraternities do so as well. One fraternity man said, "Look, if we don't have Little Sisters, the fraternities that do will get all the good pledges." Another said, "We won't have as good a rush [the period during which new members are assessed and selected] if we don't have these women around."

In displaying good-looking, attractive, skimpily dressed, nubile women to potential members, fraternities implicitly, and sometimes explicitly, promise sexual access to women. One fraternity man commented that "part of what being in a fraternity is all about is the sex" and explained how his fraternity uses Little Sisters to recruit new members:

> *We'll tell the sweetheart [the fraternity's term for Little Sister], "You're gorgeous; you can get him." We'll tell her to fake a scam and she'll go hang all over him during a rush party, kiss him, and he thinks he's done wonderful and wants to join. The girls think it's great too. It's flattering for them.*

Women as Servers

The use of women as servers is exemplified in the Little Sister program. Little Sisters are undergraduate women who are rushed and selected in a manner parallel to the recruitment of fraternity men. They are affiliated with the fraternity in a formal but unofficial way and are able, indeed required, to wear the fraternity's Greek letters. Little Sisters are not full-fledged fraternity members, however; and fraternity national offices and most universities do not register or regulate them. Each fraternity has an officer called Little Sister Chairman who oversees their organization and activities. The Little Sisters elect officers among themselves, pay monthly dues to the fraternity, and have well-defined roles. Their dues are used to pay for the fraternity's social events, and Little Sisters are expected to attend and hostess fraternity parties and hang around the house to make it a "nice place to be." One fraternity man, a senior, described Little Sisters this way: "They are very social girls, willing to join in, be affiliated with the group, devoted to the fraternity." Another member, a sophomore, said: "Their sole purpose is social—attend parties, attract new members, and 'take care' of the guys."

Our observations and interviews suggested that women selected by fraternities as Little Sisters are physically attractive, possess good social skills, and are willing to devote time and energy to the fraternity and its members. One undergraduate woman gave the following job description for Little Sisters to a campus newspaper:

> It's not just making appearances at all the parties but entails many more responsibilities. You're going to be expected to go to all the intramural games to cheer the brothers on, support and encourage the pledges, and just be around to bring some extra life to the house. [As a Little Sister] you have to agree to take on a new responsibility other than studying to maintain your grades and managing to keep your checkbook from bouncing. You have to make

> time to be a part of the fraternity and support the brothers in all they do. (The Tomahawk, 1988)

The title of Little Sister reflects women's subordinate status; fraternity men in a parallel role are called Big Brothers. Big Brothers assist a sorority primarily with the physical work of sorority rushes, which, compared to fraternity rushes, are more formal, structured, and intensive. Sorority rushes take place in the daytime and fraternity rushes at night so fraternity men are free to help. According to one fraternity member, Little Sister status is a benefit to women because it gives them a social outlet and "the protection of the brothers." The gender-stereotypic conceptions and obligations of these Little Sister and Big Brother statuses indicate that fraternities and sororities promote a gender hierarchy on campus that fosters subordination and dependence in women, thus encouraging sexual exploitation and the belief that it is acceptable.

Women as Sexual Prey

Little Sisters are a sexual utility. Many Little Sisters do not belong to sororities and lack peer support for refraining from unwanted sexual relations. One fraternity man (whose fraternity has 65 members and 85 Little Sisters) told us they had recruited "wholesale" in the prior year to "get lots of new women." The structural access to women that the Little Sister program provides and the absence of normative supports for refusing fraternity members' sexual advances may make women in this program particularly susceptible to coerced sexual encounters with fraternity men.

Access to women for sexual gratification is a presumed benefit of fraternity membership, promised in recruitment materials and strategies and through brothers' conversations with new recruits. One fraternity man said: "We always tell the guys that you get sex all the time, there's always new girls.... After I became a Greek, I found out I could be with females at will." A university official told us that, based on his observations, "no one [i.e., fraternity men] on this campus wants to have 'relationships.' They just want to have fun [i.e., sex]." Fraternity men plan and execute strategies aimed at obtaining sexual gratification, and this occurs at both individual and collective levels.

Individual strategies include getting a woman drunk and spending a great deal of money on her. As for collective strategies, most of our undergraduate interviewees agreed that fraternity parties often culminate in sex and that this outcome is planned. One fraternity man said fraternity parties often involve sex and nudity and can "turn into orgies." Orgies may be planned in advance, such as the Bowery Ball party held by one fraternity. A former fraternity member said of this party:

> The entire idea behind this is sex. Both men and women come to the party wearing little or nothing. There are pornographic pinups on the walls and usually porno movies playing on the TV. The music carries sexual overtones.... They just get schnockered [drunk] and, in most cases, they also get laid.

When asked about the women who come to such a party, he said: "Some Little Sisters just won't go.... The girls who do are looking for a good time, girls who don't know what it is, things like that."

Other respondents denied that fraternity parties are orgies but said that sex is always talked about among the brothers and they all know "who each other is doing it with." One member said that most of the time, guys have sex with their girlfriends "but with socials, girlfriends aren't allowed to come and it's their [members'] big chance [to have sex with other women]." The use of alcohol to help them get women into bed is a routine strategy at fraternity parties.

CONCLUSIONS

In general, our research indicated that the organization and membership of fraternities contribute heavily to coercive and often vio-lent sex. Fraternity houses are occupied by same-sex (all men) and same-age (late teens, early twenties) peers whose maturity and judgment are often less than ideal. Yet fraternity houses are private dwellings that are mostly off-limits to, and away from scrutiny of, university and community representatives, with the result that fraternity house events seldom come to the attention of outsiders. Practices associated with the social construction of fraternity brotherhood emphasize a macho conception of men and masculinity, a narrow, stereotyped conception of women and femininity, and the treatment of women as commodities. Other practices contributing to coercive sexual relations and the cover-up of rapes include excessive alcohol use, competitiveness, and normative support for deviance and secrecy (cf. Bogal-Allbritten and Allbritten 1985; Kanin 1967).

Some fraternity practices exacerbate others. Brotherhood norms require "sticking together" regardless of right or wrong; thus rape episodes are unlikely to be stopped or reported to outsiders, even when witnesses disapprove. The ability to use alcohol without scrutiny by authorities and alcohol's frequent association with violence, including sexual coercion, facilitates rape in fraternity houses. Fraternity norms that emphasize the value of maleness and masculinity over femaleness and femininity and that elevate the status of men and lower the status of women in members' eyes undermine perceptions and treatment of women as persons who deserve consideration and care (cf. Ehrhart and Sandler 1985; Merton 1985).

Androgynous men and men with a broad range of interests and attributes are lost to fraternities through their recruitment practices. Masculinity of a narrow and stereotypical type helps create attitudes, norms, and practices that predispose fraternity men to coerce women sexually, both individually and collectively (Allgeier 1986; Hood 1989; Sanday 1981, 1986). Male athletes on campus may be similarly disposed for the same reasons (Kirshenbaum 1989; Telander and Sullivan 1989).

Research into the social contexts in which rape crimes occur and the social constructions associated with these contexts illuminate rape dynamics on campus. Blanchard (1959) found that group rapes almost always have a leader who pushes others into the crime. He also found that the leader's latent homosexuality, desire to show off to his peers, or fear of failing to prove himself a man are frequently an impetus. Fraternity norms and practices contribute to the approval and use of sexual coercion as an accepted tactic in relations with women. Alcohol-induced compliance is normative, whereas, presumably, use of a knife, gun, or threat of bodily harm would not be because the woman who "drinks too much" is viewed as "causing her own rape" (cf. Ehrhart and Sandler 1985).

Our research led us to conclude that fraternity norms and practices influence members to view the sexual coercion of women, which is a felony crime, as sport, a contest, or a game (cf. Sato 1988). This sport is played not between men and women but between men and men. Women are the pawns or prey in the interfraternity rivalry game; they prove that a fraternity is successful or prestigious. The use of women in this way encourages fraternity men to see women as objects and sexual coercion as sport. Today's societal norms support young women's right to engage in sex at their discretion, and coercion is unnecessary in a mutually desired encounter. However, nubile young women say they prefer to be "in a relationship" to have sex while young men say they prefer to "get laid" without a commitment (Muehlenhard and Lin-

ton 1987). These differences may reflect, in part, American puritanism and men's fears of sexual intimacy or perhaps intimacy of any kind. In a fraternity context, getting sex without giving emotionally demonstrates "cool" masculinity. More important, it poses no threat to the bonding and loyalty of the fraternity brotherhood (cf. Farr 1988). Drinking large quantities of alcohol before having sex suggests that "scoring" rather than intrinsic sexual pleasure is a primary concern of fraternity men.

Unless fraternities' composition, goals, structures, and practices change in fundamental ways, women on campus will continue to be sexual prey for fraternity men. As all-male enclaves dedicated to opposing faculty and administration and to cementing in-group ties, fraternity members eschew any hint of homosexuality. Their version of masculinity transforms women, and men with womanly characteristics, into the out-group. "Womanly men" are ostracized; feminine women are used to demonstrate members' masculinity. Encouraging renewed emphasis on their founding values (Longino and Kart 1973), service orientation and activities (Lemire 1979), or members' moral development (Marlowe and Auvenshine 1982) will have little effect on fraternities' treatment of women. A case for or against fraternities cannot be made by studying individual members. The fraternity qua group and organization is at issue. Located on campus along with many vulnerable women, embedded in a sexist society, and caught up in masculinist goals, practices, and values, fraternities' violation of women—including forcible rape—should come as no surprise.

NOTE

1. Recent bans by some universities on open-keg parties at fraternity houses have resulted in heavy drinking before coming to a party and an increase in drunkenness among those who attend. This may aggravate, rather than improve, the treatment of women by fraternity men at parties.

REFERENCES

Adams, Aileen, and Gail Abarbanel. 1988. *Sexual Assault an Campus: What Colleges Can Do.* Santa Monica, CA: Rape Treatment Center.

Allgeier, Elizabeth. 1986. "Coercive Versus Consensual Sexual Interactions." G. Stanley Hall Lecture to American Psychological Association Annual Meeting, Washington, DC, August.

Blanchard, W. H. 1959. "The Group Process in Gang Rape." *Journal of Social Psychology* 49:259–66.

Bogal-Allbritten, Rosemarie B., and William L. Allbritten. 1985. "The Hidden Victims: Courtship Violence Among College Students." *Journal of College Student Personnel* 43:201–4.

Bohrnstedt, George W. 1969. "Conservatism, Authoritarianism and Religiosity of Fraternity Pledges." *Journal of College Student Personnel* 27:36–43.

Bradford, Michael. 1986. "Tight Market Dries Up Nightlife at University." *Business Insurance* (March 2): 2, 6.

Burkhart, Barry. 1989. Comments in Seminar on Acquaintance/Date Rape Prevention: A National Video Teleconference, February 2.

Burkhart, Barry R., and Annette L. Stanton. 1985. "Sexual Aggression in Acquaintance Relationships." Pp. 43–65 in *Violence in Intimate Relationships*, edited by G. Russell. Englewood Cliffs, NJ: Spectrum.

Byington, Diane B., and Karen W. Keeter. 1988. "Assessing Needs of Sexual Assault Victims on a University Campus." Pp. 23–31 in *Student Services: Responding to Issues and Challenges*. Chapel Hill: University of North Carolina Press.

Chancer, Lynn S. 1987. "New Bedford, Massachusetts, March 6, 1983–March 22, 1984: The 'Before and After' of a Group Rape." *Gender & Society* 1:239–60.

Ehrhart, Julie K., and Bernice R. Sandler. 1985. *Campus Gang Rape: Party Games?* Washington, DC: Association of American Colleges.

Farr, K. A. 1988. "Dominance Bonding Through the Good Old Boys Sociability Network." *Sex Roles* 18:259–77.

Florida Flambeau. 1988. "Pike Members Indicted in Rape." (May 19):1, 5.

Fox, Elaine, Charles Hodge, and Walter Ward. 1987. "A Comparison of Attitudes Held by Black and White Fraternity Members." *Journal of Negro Education* 56:521–34.

Geis, Gilbert. 1971. "Group Sexual Assaults." *Medical Aspects of Human Sexuality* 5:101–13.

Glaser, Barney G. 1978. *Theoretical Sensitivity: Advances in the Methodology of Grounded Theory.* Mill Valley, CA: Sociology Press.

Hood, Jane. 1989. "Why Our Society Is Rape-Prone." *New York Times*, May 16.

Hughes, Michael J., and Roger B. Winston, Jr. 1987. "Effects of Fraternity Membership on Interpersonal Values." *Journal of College Student Personnel* 45:405–11.

Kanin, Eugene J. 1967. "Reference Groups and Sex Conduct Norm Violations." *The Sociological Quarterly* 8:495–504.

Kimmel, Michael, ed. 1987. *Changing Men: New Directions in Research on Men and Masculinity.* Newbury Park, CA: Sage.

Kirshenbaum, Jerry. 1989. "Special Report, An American Disgrace: A Violent and Unprecedented Lawlessness Has Arisen Among College Athletes in all Parts of the Country." *Sports Illustrated* (February 27): 16–19.

Lemire, David. 1979. "One Investigation of the Stereotypes Associated with Fraternities and Sororities." *Journal of College Student Personnel* 37:54–57.

Letchworth, G. E. 1969. "Fraternities Now and in the Future." *Journal of College Student Personnel* 10:118–22.

Longino, Charles F., Jr., and Cary S. Kart. 1973. "The College Fraternity: An Assessment of Theory and Research." *Journal of College Student Personnel* 31:118–25.

Marlowe, Anne F., and Dwight C. Auvenshine. 1982. "Greek Membership: Its Impact on the Moral Development of College Freshmen." *Journal of College Student Personnel* 40:53–57.

Martin, Patricia Yancey, and Barry A. Turner. 1986. "Grounded Theory and Organizational Research." *Journal of Applied Behavioral Science* 22:141–57.

Merton, Andrew. 1985. "On Competition and Class: Return to Brotherhood." *Ms.* (September): 60–65, 121–22.

Messner, Michael. 1989. "Masculinities and Athletic Careers." *Gender & Society* 3:71–88.

Meyer, T. J. 1986. "Fight Against Hazing Rituals Rages on Campuses." *Chronicle of Higher Education* (March 12):34–36.

Miller, Leonard D. 1973. "Distinctive Characteristics of Fraternity Members." *Journal of College Student Personnel* 31:126–28.

Muehlenhard, Charlene L., and Melaney A. Linton. 1987. "Date Rape and Sexual Aggression in Dating Situations: Incidence and Risk Factors." *Journal of Counseling Psychology* 34:186–96.

Pressley, Sue Anne. 1987. "Fraternity Hell Night Still Endures." *Washington Post* (August 11):B1.

Rapaport, Karen, and Barry R. Burkhart. 1984. "Personality and Attitudinal Characteristics of Sexually Coercive College Males." *Journal of Abnormal Psychology* 93:216–21.

Roark, Mary L. 1987. "Preventing Violence on College Campuses." *Journal of Counseling and Development* 65:367–70.

Sanday, Peggy Reeves. 1981. "The Socio-Cultural Context of Rape: A Cross-Cultural Study." *Journal of Social Issues* 37:5–27.

———. 1986. "Rape and the Silencing of the Feminine." Pp. 84–101 in *Rape*, edited by S. Tomaselli and R. Porter. Oxford: Basil Blackwell.

St. Petersburg Times. 1988. "A Greek Tragedy." (May 29):1F, 6F.

Sato, Ikuya. 1988. "Play Theory of Delinquency: Toward a General Theory of 'Action.'" *Symbolic Interaction* 11: 191–212.

Smith, T. 1964. "Emergence and Maintenance of Fraternal Solidarity." *Pacific Sociological Review* 7:29–37.

Tallahassee Democrat. 1988a. "FSU Fraternity Brothers Charged" (April 27):1A, 12A

———. 1988b. "FSU Interviewing Students About Alleged Rape" (April 24):1D.

———. 1989. "Woman Sues Stetson in Alleged Rape" (March 19):3B.

Tampa Tribune. 1988. "Fraternity Brothers Charged in Sexual Assault of FSU Coed." (April 27):6B.

Tash, Gary B. 1988. "Date Rape." *The Emerald of Sigma Pi Fraternity*, 75(4):1-2.

Telander, Rick, and Robert Sullivan. 1989. "Special Report, You Reap What You Sow." *Sports Illustrated* (February 27):20–34.

The Tomahawk. 1988. "A Look Back at Rush, A Mixture of Hard Work and Fun" (April/May):3D.

Walsh, Claire. 1989. Comments in Seminar on Acquaintance/Date Rape Prevention: A National Video Teleconference, February 2.

Wilder, David H., Arlyne E. Hoyt, Dennis M. Doren, William E. Hauck, and Robert D. Zettle. 1978. "The Impact of Fraternity and Sorority Membership on Values and Attitudes." *Journal of College Student Personnel* 36:445–49.

Wilder, David H., Arlyne E. Hoyt, Beth Shuster Surbeck, Janet C. Wilder, and Patricia Imperatrice Carney. 1986. "Greek Affiliation and Attitude Change in College Students." *Journal of College Student Personnel* 44:510–19.

Pornography in Capitalism: Powerlessness

ALAN SOBLE

My explanation for the vast consumption of pornography appeals to both the boredom and the powerlessness yielded by capitalist work relations, the nature of labor, and the centralization of economics and politics. Pornography is a diversion, an escape from the dull, predictable world of work. Continued boredom also partially explains the quantity of pornography consumed. The sexual experience that involves visual stimuli, fantasies, and masturbation is intense (because of the hypersensitized penis), but it is short-lived and requires repetition. Visual stimuli arouse quickly but they need to be replaced with new stimuli, hence the quantity of pornography consumed and the attendant "throwaway" commodification of women's bodies. Powerlessness, however, is the more important factor. Being bored with one's wife or lover, or with life in general, is only a small part of the story. And the boredom is just a form of powerlessness or derived from it.

A common view holds that pornography causes men to have sexual thoughts, ideas, or fantasies that they otherwise would not have.[1] To a certain extent this is true; no one reading de Sade's *120 Days of Sodom* is likely to finish the book without a handful of new ideas. But probably closer to the truth is the view that pornography allows men a great deal of autonomy in constructing sexual im-ages. Goldstein and Kant defend the idea that pornography merely causes men to have sexual ideas when they distinguish between erotic daydreaming and pornography:

> *In our view erotic pictures, stories, and movies simply serve as a substitute for the self-generating daydreams of the pornography user.... The daydream comes apparently from some inner stimulation to one's imagination. In the case of erotica, the theme portrayed comes from someone else's imagination, is depicted in tangible form, and can be thought of as separate from one's own wishes and motivations.*[2]

To be sure, there is a difference between sexual daydreaming and the fantasies men have when using pornography, but Goldstein and Kant's suggestion, that in the former case the ideas come from "inside" and in the latter they come from "outside," is an oversimplification. Some of the content of our sexual daydreams comes ultimately from "outside," and the ideas entertained by users of pornography are not merely imprints from the "outside," transferred, as it were, directly and without modification from the pornographic magazine into the mind. The crude view is succinctly put by George Steiner: "Sexual relations are...one of the citadels of privacy.... The new pornographers subvert this last, vital privacy; they do our imagining for us."[3] Curiously, a defender of pornography responds to

Steiner by claiming that *this* "is exactly what all good writers have done since the birth of literature. The measure of their talent has …been their ability to *make* us see the world through their eyes."[4] But writers of good literature, even as they do show us another view of the world, do not make us—force us—to think anything, and they do not do our imagining for us.[5] One might want to insist that here we have a nice distinction between pornography and good literature: the former does our imagining for us; the latter does not.[6] For example, Joseph Slade claims that photographic and filmed pornography leave "nothing…to the imagination."[7] But Slade exposes the defect of this crude view when he later writes that "the cameraman cannot get inside the performers' minds."[8] He concludes from this that the consumers of pornography "do not know what" the performers are thinking. But it is in virtue of this feature of the camera that the consumer has freedom in actively filling in the thoughts, sensations, or feelings of the performers. The viewer can also add details or activities in his mind to those depicted.

To emphasize the causal determination of ideas by pornography is therefore one-sided. It overlooks the fact that pornography presents a partial picture of a fantasy world, that pornographic literature leaves gaps for the reader to fill in, and that pornographic films and especially photographs leave even larger gaps for the viewer to fill in.[9] The consumer of pornography uses the material not so much to learn of sexual variations but to obtain the visual and descriptive foundation upon which to build a fantasy. The brute facts provided by the photograph are transformed into a fantastic scenario, and the consumer creates a drama in which he is director, participant, or member of the audience at will. Pornography appeals to the user in virtue of this dramatic scenario; indeed, its partially undefined content, waiting to be expanded into a full script, explains why men consume it in vast quantities.

Pornography allows men to gain a sense of control. In his fantasy world the consumer of pornography is the boss: Mr. X shall screw Ms. Y in position P and at time t while she wears/disrobes/reveals/lubricates/laughs/exclaims/resists/seduces/pouts/farts in exactly the way the consumer wants. (This explanation also illuminates the appeal of prostitution: with a woman he has hired, a man can experience what he wants when he wants it.) Pornographic fantasies provide sexual experiences without the entanglements, mistakes, imperfections, hassles, and misunderstandings that interfere with pleasure and that accompany sex with a wife, lover, girlfriend, or stranger. Or, if there are to be complications, pornographic fantasy allows men to imagine the particular complications that they find arousing. Of course, no mode of sexual activity is ideal; all forms—masturbation with pornography, paying a prostitute, getting married, having sex with strange women—have their advantages and disadvantages. The vast consumption of pornography over the last twenty-five years implies that men perceive the relative benefits of masturbation with pornography as increasingly significant, enough to make that mode of sexuality a contender equal with the others.[10] And the pleasure of fantasized sexuality is not limited to the pleasure of wanting the fantasized activity to actually occur.[11] The pornographic sexual experience is not always a mere substitute for "real" sexual activity; it is often "an authentic, autonomous sexual activity."[12]

In a sense, the grab at control through fantasized arrangements is literally infantile,[13] especially if we understand maturity as a willingness to work out problems with the people one associates with. But the male user of pornography has decided, at least implicitly and for certain times or places, that maturity in this sense is not worth the loss of pleasure.[14] Men want these particular pleasures here and now, and in fantasy they have things exactly the way they want them.[15] We would be expecting far too much of people raised in an infantilizing society were we to complain about such regressions; we would be blaming the victims. The use of pornography is an attempt to recoup in the domain of sexual fantasy what is denied to men in production and politics; in this sense the use of pornography in capitalism provides substitute gratification. Pornographic fantasy gives men the opportunity, which they otherwise rarely have, to order the world and conduct its events according to their individual tastes. In the fantasy world permitted by pornography men can be safely selfish and totalitarian. The illusion of omnipotence is a relief from the estranged conditions of their lives and, with a little rationalization, can make existence in that real world, in which they have substantially less power, bearable. Men use pornography as compensation for their dire lack of power; pornography is therefore not so much an expression of male power as it is an expression of their lack of power.

The powerlessness for which pornographic fantasy compensates is not simply productive, political, and economic powerlessness. This powerlessness in capitalism can explain a tendency for people to fantasize, and it does contribute to pornographic fantasizing.[16] But if this general powerlessness were the only cause of fantasizing, we would expect not specifically sexual fantasies but Walter Mitty fantasies of astounding successes in business and politics. This kind of powerlessness explains the appeal of adventure stories and Dirty Harry movies, but it doesn't take us far enough in understanding pornography.[17] In addition, pornography compensates specifically for sexual powerlessness, the powerlessness of males in their sexual relationships with women.

In his discussion of the effects of industrialization in the early nineteenth century, Edward Shorter tells us about the

shift toward powerlessness for men in the arena of real-world politics, whereby all the little people who

had possessed some tiny stake—and feeble voice—in the governance of the traditional village community now became completely disenfranchised politically, until the advent of universal male voting toward the century's end. There has been no end of speculation, though little evidence, that the political powerlessness which men perceive is expressed in their resentment of women. If that is true, we might have further grounds for anticipating an increase in rapes in these factory-industrial regions.[18]

Supposing that the speculation contains some truth, I do not find altogether convincing the idea that an increase in rape, if understood as a *sexual* crime, is mostly due to men's *political* powerlessness. Political powerlessness should (*ceteris paribus*) lead to a political response. Therefore, to connect rape and men's powerlessness one must invoke at some point either sexual powerlessness or a reconception of rape. Shorter begins to provide the requisite sort of analysis when he discusses the increase in rape beginning in the 1960s in the Anglo-Saxon countries.[19] He suggests that rape became a political act directed at women, a response to the feminist-inspired challenge to male power. In this case the connection is made by reconceptualizing rape.

But in the case of pornography today, invoking men's sexual powerlessness is better than ignoring the sexual nature of men's interest in pornography. There are at least two sources of men's dissatisfaction in their relationships with women, dissatisfactions that can be dealt with by recouping a sense of power in the fantasy world made possible by pornography. First, men tend to be more interested in sex for its own sake than women, and they emphasize the sexual over the affectionate aspects of their relationships with women. Men who have this interest in sexual activity for its own sake to a certain extent lack control over their sexual lives and recoup this perceived loss of power in a fantasy world. There is some truth to the folk-wisdom that women can often find a sexual partner more easily than men, and that women decline an invitation to engage in sexual activity more readily than men. Pornography restores men's sense that they have control over their sexuality, by allowing them to populate their fantasy world with women who are equally interested in sex for its own sake.[20]

Second, women's accommodation to male sexuality has never been complete and is becoming less so. Earlier I explained some of women's alienation in terms of the requirements of male sexuality and the practices that socialize women or lead to their accommodation. But socialization is not omnipotent, and women can simply refuse to accommodate. Refusals to accommodate may even be entirely rational. To the extent that women refuse to fit the requirements of male sexuality, men experience frustration and powerlessness. Socialization is less effective as a mechanism for producing what men want, so they have less control over the sexuality of women. A decrease in the accommodation of women to male sexuality, which has resulted from an increase in feminist and quasi-feminist consciousness over the last twenty-five years, has contributed to male powerlessness, specifically sexual powerlessness.[21] Men whose sexual partners have not sufficiently accommodated to male sexuality, and who become sexually bored with partners over whom they have less control, turn to pornographic fantasy in which their sexual desires are satisfied by fully accommodating women.[22] If Shorter is right that rape has increased in response to the women's movement, rape can be construed as a counter-offensive, as backlash. But men who turn to pornography in response to the decreased accommodation of women are retreating, not attacking. The attempt to gain a sense of sexual control in the realm of fantasy is an admission of defeat, a resignation to the way the women's movement has changed the world.[23]

On the one hand, the use of pornography is an attempt to retain in the world of fantasy the prerogatives of masculinity that are being eroded. If sex has been, but is no longer, "a domain of activity where the individual male can conceive of himself as being plausibly efficacious,"[24] then the flight to pornography can be seen as an attempt to establish a new domain for sexual prowess under the *same* prevailing notion of masculinity. But, on the other hand, one can detect in the consumption of pornography a rejection of the prevailing notion of masculinity.[25] Masturbation violates the prevailing standards of masculinity: the real man screws real women, he does not jerk off. If the vast consumption of pornography implies that a good deal of masturbation is going on, then men are rejecting the prevailing standards of masculinity. The consumption of pornography suggests, therefore, that men are abandoning the idea that, to prove themselves, they need to seduce women. Furthermore, for men who are living alone, who are postponing or avoiding marriage, or who realize, from divorce statistics, that relationships are not the stabilizing and secure retreats from the world they once might have been, masturbation with pornography is a useful and pleasurable activity that complements the new, evolving masculine role. If pornography is used in these two ways—as adherence in the realm of fantasy to the old style of masculinity, and as embracing the trend toward a new style of masculinity— then we can again understand the consumption of pornography as a balancing act that attempts to satisfy the demands of competing pronouncements: the conservative pronouncement to be a man, and the liberal pronouncement to reject old-fashioned notions of manhood....

NOTES

1. For example, Diana Russell, "Pornography and Violence: What Does the New Research Say?" in Lederer, *Take Back the Night*, pp. 218–38.

2. Goldstein and Kant, *Pornography and Sexual Deviance*, pp. 135–36.

3. "Night Words," in Holbrook, *The Case Against Pornography*, pp. 227–36, at pp. 234–35.

4. Kenneth Tynan, "Dirty Books Can Stay," in Hughes, *Perspectives on Pornography*, pp. 109–21, at p. 119 (italics added).

5. "The good writer creates character by a cunning combination of the said and the unsaid" (Felix Pollak, "Pornography: A Trip Around the Halfworld," in Hughes, *Perspectives on Pornography*, pp. 170–96, at p. 194). Pollak defends pornography by arguing that it, too, allows the active participation of the user. See also Vidal, "On Pornography," p. 6.

6. See Davis, *Smut*, pp. 136–37.

7. "Pornographic Theaters Off Times Square," in Rist, *The Pornography Controversy*, pp. 119–39, at p. 129.

8. Ibid., p. 130.

9. See Sontag, *On Photography*, pp. 106–09.

10. Leslie Farber's reading of Masters and Johnson concludes that the perfect orgasm is "wholly subject to its owner's will, wholly indifferent to human contingency or context. Clearly, this perfect orgasm is the orgasm achieved on one's own," through masturbation (*Lying, Despair, Jealousy, Envy, Sex, Suicide, Drugs, and the Good Life*, p. 140). If the perfect orgasm is the one achieved in masturbation, then the important question is not "why do men consume so much pornography?" but rather "why do men ever bother with sex with prostitutes, wives, girlfriends, and strangers?" Davis remarks, "Considering the obstacles, one wonders how two people ever manage to copulate at all" (*Smut*, p. 20), and he answers: "Plainly, human beings must possess something sexually arousing that animal species, natural phenomena, and technological products lack. That something else is a social self" (p. 106). But one need not wax so metaphysical to explain why masturbation with pornography does not replace other modes of sexuality altogether.

Pornography cannot reproduce certain sexual sensations that can be experienced only with another person. Indeed, the ability of pornography to provide satisfaction is reduced if a person cannot use the material to conjure up fantasies based on memories of "real" sexual activity.

11. See Feagin, "Some Pleasures of Imagination," p. 51.

12. Barrowclough, Review of "Not a Love Story," p. 33.

13. Ann Snitow discusses pornography as satisfying the desire to reexperience the omnipotence of childhood, in "Mass Market Romance," pp. 153–54.

14. Nancy Hartsock argues that men enjoy pornography because it allows them to avoid the dangers of intimacy with women, that men's "fear" of intimacy drives them to reassert control through pornography (*Money, Sex, and Power*, pp. 169–70, 176, 252). But this thesis rules out altogether that for some men masturbation with pornography is a sexual activity in its own right with its own advantages. Hartsock also magnifies men's perceptions of relationships when she says they "fear" intimacy. We should not forget that "a woman without a man is like a fish without a bicycle" works both ways.

15. Molly Haskell makes the same point about women's fantasies ("Rape Fantasy." p. 85).

16. Lawrence Rosenfield explains the consumption of pornography in capitalism *entirely* as a function of political powerlessness and the powerlessness derived from noncollectivized labor ("Politics and Pornography," especially pp. 414–19).

17. Geoffrey Gorer argues that pornography is best understood by including it with "the literature of fear, the ghost story, the horror story, the thriller," and, for example, "books of wine connoisseurship," all of which invoke physical responses (*The Danger of Equality*, pp. 222–24).

18. "On Writing the History of Rape," p. 479.

19. Ibid., p. 481.

20. David Chute agrees that pornography is "a symptom of impotence rather than power," but he insists that pornography is largely consumed by young, shy, and unattractive men; hence he believes pornography is an expression only of *their*

powerlessness to entice partners ("Dirty Pillow Talk," p. 5). But consumption by these men does not explain the billions of dollars spent on pornography. Sexually active men also consume pornography, and the explanation I offer applies to them as well. Note that the President's Commission found that most patrons of adult book stores and movie theaters were white, middle-aged, middle-class men (*Report*, pp. 25–26, 157–63).

21. Consciousness-raising groups, feminist psychotherapy, and the media (e.g., *Ms.*) undoubtedly undermine socialization and encourage refusals to accommodate.

22. Heidi Hartmann ("The Family as the Locus of Gender, Class, and Political Struggle," pp. 377ff) argues against the view that the power of men over women in the home has recently been weakened. But she shows only that men have retained power over women's domestic labor, not their sexuality.

23. I think Barrett and McIntosh get it backwards when they write (*The Anti-Social Family*, p. 76): "Men would not be willing to pay prostitutes if it were not for the fact that their heterosexual desires have been indulged and accorded legitimacy and women's constructed as weak and receptive, in the interests of a male dominated marriage system. The same applies to pornography." On my account it is precisely because men's sexuality has *not* been "indulged" by not fully accommodating women that they find both prostitution and pornography inviting. (I can imagine Woody Allen's reply: men do not use pornography because there are not enough good women lovers; rather, men sleep with women because they cannot get enough good pornography.)

24. Gagnon and Simon, *Sexual Conduct*, p. 272.

25. Barbara Ehrenreich (*The Hearts of Men*, pp. 125–26) argues that men's "revolt" against the male sex role can be perceived in male-submissive sadomasochistic pornography. I extend her insight by suggesting that all pornography can be understood this way.

REFERENCES

Barrett, Michele and Mary McIntosh. *The Anti-Social Family* (London: NLB, 1982).

Barrowclough, Susan. Review of "Not a Love Story," *Screen* 23, 5 (1982): 26–36.

Chute, David. "Dirty Pillow Talk." *The Boston Phoenix*, September 23, 1980.

Davis, Murray. *Smut: Erotic Reality/Obscene Ideology* (Chicago: University of Chicago Press, 1983).

Ehrenreich, Barbara. *The Hearts of Men: American Dreams and the Flight from Commitment* (Garden City, NY: Anchor Press, 1983).

Farber, Leslie. *Lying, Despair, Jealousy, Envy, Sex, Suicide, Drugs, and the Good Life* (New York: Basic Books, 1976).

Feagin, Susan L. "Some Pleasures of Imagination." *Journal of Aesthetics and Art Criticism* 43, 1 (1984): 41–55.

Gagnon, John and William Simon. *Sexual Conduct: The Social Sources of Human Sexuality* (Chicago: Aldine, 1973).

Goldstein, Michael and Harold Kant. *Pornography and Sexual Deviance* (Berkeley: University of California Press, 1973).

Gorer, Geoffrey. *The Danger of Equality* (New York: Weybright and Talley, 1966).

Hartmann, Heidi I. "The Family as the Locus of Gender, Class, and Political Struggle: The Example of Housework." *Signs* 6 (1981): 366–94.

Hartsock, Nancy C. M. *Money, Sex, and Power* (New York: Longman, 1983).

Haskell, Molly. "Rape Fantasy." *Ms.*, November 1976.

Holbrook, David, ed. *The Case Against Pornography* (LaSalle: Open Court, 1973).

Hughes, Douglas A., ed. *Perspectives on Pornography* (New York: St. Martin's Press, 1970).

Lederer, Laura, ed. *Take Back the Night* (New York: Morrow, 1980).

Report of the Commission on Obscenity and Pornography (New York: Bantam, 1970).

Rist, Ray C., ed. *The Pornography Controversy* (New Brunswick, N.J.: Transaction Books, 1975).

Rosenfield, Lawerence W. "Politics and Pornography." *Quarterly Journal of Speech* 59 (1973): 413–22.

Shorter, Edward. "On Writing the History of Rape." *Signs* 3, 2(1977): 471–82.

Snitow, Ann B. "Mass Market Romance: Pornography for Women Is Different." *Radical History Review* 20 (1979): 141–61.

Sontag, Susan. *On Photography* (New York: Farrer, Straus and Giroux, 1973).

Vidal, Gore. "On Pornography." *The New York Review of Books*, March 31, May 12, 1966.

Wife Battering in Asian American Communities

Identifying the Service Needs of an Overlooked Segment of the U.S. Population

KIMBERLY A. HUISMAN

It is no longer a secret that violence against women transcends all boundaries. Women are raped, beaten, and mutilated around the globe regardless of factors such as their age, race, ethnicity, class, religion, education level, or sexual orientation. Despite this fact, however, most research and attention directed toward the problem of violence against women in the United States has focused on White, middle-class women, overlooking women of color and other marginalized groups. A clear example of this neglect is the scant attention that has been directed toward the problem of wife battering in Asian communities.[1] In particular, there is a discernible gap in the literature about the needs of battered Asian women, especially with regard to recently arrived immigrant and refugee women.

Drawing from interviews I conducted with 18 Asian community activists and service providers, this article examines the specific needs of Asian women who are battered and explores the various structural and cultural constraints that inhibit these women from securing help from mainstream social service agencies.

ASIAN AMERICANS: A DIVERSE AND GROWING POPULATION

The Asian population in the United States has shown steady growth in recent decades. According to the 1990 census, for example, Asians and Pacific Islanders make up 2.9% of the U.S. population, an increase of nearly 100% since the 1980 census (U.S. Bureau of the Census). However, the use of the panethnic label "Asian" presents some obvious problems. Lumping all Asian ethnic groups into one racial category is deceiving and potentially harmful because it conveys an image of a monolithic, homogeneous population and obscures the various diverse ethnic and cultural groups it represents (Espiritu, 1992). Included under this rubric are Asians who have deep historical roots in this country, such as the Chinese and Japanese populations; recently arrived immigrants, such as Filipinos, Koreans, and South Asians from India, Pakistan, and Sri Lanka; and even more recently arrived Pacific Islanders and Indochinese refugees, such as Guamanians, Samoans, Cambodians, Laotians, Vietnamese, Thai, and Indonesians.

All of these ethnic groups have their own culture, language, and history. Furthermore, there is also considerable variation within, as well as between, these various Asian ethnic groups. Although I will focus on the similarities among Asians in the United States to highlight some broader issues, I do not intend to undermine or obscure the uniqueness of each group.

WIFE BATTERING IN ASIAN COMMUNITIES

In the past few decades, there have been numerous attempts by social scientists to measure the prevalence of wife battering in the United States. These studies have produced disputed estimates, but in any event, the frequency of wife battering in Asian families is rarely mentioned or explored. To some extent this reflects the racial bias that has characterized traditional research on battered women, but it is also due in part to the difficulty inherent in obtaining reliable data on wife battering in Asian families. There are several reasons for this. First, because of the multitude of Asian languages and cultures, it is difficult for many researchers, regardless of their race or ethnicity, to do a systematic and inclusive study. Researchers are often confronted with numerous obstacles when attempting to deal with this problem. These include language barriers, cultural misunderstandings, beliefs in the myth that wife battering is not a problem among Asians who are typically stereotyped as "model minorities," and reluctance among Asians themselves to admit that wife battering exists in their communities.

Even though Asian women are grossly underrepresented in prevalence studies on wife battering, several researchers and practitioners who work with battered Asian women have estimated that wife battering occurs as frequently in the Asian population as it does in the general population (Eng, 1990; Ikeda-Vogel, Lee, & Lee, 1993; Rimonte, 1989). Some researchers have found that Asian

women who are battered are less likely than women from other racial and ethnic groups to report the abuse and those who do usually wait until the battering has reached a crisis level of severity (Bhaumik, 1988; Rimonte, 1989). This lack of reporting has been attributed to several factors, including:

> The Pacific Asian family's traditional patriarchal system and the attendant belief in the supremacy of the male; the socialization goals and processes which favor the family and community over the individual; the cultural emphasis on silent suffering versus open communication of needs and feelings; and the enormous adjustment pressures which test the limits of immigrants' and refugees' survival skills. Cultural norms and values directly or indirectly sanction abuse against women and tend to minimize it as a problem in the community. (Rimonte, 1989, p. 328)

Although patriarchy is a phenomenon that exists throughout the world, some researchers have argued that the patriarchal ideology is more oppressive and rigid in Asian communities than in the general U.S. population, particularly among recently arrived immigrants and refugees. In her comparative study of battered Asian women and battered women from other racial and ethnic groups (including White, African American, Hispanic and Latina women), Bhaumik found that Asian women were "significantly more patriarchal in their attitudes, identified more with their ethnic groups, experienced significantly less marital equality, had less social support, and suffered from more severe battering before seeking help in a shelter" (1988, pp. xiii–xiv). In an earlier study on Korean battered wives, Yim (1978) found that while length of time in the United States lessened adherence to traditional patriarchal attitudes among Korean men, "even after six years of residence in the United States, Korean men were still substantially more traditional than white American men" (p. 176).

The investment in patriarchal ideology is further compounded by other related cultural beliefs and practices that also inhibit the reporting of abuse among Asians and affect their help-seeking behavior. According to Chow (1989), there are a number of cultural dilemmas that Asian women confront in the United States. These include obedience versus independence, collective or familial interest versus individual interest, and self-control versus self-expression. These traditional cultural beliefs are rooted in rigid gender norms that may deter women from seeing themselves as battered and inhibit them from seeking help. Furthermore, these traditional cultural norms and expectations often serve as constraints by sanctioning abuse either indirectly or directly by minimizing or legitimizing violence against women (Ikeda-Vogel et al., 1993; Rimonte, 1989). For example, in traditional Asian cultures, women are often taught to obey their "male superiors." A daughter is expected to obey her father, a wife is expected to obey her husband, and a widow is expected to obey her eldest son (Chin, 1994). If a woman fails to obey her male superior, it is sometimes acceptable for him to discipline her through violent means (Yim, 1978).

Unlike the American ideal that emphasizes individual rights and freedoms, Asians generally subscribe to a more collectivist ideology in which "individual rights and freedoms are subordinated to family and community expectations and traditions" (Crites, 1990, p. 8). Based on her experience working with battered Asian women, Rimonte argues:

> A healthy family by Western standards has an open structure. Members are allowed to be individuals and to communicate their feelings freely. This ideal contrasts starkly with the controlled, conforming style of Pacific-Asians, in which a high value is placed on one's strict accountability to the family. The Pacific-Asian family has a closed structure. Communication is restricted and decision making is vertical. Power in marriage is hierarchical. (1989, pp. 329–330)

In sum, several researchers have suggested that Asian women are less likely than women of other racial and ethnic groups to report abuse and to seek help. In this article, I will discuss the specific needs of battered Asian women as well as identify the various structural and cultural barriers that compound this problem.

METHOD

The findings in this article are based on 18 interviews that were conducted in two stages between 1990 and 1993. The first group of interviews was conducted while I volunteered at a domestic violence shelter on the East Coast in 1990 and 1991. The second group of interviews took place while I volunteered at a domestic violence shelter on the West Coast in 1993.

Participants for the study were recruited in several ways. While volunteering at the East-Coast shelter, I obtained lists of other domestic violence shelters and social service organizations located throughout the United States. From these lists, I devised a new list that included shelters and agencies that were located in U.S. cities with a substantial Asian population. The list was further narrowed down by including shelters and organizations that directly worked with battered Asian women and were willing to participate in the study. While volunteering at a domestic violence shelter for Asian women on the West Coast, I recruited participants for this study from a list of people who were affiliated with the shelter and had direct experience working with battered Asian women. I also used the snowball technique by soliciting more participants from the people I interviewed.

The resultant sample consisted of 17 women and 1 man. Slightly more than half of the interviewees resided on the West Coast (7 in Los Angeles, 1 in San Francisco, and 1 in San Diego). Slightly more than 1/3 of the respondents resided on the East Coast (2 in the District of Columbia, 2 in Philadelphia, 1 in Boston, and 1 in New York City). The remaining 3 participants included 2 women in Minneapolis and 1 woman who worked at a shelter near Houston, Texas.

The race and ethnicity of the study participants varied greatly. Three were White, 2 Chinese, 2 Korean, 2 Asian Indian, 2 Cambodian, 1 Japanese, 1 Filipino, 1 Afghan, 1 African American, 1 Chinese-White, 1 Japanese-White, and 1 Japanese-Korean. All of the participants worked with battered Asian women in some capacity. Six of the interviewees worked in domestic violence shelters, 4 worked in the legal field (2 lawyers and 2 victim advocates), 4 were social workers, and the remaining 4 worked in various social service organizations.

The interviews consisted of loosely structured, open-ended questions and lasted between 45 minutes and 2 hours, with the average being 70 minutes. An attempt was made to tape-record all of the interviews; however, six were recorded by hand. The majority of the interviews were conducted face-to-face, but six took place over the phone. The quotations used in this article are taken verbatim from only those interviews that were successfully tape-recorded and transcribed.

I chose to interview people who worked with battered Asian women rather than interviewing the women themselves for several reasons. First, the people I interviewed had a great deal of exposure to wife battering in Asian communities and were generally able to elaborate on many of the issues because of their extensive knowledge and experience. Because the research was done in urban areas with diverse Asian populations, most of the interviewees had been exposed to wife battering in more than one Asian ethnic group and were able to discuss variations they had observed between different groups. Second, if I had chosen to interview battered women, I would have been limited to interviewing English-speaking women, which may have resulted in biased findings. Third, because it is generally taboo to "air your dirty laundry" in Asian cultures, it was questionable whether battered Asian women would be willing to discuss such a sensitive topic with me, a monolingual White woman.

Although I am satisfied with the results of my decision to interview people who work with battered women rather than interviewing the battered women themselves, this raises some methodological limitations. First, the interviewees were primarily exposed to Asian women who viewed themselves as being battered and had made an attempt to change their situation. Thus the interviewees' interpretations may overlook some important differences between women who define themselves as battered and those who do not. Second, the findings in this article are based on secondhand information that may reflect the perspectives and interpretations of the interviewees rather than the battered women. Third, because of the small sample size of this study, the generalizability of the findings is limited; it cannot be assumed that these findings are representative of all those who have worked with battered Asian women, and certainly not to all battered Asian women.

One final issue needs to be addressed before turning to an analysis of my findings. Because all social research involves putting people on display, I have been grappling with an unresolvable ethical dilemma while doing this research. There is inevitably some voyeurism and exploitation involved in looking at the lives of other people, particularly when the looker is White and the subjects are women of color. Given the long history of White, Western exploitation of people of color, I am deeply troubled to find myself, at some level, participating in this process. Although I have not resolved this, I do believe there are certain measures that can be taken to abate this dilemma. The research for this article was guided by a feminist perspective with my primary goal being to help improve the lives of battered women. In addition, I used a participatory method of gathering data for this article. Rather than seeing myself as the objective "knower," and "studying down," I viewed the relationship between myself and the study participants as horizontal, or being on the same plane (Harding, 1987). By using the participatory method I was able to mitigate some of these issues and obtain rich information that reflects the points of view and experiences of the study participants.

FINDINGS AND DISCUSSION

All of the interviewees reported that Asian women, particularly monolingual women and recent immigrants and refugees, have needs that differ from most women in the general population and that most existing services do not meet these needs. Furthermore, everyone I spoke with listed many constraints that make it exceedingly difficult for Asian women to obtain help. Some of these findings are consistent with the existing literature, whereas some illuminate issues that have not previously been examined. Because most of the study participants worked primarily with recently arrived immigrant and refugee women, my findings pertain mostly to these populations. First, I will discuss the unique needs of Asian women and then I will present the cultural and structural constraints. Although many of these issues overlap and are interrelated, I will attempt to separate them for the sake of clarity.

Special Needs of Asian Women

Because of a multitude of issues, many battered Asian women need specialized services. These specialized services must be culturally sensitive and must be tailored to meet their specific needs. The interviewees reported that there are many complex issues that are overlooked by mainstream social service providers. These include language and cultural issues, outreach methods, and advocacy issues. Lyn, a Chinese woman who works at one of the few shelters that provides services for Asian women located in San Francisco, sums this up well:

Asian women are not being served. The shelters that existed just did not have the capacity to handle language issues, immigration issues and the same

kind of cultural issues that Asian women would need.

Ami, a Korean social worker in San Diego, California, went as far as saying that "the conditions in mainstream shelters are scarier than the battering at home." I will address each of these issues in turn.

Language Needs.   Language is a complex issue that presents many problems for monolingual Asian women. One of the most crucial needs of monolingual Asian women is to be understood. But because there are so many Asian languages and dialects, it is often difficult for shelters to accommodate all Asian women in need. However, some of the women I spoke with who work at shelters designed to meet the needs of Asian women have developed innovative approaches to this problem. Lyn, who was quoted previously, explained that the shelter where she works has developed their own program to meet language needs, and they also use the services of two language banks in San Francisco:

One of our model projects of our program is our bilingual advocates and it's called the Multilingual Access Model and that is how we deal with all the different languages.... We have an on-call staff who are bilingual advocates; all of them are bilingual in different languages.... There's like 9 or 10 [lan-guages].... There are also 2 language banks in San Francisco.... Sometimes what happens is that our bilingual advocates are not available or we don't have that language on staff so we'll have to give them a call.

However, some of the interviewees reported that using outside interpreters can sometimes be problematic because they may not be educated about issues of wife battering and may even alter what is being said. Louise, a Korean woman who works as a victim advocate in the Los Angeles court system, reported:

Some of the interpreters that are available may not be sympathetic to the issues and may try to twist her words around.... I know some of the interpreters that are just out there in the community are completely oblivious to the issues of domestic violence and they don't know how to interpret and then they feel like, "Well I better help the person," and they won't interpret what you're trying to say to the woman. They'll just say it in other ways. And again, most of the interpreters out there are males.

Louise reported that it is often more effective to speak implicitly or indirectly about the violence when working with battered Asian women:

If you make the outreach non-threatening ... just say something about making the community better, make it very vague and non-threatening, and then you'll probably, hopefully, reach more women.... I think when I work with a lot of the domestic violence victims I don't use "violence." I don't use "domestic violence".... I usually call it a family squabble.

Although this may be an effective strategy, it is also problematic because it minimizes the abuse and obscures who is at fault. This "systems approach" to wife battering ignores issues of gender and power and may even blame the victim. This presents a dilemma because many traditional Asian cultures place the responsibility of maintaining harmony in the family upon the women. Such an approach may reinforce patriarchal and sexist practices.

I will return to some other language issues shortly. Now, however, I will turn to a discussion of other specialized needs of Asian women.

Cultural Issues. Many of the interviewees reported that for social services to be accessible to Asian women, they must be culturally sensitive. By culturally sensitive, I do not mean using culture as a justification for battering. As ridiculous as this may sound, this has been done in the U.S. legal system by employing what is known as the "cultural defense argument" to excuse Asian men from beating their wives. In the most grotesque example of

this, a Chinese man received five years' probation in New York City for beating his wife to death with a hammer; in this case, the judge ruled in favor of a cultural defense argument (Eng, 1990). Although this case may be an extreme example, it did send a powerful message to battered Asian women. Jen, a Chinese shelter worker in New York City, remembered the incident well and reported:

For Asians, there is perhaps a feeling that there is some precedence for abuse. For example, the Chen case had a tremendous impact. I think that gave Asian men the message that they could do that and get away with it because of the cultural defense argument and it gave women the message that there is no protection. It gave a very dangerous message to the community.

In contrast, by cultural sensitivity I am referring to hospitality and to providing services that will make Asian women feel most comfortable and more likely to utilize services. This includes providing outreach that will most effectively reach Asian women, providing Asian food at the shelters, and taking the time to explain things to monolingual and recently arrived Asian women that they may not be familiar with.

To better meet the needs of battered Asian women, outreach in the community must be approached differently from those methods commonly employed by mainstream agencies. For example, several participants reported that Asian women are less likely than women from other racial and ethnic groups to call a hotline. This may be due to language issues, lack of familiarity with the system, or because they live with an extended family and are afraid of getting caught. For example, Lyn observed:

They don't call the hotlines.... Oftentimes in an Asian household there is someone home all day like a grandparent which makes it frightening to make that call and we've found that they just really don't use our hotline at all.... More will come in directly in person and want to talk to someone as an individual and I think that has a lot to do with the fear of the abuser finding out while they're on the phone.

The most effective outreach methods reported include word-of-mouth, establishing trust and making contacts within the communities, and distributing literature in various Asian languages in local stores, churches, laundromats, and hair salons. Pat, a White shelter worker in Boston who works primarily with Cambodian women, stated:

Home visits work very well...educating people about domestic violence being a crime, and about the services that are available. Another thing that seems to work really well is outreach through local Asian food markets, restaurants, grocery stores. We also developed a poster about domestic violence and it's in Kmen, Vietnamese, and Chinese, which has a visual depiction of abuse and phone numbers.... I think the community-based approach, approach of word-of-mouth, is the key.

The need for a community-based approach came up during most of the interviews. The interviewees delineated various creative ways outreach is done. For example, Barbara, an African American woman who works primarily with Vietnamese, Cambodian, and Laotian women in Minneapolis found that taking the time to attend community functions pays off:

When Asian communities have cultural celebrations and holidays, members of our organization try to attend so they can gain their trust and become familiar with members of the communities. They gain trust through socializing which increases comfort when there is a problem.

A related issue is the need for advocacy. Most of the interviewees reported that there is a greater need to walk Asian women through the system and take more time to explain how things work. This is particularly the case with recently arrived immigrant and refugee women. They are more likely to be misinformed about their legal rights. Furthermore, their batterers may exploit their naïveté by telling them lies and threatening to have them deported if they leave. Karen, a Filipino victim advocate in Los Angeles, noted:

There's a greater need for advocacy for our clients because they don't speak the language and [require] specialized services. It's not like working with an English-speaking population that's familiar with the system—the legal system, the court system—so there's a greater need to spend more time to interpret, to walk people through.

Several women reported that to familiarize the women with the system, more time must be invested in each battered woman. Although most shelters have a 30-day limit of stay, Asian women often need to stay longer to work through some of these complex issues. Lyn reported:

They don't realize that in this country you have rights to everything and you can leave anytime you want to.... They need extra help to take a bus, to get to a meeting, to understand what is going on at the meeting, to understand what an attorney can do for you, to understand what the court system is, what a restraining order is.

Cultural sensitivity also includes having Asian food on hand at the shelters. Laura, a Japanese shelter worker in Los Angeles reported that, "We try and keep the place what we term 'culturally hospitable.' For instance, we always have rice. I mean we buy tons of it." Similarly, Lyn said:

We make sure that the food they eat is there so we all go shopping together. We have all different kinds of rice so we can accommodate to what they are used to. The women cook the food themselves. All the beds are futons, we have few American beds. It makes a difference because when they come to the shelter there are all these things that are familiar to her and make her feel at home.

In summary, it is clear that Asian women's needs differ markedly from women in the general population. To better meet their needs, mainstream service providers must redress their current procedures. Sarah, a White woman who works with victims of wife battering in Minneapolis, captures this well when she proclaimed that "mainstream advocates need to let go of how things *should* be done because it doesn't work in Asian communities."

Structural and Cultural Constraints

There are many cultural and structural constraints that inhibit battered Asian women from seeking help. These constraints may not apply to all Asian women in the United States; they may be contingent on factors such as length of time in the United States and proficiency in English. Cultural constraints include norms, expectations, values, and socialization processes that may sanction abuse either directly or indirectly. Structural constraints include patriarchal ideologies, language, immigration issues and laws, family, and social systems.

The present findings are consistent with the current literature on battering in Asian families (e.g., patriarchal ideology, values, norms, socialization processes) and with the literature on battering in the general population (e.g., self-blame, economic barriers, emotional dependence). In addition, some new insights on constraints have emerged from the data.

Language Constraints. One of the major constraints repeatedly mentioned throughout the interviews was language. Monolingual Asian women face a challenge with regard to language barriers. Because there are so many languages and dialects spoken between and within Asian groups, it is difficult for social service agencies to meet all of their needs. As Karen, a Filipino victim advocate, noted:

> There are so many languages in the Asian culture, to begin with. Most of the Hispanic women all speak Spanish and they can all basically, whether they're from Mexico or Spain, relate. I mean there are some differences, but they are minor differences. The African-American community all speak one language, so that's great. And the Asian culture is so difficult because you've got the Japanese, you've got the Chinese and the Chinese have dialects themselves, there's the Korean, the Vietnamese, the Cambodians, Southeast Asians.

Not only do language constraints hinder communication with social service agencies, but monolingual women have difficulty doing certain tasks that most English-speaking people take for granted. Shari, an Asian Indian social worker in Los Angeles, points out:

> A lot of them [Asian women] don't speak the language very well and you know, in fact, this lady who called the other day—she speaks very, very little English and even to get her to go and take the bus, because she has no car, and even to get her to go to social service, or go anywhere like for counseling... she can't do it because she would need to speak the language in order to call the bus or know the transit district and explain to them where she is at and tell them that she needs to go here or wherever.

Thus language barriers severely limit access to information and services and may exacerbate a woman's fear.

Most of the interviewees also reported that there was a correlation between the ethnicity of the staff workers at their organizations and the ethnicity of the women who used their services. This is also consistent with the literature (Bhaumik, 1988; Rimonte, 1989). Pat, who works in a domestic violence shelter in Boston, noticed, "There are a lot more Chinese women who call us... because a large number of our volunteers are Chinese and whatever volunteers you have, that is what community you can service."

Significantly, it may not only be monolingual Asian women who seek out service providers from their own ethnic group. Cheryl, an Asian Indian social worker in Los Angeles relayed an incident where a woman who spoke English had a strong preference to work with someone from her own ethnic group:

> I had a call from an American social worker who was working with an Indian woman, who now has

to go through a divorce, unfortunately, and she is only comfortable if she has an attorney who speaks the language even though she speaks fluent English.

Battered women may feel more comfortable discussing these issues with someone from their own ethnic group, or it may be a reflection of the availability of interpreters, or they may have learned about the available services via word of mouth in their ethnic community. Most interviewees did not think this correlation indicated that there was more abuse in certain communities. One way of overcoming this barrier is by diversifying the staff, having bilingual workers on call, and doing more outreach in the underserved communities.

Those Asian women who do overcome language constraints may still be faced with other communication barriers. For example, Eastern styles of communication vary considerably from Western styles. Generally, Western communication styles advocate being direct and straightforward, whereas Eastern styles of communication are often indirect and nonverbal (Ho, 1990). Louise, the Korean victims' advocate in Los Angeles, mentioned several times how important it is to use indirect, vague language when working with battered women and their families. For instance, she said, "When you talk to a lot of the Asian women, especially in court when we try to send the batterers to batterers' counseling, we call it education; it's again, nonthreatening ...education is a good thing and counseling is taboo."

Language barriers contribute to and compound a host of other constraints that inhibit Asian women from seeking help. These include the dissemination of misinformation, fear of authority and deportation, and the lack of awareness and education about women's legal rights in the United States.

Lack of Familiarity and Misinformation. Many battered Asian women do not reach out for help because they are afraid of what might happen. Although some of these fears are legitimate, many are based on inaccurate information. These fears include the fear of deportation, fear of ostracization from the community, and fear of law and authority.

Often, battered Asian women, particularly monolingual immigrant women, are ill-informed about laws in the United States. Some of these fears are not unfounded. One example of this, which was reported by most of the study participants, is the immigration laws that have historically discriminated against Asians. Laws such as the Immigration Reform and Control Act (IRCA) and the Marriage Fraud Act (MFA) have had an adverse effect on undocumented battered Asian women. These laws placed the burden of responsibility on battered women to prove they entered marriage in "good faith" and gave tremendous power to the batterer, who could threaten to have his wife deported. Under these laws, undocumented battered women were completely dependent on their husbands for their legal status and were often locked into abusive relationships because they had little recourse (Orloff & Kelly, 1995).

However, there has been a recent development in immigration law that may provide more protection and avenues of recourse for undocumented battered women. The Violence Against Women Act (VAWA), signed by President Clinton in September 1994, allows undocumented battered women to obtain lawful permanent resident status through either self-petitioning or suspension of deportation (Orloff & Kelly, 1995).[2]

Although this new law represents an important advancement for undocumented battered women, it is still too early to tell whether undocumented battered women are benefiting from its passage. For example, as Orloff and Kelly point out, "as of October 1995, the INS ha[d] still not issued regulations or begun processing self-petitions, and access to suspension of deportation remains limited" (1995, p. 383). Second, the conditions for inclusion under the VAWA are complex; one would need to consult an attorney or immigration law expert before filing for any relief under the VAWA (Orloff & Kelly). Finally, some Asians do not trust the legal system in the United States and, therefore, may be reluctant to pursue the protections afforded by the VAWA. In addition to the fear of deportation, some refugees are suspicious of legal authorities because in their homeland, they could not trust authorities. In fact, three of the study participants reported that this may be because women were sometimes raped by authorities in refugee camps prior to coming to the United States.

Cultural Constraints. The legitimate fear of being ostracized from her community also appears to influence an Asian woman's decision to seek help. Lyn, a Chinese social service provider for a shelter in San Francisco, discussed this:

> The community is often what keeps the women staying there. It keeps her from leaving the situation because she doesn't want her community to know; it's really shameful and scary for her to go to the community agency and say what is going on because she fears it will get out to the rest of the community.... It can be really wrong for her to leave. It will be considered the woman's fault... women are scared to leave because they won't really have their community anymore, and they have to actually literally leave the community and they don't know whether they'll be let back in.... It's pretty scary.

Similarly, Jen, a Chinese shelter worker in New York, noted:

> The options are so limited. Besides language, cultural, and economic barriers, oftentimes, a woman is only familiar with a five-block community. To leave that community and look for a job is overwhelming. By leaving she is really excommunicating herself from her identity.

However, in some situations the community can serve as a helpful support system by not tolerating abuse (Kibria, 1990). Lyn, quoted

above, also spoke about the complexity of this issue: "The communities can serve as both helpful and a hindrance because at the same time, it's really supportive to have your community there and have community agencies and some place to go."

The fear of leaving the community and the attendant fear of being ostracized is related to many other cultural issues. These issues include familial identity, economic dependency, stigma of divorce, taboo of airing dirty laundry, fear of losing face and bringing shame upon the family, and lack of awareness that wife battering is wrong. For example, Hue, a Cambodian social worker in Philadelphia, pointed out in reference to Cambodian culture, "The wife is very submissive to her husband. If she goes anywhere she has to tell her husband.... Most women don't do things for their own good, but rather they think about what people will think about them."

Tradition in many Asian cultures dictates that women must remain loyal to their family and must not air their dirty laundry. A lot of pressure is placed upon women to maintain familial harmony and ensure that the family does not lose face. Furthermore, divorce is taboo; if a woman decides to leave her husband, she will be blamed. Hue, quoted above, captures the complexity of these issues well:

> The stigma of divorce and fear of bringing shame upon the family is especially hard for them to deal with. Everything belongs to the husband, is his property—assets, wife, and kids. These beliefs are ingrained in their upbringing and values. Women are expected to be submissive, passive and dependent. They are taught to obey and not to say no. Violence is viewed as a means to control and is not seen as a problem.... When a woman is beaten it is thought of as maintaining control because she deserved it.

These beliefs and practices are often reinforced by the extended family system that is common in Asian ethnic groups. Like Asian communities, the extended family structure that exists in many Asian families can both serve as a help and a hindrance. The extended family can serve as a control mechanism or "buffer" that guards against battering. Pat, a White shelter worker in Boston, reported:

> One thing that I think makes it [wife battering] worse is that family supports are not present in this country. Women often come, especially Cambodian women, without their extended families, without the family supports that would intervene, provide support or safety, a safe place for her to go, or tell the abuser to stop, that it is not okay.

However, most of the people I interviewed spoke more about how the extended family system often positively sanctions battering against women. Lyn reported:

> Many of the women live in extended families where it is the in-laws or the kin family that is actually contributing to the abuse or is condoning or encouraging it. For example, "You have to teach her a lesson."

Similarly, Louise, a Korean victim advocate in Los Angeles, noted:

> Some extended family can be very supportive; most of them are not. The woman's family, most of them feel that once she gets married, she becomes his family so they won't have much to do with the woman, even though she goes back home to seek help, the mothers will always send them back.

This is further compounded by the fact that often, in the extended family system, the women move in with their husband's family rather than their own. This living arrangement tends to place the woman in a more vulnerable position because the husband's family typically is more likely to side with him. Jen, a Chinese shelter worker in New York, reported:

> Many women don't get the support from other family members. Usually the immigrant women we see are here alone with the husband and the husband's family, and often it is the extended family they live with, and oftentimes the women are abused not by just their husbands but also by the relatives of their husbands.

It was also reported that clergy sometimes pressure and persuade battered women to stay with their husbands. Ann, a Japanese lawyer in Los Angeles, noted:

> I remember seeing Korean ministers coming into our court trying to intervene, basically trying to pressure women not to prosecute, not to participate in the prosecution, because, they would argue, the ministers would argue, that it's against, you know, the Bible to do anything that would break up the family.

Jodi, an executive director at a shelter near Houston, Texas, who provides services primarily for Vietnamese women, recounted an incident when a pastor lied to a woman because he believed her place was in the home: "A Korean Baptist who was interpreting told a battered Asian woman that if she stayed in the shelter the government would come and take her children."

Some of the study participants also reported that religious beliefs impact help-seeking behavior of Asian women. Several of the interviewees reported that religious beliefs may deter women from seeing themselves as abused and from seeking help. Issues such as belief in reincarnation and paying dues for past lives, belief in fate and destiny, belief that suffering is virtuous, can serve to impede women from seeking help.

Several interviewees spoke about similar instances in which someone who was supposed to be helping a battered woman instead did them a grave disservice because of their own sexist beliefs. Dahlia, an Afghan woman who works at a national organization to help Third World women refugees in Washington, D.C. reported:

> One of the major problems is educating Asian men who work for social service agencies. . . . They often feel very threatened because they are told that they cannot side with the husband in domestic violence situations because the wife has certain rights.

*Many of these male social workers don't see any-
thing wrong with pushing your wife around. They
believe that the men have the right to control in the
home. This is a shocking attitude to deal with because these men take the opposite side than they are
supposed to and it is very difficult to break through
these beliefs.*

As Dahlia later pointed out, these kinds
of attitudes can have devastating effects if a
woman who has the courage to seek help is
met with someone who tells her she is the one
who is wrong.

CONCLUSION

It is clear that battered Asian women, particularly recently arrived monolingual immigrant
and refugee women, have special needs and
concerns. I have argued that there are several
internal and external forces that work in tan-
dem to keep the needs of Asian women from
being formally included in the mainstream
battered women's movement.

The internal forces that contribute to this
neglect include the cultural beliefs and practices that were pointed out in this article.
Deeply entrenched patriarchal beliefs legitimate the use of violence to "keep women in
their place" and make it difficult for battered
women to see themselves as abused. Those
who do see themselves as abused are often
afraid to leave because they fear losing face,
their children, and their community. The
stigmas of airing your dirty laundry, divorce,
and bringing shame upon the family contribute to the denial about the existence of wife
battering.

There are external forces that contribute
to the failure of mainstream organizations to
address the unique needs of battered Asian
women. These include stereotypes about
Asians such as the "model minority myth,"
lack of funding for programs for battered
Asian women, U.S. immigration laws, the historical exclusion of women of color from the
mainstream feminist movement in the United

States, and the prevalence of sexism and racism in this society.

The stereotype that depicts Asians as a
model minority is damaging on many levels.
First, this label obscures the serious problems
and injustices experienced by Asians, including wife battering. Second, "it has been used to
justify omitting Asian Americans from federal
funding and some special minority programs"
(Crystal, 1989, p. 405). Third, this stereotype
conveys the impression that "equality of opportunity and societal acceptance have been
gained, and that problems of institutional access, psychological well-being, or racial prejudice have been fully resolved" (Nakanishi,
1988, p. 164). Thus, by portraying an exem-
plary image of Asians, this myth serves to justify the exclusion of battered Asian women
from social programs and funding.

The battered women's movement in the
United States has been greatly criticized for
neglecting the issues and needs of women of
color (hooks, 1984; Lorde, 1984; Mohanty,
1991). Although there have been major strides
in recent years toward overcoming this exclusion, gaps remain. A consequence of this neglect has been that most mainstream social
service agencies do not have the knowledge
and capacity to adequately address the needs
of battered Asian women, especially those
women who do not speak English.

Finally, sexism and racism also help preserve the current system that neglects the
needs of battered Asian women. Not only do
Asian women have to deal with patriarchal
constraints within their own cultures, they are
also faced with patriarchal norms and values
specific to American culture. Images of women
as subordinate and inferior to men saturate
U.S. society. Thus battered Asian women are
confronted with sexism on two fronts, which
together may further lower their likelihood of
obtaining help.

In addition to sexism, Asian women must
deal with racism in the United States. Racism
may exacerbate a woman's fear about seeking

help outside of her community and may even promote family and community solidarity. A battered Asian woman may feel safer living with a violent husband than in a racist society. Thus issues surrounding racism may take precedence over issues surrounding sexism (Glenn, 1986). Some Asian women may have learned that to avoid racism and discrimination, it is in their best interest to remain invisible in U.S. society (Ho, 1990).

It is clear that there are multiple forces that preserve the status quo and prevent the formal inclusion of the needs of battered Asian women in mainstream organizations. But where do we go from here? I believe that to penetrate these numerous barriers and meet the needs of battered Asian women, a multilevel approach to battering must be implemented. The needs of battered Asian women must be addressed directly through mainstream social service organizations, and indirectly through education and consciousness raising. This is not an easy task. However, based on my interviews with service providers throughout the United States, there appear to be several things that can be done to improve services for battered Asian women.

First, racism and discrimination must be addressed in mainstream society as well as within social service organizations. Racism is so embedded in the fabric of our society and its institutions that it is doubtful that social service agencies are completely immune to racist and discriminatory practices. Although it may be true that social service providers are more likely than the general public to be more sensitive and aware of issues such as racism, it cannot be assumed that this is universally true. To address racism within social service organizations, more research must be done to identify if and where the problems exist. For example, do social service providers hold racist or stereotypical beliefs about Asians? Are battered Asian women treated with respect by staff and residents in shelters where they are a minority? Do shelters implement multi-

cultural outreach methods to try and reach battered Asian women in need of services? If racism is found to be a problem, measures need to be taken to condemn racist practices, to educate service providers, and to implement policies and mechanisms to help guard against racist and discriminatory practices. Service providers must adopt a written policy against racism that includes explicit measures that will be taken when violations occur. The policy should apply not only to staff and volunteers, but also to other clients. In addition, antiracism training should be required for all staff and volunteers.

Second, I think that service providers can learn a tremendous amount from each other and avoid double work. I interviewed shelter workers at three shelters that deal almost exclusively with Asian women: two in California and one in New York. Because the population of Asian women is higher in these two states than all other states in the United States, the demand for services by Asian women is higher and their needs are, perhaps, more apparent. I found that the services for battered Asian women are more developed and accessible in California and New York than in other states where the Asian population is lower. Although there is certainly communication among service providers at the national level, I believe that it can be improved. For example, annual meetings for service providers could be established where one of the goals would be to discuss approaches to meet the needs of women of color, a newsletter devoted to addressing services for women of color could be developed, and communication lines could be widened through the use of electronic mail and the internet (e.g., shelters could design their own web page).

There are broad possibilities that could result by expanding the lines of communication. For example, a service provider with little or no experience working with battered Asian women, who is in a region of the United States where the Asian population is small, could learn from a veteran service provider in San Francisco about how to address the language needs of Asian women, how to make their shelter more accessible and hospitable to Asian women, and what types of outreach and advocacy work best with battered Asian women. Whereas most service providers are undoubtedly committed to providing the best services for their clients, many have huge caseloads and little time to spend in the library hunting down the latest research. If the lines of communication were widened and information was disseminated electronically, service providers could have access to information at their fingertips, which would be much more beneficial. Until such information is available, Asian women will continue to be neglected with regard to resources, attitudes, and funding.[3]

NOTES

1. In this article, the term *Asian* includes all Asian ethnic groups residing in the continental United States, regardless of citizenship status.

2. See Orloff and Kelly (1995) for a comprehensive review of the provisions of the Violence Against Women Act that are especially relevant to immigrant and refugee women.

3. It is important to note that there is mounting evidence that there are informal mechanisms, such as women's groups, in place in Asian communities that play an important role in supporting and protecting battered women (Kibria, 1990) and in shifting wife battering from a private to a public issue (Abraham, 1995).

REFERENCES

Abraham, M. (1995). Ethnicity, gender, and marital violence. *Gender & Society, 9,* 450–468.

Bhaumik, M. (1988). *A study of wife abuse in two cultures: The American and the Asian American.* Unpublished doctoral dissertation, University of Southern California.

Chin, K. (1994). Out of town brides: International marriage and wife abuse among Chinese immigrants. *Journal of Comparative Family Studies, 25,* 53–69.

Chow, E. N. L. (1989). The feminist movement: Where are all the Asian American women? In Asian Women United of California (Eds.), *Making waves* (pp. 362–377). Boston: Beacon.

Crites, L. (1990). Cross cultural counseling in wife beating cases. *Response, 77*(4), 8–12.

Crystal, D. (1989). Asian Americans and the myth of the model minority. *Social Casework, 7,* 405–413.

Eng, P. (1990, June). *Woman battering in Asian immigrant communities in the U.S.* Paper presented at the Fourth International Interdisciplinary Congress on Women, New York.

Espiritu, L. Y. (1992). *Asian American panethnicity.* Philadelphia: Temple University Press.

Glenn, E. N. (1986). *Issei, Nisei, war bride.* Philadelphia: Temple University Press.

Harding, S. (Ed.) (1987). *Feminism and methodology.* Bloomington: Indiana University Press.

Ho, C. K. (1990). An analysis of domestic violence in Asian American communities: A multicultural approach to counseling. In L. S. Brown, & M. P. P. Root (Eds.), *Diversity and complexity in feminist therapy* (pp. 129–150). Binghamton, NY: Haworth.

hooks, b. (1984). *Feminist theory: From margin to center.* Boston: South End.

Ikeda-Vogel, L., Lee, T. & Lee, J. (1993, October). Domestic violence. *KoreAm Journal,* pp. 9–11.

Kibria, N. (1990). Power, patriarchy, and gender conflict in the Vietnamese immigrant community. *Gender & Society, 4,* 9–24.

Lorde, A. (1984). *Sister outsider.* Freedom, CA: Crossing.

Mohanty, C. T. (1991). Under Western eyes: Feminist scholarship and colonial discourses. In C. T. Mohanty, A. Russo, & L. Torres (Eds.), Bloomington: Indiana University Press.

Nakanishi, D. T. (1988). Seeking convergence in race relations research: Japanese-Americans and the resurrection of the internment. In P. A. Katz, & D. A. Taylor (Eds.), *Eliminating racism* (pp. 159–180). New York: Plenum.

Orloff, L. E., & Kelly, N. (1995). A look at the Violence Against Women Act and gender-related asylum. *Violence Against Women, 1,* 380–400.

Rimonte, N. (1989). Domestic violence among Pacific Asians. In Asian Women United of California (Eds.), *Making waves* (pp. 327–337). Boston: Beacon.

U.S. Bureau of the Census (1990). *Statistical abstract of the United States.* Washington, DC: U.S. Government Printing Office.

Yim, S. B. (1978). Korean battered wives: A sociological and psychological analysis of conjugal violence in Korean immigrant families. In H. H. Sunoo (Ed.), *Korean women in a struggle for humanization.* Memphis, TN: Association of Korean Christian Scholars in North America.